YOU MUST CHANGE

YOU MUST CHANGE YOUR LIFE
On Anthropotechnics

PETER SLOTERDIJK

Translated by Wieland Hoban

polity

First published in German as *Du mußt dein Leben ändern* © Suhrkamp Verlag Frankfurt am Main 2009.
Reprinted: 2015 (twice), 2016 (twice), 2017, 2018 (twice), 2019, 2020, 2021
This English edition © Polity Press, 2013

The translation of this work was supported by a grant from the Goethe-Institut which is funded by the German Ministry of Foreign Affairs.

Polity Press
65 Bridge Street
Cambridge CB2 1UR, UK

Polity Press
350 Main Street
Malden, MA 02148, USA

ISBN-13: 978-0-7456-4921-4
ISBN-13: 978-0-7456-4922-1 (pb)

A catalogue record for this book is available from the British Library.

Typeset in 10.5 on 12 pt Sabon
by Servis Filmsetting Ltd, Stockport, Cheshire
Printed and bound in the United States by LSC Communications

For further information on Polity, visit our website: www.politybooks.com

CONTENTS

CONTENTS

Appamādena sampādetha.
Forge ahead in vigilance!

Mahaparinibbana Sutta, 6, 7

Works, first and foremost!
That is to say, doing, doing, doing!
The 'faith' that goes with it will soon put in an appearance
– you can be sure of that!

Friedrich Nietzsche, *Daybreak*

INTRODUCTION

On the Anthropotechnic Turn

A spectre is haunting the Western world – the spectre of religion. All over the country we hear that after an extended absence, it has now returned and is among the people of the modern world, and that one would do well to reckon seriously with its renewed presence. Unlike the spectre of communism, which, when its *Manifesto* appeared in 1848, was not a returnee but a novelty among imminent threats, the present case does full justice to its revenant nature. Whether it comforts or threatens, whether it greets us as a benevolent spirit or is feared as an irrational shadow of mankind, its appearance, indeed the mere announcement thereof, commands respect as far as the eye can see – if one passes over the summer offensive of the godless in 2007, to which we owe two of the most superficial screeds in recent intellectual history: those of Chistopher Hitchens and Richard Dawkins. The forces of Old Europe have combined for a pompous welcome celebration with a gathering of unequal guests: the pope and the Islamic scholars, the American presidents and the new rulers of the Kremlin, all the Metternichs and Guizots of our time, the French curators and the German sociologists.

This attempt to restore to religion its attested rights involves the enforcement of a protocol which demands of the newly converted and fascinated that they confess to their previous errors of judgement. As in the days of the first Merovingian, who pledged allegiance to the cross because of a victorious battle, today's children of the banalized Enlightenment are likewise meant to burn what they worshipped and worship what they burned.[1] In this change of direction, long-dormant liturgical intuitions come to the fore. They demand that the novices of post-secular 'society' publicly dissociate themselves from the criticisms of religion in the theorems of the enlightened centuries. During those centuries, human self-determination seemed attainable only at the price of reclaiming the powers wasted on the world above, using them instead to improve earthly conditions as far as possible. Large quantities of energy had to be deducted from 'God' in order to get in shape at last for the world of humans. In this transference of strength lay the élan of the age that had devoted itself to the great singular 'progress'. The humanist aggression even went so far as to elevate hope to a central principle. The supplies of the desperate were to become the *primum mobile* of better times. Those who chose to advocate this first cause made the earth an immigration country in order to realize themselves there – and nowhere else. From now on, the goal was to burn all bridges to the spheres on high and invest the energy thus released in profane existence. If God existed, he would have become the loneliest figure in the universe at that point. The migration from the beyond took on aspects of a mass exodus – by comparison, the current demographically thinned-out condition of Eastern Europe seems like overpopulation. That the majority, unimpressed by ideologies of immanence, still indulged in secret excursions across the border in the time of the triumphant Enlightenment is another matter.

In the meantime, quite different drives have gained the upper hand. The situation is governed by complicated perceptions of human chances. Once it gained an awareness of itself, the Enlightenment revealed its own paradoxes and progressed to regions where life, to quote a well-known storyteller, 'becomes complex and sad'.[2] Only tired leftovers of the former unconditional forward impetus have remained in use. Things need only advance a little further and the last of the enlightened hopeful will withdraw to the countryside like the Amish of postmodernism. Other eternal progressives follow the calls of non-governmental organizations that have devoted themselves to saving the world. For the rest, the signs of the times point to revision and regress. More than a few disappointed parties seek to cling to the producers and distributors of their progressive illusions, as if there were some consumer protection for ideas to which they could appeal. The legal archetype of our age, the compensation lawsuit, extends to broad areas of life. Have its American varieties not taught us that one has to demand exorbitant sums at the outset in order to receive a vaguely satisfactory compensation at the end of the lawyers' war? The descendants of those expelled from heaven openly seek handsome reparations – in fact, they dare to dream of epochal compensations. If they had their way, the entire expropriation of the world above would be reversed. Some newly religious entrepreneurs would like nothing more than to put the disused sites of metaphysical production back into operation overnight, as if we had simply been through a recession.

European Enlightenment – a crisis of form? An experiment on a slippery slope, at any rate, and from a global perspective an anomaly. Sociologists of religion put it quite bluntly: people keep believing everywhere else, but in our society we have glorified disillusionment. Indeed, why should Europeans be the only ones on a metaphysical diet when the rest of the world continues to dine unperturbed at the richly decked tables of illusion?

Let us recall: Marx and Engels wrote the *Communist Manifesto* with the intention of replacing the myth of a spectre named communism with their own aggressive statement of true communism. Where the mere fear of ghosts had predominated, there would now be a justified fear of a real enemy of existing conditions. The present book likewise devotes itself to the critique of a myth, replacing it with a positive thesis. Indeed, the return of religion after the 'failure' of the Enlightenment must be confronted with a clearer view of the spiritual facts. I will show that a return *to* religion is as impossible as a return *of* religion – for the simple reason that no 'religion' or 'religions' exist, only misunderstood spiritual regimens, whether these are practised in collectives – usually church, *ordo*, *umma*, *sangha* – or in customized forms – through interaction with the 'personal God' with whom the citizens of modernity are privately insured. Thus the tiresome distinction between 'true religion' and superstition loses its meaning. There are only regimens that are more and less capable and worthy of propagation. The false dichotomy of believers and unbelievers becomes obsolete and is replaced by the distinction between the practising and the untrained, or those who train differently.

Something is indeed returning today – but the conventional wisdom that this is religion making its reappearance is insufficient to satisfy critical inquiries. Nor is it the return of a factor that had vanished, but rather a shift of emphasis in a continuum that was never interrupted. The genuinely recurring element that would merit our full intellectual attention is more anthropological than 'religious' in its implications – it is, in a nutshell, the recognition of the immunitary constitution of human beings. After centuries of experiments with new forms of life, the realization has dawned that humans, whatever ethnic, economic and political situation might govern their lives, exist not only in 'material conditions', but also in symbolic immune systems and ritual shells. It is their fabric that we shall discuss in the following. Why their looms are referred to with the coolly rational term 'anthropotechnics' should become self-evident in the course of their description.

3

I would like to take the first step in justifying our interest in these matters by recalling Wittgenstein's well-known demand to put an end to the 'chatter about ethics'. It has meanwhile become possible to reformulate that part of the ethical discourse which is not chatter in anthropotechnic terms. Since the 1840s, the work on this translation has – albeit under different names – formed the confused centre of modern 'cultural studies'. The ethical programme of the present came into view for a moment when Marx and the Young Hegelians articulated the theory that man himself produces man. The true meaning of this statement was immediately obscured, however, by another chatter that presented work as the only essential human act. But if man genuinely produces man, it is precisely not through work and its concrete results, not even the 'work on oneself' so widely praised in recent times, let alone through the alternatively invoked phenomena of 'interaction' or 'communication': it is through life in forms of practice. Practice is defined here as any operation that provides or improves the actor's qualification for the next performance of the same operation, whether it is declared as practice or not.[3]

Anyone who speaks of human self-production without addressing the formation of human beings in the practising life has missed the point from the outset. Consequently, we must suspend virtually everything that has been said about humans as working beings in order to translate it into the language of practising, or self-forming and self-enhancing behaviour. It is not only the weary *Homo faber*, who objectifies the world in the 'doing' mode, who must vacate his place on the logical stage; the time has also come for *Homo religiosus*, who turns to the world above in surreal rites, to bid a deserved farewell. Together, workers and believers come into a new category. It is time to reveal humans as the beings who result from repetition. Just as the nineteenth century stood cognitively under the sign of production and the twentieth under that of reflexivity, the future should present itself under the sign of the exercise.

The stakes in this game are not low. Our enterprise is no less than the introduction of an alternative language, and with the language an altered perspective, for a group of phenomena that tradition tended to refer to with such words as 'spirituality', 'piety', 'morality', 'ethics' and 'asceticism'. If the manoeuvre succeeds, the conventional concept of religion, that ill-fated bugbear from the prop studios of modern Europe, will emerge from these investigations as the great loser. Certainly intellectual history has always resembled a refuge for malformed concepts – and after the following journey through the

4

various stations, one will not only see through the concept of 'religion' in its failed design, a concept whose crookedness is second only to the hyper-bugbear that is 'culture'. Then one will also understand why, in the light of the altered expositions, it would be equally futile to take the side of the negative bigotry that has presented itself in our climes for almost two centuries as a simplistic atheism – a Gessler's hat[4] that elegant intellectuals were happy to salute every time they passed it, and not without taking the opportunity to claim for themselves the distinction 'intellectually honest', or sometimes 'critical' or 'autonomous'. Now it is a matter of turning the whole stage by ninety degrees until the religious, spiritual and ethical material becomes visible from a revealing new angle.

Let me repeat: the stakes are high. We must confront one of the most massive pseudo-evidences in recent intellectual history: the belief, rampant in Europe since only two or three centuries ago, in the existence of 'religions' – and more than that, against the unverified faith in the existence of faith. Faith in the existence of 'religion' is the element that unites believers and non-believers, in the present as much as in the past. It displays a single-mindedness that would make any prefect of the Congregation for the Doctrine of the Faith in Rome green with envy. No one who overcame religion ever doubted its existence, even if they opposed every single one of its dogmas. No denial ever confronted the denier with the question of whether its name was justified, and whether it had any lasting value in such a form. It is only because society has grown accustomed to a comparatively recent fiction – it did not come into use until the seventeenth century – that one can speak today of a 'return of religion'.[5] It is the unbroken faith in religion as a constant and universal factor which can vanish and return that forms the foundation of the current legend.

While psychoanalysis relied on the return of repressed feelings as its central theorem, an analysis of ideas and behaviour such as the present one is based on the return of what is not understood. Rotation phenomena of this kind are inevitable as long as the element that was there disappears and resurfaces without being adequately understood in its particularity. The aim of getting to the heart of the matter oneself can only be made fruitful if one neither affirms nor rejects the object of examination, and begins instead with a more fundamental explication. This is a project that was set in motion by a vanguard of researchers in the nineteenth and early twentieth centuries, albeit using methods whose inadequacy has long been apparent – I am thinking of such authors as Feuerbach, Comte, Durkheim and

Weber. In their investigations, at least, so-called religions gradually gained clearer profiles as symbolically structured behavioural systems – though none of them sufficiently formulated the practice nature of 'religious' behaviour and its foundation in autoplastic procedures. It was only the later Nietzsche, in his dietological reflections of the 1880s – recall the corresponding pages in his self-crucifixion text *Ecce Homo* – who offered points of departure for a doctrine of life practice, or a general ascetology. Though they have been misunderstood by inattentive readers as a withdrawal of philosophy to the apothecary level,[6] whoever studies them sufficiently closely can discover in them the seminal ideas for a comprehensive theory of practising existence.

The translation suggested here of the religious, spiritual and ethical facts into the language and perspective of the general theory of practising defines itself as an Enlightenment-conservative enterprise – a conservatory one, in fact, in the matter itself. It rests on a twofold interest in preservation: firstly, it declares its allegiance to the continuum of cumulative knowledge that we call Enlightenment, and which, despite all rumours of having entered a new 'post-secular' state, we in the present continue as a context of learning meanwhile spanning four centuries; and secondly, it takes up the threads, some of them millennia old, that tie us to early manifestations of human knowledge about practice and animation – assuming that we are prepared to follow on from them in an *explicit* fashion.

With this, we have introduced the key term for everything that will be read in the following: the world 'explicit', applied to the objects in question, contains the present book *in nuce*. The aforementioned rotation of the intellectual-historical stage means nothing other than a logical manoeuvre to render explicit circumstances that, in the masses of tradition, are present in 'implicit' – that is, inward-folded and compressed – forms. If Enlightenment in a technical sense is the programmatic word for progress in the awareness of explicitness, one can say without fear of grand formulas that rendering the implicit explicit is the cognitive form of fate. Were this not the case, one would never have had cause to believe that later knowledge would necessarily be better knowledge – for, as we know, everything that has been termed 'research' in the last centuries has rested on this assumption. Only when the inward-folded 'things' or facts are by their nature subject to a tendency to unfold themselves and become more comprehensible for us can one – provided the unfolding succeeds – speak of a true increase in knowledge. Only if the 'matters' are spontaneously prepared (or can be forced by imposed examination) to come to light in magnified and better-illuminated areas can one seriously – which here means with ontological emphasis – state that there is science in progress, there are real knowledge gains, there are expeditions in which we, the epistemically committed collective, advance to hidden continents of knowledge by making thematic what was previously unthematic, bringing to light what is yet unknown, and transforming vague cognizance into definite knowledge. In this manner we increase the cognitive capital of our society – the latter word without quotation marks in this case. In earlier times, one would probably have said that conceptual work leads into a 'production'. Hegel went so far as to say that the truth is essentially a result – and thus, inevitably, only appears at the end of its drama. Where it reveals itself in a finished state, the human spirit celebrates the Sunday of life. As I do not wish to examine the concept of the concept here, and have other things in mind with the principle of work, I shall content myself with a somewhat less triumphant, but no less binding thesis: there is nothing cognitively new under the sun.

The novelty of the new, as noted earlier, stems from the unfolding of the known into larger, brighter, more richly contoured surfaces. Consequently, it can never be innovative in an absolute sense; in part, it is always the continuation of the cognitively existent by other means. Here, novelty and greater explicitness amount to the same thing. We can therefore say that the higher the degree of explicitness, the deeper the possible, indeed inevitable disconcertment caused by the newly acquired knowledge. I have previously accepted as a conventional fact that this table is made of cherrywood; I acknowledge with the tolerance of the educated that the cherrywood consists of atoms, even though these oft-cited atoms, these epistemological contemporaries of the twentieth century, possess no greater reality for me than unicorn powder or Saturnian influences. That these cherrywood atoms dissolve into a mist of sub-atomic almost-nothings upon further explication – this is something that I, as an end consumer of physical Enlightenment, must accept, even if it goes decisively against my assumptions about the substantiality of substance. The final explanation illustrates most emphatically how the later knowledge tends to be the more disconcerting.

Among the wealth of cognitive novelties under the modern sun, none are remotely comparable in their far-reaching consequences to the appearance and propagation of immune systems in the biology of the late nineteenth century. From that point on, none of the scientific integrities – animal organisms, species, 'societies' or cultures – could remain the same. Only hesitantly did people begin to understand that the immune *dispositifs* are what enable systems to become systems, life forms to become life forms,[7] and cultures to become cultures in the first place. It is only by virtue of their immunitary qualities that they ascend to the level of self-organizing unities, preserving and reproducing themselves with constant reference to a potentially and actually invasive and irritating environment. These functions are performed to an impressive degree in biological immune systems – whose discovery resulted from the investigations of Ilya Mechnikov and Robert Koch's student Paul Ehrlich at the end of the nineteenth century. There one finds the baffling idea that even relatively simple organisms like insects and molluscs have a native 'foreknowledge' of the hazards that accompany a typical insect or mollusc life. Consequently, immune systems at this level can be defined *a priori* as embodied expectations of injury and the corresponding programmes of protection and repair.

Viewed in this light, life itself appears as a dynamics of integration that is equipped with auto-therapeutic or 'endo-clinical' competencies and refers to a species-specific space of surprise. It has an equally innate and – in higher organisms – adaptively acquired responsibility for the injuries and invasions it regularly encounters in its permanently allocated environment or conquered surroundings. Such immune systems could equally be described as organismic early forms of a feeling for transcendence: thanks to the efficiency of these devices, which are constantly at the ready, the organism actively confronts the potential bringers of its death, opposing them with its endogenous capacity to overcome the lethal. Such functions have earned immune systems of this type comparisons to a 'body police' or border patrol. But as the concern, already at this level, is to work out a *modus vivendi* with foreign and invisible powers – and, in so far as these can bring death, 'higher' and 'supernatural' ones – this is a preliminary stage to the behaviour one is accustomed to terming religious or spiritual in human contexts. For every organism, its environment is its transcendence, and the more abstract and unknown the danger from that environment, the more transcendent it appears.

Every gesture of 'suspendedness' [*Hineingehaltensein*] in the open, to use Heidegger's term, includes the anticipatory preparedness of the living system for an encounter with potentially lethal powers of irritation and invasion. 'The creature gazes into the open with all its eyes', Rilke states at the beginning of the eighth *Duino Elegy* – life itself is an exodus that relates inner matters to the environment. The tendency into the open emerges in several evolutionary steps: though virtually all organisms or integrities transcend into the first-level spaces of surprise and conflict that are assigned to them as their respective environments (even plants do this, and animals all the more so), only very few – only humans, as far as we know – achieve the second level of transcendent movement. Through this, the environment is de-restricted to become the world as an integral whole of manifest and latent elements. The second step is the work of language. This not only builds the 'house of being' – Heidegger took this phrase from Zarathustra's animals, which inform the convalescent: 'the house of being rebuilds itself eternally'; it is also the vehicle for the tendencies to run away from that house with which, by means of its inner surpluses, humans move towards the open. It need hardly be explained why the oldest parasite in the world, the world above, only appears with the second transcendence.

I shall refrain from touching on the consequences of these reflections for the human realm at this early stage. For now it is sufficient to note that the continuation of biological evolution in social and cultural evolution leads to an upgrading of immune systems. In the case of humans, we have reason to expect not only a single immune system – the biological one, which is the first in evolutionary terms, but the last in terms of its discovery history. The human sphere contains no fewer than three immune systems, which function layered on top of one another in close collaborative interaction and functional augmentation. In the course of man's mental and socio-cultural evolution, two complementary systems have developed for the pre-emptive processing of injuries: firstly the socio-immunological methods, especially legal and solidaristic ones, but also the military ones by which people resolve their confrontations with distant and foreign aggressors and insulting or harmful neighbours;[8] and secondly the symbolic or psycho-immunological practices on which humans have always relied to cope – with varying success – with their vulnerability through fate, including mortality, in the form of imaginary anticipations and mental armour.[9] It is one of the ironies of these systems that their dark sides are capable of explication, even though their existence depends on consciousness from the start and they consider themselves self-transparent. They do not function behind the backs of subjects, being entirely embedded in their intentional behaviour – nonetheless, it is possible to understand this behaviour better than it is understood by its naïve agents. This is what makes cultural science possible; and it is because a non-naïve approach to symbolic immune systems has itself become vital to the survival of 'cultures' today that cultural science is necessary.[10]

9

In this book, we will naturally be dealing primarily with the manifestations of the third level of immunity. I gather material on the biography of *Homo immunologicus*, guided by the assumption that this is where to find the stuff from which the forms of anthropotechnics are made. By this I mean the methods of mental and physical practising by which humans from the most diverse cultures have attempted to optimize their cosmic and immunological status in the face of vague risks of living and acute certainties of death. Only when these procedures have been grasped in a broad tableau of human 'work on oneself' can we evaluate the newest experiments in genetic engineering, to which, in the current debate, many have reduced the term 'anthropotechnics', reintroduced in 1997.[11] What I have to say on this matter from today's perspective will be woven *ad hoc* into the further course of this study. The tendency of my position is already manifest in the title of this book: whoever notes that it reads 'You Must Change *Your* Life' rather than 'You Must Change *Life*' has immediately understood what is important here.[12]

The hero of the following account, *Homo immunologicus*, who must give his life, with all its dangers and surfeits, a symbolic framework, is the human being that struggles with itself in concern for its form. We will characterize it more closely as the ethical human being, or rather *Homo repetitivus*, *Homo artista*, the human in training. None of the circulating theories of behaviour or action is capable of grasping the practising human – on the contrary: we will understand why previous theories had to make it vanish systematically, regardless of whether they divided the field of observation into work and interaction, processes and communications, or active and contemplative life. With a concept of practice based on a broad anthropological foundation, we finally have the right instrument to overcome the gap, supposedly unbridgeable by methodological means, between biological and cultural phenomena of immunity – that is, between natural processes on the one hand and actions on the other.

It has been stated often enough in endless discussions on the difference between natural and cultural phenomena – and the methods of their scientific investigation – that there are no direct routes from the one sphere to the other. The demand for a direct connection, however, is a superfluous nuisance to which one should pay no heed. It is revealing that it is made primarily by those who claim a reservation, enclosed by metaphysical fences, for what are known here as the humanities.[13] Some defenders of the world of the spirit seek to make the divide between natural events and works of freedom as deep as possible – if need be, down to the very depths of an ontological dualism, supposedly to preserve the crown colonies of the intellectual from naturalistic interference. We will see what is to be thought of such efforts.

In truth, the crossing from nature to culture and vice versa has always stood wide open. It leads across an easily accessible bridge: the practising life. People have committed themselves to its construction since they came into existence – or rather, people only came into existence by applying themselves to the building of said bridge. The human being is the pontifical creature that, from its earliest evolutionary stages, has created tradition-compatible connections between the bridgeheads in the bodily realm and those in cultural programmes. From the start, nature and culture are linked by a broad middle ground of embodied practices – containing languages, rituals and technical skills, in so far as these factors constitute the universal forms of automatized artificialities. This intermediate zone forms a morphologically rich, variable and stable region that can, for the time being, be referred to sufficiently clearly with such conventional categories as education, etiquette, custom, habit formation, training and exercise – without needing to wait for the purveyors of the 'human sciences', who, with all their bluster about culture, create the confusion for whose resolution they subsequently offer their services. It is in this 'garden of the human' – to recall a well-chosen non-physical formula by the physicist Carl Friedrich von Weizsäcker[14] – that the following investigations will find their objects of examination. Gardens are enclosed areas in which plants and arts meet. They form 'cultures' in an uncompromised sense of the word. Whoever enters the gardens of the human encounters the powerful layers of orderly internal and external actions with an immune-systemic tendency above biological substrates. In the face of the worldwide crisis of cultures, which also includes the ghostly neo-religious episodes mentioned at the start, it is more than a mere academic pleasure if the explication of this domain is placed on the agenda of civilization parliaments.[15]

For internal reasons, a practice-anthropological study cannot possibly be carried out in a detached, unbiased fashion. This is because sooner or later, every discourse on 'man' exceeds the limits of mere description and pursues normative goals – whether these are revealed are not. At no time was this more clearly recognizable than in the early European Enlightenment, when anthropology was founded as the original 'civil science'. At that time, the new science of human beings began to push itself in front of the traditional disciplines of logic, ontology and ethics as the modern paradigm of philosophy. Whoever entered the debate on man did so in order to assert – as a 'progressive' – the equation of citizen and human, either with the intention of abolishing the nobles as secessionists of humanity or elevating humanity as a whole to nobility, or – as a 'reactionary' – to portray man as the originally sinful, corrupted and unstable animal that one should, for one's own sake, never release from the hand of its taskmasters – or, medievally put, its *correctores*.

The insurmountable bias of anthropological theory is closely interwoven with the nature of its object. For, as much as the general talk of 'man' may be infused with an egalitarian pathos, whether it concerns the real or stated equality of humans against their biological background or the virtual equal value of cultures before the court of survival-worthiness – it must always take into account that humans are inescapably subject to vertical tensions, in all periods and all cultural areas. Wherever one encounters human beings, they are embedded in achievement fields and status classes. Even the outside observer cannot entirely escape the binding nature of such hierarchical phenomena, as much as they might try to view their tribal idols in isolation. Quite obviously there are certain meta-idols whose authority exceeds cultural boundaries – clearly there are universals of achievement roles, status recognition and excellence from which no one can be emancipated, neither in their own context nor in a foreign one, without finding themselves in the position of the barbarian.

Fatally, the term 'barbarian' is the password that opens up the archives of the twentieth century. It refers to the despiser of achievement, the vandal, the status denier, the iconoclast, who refuses to acknowledge any ranking rules or hierarchy. Whoever wishes to understand the twentieth century must always keep the barbaric factor in view. Precisely in more recent modernity, it was and still is typical to allow an alliance between barbarism and success before a large audience, initially more in the form of insensitive imperialism, and today in the costumes of that invasive vulgarity which advances into virtually all areas through the vehicle of popular culture. That the barbaric position in twentieth-century Europe was even considered the way forward among the purveyors of high culture for a time, extending to a messianism of uneducatedness, indeed the utopia of a new beginning on the clean slate of ignorance, illustrates the extent of the civilizatory crisis this continent has gone through in the last century and a half – including the cultural revolution downwards, which runs through the twentieth century in our climes and casts its shadow ahead onto the twenty-first.

As the following pages deal with the practising life, they lead – in accordance with their topic – to an expedition into the little-explored universe of human vertical tensions. The Platonic Socrates had opened up the phenomenon for occidental culture when he stated *expressis verbis* that man is a being potentially 'superior to himself'.[16] I translate this remark into the observation that all 'cultures', 'subcultures' or 'scenes' are based on central distinctions by which the field of human behavioural possibilities is subdivided into polarized classes. Thus the ascetic 'cultures' know the central distinction of complete versus incomplete, the religious 'cultures' that of sacred versus profane, the aristocratic 'cultures' that of noble versus common, the military 'cultures' that of brave versus cowardly, the political 'cultures' that of powerful versus powerless, the administrative 'cultures' that of superior versus subordinate, the athletic 'cultures' that of excellence versus mediocrity, the economic 'cultures' that of wealth versus lack, the cognitive 'cultures' that of knowledge versus ignorance, and the sapiental 'cultures' that of illumination versus blindness.[17] What all these differentiations have in common is the espousal of the first value, which is considered the attractor in the respective field, while the second pole consistently functions as a factor of repulsion or object of avoidance.

What I here call attractors are, in their mode of effect, the yardstick for vertical tensions that provide orientation in mental systems. Anthropology can no longer ignore the reality of such elements unless it wishes to talk around the decisive vectors of the human condition. Only from the angle of the attractive forces acting 'from above' can one explain why and in what forms *Homo sapiens*, whom the palaeontologists deliver directly to the entrance of the humanities faculty for us, was able to develop into the upward-tending animal described more or less in unison by the historians of ideas and world travellers. Wherever one encounters members of the human race, they always show the traits of a being that is condemned to surrealistic effort. Whoever goes in search of humans will find acrobats.

The reference to the pluralism of central distinctions is not meant only to draw attention to the multifarious 'cultures' or 'scenes'. Such a pluralism of central distinctions also implies an explanation of how, in the history of 'cultures', especially in their more intense and creative phases, there could be superimpositions and mixtures of initially separate areas, reversals of values and intersections of disciplines – phenomena, then, that underlie the forms of spirituality and sophistication still attractive today. It is because the central distinctions can migrate from their original field and settle successfully in foreign zones that we have the spiritual chances which still fascinate us as the higher and highest possibilities of human beings: these include a non-economic definition of wealth, a non-aristocratic definition of the noble, a non-athletic definition of high achievement, a non-dominatory definition of 'above', a non-ascetic definition of perfection, a non-military definition of bravery and a non-bigoted definition of wisdom and fidelity.

To conclude these preparatory remarks, I would like to say a few words on the partiality of the present book and warn of a misunderstanding that could easily occur. The following investigations take their own result as the point of departure: they testify to the realization that there are objects which do not permit their commentator a complete *epoché*, no withdrawal into disinterestedness, even if the project is theory – which presupposes an abstinence from prejudices, caprices and zealous obsessions. We are dealing here with an object that does not leave its analyst alone; it would not be appropriate to the topic if the author were to remain entirely behind the fence of non-intentionality. The matter itself entangles its adepts in an inescapable self-referentiality by presenting them with the practising – the 'ascetic', form-demanding and habit-forming – character of their own behaviour. In his treatise on the battles between the gods underlying ancient Dionysian theatre, the young Nietzsche notes: 'Alas! The magic of these struggles is such, that he who sees them must also take part in them!'[18] Similarly, an anthropology of the practising life is infected by its subject. Dealing with practices, asceticisms and exercises, whether or not they are declared as such, the theorist inevitably encounters his own inner constitution, beyond affirmation and denial.

The same applies to the phenomenon of vertical tensions, without which no purposeful practising is possible. With reference to tensions of this kind, the theorist will do nothing to fend off their bias – aside from the usual willingness to clarify that which causes it. Anthropological study understands an affection by the matter itself as a sign of its philosophical orientation. In truth, philosophy is the mode of thought shaped by the most radical form of prejudice: the passion of being-in-the-world. With the sole exception of specialists in the field, virtually everyone senses that anything which offers less than this passion play remains philosophically trivial. Cultural anthropologists suggest the appealing term 'deep play' for the comprehensively absorbing preoccupations of human beings. From the perspective of a theory of the practising life we would add: the deep plays are those which are moved by the heights.

14

Finally, a word of warning about the misunderstanding that, as stated above, could easily occur. It follows from the fact that at present a large number of people with 'religious' interests are taking part in a large-scale anti-naturalistic mobilization that seeks to fend off the alleged and genuine interventions of the reductive sciences in the hallowed regions of what is experienced and qualitatively felt. It is immediately clear how the arguments against naturalism serve an early epistemological defence of the facts of faith. Whoever transfers what they experience to an inner fortress that cannot be conquered by the scientistic Saracens of today or tomorrow can, initially at least, believe they have done enough to place these delicate treasures under philosophical protection. This at least secures the conditions of the possibility of religiosity, if not the actual tenets of faith. The criticism levelled at naturalists – represented mostly by assertive neurologists today – rightly on the whole, concerns the tendency, conditioned by their field, to view the facts of consciousness in functional distortion and external reflection, without being able to do justice to the irre-solvable single-mindedness of the ideational elements that appear in the first-person perspective.

To those who deal with these thought figures,[19] I would like to say that at their core, the following investigations serve neither natural-istic nor functionalistic interests, although I consider it desirable to keep open the possibility of drawing on the results of such research from the 'spirit side' too – especially under the aforementioned immunological aspect. If my intention leads to a defamiliarization or, at times, a provocative re-description of the objects of analysis, it is not because external systems of logic are applied to them – as one can observe when neuroscientists talk about Christology[20] or geneticists discuss the DNA of monotheists.[21] The defamiliarization resulting from my theoretical exercises, if it is perceived as such, rests entirely on internal translations by which the internal anthropotech-nic languages are made explicit in the spiritual systems themselves. What I refer to here as 'internal languages' are, as can be shown, already contained in the countless 'religiously' or ethically coded practice systems, so making them explicit does not cause any foreign infiltration. With their help, the things inherently expressed by the holy texts and time-honoured rules are restated in a closely connected alternative language. Repetition plus translation plus generalization results, with the correct calculation, in clarification. If there is such a thing as 'progress in religion', it can only manifest itself as increasing explicitness.

The Planet of the Practising

— 1 —

THE COMMAND FROM THE STONE

Rilke's Experience

I will first of all present an aesthetic example to explain the phenomenon of vertical tensions and their meaning for the reorientation of
the confused existence of modern humans: the well-known sonnet
'Archaic Torso of Apollo', which opens the cycle *New Poems: The
Other Part* from 1908. Beginning with a poetic text seems apposite
because – aside from the fact that the title of this book is taken from
it – its assignment to the artistic field makes it less likely to provoke
those anti-authoritarian reflexes which follow almost compulsively
from any encounter with statements made dogmatically or from
above – 'what does "above" mean anyway!' The aesthetic construct,
and nothing else, has taught us to expose ourselves to a non-enslaving
experience of rank differences. The work of art is even allowed to
'tell' us, those who have run away from form, something, because
it quite obviously does not embody the intention to confine us. 'La
poésie ne s'impose plus, elle s'expose.'[1] Something that exposes itself
and proves itself in this test gains unpresumed authority. In the space
of aesthetic simulation, which is at once the emergency space for the
success and failure of the artistic construct, the powerless superiority
of the works can affect observers who otherwise take pains to ensure
that they have no lord, old or new, above them.

Rilke's 'Torso' is particularly suited to posing the question of the
source of authority, as it constitutes an experiment about allowing
oneself to be told something. As we know, Rilke, under the influence
of Auguste Rodin, whom he had assisted between 1905 and 1906 in
Meudon as a private secretary, turned away from the art nouveau-
like, sensitized-atmospheric poetic approach of his early years to
pursue a view of art determined more strongly by the 'priority of
the object'. The proto-modern pathos of making way for the object

19

without depicting it in a manner 'true to nature', like that of the old masters, led in Rilke's case to the concept of the thing-poem – and thus to a temporarily convincing new answer to the question of the source of aesthetic and ethical authority. From that point, it would be the things themselves from which all authority would come – or rather: from this respectively current singular thing that turns to me by demanding my full gaze. This is only possible because thing-being would now no longer mean anything but this: having something to say.

In his field, and with his means, Rilke carries out an operation that one could philosophically describe as the 'transformation of being into message' (more commonly, 'linguistic turn'). 'Being that can be understood is language', Heidegger would later state – which conversely implies that language abandoned by being becomes mere chatter. When, and only when, being contracts in privileged things and turns to us via these things can we hope to escape the increasing randomness, both aesthetically and philosophically. In the face of the galloping inflation of chatter, it was inevitable that such a hope would draw in numerous artists and people of 'spirit' around 1900. In the midst of the ubiquitous dealings with prostituted signs, the thing-poem was capable of opening up the prospect of returning to credible experiences of meaning. It did this by tying language to the gold standard of what things themselves communicate. Where randomness is disabled, authority should shine forth.

It is clear enough that not every something can be elevated to the rank of a thing – otherwise everything and everyone would be speaking once more, and the chatter would spread from humans to things. Rilke privileges two categories of 'entities' [*Seienden*], to express it in the papery diction of philosophy, that are eligible for the lofty task of acting as message-things – artifices and living creatures – with the latter gaining their particular quality from the former, as if animals were being's highest works of art before humans. Inherent to both is a message energy that does not activate itself, but requires the poet as a decoder and messenger. This underlies the complicity between the speaking thing and Rilke's poetry – just as, only a few years later, Heidegger's things would conspire with the 'legend' of a contemplative philosophy that no longer wants to be a mere scholastic discipline.

These somewhat accelerated remarks outline a framework in which we can attempt a brief reading of the 'Torso' poem. I am assuming that the torso mentioned in the sonnet is meant to embody a 'thing' in the eminent sense of the word, precisely because it is merely the leftover of a complete sculpture. We know from accounts of Rilke's life that his stay in Rodin's workshops taught him how modern sculpture had advanced to the genre of the autonomous torso.[2] The poet's view of the mutilated body thus has nothing to do with the previous century's Romanticism of fragments and ruins; it is part of the breakthrough in modern art to the concept of the object that states itself with authority and the body that publicizes itself with authorization.

ARCHAIC TORSO OF APOLLO

We never knew his head and all the light
that ripened in his fabled eyes. But
his torso still glows like a gas lamp dimmed
in which his gaze, lit long ago,

holds fast and shines. Otherwise the surge
of the breast could not blind you, nor a smile
run through the slight twist of the loins
toward that centre where procreation thrived.

Otherwise this stone would stand deformed and curt
under the shoulders' transparent plunge
and not glisten just like wild beasts' fur

and not burst forth from all its contours
like a star: for there is no place
that does not see you. You must change your life.[3]

Whoever absorbs anything vaguely concrete upon first reading has understood this much: the poem is dealing with perfection – a perfection that seems all the more binding and mysterious because it is the perfection of a fragment. It is reasonable to suppose that this work was also an expression of thanks to Rodin, his master in his Paris days, for the concept of the autonomous torso, which he had encountered in his workshop. The reason for the existence of the perfection conjured up in these fourteen lines is that it possesses – independently of its material carrier's mutilation – the authorization to form a message that appeals from within itself. This power of appeal is exquisitely evident in the object evoked here. The perfect thing is that which articulates an entire principle of being. The poem has to perform no more and no less than to perceive the principle of being in the thing and adapt it to its own existence – with the aim of becoming a construct with an equal power to convey a message.

Rilke's torso can be experienced as the bearer of the attribute 'perfect' because it brings along something that permits it to snub

21

the usual expectation of a morphological whole. This gesture is one of the motifs of modernity's turn against the principle of imitating nature, that is to say, imitating predefined morphological expectations. It is still capable of perceiving message-totalities and autonomous thing-signals when no morphologically intact figures are left – indeed, precisely then. The sense for perfection withdraws from the forms of nature – probably because nature itself is in the process of losing its ontological authority. The popularization of photography also increasingly devalues the standard views of things. As the first edition of the visible, nature comes into discredit. It can no longer assert its authority as the sender of binding messages – for reasons that ultimately come from its disenchantment through being scientifically explored and technically outdone. After this shift, 'being perfect' takes on an altered meaning: it means having something to say that is more meaningful than the chatter of conventional totalities. Now the torsos and their ilk have their turn: the hour of those forms that do not remind us of anything has come. Fragments, cripples and hybrids formulate something that cannot be conveyed by the common whole forms and happy integrities; intensity beats standard perfection. A hundred years after Rilke pointed to this, we probably understand it better even than his own contemporaries, as our perceptual capacity has been numbed and plundered by the chatter of flawless bodies more than in any preceding generation.

These observations will have made it clear how the phenomenon of being spoken to from above embodies itself in an aesthetic construct. To understand an appeal experience of this kind, it is not necessary to address the assumption, accepted by Rilke, that the torso he describes was once the statue of a god – of Apollo, the curators of the day believed. One cannot entirely rule out an element of art nouveau-esque reverence for education in the poet's experience of the sculpture; it is said that Rilke encountered the poem's real-life model during a visit to the Louvre, and as far as we know, it would have been a piece from the classical period of Greek sculpture rather than an archaic work of art. What the poet has to say to the torso of the supposed Apollo, however, is more than a note on an excursion to the antiques collection. The author's point is not that the thing depicts an extinct god who might be of interest to the humanistically educated, but that the god in the stone constitutes a thing-construct that is still on air. We are dealing with a document of how newer message ontology outgrew traditional theologies. Here, being itself is understood as having more power to speak and transmit, and more potent authority, than God, the ruling idol of religions. In modern times, even a

God can find himself among the pretty figures that no longer mean anything to us – assuming they do not become openly irksome. The thing filled with being, however, does not cease to speak to us when its moment has come.

We are approaching the critical point: the final two lines have always captivated readers. They awaken feelings of significance that virtually unhinge the entire lyric construct – as if it were merely the path towards a climax for which the rest is laid out. And indeed, the two closing sentences – 'for there is no place / that does not see you. You must change your life.' – almost began an independent career, imprinting themselves on the memories of the educated in general, not only Rilke admirers and poetry fanatics. I admit: on this particular occasion, I am inclined to agree with the need to take lines out of their context, not least because the popular taste for the beautiful places sometimes contains a valid judgement on authentic moments of climax. One does not need to be an enthusiast to understand why those closing lines have developed a life of their own. In their dignified brevity and mystical simplicity, they radiate an art-evangelical energy that can scarcely be found in any other passage from recent language art.

At first glance, the initial statement seems the more enigmatic one. Whoever understands or accepts it, or allows it to apply in the lyric context – which amounts to the same in this case – is immediately affected by an almost hypnotic suggestion. By seeking to 'understand', one gives credit to a turn of phrase that reverses the everyday relationship between the seer and the seen. That I see the torso with its stout shoulders and stumps is one aspect; that I dreamily add the missing parts – the head, the arms, the legs and the genitals – in my mind and associatively animate them is a further aspect. If need be, I can even follow Rilke's suggestion and imagine a smile extending from an invisible mouth to vanished genitals. A completely different aspect, however, the thoroughly incommensurable one, lies in the imposition of accepting that the torso sees me while I observe it – indeed, that it eyes me more sharply than I can look at it.

The ability to perform the inner gesture with which one makes space for this improbability inside oneself most probably consists precisely in the talent that Max Weber denied having. This talent is 'religiosity', understood as an innate disposition and a talent that can be developed, making it comparable to musicality. One can practise it, just as one practises melodic passages or syntactic patterns. In this sense, religiosity is congruent with a certain grammatical promiscuity. Where it operates, objects elastically exchange places with subjects.

Therefore, if I accept that there are – on the shimmering surface of the mutilated stone – numerous 'places' that amount to eyes and see me, I am performing an operation with a micro-religious quality – and which, once understood, one will recognize at all levels of macro-religiously developed systems as the primary module of a 'pious' inner action. In the position where the object usually appears, never looking back because it is an object, I now 'recognize' a subject with the ability to look and return gazes. Thus, as a hypothetical believer, I accept the insinuation of a subject that dwells inside the respective place, and wait to see what this pliable development will make of me. (We note: even the 'deepest' or most virtuosic piety cannot achieve more than habitualized insinuations.) I receive the reward for my willingness to participate in the object–subject reversal in the form of a private illumination – in the present case, as an aesthetic movedness. The torso, which has no place that does not see me, likewise does not impose itself – it exposes itself. It exposes itself by testing whether I will recognize it as a seer. Acknowledging it as a seer essentially means 'believing' in it, where believing, as noted above, refers to the inner operations that are necessary to conceive of the vital principle in the stone as a sender of discrete addressed energies. If I somehow succeed in this, I am also able to take the glow of subjectivity away from the stone. I tentatively accept the way it stands there in exemplary radiance, and receive the starlike eruption of its surplus of authority and soul.

It is only in this context that the name of the depicted has any significance. What appears in the former statue of Apollo, however, cannot simply be equated with the Olympian of the same name, who had to ensure light, contours, foreknowledge and security of form in his days of completeness. Rather, as the poem's title implies, he stands for something much older, something rising from prehistoric sources. He symbolizes a divine magma in which something of the first ordering force, as old as the world itself, becomes manifest. There is no doubt that memories of Rodin and his cyclopian work ethic had an effect on Rilke here. During his work with the great artist, he experienced what it means to work on the surfaces of bodies until they are nothing but a fabric of carefully shaped, luminous, almost seeing 'places'.[4] A few years earlier, he had written of Rodin's sculptures that 'there were endless places, and none of them did not have something happening in them'.[5] Each place is a point at which Apollo, the god of forms and surfaces, makes a visually intense and haptically palpable compromise with his older opponent Dionysus, the god of urges and currents. That this energized Apollo embodies a manifestation of Dionysus is indicated by the statement that the stone glistens 'like wild beasts' fur': Rilke had read his Nietzsche. Here we encounter the second micro-religious or proto-musical module: the notorious 'this stands for that', 'the one appears in the other' or 'the deep layer is present in the surface' – figures without which no religious discourse would ever have come about. They tell us that religiosity is a form of hermeneutical flexibility and can be trained.

'For there is no place / that does not see you. You must change your life.' It remains to be shown why the second sentence, which seemingly requires no interpretation, is actually far more enigmatic than the first. It is not only its lack of preparation, its suddenness that is mysterious. 'You must change your life' – these words seem to come from a sphere in which no objections can be raised. Nor can we establish from where they are spoken; only their verticality is beyond doubt. It is unclear whether this dictum shoots straight up from the ground to stand in my way like a pillar, or falls from the sky to transform the road before me into an abyss, such that my next step should already belong to the changed life that has been demanded. It is not enough to say that Rilke retranslated ethics in an aestheticizing fashion into a succinct, cyclopian, archaic-brutal form. He discovered a stone that embodies the torso of 'religion', ethics and asceticism as such: a construct that exudes a call from above, reduced to the pure command, the unconditional instruction, the illuminated utterance of being that can be understood – and which only speaks in the imperative.

If one wished to transfer all the teachings of the papyrus religions, the parchment religions, the stylus and quill religions, the calligraphic and typographical, all order rules and sect programmes, all instructions for meditation and doctrines of stages, and all training programmes and dietologies into a single workshop where they would be summarized in a final act of editing: their utmost concentrate would express nothing other than what the poet sees emanating from the archaic torso of Apollo in a moment of translucidity.

'You must change your life!' – this is the imperative that exceeds the options of hypothetical and categorical. It is the absolute imperative – the quintessential metanoetic command. It provides the keyword for revolution in the second person singular. It defines life as a slope from its higher to its lower forms. I am already living, but something is telling me with unchallengeable authority: you are not living properly. The numinous authority of form enjoys the prerogative of being able to tell me 'You must'. It is the authority of a different life in this

25

life. This authority touches on a subtle insufficiency within me that is older and freer than sin; it is my innermost not-yet. In my most conscious moment, I am affected by the absolute objection to my status quo: my change is the one thing that is necessary. If you do indeed subsequently change your life, what you are doing is no different from what you desire with your whole will as soon as you feel how a vertical tension that is valid for you unhinges your life.

As well as this ethical-revolutionary reading, there are also somewhat more concrete and psychologically accessible interpretations of the torso poem. There is no need to limit our commentary to lofty art-philosophical and being-philosophical positions; the experience of authority that binds the poet for a moment to the ancient statue can perhaps be reconstructed more plausibly on a more sensual, aesthetically comprehensible level. This raises the somatic, or, more precisely, the auto-erotic and masculine-athletic, impressions of the sculpture, which must have provoked in the poet (who, in the language of his time, was a neurasthenic and a weak-bodied introvert) an empathetic experience of the antipodal mode of being that is native to strong 'body people'. This is in keeping with a fact that did not escape Rilke, namely that, in the immeasurably rich statue culture of the ancient Greeks, there was a dominant system of physical and mental kinship between gods and athletes in which resemblance could reach the level of identity. A god was always a form of sportsman too, and the sportsman – especially the one celebrated in a hymn of praise and crowned with a laurel wreath – was always also a god of sorts. Hence the athlete's body, which unifies beauty and discipline into a calm readiness for action, offers itself as one of the most understandable and convincing manifestations of authority.

The authoritative body of the god-athlete has an immediate effect on the viewer through its exemplarity. It too says concisely: 'You must change your life!', and in so doing simultaneously shows what model this change should follow. It displays how being and being exemplary converge. Every classical statue was a petrified or bronze-cast teaching permit in ethical matters. What was known as Platonism, an otherwise rather un-Greek affair, could only find its home in Greece because the so-called ideas had already established themselves in the form of statues. Platonic love was already widely anchored in society some time before Plato, as a training affect in exercises between the somatically perfect and the beginners, and this eros worked in both directions – from the model to his emulators and from the desirer to his model. Now, I certainly do not wish to posit any narcissistic relationship between Rilke and a fragment of ancient Greek art exhibited in the Louvre glorifying the male body cult. It is plausible, however, that the author of the sonnet saw some of the radiance of ancient athletic vitalism and the muscular theology of the wrestlers in the palaestra in the real torso he viewed. The difference of vitality between the elevated and profane bodies must have spoken to him directly, even when faced with a mere relic of idealized masculinity.

With this way of feeling, the poet would have been no more or less than a sensitive contemporary of the late renaissance in Europe, which reached a critical stage around 1900. Its defining trait is the return of the athlete as the key figure of ancient somatic idealism. With this, the process of post-Christian cultural reorganization that had begun around 1400 as a philological and artistic Renaissance entered its mass-cultural phase. Its foremost characteristic is sport, and it can never be emphasized too much how deeply it affected the ethos of the moderns. The restarting of the Olympics (and the excessive popularization of soccer in Europe and South America) marked the beginning of its triumph, whose end is barely in sight, unless one interprets the current doping corruption as the indication of an imminent breakdown – though no one can say at present what might replace athletism. The cult of sport that exploded around 1900 possesses an outstanding intellectual-historical, or rather ethical-historical and asceticism-historical, significance, as it demonstrates an epochal change of emphasis in practice behaviour – a transformation best described as a re-somatization or a de-spiritualization of asceticisms. In this respect, sport is the most explicit realization of Young Hegelianism, the philosophical movement whose motto was 'the resurrection of the flesh in this life'. Of the two great ideas of the nineteenth century, socialism and somatism, it was clearly only the latter that could be widely established, and one need not be a prophet to assert that the twenty-first century will belong to it completely, even more than the twentieth.

After all we have said, it does not seem inappropriate to suggest that Rilke had some participation in the somatic and athletic renaissance, even though his connection was obviously indirect and mediated by artefacts, namely the category of 'things' discussed above. Rilke certainly made no secret of feeling stimulated by Nietzsche, and he equally – in the 'Letter of the Young Worker'[6] – took up the timely cause of reclaiming sexuality from the crippling tradition of Christian 'renunciation of instincts'.

The presence of the athletic *mana* in the torso, still shining and licensed to teach, contains an element of orientational energy that I shall term – even if the phrase initially seems inappropriate – 'trainer authority'. In this capacity and character, it addresses the present-day weaklings of the body and of life with words of an unmistakably sport-ethical nature. The statement 'You must change your life!' can now be heard as the refrain of a language of getting in shape. It forms part of a new rhetorical genre: the coach discourse, their changing-room lecture to a weakly performing team. Whoever speaks to teams must address each individual player as if speaking to them alone. Such speeches cannot be tolerated in company, but they are constitutive for teams.

Give up your attachment to comfortable ways of living – show yourself in the gymnasium (*gymnos* = 'naked'), prove that you are not indifferent to the difference between perfect and imperfect, demonstrate to us that achievement – excellence, *areté*, *virtù* – has not remained a foreign word to you, admit that you have motives for new endeavours! Above all: only grant the suspicion that sport is a pastime for the most stupid as much space as it deserves, do not misuse it as a pretext to drift further in your customary state of self-neglect, distrust the philistine in yourself who thinks you are just fine as you are! Hear the voice from the stone, do not resist the call to get in shape! Seize the chance to train with a god!

— 2 —

REMOTE VIEW OF THE
ASCETIC PLANET

Nietzsche's Antiquity Project

The term 'late renaissance', which I have suggested to characterize the still inadequately understood sport cult phenomenon that appeared after 1900, proves helpful in dating Nietzsche's intervention in the midst of the discourses of the Enlightenment as it changed into modernity. In truth, any attempt to understand Nietzsche must begin with a reflection on his date. With this thinker, it is not sufficient to cast a glance at his dates of birth and death in order to know when he was living and thinking. One of the enormities of this author is the impossibility of identifying him as a child of his time. Naturally it is easy to point to the aspects of his work that are typical of the time. One can show how, as an artist, he made the transition from Biedermeier-weakened Romanticism to a late Romantically tinged modernity; as a publicist, the leap from Wagnerism to a prophetic elitism; as a thinker, the change of position from symbolist late idealism to perspectival naturalism – or, expressed in names, from Schopenhauer to Darwin. If only the aspects of Nietzsche that were indebted to his epoch were significant, the reception of his work would not have lasted beyond 1914 – the turning point from which the moderns, once and for all, had other concerns; and as early as 1927, Heidegger was already elevating these 'other concerns' to the level of concern [*Sorge*] itself, concern *sans phrase*.

In truth, Nietzsche's impulses only began to unfold in that age of 'other concerns', and there is no end to this work of unfolding in sight. The author of *The Genealogy of Morals* is the most philosophically observant contemporary of the processes referred to with the concept of the 'somatic or athletic renaissance' introduced above. In order to gain a suitable idea of their thrust and their pull, it is indispensable to reread his writings on the art of living, which pose the question of

29

the true date of Nietzsche's intellectual existence for strong objective reasons.

One can believe without further investigation the claim that the author occasionally thought of himself as someone from the Renaissance who had ended up in the wrong period. What is relevant in our context is not the sense of an elective past, or some homesickness for a bygone golden age for art and uncompromising methods. The decisive aspect is rather the fact that Nietzsche was himself an actor in a genuine renaissance, and that the only reason he did not identify himself accordingly is that his notion of renaissance was too dependent on art-historical conventions. It is not for nothing that the young Nietzsche was one of the most intensive readers of Jacob Burckhardt's epoch-morphological masterpiece *Die Kultur der Renaissance in Italien* (1860), a work in which the historian gathered together several centuries' worth of culture to form a single giant mural. Stepping back from this huge picture, the art-recipient of the late nineteenth century had no choice but to long for times past and project himself into a suitable part of the painting. Everything suggests that Nietzsche was no stranger to such exercises. He may have transported himself to the army camp of Castruccio Castracani to experience heroic vitalism up close, or gone for a walk along the Lungotevere, dreaming of becoming a Cesare Borgia of philosophy.

Nonetheless, it would have sufficed for the wanderer of Sils Maria to abandon the art-historically confined notion of renaissance and advance to a process-theoretical one; then he would inevitably have reached the conclusion that the age of 'rebirth' had by no means ended with the artistic and cultural events of the fifteenth and sixteenth centuries. From a processual perspective, Nietzsche would have recognized himself at the current pivot of an advancing renaissance that was in the process of outgrowing its educated middle-class definitions. Via the mediation of the Enlightenment, this movement had changed from a hobby among a tiny literate elite and their secretaries, an ostentatious amusement among princely and mercantile art patrons and their masterly suppliers (who established a first 'art system'[7]), into a national, a European, indeed a planetary matter. In order to spread from the few to the many, the renaissance had to discard its humanistic exterior and reveal itself as the return of ancient mass culture. The true renaissance question, reformulated in the terminology of practical philosophy – namely, whether other forms of life are possible and permissible for us alongside and after Christianity, especially ones whose patterns are derived from Greek and Roman (perhaps even Egyptian or Indian) antiquity – was no longer a secret discourse or an academic exercise in the nineteenth century, but rather an epochal passion, an inescapable *pro nobis*. Hence one must beware of the false conclusion that the topic of the 'life reform', which was in the air from the Romantics and early socialists on, though it only reached its charismatic peak after 1900, was a mere sectarian quirk – with the 'reform houses'[8] as an endearingly old-fashioned relic. The life reform is rather the renaissance programme itself, transferred from bourgeois art history to the arena of battles for the true *modus vivendi* of the moderns. Placing Nietzsche in this arena means dating him correctly, for the time being.

This expansion of the renaissance zone is no more than a first step, however. If one left it at that, one would only have re-dated Nietzsche semi-correctly at best. One would certainly have done him justice by assimilating his present into a past of his choosing; as far as his more radical 'chronopolitics' is concerned, however, his striving to break out of the Modern Age as such, one would not really be taking him seriously. This attempt to break out is what holds the far greater provocation and the far more potent food for thought. Dealing with it also demands more than the re-dating suggestion that has been common for some time, which posits that Nietzsche belongs not to modernity but to postmodernity, as one of its founding fathers. Nietzsche's position cannot be defined in terms of a choice between modern and postmodern – in fact, it does not even show up on this field. Nietzsche's departure to a period that suited him did not, as some would have it, take him into an era 'after modernity', whatever that might mean. What he envisaged was not a modernization of modernity, no progress beyond the time of progress. Nor did he, by any means, break up the one historical narrative into several, as seemed plausible to critical minds working on the self-investigation of the Enlightenment during the late twentieth century. Nietzsche was concerned with a radical allochrony, a fundamental other-timeliness in the midst of the present.

His true date is therefore antiquity – and, because antiquity can only exist in modern times as repetition, neo-antiquity. The neo-ancient antiquity in which Nietzsche locates himself is not meant as a mere programme, something that could be placed on the agenda to meet the needs of today. An arranged antiquity would go against Nietzsche's intentions, as its reservation on the daily agenda would itself be an unwelcome act of modernism. Agendas provide the forms of work that modernity uses to arrange its steps on the timeline to the future, whether one interprets them as a meaningful or empty forward motion. What Nietzsche had in mind was not a repetition

31

of ancient patterns on the model of fashion, whose antiquity is never more than a few years ago; the question of whether fashions rotate in decades or millennia was of no consequence to him. His concept of allochrony – initially introduced shyly as 'untimeliness', then later radicalized to an exit from modernity – is based on the idea, as suggestive as it is fantastic, that antiquity has no need of repetitions enacted in subsequent periods, because it 'essentially' returns constantly on its own strength. In other words, antiquity – or the ancient – is not an overcome phase of cultural development that is only represented in the collective memory and can be summoned by the wilfulness of education. It is rather a kind of constant present – a depth time, a nature time, a time of being – that continues underneath the theatre of memory and innovation that occupies cultural time. If one could show how recurrence defeats repetition and the circle makes a fool of the line, this would not only demonstrate an understanding of the point of Nietzsche's decisive self-dating; it would also fulfil the precondition for any judgement on whether, and in what sense, Nietzsche is our contemporary, and whether, and to what extent, we are or wish to be his contemporaries.

This much should be clear by now: the term 'renaissance' can only remain fruitful and demanding as long as it refers to a far-reaching idea: that it is the fate of Europeans to develop life and forms of life according to and alongside the Christian definitions of life and forms of life. From Nietzsche's perspective, it is not a matter of imitating ancient patterns, but rather – before all revivals of specific content – of revealing antiquity as a mode of non-historical, non-forward-directed, non-progressive time. This calls for no less than the suspension of Christian cultural time, whether it is envisaged as an apocalyptic acceleration of the end or a patient pilgrimage through the world – or as a church-politically prudent combination of both modes. It goes without saying that enlightened cultural time, the time of progress and the time of capital are also affected by this suspension.

Only in this context is there any point in re-examining Nietzsche's overexcited confrontation of Christianity. From today's perspective, it is a somewhat unpleasant chapter to which one only returns because the reasons for doing so are stronger than the reservations. One could pass over it as an episode of *fin-de-siècle* neurosis, not least out of sympathy for the author, were it not simultaneously the vehicle for Nietzsche's most valuable and enduring insights. The anti-Christian polemic shows its productive side if one transfers it to the context of Nietzsche's 'antiquity project', which, as we have seen, is devoted to a regeneratively intended return to the pre-Christian era (and hence an emancipation from the schema antiquity–Middle Ages–Modern Age). Wanting to go back to a time before Christianity here means situating oneself prior to a *modus vivendi* whose binding nature has meanwhile been undone and now only seems effective in inauthentic adaptations, culturally Christian translations and pity-ethical (as well as pity-political, including self-pity-political) re-stylizations. In leaping back to before the cultural period of Christianity, he is by no means espousing its humanistic reform – this had been the programme of compromise in Modern Age Europe, which created the enormous hybrid of 'Christian humanism' through centuries of literary, pedagogical and philanthropic work – from Erasmus to T. S. Eliot, from Comenius to Montessori, and from Ignatius to Albert Schweitzer. What occupies him does not concern the conditions of the possibility of an amalgam, but rather the preconditions for a radical break with the system of half-measures. In Nietzsche's usage, the word 'Christianity' does not even refer primarily to the religion; using it like a code word, he is thinking more of a particular religio-metaphysically influenced disposition, an ascetically (in the penitent and self-denying sense) defined attitude to the world, an unfortunate form of life deferral, focus on the hereafter and quarrel with secular facts – in *The Antichrist*, Nietzsche inveighed against all this with the fury of a man who wanted to bring the pillars of the Western religious tradition, and hence also of his own existence, crashing down.

All this can be used to support my thesis, which connects these reflections to the subject of the book: in his role as the protagonist and medium of a differently understood antiquity, Nietzsche becomes the discoverer of ascetic cultures in their immeasurable historical extension. Here it is relevant to observe that the word *áskesis* (alongside the word *meléte*, which is also the name of a muse) simply means 'exercise' or 'training' in ancient Greek. In the wake of his new division of ascetic opinion, Nietzsche not only stumbles upon the fundamental meaning of the practising life for the development of styles of existence or 'cultures'. He puts his finger on what he sees as the decisive separation for all moralities, namely into the asceticisms of the healthy and those of the sick, though he does not show any reservations about presenting the antithesis with an almost caricatural harshness. The healthy – a word that has long been subjected to countless deconstructions[9] – are those who, because they are healthy, want to grow through good asceticisms; and the sick are those who, because they are sick, plot revenge with bad asceticisms.

This can only be called a hair-raising simplification of the situation.

Nonetheless, one has to admit: hammering home these arguments does bring something to light that must be acknowledged as one of the greatest discoveries of intellectual history. Nietzsche is no more or less than the Schliemann of asceticisms. In the midst of the excavation sites, surrounded by the psychopathic rubble of millennia and the ruins of morbid palaces, he was completely right to assume the triumphant expression of a discoverer. We know today that he had dug in the right place; what he dug up, however – to continue the metaphor – was not Homer's Troy, but a later layer. And a large number of the asceticisms to which he referred polemically were precisely not expressions of life-denial and metaphysical servility; it was rather a matter of heroism in a spiritual disguise. Nietzsche's occasional misinterpretations cannot detract from the value of his discovery. With his find, Nietzsche stands fatally – in the best sense of the word – at the start of modern, non-spiritualistic ascetologies along with their physio- and psychotechnic annexes, with dietologies and self-referential trainings, and hence all the forms of self-referential practising and working on one's own vital form that I bring together in the term 'anthropotechnics'.

The significance of the impulse coming from Nietzsche's new view of ascetic phenomena can hardly be overestimated. By shifting himself to a 'supra-epochal' antiquity that waits beneath every medieval and modern non-antiquity, and under every future, he attained the necessary level of eccentricity to cast a glance, as if from without, at his own time and others. His alternative self-dating allowed him to leap out of the present, giving him the necessary eyesight to encompass the continuum of advanced civilizations, the three-thousand-year empire of mental exercises, self-trainings, self-elevations and self-lowerings – in short, the universe of metaphysically coded vertical tension – in an unprecedented synopsis.

Here we should quote especially those sections from Nietzsche's central morality-critical work *The Genealogy of Morals* that deal with their subject in a diction of Olympian clarity. In the decisive passage he discusses the practice forms of that life-denial or world-weariness which, according to Nietzsche, exemplifies the morphological circle of sick asceticisms in general.

> The ascetic [of the priestly-sick type] treats life as a wrong path on which one must walk backwards till one comes to the place where it starts; or he treats it as an error which one may, nay *must*, refute by action: for he *demands* that he should be followed; he enforces, where he can, *his* valuation of existence. What does this mean? Such a monstrous valuation is not an exceptional care, or a curiosity recorded in human history: it is one of the broadest and longest facts that exist.

Reading from the vantage point of a distant star the capital letters of our earthly life would perchance lead to the conclusion that the earth was the truly *ascetic planet*, a den of discontented, arrogant, and repulsive creatures, who never got rid of a deep disgust of themselves, of the world, of all life, and did themselves as much hurt as possible out of pleasure in hurting – presumably their one and only pleasure.[10]

With this note, Nietzsche presents himself as the pioneer of a new human science that one could describe as a planetary science of culture. Its method consists in observing our heavenly body using 'photographs' of cultural formations as if from a great altitude. Through the new image-producing abstractions, the life of the earthlings is searched for more general patterns – with asceticism coming to light as a historically developed structure that Nietzsche quite legitimately calls one of 'the broadest and longest facts that exist'. These 'facts' demand a suitable cartography and a corresponding geography and basic science. That is all the genealogy of morals seeks to be. The new science of the origins of moral systems (and *eo ipso* of morally governed forms of life and practice) is the first manifestation of General Ascetology. It begins the explication history of religions and systems of ethics as anthropotechnic praxes.

We must not let ourselves be distracted by the fact that, in this passage, Nietzsche is referring exclusively to the asceticisms of the sick and their priestly minders. The ascetic planet he sights is the planet of the practising as a whole, the planet of advanced-civilized humans, the planet of those who have begun to give their existence forms and contents under vertical tensions in countless programmes of effort, some more and some less strictly coded. When Nietzsche speaks of the ascetic planet, it is not because he would rather have been born on a more relaxed star. His antiquity-instinct tells him that every heavenly body worth inhabiting must – correctly understood – be an ascetic planet inhabited by the practising, the aspiring and the virtuosos. What is antiquity for him but the code word for the age in which humans had to become strong enough for a sacred-imperial image of the whole? Inherent in the great worldviews of antiquity was the intention of showing mortals how they could live in harmony with the 'universe', even and especially when that whole showed them its baffling side, its lack of consideration for individuals. What one called the wisdom of the ancients was essentially a tragic holism, a self-integration within the great whole, that could not be achieved without heroism. Nietzsche's planet would become the place whose inhabitants, especially the male ones, would carry the weight of the world anew without self-pity – in keeping with the Stoic maxim that

35

the only important thing is to keep oneself in shape for the cosmos. Some of this appeared not much later in Heidegger's doctrine of concern, at whose call mortals must adjust to the burden character of Dasein (after 1918, the mortals were primarily the wounded and non-fallen, who were meant to keep themselves ready for other forms of death on other fronts). Under no circumstances could the earth remain an institution in which the *ressentiment* programmes of the sick and the compensation-claiming skills of the insulted determined the climate.

In his differentiation between asceticisms, Nietzsche posited a clear divide between the priestly varieties on the one side, illuminated by his vicious gaze, and the disciplinary rules of intellectual workers, philosophers and artists as well as the exercises of warriors and athletes on the other side. If the former are concerned with what one might call a *pathogogical* asceticism – an artful self-violation among an elite of sufferers that empowers them to lead other sufferers and induce the healthy to become co-sick – the latter only impose their regulations on themselves because they see them as a means of reaching their optimum as thinkers and creators of works. What Nietzsche calls the 'pathos of distance'[11] is devoted entirely to the division of asceticisms. Its intention is to 'keep the missions separate' and set the exercises whereby those who are successful, good and healthy can become more successful, good and healthy apart from those which enable resolute failures, the malicious and the sick to place themselves on pedestals and pulpits – whether for the sake of perversely acquired feelings of superiority or to distract themselves from their tormenting interest in their own sickness and failure.[12] Needless to say, the opposition of healthy and sick should not be taken as purely medical: it serves as the central distinction in an ethics that gives a life with the 'first movement' ('be a self-propelling wheel!' [*Thus Spoke Zarathustra*]) priority over a life dominated by inhibited movement.

The extension of the moral-historical perspective makes the meaning of the thesis of the athletic and somatic renaissance apparent. At the transition from the nineteenth to the twentieth century, the phenomenon labelled the 'rebirth of antiquity' in the language regulations of art history entered a phase that fundamentally modified the motives of our identification with cultural relics from antiquity, even from the early classical period. Here, as we have seen, one finds a regression to a time in which the changing of life had not yet fallen under the command of life-denying asceticisms. This 'supra-epochal' time could just as easily be called the future, and what seems like a regression towards it could also be conceived of as a leap forwards. The manner in which Rilke experienced the torso of Apollo testified to the same cultural shift that Nietzsche was pursuing when he pushed his reflections on the establishment of the priestly, 'bio-negative', spiritualistic asceticisms to the point where the paradoxical struggle of the suffering life against itself became apparent. In discovering the ascetological foundations of higher human forms of life, he assigned a new meaning to 'morality'. The power of the practice layer in human behaviour is sufficiently broad to span the contrast between affirmative and denying 'moralities'.

Let us emphasize once again: this disclosure of 'one of the broadest and longest facts that exist' concerns not only the self-tormenting approaches to shaping one's self-dealings; it encompasses all varieties of 'concern for oneself' as well as all forms of concern for adaptation to the highest. Aside from that, the jurisdiction of ascetology, understood as a general theory of practising, doctrine of habit and germinal discipline of anthropotechnics, does not end with the phenomena of advanced civilization and the spectacular results of mental or somatic vertical ascent (leading into the most diverse forms of virtuosity); it closes every vital continuum, every series of habits, every lived succession, including the seemingly most formless drifting and the most advanced neglect and exhaustion.

One cannot deny a marked one-sidedness in Nietzsche's late writings: he did not pursue the positive side of his ascetological discoveries with the same emphasis as that he displayed in his explorations of the morbid pole – undoubtedly because of a stronger inclination towards examining the therapeutic purpose of negative ascetic ideals than the athletic, dietological, aesthetic and also 'biopolitical' purpose of positive practice programmes. Throughout his life, he was sufficiently sick to be interested in possibilities of overcoming sickness in a meaningful way, and sufficiently lucid to reject the traditional attempts to bestow meaning upon the senseless. That is why he exhibited a combination of reluctant respect for the attainment of ascetic ideals in the history of mankind to date and reluctance to draw on them himself. In Nietzsche's case, this fluctuation between an appreciation of self-coercive behaviour and scepticism towards the idealistic extravagances of such praxes led to a new attentiveness towards the behavioural area of asceticism, practice and self-treatment as a whole. It is the re-description of this in terms of a general theory of anthropotechnics that is now called for.

There are three points to bear in mind that make the discovery of the 'ascetic planet' as far-reaching as it is problematic. Firstly: Nietzsche's new view of the ascetic dimension only become possible in a time when the asceticisms were becoming post-spiritually somatized, while the manifestations of spirituality were moving in a post-ascetic, non-disciplined and informal direction. The de-spiritualization of asceticisms is probably the event in the current intellectual history of mankind that is the most comprehensive and, because of its large scale, the hardest to perceive, yet at once the most palpable and atmospherically powerful. Its counterpart is the informalization of spirituality – accompanied by its commercialization in the corresponding subcultures. The threshold values for these two tendencies provide the intellectual landmarks for the twentieth century: the first tendency is represented by sport, which has become a metaphor for achievement as such, and the second by popular neo-mysticism, that *devotio postmoderna* which covers the lives of contemporary individuals with unpredictable flashes of inner emergency.

Secondly: on the ascetic planet, once discovered as such, the difference between those who make something or a great deal of themselves and those who make little or nothing of themselves becomes increasingly conspicuous. This is a difference that does not fit into any time or any ethics. In the monotheistic age, God was viewed as the one who causes and does everything, and hence humans were not entitled to make something, let alone a great deal, of themselves. In humanistic epochs, by contrast, man is considered the being responsible for causing and doing everything – but consequently no longer has the right to make little or nothing of himself. Whether people now make nothing or much of themselves, they commit – according to traditional forms of logic – an inexplicable and unpardonable error. There is always a surplus of differences that cannot be integrated into any of the prescribed systems of life-interpretation. In a world that belongs to God, human beings make too much of themselves as soon as they raise their heads; in a world that belongs to humans, they repeatedly make too little of themselves. The possibility that the inequality between humans might be due to their asceticisms, their different stances towards the challenges of the practising life – this idea has never been formulated in the history of investigations into the ultimate causes of difference between humans. If one follows this trail, it opens up perspectives that, being unthought-of, are literally unheard-of.

And finally: if the athletic and somatic renaissance means that de-spiritualized asceticisms are once more possible, desirable and vitally plausible, then Nietzsche's agitated question at the end of his text *The Genealogy of Morals*, namely where human life can find its bearings after the twilight of the gods, effortlessly answers itself. Vitality, understood both somatically and mentally, is itself the medium that contains a gradient between more and less. It therefore contains the vertical component that guides ascents within itself, and has no need of additional external or metaphysical attractors. That God is supposedly dead is irrelevant in this context. With or without God, each person will only get as far as their form carries them.

Naturally 'God', during the time of his effective cultural representation, was the most convincing attractor for those forms of life and practice which strove 'towards Him' – and this towards-Him was identical to 'upwards'. Nietzsche's concern to preserve vertical tension after the death of God proves how seriously he took his task as the 'last metaphysician', without overlooking the comical aspect of his mission. He had found his great role as a witness to the vertical dimension without God. The fact that he did not have to fear any rivals during his lifetime confirms that his choice was right. His aim of keeping the space above the dead free was a passion that remained understandable to more than a few fellow sufferers in the twentieth century; this accounts for the continued and infectious identification of many readers today with Nietzsche's existence and its unliveable contradictions. Here, for once, the epithet 'tragic' is appropriate. The theomorphism of his inner life withstood his own exercises in God-destruction. The author of *The Gay Science* was aware of how pious even he still was. At the same time, he already understood the rules in force on the ascetic planet well enough to realize that all ascents start from the base camp of ordinary life. His questions – transcend, but where to; ascend, but to what height? – would have answered themselves if he had calmly kept both feet on the ascetic ground. He was too sick to follow his most important insight: that the main thing in life is to take the minor things seriously. When minor things grow stronger, the danger posed by the main thing is contained; then climbing higher in the minor things means advancing in the main thing.

— 3 —

ONLY CRIPPLES WILL SURVIVE

Unthan's Lesson

That life can involve the need to move forwards in spite of obstacles is one of the basic experiences shared by the group of people whom, with a carefree clarity, one formerly called 'cripples', before younger and supposedly more humane, understanding and respectful spirits of the age renamed them the handicapped, those with special needs, the problem children, and finally simply 'human beings'.[13] If, in the following chapter, I persist in using the old term, which has meanwhile come to seem tactless, it is purely because it had its traditional place in the vocabulary of the time that I am recalling in these explorations. Abandoning it for the sake of sensitivity, and perhaps merely oversensitivity, would cause a system of indispensable observations and insights to disappear. In the following, I would like to demonstrate the unusual convergence of human and cripple in the discourses of the generation after Nietzsche in order to gain further insights into the structural change of human motives for improvement in recent times. Here it will transpire to what extent references to the human being in the twentieth century are rooted in cripple-anthropological premises – and how cripple anthropology changes spontaneously into an anthropology of defiance. In the latter, humans appear as the animals that must move forwards because they are obstructed by something.

The reference to rooting provides the cue, albeit indirectly, for the reflections with which I shall continue the explorations on the planet of the practising stimulated by Nietzsche – and, in a sense, also the contemplations on torsos introduced by Rilke. In 1925, two years before Heidegger's *Being and Time*, three years before Scheler's *The Human Place in the Cosmos*, the Stuttgart publisher Lutz' Memoirenbibliothek printed a book with the simultaneously amusing and shocking title *Das Pediskript: Aufzeichnungen aus dem*

Leben eines Armlosen, mit 30 Bildern [The Pediscript: Notes from the Life of an Armless Man, with 30 Illustrations]. It was 'penned' by Carl Hermann Unthan, who was born in East Prussia in 1848 and died in 1929 – in truth, it was written on a typewriter whose keys were pressed using a stylus held with the foot. Unthan unquestionably deserves a place in the pantheon of reluctant virtuosos of existence. He belongs to those who managed to make a great deal of themselves, even though his starting conditions suggested that he would almost certainly make little or nothing of himself. At the age of six or seven the boy, born without arms, discovered by chance the possibility of playing on a violin fastened to a box on the ground. With a mixture of *naïveté* and tenacity, he devoted himself to improving the method he had discovered for playing the violin with his feet. The right foot played the part of the left hand, fingering the notes, while the left foot moved the bow.

The young man pursued his exercises with such determination that after attending secondary school in Königsberg, he was accepted as a student at the Leipzig Conservatory. There, mastering an enormous practice workload, he reached a notable level of virtuosity. He expanded his repertoire, soon also including showpieces of the highest difficulty. Naturally the handicapped man's violin playing would never have attracted such attention far and wide if it had been carried out in the usual form, without the element of acrobatic improbability. Before long, a vaudeville entrepreneur showed interest in Unthan. In 1868, still a minor, he began to go on concert tours, which, after stops in rural towns, took him to the European capitals, and later even across the ocean. He performed in Vienna, where he was introduced to the conductors Johann Strauss and Michael Zierer. In Munich he impressed the Hungaro-Bavarian military band leader and waltz king Josef Gungl by playing Gungl's brand new composition, the 'Hydropathen-Walzer'; he was especially flabbergasted by Unthan's execution of double stops with his toes. After a concert at the 'overcrowded grand ballroom' in Budapest, he was reportedly congratulated on his virtuosic performance by Franz Liszt, who had been sitting in the first row. He patted him 'on the cheek and shoulder' and expressed his appreciation. Unthan notes on this incident: 'What was it that made me doubt the authenticity of his enthusiasm? Why did it seem so artificial?'[14] One can see: in this note, Unthan, who was already over seventy by the time he wrote *Das Pediskript*, was not simply touching on imponderabilities in relationships between older and younger virtuosos. Those questions, written down half a century after the scene they describe took place, were significant as a symptom: they reminded the author of a distant time when the illusion that he could be taken seriously as a musician, not merely a curiosity, was still intact. Even fifty years later, the author still felt the cold breeze of disillusionment in Liszt's paternally sympathetic gesture; Liszt, a former prodigy himself, knew from experience what kind of life awaits virtuosos of any kind. So he would have known all the better what future lay before a young man who was to travel the world as a victor over a quirk of nature.

There is a widespread cliché among biographers: that their hero, who often has to go through arduous early years first, 'conquers the world for himself'. In his mode of self-presentation, Unthan takes up this figure by following each anecdote with another and recounting the saga of his successful years as a drawn-out travelogue, moving from city to city and continent to continent. He tells the story of a long life in constant motion: on Cunard steamers, on trains, in hotels of every category, in prestigious concert halls and dingy establishments. He probably spent the majority of his career on dubious vaudeville stages, from which he would blow the baffled audience kisses with his feet at the end of his performances.[15] The dominant sound in Unthan's public life seems to have been the cheering and applause of those surprised by his presentations. Unthan's 'notes', which can neither be called an autobiography nor memoirs – the closest category would be that of curiosities – are written in a language at once naïve and sentimental, full of stock phrases, echoing the diction of the factual account in the mid-nineteenth century; one can imagine the author's tongue in the corner of his mouth while writing.

On every page of *Das Pediskript*, Unthan demonstrates his conviction that the success of his life is revealed through an overflowing collection of picturesque situations he has experienced. Unthan lays out his treasures like a travel writer of the bourgeois age – his first concert, his first bicycle, his first disappointment. These are accompanied by a host of bizarre observations: a bullfight in which the bull impaled several toreros; a sword-swallower who injured his throat with an umbrella; garishly made-up females of all ages in Havana in 1873, with 'an odour of decay hovering over everything', with dancing negresses: 'We saw the most forbidden things imaginable'; a lizard-eating event in Mexico; 'sold out' in Valparaiso, with the recollection that 'the sun slowly sank into the still ocean. As if it were finding it difficult to leave . . .' Seven hours of brisk swimming 'without turning on my back', and heavy sunburn as a result; his encounter with an armless portrait painter in Düsseldorf, a comrade in fate who painted with one leg – 'there was no end to the questions and answers', 'he was full of vitality and good cheer. But most of our chats touched on deep matters nonetheless.' His mother's death: 'there was a praying inside me, though I did not and do not know what it was praying'. Appearances in the Orient, where people are more distinctive: 'a list of my most striking experiences alone would fill entire volumes'. Disappointment at the Holy Sepulchre, where 'the most degenerate riffraff' appeared to have gathered; arrest in Cairo, nicotine poisoning in Vienna, rifle shooting with his feet in St Petersburg, in the presence of Tsar Alexander III, guest appearance in Managua – 'the city of León bore the character of decline'; a comet over Cuba; participation in a film entitled *Mann ohne Arme* [Man Without Arms]. On board the *Elbe* to New York as a fellow passenger of Gerhart Hauptmann, who has a brief conversation with the artiste. Then the New World: 'Americans show a stimulating understanding in the face of the extraordinary.' '"You're the happiest person I know", said a man they called John D. "And what about you, with your money, Mr Rockefeller?", I asked him. "All my money can't buy your zest for life . . ."'

Das Pediskript could be read as a sort of 'life-philosophical performance', using the latter word in its popular sense. Unthan steps before his audiences in the posture of an artiste whose special virtuosity on the violin, and later with the rifle and the trumpet, is embedded in an overall virtuosity, an exercise in the art of living that pervades all aspects of life – it is no coincidence that the picture section of the book primarily shows the author carrying out such everyday actions as opening doors and putting on his hat.

If one wanted to translate Unthan's more general intuitions into a theoretical diction, his position would have to be defined as a vitalistically tinged 'cripple existentialism'. According to this, the disabled person has the chance to grasp their thrownness into disability as the starting point of a comprehensive self-choice. This applies not only to the basic auto-therapeutic attitude as expressed by Nietzsche in *Ecco Homo*, in the second section under the heading 'Why I Am So Wise': 'I took myself in hand, I made myself healthy again.' Unthan's choice applies to his own future. He places the following words in the mouth of the twenty-one-year-old who felt he had been released into independence: 'I will seize myself with an iron first to get everything out of myself.'[16] He interprets his disability as a school for the will. 'Anyone who is forced from birth to depend on their own experiments and is not prevented from performing them [. . .] will develop a will [. . .] the drive towards independence [. . .] constantly stimulates further experiments.'[17]

The consequence is emotional positivism, which is accompanied by a rigorous prohibition of melancholy. Unthan's aversion to every form of pity recalls similar statements in Nietzsche's moral philosophy. Only constant pain, for example, might be capable of wearing down someone handicapped: 'All other obstacles are defeated by the will, which forges ahead into the sunshine.'[18] The 'sunny attitude to life' of the cripple who was able to develop freely leads, we are told, to a 'higher percentage of zest for life' than is the case for a 'fully able person'.[19]

Unthan ends his account with a summary in which he presents his confession:

> I do not feel lacking in any way compared to a fully able person [. . .] I have never found anyone with whom, taking all conditions into account, I would have wanted to exchange places. I have certainly struggled, even more with myself than with my surroundings, but I would not give up those exquisite pleasures of the soul, which came about precisely through the struggles caused by my armlessness, for anything in the world.[20]

So it is ultimately only a matter of giving the cripple a chance to develop freely: this thesis is the culmination of Unthan's moral intuitions, which fluctuate between the urge for emancipation and the longing to participate. This free development should not be mistaken for a licence to aesthetic excesses, as called for in the Bohemian ideologies appearing at the same time. Allowing the cripple 'enough light and air in his development'[21] rather means giving him a chance to participate in normality. For the handicapped person, this reverses the relationship between bourgeois and artistes. Unlike bourgeois rebels against the ordinary, he cannot dream of following the people in the green caravan.[22] If he wants to be an artist, it is in order to be a bourgeois. For him, artistry is the quintessence of bourgeois work, and earning a living through it is what gives him a sense of pride. On one occasion, the author remarks that he would not want to receive a fur coat for the winter as a gift from a noble sir, as Walther von der Vogelweide did: 'I would rather earn the fur coat with my feet.'[23]

At the ethical core of Unthan's cripple existentialism one discovers the paradox of a normality for the non-normal. What makes this existentialist in the stricter sense of the word is a group of three motifs whose development only took place in the twentieth century: firstly, the figure of self-choice, whereby the subject makes something out of that which was made out of it; secondly, the socio-ontological constraints affecting anyone who exists under 'the gaze of the other'

– this produces the impulse of freedom, the stimulus to assert oneself against the confining power coming from the foreign eye; and finally the temptation of insincerity, with which the subject casts its freedom away to play the role of a thing among things, an in-itself, a natural fact.

From the perspective of French existentialism, Unthan did everything right. He chooses himself, he asserts himself against the enslaving pity of the others, and remains the perpetrator of his own life rather than becoming a collaborator with the allegedly dominant circumstances. But the reason he does everything right – perhaps more right than can be expressed in any philosophical jargon – cannot be sufficiently illuminated with the thinking methods found left of the Rhine. The inadequacy of the French approach lies in the fact that the existentialism which developed in France after 1940 formulated a philosophy for the politically handicapped (in this particular case, for the people of an occupied country), while in Germany and Austria, the last third of the nineteenth century had seen the growth of a vitalistic-therapeutically coloured philosophy for the physically and mentally handicapped, namely neurotics and cripples, that charged itself up with political, social-philosophical and anthropological ideas after 1918. While the occupation taught the French to associate existence (and existential truth) with resistance and freedom in the underground, Germans and Austrians had begun two generations earlier to equate existence (and existential truth) with defiance and compensatory acts. Thus the drama of 'continental philosophy' – to draw this once on the laughable classification of content-oriented thought by formalists across the water – in the first half of the twentieth century can only be understood if one bears in mind the contrasts and synergies between the older and more comprehensive Central European existentialism of defiance and the younger, more politically restricted Western European existentialism of resistance. The first goes back to pre-Revolution times, for example the work of Max Stirner, and continues – after its culmination in Nietzsche – until the systems of Freud, Adler and the later compensation theorists who became active in Germany; the second, as noted above, took shape under the 1940-4 occupation, with a history extending back via the revanchism of the Third Republic to the anger collection movements among the losers of the French Revolution, that is to say the early socialists and communists. Once one has understood the German model, one will easily recognize it in its caricatured forms left of the Rhine. What circulated on the *Rive Gauche* after 1944 as the doctrine of the Anti was the political adaptation of German cripple existentialism, whose adherents were committed to the ethics of the Nonetheless.

Unthan undoubtedly belongs to the earlier defiance-existentialist movement. Because of the special nature of his circumstances, however, he was not fully subsumed under this tendency. What sets him apart is a special form of 'living nonetheless' that isolates him from the heroistic mainstream and brings him into the company of artistes. His heroism is that of a striving for normality. Part of this is the willingness to be not simply an involuntary curiosity, but a voluntary one. One could therefore define his position as that of a vaudeville existentialist. Its starting point is the cunning of fate that commands him to make an artistic virtue out of an anomalous necessity. Driven along by strong initial paradoxes, the vaudeville existentialist searches for a way to achieve a form of 'decent exhibitionism'. For him, normality is to become the reward for abnormality. In order to be at peace with himself, he must therefore develop a form of life in which his pathological oddity is transformed into the precondition for a successful assimilation. Hence the 'armless fiddler', as Unthan was known on American stages, could under no circumstances perform as a mere cripple, as was the custom in the European circus and even more in the freakshows across the Atlantic. He had to present himself as the victor over his disability and beat the gawking industry at its own game.

The achievement of this success confirms Unthan's unusual position, which is once more occupied by various outstanding artists today. By managing to develop the paradoxes of their mode of existence, the handicapped can become convincing teachers of the human condition – practising beings of a particular category with a message for practising beings in general. What Unthan conquered for himself was the possibility of becoming, as a cripple virtuoso, a subject that can be beheld and admired to the same extent as it can be exhibited and gawked at – exhibited primarily by the impresarios and circus directors often mentioned, seldom favourably, in *Das Pediskript*, stared at by an audience whose curiosity often gives way to moved enthusiasm within a short time. When the existentialism of defiance is heightened into its vaudeville form, we see the emergence of the cripple artiste who has chosen himself as a self-exhibitable human. In the race against the voyeuristic curiosity of the normal, which must constantly be won anew, his self-exhibition pre-empts mere sensation. For him, the dichotomy between life and art no longer exists. His life is nothing other than the hard-won art of doing normal things

46

like opening doors and combing one's hair, as well as less normal things such as playing the violin with one's feet and dividing pencils in the middle through a gunshot triggered with the foot. The virtuoso of the ability to be normal can rarely indulge in the luxury of depressive moods. Living in the Nonetheless imposes an ostentatious zest for life on those who are determined to succeed. The fact that things may be different on the inside is no one's business. The land of smiles is inhabited by cripple artistes.

I would add that Hugo Ball, the co-founder of Dadaism and co-initiator of the Cabaret Voltaire in Zurich in 1916, was, alongside Franz Kafka, the most significant German-language vaudeville existentialist, both in his Dadaist phase and in his Catholic period. In his 1918 novel *Flametti oder: Vom Dandysmus der Armen* [Flametti, Or, The Dandyism of the Poor] he assembles a pandemonium of marginal figures from the sideshow and circus milieu and has a speaker declare that these people are truer humans than the ordinary citizens who seemingly manage to keep to the middle. The vaudeville people know more about 'real life' because they are those who have been thrown to the margins, the fallen and the battered. These 'jostled humans' are perhaps the only ones who still exist authentically. In a time when normal people have devoted themselves to madness, they remember – as broken as they are – the better possibilities of being human. They are the non-archaic torsos who keep themselves in shape for unknown tasks. Thanks to them, the circus becomes an invisible church. In a world of fellow travellers complicit in the collective self-deception, the circus performers are the only ones who are not swindlers – someone walking the tightrope cannot pretend for a moment. A little later, Ball stumbles on the trail of a sacred acrobatics to which he erected a monument in strictly stylized, neo-Catholically aroused studies: *Byzantinisches Christentum: Drei Heiligenleben* [Byzantine Christianity: Three Saints' Lives] (1923). It is dedicated to three heroes of the early Eastern church: John Climacus, Dionysius the Areopagite and Simeon Stylites, and constitutes one of the central works from the twilight of the ascetological age.

This brings us to a new development in our account of the phenomenon of practising. By investigating the forms of life among the disabled, a class of practising persons comes into view among the inhabitants of the ascetic star where more particular motives gain the upper hand. They do not follow their asceticisms for God's sake – or if they do, like Ignatius of Loyola, who was crippled by cannon fire, it is because Christ impresses them as a model for the neutralization of their defect.

It is not without reason that Christ was recommended for imitation by the founder of the Jesuit order as the captain of all who suffer. The visibly handicapped, however, only formed a marginal group among the ranks of the holy self-tormentors whom Nietzsche saw marching through the centuries like hoarse choirs of pilgrims. They are not sick in the usual sense of the word, though Nietzsche did voice the suspicion that they were psychologically ill. Incidentally, both psychoanalysis and the official cripple pedagogy of the 1920s found among the disabled a propensity for envy complexes towards the able-bodied – the very thing from which Unthan insists he never suffered in the slightest. For them, leading a practising life is a response to the stimulus that lies in the concrete disability; it provides the incentive of inhibition that sometimes provokes an artiste's answer. As Unthan notes, one must grant the handicapped 'freedom' in the form of 'light and air' in their development, until the blow suffered has been overridden by self-will and integrated into a life project. Thus, through the phenomenon of inhibited and handicapped life, General Ascetology now faces its trial by fire.

Now it remains to show how an entire system of insights into the laws of defiant existence emerged from the analytics of inhibitions. This requires an excursion into the catacombs of intellectual history. The most significant document of the existentialism of defiance is in fact of German origin; it is simultaneously the manifesto of the earlier discipline of cripple anthropology, completely forgotten in the philosophical and pedagogical fields. I am referring to the book *Zerbrecht die Krücken* [Break the Crutches] by Hans Würtz, the Nietzsche-inspired initiator of state-run special education, a work that appeared in the early 1930s without eliciting the slightest reaction – for reasons we shall discuss shortly. The book is not mentioned in any history of philosophy, it is not covered in any anthropological textbook,[24] and its existence is unknown even among Nietzsche experts – even though Nietzscheans, be they academic or not, would have every reason to examine the reception of Nietzsche's ideas among cripple pedagogues before and after 1918. One cannot possibly gain an adequate understanding of Nietzsche, however, without contemplating the effects and echoes of his work among cripples and their spokesmen.

The reason for the book's oblivion lies above all in the political implications of its subject – and the time of its publication. Appearing in 1932, a work with the title *Break the Crutches* was not timely in Germany – not because the idea of breaking crutches would have been unpopular, however, but rather because the motto of the title attracted too many sympathizers, though they were admittedly not interested in the real handicapped people. Larger libraries list this rare work under its complete title: *Zerbrecht die Krücken: Krüppel-Probleme der Menschheit. Schicksalsstiefkinder aller Zeiten in Wort und Bild* [Break the Crutches: Cripple Problems of Mankind. The Stepchildren of Fate from All Times in Words and Images], published in Leipzig in 1932 by Leopold Voss. The author, who was born in the Holsteinish town of Heide in 1875 and died in Berlin in 1958, was orphaned early on and began his career as a primary school teacher in Hamburg-Altona, then Berlin-Tegel. From 1911 onwards he worked as educational inspector at the Oskar-Helene Home in Berlin-Zehlendorf, which had previously been the sanatorium and school for cripples in Berlin-Brandenburg. Under the young idealist's direction, this institution became a state-funded Mecca of cripple care and gained an international reputation. Together with Konrad Biesalski, an orthopaedist, Hans Würtz turned the Zehlendorf institution into a focus for this new form of philosophical practice. The Würtz-Biesalski cripple institution maintained its position as a stronghold of the existentialism of defiance for two decades, before new directors with Nazi ties adapted it to the party line. Here Nietzsche's ideas on the equivalence of life and the will to power were to be put to the test in daily dealings with the handicapped.

In the Reichstag elections in July 1932, the NSDAP had won 37.3 per cent of votes, making it the largest parliamentary group in the Reichstag by some distance. The vociferous party was met with strong support among the newly disabled from the First World War – an estimated 2.7 million in Germany alone. As far as the motto 'break the crutches' is concerned, then, Würtz should have received a favourable response – the widespread desire in Germany at the time was that people would be able to live without the irksome auxiliary constructions of the care system – on a small and a large, even the largest, scale. The hour of moved emotions had struck. Only someone who could credibly promise the abolition of prevailing disability systems could appear as the leader of a movement with a significant number of followers. The prospect of a crutchless existence appeared on the horizon and became a guiding image for all who felt insulted, handicapped and confined by their circumstances. The hour of people's anarchisms had arrived.

Since its beginnings, anarchy had been the philosophy of the Without. It sought to make its audience realize how many tools one finds in the modern order of things that can be dispensed with if one only believes in a life without masters or domination: without the state (the political crutch), without capitalism (the economic crutch),

49

without the church (the religious crutch), without the nagging conscience (the Judaeo-Christian crutch of the soul) and without marriage (the crutch on which sexuality hobbles through the years). In the context of the Weimar Republic, this meant above all without the Treaty of Versailles, which had become a fetter causing increasing anger. Beyond this, many at the time even wanted to dispense with democracy: many contemporaries considered it no more than a way for the people to be ridiculed by their own representatives – so why not bring in the populists and try out ridiculing the people's representatives instead? Breaking crutches was in the process of becoming the heart of revolutionary politics – indeed the motor of up-to-date revolutionary ontology. Beyond politics and everyday life, the call was heard for a revolt against everything that disturbs us through its mere existence. The crutch-weary wanted to shake off no less than the yoke of the real. All politics was transformed into politics for the handicapped in turmoil. Whoever wanted to channel the general anger at the 'given' and 'prevailing' circumstances could be sure that the majority of their contemporaries were prepared to recognize, in all manifestations of the institutional, crutches that were waiting to be broken. The twentieth century belongs to the people's fronts against auxiliary constructions.

Naturally the NSDAP could never appear openly under the sign of the cripple problem that needed to be solved, even though it was essentially nothing other than a militant response to the question of cripples and crutches. The party resolved the contradiction it embodied by placing the dangerous subject of lives that were 'unworthy of life' [*lebensunwertes Leben*] on its programme: with this gesture it succeeded in radically externalizing its innermost motive. Otherwise, the movement's leaders would have had to out themselves as crippled leaders of cripples, as the disabled special needs educator Otto Perl did around the same time. They would have had to disclose what competencies and delegation structures made them eligible to stand at the forefront of the national revolution: Hitler as an emotional cripple who sought to merge with the people's community in ecstatic moments, Goebbels as a clubfooted man longing to walk across elegant floors, and Göring as a drug addict who saw Nazi rule as a chance for him and his co-junkies to have a massive party – they could all have told the people about their struggles, their dreams and their great Nonetheless. The inopportunity of such confessions is obvious enough, to say nothing of their psychological improbability. 'Movements' of this type live off the fact that their *primum mobile* remains in latency. The political space in those years was undeniably steeped in descendants of the cripple problem – not least because Emil Ludwig had made the disability of Wilhelm II a central psychopolitical focus for a wider audience in his biography of 1925. The public sphere was echoing with questions about giving meaning to a handicapped existence – and the compatibility of power and disability. Can the handicapped be allowed to come to power? What is power in any case, if it can be attained by the handicapped? What happens to us if the handicapped are already in power? Nietzsche's meditations from the 1880s, seemingly removed from the real world, had become part of the fiery nucleus of politics within a short time. Hans Würtz skilfully updated Nietzsche's perspectives by showing how disability, with the right 'schooling', can lead to a surplus of will to success in life.

'The material has been collected without any prejudice', we are told in the introduction to his book, which offers an encyclopaedic overview of practically all significant cultural figures with known disabilities in Europe. Würtz thus also mentions his contemporary Joseph Goebbels in his summaries and charts on the human history of the cripple problem: he lists the Nazi propagandist twice in the category of clubfooted cripples, where he did not *a priori* have to fare badly alongside figures such as Lord Byron – once in the list of nations,[25] and once in the list of functions, with the classification 'revolutionary politician'.[26] Thanks to the cripple educator Würtz, the chief agitator of the NSDAP is mentioned in a *Who's Who* of humanity containing almost five hundred names, featuring the great and greatest, as well as figures like Unthan, whom Würtz lists together with numerous comrades in fate in the broadly represented category 'show cripples and cripple virtuosos'.[27]

What the protagonists of this work shared was the ability to make the philosophy of the Nonetheless a reality. That Würtz's lists feature persons such as Jesus, who recent findings suggested was 'crippled by ugliness', and Wilhelm II – who had a crippled arm, but within whom there was also a 'cripple psychopath',[28] like the handicapped doll inside the handicapped doll – shows the magnitude and the explosiveness of this problem complex. Naming such great figures illustrated the theory, leading from the philosophy of life to that of spirit, that disabled persons can transcend their afflictions and anchor themselves in the realm of transpersonal values.[29] In fact, Wilhelm had more than plainly neurotic political decisions to answer for; he had also developed stage sets for the Bayreuth Festival and attempted various other transitions into the objective. As for Jesus' breakthrough from the sphere of his assumed handicaps to the spiritual

51

sphere, its results have long since been worked into the ethical foundations of occidental culture. In Max Scheler's philosophy of values, which Würtz presumably did not know, there was a parallel attempt to show the autonomous rules of the value sphere in relation to its 'basis' in the tensions of life. Würtz calls the epitome of action that leads to the transpersonal 'work' – we understand that this word is only one of the pseudonyms under which the phenomenon of practising continues to emerge.

'Overcome inhibition is the mother of all unfolded [...] movement.'[30] According to Würtz, the movement here termed 'unfolded' is not simply compensatory, but in fact overcompensatory movement: the reaction exceeds the stimulus. With this, the author had formulated a theorem whose ambit extends to asymmetrical movement complexes of all kinds – organic and intellectual, mental and political – even if he restricted himself in his book to demonstrating his thesis using the phenomenon of physical disability. These applications were demanding enough: through intensive collaboration based on scientific research, he insisted, German doctors, educators and pastors should unite in the 'goal-setting collective for cripple elevation' [Zielsetzungsgemeinschaft der Krüppelhebung]. As high as he aimed, however, Würtz remained unaware of the political potential of his reflections. Certainly he had stated in general terms that surplus energy from overcoming obstacles turns into a dynamic forwards thrust: 'the lame Ignatius of Loyola and Götz von Berlichingen were always on the move',[31] as were the restless epileptics St Paul and Caesar. And there is no shortage of references to the 'short, crooked-necked Alexander the Great' and the equally 'crooked-necked', 'short, mongoloid-ugly Lenin', as well as the 'small and hip-lame' Rosa Luxemburg.[32]

And yet: for Würtz, the cripple-psychological universals of 'sorrow and defiance' retain a purely individual-psychological meaning. A radical political change like the völkisch socialism of 1933, however, which boasted above all of bringing movement, attack and revolution – what was this if not an external application of the law of compensation? If overcome inhibition is the mother of all unfolded movement, which 'maternal urges' form the origin of the inclination towards self-aggrandizement through celebration and terror? What does it mean to go to the 'mothers' if the word describes the product of inhibition and overcoming? If overcompensation for disability transpired as the secret of success, should one conclude that most people are not sufficiently disabled? These questions may be rhetorical, but they nonetheless show one thing: the path to a great theory of compensation is paved with awkwardnesses.[33]

As far as Goebbels is concerned, he was obviously not interested in the progress of this clarification. He showed little enthusiasm about his acceptance into the pantheon of the handicapped. Being listed alongside great figures such as Kierkegaard, Lichtenberg, Kant, Schleiermacher, Leopardi, Lamartine, Victor Hugo and Schopenhauer, to name only a few, did not induce him to out himself. Making his psyche available to science during his lifetime would probably have been the last thing he was considering. Nor would the central orthopaedic principle of the institute in Zehlendorf have appealed to him: 'The stump is the best prosthesis.' In Würtz's four-group classification – growth cripples (anomalies of size), deformity cripples, latent cripples (incorrect posture) and ugliness cripples (disfigurement) – he would undoubtedly have had had to join the second, perhaps also the fourth, as well as the subgroup 'complex cripples',[34] which leads over into the psychological field.

Goebbels had other plans: supposedly, all copies of *Zerbrecht die Krücken* not yet in distribution were confiscated on his orders. The further course of history speaks for itself. Not long after January 1933, Würtz was denounced at his own institute as an enemy of the people; his critics suddenly claimed to have discovered in him an armchair communist and philo-Semite. Owing to a well-timed accusation of abuse of office and embezzlement of donations, he was dismissed without notice and without any claim to a pension; allegedly he had used some of the donations received by the society for the promotion of the Oskar-Helene Home for the publication of *Zerbrecht die Krücken* – as if the book were merely the author's private matter, unconnected to the work of the institution he co-directed.

It is not difficult to recognize in the allegations against Würtz a conflict between the institution's fieldworkers and the publishing alpha leader. His accusers, ambitious colleagues, took over leading positions following his removal – as if to make it clear that a successful revolution cares for its children rather than devouring them. Würtz remained naïve enough to believe that he could prove his innocence under the prevailing conditions. He therefore returned to Germany from exile in Prague for his trial, at the end of which a Berlin court gave him a suspended sentence of one year's imprisonment. He subsequently left Germany, finding refuge in Austria until the end of the war. In 1947 he achieved complete legal and professional rehabilitation. He was buried in July 1958 in the Berlin-Dahlem Waldfriedhof [forest cemetery].

It is instructive for our further reflections to examine the connections between Nietzsche's efforts towards the analytics of the will and

Würtz's deliberations on special education. Each author could have referred to the other to illustrate his axioms – which, in the case of the younger in relation to the older, indeed occurred. From the perspective of the Berlin disability expert, Nietzsche offers an example of his concept of 'overcome inhibition'. He classifies the philosopher, without whose ideas his own work would scarcely be imaginable, somewhat cold-bloodedly as the 'psychopathically handicapped growth cripple Nietzsche'.[35] At least the latter, he admits – through a combination of the laws of compensation, great talent and hard work on himself – managed to overcome his handicap partially, which is why his work should be acknowledged as an attempt to cross over into the trans-pathological sphere of values.

Reversing the perspective produces a more complex picture. Nietzsche would recognize in the special needs educator from Berlin the phenomenon of the pupil, which he viewed with some suspicion, and about which we need only say here that they frequently display the weaknesses of their masters, and in compromising magnifications, rather than their virtues. A second glance would show what concrete form the priestly syndrome attacked by Nietzsche took in Würtz's case. The main characteristic of this phenomenon is the tendency, found among the stronger sick, to assume leadership of a following composed of weak existences. The literature I have consulted does not mention any disability on Würtz's own part, so it remains unclear whether Nietzsche's diagnoses of the dynamics of the priestly-ascetic ideal apply in the personal case of his emulator. The style of Würtz's publications, which culminate in hymns to 'victorious fighters for life',[36] certainly suggests a spokesman syndrome; the manner in which he is ignited by his own mission would support this. The proximity to the priestly type reveals itself in Würtz's quasi-imperial taste for bringing increasingly large parts of mankind into his jurisdiction. Here the usual dynamic of the alpha leader becomes visible: for Nietzsche, an unmistakable manifestation of the will to power.

Nonetheless, everything we know today suggests that for Würtz, his work at the Oskar-Helene Home in Berlin was the focal point of his commitment. Outside observers are in no position to question the seriousness of his lifelong dedication to the welfare of his patients – even if his authoritarian approach is less appealing today, and, at least on paper, one would sooner sympathize with the self-determination model of the alternative special needs educator Otto Perl.[37] For its educational inspector, the Berlin institution additionally served as the pulpit from which he announced his suggestions for solving the riddle of mankind to a somewhat reluctant audience.

These consisted mostly of modal transformations: you can do what you want; you should want what you must do – you should be able to want and you are able, assuming there is someone at your side who wants you to want. The last variation is particularly significant: it defines not only the figure of the will-trainer for the handicapped, but in fact the trainer's function as such. My trainer is the one who wants me to want – he embodies the voice that can say to me: 'You must change your life!'[38]

The phenomenon of caring for the handicapped in the spirit of a philosophy of the will that urges cripples to work on themselves belongs unmistakably within the radius of the major event described above: the de-spiritualization of asceticisms characteristic of the nineteenth and twentieth centuries. Its counterpart on the 'religious' side is the de-heroization of priesthood, temporarily offset from the 1920s onwards by the over-elevation of the sacred that was typical of the *renouveau catholique* and the pious branch of phenomenology – with delayed effects that can be identified among such authors as the ecologist Carl Amery and that para-Catholic phenomenon of elegance, Martin Mosebach.

While insisting on the jargon of heroism as an educator of the will, Würtz ironically overlooked the pioneering element in the turn of the ascetological era to which his work belongs. For all his heroistic suggestion, it is his pragmatic focus on a programme for toughening up the disabled and inhibited that is decisive. His pseudo-priestly manner should not be taken at face value. Behind it lies a phenomenon foreshadowed in Nietzsche's dietological theses: I shall call it the emergence of the general training consciousness from the particular case of education for the sick and disabled. Training naturally involves, alongside the trainee and the training programme, the trainer – it is this seminal figure that gained a profile under the late Wilhelminian, life-philosophical and will-philosophical attire of Würtz's declarations.

With the appearance of the trainer figure – or, more precisely, its reappearance after its co-downfall with the decline of ancient athletic culture – the somatic and athletic renaissance at the turn of the twentieth century entered its concentrated phase. It would not be insulting to call Hans Würtz an imperial trainer of the handicapped – the Trapattoni of cripples, as it were.[39] He stands in a line of trainer-authors extending back to Max Stirner, author of *The Ego and Its Own* (1845). Needless to say, Würtz, with his sure instinct for team selection, counted the latter among his exemplary clients. In his function as the trainer of one's own uniqueness, Stirner was one of the first to realize that the metaphysically overweight do not cut a fine figure on the playing field of existence. The removal of ideological rafters in people's heads that he recommended in his book was already nothing other than an explicit mental fitness programme. With regard to this patriarch of egotism, Würtz managed to formulate a generalization of considerable scope: 'In keeping with his psychological structure, the cripple Stirner sees all other people as unconscious and involuntary fighters for the value of the ego.'[40] For Würtz, this confirms his initial assumption: being aware of one's uniqueness and being a 'fighter for life' converge. Today one would phrase it more carefully: disabilities lead not infrequently to sensitizations, and these can bring about increased efforts – which, under favourable conditions, result in greater life achievements. While Stirner's uniqueness remained trapped within neurosis, as Würtz regretfully points out, constructive work with the handicapped should aim 'to free the problematic cripple to become a person of character'.[41] We would no longer formulate it in this way today, whether speaking about pre-Revolution philosophers or other problematic natures.

The hypothesis that the special educator, in his practical and moral-philosophical profile, embodies one of the first instances of the modern trainer can be substantiated through numerous of the author's own statements. In Würtz's case it is clear: the trainer is the timely partner in non-metaphysical vertical tensions, which give the trainee's life a secure sense of above and below. He is responsible for ensuring that 'medically prescribed exercises give this ability (acquired by the client) a rooting in his powers', so that 'his will to survive also finds a concrete basis'.[42] With a clarity that would be an asset to an analytic philosophy of sport, Würtz declares at the training-theoretically decisive point, referring to the disabled person:

> His will thus gives his life an inner gradient if he compares his earlier state of powerlessness with the abilities he has triumphantly acquired, and measures the success he has already achieved against the goal of his regimen. His striving gains a forward drive. Overcoming the earlier sense of powerlessness is simultaneously an ethical victory [. . .]. The carefully mediating character of the education must not be burdened with a fear of excessive strain. [. . .] We therefore demand a life-affirming attitude in those who educate the handless [. . .].[43]

There cannot be many statements in recent literature that encapsulate the post-metaphysical transformation of vertical tension – that is, of the inherent awareness of vital asymmetry – so explicitly. For this gain in explication one has to take a few heroistic phrases in one's stride; in their content, however, they are simply the mask of the athletic renaissance. One can, incidentally, also observe the de-heroization of the trainer's role in the sporting history of the twentieth century. There is, however, a counter-movement in the field of sport – analogous to the developments in the religious field – that could be called the *renouveau athlétique*: here the extreme athlete is raised aloft as the spiritually empty counterpart of the saint.

The philosophical anthropology of the twentieth century ignored the contributions of special education – but nonetheless arrived at related observations from similar conceptual points of departure. With its own means, the anthropology of the ordinary person forged a path to an even more general disability awareness than the special needs educators could have dreamt of – its practical conclusions, however, were diametrically opposed to those of heroic cripple didactics. Its maxim: do not break the crutches under any circumstances! One can already hear this warning in Viennese psychoanalysis, when Freud describes man as a 'prosthetic God' who could not survive without the support of civilizatory provisions for existence. With his Oedipus legend, one might add, Freud managed to incorporate the male half of humanity into the family of clubfeet while diagnosing the female half with genital crippledom in the form of inborn penislessness. One hears the warning call even more loudly in Arnold Gehlen's doctrine of supportive institutions, which states that the delusional boundlessness of unleashed subjectivity can only be saved from itself through a protective framework of transpersonal forms. Here the crutches reappear as the institutions, and their significance becomes all the greater because the anarchists of the twentieth century – on the left and the right – had called rather too successfully for their destruction. Gehlen was extremely concerned when he witnessed the emergence of a new Without movement among the young people of the West in the 1960s. In his anthropological justification of institutions one finds a culmination of the anti-Rousseauism of the twentieth century, condensed in the warning that human beings always have much more to lose than their chains. He asks whether all political culture does not begin with the distinction between chains and crutches. This advocation of existence with compulsory crutches reaches its most dramatic form in the statements of biological palaeoanthropology in the work of Louis Bolk and Adolf Portmann: according to them, *Homo sapiens* is constitutively a cripple of premature birth, a creature condemned to eternal immaturity that, because of this condition (which biologists term neoteny, a retention of juvenile and foetal traits), is only capable of survival in the incubators of culture.[44]

These highly generalized statements of modern anthropology present a functional explication of the holistic pathos that was characteristic of older cultures – those cultures that insisted intransigently on the priority of tradition and custom (the established incubator) over the whims of individuals eager for innovation. Every orthodoxy, whether it draws its validity from religion or from being venerable and ancient, is a system for preventing mutations of the structures that ensure stability. In this sense, the ancientness of the ancients is self-validating. While a tradition, as long as it appears old enough, provides evidence of its viability and its compatibility with other stock elements, a new idea and its subjective deviation must first prove their repeatability – assuming they are interested in doing so. In the anti-mutation traditionalist systems, however, the presupposition is that even permitting the attempt to prove the usability of something new is never worthwhile. Periods with a greater openness for innovation, on the other hand, rely on the observation that even after far-reaching moral revaluations and technical innovations, a sufficient number of stabilizations are still possible in order to redirect our *modus vivendi* towards a more pleasant state. But the innovations must always be assessed in terms of their agreement with the need for stability in care systems for premature birth cripples (commonly known as cultures).

Wherever humans appear, their crippledom has preceded them: this insight was the chorus of philosophical discussions on the human being in the previous century, regardless of whether, as in psychoanalysis, one speaks of humans as cripples of helplessness who can only hobble towards their goals;[45] or, like Bolk and Gehlen, views them as neotenic cripples whose chronic immaturity can only be balanced out by rigid cultural capsules; or, like Plessner, as eccentric cripples chronically standing beside themselves and observing their lives; or, like Sartre and Blumenberg, as visibility cripples who must spend their lives coming to terms with the disadvantage of being seen.

Beyond these forms of constitutive crippledom, historically acquired variants also come into view – most of all, if one believes Edmund Husserl, among modern Europeans. In their effects to achieve the intellectual conquest of reality, they have fallen into two dangerously misguided positions of enormous dimensions – in almost pathographical formulations, he calls them physicalist objectivism and transcendental subjectivism.[46] Both are modes of thinking being-in-the-world that amount to comprehensive misreadings of the world and reality.

If one considers that our existence in the 'lifeworld' constitutes the original relationship termed 'being-in-the-world' since Heidegger, one reaches an ironic conclusion: due to laboriously acquired misconditionings, we chronically confuse the first world with the second world of physicists, philosophers and psychologists. The ageing Husserl had adopted this precarious view of the civilized European as a cripple of world-misreading from his renegade pupil Heidegger, for whom man begins in most cases as a cripple of inauthenticity – and ends in the same state, unless he is lucky enough to happen upon a trainer who will put his orthopaedic data of existence in order. Among the acquired disabilities, the neo-phenomenologist Hermann Schmitz recently uncovered a new one, habitual irony: it robs the ironist of the ability to be fulfilled in shared situations. Here the focus of investigation shifts to a crippledom of distance, emerging from an impairment of the capacity for participation through the compulsion to chronic elegance. And indeed, the role of irony in the history of reality-misreadings has not yet been sufficiently acknowledged.

The implications of these observations are as diverse as the diagnoses themselves. They have one thing in common, however: if humans are cripples, without exception and in different ways, then each one of them, in their own particular way, has good reason to understand their existence as an incentive for corrective exercises.

We recall that in Würtz's schema of crippledoms, short persons were classified as 'growth cripples'. In later times, the same people were termed 'disabled in terms of growth'. When it even became offensive to speak of 'disability', the small became those who have different abilities in terms of their format. In the 1980s, politically correct Americans found the most up-to-date name for people who often have to look upwards: 'vertically challenged people'. This turn of phrase cannot be admired enough. It constitutes a terminological creation that outgrew its inventors without their even noticing what they had achieved. We can laugh at this formulation twice: once at the correct preciousness of its authors and once at ourselves. We have every right and reason to laugh, for we have an absolute majority in the assembly of those who are challenged by verticality. The formula has been valid since we began to practise learning to live – and, as I am seeking to show, one can neither *not* practise nor *not* learn to live. Even being a poor student must first be learned.

In short, people had to speak about the handicapped, the differently constituted, to stumble on a phrase that expresses the general constitution of beings under vertical tension. 'You must change your life!' means, as we saw in Rilke's torso poem: you must pay attention to your inner vertical axis and judge how the pull from its upper pole affects you! It is not walking upright that makes humans human; it is rather the incipient awareness of the inner gradient that causes humans to do so.

— 4 —

LAST HUNGER ART
Kafka's Artistes

The inclination of anthropologists to seek the truth about *Homo sapiens* among the handicapped, typical of our time, is mirrored widely in the literature of modernity. Our reference to the armless violinist Unthan demonstrates that in certain cases, it is only one step from the existentialism of the handicapped to that of acrobats. It now remains to show why the transition from the condition of the disabled to acrobatism was not merely an idiosyncrasy among marginal figures, as Unthan developed in reaction to his innate stimulus, or as evident in Hugo Ball, author of the biographies of Christian ascetics, when he attempted to transcend the spiritual deformations of the World War era by 'fleeing from the time'. This revolt against the century brought him into the company of the hermits who had fled their own time 1500 years earlier.

In the following I shall discuss, initially using a literary model and later in a psychological and sociological context, how acrobatism became an increasingly far-reaching aspect of modern reflection on the human condition: this occurred when, following the trail of the ubiquitous Nietzsche, peopled discovered in man the unfixed, unleashed animal that is condemned to perform tricks. This shift of view to the acrobat brought to light a further aspect of the epochal turn that I would describe as a trend towards the de-spiritualization of asceticisms. We have adopted Nietzsche's identification of the ascetological twilight, and assured ourselves that the desirable decline of repressive ascetic ideals by no means occasions the disappearance of the positive practising life. It may only be the twilight of the ascetics, as which understand the turn of the twentieth century, that reveals – retrospectively and very differently illuminated – the three-thousand-year empire of metaphysically motivated asceticisms in its full dimensions. There is much to support this: whoever looks for humans will find ascetics, and whoever observes ascetics will discover acrobats.

To substantialize this suspicion, whose earliest formulations go back to the morality-archaeological digs of the other Schliemann, I would like to call Kafka as a witness of the time. Considering his research approach, it is natural to suppose that he had already absorbed the impulse coming from Nietzsche early in life, and internalized it to such a degree that he forgot the origin of his interrogations – which is why Kafka's work contains virtually no explicit references to the author of *The Genealogy of Morals*. He further developed the impulses in the direction of a progressive lowering of the heroic tone, while simultaneously reinforcing the awareness of the universal ascetic and acrobatic dimension of human existence.

To mark the moment at which Nietzsche passed the baton on to Kafka, I point to the well-known tightrope episode in the sixth part of the prologue to *Thus Spoke Zarathustra*, where Zarathustra takes the acrobat as his first pupil after the latter's ultimately fatal fall – or, if not as his pupil, then at least his first kindred spirit among the people of the plains. He consoles the dying man by enlightening him as to why he has nothing more to fear – no devil will come for him to sour his life after death. Upon this, the acrobat gratefully replies that merely losing his life is no great loss:

'I am not much more than a beast that has been taught to dance by being dealt blows and meagre morsels.'[47]

This statement constitutes the first confession of acrobatic existentialism. The minimalistic assertion is tied inseparably to Zarathustra's response, which holds up a noble mirror to the victim of this accident:

'Not so,' said Zarathustra. 'You have made danger your calling: there is nothing in that to despise. Now your calling has brought you down: therefore will I bury you with my own hands.'[48]

The point of this dialogue cannot be missed. It has the meaning of a primal scene, as it describes the constitution of a new type of *communio*: no longer a people of God, but travelling people; not a community of saints, but one of acrobats; not paying contributors to an insured society, but members of an organization of those living dangerously. The animating element of this – for the time being – invisible church is the pneuma of affirmed danger. It is no coincidence that the acrobat who has fallen from his tightrope is the first to move towards Zarathustra's doctrine. In the final moment of his life, the tightrope artiste feels that the new prophet has understood him as no one has before – as the being that, even if it was scarcely more than an animal that was taught to dance, had made danger its profession.

After this prologue to the acrobat's novel, it was Kafka who wrote the next chapter. In his case, the dawn of the acrobats is already several degrees brighter and clearer, which is why one can make out the scenery in something close to daylight. There is no need to explain in detail here that Kafka was an advocate of gymnastic exercises, vegetarian diets and ideologies of hygiene that were typical of the time.[49] In the collection of statements he excerpted from his octavo notebooks and arranged in a numbered list (later edited and published by Max Brod under the title *Betrachtungen über Sünde, Leid, Hoffnung und den wahren Weg* [Observations on Sin, Suffering, Hope and the True Path]), the first entry reads:

> The true path is along a rope, not a rope suspended way up in the air, but rather only just over the ground. It seems more like a tripwire than a tightrope.[50]

No one would claim that this note is self-explanatory. The two sentences become transparent if one reads them as a continuation of the scene opened by Nietzsche – albeit in a direction that markedly deviates from Nietzsche's heroic and elevating intentions. The 'true path' is still connected to the rope, but it is shifted from a high altitude almost to the ground. It serves less as a device for acrobats to demonstrate their sureness of step than as a trap to trip them up. This seems to convey the message that the task of finding the true path is difficult enough already for one not to have to climb high in order to live dangerously. The rope is no longer meant to test the ability to keep your balance on the slimmest foundation; its function is more to prove that if you are too sure of yourself, you will fall if you simply walk forwards. Existence as such is an acrobatic achievement, and no one can say with certainty what training provides the necessary skills to master this discipline. Hence the acrobat no longer knows what exercises keep him from falling – aside from constant vigilance. This fading level of artistedom by no means indicates a loss of this phenomenon's significance; on the contrary, it reveals how aspects of the artiste spread to affect all aspects of life. The great subject of the arts and philosophies of the twentieth century – the discovery of the ordinary – draws its energy from the dawn of the acrobats, which ensues in parallel with it. It is only because the esotericism of our time exposes the equivalence of ordinariness and acrobatics that its investigations produce non-trivial results.

Kafka's hermetic note can also be assigned to the complex of developments that I call the de-spiritualization of asceticisms. It shows that the author is part of the great unscrewing of the moderns from a system of religiously coded vertical tensions that had been in force for millennia. Countless people were trained as acrobats of the world above in this era, practised in the art of crossing the abyss of the 'sensual world' [*Sinnenwelt*] with the balancing pole of asceticism. In their time, the rope represented the transition from immanence to transcendence. What Kafka and Nietzsche have in common is the intuition that the disappearance of the world above leaves behind the fastened rope. The reason for this would be completely opaque if one could not demonstrate a deeper *raison d'être* for the existence of ropes, a rationale that could be separated from their function as a bridge to the world above. There is in fact such an explanation: for both authors, the rope stands for the realization that acrobatism, compared to the usual religious forms of 'crossing over', is the more resistant phenomenon. Nietzsche's reference to 'one of the broadest and longest facts that exist' can be transferred to it. The shift of focus from asceticism to acrobatics raises a universe of phenomena from the background that effortlessly encompasses the greatest oppositions in the spectrum from wealth of spirit to physical strength. Here charioteers and scholars, wrestlers and church fathers, archers and rhapsodists come together, united by shared experiences on the way to the impossible. The world ethos is formulated at a council of acrobats.

The rope can only function as a metaphor for acrobatism if one imagines it stretched out; one must therefore pay attention to the sources of tension, its anchors and its modalities of power transfer. As long as the rope's tension was produced with metaphysical intentions, one had to suppose the existence of a pull from the world above to explain its particular form of intensity. Ordinary existence came into contact with this pull from above through the ubiquitous example of the saints, who, owing to efforts that people liked to term superhuman, were occasionally permitted to approach the impossible. We must not forget that *superhomo* is an arch-Christian word in which the high Middle Ages uttered its most intense concern – it was first used for the French king St Louis IX in the late thirteenth century! The exhaustion of such an otherworldly pole becomes most apparent in the fact that ever fewer people strive to walk the tightrope. In keeping with an egalitarian zeitgeist of neighbourly ethics, one is now content with an amateurish, at best floor-gymnastic interpretation of Christianity. Even a holy hysteric like Padre Pio had so little faith in the transcendent origin of his wounds that, it is alleged, he yielded to

the temptation to bring about his bloody palms with the aid of cor-
rosive acids and renew them as required.[51]

Since the nineteenth century, the assembly of an alternative generator for the build-up of high existential tension has been on the agenda.
In truth, this generator is set up by demonstrating the existence of an
equivalent dynamics in the interior of the existence that understands
itself correctly. We must once again invoke the name of Nietzsche,
for it was he who succeeded in revealing an *a priori* asymmetry with
a strong pull between being able and being more able, wanting and
wanting more, and between being and being more – as well as uncovering the aversive or bionegative tendencies that not infrequently aim,
under the pretext of humility, for the wanting of not-wanting and of
always-wanting-to-be-less. Talk of the will to power and of life as
constant self-overcoming, by now all too commonplace, provides the
formulas for the inherent differential energetics of the existence that
works on itself. As hard as the circulating ideologies of relaxation
might try to conceal these circumstances, the modern protagonists
in the search for the 'true path' have not tired of drawing our attention to the elementary facts of the life demanded from above, as they
were before being covered up by trivial moralities, humane chum-
miness and wellness programmes. That Nietzsche presented them in
heroistic codings, while Kafka favoured the lowly and paradoxical
figures, does not change the fact that the two were working towards
the same cause. Whether Zarathustra says in his first speech that 'man
is a rope, stretched between beast and *Übermensch*' or Kafka has the
rope set up close to the ground as a tripwire for the self-righteous –
it is neither the same rope nor the same trick in both cases, but the
ropes come from the same factory, which has been making equipment
for acrobats since time immemorial. The technical observation that
Nietzsche tended towards an acrobatics of strength and wealth while
Kafka preferred that of weakness and lack does not require further
exposition here. This difference could only be discussed within a
general theory of good and bad habits and a consideration of the sym-
metries between strengthening and weakening forms of training.

Kafka objectified his intuitions about the meaning of acrobatics
and asceticism in three tales that have become classics: 'A Report to
an Academy' (1917, first published in the journal *Der Jude*, edited
by Martin Buber), 'First Sorrow' (1922, first published in the journal
Genius) and 'A Hunger Artist' (1923, first published in *Die Neue
Rundschau*).

The first of these contains the autobiography of an ape that became
human by means of imitation. What Kafka presents is no less than

a new depiction of the hominization process from the perspective of an animal. The motif of this transformation is found not in the usual combination of evolutionary adaptations and cultural innovations. Instead, it results from a fatal facticity: the circumstance that the animal-catchers of the Hagenbeck Circus capture the ape in Africa and abduct it to the world of humans. The implied question is not made explicit: why do humans, at the present end of their development, create both zoos and circuses? Presumably because both places confirm the vague feeling that they could learn something there about their own being and becoming.

The ape already realizes aboard the ship which takes it back to Europe that, as far as its future fate is concerned, the choice between the zoo and vaudeville leaves only the latter as a tolerable option. Only there can it see a chance to preserve some remainder, however small, of its legacy. This legacy lives on within it as the feeling that there must always be some way out for an ape – ways out are the animal raw material for what humans pompously call 'freedom'. In addition, the ape arrives in the human world with its natural mobility impaired, marked by two gunshots fired during its capture – one at the cheek, leaving a scar that causes its captors to call it 'Red Peter', and one below the hip, turning it into a cripple and allowing it to walk only with a slight limp. Hans Würtz should have included Red Peter alongside Lord Byron and Joseph Goebbels in the class of 'deformity cripples', the limping and misshapen, and partly also next to Unthan, the armless fiddler, who states at one point in his memoirs that he started limping without any organic cause for a time, but managed to give up this incorrect posture again through intensive training.

Because the vaudeville path is the only one still viable, the ape's humanization leads directly to the acrobatic trail. The first trick Red Peter learns – unaware that it marks the beginning of his self-training – is the handshake, the gesture with which humans communicate to their kind that they respect them as equals. While social philosophers of Kojève's type attribute humanization to the duel, in which the opponents risk their life on the basis of a feeling that some inadequately call boisterousness, Kafka's acrobatic anthropology contents itself with the handshake, which renders the duel superfluous: 'a handshake betokens frankness'.[52] This gesture is the realization of the first ethics – an ape had to perform it so that the provenance of the ethical from conditioning would become apparent, in this case a conditioning towards similarity. Even before the handshake, Red Peter had acquired a mental attitude that would provide the foundation for all further learning – the forced peace of mind based on the realization that attempting escape would only worsen its situation. Having understood that becoming a member of mankind is the only way out for the displaced animal, it can do anything it wants – except breaking the crutches on which it limps towards its goal. Between the freedom of apes and humanization lies a spontaneous stoicism that keeps candidates from 'desperate acts', as Red Peter puts it.

The next tricks develop further what was implicit in the first: Red Peter learns to spit in people's faces for fun, and to be good-naturedly amused when they reciprocate. This is followed by pipe-smoking, and finally by dealing with bottles of liquor, which present the first major challenge for its old nature. The implication of these two lessons is clear: humans cannot become what they are meant to represent in their sphere without stimulants and narcotics. From that point on, Red Peter gets through a series of teachers on his way to the heights of vaudeville aptitude – including one who is so confused by his dealings with his pupil that he has to be admitted to an asylum. In the end, 'with an effort which up till now has never been repeated', he manages to reach 'the cultural level of an average European',[53] which means nothing in one sense, but something significant in another sense, as it opens a way out from the cage, 'the way of humanity'.[54] Summing up, the humanized ape places value on noting that his account is a neutral reproduction of genuine events: 'I am only making a report. To you also, honoured Members of the Academy, I have only made a report.'[55]

At the next stage of Kafka's vaudeville-existentialist investigations, the human personnel steps into the foreground. In the short tale 'First Sorrow', which Kafka described as a 'revolting little story' in a letter to Kurt Wolff, he tells of a trapeze artist who has become accustomed to remaining up inside the circus dome instead of descending after his performances. He settles in under the tent roof, forcing those around him to look after him up there. Having grown accustomed to an existence far above the ground, he finds moving between the cities in which the circus makes its guest appearances increasingly torturous, such that his impresario does his best to make the shifts easier for him. In spite of this, his suffering becomes ever greater. He can only survive the inescapable travels in the fastest of cars or by hanging from the luggage racks of train compartments. One day, he surprises his impresario with the announcement that he requires a second trapeze at all costs – in tears, he asks himself how he could ever have made do with a single bar. He then falls asleep, and the impresario discovers the first wrinkles in the sleeper's face.

This tale presents fundamental statements of vaudeville

existentialism compressed into a very short form. They all concern the internal dynamics of the artiste's existence, starting with the observation that the artiste increasingly loses touch with the world on the ground. By wanting to settle exclusively in the sphere in which he performs his tricks, he ends his relationship with the rest of the world and withdraws to his precarious height. Such lines read like an earnest parody of the idea of anachoresis, the religiously motivated renunciation of the profane world. Kafka's trapeze artist thus does away with the tension that accompanies a double life as 'artist and citizen', as described in the temporally and conceptually close statements of Gottfried Benn and Thomas Mann: he opts for the complete absorption of his existence by the one. His demand for the second trapeze indicates the innate tendency in all radical artistry towards a constant raising of its standards. The urge to go further is as inherent in art as the will to transcend reality in religious asceticism: perfection is not enough. Nothing less than the impossible is satisfactory.

We here encounter a further mental module[56] seldom missing from the composition of religious systems: it encompasses the inner operations that present the impossible as achievable – in fact, they assert that it has already been accomplished. Wherever they are carried out, the boundary between the possible and the impossible vanishes. This third building block enables the rehearsal of a hubristic conclusion: the impossibility of x proves that it is possible. In a peculiar fashion, the artiste who demands a second bar is repeating the *credo quia absurdum* with which Tertullian formalized the new syllogism in the third century.[57] Needless to say, this constitutes the true surrealistic religious module. Its execution involves an inner operation that Coleridge – in an aesthetic context – termed a 'willing suspension of disbelief'.[58] With this, the believer ruptures the system of empirical plausibility and enters the sphere of the actually existing impossible. Whoever trains this figure intensively can attain the mobility in dealing with the unbelievable that is typical among artistes.

Kafka makes his decisive discovery in the form of an implicit clue. He uncovers the fact that there is no artistry whose one-sidedly absorbing training duties do not lead to an unmarked second training. While the first is based on toughening exercises, the second amounts to a course of un-toughening, and simultaneously moulds the artiste on the rope into a virtuoso of the inability to live. That he must be taken no less seriously in this state than in his first function is shown by the impresario's behaviour: he meets his charge's needs in both respects, on the one hand with new apparatus for his high-altitude performance, and on the other hand with all the life-facilitating equipment required especially in the critical moments of transition. We now understand that this equipment too has the character of training devices, devices used by the acrobat to train his increasing remoteness from life. The impresario would have had every reason to be concerned about this second movement towards the limits of possibility. At the same time, however, it proves the artiste's radical artistry – an artiste who remained suited to life would only reveal that he had time for dealing with non-art alongside his art, which would automatically eliminate him from the ranks of the great. Kafka can therefore be considered the inspirer of a negative theory of training.

The author's most significant impulses are to be found in the short tale 'A Hunger Artist'. Here, he augments his observations on the existence of artistes with a statement about their future fate. The opening sentence already makes the tendency clear: 'During these last decades the interest in hunger artists has markedly diminished.'[59] The contemporary audience, we are told, no longer derives much amusement from the performances of such virtuosos, while observers were spellbound in earlier times. In the heyday of the art, there were subscribers who would sit in front of the cage for days – in fact, the attention of the whole town was fixed on the ascetic, and 'from day to day of his fast the excitement mounted'.[60] While demonstrating his art, the faster wore a black top that greatly emphasized his ribs. He was kept in a cage lined with straw in order to guarantee the full monitoring of his activities. Wardens ensured the strict observance of the fasting rules, preventing him from eating anything in secret. He would never have resorted to dishonest means, however. Occasionally he even had an opulent breakfast served for the guards, paid for out of his own pocket, as a token of his gratitude for their services. Nonetheless, suspicion towards his art was a constant companion.

In better times, hunger performances could be displayed as a self-sufficient sensation in the world's largest venues. The impresario set a limit of forty days for each fasting period – not for the sake of any biblical analogy, but because experience had shown that the audience's interest in large cities could only be held for that long, and began to dwindle if the event continued. The hunger artist himself was always dissatisfied with this temporal restriction, as he felt an urge to prove that he could even outdo himself with 'a performance beyond human imagination'.[61] When he collapsed after his forty-day performance it was by no means because he was exhausted from fasting, as his impresario, confusing cause and effect, claimed, but rather out of frustration that he had been prevented yet again from overstepping the boundary of what was thought possible.

When the waning of public interest in hunger art noted at the start of the tale began, the artist, after some vain attempts to revive the dying genre, decided to dismiss his impresario and join a large circus; here, he knew, he would by no means be a prestigious performer, only a marginal curiosity. His cage was set up near the stalls for the circus animals, so that the visitors who came in throngs to see the animals in the intervals would cast a passing glance at the emaciated ascetic. He had to face the facts, even the bitterest one: he was now no more than 'an impediment on the way to the menagerie'.[62] True, he could now fast for as long as he had always wanted, because he remained unobserved and therefore unrestrained, but his heart was heavy, for 'he was working honestly, but the world was cheating him of his reward'.[63] Concealed among his straw, he set records that went unnoticed.

When he felt his death growing near, the hunger artist made his artistic confession to the warden who had found him by chance curled up in the straw:

> 'I always wanted you to admire my fasting,' said the hunger artist. 'We do admire it,' said the overseer, affably. 'But you shouldn't admire it,' said the hunger artist. 'Well then we don't admire it,' said the overseer, 'but why shouldn't we admire it?' 'Because I have to fast, I can't help it,' said the hunger artist. 'What a fellow you are,' said the overseer, 'and why can't you help it?' 'Because [. . .] I couldn't find the food I liked. If I had found it, believe me, I should have made no fuss and stuffed myself like you or anyone else.'[64]

After his death, the cage was given to a young panther that leapt about splendidly. The narrator conveys the essence of its existence by telling us that 'it lacked for nothing'.

I do not intend to comment on this oft-interpreted masterpiece from an artistic perspective. In our context, an anartistic reading that takes the text as an intellectual-historical document is sufficient. What is important is to take Kafka's reflection further and arrive at a general ascetological model. What began as a vaudeville philosophy can now be developed into an explication of classical asceticisms. This is due to the choice of discipline: fasting. It is not an artistic discipline like any other; it is the metaphysical asceticism *par excellence*. From time immemorial it has been the exercise by which, if it succeeds, the ordinary human who is subject to hunger learns – or observes in others – how one can beat nature at its own game. The fasting of ascetics is the skilled form of the lack that is otherwise always experienced passively and involuntarily.[65] This triumph over need is only accessible to those who are assisted by a greater need: when the old master ascetics say that hunger for God or enlightenment[66] must overrule every other desire if it is to be sated, they are presupposing a hierarchy of privations. The pious language game takes up the possibility of doubling oral abstinence in order to counter profane hunger with a sacred one. In truth, sacred hunger is not a longing to be filled, but rather the search for a homeostasis for which 'satisfaction of hunger' is only a spiritual-rhetorically established metaphor.[67]

The decisive aspect of Kafka's asceticism parable is the artiste's admission that he did not deserve admiration, because his fasting was simply a consequence of his innermost inclination – or rather disinclination: all he was doing was obeying his aversion to the imposition of having to consume the food that was available. The statement 'But you shouldn't admire it' is the most spiritual European pronouncement during the last century; we have yet to hear the analogous injunction: you should not sanctify it. What Nietzsche generally described as the negativism of the vitally handicapped now returns specifically as an aversion to nutrition. Hence Kafka's artiste never overcomes himself; he follows an aversion that works for him, and which he only needs to exaggerate. In the final analysis, the most extreme artistedom turns out to be a question of taste. 'I do not like the taste of anything' – thus the verdict pronounced at the Final Judgement on what existence has to offer. The rejection of nourishment goes even further than the message of 'don't touch me' conveyed by Jesus to Mary of Magdalene in John 20:17; it gesturally communicates 'don't enter me' or 'don't stuff me full'. It moves from the prohibition of contact to the refusal of metabolic exchange, as if any collaboration with the absorptive tendencies of one's own body were a depraved risk.

What makes Kafka's experiment meaningful is the fact that he works consistently under the 'God is dead' premise. This enables hunger art to reveal what remains of metaphysical desire when its transcendent goal is eliminated. What transpires is a form of beheaded asceticism in which the supposed tensile strain from above proves to be an aversive tension from within; then the torso is everything. Kafka experiments with leaving out religion – to test out a final religion of leaving out everything that previously characterized it: what remains are the artiste's exercises. The hunger artist is therefore speaking truthfully when he asks not to be admired. The withdrawal of the public's interest in his performances comes at exactly the right moment – as if the crowd, without knowing, were following the inspirations of a zeitgeist that wants to speak the final word on the world of hunger: over and finished. Now the time has come for those who lack for nothing, be they panthers, inhabitants of workers' and farmers' republics or followers of a social market economy. What was once the most spiritual of all asceticisms is now, in truth, no more than 'an impediment on the way to the menagerie'.

Ten years after the publication of 'A Hunger Artist', Joseph Stalin put an end to hunger art by other means when, during the winter of 1932–3, he sent innumerable Ukrainian farmers – counts vary between 3.5 and 8 million – to their death through a hunger blockade; they too were untimely, impediments on the way to abundance.[68]

Even Stalin was not able to achieve the profanation of hunger completely. The hunger artist actually existed in his time – not in Prague but in Paris, a few years after Kafka's death; not as a man in a black top with bulging ribs, but as a very skinny young woman in blue stockings. She too was an artiste in the field of weight loss for the sake of the entirely other: the greatest thinker of anti-gravitation in the twentieth century, born in 1909, an anarchist of Jewish descent, converted to Catholicism, an insider on all magic mountains of worldlessness and simultaneously a searcher for a rooting in authentic community, resistance fighter and defiance existentialist, who wanted to starve alongside the workers in order to ennoble her lack of appetite and humble her nobility. Simone Weil managed to die in British exile at the age of thirty-four of a twofold cause: tuberculosis and voluntary starvation.

— 5 —

PARISIAN BUDDHISM

Cioran's Exercises

The last figure I wish to present in these introductory reflections, the Romanian aphorist Emile M. Cioran, who was born in 1911 and lived in Paris from 1937 to 1995, is likewise part of the great turn that is at issue here. He is an important informant for us, because one can see in his work how the informalization of asceticism progresses without a loss of vertical tension. In his own way, Cioran too is a hunger artist: a man who fasts metaphorically by abstaining from solid food for his identity. He too does not overcome himself, rather – like Kafka's protagonist – following his strongest inclination, namely disgust at the full self. As a metaphorical faster, all he ever does is to show that refusal is the foundation of the great, demonstrating the unfolding of scepticism from a reservation of judgement to a reservation about the temptation to exist.

To approach the phenomenon of Cioran, it is best to take two statements by Nietzsche as a guideline:

Whoever despises himself still respects himself as one who despises.[69]

Moral: what sensible man nowadays writes one honest word about himself? He must already belong to the Order of Holy Foolhardiness.[70]

The latter remark refers to the almost inevitably displeasing nature of all detailed biographies of great men. Even more, it describes the psychological and moral improbability of an honest self-portrayal. At the same time, it names the one condition that would make an exception possible; one could, in fact, view Cioran as the prior of the prospective order imagined by Nietzsche. His holy foolhardiness stems from a gesture that Nietzsche considered the most improbable and least desirable: a rejection of the norms of discretion and tact,

73

to say nothing of the pathos of distance. Nietzsche only approached this position once in his own work, when he practised the 'cynicism' necessary for an honest self-portrayal in the 'physiological' passages of *Ecce Homo* – immediately labelling this gesture as 'world-historical' to compensate for the feeling of embarrassment through the magnitude of the matter. The result was more like baroque self-praise than any indiscretion towards himself, however – assuming that self-praise was not a deeper form of exposure on this occasion. The rest of the time, Nietzsche remained a withdrawn prophet who only perceived the disinhibitions he foresaw through the crack of a door.

Whoever, like Cioran, dated themselves after Nietzsche was condemned to go further. The young Romanian followed Nietzsche's lead not only by heading the Order of Holy Foolhardiness, along with other self-exposers such as Michel Leiris and Jean-Paul Sartre; he also realized the programme of basing the final possibility of self-respect on contempt for oneself. He was able to do this because, despite the apparently unusual nature of his intention, he had the zeitgeist on his side. The epochal turn towards making the latent explicit took hold of him, and led him to commit thoughts to paper that no author would have dared formulate a few years earlier. In this turn, the 'honest word about himself' postulated yet excluded in practice by Nietzsche became an unprecedented offensive power. Mere honesty becomes a mode of writing for ruthlessness towards oneself. One can no longer be an autobiographer without being an autopathographer – which means publishing one's own medical file. To be honest is to admit what one lacks. Cioran was the first who stepped forward to declare: 'I lack everything – and for that reason, everything is too much for me.'

The nineteenth century had only pushed the genre of the 'honest word' to its limits once, in Dostoyevsky's *Notes from Underground*, published in 1864. Nietzsche's reaction to this work is well known. Cioran worked for half a century on his notes from the attic, in which he treated his only subject with admirable monotony: how to continue when one lacks everything and everything is too much. Early on, he saw his chance as an author in donning the coat offered by Nietzsche; he had already slipped into it during his Romanian years, and never took it off again. If Nietzsche interpreted metaphysics as a symptom of suffering from the world and an aid to fleeing from it, Cioran accepted this diagnosis without the slightest attempt to formulate an opposing argument. What he rejected was Nietzsche's flight in the opposite direction: the affirmation of the unaffirmable.

For Cioran, the *Übermensch* is a puerile fiction, a puffed-up caretaker who hangs his flag out of the window while the world is as unacceptable as it always has been. Who would speak of the eternal recurrence, when existing once already means existing once too often?

In his student years, Cioran had experimented for a time with the revolutionary affirmations typical of the time and drifted about in the circles of Romanian right-wing extremists. He took to the fashionable mysticism of general mobilization and to political vitalism, which was praised as a cure for scepticism and an excessive preoccupation with one's inner life. All this invited him to seek salvation in the phantasm of the 'nation' – a close relative of the spectre now active as 'returning religion'.

Cioran abandoned this position – assuming it ever was one – before long. In time, his increasing disgust with its hysterical excursions into positivity restored his clear-sightedness. When he moved to Paris in 1937 to begin an almost sixty-year period of hermit-like existence there, he was not entirely cured of the temptation to participate in great history, but he did increasingly leave behind the exaltations of his youth. The basic aggressive-depressive mood that had always characterized him was now expressed in other forms. During this phase, Cioran succeeded in gaining a lasting foothold in the genre of the 'honest word about himself'.

> The impossibility of killing or killing myself caused me to stray into the field of literature. It is this inability alone that made a writer out of me.[71]

Never again would he use the language of commitment he had adopted in his Romanian days with the talent of the pubescent imitator. The blind admiration he had once felt for Germany and its brutal shift disappeared with it. 'If there is one illness of which I have been cured, it is that one.'[72] For the cured man, part of speaking an honest word about his own illness is the admission that he sought to heal himself by dishonest means. Liberated from this evil once and for all, he devoted himself to the task of inventing the writer Cioran, who would set up a business using the psychopathic capital he had discovered in himself as a youth. The figure that created itself in those days could have come from one of Hugo Ball's novels: it presents a 'jostled human', the vaudeville saint, the philosophical clown who expands despair and the disinclination to make anything of himself into a theatre revue.

The secularization of asceticisms and the informalization of spirituality can be observed in Cioran's 'life's work' in the most concentrated form possible. In his case, the Central European existentialism of defiance was expressed not in an existentialism of committed resistance, but rather in an endless series of acts of disengagement. The œuvre of this existentialist of refusal consists of a succession of rejection letters to the temptations to involve oneself and take a stance. Thus his central paradox crystallizes ever more clearly: the position of the man with no position, the role of the protagonist with no role. Cioran had already attained stylistic mastery with the first of his Parisian books, the 1949 text *Précis de décomposition* – translated into German by Paul Celan in 1953 under the title *Lehre vom Zerfall* [English title: *A Short History of Decay*]. Cioran had certainly absorbed the spirit of the Without period to lasting effect; the crutches he wanted to break, however, were those of identity, belonging and consistency. Only one basic principle convinced him: to be convinced by nothing. From one book to the next he continued his existentialist floor gymnastics, whose kinship with the exercises of Kafka's fictional characters is conspicuous. His number was fixed from the start: it is that of the hungover marginal figure who struggles not only through the city, but rather in the universe as a homeless (*sans abri*), stateless (*sans papier*) and shameless (*sans gêne*) individual. It is not for nothing that his impressive collection of autobiographical utterances is entitled *Cafard* [Snitch/Cockroach/Moral Hangover] in the German edition.[73] As a practising parasite, Cioran followed on from the Greek meaning of the word: *parásitoi*, 'people who sit at a spread table', was what Athenians called guests who were invited to contribute to the company's entertainment. The Romanian emigré in Paris did not find it difficult to fulfil such expectations. In a letter to his parents he wrote: 'Had I been taciturn by nature, I would have starved to death long ago.'[74] Elsewhere he states: '*All our humiliations come from the fact that we cannot bring ourselves to die of hunger.*'[75]

Cioran's aphorisms read like a practically applicable commentary on Heidegger's theory of moods, that is to say the atmospheric impregnations of the individual and collective 'thymos' that 'lend' existence an *a priori* pre-logical tinge. Neither Heidegger nor Cioran went to the trouble of discussing the lending and the lender of moods as extensively as the significance of the phenomenon would demand – presumably because both tended to break off psychological analysis and move on quickly to the sphere of existential statements. In truth, Cioran accepts his aggressive-depressive disposition as the primal atmospheric fact of his existence. He accepts that he is fated to experience the world primarily in dystonic timbres: weariness, boredom, meaninglessness, tastelessness, and rebellious anger towards everything that is the case. He frankly confirms Nietzsche's diagnosis that the ideals of metaphysics should be viewed as the intellectual products of physical and psychophysical illness. By taking the approach of speaking 'an honest word about himself' further than any author before him, he openly admits that his concern is to offset the 'failed creation'. Thinking does not mean thanking, as Heidegger suggests; it means taking revenge.

It was only with Cioran that the thing Nietzsche had sought to expose was fulfilled as if the phenomenon had existed from time immemorial: a philosophy of pure *ressentiment*. But what if such a philosophy had only become possible through Nietzsche's influence? Here the German-born existentialism of defiance changes – bypassing the French existentialism of resistance, which Cioran despised as a shallow trend – into an existentialism of incurability with crypto-Romanian and Dacian-Bogomilian shades. This shift only came to a halt at the threshold of Asian inexistentialism. Though Cioran, marked by European *vanitas*, played throughout his life with a feeling of all-encompassing unreality, he could never quite bring himself to follow Buddhism in its abandonment of the postulation of reality, and with it that of God. The latter, as is well known, serves to guarantee the reality we know through a 'last reality' that is hidden from us.[76] Though he felt drawn to Buddhism, Cioran did not want to subscribe to its ontology. He not only loathed the reality of the world, but also intended to take advantage of it; he therefore had to accept the reality of reality, even if it was only sophistically. He neither wanted to save himself nor to let anyone else save him. His entire thought is a complaint about the imposition of requiring salvation.

One could pass over all this as a bizarre breeding phenomenon in the biotopes of Parisianism after 1945, were it not for the fact that it brings to light a generally significant tendency that forces a radical change of conditions on the planet of the practising. Cioran, as noted above, is a key witness to the ascetologically far-reaching shift that we are thematizing as the emergence of anthropotechnics. This shift draws our attention to the informalization of spirituality that I said we should grasp as a complementary counter-tendency to the de-spiritualization of asceticisms. Cioran is a new type of practising person whose originality and representative nature are evident in the fact that he practises rejecting every goal-directed way of practising. Methodical exercises, as is well known, are only possible if there is a fixed practice goal in sight. It is precisely the authority of this goal that Cioran contests. Accepting a practice goal would mean believing

– and 'believing' refers here to the mental act whereby the beginner anticipates the goal.

This running forwards to the goal is the fourth module of the 'religious' behavioural complex.[77] The anticipation generally takes place as follows: one looks at someone perfect, from whom one receives, incredulous and credulous at once, the message that one could be the same one day. We will see in later chapters how the use of this inner operation set armies of practising humans in motion over millennia.[78] Without the module of running forwards to the goal there can be no *vita contemplativa*, no monastic life, no swarm of departures to other shores, no wanting to be the way someone greater once was. One can therefore not emphasize enough that the most effective forms of anthropotechnics in the world come from yesterday's world – and the genetic engineering praised or rejected loudly today, even if it becomes feasible and acceptable for humans on a larger scale, will long remain a mere anecdote compared to the magnitude of these phenomena.

The believer's running-ahead into perfection is not Cioran's concern. He certainly has a passionate 'interest' in the religious texts that speak of perfection and salvation, but he will not carry out the believing operation as such, the anticipation of one's own being-ready-later. His non-belief thus has two sides: that of not being able, because his own prevailing mood corrodes the *naïveté* required for the supposition of perfection,[79] and that of not being willing, because he has adopted the stance of the sceptic and does not want to abandon this definitive provisional state in favour of a position. His only option, then, is to experiment with the leftovers. He is forced to play on an instrument for which any purposeful training would be futile – the detuned instrument of his own existence. Yet it is precisely his performance on the unplayable instrument that shows the unsuppressible universality of the practising dimension: for, by practising in the absence of a suitable instrument, the 'anti-prophet' develops an informal version of mastery.

He becomes the first master of not-getting-anywhere. Like Kafka's hunger artist, he turns his aversion into a virtuoso performance and develops the corresponding form of skill for his *cafard*. Even in this form one hears the appeal that returns in all artistedom: 'I always wanted you to admire it . . .' While Kafka's fasting master waits until the end before uttering the contrary injunction 'you shouldn't admire it', Cioran provides the material for demystifying his art from the outset by revealing it on almost every page as the act of letting oneself go under the compulsion of one's prevailing mood. It is this mood speaking when Cioran remarks: 'I am incapable of not suffering.'[80] 'My books express an *attitude to life*, not a vision.'[81] He felt a contemptuous suspicion towards the possibility of therapeutically modifying attitudes towards life; he lived off the products of his disposition, after all, and could hardly have afforded an attempt to change it.

In contributing to the discovery that even letting oneself go can be art, and that, if it is accompanied by the will to skill, it also requires training, Cioran helped the Order of Holy Foolhardiness to find a set of rules. It is preserved in his *Précis de décomposition*, this book of peculiar exercises that, as I intend to show, formulates the true charter of modern 'culture' as an aggregate of undeclared asceticisms – a book that exceeds any binding. The extent of Cioran's own awareness of his role in translating spiritual habitus into profane discontent and its literary cultivation is demonstrated in *A Short History of Decay* (whose title could equally have been rendered as 'A Guide to Decay'), the work that established his reputation. Originally this collection was to be entitled *Exercices négatifs* – which could refer both to exercises in negation and anti-exercises. What Cioran presented was no less than a set of rules intended to lead its adepts onto the path of uselessness. If this path had a goal, it would be: 'To be more unserviceable than a saint . . .'.[82]

The tendency of the new set of rules is anti-stoic. While the stoic manner does everything in its power to get into shape for the universe – Roman Stoicism, after all, was primarily a philosophy for civil servants, attractive for those who wanted to believe that it was honourable to hold out in the place assigned by providence as a 'soldier of the cosmos' – the Cioranian ascetic must reject the cosmic thesis as such. He refuses to accept his own existence as a component of a well-ordered whole; it should rather serve to prove that the universe is a failure. Cioran only accepts the Christian reinterpretation of the cosmos as creation to the extent that God comes into play as the impeachable cause of a complete fiasco. For a moment, Cioran comes close to Kant's moral proof of God's existence, albeit with the opposite result: the existence of God must necessarily be postulated because God has to apologize for the world.

The procedure Cioran develops for his anti-exercises is based on the elevation of leisure to a practice form for existential revolt. What he calls 'leisure' is actually a conscious drift through the emotional states of the manic-depressive spectrum unencumbered by any form of structured work – a method that anticipates the later glorification of the *dérive*, the act of drifting through the day espoused by the situationists of the 1950s. Conscious life in a state of drift amounts to a practising reinforcement of the sense of discontinuity that belonged to Cioran's disposition because of his moodiness. The reinforcing effect is further heightened dogmatically by the bellicose thesis that continuity is a 'delusional idea'[83] – it would have sufficed to call it a construct. Hence existence means feeling ill at ease at constantly new now-points.

The literary form that corresponds to the punctualism of Cioran's self-observation, which alternates between moments of contraction and diffusion, is the aphorism, and its publicistic genre the aphorism collection. The author establishes a relatively simple and stable grid of six or eight themes early on, using it to comb his states in the drift and move from an experiential point to a corresponding thematic node. With time, the themes – like partial personalities or editorial offices working alongside one another – develop a life of their own that enables them to continue growing self-sufficiently without having to wait for an experiential occasion. The 'author' Cioran is merely the chief editor who adds the finishing touches to the products of his typing rooms. He produces books by compiling the texts provided by his inner employees. They present their material in irregular sessions – aphorisms from the blasphemy department, observations from the misanthropy studio, gibes from the disillusionment section, proclamations from the press office of the circus of the lonely, theses from the agency for swindling on the edge, and poisons from the editorial office for the despisal of contemporary literature. Formulating the thought of suicide is the only job that remains in the chief editor's hands; this involves the practice on which all further sequences of repetition depend. This thought alone permits, from one crisis to the next, the restoration of the feeling that one is still sovereign even in misery – a feeling that provides discontented life with a minimum of stability. In addition, those responsible for the different themes know what the neighbouring offices are producing, meaning that they increasingly quote and align themselves with one another. The 'author' Cioran simply invents the book titles that hint at the genre – syllogisms, curses, epitaphs, confessions, lives of the saints or guidelines for failure. He also provides the section headings, which follow a similar logic. In everyday life he is much less of a writer than a reader, and if there was one activity in his life that, from a distance, resembled a regular employment or a formal exercise, it was the reading and rereading of books that served as sources of comfort and arguments to be rebutted. He read the life of St Teresa of Ávila five times in the original Spanish. The numerous readings are inserted into the process of the anti-exercises and, together with memories of his own words, form a bundle of interactions to the nth degree.

The 'negative exercises' of the Romanian 'trumpery Buddha' – as he terms himself in *All Gall Is Divided* – are landmarks in the recent history of spiritual behaviour. All they require now is explication as valid discoveries, beyond the chummy comments about the prevailing mood that have dominated the reception of his work thus far. The scepticism attributed to the author in accordance with some of his own language games is anything but 'radical' – it is virtuosic and elegant. Cioran's approach may seem monotonous, but it almost never leads to the dullness that characterizes radicalisms. What he says and does serves to raise his suffering to the level of skill that corresponds to his abilities. Cioran's work appears far less self-contradictory as soon as one notes the emergence of the practice phenomenon – so once again we have 'one of the broadest and longest facts that exist' in an unusual declination. Even if his prevailing mood was that of a 'passive-aggressive bastard' – as group therapists occasionally put it in the 1970s – his ethos was that of a man of exercises, an artiste who even made a stunt out of sluggishness, who turned despair into an Apollonian discipline and letting oneself go into an étude almost classical in manner.

The effective history of Cioran's books shows that he was immediately recognized as a paradoxical master of exercises. Naturally they only spoke to a small number of readers, but resonated very strongly with them. The small band of intensive recipients even discovered in the writings of this infamous author something whose existence he would probably have denied – a brotherly vibration, a hidden tendency to give the 'Trappist Order without faith', of which he playfully and irresponsibly considered himself a member, a slightly denser consistency. There was a secret readiness in him to give advice to the despairing who were even more helpless than himself – and a far less concealed inclination to become famous for his exercises in escape from the world. While he may have resisted the *tentation d'exister* more or less resolutely – even in brothels, even in chic society – he was willing, with all due discretion, to succumb to the temptation of becoming a role model. It is thus not unreasonable to see in Cioran not merely the apprentice of an informalized asceticism, but also an informal trainer who affects others from a distance with his *modus vivendi*. While the ordinary trainer – as defined above – is the one 'who wants me to want',[84] the spiritual trainer acts as the one who does not want me not to want. When I want to give up, it is he who advises against it. Aside from that, I will only point out that Cioran's books provided an effective form of suicide prevention for numerous readers – something that is also said of personal conversations with him. Those seeking advice may have sensed how he had discovered the healthiest way of being incurable.

I read Cioran's output of 'negative exercises' as a further indication that the production of 'high culture', whatever that may mean in specific terms, has an indispensable ascetic factor. Nietzsche made it visible by reminding his readers of the immense system of rigid conditioning on which the superstructure of morality, art and all 'disciplines' is based. This asceticism-based thought only becomes clearly visible when the most conspicuous standard exercises in culture, known as 'traditions', find themselves in the difficult situation of Kafka's hunger artist – as soon as one can say that interest in them 'has markedly diminished during these last decades', the conditions of possibility of their survival will themselves become conspicuous. When interest in a form of life dwindles, the ground on which the visible parts of the constructions erected themselves is revealed here and there.

TRANSITION
RELIGIONS DO NOT EXIST:

From Pierre de Coubertin to L. Ron Hubbard

It is time to draw our conclusions from the indications we have discussed about an anthropotechnic re-description of the religious, ethical and ascetic-artistic phenomena. I will therefore return to the two main practice- and mentality-historical tendencies of the last century: the rise of the neo-athletic syndrome around 1900 and the explosion of informal mysticism, regardless of whether it manifests itself *privatissime* or in the network operations of psychotechnic sects. It is with reference to both of these that the hypothesis of the spectral 'return of religion' can be rendered more precise. I will begin by using the example of the neo-Olympic movement founded by Pierre de Coubertin to show how an undertaking initiated as a cult religion outgrew its religious design to become the most comprehensive organizational form for human behaviour of effort and practice that could always be observed outside the worlds of work and war – compared to the dimensions of the neo-Olympic sport cult, even the pilgrimages of the Middle Ages and the excesses of Spanish monastic culture in the seventeenth century (when a substantial part of the populace flooded the prison cells to rid themselves of their selves by all available means) are of a merely episodic character. Then, using the example of the Church of Scientology, founded by the science fiction author Lafayette Ron Hubbard, I will investigate what we can learn when a company for distributing well-known methods of auto-suggestion manages to expand into a worldwide psychagogic firm that claims to be a religion.

I will present the conclusions in advance: the fate of Olympism and the business of the Scientological 'churches' show that 'religion', as understood by those who exploit the notion, does not exist – and never has. Both de Coubertin and Hubbard fell for a modern mirage

83

whose examination gives insights into the fabrication and constitution of 'religion' in general. Both wanted to found or contribute to something that cannot be, and which therefore, once 'founded', inevitably transpires as something other than what its founder thought it should be or should seek to become. Both founders made the same mistake in opposite ways: actual Olympism refused to become the religion planned by de Coubertin, while the Scientology movement resists being viewed merely as the psychotechnic firm that it in fact is. In the first step of analysing these two refusals, I will clarify the meaning of my claim that religion does not exist. What we are actually dealing with – on a scale whose measurement has scarcely begun – are variously misinterpreted anthropotechnic practice systems and sets of rules for moulding one's inward and outward behaviour. Under the shelter of such forms, the practising work on improving their global immune status[85] – which, both on European soil and in Asia, highlights the paradox of how destroying physical immunity has not infrequently been praised as the royal road to boosting metaphysical immunity (immortality): recall St Francis of Assisi's exercises of deliberate attrition for 'brother donkey' – as he was wont to call his body – and certain parasuicidal practices that brought notoriety to Tibetan and Mongolian Buddhism and Lamaism.

Cioran's *All Gall Is Divided* contains the following remarks under the heading 'religion':

> Without the vigilance of irony, how easy it would be to found a religion!
> Merely allow the gawkers to collect around our loquacious trances.[86]

This note is instructive, for despite its modern sarcasm, it testifies to a premodern understanding of the phenomenon known as 'religion'. With his micro-theory of the genesis of religion from the commotion around ecstasy, Cioran, the son of an Orthodox priest, continues the line of Old European theories of supply.[87] The two components or 'raw materials' whose combination produces religion are thus an ecstatic performance by an individual and a corresponding curiosity among the masses. The first naturally takes priority, as it contains the more precious element. If one further interprets Cioran's observation, religion only comes about when the rare – the ecstatic offering – approaches the common – profane curiosity – and allows it to gather around it. It is plain that Cioran here reproduces, albeit on a cruder level, the conviction of the classical monotheisms that it is ultimately God, and God alone, who provokes and permits the assemblages whose congealed form we call churches. He organizes the assemblage by, as they say, revealing Himself to humans.

In typological terms, the supply-theoretical interpretation of the religious phenomenon corresponds to the Catholic position, in so far as the latter is based on a strictly hierarchical line of offer-conveyance running from God to humans, from the priests to the laypersons. The primacy of the giver and the priority of the gift remain unassailable in this universe. The believers here appear exclusively on the taking side, like the hungry at a soup kitchen.[88] In clericocratic times, the 'word of God' was not simply a sublime gift; it was simultaneously the model of an offer one cannot refuse. That is why the most Catholic of the Catholics still insist on the Latin mass today: it presents the diamond core of the religion of supply. It asks not what humans can understand, but rather what God wants to show. For the religion's followers, the Most High is most present when the priest carries out his Latin mystery play with his back to the congregation – church Latin is the petrified form of the 'loquacious trances'. Cioran indicates quite openly that he often found himself in states that would have induced more naïve natures to take church-founding steps.

Demand-theoretical interpretations of the religious phenomenon take us onto the soil of modernity. Here, to take up our image again, the crowd now takes precedence, and one asks oneself how best to meet the needs of the masses. Now there can no longer be any talk of permitting, from above, the common to be present at the appearances of the rare. Rather, it is a matter of giving the many what they want – or what they will want once they have been shown what they are entitled to expect. Those who wish to can see a democratic shift in this. Its consequence is the task of interpreting the assemblage as a demand and responding to it by offering an appropriate supply. To take up this position one must read faith as the updated version of a disposition that is inherent in human existence. Aside from that, it is plain enough why the priority of the demand means that the supplying side must be flexible and refrain from adopting any threatening tone.

This brings us into the field of Protestant practices, where, *summa summarum*, the meeting of demands – for a just God, an address for metaphysical needs, or a helper for a successful life – is the central concern.[89] This applies less in empirical than in typological terms, however; early Protestantism, especially in its Puritan variety, loved the apocalyptic communications characteristic of heartily fist-waving religions of supply. In truth, the Reformation had got under way as a restoration of the offer-theological motif against Catholic inefficiency. It only showed its demand-theoretical quality when the congregations changed into a religiously interested audience. Furthermore, modern

Protestant theology – the work of Karl Barth, for example – is responsible for the most radical formulation of the supply principle, combined with the harshest rejection of the humanely and undogmatically dissolving religiosity of demand that had defined the situation since the eighteenth century. Barth had recognized Schleiermacher, the wooer of the educated among those who despised religion, as the master theologian of the religion of demand – or worse still, the religion of talent – and devoted himself to opposing him as firmly as possible.[90]

It was the same Karl Barth who arrived at the thesis – unheard-of in its time – that Christianity is *not* a religion, because 'religion is unbelief'. He had the right idea, but made the wrong point and presented the most unsuitable of all possible justifications: that the 'word of God' strikes through the fabric of cultural machinations vertically from above, while mere religion is never more than a part of the system of humanities and all-too-humanities set up from below. The argument may seem impressive as a catastrophe-theological intensification of the situation after 1918, but as a description of the overall situation it would be misleading – for modernity is simply not known for being a time in which God shows Himself vertically to humans. This century the earth was struck by meteorites, plummeting down from the outermost and highest places; but there were no gods among them. Had Barth's claim been true, he would have been right in his resolute enmity towards all natural theologies. He would have had good reason to discard any derivation of religion from the structures of consciousness – and likewise any dissolution of Christianity into enlightened ethics. The reason why his thesis was wrong becomes evident upon closer inspection of the 'vertically from above' motif. We know from the phenomena described above that the entire complex of verticality in modernity is revised into a new version that permits a deeper understanding of the emergence of embodied improbability – Barth, however, did not participate sufficiently in its developments. He fell prey to the error that theologians are *ex officio* constrained to make: simply co-opting the dimension of vertical tensions for the 'call from above' in its Christian decoding.

Nonetheless, Barth must be considered the most important recent 'observer' of verticality after Nietzsche. He succeeded in producing a new presentation of Christian doctrine that presupposes the absolute precedence of God's self-representation. This means that the situation of humans can only be understood in the steepest vertical terms: the true God is the one who uncompromisingly overtaxes humans, while the devil meets them at their own level. Even Barth, however, did not deny the existence of 'religions' when he contrasted them with the non-religion of Christianity. He missed the fact that the former were no more 'religions' than his favoured Christian brand. Whether Christian or non-Christian, all of them are both materially and formally nothing other than complexes of inner and outer actions, symbolic practice systems and protocols for regulating traffic with higher stressors and 'transcendental' powers – in short, forms of anthropotechnics in the implicit mode. They are constructs which, for purely pragmatic reasons – initially out of Roman-Christian opportuneness, then later due to Protestant confessional polemics and enlightened systematics – were given the name *religio*, a term dragged along from the millennium of Latinity, referring back both compulsively and arbitrarily to the language games and cultic pursuits of Roman state bigotry.[91] What *religio* (literally 'reverence') meant for the Romans, before St Augustine took the word out of their mouths and spoke of *vera religio*, can best be learned from a detail: that some of the most important Roman legions were allowed to bear the honorific *pia fidelis*, on the model of the *Legio tertia Augusta*, stationed in North Africa, which existed from the middle of the first century BC to the fourth century AD, as well as the *Legio prima adiutrix*, based first in Mainz and later in Pannonia, which existed from Nero's day until the middle of the fifth century. Owing to Christian alterations of meaning, Caesar's piously faithful followers became the legionaries of Christ, known in French as *fidèles* to this day.

Recalling Pierre de Coubertin's neo-Olympism and Ron Hubbard's Church of Scientology raises several questions: what is religion anyway, if the people next door can simply found one? What does religion mean if a Hellenophile educator with a taste for men's bodies in battle and a beaming smart aleck, known until then mainly as the author of cunning space crime novels, believed in all seriousness and unseriousness that they had called one into existence before our eyes? Would that not mean that the safest method of exposing all 'religions' is to found one's own? What do we learn about 'religion' in general by studying the blueprints of newly founded cults and observing their *modus operandi* in their long-term activities? Naturally these questions do not only arise with the two examples highlighted here. They could equally validly be directed at every one of the many recent religious experiments that have drawn attention to themselves since the French Revolution – from the cult of the Supreme Being founded in 1793[92] via Saint-Simonism, Auguste Comte's sociological religion, Mormonism, theosophy and anthroposophy to the makeshift neo-Hindu cults and manifold networks of psychotechnic sects spanning the globe today. All these enterprises already came about under the eyes of the Enlightenment, and could have been studied *in vivo* and *in vitro* if there had been corresponding interest in doing so with the suitable optics and methods.

As far as de Coubertin's neo-Olympism is concerned, its history has been recounted sufficiently often – most recently on the occasion of the centenary celebrations for the modern Olympic Games in 1996 – for there to be no need for me to reproduce more than some rudimentary aspects here. Three sources and elements of de Coubertin's sport-religious system have also been amply acknowledged: they can be found in John Ruskin's gymno-philosophical ideas on eurhythmics,[93] in Dr Brooke's neo-Hellenistic Olympic Games in Shropshire (held from the mid-nineteenth century on) and in Wagner's Bayreuth Festival, where the archetype of a modern elitist-communitary edification cult was taken up in its full articulation – six thousand foot away from everyday industrial life and class divisions. Some have also referred to the inspiring effect of the Parisian *Exposition universelle* of 1889 in order to explain the transfer of the totalizing impulse. Viewed in this light, Olympism appears as a timely globalization of sport in action.[94]

The famous Sorbonne congress of 1894 for the 'Reinstatement of the Olympic Games' had already gathered these ingredients together – augmented by de Coubertin's own socio-therapeutic and pedagogical motifs – to form an effective mixture. De Coubertin recounts in his memoirs that at the opening session at the Sorbonne on 16 June, Gabriel Fauré's *Hymn to Apollo* op. 63 for voice, harp, flute and two clarinets, specially composed for the occasion and based on an inscription found shortly beforehand at the Athenian Treasury at Delphi, was premiered before two thousand 'enchanted listeners':

> A subtle feeling of emotion spread through the auditorium as if the antique eurhythmy were coming to us from the distant past. In this way, Hellenism infiltrated into the whole vast hall.[95]

At the same time, the Paris congress laid down the fundamental aspects of the games and the organization carrying them: the four-year rhythm, which would create a temporal structure for all future times like a new religious calendar; the enlightened dictatorship of the IOC presidency, later consolidated by the election of de Coubertin as president for life; modernism in the definition of sport; equality of different sports; exclusion of children; the principle of circulating games; amateurism (which remained controversial, however, and was suspended in 1976); internationalism and the principle of *pax olympica*. Furthermore, Athens was chosen as the location of the first games and Paris as that of the second in order to draw sufficient attention to their place of birth and their place of rebirth. Little did those in charge know that the Paris Olympics of 1900 would be the low point in the history of Olympism: they were barely noticed alongside the simultaneous *Exposition universelle*. The lesson from this was that two world festivals at the same time are not feasible.

The first Olympic Games of the Modern Age were held in Athens a mere two years later, with great ceremony, under the patronage of the king of Greece – as a purely andrological festival, for the enthusiastic baron had a famously low opinion of women's sports; he wanted the female role in the games to be restricted to handing the winner the olive branch or placing the wreath on his head. De Coubertin's failure to establish his *taceat mulier in arena* was only the first of many in the practical realization of his 'muscle religion'. One of the most far-reaching consequences of the first games was that thanks to the donation of a major patron, the Panathenaic Stadium of Athens, from the time when Greece was a Roman province, could be restored and used again. This initiated the stadium and arena renaissance of the twentieth century, which is still producing ever new event architectures based on ancient primary forms to this day.[96] Even the monks of Mount Athos supposedly contributed money to the Olympic subscription, as if following the revelation that in distant Athens, the modern replicas of their own blurred archetypes were entering the stage again – had the first monks of Eastern Christianity not called themselves the 'athletes of Christ', and joined forces in training camps called *asketería*?

The notable and unforeseen climax of the Athenian games was the first marathon. The idea for this came from the French classical scholar and Hellenophile Michel Bréart, who, at the closing banquet of the Sorbonne conference, had praised the establishment of a marathon trophy for the first winner in the new discipline. When the victor of the race, a twenty-three-year-old Greek shepherd by the name of Spiridion Louys, entered the shining white marble stadium on 10 April 1896 wearing the *fustanella*, the traditional dress (the winning time was given as 2 hours, 58 minutes and 50 seconds), a state came about that it would scarcely be adequate to call 'exceptional'. It was as if a new form of energy had been discovered, a form of emotional electricity without which the way of life in the subsequent era would no longer be imaginable. What happened that scorching afternoon in the Panathenaic Stadium at around five o'clock must be classed as a new kind of epiphany. A previously unknown category, the gods of the moment, introduced itself to the modern audience – gods that require no proof because they only exist for the duration of their manifestation and are not believed in, but experienced. In that hour a new chapter in the history of enthusiasm was opened – and whoever is unwilling to speak of this history must remain silent about the twentieth century.[97] The Greek crown princes ran the last metres of the race alongside the athlete amid the ecstatic cheering of almost 70,000 people; after he had crossed the finishing line, they carried him aloft before the king, who had stood up from his stadium throne. Had one wanted to prove that a new age of inverted hierarchies had begun, this would have provided the most spectacular evidence. For a moment, an athletic shepherd became king over the king – for the first time, one could witness the majesty, indeed the power of the monarch being transferred to the runner; in later decades, there was even a growing feeling that shepherds and their ilk were striving to rule the country alone. A sustained wave of rapture swept over the whole country; an enthusiastic barber promised to shave the victor for free for the rest of his life. An olive branch and a silver medal were the official marks of honour, and these were followed by a flood of gifts.

It is still unclear how Spiridion Louys acquired the necessary stamina; the shepherd boy had supposedly worked for an officer as a messenger or water-carrier and become accustomed to long distances as a result. In a test run two weeks before the games, he had come fifth. He would hardly ever have encountered the word 'training' until then – I take that as supporting my hypothesis that most varieties of practice behaviour take the form of undeclared asceticisms.[98] For the brothers on Mount Athos, it may have seemed like a confirmation of their intuitions when, not long afterwards, the rumour began to circulate that the runner had spent the night prior to the race in prayer before icons – even de Coubertin took this information seriously enough to begin reflecting on the mental and spiritual components of the greatest sporting achievements. Like Friedrich Nietzsche, Carl Hermann Unthan and Hans Würtz, the founder of the games was also convinced that the will ultimately leads to success and victory. De Coubertin therefore made no secret of his aversion to the positivism of sports physicians, who were too 'philistine' in their thinking to grasp the higher dimensions of sport in general and the new movement in particular.[99]

Pierre de Coubertin believed that what he was invoking under the name of Olympism would amount to no less than a fully valid new religion. He thought that he could support this view by drawing on the religious embedding of the ancient games. During their thousand-year existence they had always been held *coram deis*; in fact, they not only took place before the gods, but also with their approval, perhaps even their participation – in so far as one can interpret the victories of athletes in the stadium and the palaestra as events that never took place without the consent of the divine, and why not their intervention too? De Coubertin's yet-to-be-created 'religion of the athlete' did not follow on directly from Greek mythology, however – the founder of the games was too educated not to know that the gods of Hellenism are dead. Its point of departure was the modern art religion of the Wagnerian variety, which had been conceived as a sacred act to reconcile the torn 'society' of the day. As every complete religion has an ordained clergy alongside its dogma and rituals, its embodiment became the function of the athletes. It was they who would administer the muscular sacraments to the ecstatic masses. This is my body, my struggle, my victory. Thus de Coubertin's Olympic dream unified Romantic Graecophilia, as well as the pedagogical pathos of the nineteenth century, with the aesthetic heathendom of the body cult to form an amalgam that would meet modern standards.

What de Coubertin expected from an effective new 'religion' can be seen in a memoir note on a visit to the Bayreuth Festival. Here he draws parallels between the two seemingly disparate spheres:

> Music and sport have always been the most perfect 'isolators', the most fruitful aids to reflection and vision, as well as powerful stimuli, like 'massage of the will', encouraging me to persevere. In fact, after a period of difficulties and perils, all immediate worries were suddenly removed.[100]

With the notable word 'isolator', de Coubertin points to the ability of 'religion' to divide reality into ordinary and extraordinary situations. Wherever one finds sport and music, therefore, one also finds religion, in so far as their key characteristic – the effect of transcending everyday life and eliminating worries – is present. If one develops the term 'isolator' further, one arrives at the following statement: that which brings about an exceptional state is religious. For de Coubertin, religion is the attainment of the 'other condition' by sporting means – here begins one of the paths leading to event culture. As is customary for threshold states, these means must simultaneously be released and kept under control; the fully developed athletes' religion would have to carry out both tasks. The athletic exercises prepare the exceptional state in the competitions, and the stadium cult steers the mounting arousal in the prescribed directions. In the 'isolator' of Bayreuth, de Coubertin realized once and for all why nothing short of a newly founded religion could do justice to his intentions. Like Richard Wagner, he wanted to propel people out of their ordinary lives for a few incommensurable moments before releasing them back into the world transformed, elevated and purified. De Coubertin found an affirmation of his basic position in the esoteric climate of the Wagner festival. Just as the boldest form of art-religious offer was at home in Bayreuth, the analogous manifestation of sport religion would find its base in Olympism. Comparable to a nineteenth-century Malraux, de Coubertin declared that the twentieth century would be Olympic or would not be at all.

Against this background, one can understand in what sense the success story of the Olympic idea was simultaneously the failure story of de Coubertin's original aims. However one chooses to interpret Olympism, it is clear that it resulted in anything but the triad of sport, religion and art that de Coubertin wanted to transpose from antiquity to the Modern Age. His failure as the founder of a religion can be summed up quite simply: he had called into being a system of exercises and disciplines that was perfect for refuting the existence of 'religion' as a separate category of human action and experience. What in fact came about and became ever more solid in its consistency was an organization for the stimulation, guidance, care and management of primarily thymotic (pride- and ambition-based) and secondarily erotic (greed- and libido-based) energies. The former were by no means restricted to the athletes, but were equally present among the newly created functionaries without whom the new cult could not be put into action. For them, the indispensable parasites of sport, this was the start of a golden age, because the Olympic movement spontaneously followed the most important of all organizational secrets: to create as many functions and honorary offices as possible, in order to guarantee the thymotic mobilization of the members and their pragmatic binding to the sublime cause. De Coubertin, who liked to move in old aristocratic circles, had nonetheless realized that modernity is the era of the *nouveau riche* and the *nouveau important*. For the latter in particular, his movement was an ideal field of activity. As well as the ambition-political incentives, greed-related rewards were not neglected; Olympism produced many new fortunes, some resulting from the direct flow of donations from applying cities into the bank accounts of IOC members. The pragmatic foundation for both forms of incentive was provided by the clubs, the natural matrices of sporting exercises and the alliances between trainers and the practising; they experienced their most impressive presentation in the competitive games themselves. The time was clearly right for this order of disciplines. If the age belongs to the competitive economy, then competitive sport is the zeitgeist itself.

The overall outcome of de Coubertin's efforts, then, could not have been more ironic: he failed as a religious founder because he exceeded every foreseeable level of success as the initiator of a practice and competition movement. The initiator of the games missed what became the alpha and omega for the next generation functionaries in their further undertakings: the glaringly obvious fact that the Olympic idea would only survive as a secular cult without a serious ideological superstructure. The small elements of fairness-pathos, youth ceremony and internationalism that had to be kept as a matter of form could also be summoned up without a great lifting of souls. Often enough, a mere wink was all that remained of de Coubertin's noble pacifism among his pragmatic heirs. The games had to integrate themselves amid the excesses of mass culture, changing into a profane event machine more resolutely at every repetition. On no account should they present themselves too loftily – least of all with the 'Catholic' or offer-theological trait that characterized de Coubertin's approach. Where higher things could not entirely be avoided, as in the obligatory opening celebration, they would go no further than the ceremonious entrance of the athletes, the hymn, the flame and the appeal to the youth of the world. The post-war games in Antwerp in 1920 featured, for the first time, a separate High Mass in the cathedral, with a chilling moment when the names of Olympic icons killed in the war were read out. The Olympic idea never had a chance as a 'heathen' form of a religion of offer from above. Disenchanted into an athletes' summit, it became an irresistible magnet for the masses.

The pragmatic turn did not even demand of its protagonists a betrayal of de Coubertin's vision; it was entirely sufficient not to comprehend the old man's lofty intentions. Soon no one knew any more what his dream of a religious synthesis of Hellenism and modernity had once meant. It is no exaggeration to say that the Olympic idea triumphed because its followers at all levels, from the board members of the IOC to the local clubs, had soon lost any inkling of it – even when tears were flowing at the presentation ceremony. The valiant Willi Daume, who, as long-standing chairman of the German National Olympic Committee, had access to the sources, could only shake his head about the ideational motives of the Olympic cause. Referring to the 'religion of the athlete', he notes in flawless functionaries' prose: 'Here things become slightly confused.'[101]

Through its de-spiritualization, the Olympic movement of the twentieth century shows how a 'religion' can spontaneously regress to the format of its true substance – the anthropotechnic basis, as embodied by a graduated system of exercises and diversified disciplines, integrated into a superstructure of hierarchized adminstrative acts, routinized club relationships and professionalized media representations. None of the structural characteristics of an elaborated 'religion' remain except for the hierarchy of functionaries and a system of exercises that, in keeping with their secular nature, are referred to as 'training units'. The only function of the IOC Vatican in Lausanne is to administer the fact that God is olympically dead too.

In this respect, one can say that the 'religion of the athlete' is the only phenomenon in the history of faith that disenchanted itself by its own means – only a few intellectual strains of Protestantism in Europe and the USA have achieved anything comparable. As the non-religion longed for by countless people, the athletic renaissance was able to spread over large parts of the world. Its development shows the change from a zeal into an industry. Small wonder that the young science of sport showed no interest in becoming the theology of this cult movement, which had barely been founded before its spirit was driven out. But the response among anthropologists was also reserved; to this day, they are interested neither in the artificial tribes of professional athletes nor in the fact that the emergence of the sport functionaries marked the appearance of a new sub-species no less deserving of attention than Aurignacian man.

There is no stronger example in the twentieth century of the tendency towards a phenomenon I have mentioned several times, namely the de-spiritualization of asceticisms, than the Olympic movement. As far as the opposing tendency is concerned, the worldly appropriation of the spiritual, the Church of Scientology founded by the novelist and DIY psychologist L. Ron Hubbard is just one example among many – but an outstandingly informative one. In the following, I would like to honour the inventor of Dianetics as one of the greatest enlighteners of the twentieth century, as he decisively increased our knowledge about the nature of religion, even if largely involuntarily. He earned himself a place in the pantheon of science and technology, as he successfully performed a psychotechnic experiment whose results were significant for culture as a whole. After Hubbard, it is clear once and for all that the most effective way of showing that religion does not exist is to establish one's own.

Whoever wishes to found a religion can essentially operate on one of two assumptions. The first is that many religions already exist, but the true one is not among them; now new insights have finally made it possible and necessary to call it into existence. Christianity followed this schema to set itself apart from Judaism, just as Augustine later did the same in relation to Manichaeism and the Roman cult, and, even later, Mohammed drew the line between Islam and its two monotheistic predecessors. An analogous approach was taken by the Enlightenment thinkers, who wanted to found the 'religion of reason' from the seventeenth century onwards by breaking away from the historical religions.[102] Such initiatives seek to draw authority from the progressive disclosure of the truth, which dictates the content for which the suitable form then has to be found. The new content lies in a message that, so the founders believe, holds more salvific power than previously known cults; one can therefore call this type of religion-founding content-religious. Its protagonists are usually naïve, in a value-free sense of the word. They think they believe that they believe what they believe. If they are not naïve they would like to be, and regret their weakness of faith. The wiser among the weak of faith elevate doubt itself to an organ of faith for an ascetologically plausible reason: chronic doubt is the most effective exercise for keeping alive that which is doubted.

The second assumption under which a new religion can be started is that the previous religions are inadequate because they cling too much to their content, whereas in future the concern will rather be to foreground the form or 'mood' of religion. This turn towards the formal side involves a dramatic bifurcation: the first option is for the new religion to be born as a free-floating meta-religion that no longer knows any dogmatic precepts, yet wants to preserve the dimension of the religious 'in itself' *bona fide* in a content-neutral form – this is roughly what is done by most modern confessionless people, who believe that there might be something after all in the thing they do not believe in. The advantage of this position is that it defuses the tensions between salvific knowledge and secular knowledge, between theology and ethics. Romantic Protestantism had already approached the self-dissolution of positive religion in polyvalent emotional culture, as is evident when Schleiermacher states in his second speech *On Religion*: 'It is not the person who believes in a Holy Scripture who has religion, but rather he who requires none and could probably make one himself.' Or the new religion could exclusively take the formal side of religion to convey foreign content. This was the case with Pierre de Coubertin, among others, who wanted to tie the content of sport to the form of religion – with the results discussed above.

If one goes a step further along the form-religious path, it becomes apparent how religion can be employed as a mere vehicle to realize alien content *mala fide*. The 'political theologies', whereby religion is used as a psychosocial support system for state success and which are once more enjoying considerable attention, are the inescapable example of this. To clarify this attitude through examples, one need only think of popes who enlarged the church state while leading their troops, or French cardinals who formed alliances with the Muslim Turks to harm the Christian rulers of Austria. In both distant and recent times, entire peoples and nations have also appeared in the guise of religious communities. The empirical political reality of the twentieth century illustrates to the point of overkill how revolutionary movements can garnish themselves with messianic trappings, as if the activists had wanted to give the lie to Friedrich Engels's careless claim from 1844 that 'all the possibilities of religion are exhausted'.[103] As soon as the form-religious view becomes radicalized, the abstraction progresses to the point where any content can potentially take on a religioid design if the content provider so desires. Religion then appears as a rhetorical-ritual mode and an immersion procedure that can serve any project – be it political, artistic, industrial, sporting or therapeutic – as a medium of self-distribution. It can very easily be transferred back to old content-based religions.[104]

In the following, I will show how Lafayette Ron Hubbard's entrepreneurial and literary-rabulistic genius drew profit from the form-religious principle in its most abstract manifestation during the promotional campaign for a product called 'Dianetics' in 1950, only to convert it soon afterwards into the Scientological 'church' through a religioid upgrading. The starting point for Hubbard's campaign lies in the cultural crisis of the late 1940s, which also marked a period of personal setbacks for the author. At the time, he could presume a market for life counselling and self-help literature with considerable growth potential and a tangle of psychoanalytical, life-philosophical, pastoral, business consulting, psychagogic, religioid, dietary and fitness-psychological motifs. Hubbard's ingenious approach consisted in bringing all these forms of demand together into a single point. He placed himself in the tradition of modern charlatans, taking this word too in a value-free sense, who seek to combat all illnesses with a single medicine – or all problems with one solution. One can observe this habitus in countless concrete forms between the sixteenth and twentieth centuries – from the zero-point thought of modern philosophy to the political idea of total revolution. According to the great charlatans, the art of arts has always been to distil the one essence, the panacea, the universal agent, regardless of whether this is carried out in physical or moral flasks. As a rule, the distillation produces a simple substance, a final element, or a simple action and a final operation. Whoever has it or is capable of it has and is capable of everything.

Hubbard's product was conceived as a mental panacea and brought onto the agitated life-counselling market. At first glance, his 'Dianetics' of 1950 seemed to be no more than a new method, praised with much ado, to clean the misted windowpanes of our consciousness – a product, to be sure, whose already conspicuously high sales in the first year proved that five years after the first atomic bombs fell, a large number of Americans were prepared to follow spiritual and intellectual suggestions for the simplest solution to the world's problems. There was no time left for complicated esoteric systems, the author announced; one had to change the world from the ground up – rapidly enough to make sure that the bomb did not beat everyone to it. 'Survival' had become the watchword of life counselling. It forms the American counterpart to early Christian metanoia in the face of time running out. Against the background of the incipient nuclear arms race between the USA and the Soviet Union, 'Dianetics' initiated an alternative course of the world – between itself and the world system of war, mental illness and crime. Confronted with such a scenario, who would have refused to join the camp of those who claimed self-assuredly that they had the solution to the world's problems?

The solution lies in the name of the method: the word 'Dianetics' supposedly comes from the two Greek components *dia* (through) and *nous* (mind) and denotes the science of what happens 'through the mind' – occasionally a word such as *dianoua* is also named as a source, though unfortunately this does not exist in Greek. One can intuit the point, namely that everything happens through the mind – though the precise sense of 'through' remains unclear. One cannot yet tell how the system reworks the old contrast between mind and matter – 'scientifically' on the surface and gnostically in its deep structure. Dispensing with false modesty, Hubbard's new hyper-method presents itself as the 'modern science of mental health' and promises to offer the simplest solution to all problems that had hitherto seemed insoluble. Like a Californian avatar of Johann Gottlieb Fichte, Hubbard praises his science of knowledge as ending the era of mere preliminary attempts. While traditional solutions in turn became part of the problems, whether they presented themselves as religions, philosophies, therapies or politics, Dianetics proclaims the solution to all problems in a definitive clarity. This solution, we are assured, will not end up drifting to the problem side again – which is why none but malicious and mentally disturbed people could have any interest in the prevention of Dianetics. This provides, from now on, a new criterion for the rapid diagnosis of psychopathic dispositions: indifference or hostility to the offers of Dianetics. A disproportionate polemic against what Hubbard called 'conventional psychiatry' is a running thread through his entire work – and that of his students. He undoubtedly knew what experts would say about him and his activities. He made them pay dearly for his intuitions.[105]

As far as its actual content goes, Dianetics initially offers no more than a simplified and technified variation on the basic assumptions of psychoanalysis: it merrily replaces Freud's distinction between the systems or field states of conscious/unconscious with Hubbard's distinction between the analytical mind (with its clear memory bank) and the reactive mind (with its pathological memory bank). The latter holds the sum of all problems, while the former offers the solution to all problems. With this starting situation, it seems like the natural task of the analytical mind to clear up the reactive mind until only clear ideas are left. Whoever managed to empty their pathological store would bring about the sole dominion of the analytical mind and could henceforth call themselves 'clear'. All 'processing' follows the maxim that wherever there was a reactive mind, there will now be an analytical one. The task of Dianetic procedures is no less than the production of the clear. They lead clients, regardless of their specific ailments, along inner 'time tracks' and back to the 'engrams' in their pathological memory – often with 'locks' on the pathogenic stores that must first be opened. This takes place on the more or less fantastic assumption that the old engrams can be 'erased' through recall and the 'aberrations' they have caused eliminated – an assumption that had already been popularized by psychoanalysis and Alfred Hitchcock in Hubbard's early days, although it never managed to achieve more than pseudo-plausibility.

If this were all there is to say about Hubbard's approach, one could content oneself with the conclusion that Dianetics is a more or less amusing chapter in the epic of the Americanization of psychoanalysis. This epic relates how the partisans of ego psychology took advantage of the psychology of the unconscious – or how the healthy soul of the esoteric West Coast triumphed over the morbid psyche of the East Coast. In truth, however, the Dianetics/Scientology episode belongs to a broader intellectual-historical movement that I would like to term the techno-gnostic turn in Western psychology. This is characterized by a new, wholesale defamiliarization of mankind's store of mental and spiritual traditions. The distortive energy comes from a technology-historical event that must be viewed as the greatest caesura since the implementation of vowel-alphabetical scripts around 700 BC: the advent of computer culture. Its unfolding around the middle of the twentieth century forced a revision of the time-honoured mind–body dichotomy by showing, through the construction of computers or 'mind machines', that many of the phenomena one had previously attributed to the mind-and-soul side of the totality of being in fact belonged on the mechanical-material side. Reflection is a property of matter, not a privilege of human intelligence. Since then, the redistribution of the world under the pressure of the new cybernetic centre has defined the drama of contemporary thought. In this process it becomes clear why idols fall. The philosophy of cybernetics renders it possible to formulate a general theory of twilights of the gods.[106]

The Hubbard phenomenon unmistakably belongs to the turbulences set off by the irruption of cybernetics into the domains of metaphysical classicism. As a contemporary of the first generation of cybernetics and an author of science fiction novels (viewed not entirely unfavourably by connoisseurs of the genre), he had the advantage of privileged early access to the new world of inner technologies. One should take care to avoid the fallacy that Hubbard's 'former life' in science fiction was something negative. Gotthard Günther, still the most significant philosophical commentator on the event of the computer, has argued convincingly that the science fiction novel should be viewed as the laboratory for the philosophy of the technical age – a claim that seems entirely legitimate if one considers the work of authors like Stanisław Lem and Isaac Asimov, to name only the greatest.

There is every indication that the novelist Hubbard never abandoned his original genre – he merely expanded it. Showing great consistency, his first step beyond the confines of science fiction led him to Dianetics, which, in its cognitive status, is nothing other than psychology fiction. This is in keeping with the accounts of those close to him that Hubbard wrote his 500-page book *Dianetics* in Bayhead, New Jersey, in a mere month – and completely 'off the top of his head', without drawing on any scientific research. The experimental foundation he invokes – 'hundreds of case studies' – is itself part of the invention. This observation casts a retroactive light on the systems of Freud and C. G. Jung; once one has grasped the schema of psychology fiction in its outlines, one also recognizes its characteristics in the alternative versions.

In the present context, Hubbard's second step is especially instructive: the movement that expanded the psychology fiction of Dianetics into the religion fiction of Scientology. Observing this transition, one witnesses the debut of the religion of the technical age.[107] When the success of Hubbard's book *Dianetics: The Modern Science of Mental Health* sent him the message from the real world that applied fiction 'works', he took this as the go-ahead for his ambitions. With the same élan that had carried him towards his first expansion of science fiction's boundaries, he performed the second and opened, after the psychotherapeutic front, the religious one. The response from the real world showed that this time too, it had 'worked' – the religion fiction materialized in a very short time and took the form of an actually existing 'church'. There was an unmistakable element of taking the bull by the horns at work, as Hubbard had reason to fear the reaction of the organized medical profession after the disproportionate success of his self-help therapy book. To the extent that the establishment denied that his 'magical' methods were in any way effective, and accused him of dealing irresponsibly with the hopes of the suffering, many of them incurable, it seemed natural to flee to the immunity of the religious sphere. Incidentally, it was never a secret in the inner organizational circle of the time that the ecclesiastical camouflage of the new anti-professional healing method was simply a way of misleading the tax authorities.

When Hubbard developed the Church of Scientology in 1954, he applied the form-religious strategies: he surrounded the profane content of Dianetics®, and later of Hubbard books, Hubbard speeches, Hubbard counselling techniques etc., with the apparatus of sacred techniques typically found in religion. Its basis is a founder cult without boundaries: the celebration of the master as the awakener of humanity runs through the entire media sphere of Scientology. It constitutes one of the most airtight systems of self-praise in recent intellectual history – like a space station, it recycles its own system-inherent operating data. This was augmented by a sharp propaganda of urgency, the strategic version of the apocalyptic: it explained to clients that the only choice was between Scientology and suicide. This ensured total immersion in Hubbard's theme park. In addition, the sect created countless internal functional roles such as 'auditors', 'registrars', 'ethics officers', and a wealth of new importances in the form of supervisory and regulatory tasks – the imaginative replicas of a church hierarchy – as well as institutes, business centres, clinics, and even colleges where one could acquire heterodox academic titles, including Doctor of Theology. One can hardly say that no provision was made in this far-sighted enterprise for the newly important and those who wanted to join them. Internal communications were refined through the introduction of an insider language whose use gave the divide between members and non-members the desired depth. A system of mutual regulations stabilized the business; the discreet observation of members for an early diagnosis of scepticism rounded off the package of church-imitating measures. The design of the Scientological community was also original: the intention was that each new believer would also be a new customer. One has to go back to the Catholic trading of indulgences in the sixteenth century to find a similarly close and elegant connection between salvific and monetary transactions.[108]

Hubbard already deserves the greatest acknowledgement for these achievements in the recreative reconstruction of the church phenomenon alone, as his form-religious imitation procedure provided valuable insight into the general conditions of religion-founding, whether historically grown or currently synthesized. The loss of aura in his artefact of religion clearly did not worry him. What the new church lacked in venerability it balanced out through the carefreeness with which it presented itself as the summit of humanity's quest for truth that had been conquered late, but still in time. Scientological theology candidly allows the religious founders of the past to look up to him, the finisher – Buddha, Lao Tzu, Jesus, Mohammed, but also authors such as Aristotle, Kant, Schopenhauer, Freud, Bergson and whoever else is entitled to candidacy in the colourful list of precursors. All of them can rejoice that Hubbard has completed what they could only strive for with inadequate means. A certain Dharma is also said to have been very close to the truth in days gone by, supposedly an Asian monk of antiquity. Evil to him who evil thinks – after all, does the New Testament not also contain details that do not stand up to historical criticism? I am not sure one can claim that Hubbard was attempting, with his less successful claims, to show that a complete church should also include signs of its own fallibility.

The question of whether Hubbard wanted to go beyond psychology fiction and religion fiction and create a form of politics fiction will remain unanswered here.[109] Depending on one's attitude and mood, one can take the corresponding statements by the master – especially the notorious equation of democrats and apes – either as Dadaistic or as pre-fascistic. There is a parodistic quality that runs through the entire spectrum of Scientological themes and leaves nothing that Hubbard ever touched unchanged or untwisted. Whatever symbolic traditions he appropriated reappeared as technically repeatable phenomena. Clearly, nothing is more suited to translation into the universe of technical images than 'religion', as it aims by definition for the production of special effects.

Hubbard's achievements as a parodist of religion were outstanding, not least as a parodist of the hierarchical principle – recall his amusing 'Operating Thetan', levels one to eight – but also as a parodist of the mystical idea that the soul (now 'Thetan') recognizes God within its innermost self. The insight that fragile psyches can be replaced by high-class Thetan implants would itself have earned Hubbard a Nobel Prize. Scientology's way of dealing with its apostates is also of great parodistic value – here the classic condemnation of infidels is travestied in the systematic molestation of ex-Thetans. This would be even more comical, were it not for the fact that it meant subjecting their targets to vicious psychological terror. The old missionary cults followed the principle that one wins over the people by converting the king; translated into modern terms, this means that one must first of all court celebrities.[110]

With the help of these techniques, Hubbard managed to establish an intellectual-historical Las Vegas based on quotations without boundaries in a few decades. He led the 'church' into the age of its technical producibility. Unease in the face of this complex of compromising imitations may be one of the reasons why followers of the 'original religions' prefer to avoid it. The attention of the organs of German intelligence to the ambiguous organization is all the greater, however – in the USA, the FBI had it in their sights for a time. Its suspicious appearance is a consequence of its design, as it almost openly displays its principle of production. This has to be the case, as Scientology offers the model for the form-religious staging of foreign content.

In April 2007, the European Court of Human Rights confirmed the right of Scientology – despite its sometimes dubious, at times even manifestly criminal economic activities[111] – to present itself as a religious community. This verdict merits the closest attention, because it is a disturbing indication of the increasing illiteracy of our legal system in 'religious' matters. Despite all appearances, it does not contain any statement about the religious quality of the enterprise; it merely points out the inalienable right of every person to avow a functioning fiction. The judges took the Scientological organization's claim of pursuing spiritual, 'religious' and humanistic goals at face value. On closer inspection, the Strasbourg verdict was no more than a statement by the court about itself, in that it declared questions of parody outside its jurisdiction. A similar logic applies to airport security staff, who are categorically obliged to prevent a joker claiming to have a bomb in his hand luggage from entering the departure zone – one cannot, after all, expect them to take such statements anything but literally.

It is thus decreed by the supreme court: in our time, all that is required to be a religion is for a business to claim that it is one. A person with religion in their hand luggage can proceed to the gate. It did not occur to the judges that Jesus himself would not have been able to sue for recognition as a religious founder at the European Court of Human Rights because he did not know the word 'religion'. Nor was the concept of human rights available to Jesus, least of all the inviolable right of modern people to the free cultivation of illusions. The Strasbourg judges did not realize how close they were to Hubbard: if he could found a religion, they could allow one. At least the judges – assuming there were no undercover Scientologists among their ranks – attempted to pass judgement in good faith, while Hubbard knowingly built his 'church' on an abyss of ironies. In addition, the Scientology lawyers have been working for decades on transforming the legal systems of their host countries into locations for jurisprudence fiction – with impressive success. Without the taste for lawsuits among American lawyers, whose effects also reach across to Europe, it is clear that Scientology would long have disappeared from the market.

My conclusion from the dispute over the religious status of this psychotechnic group is that it proved once and for all that religion does not exist. If one looks to the heart of the fetish of religion, one exclusively finds anthropotechnic procedures (this applies analogously to the second large-scale fetish of the present, 'culture'). The word 'religion', both here and elsewhere, represents two things: inwardly, it is a password to unlock the more yielding zones of the psyche, those in danger of exploitation, and outwardly it is a badge that one shows in order to be admitted to the world of the respectable semblance. In the context of a genetic theory of culture one would call this effect pseudo-transcendence. It comes about as soon as the origins of mental fabrications disappear behind a 'veil of ignorance' and are treated by clients as a venerable legacy.[112] As one can see, a few years are now sufficient to create pseudo-transcendent effects.

In summary, we can say that the indirectly enlightening dynamic of Hubbard's Scientological doctrine, and even more the instructive implications of his organizational art, are connected to the unprecedented shamelessness of his eclecticism. In this, Hubbard dwarfs even Rudolf Steiner – and God knows Steiner was no shy man. Hubbard's ruthless drive towards self-establishment shows the signature of his time in so far as it shows, in its way, the transition from 'the truth of thought to the pragmatics of action'.[113] All the Hubbard system knows about what was termed the 'spirit' or 'soul' in tradition is that these too must now become sites of survival. In his thought, the principle of survival has pervaded the beyond and subjugated everything that was ever viewed as exceeding physical life spiritually or intellectually. Thus Scientology offers pragmatism from beyond for the world here, and vice versa. In so doing, it provides the metaphysical justification of greed for higher positions in the pyramid game of life. In games of this kind, new members always pay the expenses for the rise of the older members. The circumstance that evil is also directly good, that dangerous insight anticipated by Nietzsche, has the chance to unfold fully in such games. This is the foundation of the gnostic irony where everything is merely a game. In Los Angeles, where Scientology is most deeply anchored, this was translated into the thesis that everything is a film relating to earlier films. The main thing is to be in the producers' camp.

If one reduces this 'religion' to its essentials, one finds three irreducible complexes, each of which shows a clear connection to the anthropotechnic dimension. Firstly, on the dogmatic side: a tightly organized illusion-practising society whose members are impregnated ever more deeply over time with the concepts of the milieu. Then, on the psychotechnic side: a set of training instructions for the exploitation of all chances in the transcendent struggle for survival. If one turns finally to the head of the organization, the last thing one can see is any 'religious founder': before us stands a radically ironic, universally flexible business trainer who will stop at nothing, and demonstrates to his progeny what techniques one requires to survive in the jungle battle of egotisms. This does not mean, incidentally, that the matter does not occasionally have a certain charm. Even well-meaning and not entirely unintelligent people can find a temporary home there, as long as they firmly resolve to keep their doubts at bay – the 'willing suspension of disbelief', to quote Coleridge once again, is always the believers' most intimate contribution to the survival of suspicious constructs. In systemic terms, this confirms the rule that a perverse whole can appropriate the relative integrity of its parts without corrupting them entirely. Without this effect, admittedly, the complete religious history of mankind would be unimaginable.

To close with an *ad personam* argument, I would like to note that only three figures in recent intellectual history can be compared to

Hubbard from a typological perspective: the Marquis de Sade, the pioneer of philosophy fiction, who espoused the release of a sexualized will to power; the Russian faith healer and Bohemian monk Rasputin, whose maxim was 'strength is truth'; and the British occultist Aleister Crowley, who spent his life with experiments in malevolence and narcotic excesses, and claimed to be Satan, the Antichrist, and the beast of the apocalypse whose number is 666. I will not investigate here whether Crowley's games with occult traditions could be taken as a feral version of the rehabilitation of matter – the analogy between black magic and historical materialism is relatively obvious.

In this infernal foursome, the youngest member was surely the most successful. According to Hubbard's eldest son, L. Ron Hubbard Jr, his father was fascinated by Crowley early on. Through one of his pupils, the rocket scientist Jack Parsons of the Californian Institute of Technology, he had come into contact with the notorious Ordo Templi Orientis and been introduced to black-magical ways of thinking.[114] There he supposedly learned that the will is everything and may do anything. From this school he took away the most secret of the illuminations underpinning his system: anyone can triumph, no one must die. Whoever wants to become God can do so in a few sessions. Hubbard knew at first hand that the beast from the deep was speaking through these words – in free translation: the revenge of matter for three thousand years of misjudgement and resentment. After Crowley's death in 1947, Hubbard supposedly believed that his position was vacant and awaiting a worthy successor.

L. Ron Hubbard Jr, a knowledgeable, albeit not entirely neutral witness, also states that his father, with whom he worked together in all areas during the founding years of the 'church', was a mental and physical wreck from the mid-1960s on, a victim of his own fictions and a casualty of his addiction to drugs and medications. He therefore withdrew to a luxury yacht to hide from his followers, guiding his company from the high seas for many years. During the last years of his life he was caught in his own trap, lost like a prisoner in an exploding fireworks factory, plagued by hypochondria, overcome by fits of rage and filled with the wish to destroy 'oppressive persons' who dared to criticize his work. He withdrew from the public eye to avoid showing his disciples where his methods could lead.

I

The Conquest of the Improbable
For an Acrobatic Ethics

'. . . jump through the burning hoop of the world'

Ingeborg Bachmann

PROGRAMME

After the partly narrative, partly analytical introduction to the 'planet of the practising', the terrain of the following investigations should be sufficiently familiar in its rough outlines; now it is time to survey the ascetological field more precisely. This assumes that we keep our distance from the chimeras of 'philosophical anthropology' – regardless of whether it sides with Scheler in attempting to explain 'the human place in the cosmos' or, taking up Blumenberg's trail, resolves to give an accurate perspective on man as the animal that sees itself being seen. I am not saying that someone who sees chimeras has not seen anything. But they only recognize what their method allows them to perceive – the specialist interests in a personified form: the philosophy professor himself, who swings over from the savannah to the seminar as a model for all evolution. And when Scheler says that man is the Catiline of nature, the eternal troublemaker, *rerum novarum cupidus*, such a perspective even adds a political and criminological colour – one expects Cicero to appear at once and ask the eternal man how long he will continue to abuse our patience.

A material anthropology at the standard of our present knowledge can only be developed in the form of a general anthropotechnology. This describes humans as the creatures that live in the enclosure of disciplines, involuntary and voluntary ones alike[1] – from this angle, anarchisms and chronic indisciplines too are simply disciplines in alternative enclosures. The word 'anthropotechnics' points to a universe on which such authors as Arnold Gehlen (with his insistence on the necessity of tying the individual to 'institutions' to avert a descent into wildness), Jacques Lacan (with his espousal of a 'symbolic order', understood in terms of paternal law) and Pierre Bourdieu (with his attentiveness to the basis of class-specific behaviour in the 'habitus') have already formulated partial views. Ethnolinguists inspired by Wittgenstein, structuralist ritual researchers and Foucauldian discourse historians also set foot on this terrain some time ago.

Any unwillingness to learn from these authors would be unwise. Anyone who has taken a cue from Nietzsche and started to develop a notion of one of the 'broadest and longest facts that exist', however, cannot avoid re-examining the entire human field in the light of this General Ascetology. Its object, the implicit and explicit practice behaviour of humans, forms the core of all historically manifest varieties of anthropotechnics – and it is questionable whether genetics will ever contribute more than an external modification to this field, which has long been practically constant in its power. If I am arguing for an expansion of the practice zone, I am doing so in the face of the overwhelming evidence that humans – on this side and the other side of 'work and interaction', and on this side and the other side of 'active and observing life' – have an effect on themselves, work on themselves and make examples of themselves.

In the following, I will demonstrate the autoplastic constitution of the essential human facts. Being human means existing in an operatively curved space in which actions return to affect the actor, works the worker, communications the communicator, thoughts the thinker and feelings the feeler. All these forms of reaction, I would argue, have an ascetic, that is to say a practising character – although, as stated above, they largely belong to the undeclared and unnoticed asceticisms or the occulted training routines. It is only with the first expressly practising humans that the ascetic circle of existence is explicitly rendered visible. They create the self-referential relationships that commit the individual to participating in its own subjectification. They all have authority for us in anthropological questions, whether they are farmers, workers, warriors, writers, yogis, athletes, rhetoricians, circus artistes, rhapsodists, scholars, instrumental virtuosos or models.

— 1 —

HEIGHT PSYCHOLOGY

The Doctrine of Upward Propagation and the Meaning of 'Over'

Marriage from an Evolutionary Perspective

No one who has been willing to follow my deliberations this far should be surprised if I turn once again to Nietzsche, the rediscoverer of the ascetic field in all its breadth and layers, to provide the first keyword for the elaboration of a practice-anthropological view of the complex of human facts.[2] In the section 'On Children and Marriage' from the first part of *Thus Spoke Zarathustra* (1883), the new prophet tries his hand at life counselling for higher human beings:

> I have a question for you alone, my brother: I cast this question like a sounding-lead into your soul, that I may know how deep it is.
>
> You are young and wish for a child and marriage. But I ask you now: are you a human being with the *right* to wish for a child?
>
> Are you the victor, the self-compeller, commander of the senses, master of your virtues? Thus I ask you.
>
> Or is it the beast and dire need that speak out of your wish? Or isolation? Or discord with yourself?
>
> I would that your victory and your freedom might yearn for a child. Living monuments shall you build to your victory and your liberation.
>
> Over and beyond yourself shall you build. But first you must be built yourself, four-square in body and soul.
>
> Not only onwards shall you propagate yourself, but upwards! May the garden of marriage help you to do so!
>
> A higher body shall you create, a first movement, a self-propelling wheel – a creator shall you create.
>
> Marriage: thus I call the will of two to create the one that is more than those who created it.[3]

111

As always when reading *Zarathustra*, one should not be misled by the evangelizing tone. These are not neo-religious instructions, but rather directions for the neo-ascetic trainer. In the present case they refer not to physical exercise of a gymnastic or athletic nature, but rather to the sexual diet, or more precisely the inner attitude that should be reached before the natural consequences of human reproductive activity can be affirmed. What Nietzsche's prophetic double presents is no less than a critique of the linear sequence of generations. Thus children who resemble their parents in the status quo are superfluous, or more precisely superfluous replicas of superfluous originals. We shall hear more about the reason for their superfluity shortly.

From the perspective of the new procreation trainer, every marriage must be considered a *mésalliance* brought about simply by natural automatism or the social mechanics of the desire for children. Because the man, as Nietzsche presumed to know, had thus far been merely a means to a child for the 'real woman', this well-trained female sympathizer and duped fulfiller of feminine wishes, must in future be assisted by an adviser who will encourage him to look out for other women – ones on an equal footing who do not want to make the husband 'the maid of a woman', but rather form a partnership for the pursuit of nobler aims. It should not unsettle us that the primary goal of better marital partnerships is defined a few verses later with the later politically and mass-culturally charged term *Übermensch* (Walter Kaufmann, the man who introduced Zarathustra to an American audience, renders it undauntedly as 'superman'). It would not be the first word from the dictionary of philosophical art nouveau to regain acceptable meanings after a systemic and sporting translation – recall such wilted articles as *élan vital*, *fluidum*, giving meaning to the meaningless, the creative pause etc., which are awakening today to a second, third, nth life thanks to new company plaques.[4]

It is not my aim here to examine the relationship between genetics, pedagogy, dietetics and artistry in Nietzsche's call for 'upward propagation'. I shall content myself with the observation that the biological part in this project can practically be overlooked alongside the three other elements. There is no 'eugenics' in Nietzsche – despite occasional references to 'breeding' – at least no more than is implicit in the recommendation to choose a partner under decent lighting conditions and with one's self-respect intact. Everything else falls under training, discipline, education and self-design – the *Übermensch* implies not a biological but an artistic, not to say an acrobatic programme. The only thought-provoking aspect of the marriage recommendations quoted above is the difference between onward and upward propagation.[5] This coincides with a critique of mere repetition – obviously it will no longer suffice in future for children, as one says, to 'return' in their children. There may be a right to imperfection, but not to triviality.

What Does 'Upwards' Mean? For a Critique of the Vertical

The quoted passage brings into play Nietzsche's speciality, his attentiveness to questions of verticality in human matters of values, rank and achievement, to particular effect. It can be taken as the starting point for the central questions of General Ascetology: what is the business of the practising life, and to what end is it pursued? In what sense can we distinguish here between horizontality and verticality, whether the concern is the ascending line from parents to children in particular or the gradation between the levels of the practising life in general? Whence does Nietzsche draw his conviction that the kinetic attribute 'onward' has less value than 'upward'? From what sources does he acquire his knowledge of what above and below mean in such contexts? How can one form of life, one mode of being, be located *over* another in this field anyway? Where do the criteria for judgements of 'over' come from? Are they immanent in circumstances, or are they introduced from without? Why is continuing horizontally no longer the highest goal for Nietzsche – as it is for the majority of seasoned traditionalists in all times and peoples – and what motives underlie his conviction that a continuation of the game of replications is only affirmable and non-trivial if it brings about an enhancement?

It is clear from these questions that we will not advance any further in these reflections on the nature of practice directions without a 'critique of the vertical'. For the pedagogical, athletic, acrobatic, artistic, and ultimately any symbolic or 'culturally' mediated interpretation of the words 'above' and 'over' obviously addresses a second spatial meaning overlying the primary orientations in the physical or geographical space. These two spatial meanings are of the same evolutionary age – indeed, one cannot rule out the possibility that what we are here terming the second meaning should, at least in development-psychological terms, be given priority over the first. The reason for this is not an esoteric one: in its relationship with its mother, every infant experiences a pre-symbolic and supra-spatial Above to which it looks up before it learns to walk. Fathers and grandparents are likewise 'up there', long before the child begins to build towers from blocks and place one piece on top of the others as the uppermost. Then it can knock over its edifices and learn that one always remains superior to self-made constructs. It is sufficient to observe how the highest block returns to its original position on the ground following the collapse. This provides an experience of primitive sovereignty whose development continues into the games of critique among adults – every deconstruction is a game of little towers with the classics. By contrast, the child cannot similarly overturn the established polar situation with the parents up there and itself down there. At the experiential level, it remains – barring psychotic deregulations – embedded in a stable vertical tension, possibly until old age, when it has long since physically outgrown its progenitors. The 'looking up' of children to their parents and adults in general, especially to cultural heroes and transmitters of knowledge, gives rise to a psychosemantic system of co-ordinates with a pronounced vertical dimension. One could almost describe the world of the early psyche as monarchic.

In *Zarathustra*, Nietzsche presupposes the decline of the four-thousand-year empire of monarchies as a fact. The psychopolitical situation in which he wants to make himself useful as a procreation adviser is thus informed not only by the statement 'God is dead', but equally by the assertion 'the king is dead'. While the first claim must be augmented by the supplement 'God remains dead' – this is the novelty in the message of the madman [*der Tolle Mensch*], whether one hears it as bad news or welcomes it as a gospel – the second, in keeping with the old ritual law, is followed by the proclamation 'Long live the king!' Nietzsche also yields to this law, but not without raising it to a more abstract level. Though empirical kings have ceased to be impressive and are only 'above' others from the perspective of protocol and the tabloid press, the royal function as such, understood as a pole of attraction to the pure Above, Over and Upwards, remains imaginarily intact in many individuals despite real circumstances, and demands a new interpretation. The replacement of kings with presidents and celebrities does not provide any solution to the task at hand. It deals with the problem on the surface, without even noticing the necessity of redefining the pre- of presidency and the pro- of prominent.

The Time of Artistes

Only within the framework of a comprehensive reform in the vertical system, with all its psychosemantic and culture-dynamic aspects, can one do justice to Zarathustra's critique of profane reproduction. The death of 'God' was at once that of His vassal, the previous human being, and whoever would declare a successor must acknowledge that man, the conventional representative of the 'symbolic species' governed by notions of God, 'remains dead'.[6] If one wanted to follow the ritual law and proclaim a living king under the new conditions, one would have to find a candidate who was neither king or man in the conventional sense. The only suitable being would be one with special traits that placed it outside the horizon of ordinary human existence – a creature sufficiently inhuman or post-human to meet the requirements of this bizarre line of succession. Going by everything we know about human forms of life in general and Nietzsche's view of them in particular, only a figure from the pandemonium of the human is suitable for this role: the artiste, or more precisely the acrobat. The undermining of the human through the radically artificial began long ago with his emergence – could he be the figure for whom great times are now beginning?

We recall: Zarathustra's first conquest on his way from the mountains to the cities was a fallen tightrope walker who said that he was never much more than an animal trained with blows and fodder. If one accepts a first pointer from him towards possible meanings of the provocative word *Übermensch*, an image forms of a living being that is subjected to constant grooming and physically experiences adaptations to the improbable. Such an *Übermensch* is closer to animality than the educated bourgeois because of the physical dimension of its art, yet simultaneously closer to an extra-human dimension by virtue of its removal from the everyday sphere through its daily occupational hazards. Someone who balances on the high wire lives from giving the audience a reason to look up. No one would do so without effective attractors: the danger that constantly accompanies the artiste, the embodied bravura that saves him at every step, and the overcoming of impossibility that enables its conqueror to walk between the precipice on the right and the precipice on the left as the ordinary person walks from their front door to the parlour. Thus the *Übermensch*'s other qualities are not important; he brings traits that distinguish him from previous humans in the same way the tightrope walker differed from his audience. Thomas Mann, incidentally, in the chapter on the Parisian circus in his *Confessions of Felix Krull*, had already put a vehement denial of the artiste's membership of the ordinary human race in the mouth of his protagonist. One reads that the trapeze artist Andromache, 'daughter of the air', is neither a woman in the conventional sense of the word nor even a human being at all. Her true nature is that of a 'solemn angel of daring'. Jean Genet voices similar sentiments: 'Does anyone in his right mind walk on a wire or express himself in verse? It's sheer madness. Man or woman? Unquestionably a monster.'[7]

Initially, the '*über*' [over] in *Übermensch* refers only to the altitude at which his rope is fastened above the heads of the spectators. I do not think it an affront to Nietzsche if we note that beneath the Romantic mask of his most oft-cited idea lies, initially, nothing other than a fantasy of prominence,[8] in so far as one takes prominence as the category of people worth seeing – worth seeing according to criteria that remain to be discussed. Whether the protruders and outstanders (Latin *prominere*, 'to protrude' and *eminere*, 'to stand out') walk over tightropes, catwalks or red carpets is merely a technical difference. What matters is the position of the monster (from the Latin *monere*, 'to warn'), in which the skill increased through strict training and its exposition in total visibility are drawn together into a single complex. In this sense prominence, after artistry and in alliance with it, provides the second impulse for the subversion of the human being through a non-human principle. Ultimately, with his hysteroid *Übermensch* propaganda, Nietzsche simply ensures the possibility of fastening new ropes overhead that are worth looking up to. The 'over' here refers to the dimension of looking upwards. The human of the 'over' is the artiste who draws our gaze to wherever he is active. For him, being there means being up there.[9]

At this point one could raise the objection that the artiste Nietzsche was primarily an evolutionist, even a biologist of the worst kind whose work exemplifies the fatal gesture of his century – the betrayal of the world of the intellect in the name of a naturalism without limits. What else could the desire to 'translate man back into nature' mean? Had Nietzsche not genuinely undergone a dangerous conversion that estranged him from his beginnings? Had he not turned away from Schopenhauer, the last thinker of renunciation, to join the camp of Darwin, the master thinker of affirmation through adaptation? Did he not, in fact, push the idea of success in life through adaptation further, arriving at the even more dangerous doctrine of success through conquest – with this inversion of the adapting direction entirely following the line of a biologically founded, metabiologically over-elevated concept of power? When Nietzsche, in the prologue to *Thus Spoke Zarathustra* quoted above, lets the prophet say to the city-dwellers in his first speech that 'man is a rope, stretched between beast and overman [*Übermensch*] – a rope over an abyss', are we not hearing, above all else, the voice of the biologist insisting that the last word on the evolution of *Homo sapiens* has not yet been spoken?

Nature Acrobatics on Mount Improbable

This objection to the artistic-acrobatic understanding of the term *Übermensch* does not hold up, because the artistic dimension does not conform to the exhausted separation of nature and culture. Evolutionary biology, for its part, only makes sense if viewed as a doctrine of nature's artistry. With Darwin's optics, nature itself is transformed into a circus in which species work their way upwards to the most incredible performances through a never-ending repetition of the simplest procedures known as variation, selection and heredity, generally in a co-evolutionary and co-opportunistic manner and in trans-species ensembles – one need only recall the 900 species of figs that exist worldwide: each one of these has its own exclusive species of fig fly that lives in the fruits, and without which none of the fig species could reproduce.[10] Among the artiste-like inventions of culture, Nietzsche mentions those equalling the natural work of art 'a woman's breasts', this masterpiece of pre-human evolutionary artistry that is 'useful and at the same time pleasing'.[11] Viewed through the opera glasses of evolutionary theory, the thing we call life is nothing other than a vaudeville with an immeasurable wealth of forms in which every branch of artistry, that is to say every species, attempts to perform the feat of all feats: survival. There is no species that has not, like Nietzsche's tightrope walker, made danger its profession in some way. If one hears from natural historians that well over 90 per cent of the countless species that have lived on the earth have died out (for example, 150 of the 9,800 known species of birds in the last few centuries alone), the phrase 'occupational hazards' takes on a non-trivial meaning. From this perspective, biology becomes historical thanatology.

If, on the other hand, one speaks of current life forms, one must, especially as a naturalist, be able to recount their success story and illuminate the principles of their continuation – which means saying how they succeeded in staying on the survivors' side to this day. The star biologist Richard Dawkins took on a project of this kind over a decade ago when he recounted, in a popular lecture series at the Royal Institute – broadcast by the BBC under the seemingly child-friendly title *Growing Up in the Universe* – the history of life and its most imposing success forms. The title of the resulting book, *Climbing*

Mount Improbable, once more demonstrates Dawkins's ability to popularize his field with vivid formulations.[12] In this particular case he surpassed his own aims. Natural history – described as a climbing tour in the mountains of improbabilities – directly becomes a nature-artistic affair in which one cannot decide, and fortunately does not have to, whether the ascent of 'Mount Improbable' is carried out by the different species or the biologist who studies them. The image of climbing this peak of improbability is itself most likely to be inadequate, as the rise of species cannot be understood as the conquest of a pre-existing summit. Rather, its development constitutes the folding-out of the mountain to its current altitude. Behind the image of the ascent to the mountain of the improbable lies a deeper figure, namely the emergence of a peak that is raised from the more probable to the more improbable by trivial evolutionary forces. Whether one takes the path to the summit as a climbing or a lifting of the entire rock mass, however, natural history takes on an immanent artiste-like dimension through this observation. 'Survival' is a code word for nature acrobatics. The question of who watches nature perform its feats cannot be answered from a human perspective – the only observer we can point to is the biologist, who enters the theatre of evolution with a delay of hundreds of millions of years.

In the light of these reflections, it would seem logical to relate the 'over' in *sur*vival [*Überleben*] and the 'over' in Über*mensch* to the dimension of growing improbabilities.[13] While dying out would always be the more probable result of a species's attempts to live, and the stagnation of humans in a final form of human existence would certainly be the more probable end to human history – an end that is not espoused without some self-satisfaction by the proponents of a supposed 'right to imperfection' – survival and over-humanization together embody the tendency towards the rise of the probable to the less probable. A surviving species embodies the current link in a chain of replications that has succeeded in stabilizing its improbability. If one assumes that a stabilized improbability immediately becomes a base for further ascents, this provides the basic principles for an understanding of the evolutionary drift towards the summit of Mount Improbable.

The biologist's reference to peaks of the improbable thus offers an answer to the question posed above as to the meaning of 'upwards' in Zarathustra's command – 'Not only onwards shall you propagate yourself, but upwards!' – that is plausible in the context of current knowledge. This response assumes that evolution as such always moves 'upwards', in the sense that it establishes a continuum of life form experiments at constantly rising levels of stabilized improbability. That is not a planned progress, of course; yet, as a movement towards increasing complexity, it is an unmistakably directed process. The contrast between 'onwards' and 'upwards' disappears of its own accord in the succession of generations, because, when viewed diachronically over extended periods, all species that seem to embody stable final forms transpire as momentary states within a genetic drift that is unpredictable in its details, but points 'upwards' overall. The global drift in the fitness current shows an increase in those species rewarded with survival, and it is precisely this tendency – that the current runs uphill counter-intuitively – that Dawkins illustrates with the image of climbing the heights of the improbable.

> the evolutionary high ground cannot be approached hastily. Even the most difficult problems can be solved, and even the most precipitous heights can be scaled, if only a slow, gradual, step-by-step pathway can be found.[14]

This pathway is sought by the 'selfish' genes, which are simultaneously passed onwards and upwards in the constant reality test of species life.

Nietzsche's 'artiste metaphysics' can follow on effortlessly from the tenets of Darwinist biology. In terms of their improbability, natural species and 'cultures' – the latter defined as tradition-capable human groups with a high training and skill factor – are phenomena along the same spectrum. In the natural history of artificiality, the nature–culture threshold does not constitute any particularly notable caesura; at most, it is a hump in a curve which rises more rapidly from that point on. The only privilege of culture in relation to nature is its ability to speed up evolution as a climbing tour on Mount Improbable. In the transition from genetic to symbolic or 'cultural' evolution, the shaping process accelerates to the point at which humans become aware of the appearance of the new in their own lifetime.[15] From that point, humans adopt a stance on their own capacity for innovation – and, until recently, almost always one of rejection.

Primary Conservatism and Neophilia

During the last forty thousand years of human evolution, the standard reaction to the increased conspicuity of additional improbability was, as far as one can see, an unconditionally defensive one. On their habitual surfaces, all old cultures, extending back to their early Palaeolithic forms, are consummatively conservative. They seem infused with a visceral enmity towards innovation, presumably because the task of transferring their conscious content, their symbolic and technical conventions to subsequent generations with consistent intensity already taxes them to the limits of their capacity. Cultures as such are consistently based on the fundamental contradiction between the acquired neophilic attitude of *Homo sapiens* and the – at first – inevitably neophobic constitution of their rule apparatuses. Because the reproduction of their ritual and cognitive content is its first and only concern, its path through the ages is massively neoclastic – the shattering of the new in general precedes the iconoclasms in particular by many millennia. For every Cataline, every *rerum novarum cupidus*, there are ten thousand preservers of the old like Cato. As even the most stable cultures are constantly infiltrated by symbolic and technical innovations, however, whether inventions of their own or infections through contact with the arts of neighbouring cultures, they employ the trick of camouflaging the novelty of what has been newly absorbed, adapting the elements integrated *nolens volens* to the store of their own oldest material as if they had always belonged to their domestic cosmos. Such an integration of the new into the archaic is one of the primary functions of mythical thought: making experienced improbabilities, whether events or innovations, invisible as such and backdating the invasive, unignorable new to the 'origin'. The preference of metaphysics for the substantial and its resentment towards the accidental are unmistakably still offshoots of the mythical thought form.

One cannot emphasize enough how significantly the later positivization of the new that began in Europe in the fifteenth century impacted the mental ecosystems of threshold peoples.[16] It amounts to the revaluation of all values, because it turned the oldest civilizatory paradox – that neophilic individuals lived in neophobic social structures – on its head. Over the centuries, it forced most people into an involuntarily neophobic position from which they were scarcely able to keep up with the ecstasy of innovation in the surrounding civilization. This change breaks with the majesty of the old and transfers the kingly function to those who bring the new. Now, whoever calls out 'Long live the king!' must be referring to innovators, authors and multipliers of the cultural patrimonium. Only because the Modern Age opened the era of neolatry was Nietzsche able to risk pushing this trend even further and suggesting radically modified rules for procreation. While procreation had previously always been dictated by the reproducing side, and its criterion for success was the return of the old in the younger, the child was now to take priority – which it achieves when, as Nietzsche unambiguously states, it becomes the one that is *more* than the two who created it. Those who oppose this are the last humans.

Artiste Metaphysics

The evolutionary preconditions for this turn can be clearly named, even if the consequences remain unforeseeable: they lie in the neolatric valuations of the European Renaissance, which ultimately go back to the reinterpretation of the Christian Trinity in favour of the creative spirit and the shifting of the *imitatio Christi* to the *imitatio Patris Spiritusque*. Against this background, Nietzsche did not have to do much more than tear away the husks of convention from the cult of the new, which was already fully developed in his time, and embrace the dogma of innovation without limits. He was one of the first who was able to perceive Mount Improbable emerging from the mist. At the same moment he realized the relativity of height, for he observed that even high mountain ridges seem flat when one stands and walks on them. Only thus could he arrive at the opinion that the mountain of evolution was not yet high enough – he wanted to place a second mountain on the first, and a third on the second. Accordingly he wrote: 'fewer and fewer climb with me on ever higher mountains – I build a mountain range from ever more sacred mountains'.[17] Above every mountain range of results, there is a mountain range of tasks to be unfolded upwards. Only erecting new steep faces can compensate for the flattening out of the mountain resulting from the habit of living on it.

One must realize how much Nietzsche is speaking here as an artist: the desire to push improbability further to a mountain range of mountain ranges articulates the highest level to which an artiste's confession can advance. Only the artistic will to transform the future into a space of unlimited art-elevating chances enables us to understand the core of the procreation rule: 'a creator shall you create [. . .] a self-propelling wheel, a first movement'. This rule contains no less than Nietzsche's theology after the death of God: there will continue to be a God and gods, but only humanity-immanent ones, and only to the extent that there are creators who follow on from what has been achieved in order to go higher, faster and further. Such creators never work *ex nihilo*, of course, contrary to a scholastic misconception; they take up results of earlier work and feed them into the process once again. Creation is a resumption of the first movement, the return into the flame that burns upwards, or the turning of the 'self-propelling wheel' that moves 'from within itself' [*aus sich*] – this formulation brings into play the better form of scholasticism, where the from-within-itself constitutes the kinetic dimension of the in-itself and the for-itself.

The creator follows a metaphysical assignment: if life itself is already a vibrating mountain of improbabilities, one can only prove an affirmation by piling that mountain up even higher. That is why upward procreation is meant to create a creator. By producing additional increasers of the improbable, one acclaims the dynamic of improbability increase as a whole. Hence the demand for a human being who has overcome their own obstacles in life and is free of resentment towards creativity. Only such a person would no longer take themselves – let alone their ancestors – as a yardstick for the becoming of the next generation. Only they could affirm without neophobic reflexes the idea that the cultural mountain range of improbability must, in future, be unfolded a level higher with each generation; they would not turn their own imperfection into an obligation for their descendants. They would rather die out than return unchanged. They understand and welcome the fact that according to the law of the normalization of the improbable, earlier peaks present themselves as mere hills or plains in the perception of later generations. One also finds this law among parasitic and flattened-out forms – in the law of increasing jadedness on the art market, for example, or the escalation trends in the hardcore erotic sector.

For the 'creative' (a word that died a heat death in less than a century) person, the comparative – in the form Indo-Germanic languages place in their speakers' mouths – is more than simply a grammatical function. The elementary triads *big – bigger – biggest*, *bonus – melior – optimus*, or *potens – potentior – potentissimus* give a primitive impression of life's graduated acts of enhancement. One need only undo the theological blockage of the superlative in order to understand that the *maxima* have always left room for increase, even when they are secured with *nec-plus-ultra* fences. It is the very cultural process of life that presents what was great yesterday as smaller, and passes off the greater of earlier times as normality only a short time later. It transforms the insurmountable difficulties of yesterday into paths on which, soon afterwards, even the untrained will advance with ease. For those who have lost faith in the omnipotence of obstacles – and what was classical ontology if not a faith in large-scale obstacles? – the previous state is the base camp for the next outing. From that point on, the acrobatic path is the only viable one.

Making Asceticism Natural

On closer inspection, what people sought to call Nietzsche's 'biologism' – and 'biologism', as some diagnosticians of imperialism suppose, is the mystified form of capitalist competition – transpires as a generalized acrobatism: a doctrine of the processual incorporation of the nearly impossible. This has less to do with economy than with an amalgam of artistry, artistedom, training science, dietology and ascetology. This combination explains the programmatic statement entrusted to a notebook by the author of *The Genealogy of Morals* in the autumn of 1887:

> I also want to make asceticism natural again: in place of the aim of denial, the aim of strengthening.[18]

The existence of tomorrow's humans is thus to be based entirely on practice and mobility, including a gymnastics of the will and tests of courage for one's own powers. Nietzsche even envisages a training for moral virtues in which one can prove one's 'strength in being able to keep one's word'.[19]

For the philosophical acrobat, making asceticism 'natural' involves basing anti-naturalism on nature – which means that the body must always be taken along, from the bottoms to the tops of the acrobatic figures. When the artistes of the Chinese State Circus show in one of their pyramid stunts how five, six or seven artistes climb up one another such that the uppermost is standing on the shoulders of countless others lower down, and he then performs a one-handed handstand while, to top it all, balancing glasses of water on a tray placed on the sole of his left foot – then philosophers too should realize (assuming they go to the circus) what Nietzsche observed with such pathos: that there is no less corporeality involved at the highest point than in the middle or at the bottom.[20] It is also clear how the acrobatic figure provides its own commentary on the topos 'mind over matter'. Artistedom is the somatization of the improbable.

Nothing More Monstrous than Man: Existence at High Altitude

This viewpoint is not entirely contemporary. It is foreshadowed in older bodies of wisdom literature – in the European context, probably most decisively in the oft-discussed choral song from *Antigone* by Sophocles, in which 'man' is described as the most wondrous (*deinóteron*) of all beings,[21] the most monstrous of the 'monstrous' [*des Ungeheuren*], as Hölderlin rendered it strikingly, but also tendentiously. He is a danger-seeking monster of disturbance that slanders the status quo and leaves nothing as it was: as a seafarer who explores the most perilous zones of the sea; as a desecrator of the holy soil who weakens it with his plough; as a bird-catcher who lays out treacherous nets; as an extravagant big-game hunter in the mountains; as a state-builder and lawmaker; as a doctor who pushes back suffering – in all of these, then, an artiste: 'Skilful beyond expectation are the contrivances of his art' – at a loss only before the inevitability of death. With such a nature, arrogance is to be expected – the acrobat's pride over the heads of the crowd, and hubris outside of the common rules. Sophocles has a splendid word for this disposition towards immoderation: *ápolis*, 'cityless', overstepping the *polis*, 'apolitical' in the sense of a sacrilegious non-participation in the citizen's religion of golden mediocrity – one cannot help thinking of the Athenian model monster, the over-gifted Alcibiades, who danced on more than one tightrope.[22]

Sophocles here brings up a principle by which the subversion of humanity comes from within humans themselves: it was conventionally termed 'hubris'. This interpretation is short-sighted, not to say bigoted, because it remains compulsively bound to a praise of the middle – even if the *meson*, as the ancients viewed it, was something quite different from what the word means today. The advantage of this reading, at least, is that it brings up the vertical tension that is inseparable from human existence – even if it is only by defining humans as beings endangered by a harmful height. The Old European critique of hubris thus represents the basic form of what was known in the twentieth century as 'height psychology'. In modernity, admittedly, hubris has changed its approach: it no longer appears as self-elevation, but rather as the presumption of a lowness to which, on closer consideration, no one can lay claim.

Max Scheler arrived at the phrase 'height psychology' in the 1920s to express his dissatisfaction with the psychology of the unconscious propagated by Freud, Jung and others and, for a time, known as 'depth psychology'. In Scheler's view, it explained humans one-sidedly 'downwards', oriented towards the mental mechanism, whether drive-theoretically or neuro-theoretically underpinned.[23] He believed that the psychologies of modernity excessively biologized humans, underestimating or entirely neglecting their involvement in a register of metabiological realities, the sphere of intellectual and spiritual 'values'. The word *Geist* – denoting both the spirit and the mind – is taken by Scheler as indicating the partial release of humans from the absolutism of organismic life: what idealistic philosophers once called 'participation', after all, simply meant an access to higher objects while retaining one's organic shackles. Humans project into this 'other world', the spiritual or metabiological (some authors call it 'bionegative') zone of values, by attempting to reach the more-than-natural by natural means. Under Nietzsche's influence, Scheler had understood that the body must be taken along in the transition to the higher register; this distinguishes him favourably from spiritualists and dualists.

He also knew this: the task faced by modern height psychology is the opposite of that dictated to its Old European precursors. While the ancients had to bring 'extravagant' back to the *meson*, the healthy middle, the moderns have to remind their contemporaries of the region of height as such, assuming these are humans of the type who feel most comfortable at the average level and below. Left to their own devices, they chronically excuse themselves downwards, and prefer to follow models which prove that downhill paths are more likely to be successful than steep climbs. The modern human being can therefore only be 'sub'verted from a height, from the overground. The hidden overground, however, lies – and this is new – more in artistedom than in 'religion', in that 'religions', as hinted above, can be co-opted much more easily for artistic purposes (with their branches of asceticism, ritualism, ceremonialism) than vice versa. Artistedom is subversion from above, it *super*verts the 'existing'. The subversive, or rather superversive, principle lies not in the 'height' of haughtiness, the *hypér* of *hybris* or the *super* of *superbia*; it is concealed in the 'acro' of acrobatics.

The word 'acrobatics' refers to the Greek term for walking on tiptoe (from *akros*, 'high, uppermost' and *baínein*, 'to go, walk'). It names the simplest form of natural anti-naturalness. Before the nineteenth century, the term was used almost exclusively for tightrope acrobatics and later expanded to include most other forms of bodily wizardry, such as advanced gymnastics and the corresponding circus routines. The athletisms and extreme sports, on the other hand, for reasons that remain to be established, sought to avoid any association with acrobatics, as obvious as their kinship might seem – to say nothing of their joint campaign to make the mountains of improbability higher.

Jacob's Dream, Or, The Hierarchy

The central document of the subversion, or rather supraversion, of humanity through artistry far predates Sophocles' references to the techno-hubristic constitution of the human sphere. I am referring to the dream vision of Jacob as recounted in the patriarchal stories in the book of Genesis, here in chapter 28:

> [10]Jacob left Beersheba and set out for Haran. [11]When he reached a certain place, he stopped for the night because the sun had set. Taking one of the stones there, he put it under his head and lay down to sleep. [12]He had a dream in which he saw a stairway resting on the earth, with its top reaching to heaven, and the angels of God were ascending and descending on it. [13]There above it stood the Lord, and he said: 'I am the Lord, the God of your father Abraham and the God of Isaac. I will give you and your descendants the land on which you are lying.'[24]

The Old European tradition does not know any image for the interpretation of human ties to vertical forces that has a comparably powerful effect. Here too we find over-humans, though not of the species coming from humans, but rather those who are created thus by God. The work carried out here by angels is that of acrobats from the start: they climb up and down a ladder – in some translations a staircase – between heaven and earth. This is meant to demonstrate a fact that should be pointed out very plainly: the sphere in which humans lead their lives forms the midpoint between worlds above and below it. Every human operation, even the most skilled and meaningful, whether profane or sacred, is overarched by a higher world of transcendental actors whose agents are the angels. Whatever humans are capable of doing can be done better at the over-human level. Thus, since time immemorial, angels have been making their own contribution to an artistic superversion of the human.

There is good reason to claim that the history of Old Europe is, in many respects, the history of translations of Jacob's Ladder from the dream sphere into daily culture. It constitutes the shared history of hierarchy and acrobatics – in so far as one transfers the initial *akro bainein*, the 'walking high up on tiptoe', onto walking and standing on the steps of a ladder between the earth and the Highest, and onto the many ranks of nobility between the king and the people. Incidentally, ladder acrobatics in the circus constitutes a transitional form to aerial acrobatics – as with angels, whom one imagines not only as rung-climbers, but also as a flying company.[25] It makes good sense, therefore, when Jacob builds the first house of God, Bethel, in the very place where the angels' ladder touched the earth. For the first brick, he takes the stone that he used as a pillow on the critical night. When an old nomadic people territorializes itself, the best place to do so is one from which the route continues vertically.

Where there was dream hierarchy there shall be real hierarchy. Just as the angels stand above one another in ten ranks, from the worshipping seraphim to the executive angels of the basic courier service, the members of the actually existing church should also stand above one another, according to Pseudo-Dionysius the Areopagite – and likewise the functionaries of actual administrations and the all-too-actual corporations of bureaucrats; whether the Old European nine-level secondary school [*Gymnasium*] also contains a distant projection of the Neoplatonic-Christian choir levels is an open question.[26] What Jacob, the patriarch of the hierarchy thinkers, dreams up is an artistic pyramid of subtle bodies. Unlike in the circus, its sight results not in storms of applause as soon as it persists for a minute; it is meant to last for millennia – at least, that is how Pseudo-Dionysius translated the ladder vision into his system. That the Areopagite thus simultaneously created a symbol of the acrobatization of both heavenly and ecclesiastical hierarchies, however, can only be noted from the current pole of history, once the dissolution of traditional hierarchical systems provokes a new reflection on the reasons, modes of operation and metamorphoses of verticality.

It testifies to the power of the ladder tradition that even Nietzsche was still under its influence when he lets Zarathustra say to his friend that he wants to show him 'all the stairways to the *Übermensch*'.[27] What is notable here is the paradoxical construction whereby the stairway is to continue existing, even if there is no longer anything above it to lean against. The old world's most powerful symbol of verticality mysteriously survives the atheistic crisis. It continues to indicate a tension coming from the heights, even though it is no longer consolidated by any transcendental opposing camp. The problematic motif of the transcendence device that cannot be fastened at the opposite pole also returns in Zarathustra's declaration that 'man is a rope, stretched between beast and *Übermensch*' – whether ladder or rope, one can no longer tell with this imagery where the upward tension is supposed to come from. This difficulty remains irresolvable at the level of traditional imaginations; indeed, it would have ruined the entire structure, had Nietzsche not long since adapted implicitly to the completely different kind of evolutionary enhancement of improbability. With its help, the transformation of angels into artistes succeeds almost unnoticed. In the same way the former served as God's messengers, the latter act as messengers of art. They convey the good and alarming news that people are piling up ranges of ever higher and more sacred mountains.

Over-Words

Finally, it should be noted that Nietzsche, though the most radical analyst of the newly broached problematics of verticality, was not alone in his time. One could say that the most contemporary thinkers in the nineteenth and twentieth centuries were those who added at least one term to modernity's vocabulary of verticality: Marx speaks of superstructure and overproduction, his brother-in-law Lafargue of overconsumption, Darwin of survival, Nietzsche of the *Übermensch*,[28] Freud of the superego, Adler of overcompensation, and Aurobindo of the supermind and the supramental.[29] We owe the word 'overkill' to an astute nuclear strategist, 'hypertonia' to an obscure doctor, 'over-population' to an obscure demographer, 'supermarket' to an obscure wholesaler, and 'superstar' to an obscure journalist. One must go as far back as the fifth century to find an analogous wave of new verticality words; they were introduced almost exclusively by the master thinker of hierarchism, the aforementioned Pseudo-Dionysius, who stirred up the vocabulary of Christian-Platonic theologians for the next thousand years with his numerous neologisms using the prefix 'hyper-'.[30]

If there is a word missing from the dictionary of the twentieth century, even though the matter itself was ubiquitous, it is the word *Übermörder* [super-murderer] – it would apply to the group of dictators who capitalized on the vertically blind and anti-hierarchical affects of mass culture to make great politics, usually under socialist pretences. As far as Nietzsche's ominous *Übermensch* is concerned, I cannot refrain from ending my reflections on this concept with an ironic note. One thing is clear: in the dating of the era of the *Übermensch*, its inventor fell prey to the greatest of all possible optical illusions – which is astounding, for nothing seems more obvious than the fact that the age of the *Übermensch* lies not in the future, but in the past. It is identical to the epoch in which humans sought to elevate themselves above their physical and mental status by the most extreme methods for the sake of a transcendent cause. Christianity undeniably has a share of the copyright on the word *Übermensch*, incurring royalties even when it is used for anti-Christian purposes.[31]

No Slave Revolt in Morality: Christian Athletism

I part ways most importantly with Nietzsche in his interpretation of the difference between master morality [*Herrenmoral*] and slave morality [*Sklavenmoral*]. I concede that I am unsure whether a major event such as the 'slave revolt in morality' invoked so forcefully by Nietzsche ever occurred. I tend more towards the view that this supposed revaluation of all values, this most far-reaching distortion of all that was naturally right in the history of the spirit, was a fiction in which the author elevated a number of very significant and correct observations to an untenable construct. His motive lies in the fact that Nietzsche, though not intending to found his own religion, did intend to de-found traditional Christianity with holy fury.

It is precisely the ascetological perspective reopened by Nietzsche that highlights the continuity in the transition from 'heathen' antiquity to the Christian world, especially in the area most relevant here: the transference of athletic and philosophical asceticism to the monastic and ecclesiastical *modus vivendi*. Had this not been the case, the early monks of Egypt and Syria would not – citing Pauline images of the apostles' *agon* – have called themselves the 'athletes of Christ'. And were monastic asceticism not an internalization of the regimen of physical warriors as well as an adoption of philosophical doctrines of the art of living from a Christian perspective, monastic culture – especially in its West Roman and Northwest European manifestations – could not possibly have led to the unfolding of powers on all cultural fronts – charitable, architectural, administrative, economic, intellectual and missionary powers – that took place between the fifth and eighteenth centuries. What actually happened, then, was a displacement of athletism from the arenas to the monasteries; or, more generally speaking, a transference of proficiency from declining antiquity to the burgeoning Middle Ages – to mention only the periods, and not name each of the old and new carriers of competence, the aretological collectives of that time and later times.[32]

Hugo Ball put his finger on the essence of these shifts when he emphasized, in his book *Byzantinisches Christentum* (1923), that the intellectual heroism of the monks constituted a superior counterproject to the 'nature heroism' of warriors.[33] It is obvious that this great transfer led to distortions under the influence of *ressentiment*. But even as tendentious a statement as 'But many who are first will be last, and many who are last will be first' (Matthew 19:30), which Nietzsche mercilessly exposed, could also be read from the perspective of the great shift of *areté*. It could be saying that the hierarchy resulting from the conditions of power and ownership should not remain the only permissible view – in fact, not even the central one – of intellectual rankings.

Aristocracy or Meritocracy

I repeat: a slave revolt of morality did not, in my view, take place at any time in the Old Europe. In reality, a revaluation of values occurred in the separation of power and virtue (*areté, virtù*) that would have been inconceivable for the ancient Greeks – a separation whose effects continued into the woolly endgames of European aristocracy in the nineteenth century. The Old European social order committed its true sin against the spirit of positive asceticism not through its Christianization, but rather through the Faustian pact with a class system that saw a nobility without *virtù* reaching the top in many places. This enabled the consolidation of a non-meritocratic exploitative aristocracy whose only achievement lay in the identical transference of its inflated self-image to equally useless descendants, often over several centuries. One gains a clearer picture of this chronic European disgrace, the hereditary nobility, by comparing conditions in the ancient scholarly culture of China, which pushed back the hereditary nobility with an educated nobility for over two thousand years. The indicated revaluation of values did not bring to power the *ressentiments* of sick little people, as Nietzsche suggests; rather, the mixture of laziness, ignorance and cruelty among the heirs to local power was expanded into a psychopolitical factor of the highest order; the court of Versailles was only the peak of an archipelago of noble inutility that spread over Europe. It was only the neo-meritocratic renaissance between the fifteenth and nineteenth centuries, borne by the middle class and the virtuosos, that gradually put an end to the grotesque of hereditary aristocracy in Europe – leaving aside the still-virulent phantoms in the yellow press.

Only since then have we been able to say once more that politics as a European form of life means the struggle and the concern for the framework of institutions in which the most important of all emancipations can take place – the emancipation of the differences that arise from achievements and are controlled from the differences created and passed on through subjugation, power and privilege. Needless to say, the aforementioned group of *Übermörder* were not politicians, but rather exponents of an oriental power concept that does not acknowledge any discipline except the art of domination. They had no interest in the European definition of the political, for all they got to see of the range of differences was the portion that could be explained by theories of class and race. Such theories have always been blind as soon as the birth of difference from levels of proficiency came into focus.

— 2 —

'CULTURE IS A MONASTIC RULE'

Twilight of the Life Forms, Disciplinics

Non-Dominatory Gradations

After the first excursions into the preliminaries of an analysis of vertical tensions, it should be appreciable why any theory of culture must be viewed as half-blind if it does not pay attention to the tendencies in cultural life to form internal multi-storey structures – and not only ones dependent on political hierarchies. This thesis is not intended to rekindle the tiresome debate on so-called 'high culture', which, for various reasons, has become conspicuously quiet in recent decades. My concern is rather to develop a more ethically competent and empirically adequate alternative to the heavy-handed attribution of all hierarchy effects or gradation phenomena to the matrix of power and subjugation.

The necessity of such an undertaking has become apparent since modern 'society', after two hundred years of experimenting with egalitarian and neo-elitist motifs, entered a phase in which it is possible to draw conclusions from these attempts as a whole and assess their results. A paradigmatic phenomenon for the new situation is the emergence of the sport system in the twentieth century – what I termed the 'athletic renaissance' above – which enables a wealth of conclusions about a non-dominatory dynamic of gradations. An equally significant stimulus came from the formation of a non-aristocratic economy of prominence, whose investigation is indispensable for an understanding of the driving forces behind the vertical differentiation of modern large-scale groups in the public sphere. The gradation phenomena within the worlds of science, administration, school, health and political parties, to name only these few areas, lie far outside what can be grasped with the crude claw arms of a theoretical set-up

131

governed by insinuations of dominance. I recently presented some moderately extensive reflections towards a more general definition of the step-forming forces as figures in the field of a political psychology of *thymós* (pride, ambition, will to self-assertion), in my book *Rage and Time*.[34] Neo-thymotic analysis, which incorporates Platonic, Hegelian and individual-psychological motifs, describes the social field as a system driven in equal measure by pride and greed. Pride (*thymós*) and greed (*éros*) can form alliances despite their antithetical natures, but the rewards of pride – prestige and self-respect – and greed – appropriation and enjoyment – belong to clearly separated areas.

In the following, I will show in broad terms how the shift from a theory of class society (with vertical differentiation through dominance, repression and privilege) to a theory of discipline society (with vertical differentiation through asceticism, virtuosity and achievement) can take place. For the first round of this operation I shall take Ludwig Wittgenstein and Michel Foucault as philosophical and idea-historical mentors – the former because his attentiveness to the integration of language into behavioural figures ('language games') provided modern sociology with an effective instrument for revealing manifest and latent ritual structures, and the latter because his investigations into the interlocking structures of discourses and disciplines led him to a breakthrough in reaching an understanding of power beyond simple denunciation – and thus an exit from a long history of ideological misunderstandings that ultimately refer back to pathogenic legacies of the French Revolution. This double stimulus at once clarifies the direction in which the next steps have to be taken: beyond Wittgenstein, by moving on from the language game theory to a universal theory of practice and asceticism, and beyond Foucault, by developing his analysis of discursive forms further into a de-restricted disciplinics.

Wittgenstein's Monastic Rule

Our starting point is a brief, at first glance somewhat mysterious note that Wittgenstein entrusted to one of his notebooks in January 1949, two years before his death: 'Culture is a monastic rule. Or it at least presupposes a monastic rule.'[35] The appearance of a term such as 'monastic rule' in the philosopher's vocabulary might initially take the reader aback. His way of life in Cambridge contained little that would justify monastic analogies, unless one's definition included the imperishable academic rituals. The striking phrase appears somewhat less astounding in the light of recent biographical studies, which show to what extent Wittgenstein's life was infused with religious motifs, and how profound his efforts were to achieve ethical perfection. 'Of course I want to be perfect!' he supposedly said as a young man in reply to a critical question from a female friend.[36] In a New Year's letter to Paul Engelmann, his friend during his Vienna years, he wrote in 1921: 'I should have changed my life for the better and become a star. But I stayed put on the earth, and now I am slowly wasting away.'[37] According to Bertrand Russell, Wittgenstein was toying with the idea of entering a monastery around 1919; he had completed the *Tractatus* a year earlier, and realized that he could scarcely expect much of an echo. In 1926 – after his humiliating failure as a primary school teacher in rural Austria – he did indeed work as a gardener at the monastery of the 'Barmherzige Brüder' [Compassionate Brothers] in Hütteldorf, near Vienna. Wittgenstein's most revealing statement on religious matters is contained in a note from 1948:

> The honest religious thinker is like a tightrope walker. It almost looks as though he were walking on nothing but air. His support is the slenderest imaginable. And yet it really is possible to walk on it.[38]

I shall now combine these isolated observations to form the thesis that Wittgenstein is a rare example of an inverse acrobat, one who found the easy more difficult than the impossible. Naturally his art was also located on a vertical axis; if one were to place him somewhere on Jacob's Ladder, however, this thinker would undoubtedly belong to the group of descending angels (we shall omit the fallen ones). When the thirty-two-year-old author writes in a letter to Engelmann that he should have become a star, one could perhaps read 'become' as 'remain'. Who would want to become a star without some prior conviction that they had once been one? This strong observer comes from very far above – with time, he realizes that it is a mistake to remember overly lofty origins if one is fated to exist on the ground.

One statement in a letter to Engelmann from 1926 reveals what existence on the ground can mean: 'I am not happy, and not because my swinishness troubles me, but within my swinishness.'[39] Wittgenstein's oft-cited 'mysticism' is the trace of a disconcertion upon arrival that never entirely ended – in the inelegant terminology of psychiatry one would presumably speak of a schizoid structure. Such an immigrant would not simply find one or two aspects of what is the case here astounding, but rather the totality of what he encountered. His existence curve describes the long struggle for a bearable arrival after being brought back down to the factual earth – without an overly great loss of the lucidity he brought along with him. Grasping things as they are and performing the unavoidable acts of life as they happen to be dictated by the local grammar, without getting even deeper into 'swinishness' – that may have been the goal of Wittgenstein's exercises. Hence the obstinately resigned note from 1930: 'I might say, if the place I want to reach could only be climbed up to by a ladder, I would give up trying to get there. For the place to which I really have to go is one that I must actually be at already. Anything that can be reached with a ladder does not interest me.'[40]

An entry from 1937 shows how strongly Wittgenstein wanted to persuade himself to adopt a floor-gymnastic interpretation of existence: 'You write about yourself from your own height. You don't stand on stilts or on a ladder but on your bare feet.'[41] On the other hand, the author can imagine what it would be like to be saved (from sin, from reality or from gravity): then you would no longer stand on the earth but hang from the sky – though an outside observer would not easily distinguish between the two, as hanging from the sky and standing on the earth look practically the same from the outside.[42] Wittgenstein remains convinced to the end that the goal is to become as happy after the descent into existence as one destined for despair can be: 'Never stay up on the barren heights of cleverness, but come down into the green valleys of silliness.'[43] Such premises no longer permit a philosophical project in the usual sense of the word, in so far as philosophers had, until then, always wanted to keep the ascending angels on the ladder company. For Wittgenstein, this was obvious; it would have been helpful if those who plundered his ideas in the strongholds of Analytic Philosophy had seen it with the same clarity.

If, under these conditions, one asks as to the meaning of the statement 'Culture is a monastic rule. Or it at least presupposes a monastic rule' – penned by a sixty-year-old – one notices first of all how casually, almost carelessly, the author uses the word 'culture' – he of all people, who always displayed a seventh sense for seeking out hidden ambiguities beneath identical surface formulations. Everything suggests that he was, at that moment, less concerned with the word 'culture', under which he would immediately have sensed the lacunas if he had been interested in looking more closely, than with the phrase 'monastic rule' [Ordensregel]. This, despite its unusual sound, is unmistakably where the greater analytical emphasis lies. Its meaning was clearer to Wittgenstein: such a rule expresses one of the most suggestive attempts to approach what a grammar meant for him – it forms a set of dictates that require no further justification, and whose sum produces a form of life, the monastic way of life, whether in the Pachomian, Augustinian, Cassianic, Benedictine, Franciscan or any other style. To understand what it means to follow a rule – and this is the chronically recurring question in later Wittgenstein – it is sufficient to imagine how one would live if one entered a religious order. What gives it its specific character, and how the rule affects those who follow it, is only revealed to those who make it their own by choosing the monastic way of life themselves. The Wittgensteinian monk, however, would be condemned to playing the role of ethnologist in his order, as he would remain incapable of absorption into the collective form of life for psychological reasons. He would, furthermore, be an ethnologist who is tricked by the natives – for he would be joining a tribe that contained no natives, only joined members like himself.

The particularity of a monastic rule – and this is where Wittgenstein's statement becomes problematic – is that whatever the individual prescriptions, it requires the monks (the author would scarcely have been thinking of nuns) to carry out every step, every action in meditative contemplation and choose every word carefully. Whether it is the form of the tonsures, the dress code, the regulations for setting up the sleeping quarters and the behaviour of the older and younger monks in them, the allocation of sleeping times, the holy readings, the gatherings to prayer, the work in the scriptoria, the arrangement of the storerooms and dining rooms, and so on – all the concrete rules are embedded in the rule of all rules, which states that the monk must not carry out the slightest action out of mere dull habit, but rather be prepared for interruption by orders from his superior at any moment – as if constantly expecting the Saviour to enter the premises. St John Cassian insisted that a scribe called to the door by his superior should not even finish the letter he had begun: he should rather leap up to be fully ready for the new assignment.[44]

Monastic life thus differs from ordinary life in three ways: firstly, entering an order implies compliance with the artificial system of carefully written rules that animate the monastic life of whatever observance. In the case of ordinary culture, by contrast, one grows into it without ever being asked if one wishes to accept its rules – indeed, most never reflect on whether there is any *regula* for the local forms of life at all. Secondly, living behind monastery walls creates a special climate of vigilance and readiness for any given tasks that is not found in any form of life in the non-monastic sphere – 'obedience' and 'piety' are metaphors for total availability. The basic rhythm of monastic existence is created from a calculated interplay of practical tasks and cultic interruptions; in this way, the hands testify to the monastic-communist maxim that work is good, but prayer is better. In monastic culture, after all, the strongest characteristic of profane culture disappears – the division of labour between the sexes, and the concern for the transference of existing forms of life to the little bar-barians who emerge from the intercourse between the sexes.

Culture Arises from Secession

Wittgenstein's point was clearly a different one. When he notes 'Culture is a monastic rule', the meaning of 'culture' here has shrunk to a finely sieved residue. By no means should every form of life that appears in 'societies' be considered culture, only those comparable to existence under a monastic rule in terms of explicitness, strictness, vigilance and reduction to the essential – and which permit a *modus vivendi* whose first and last criterion is relief from the consequences of sexuality. It is insignificant here that the monastic rules, in their sacral transparency and elitist unambiguity, are ultimately no less arbitrary than the fixed regulations of any grammar among natural languages. All that matters is the separatist dynamic of life under the rule. Wittgenstein's use of the term 'culture' leaves no doubts: for him, culture in the substantial sense of the word only comes about through the isolation of the truly cultivated from the rest of so-called 'culture', this muddled aggregate of better and worse habits whose sum is barely more than the usual 'swinishness'.

From this perspective it is easier to explain why Wittgenstein is one of the few authors of modernity – perhaps the only one of real distinction in the period between Nietzsche and Foucault, except for Heidegger – whose work displays the transformation of philosophy from a school subject back to an engaging discipline. His example shows what happens when study becomes exercise. The reason for this change can be found in his secessionist understanding of culture. It is easy to show that this was part of Wittgenstein's Austrian legacy, which he never abandoned.

Wittgenstein knew from childhood what a secession is, as the breaking away of the group of artists around Gustav Klimt, Koloman Moser and Josef Hoffmann from the historicistically inclined con-servative Vienna *Künstlerhaus* in 1897 had been one of the main events in *fin-de-siècle* Vienna. Karl Wittgenstein (1847–1913), the philosopher's father, a steel industrialist and music patron, was one of the secession's most important sponsors – not only for the construction of the building on the Karlsplatz, but also through personal support for individual artists. The young Wittgenstein was sixteen when Klimt staged his next act of self-removal by leaving the secession, and nineteen at the publication of Adolf Loos's epoch-making essay *Ornament and Crime*. One can assume that from that moment on at the latest, the concept of culture had merged irreversibly with the secession phenomenon – for the young man and the young Viennese culture scene in equal measure. This included the experience that a secession is not sufficient in order to remain faithful to the impulse to break away from the usual. Only a constant progression in distancing oneself from the misery of conventions can preserve the purity of the modernizing project – hence the never-ending rhythm of secession in the art of the twentieth century, which remains in motion until there is nothing left from which to secede. In fact, Loos was one of the strongest critics of the first aesthetics of secession. He saw it as no more than the replacement of one form of kitsch with another – of the vulgar ornament with a select one.

As Allan Janik and Stephen Toulmin have shown, Viennese modernity as a whole was characterized by secessionist motifs in the broadest sense. For its protagonists, the culture-founding gesture consisted in exiting from the system of conventions in which the aristocratic-bourgeois audience in the imperial capital revelled. Regardless of whether it was architecture, painting, music or language, the group of moderns constituted itself through a secessionist operation in every field – through the separation of the purists from the ornamentalists, the constructivists from the indulgent, the logicians from the journalists and the grammarians from the chatterers. What united the new artists was an aversion to every form of excess. In their view, culture and art could only progress through a radical opposition to what Karl Kraus called the 'debasement of practical life by ornament, demonstrated by Adolf Loos'.[45] The equation of ornament and crime presented by Loos in his essay perfectly expresses the new ethos of formal clarity determined by the true use of things – it also reminds us that functionalism was initially a form of moralism, or more precisely an ascetic practice that sought to come closer to the good by dispensing with what could not be justified. It would not be difficult to pinpoint the Loos factor in detail in Wittgenstein's logical habitus, for example when the philosopher notes: 'I assert that use is the form of culture, the form which makes objects.'[46] The polemical atmosphere in which the search for the 'form of culture' took place is demonstrated in an aphorism by Karl Kraus:

Adolf Loos and I, he literally and I in language, have done no more than to show that there is a difference between an urn and a chamber pot, and that culture only has room to move within this difference. The others, however, the positives, are divided into those who use the urn as a chamber pot and those who use the chamber pot as an urn.[47]

Wittgenstein's late note 'Culture is a monastic rule' still presupposes the aggressive ethic of reduction and the future-postulating tenor of the formal purism characterizing early Viennese modernity. The bizarre overtones accompanying his remark make sense when one grasps the paradox underlying the basic secessionist stance: that a credible ascent within culture can only be achieved through a descent to elementary forms. For these form zealots, the simple stood above the complicated. For the participants in the great exodus from the 'debased' sphere, the calls to return 'to the things', 'to the elementary life forms' or 'to real use' were synonymous. Through these campaigns, the phenomenological as well as the functionalistic, the reductionistic as well as the postivistic, entire worlds of 'ornaments' – or whatever one wishes to call the superfluous elements – fell by the wayside. What would count in future was the study of primary forms, grammars and their constructive principles. The participants in the course of study that enabled and justified 'culture' in the new sense were a group of artist-ascetics living under an explicit rule. For them, ethics, aesthetics and logic pointed in the same direction. The Viennese monastic rule was only decisive for the growth of a new 'culture' because it took an opposing stance to the predominance of debased conditions in every single one of its tenets. The style was neo-Cistercian and *dépourvu*, founded on the trinity of clarity, simplicity and functionality.

Form and Life

I would not have to remind readers of these connections if the figure of secession, independently of its Viennese history, were not to become significant for everything that will be said in the following about the organizational forms of the practising life, in its earlier and earliest manifestations too. The secession gesture as such already expresses the imperative without which there could never have been any monastic 'order', any reform or any revolution: 'You must change your life!' This presupposes that life has something about it which the individual has – or can acquire – the competence to change. In 1937, Wittgenstein noted: 'The fact that life is problematic shows

138

that the shape of your life does not fit into life's mould. So you must change your life and, once your life does fit into the mould, what is problematic will disappear.'[48]

The belief in the possibility of a better 'fit' between form and life is based on a concept of form that can be traced back to the founding phase of philosophy in the work of Socrates and Plato, and to the early period of Brahmanic asceticisms. It expresses the conviction that there is a 'good form' of life, regardless of whether it comes from the Viennese workshops, the Athenian school or the monasteries of Benares – a form whose adoption would necessarily lead to the elimination of disturbances in existence. Finding the good form is a design task that includes a moral-logical exercise. It is only because philosophy itself implies such a task from the outset that it can catch on as a 'school'; the school as such is itself a secession phenomenon – as much in the case of Plato, the founder of the Academy, as among the Viennese moderns. Where there is secession, the reformers have run out of patience with the pre-existing facts. They no longer want to see either the conventional conditions or their reproductions; the hour of a return to the original models has struck. The model does not represent life; it precedes it. One can virtually speak of the birth of philosophy from the spirit of secession to models. It is not quite by chance that Platon's Athenian Academy, founded in 387 BC – and consistently in use until its destruction by Sulla in 86 BC – was located out of the way, almost a mile to the northwest of the city centre, though very appropriately next to a larger sports venue, the gymnasium, which was soon incorporated into the educational system.

The founding of a school implies a rejection of fate kitsch – be it late Athenian or late Habsburg. It requires the conversion of questions of fate into tasks of discipline. Plato had already rejected tragedy because he sensed a moral 'debasement' in it: instead of watching comfortably and sentimentally as other people perish in their entanglements, he considered it more commendable to tend to one's own mistakes and, once aware, to correct them to the best of one's ability. One could almost say that the school is based on the invention of the 'mistake' – the mistake is a secularized, revisable misfortune, and a pupil is someone who learns from mistakes and attempts to eliminate them. What is conspicuous here is the convergence of the basic Socratic position, as developed by Nietzsche in his early writings, and Wittgenstein's approach to continuous self-clarification. For the latter too, the language analyst, there is nothing tragic, 'and conflict [does] not become something splendid but a *mistake*'.[49]

Let us be open about the point of these reflections: in showing

139

that Wittgenstein's concept of culture involves a strongly secessionist understanding of 'work' on one's personal mistakes and the mistakes of collective sensibility, one removes every possibility of co-opting him for the egalitarian and relativist ideology that accompanies the numerous varieties of Anglo-American Analytic Philosophy. In reality, Wittgenstein's 'work' is probably the harshest manifestation of ethical elitism in the twentieth century – perhaps excepting Simone Weil, as the only reform elitist of equal stature. His secessionist-elitist approach extends so deep that the author even wished he could have withdrawn from himself and his various forms of 'swinishness', had this been possible. Once Wittgenstein's unbending elitism – which, incidentally, is as radical as it is apolitical and ahistorical – is revealed, this not only affects our understanding of his most successful theorem, that of 'language games'; it also casts a very different light on Wittgenstein's role as a teacher.

Language Games Are Exercises: The Deception of 'Ordinary Language'

Now it becomes directly apparent that the 'language games' cited *ad nauseam* in reality constitute asceticisms, or rather micro-ascetic modules: verbally articulated practical exercises whose performance is usually acquired via imitation – without anyone to tell us whether it is worthwhile or desirable to carry out these games. Evidently the cultures themselves do not enlighten us here – they are condemned to affirmation in these matters. What is less acceptable is that the language game theory also answers these questions evasively. It thus conceals the fact that an imitation of ordinary 'swinishnesses' is inherent in most language games, while the most important thing, namely participation in secession, usually remains unspoken or uncomprehended. In the conventional language game, one practises something that is not actually worth practising. One practises it *nolens volens* by doing what everyone does without considering whether it is worth doing. A conventional language game is the everyday, not explicitly declared training of the 'swine', and hence of those who do not care whether their form of life stands up to examination.

Only in the rarest of cases is the ability to participate in language games acquired through a voluntary adoption of a clarified secessionary form of life. This, as Wittgenstein emphasizes in the second half of his statement, would presuppose an explicit 'monastic rule' – although the word 'explicit' refers to a form knowledge or asceticism knowledge that was either distilled in the course of long experiments with the practising life (as in the era of the *regula* authors from Pachomius to Isidore of Seville, or in the Brahmanic and Yogic traditions) or had to be newly developed amidst a cultural crisis (as in *fin-de-siècle* Vienna) through a radicalized design. Then, however, and only then, practising means assimilating the practice-worthy via declared asceticisms. Exercises of this level lead to language games and forms of life for non-swine. As elementary as they might seem, they constitute the perfect impregnation of everyday life through artistry. The perfect depiction of normality thus becomes an acrobatic exercise. For Wittgenstein, the ethical miracle takes place at the summit of Mount Improbable: the miracle that forms of life can be clarified through logical analysis and technical reconstruction.

For all his efforts at humility, one cannot help but note a certain hypocrisy in late Wittgenstein, because he usually pretended not to know that his language game theory contained a murky concession to existence in the trivial and 'swinish' dimension, even though he had always striven to keep away from it. For himself, he kept an eye out for clarified monastic rules under which exceptional humans of his cast and secessionists of equal stature would want to live – and would, perhaps, also be able to live according to their standards. These forms are also known as 'language games', but one can tell that the robes are of the finest cloth. When the once-fashionable movement of ordinary language philosophy invoked Wittgenstein as an influence, it fell prey to a deception of which the master himself was far from innocent. He was never interested in the ordinariness of 'ordinary language'; the art would have been to sense something of the perfectionism of the Viennese workshops coming through the word 'ordinary'. People forgot to remind the English patients that they should not be too hasty in their eagerness to praise the everyday. It was in the spirit of great reform to say 'ordinary' while meaning 'extraordinary'. One would have had to explain to the interested what the search for the quintessential form of use actually meant, at the risk of spoiling the party for the ordinarists. Anyone who has hung their coat on a hook designed by Adolf Loos has a standard that will remain unforgotten. If one then sees where one's British and American colleagues hang their things, one can never take them seriously again.

The subtle mendacity of language game theory is undoubtedly the secret of its success. It also reveals something that otherwise only 'shows itself' in Wittgenstein's habitus as a 'teacher'. He knows that teaching means demonstrating, but what he is able to demonstrate as a virtuoso – the logical analysis of language – is worlds apart from what he actually wanted to demonstrate: the saint's form of life. What 'shows itself' in Wittgenstein's teaching is that he does not show what he is concerned with – and that he cannot do what he wants, and never stops wanting to do what he cannot. The established Wittgenstein hagiography has long since admitted that its hero more or less failed miserably in his role as primary school teacher in Austria between 1920 and 1926. But no one dares utter the fact that he failed equally – and even worse, as there were consequences to this failure – as a university lecturer, presumably because, in secret, people exculpate the author psychologically, as well as believing that by becoming a global celebrity, he achieved more than a *Homo academicus* could dream of anyway. When Wittgenstein wrote in 1946, shortly before leaving the teaching profession, 'I am showing my pupils details of an immense landscape which they cannot possibly know',[50] he was implicitly admitting to keeping his audience in the dark as to his real preferences. He could have done more to illuminate those parts of the landscape that concerned him, but he preferred to offer noble disorientation – as if his Christian perfectionism were as much of an undisclosable private matter in Cambridge as his homosexuality, something that was not appreciated at that time.

What Shows Itself

In my view, the absence of any explicit criticism of Wittgenstein's role as a university lecturer indicates that his students turned a blind eye to their teacher's ambiguity and contented themselves with half the lesson. What one could achieve with half the lesson is demonstrated by the trends that have dominated university philosophy for over fifty years on both sides of the Atlantic. The paradigm of the mental athlete and arrogant epistemologist, bursting with acumen, to which Wittgenstein himself had contributed through his academic persona, became dominant everywhere, while the things that truly mattered to the thinker all but disappeared from the curricula of analytic seminars. Wittgenstein must have noticed that on the path of 'it shows itself', something quite different from what he desired was coming to light. The idea of having any direct effect as a role model had long since collapsed when he noted in 1947: 'Most likely I could still achieve an effect in that, above all, a whole lot of garbage is written in response to my stimulus and that perhaps provides the stimulus for something good.'[51]

It would be impossible to find another example in the history of philosophy of a thinker who foresaw his own effects so precisely. At the same time, the statement also sums up the intellectual catastrophe of the second half of the twentieth century. The 'garbage' that Wittgenstein knows he will provoke soon or posthumously is no different from the 'swinishness' into whose hands he would play with his official later theory, the pseudo-neutral language game principle. Wittgenstein's late ambiguity does not, admittedly, express merely a private complex; it testifies to an objective difficulty that he was unable to overcome. For him, the survivor of the late Habsburg world, the clocks had stopped in November 1918 – and would remain immobile for the rest of his life. Until then, like the other protagonists of Viennese modernity, he had been ahead of his time – part of the ascetic-formalist problem community of those who embarked on the great reform. After the collapse of the Austrian world he lost all connection to the topics of the present, navigating in a space of undated and unaddressed problems – in this perhaps comparable only to Emile Cioran, who, after breaking with the hysterical exaggerations of his early 'committed' phase, had also moved towards a form of exiled and decontextualized resistance to the conventionalities of existence. It would be a worthwhile undertaking to examine Wittgenstein and Cioran alongside each other with reference to their anachronistic exercises – both invented something aptly summarized by the younger in his discarded book title *Exercices négatifs*.[52] The sum of Wittgenstein's achievements during his British years (1929–51) is a tragic testimony to the immobilization of the Kakanian *reformatio mundi* caused by the war.

Since the amputation of its world, Austria has been a country without reality, and Wittgenstein's re-imported philosophy its great lie. Before 1918, Wittgenstein's defection from late Habsburg Austrianhood to a designer Christianity à la Tolstoy may have symbolized part of the inevitability of radical reform sensed by the best; after 1918, however, such an option only formed part of the almost universal failure in formulating the rules for life in a post-dynastic world. Had Wittgenstein already believed then that culture was a monastic rule, the emergency of the time would have led him either to write one or to participate in its production – even if it were only in the inelegant form of a party programme or an educational plan for post-feudal generations. Instead, he fled to the obsolete world of rural Austrian primary schools – a Narodnik who had chosen the wrong century. Later on, his philosophical analyses contributed to popularizing the Austrian modus of flight from reality by way of England. The lie of language games began its triumphal march through the institutions of the Western world without anyone noticing the basis of the deception. It was as if American hardware stores had decided to stock only products of aristocratic formalism à la Loos – ignoring the fact that hardware stores inevitably restrict themselves to a standard inventory. Through the manner in which he stood still in 1918, Wittgenstein was one of the ideological contributors to the intellectual standstill in the Anglophone world after 1945: on the outside a seeming equality of all forms of life, analytic fitness and a liberal 'anything goes' mentality, but on the inside a homesick longing for the green valleys of silliness and feelings of hierarchy belonging to an elite from times past.

Declared Exercises

I do not want these diagnoses to be misunderstood as destructive criticism; on the contrary, correcting the distortions caused by Wittgenstein is no insoluble task. A reminder of the secessionist dynamic of searching for the good form is sufficient to understand that the language game theory is really a training theory based on the – itself undeclared – difference between declared and undeclared asceticisms. The individual language games are micro-ascetic modules normally carried out by the players without knowing, let alone reflecting upon what they are doing. If they act as they have been taught, they are possessed by the grammar, as it were, even if it is only a mild possession by habits of sentence structure. Nonetheless, possession by an unconsciously or semi-consciously followed rule cannot be the right way for humans to act in relation to the right and the true. True as it might be that the meaning of a word is determined by its real usage, the decisive factor is the refinement of that usage. Did Adolf Loos not study the independent life of everyday things in minute detail, then replacing the most trivial objects with utensils of the most ingenious simplification and the greatest material purity? And Wittgenstein himself – did he not, in the house in Vienna that he designed for his sister, even abandon the seemingly definitive shapes of door-handles and supplant them with his own, handles whose shape indicated whether the door opened inwards or outwards?

The conclusions to be drawn from these analogies are far-reaching: many undeclared exercises can and should, in fact, be concerted into declared ones and clarified in the process. The asymmetry between the undeclared and the declared exercise is itself one of the first ethical facts. This difference justifies Wittgenstein's assertion – directed against the Enlightenment-style instrumentalization of clarity for the sake of 'progress' – of 1930: 'For me on the contrary clarity, perspicuity are valuable in themselves.'[53] This supposed end in itself is, in truth, the medium in which the conversion of possessed rule-applications to free exercises takes place.

For the primal ethical imperative 'You must change your life!' to be followed, therefore, it is initially necessary for the practising to become aware of their exercises as exercises, that is to say as forms of life that engage the practising person. The reason for this is self-evident: if the players are themselves inescapably affected by what they play and how they play it (and how it has been drilled into them to play it), they will only have access to the bridge of their self-change by recognizing the games in which they are entangled for what they are. Consequently, the language game theory is not an expression of 'therapeutic positivism', as the American philosopher Brian Farell claimed in 1946 with the insensitivity of the hardware store customer – one can understand why Wittgenstein was extremely displeased by this. It is the working form of transformative asceticism, and hence aesthetic secessionism in action. It is carried out with the aim of choosing between the muddle of life forms dictated, absorbed under situative compulsion and inevitably close to 'swinishness' to find those that can be taken up into the clarified 'monastic rule'. Every thing is a 'language game', living crystal and swinishness alike – what matters is the nuance.

Whereof One Should Not Be Silent

This takes care of the chatter, rampant among Wittgensteinians, of the silence that must allegedly be maintained about everything that truly matters in life. One does not keep silent when it is a matter of preferences. Here too, looking for the source of the confusion leads us to Wittgenstein himself. On this sensitive point he fell for his own ideology by amalgamating the Jesuan and monastic habitus of silence, which had already been attractive for him early on, with his logically weak denial of the possibility of metalanguage – had his entire output not been one great breaking of the rule of silence, a speaking, scattered over the decades, about the what and the why of speaking?

All that remains of the talk about silence is as much as is required to show a practising person that the main thing is to carry out the exercise, not to reason over it. One can only carry out a throw of the discus by throwing it; no amount of chatter about discuses and the right way to throw them can replace the throw itself, and neither the biographies of throwers nor the bibliography of throwing literature will lead a single step further. This by no means changes the fact that 'discology' could become a discipline carried out in keeping with the standards of the art, assuming it existed. Its performance would consist in carrying out the language games belonging to this -ology *lege artis* – why not in a special department for throwing research and human projectile studies? Whether it would be better to be a discus-thrower or a discologist is another matter. It forces one to choose between two disciplines, each of which requires its own form of expertise – or it results in a combination of subjects and leads to the emergence of the *athleta doctus*.

Taken on its own, Wittgenstein's silence-posturing has no deeper meaning than Erich Kästner's verse 'Nothing good happens unless you do it.' One could, if one liked, also associate it with the *Regula Benedicti*, which states in the section 'What Kind of Man the Abbot Ought to Be': 'Therefore, when anyone receives the name of Abbot, he ought to govern his disciples with a twofold teaching. That is to say, he should show them all that is good and holy by his deeds even more than by his words.'[54] Wittgenstein's habitus becomes 'religiously' charged because the primal scene of 'silently embodying the truth', like Jesus standing before Pilate, shines through him. The philosopher's behaviour perhaps becomes easier to understand if one imagines him standing constantly before Pilate. This provides a pictorial commentary on the statement 'But Wittgenstein was silent.' In reality, he was not silent; on the contrary, he gave lectures through a behaviour befitting a man who is convinced that the world is the ideal place to show something. But he was never entirely sure about the content of what had to be shown; he was neither able to take the step of adopting a formal teaching and training role nor that of choosing a manifest guru or messiah role. He remained indecisive in the most important question, partly for mental reasons and partly because, within his doctrine of silent showing, he did not separate two tasks: providing examples as a technical master and setting an example as a life teacher.

The Ascetological Twilight and the Gay Science

Wittgenstein's inability to explicate the difference between asceticism and aesthetics – and the resulting confusion between the demonstrative performance of an exercise and a silent embodiment of the 'ethical' – may have caused half a century of bewilderment in the camp of analytic opportunism, but it is not in itself an incurable ailment. To put it in the terms of the attempt developed here, Wittgenstein's work, like that of all the authors treated so far, belongs to the movement that began in the late nineteenth century and which I call the ascetological twilight. We must draw the necessary conclusions from it – and I repeat my claim that they will culminate in a general anthropotechnics. What the author left behind is a wealth of coherently incoherent studies on the clarification of the purpose of a practising behaviour. Strangely enough, his active vocabulary shows a gap in the decisive place – at least, I do not know of any passage in his writings where the word 'practise' is used in more than a passing fashion. Nor do I find any indication that Wittgenstein was aware of the etymological equivalence of *áskesis* and 'exercise'. One can, therefore, perhaps say that Wittgenstein's 'work' was arranged around a blind spot, the missing central concept of *áskesis*. His explicit sense of the grammatical cannot be separated from his implicit understanding of the ascetic.

Wittgenstein's investigations into the diversity of language games should therefore be read as contributions to General Ascetology – as collected references to the ubiquity of the practical-practising motif in all fields of human behaviour. Micro-asceticism is always current. It remains involved in all that humans do – indeed, it even extends to the pre-personal zone, into the idiolects of all body parts, each of which has its own history. There is no escape from the games and language games because the law of practice misses nothing, whether it happens deliberately or in ego-remote and non-intentional chains of repetitions. That everyday life and practice are identical is one of the strongest intuitions of language game thinking. It needs to be made clear, however – against the mainstream of evened-out language game chatter – that not all everyday things are acceptable *per se*, and that not every repetition of a well-worn language game helps the practising person to progress, or is even of use to them at all. What is more, it is untrue that philosophy is a sickness of language that can be cured by regressing to everyday usage. If anything, listening closely to ordinary language teaches us the opposite: it is often far sicker than the philosophy it claims to cure.

In my view, everything Wittgenstein put down on paper as a language ethicist and logical reformer only makes sense if understood as the most serious resumption at that time of Nietzsche's programme of the *Gay Science*. This science is gay to the extent that it advances its clarifications to the detriment of stupidity, without succumbing to the tendency towards fundamentalist moroseness that is usually connected to reformist polemicism. I shall therefore take the liberty of regarding Wittgenstein as an occult Nietzschean – not only on the tactical or formal level (for, like the author of *Human, All Too Human*, he recorded the best part of his insights in small attacks) but also strategically, in that he, like Nietzsche, gave philosophy a guerrilla form and developed an existentially binding transformative analysis with the aim of bringing about a clarifying change in the form of life, and thus changing life itself from the ground up.

Foucault: A Wittgensteinian

If Wittgenstein was an occult and involuntary Nietzschean, Michel Foucault emerged from the outset as his manifest and voluntary counterpart. Nonetheless, one can say that Foucault started from where Wittgenstein left off: showing that entire branches of science or epistemic disciplines are nothing other than complexly structured language games, also known as discourses or discursive practices. Just as Wittgenstein had broken with the cognitivist prejudice in language theory to show how much speaking is an act rather than knowledge, Foucault broke with the epistemist prejudice in the theory of science in order to explain how much the disciplines he examined are performative systems rather than 'reflections' of reality. His choice in the book *The Order of Things* to refer to the group of disciplines whose performativity of scientific knowledge or of knowledge effects he demonstrates as the 'episteme', of all things, is a case of exquisite irony – comparable in this only to the psychoanalytical use of the word 'rationalization' to describe the 'logical' explanations of neurotics dictated by wishful thinking. Analogously, the disciplines of the 'episteme' constitute the discursive pseudo-explanations of those who dominate theory, be they psychiatrists, doctors, biologists, economists, prison directors or jurists by profession. Owing to their performative status, the 'discourses' at any time in the history of practical power are an amalgam of knowledge effects and executive competencies.

One could therefore describe Foucault's work as it developed between the late 1950s and the mid-1970s as a Wittgensteinianism intensified via Heidegger – and hoisted up further with surrealisms – that grew, curiously enough, without any closer knowledge of German or British sources, just as French culture after 1945 in general offered no fertile ground for the ideas of the analytic tradition. Naturally, Foucault's attempts had little to do with the fashion of Parisian structuralism – aside from certain parallels in the stance against the dictates of 'hyper-Marxism'.[55]

Tragic Verticality

His work, however, is too varied and too flamboyant to be summed up from a single perspective. I shall focus on two aspects with an obvious connection to our inquiries: firstly, Foucault's laconic and prescient early contributions to a redefinition of the vertical dimension in human existence, and secondly, his richly varied late studies on the autoplastic or self-sculptural life techniques of antiquity. I would consider the first relevant document to be Foucault's lengthy introduction to Ludwig Binswanger's book *Dream and Existence* (1954), in which he addresses the 'tragic verticality' of existence; the other sources are from the group of studies he pursued during his hiatus from writing between 1976 and 1984, which organize the posthumously edited body of work around such figures as 'self-concern', 'self-culture' and 'struggle with oneself'.

The 'acrobatic' dimension – as a stance taken by existence upon the appearance of its inherent vertical tension – is unmistakably visible at both poles. I shall pass over Foucault's reflections on the horizontal phenomenon, the oft-cited historical formations of 'discourses', as they are not productive for our line of questioning, and because they exhibit the same seductive ambiguity as Wittgenstein's language game theorem; they have the effect of traps into which intellectuals like to walk in order to confirm their critical reflexes – when Foucault himself especially emphasized that he had never met an 'intellectual' in his life, only people who write novels, people who work with the sick, people who teach, people who paint and people 'of whom I have never really understood what they do ... But intellectuals? Never.'[56]

One thing that has scarcely ever been noted among the turbulences of Foucault's reception after the breakthrough of *The Order of Things* in 1966 is that the author's emergence twelve years earlier had begun with a grand anti-psychoanalytical gesture: with amazing self-confidence, he pushed aside the mechanics of deformation described in Freud's dream analysis, the 'dream work' [*Traumarbeit*], defining the dream as the decisive manifestation of the tragic truth about human beings:

149

> If the dream is the bearer of the deepest human meanings, this is not insofar as it betrays their hidden mechanisms or shows their inhuman cogs and wheels, but on the contrary, insofar as it brings to light the freedom of man in its most original form.[57]

While sleep denies death by simulating it, dreams – especially the dream of death – speak the truth. It thus achieves a form of 'self-fulfilment' by causing the 'emergence of what is most individual in the individual'.[58] 'But in every case death is the absolute meaning of the dream'.[59]

If this is true, the structure of existence can only be elucidated through the analysis of dreams. It is in dreams that humans enter the true Dionysian theatre – but not to become a new Oedipus. When we dream, we move within a directed spatiality more originary than geometry and the clear disposition of things in bright spaces. The character of the vertical axis in the existential spatiality of dreams is completely different from those in mathematics or architecture. It provides enthusiasm with the direction of its ascent – up until the calm at the summit, close to the divine. At the same time,

> The vertical axis can also be the vector of an existence that has lost its place on earth and, like Solness the Builder, is going to resume, up above, its dialogue with God. Then it indicates flight into excess, and from the start is marked by the vertigo of a fall.[60]

Binswanger had already asserted the anthropological priority of the vertical dimension because for him, the essential temporality of existence revealed itself in the dramas of ascent and fall. Foucault adopts Heidegger's definition of 'transcending' on the vertical axis as 'breaking away from the foundations of existence'; the complementary movement reveals itself as a tragic 'transdescendence', the fall from a pinnacle whose only purpose seems to be that of supplying the extravagant with the necessary altitude for fatal plunges.

It would take some twenty-five years for the paths of Foucault's thought to return to the place he had touched on in his Binswanger commentary. From that point on, he knew that work on verticality is not simply a matter of the originary imagination discussed in the early reflections. Now it meant a power of self-shaping in which the ethical competence of the individual is concentrated. Just as the young Foucault – who survived two suicide attempts in his early twenties – interprets suicide as the regained original gesture 'in which I make myself world',[61] the older Foucault discovers practising self-shaping as the movement arising from one's ownmost possibility of existence: beyond oneself with oneself.

This discovery awakened the thinker's enthusiasm primarily because it allowed him to put his cards on the table and show himself as a man of the vertical, without arousing any suspicions that he secretly wanted to return to the well-trodden paths of a run-of-the-mill transcendence in the Christian-Platonic style.[62] In the same act, he clarified his relationship with Nietzsche by correcting the temptation to excess emanating from the latter's work through Nietzsche's own late asceticism – or, more precisely, through its pre-Christian patterns, of which Nietzsche had dreamed when he declared his aim to 'make asceticism natural again'. Foucault had understood that the Dionysian fails if one does not implant a Stoic inside him. The latter admits entertaining the misconception that getting beside oneself already means going beyond oneself. The 'beyond' in the practising going-beyond-oneself[63] is now only seemingly the same as the one discussed upon the early discovery of tragic or Icarian verticality.[64] It is, in truth, the 'beyond' of superior maturity, acquired on the rungs of the practice ladder.[65]

The transgressive kitsch that Foucault had picked up from Bataille many years beforehand, and to which his mimetic talent enabled him to contribute a few precarious specimens of his own, stepped into the background. In retrospect it would prove no more than an episode on the way to a more general understanding of the self-forming constitutions of practising life. Needless to say, the last connections to the *ressentiment*-driven leftist milieu in France were now also severed. Foucault had distanced himself from its fabrications long ago, and when he stated in a 1978 interview that 'nothing is more foreign to me than the idea of a "Master" who imposes his own law. I accept neither the notion of domination nor the universality of the law',[66] he voiced a conviction that had estranged him from the Stalinist, Trotskyist and Maoist wings of the French intellectual scene for over two decades – to retain only a few connections to anarcho-liberal and left-Dionysian tendencies.

More importantly, he had now also liberated himself from the paranoid leftovers of his own studies in power. It was only the attitude of methodical calmness, acquired late on, that enabled him to formulate a concept of regimen, disciplines and power games devoid of all compulsively anti-authoritarian reflexes. When he states sententiously in the same interview, recalling his beginnings in abstract revolt, 'One not only wanted a different world and a different society, one also wanted to go deeper, to transform oneself and to revolutionize relationships to be completely "other"',[67] he is already speaking as someone genuinely changed who, light years away from his beginnings, remembers his confused longing for complete otherness. With this turn of phrase he is beyond irony, even beyond humour. In his way, Foucault repeated the discovery that one cannot subvert the 'existing' – only supervert it. He had stepped out into the open and become ready to perceive something strictly invisible for an intelligence conditioned in French schematicisms: the fact that human claims to freedom and self-determination are not suppressed by the disciplines, regimes and power games, but rather enabled. Power is not an obstructive supplement to an originally free ability; it is constitutive for ability in all its manifestations. It always forms the ground floor above which a free subject moves in. Hence one can describe liberalism as a system of disciplinary checks and balances without glorifying it in the slightest – but without denouncing it either. With the calm severity of a civilization trainer, Foucault states: 'Individuals could certainly not be "liberated" without educating them in a certain way.'[68]

Language Games, Discourse Games, General Disciplinics

This cleared the way for a General Disciplinics. Foucault had gone a certain distance along this path by newly covering the universe of ancient philosophical asceticisms in a series of meticulous rereadings of mostly Stoic authors – unimpeded by the ubiquitous barriers of critical kitsch, which sees domination in every form of 'self-control', and immediately suspects any discipline in one's way of life of being a self-repression that doubles an external repression. We recall, to name one of the best-known examples, the discrepancies read into the Sirens chapter of the *Odyssey* by Adorno and Horkheimer in the *Dialectic of Enlightenment*, where the Greek seafarer becomes a bourgeois with suppressed drives who instantly advances to the prototype of the European 'subject'. One thinks back with trepidation to the times in which a younger generation of intellectuals viewed such gaucheries as the *non plus ultra* of critical thought.

The attraction of Foucault's late writing lies in the undisguised expression of wonder at the regions into which his study of ancient authors led him. He claims the status of a 'philosophical exercise' for his expedition into the history of asceticisms or 'self-techniques':

> There is irony in those efforts one makes to alter one's way of looking at things. [. . .] Did mine actually result in a different way of thinking? Perhaps at most they made it possible to go back through what I was

already thinking, to think it differently, and to see what I had done from a new vantage point and in a clearer light. Sure of having travelled far, one finds that one is looking down on oneself from above.[69]

The proximity between Wittgenstein's clarification of form and Foucault's philosophical exercise is remarkable. The analogies between the 'language games' and 'truth games' are also unmistakable. The essential differences between the two thinkers of the practising life, on the other hand, become clear when one compares their interpretations of the stay at the summit of Mount Improbable. While Wittgenstein finds it amazing enough if forms of life can be clarified to the point where existence on a plateau is identical to a stay at a Tibetan mountain monastery, Foucault hurls himself into the role of the mining engineer who, through deep drilling at different points, reveals the height of the mountains and the number of concealed folds within them. For him, the mountain of improbability is an archive, and the most plausible way to inhabit it is by penetrating the old corridors in order to study the physics of the archive. His intuition, admittedly, tells him that the mountain culminates in each individual that inhabits it, which is why the ethics of these studies seeks to make it clear that what looks like a rock mass is in truth an accumulation of respectively singular culminations – even if these do not, for the most part, sense themselves as such. Here the imperative 'You must change your life!' means: 'You yourself are the mountain of improbability, and as you fold yourself, thus will you tower up.'

The objective parallels between Wittgenstein and Foucault are impressive, even if we leave aside the psychodynamic aspect of the *bioi paralleloi* of two precocious homosexuals who, after a phase of advanced self-destruction attempts, managed to arrive at a form of self-therapy. To my knowledge, Wittgenstein's note from 1948 – 'I am too soft, too weak, and so too lazy to achieve anything important. The industry of the great is, amongst other things, a sign of their *strength*, quite apart from their inner wealth'[70] – has not yet been examined in the light of Foucault's studies on confessional practices. One could easily imagine those lines being written after an encounter between Wittgenstein and Foucault – though Wittgenstein would have felt more disgust than admiration for Foucault's work up to 1975, as he would have found his early and middle style unbearable. But he would probably have read the posthumous writings as the marvels of mannerism-free clarity that they are.

It is in the effective histories of the two thinkers, however, that their kinship is strongest. For both, it was the point of highest imitability that triggered academic success, because in both cases it constituted the point of the most suggestive misunderstandability. We have seen how Wittgenstein's language game theory turned into the misdirection of 'ordinary language'; in Foucault's case, it is easy to understand why his discourse theory seemed an easy target for critical conformism. People took all those analyses of asylums, clinics, police institutions and prisons for a slightly outlandish form of social critique and lavished praise on its lyrically drugged fastidiousness. None of his readers understood that they were always also ascetic exercises in self-shaping in place of a third suicide attempt, and possibly even the author himself was not always aware of it. His insistence on the anonymity of authorship aimed in the same direction: if no one is there, no one can kill themselves. The bafflement was therefore great when the older Foucault sidestepped with the irony of one who had detached himself, shaking off his critical and subversive followers. Whoever still wanted to remain on his trail after that comforted themselves with the oft-repeated assurance that philosophy is not a discipline, but an activity that 'crosses' disciplines. Thus he offered anarcho-criticistic kitsch – or, to tell the truth, the laziness that likes to think of itself as a subversive power – a final refuge.

Philosophical Multisport: The Subject as Carrier of Its Exercise Sequences

In reality, he had completed the breakthrough to a conception of philosophy as exercise and trained off the last remnants of excess surrealistic weight. He had realized that aestheticism, activistic Romanticism, constant irony, talk of transgression and subversionism are but dreamy and sluggish pursuits that conceal with difficulty a lack of form. He had long since understood: whoever speaks of subversion and effuses about becoming belongs in the beginners' class. Foucault had turned himself into something of which Nietzsche had provided a first notion in his last 'physiological' notes: the carrier of an intelligence that had become pure muscle, pure initiative. Hence the complete absence of mannerisms in his late style. The replacement of extravagance with manneredness – the secret of his middle period that can be unlocked through Binswanger – had become superfluous.

According to Foucault, philosophy can once more imagine becoming what it was before the cognitivist misconception threw it off course: an exercise of existence. As the ethos of the lucid life, it is pure discipline and pure multisport – in its own way, it entails the restoration of the ancient *panathlon* without restricting itself to a fixed group of *agones*. The analogy between forms of sport and forms of discourse and knowledge should be taken as literally as possible. The philosophical intelligence practises the discipline that it is primarily in the individual disciplines in which it immerses itself; if need be, even in 'philosophy'. A word of warning about 'crossing': in 99 per cent of cases, it falls prey to beginners' mistakes. There is no meta-discipline, of course – and hence no introduction to philosophy that is not itself the decisive exercise from the outset.

It seems to me that one can only do justice to Foucault by taking his impulse together with that of Pierre de Coubertin. The completion of the renaissance through the return of the athlete around 1900 encompasses the return of the wise man: in the *panathlon* of intelligence, he makes his own contribution to clarifying the form in which that renaissance continues today. Whatever the answer, the term can no longer be reduced to its art-historical and educated middle-class meanings. It indicates an indefinitely far-reaching unleashing of ability and knowledge forms beyond the Old European guild- and estate-based societies. By producing new configurations between contemplation and fitness, the current 'renaissance' enables new festivals on the plateau of the mountain of improbabilities. Anyone who has ever taken part in such a festival knows that neither a 'knowledge society' nor an 'information society' exists, as much as the new mystifiers might speak of them. What has constantly been arising since the renaissance is a multi-disciplinary and multi-virtuosic world with expanding limits of ability.

View of an Immense Landscape

Once free from the phantom of a 'philosophical activity' beyond discipline and disciplines, one can experience in Foucault's world the moment in which the whole scene is in open view. It can best be described with Wittgenstein's reference to showing his pupils an 'immense landscape which they cannot possibly know'.[71] It is the inconceivably wide landscape of disciplines; its sum forms the basis for the routines of all cultures and all trainable competencies. Here we have, both *de facto* and *de jure*, the 'broadest and longest fact that exists'. The path followed in exemplary fashion by Foucault leads, if pursued far enough, to a General Disciplinics as an encyclopaedia of ability games.

The discourse formations and knowledge games examined by

Foucault form only a narrow segment of these, albeit one of great paradigmatic energy. The consequences of Foucault's suggestions will only be appreciated if there is one day a fully worked-out form of General Disciplinics – which would probably take a century to develop. Its implantation would require a suitably contemporary transformation of universities and colleges, both in the structuring of the so-called 'subjects' or 'courses' and in the basic assumptions of academic pedagogy – which, against its better judgement, still clings to the briefcase-and-box theory, where teaching and learning is nothing but transferring knowledge from the professor's briefcase to the students' file boxes, even though it has long been known that learning can only take place through a direct participation in the disciplines. Establishing an academic system with discipline-based content and methods would at once be the only realistic way to counteract the atrophy of the educational system, founded on a reformed idea of the subjects and tasks of a Great House of Knowledge.

In the course of such a rearrangement, the effective geology of the man-made Mount Improbable would come to light. This *universitas* of disciplines embodies the real cultural science after the dissolution of cultural phantoms into the wealth of competency systems and trainable ability units. The over-discussed question of the subject is reduced to this compact formulation: a subject is someone who is active as the carrier of a sequence of exercises – which, furthermore, means that intermittently popular thought figures such as excess, decentring and the death of the subject are at best parasitic supplementary exercises to the qualifying ones; they can be assigned to the category of advanced mistakes.

In this context, I can only hint very cautiously at what elements might come together in General Disciplinics. This would certainly no longer be a mere theory of discourses, or groups of statements including corresponding asceticisms and executives. It would integrally encompass the spectrum of ability systems composed of knowledge and practical acts. This spectrum extends from (1) acrobatics and aesthetics, including the system of art forms and genres – NB: in the post-university House of Knowledge, the *studium generale* consists of artistry, not philosophy – via (2) athletics (the general study of sporting forms) to (3) rhetoric or sophistry, then (4) therapeutics in all its specialized branches, (5) epistemics (including philosophy), (6) a general study of professions (including the 'applied arts', which are assigned to the field of *arts et métiers*) and (7) the study of machinistic technologies. It also includes (8) administrativics, which constitutes both the static

156

substructure of the political or governmental and the universe of legal systems, as well as (9) the encyclopaedia of meditation systems in their dual role as self-techniques and not-self-techniques (the distinction between declared and undeclared meditations comes into play here), (10) ritualistics (as humans, according to Wittgenstein, are ceremonial animals and the ceremonies form trainable behavioural modules whose carriers appear as 'peoples' – which is why the linguistic sciences, like the theory of games and 'religions', form a sub-discipline of ritualistics), (11) the study of sexual practices, (12) gastronomics and finally (13) the open list of cultivatable activities, whose openness means the interminability of the discipline-forming and thus subjectification-enabling field itself. One can see from this list that Foucault's interventions touch on fields 1, 3, 4, 5, 8, 10 and 11. Ordinary philosophers restrict themselves to field 5, with occasional excursions to 8 or 1 and 3, which tells us enough about Foucault's panathletic qualities.

By way of precaution, I would point out that this first view of the thirteen-headed monster of disciplinics lacks the phenomena of war and 'religion', which are imposing ones for the everyday consciousness. There is a sound methodological reason for this: war is not a discipline of its own but an armed sophistry (a continuation of the art of being right by other means) that incorporates elements of athletics, ritualistics and machine technology. Nor is 'religion' a clearly demarcated discipline, but rather – as already hinted – an amalgam of rhetoric, ritualistics and administrativics, with the occasional addition of acrobatics and meditation.

Between Disciplines

Finally, I would like to point out how the question of the 'critical' dimension is inherent in each of the fields and oversteps each one of them: in every single area there is a constant practical crisis that leads to a separation of the right and the wrong in the execution of the discipline – often with immanently controversial results. Hence each individual discipline possesses a vertical tension that is unique to it and only comprehensible from within it. The status of an achiever in a given field does not tell us anything about their ranking in other areas. From a moral-philosophical perspective, it is decisive that the internal differences within a field form the dimension subject to Nietzsche's distinction between good and bad – which also means that there can be bad things within a discipline, but not evil ones.

157

On the other hand, there is a constant external observation of disciplines by authorities and individuals that are remote from them; these value or frown upon the results of exercises in foreign spheres according to their own standards. Outside observers can find what athletes do unimportant and what jewellers do superfluous without having to worry about whether the athletes or jewellers are the best in their field. External observers are even free to say that it would be better if this or that discipline, or even an entire complex of disciplines, did not exist – indeed, that the existence of some disciplines as such is a reprehensible aberration. Thus early Christians were convinced that gladiatorial fights were evil, even if the fighters were masters of their field, and the whole system of bread and circuses was nothing but a loathsome perversion. These negative assessments prevailed in the long term – which, to my knowledge, no one regrets. The decisive factor in their success was the fact that they precisely introduced alternative disciplines and surrounded these with positive evaluations. Some people today, by contrast, are of the opinion that parliamentary democracy, orthodox medicine or large cities should be abolished, as nothing good can come of them. These critics will not prevail because they do not show what should be done instead. The operative distinction here is between good and evil. What is evil should not be; one cannot improve it, only eliminate it. Just as the first distinction works with a withdrawal of value, the second works with a withdrawal of being.

Clearly only the first distinction is significant for the disciplinicist. For them, the wealth of disciplines itself is Mount Improbable, and one does not criticize mountains – one climbs them or stays at home. Nietzsche was probably the first to understand what conventional moralism is: the criticism of mountains by non-climbers. One can indeed resolve to turn one's back on the 'world' as the epitome of unaffirmable exercises and practise something other than life 'in the world' to the point of perfection – this is precisely what the escapists of late antiquity had in mind. There is, however, a notable difference between early Christians and modern radicals in this respect. The Christian bishops wrote monastic rules for life on other mountains, rules under which people could live for 1,500 years – in some cases to this day. The latter faction, by contrast, reacts to whatever is the case by standing around and finding it unfair. To them, all mountains are evil.

Foucault had grasped that 'subversion', 'stupidity' and 'unfitness' are three words for the same thing. When two journalists from *Les*

Nouvelles Littéraires asked him in 1984, 'Does your return to the Greeks participate in a weakening of the ground on which we think and live? What did you want to destroy?', his laconic response to the subversion parrots was: 'I did not want to destroy anything!'[72] Together with his declaration of 1980 – 'From this point of view all of my investigations rest on a postulate of absolute optimism. [. . .] I say certain things only to the extent to which I see them as capable of permitting the transformation of reality'[73] – this rejection of a two-hundred-year folklore of destruction constitutes Foucault's philosophical testament. His response in 1984 was almost literally his last word; a few days after the interview, conducted in late May, he collapsed in his apartment and died three weeks later, on 25 June, at the Pitié-Salpêtrière Hospital, whose former functions he had described in his book *The History of Madness*.

── 3 ──

SLEEPLESS IN EPHESUS

On the Demons of Habit and Their Taming
Through First Theory

The Cure for Extravagance: Discourse Analysis

Ludwig Binswanger was probably the only psychiatrist who Foucault knew understood, not to say predicted him – in the sense that he found in Binswanger's writings the most important elements for a language of endangered life, both in general and in his own particular case. In those writings he became acquainted with the tragic interpretation of verticality, in which the 'extravagance' of existence means being stuck too high up on the existential ladder. It was also clearly from Binswanger that he adopted the reference to Henrik Ibsen's play *The Master Builder* (premiered in 1892) – it portrays a manic architect who 'builds higher than he can climb' and ultimately falls to his death from the unliveable height of his tower.[74] Most of all, Foucault owed to Binswanger his early insights into the basic problem of his own existence, which the Heidegger-inspired psychiatrist had summarized in space-analytical terms: as a disproportion between width and height – or discourse and flight. This imbalance can, as Binswanger explained in his 1949 essay 'Extravagance', manifest itself either as a manic volatility and rapid digression through ideas in the *vols imaginaires*[75] or as a schizoid scaling of heights that do not stand in any productive relation to the narrowness of the experiential horizon;[76] in this sense, extravagance is the disease of the talented youth. The therapy consists of a form of mountain rescue intervention: the aim is to bring the lost climber back to the valley and explain the terrain to them until they feel able to respect the circumstances on their next climb. Understanding those circumstances involves knowing the relation between the difficulty of the slope and the training level of the peak conqueror.

Existence-analytical therapeutics is thus more an ethics than a form of medicine: it offers guidance in proportion-aware behaviour within the existential space. This space is existentially structured in so far as verticality and horizontality here have an ethical, not a geometric meaning: hence the horizontal stands for experience and 'discursivity'[77] – possibly this is where Foucault drew the idea of discourse analysis as an acquisition of the ability to navigate in the horizontal space – and the vertical for height of rank and decisiveness, assuming that existential height implies the ability to make decisions.

This brings into view an ethics that does not have values, norms and imperatives at its centre, but rather elementary orientations in the 'field' of existence. In the orientation-ethical approach to the how, the whither and the wherefore of existence, it is assumed that the 'subjects' – the existing parties as those able and unable to live their lives – are 'always already' immersed in a field or milieu that provides them with basic neighbourhoods, moods, and tensions in certain directions. That is why ethics is the theory of the first disclosednesses and movednesses – and thus First Science. The first things are not givens, but rather aspects of tendencies between extremes: complications, facilitations, narrowings, widenings, inclinations, disinclinations, lowerings, raisings. They form – as the matrix of the 'moods' [*Stimmungen*] that Heidegger disclosed for philosophy – a complex of pre-logical insights and orientations which the logical, concrete and evaluating world-relations are hooked into.

The First Ethical Distinction in Heraclitus

The earliest reference in the Old European space to a mode of thought that formulates an ethics of the kind touched on above can be found in a collection of fragments attributed to the Ionian proto-philosopher Heraclitus, who lived at the turn from the sixth to the fifth century BC. I am thinking in particular of the equally well-known and enigmatic Fragment 119 quoted by Stobaeus: *ēthos anthrópo daímon*, conventionally translated as 'Man's character is his fate.' Heidegger famously expressed his dissatisfaction with this trivial translation in the 'Letter on Humanism' addressed to Jean Beaufret in 1946. He accuses it of being thought in modern, not Greek terms – an objection that still applies to the slightly modified, Swabian-tinged version 'Man's particularity is his demon.' In order to shift things into place, Heidegger feels it necessary to bring out the heavy fundamental-ontological artillery: he treats the seemingly unassuming terms *ēthos* and *daímon* like funds deposited in an idea-historical bank that, even with the lowest possible interest rate, have now, over two thousand years later, grown into an enormous fortune. In his view, only fundamental ontology is entitled to make withdrawals from this ancient meaning account, for it alone is capable of thinking pre-Socratically and post-metaphysically at once. I will now show how, as exaggerated as his suggestion may be, he was not entirely wrong.

Heidegger's Cunning

In order to gain access to the treasure of meaning, Heidegger uses a hermeneutical trick: he brings the *ēthos daímon* statement together with the anecdote, related by Aristotle, in which Heraclitus, the philosopher from Ephesus in Asia Minor, is visited by a group of hesitant strangers who find him warming himself by the oven and bids them enter with the words 'Here too the gods are present.' The contextualizing strategy is as simple as it is effective. Just as the oven anecdote is meant to remind us that even in the ordinary, the unusual shines through, that the divine is present even in the most unassuming, the fragment to be interpreted seeks to express that the unknown is present in the known and the supra-real in the everyday. Hence the saying, if one translates *ēthos* with 'stay' or 'abode' (which is problematic) and *daímon* with 'God' (which is probably a little too lofty), would mean: 'Man dwells, in so far as he is man, in the nearness of God.'[78]

Although I consider this first translation by Heidegger unsuccessful, both philologically and philosophically, it has a stimulating element. For living in the nearness of God means discovering a form of vertical neighbourhood in which it is even more important to find a *modus vivendi* with the resident of the apartment above than with one's next-door neighbour. One can work with this point, even if the rest is unconvincing. But that is not the end of it: Heidegger then makes a second translation suggestion, in which he turns the problematic into the grotesque by augmenting the motif of neighbourhood with that of uncanniness. Now the three little words *ēthos anthrópo daímon* supposedly mean: 'The (familiar) abode is for man the open region for the presencing of god (the unfamiliar one).'[79] If that were truly the meaning of this statement, it would make Heraclitus the most profound commentator on Heidegger's work ever to come from ancient Greece.

Nonetheless, Heidegger did understand one aspect of Heraclitus' epigram correctly. The word *ēthos*, which should probably be taken in a more down-to-earth sense, and translated somewhat less preciously as 'behaviour' or 'habit', is placed in a state of 'upward' tension through its combination with the word *daímon*. Here, instead of thinking of 'the god', it is sufficient to imagine some higher spirit force that could tend equally towards good or evil.[80] Nor does this power simply border externally on the human *ēthos* complex, for it is capable of overpowering it from within and sucking it up.

What the *Daímon* Brings About: The Ethical Distinction

If one leaves aside the curious aspects of Heidegger's consideration of Heraclitus, something remains that is more than a mere projection: every complex of human behaviour contains a certain tension between height and depth. It consists, if the image is permissible, in an ontological two-storey structure that is explicitly noted from now on – in so far as one can equate noting with describing. It entails that the lower, the habitual foundation, and the upper, the demonic, are capable of absorbing each other – in both directions, one should note. Firstly, if a bad *ēthos* pulls man cacodaemonically downwards until he keeps the swine company, as Heraclitus tirelessly asserts in a series of drastic animal comparisons – the language game 'man equals swine' evidently runs through from Heraclitus' Ephesus to Wittgenstein's Vienna – or secondly, if a good *ēthos* lifts him up agathodaemonically, so that he approaches the sphere of the divine (*theion*). This corresponds to the saying of Heraclitus quoted by Celsus (Fragment 78), which states that ordinary human behaviour (*ēthos anthrópeion*) has no valid insights (*gnómas*), whereas that of the gods (*theion*) does.

No talk, then, of the familiar human 'abode' transcending towards the 'unfamiliar' of its own accord. Heraclitus' opinion is more along these lines: as long as man remains in his average *ēthos*, he has nothing that connects him to the realm above. If it were true that Fragment 119 implicitly adopts any stance concerning the 'place' or 'abode' of humans, it would be this: where we are, the animal confinement of the many to their habits collides with the openness of the few to the logos. This is completely in keeping with the tendency of numerous other statements attributed to Heraclitus, which leave no doubt as to how he, whom tradition portrays as a melancholic and *eo ipso* a man of distance, judged the forms of life among the masses. That this 'misanthropic' thinker should have stated that 'man' as such in his habitual circumstances should be open to the divine, as Heidegger suggests, is quite simply unthinkable.

Nonetheless, Heidegger was right to note a fundamental problematics of verticality in Heraclitus' use of the word *ēthos*. This does not concern the alleged transcendence of 'man' towards the divine, regardless of whether one calls it the super-*ego*, the super-*tu* or the super-*id*. Heraclitus was an ethicist, not an anthropologist. The first ethics deals with a difference among humans that first becomes explicit through thought – or perhaps one should call it becoming aware of the logos dimension. Heraclitus' misanthropy is the fanfare that opens the explication. It shows how the difference within each human manifests itself as a difference between humans. If Heraclitus places the many and the few in stark opposition to each other, it is not because his thought is elitist, but rather because he is among the first of those who became specifically aware of the thought that has always been acting unnoticed within us – and who thus actualized the difference between the thinking, or more precisely those attentive to the logos, and the others, the inattentive ones, in the first place. He could not have done this if he had not first established within himself the predominance of thought over non-thought – or rather of having good sense (*sophronein*), which Fragment 112 thus terms the greatest virtue (*areté megíste*).

It is precisely from this gesture, the subordination of non-good sense to good sense, that ethics comes about as First Theory. Consequently, ethics can only take the form of a duel between man and himself – though this duel can be externalized as a provocation of those who evade it. From its first word, the first ethics already deals with the difference between that which is above and that which is below, yet usually strives to reach the top. This 'ethics' as a primary orientation has an immediate 'ontological' sense, provided it contains the thesis '*sophronein* exists'. It would be a theoreticistic reduction of this statement, however, if it were used to express no more than its propositional content. It is an authoritative, spurring and tonic statement that confronts its addressees with the challenge: 'Give precedence to *sophronein*!' The oldest version of the metanoetic imperative already demands that humans distinguish between the upper and the lower within themselves.

Being Superior to Oneself

That the primal ethical directive 'You must change your life!' becomes acute in the pre-Socratic word *sophronein* – and with a manifestly practice-theoretical tendency – can be explained with reference to a thought formulated by Plato a hundred years after Heraclitus in a greatly admired passage from book four of the *Republic* (430e–432b), dealing with prudence (*sophrosyne*) in the individual and in the polis. There, prudence is defined first of all as 'dominance over the desires' (*epithymion epikráteia*) – though I cannot say at this point what these 'epithymic' feelings known as 'desires' are, or what is meant by 'dominance'. Then Socrates draws our attention to the peculiarity of the self-relationship to which this refers: if prudence is related or identical to dominance over affects or passions, it manifests an inner asymmetry within humans – a dramatic difference from themselves that can be evaded, but not neutralized. This is demonstrated by the figure of speech that someone is 'stronger than themselves' (*kreitto hautou*) – which is also translated as 'superior to oneself'.

At first glance, Socrates says, such a phrase seems ridiculous, and paradoxical to boot: 'For the man who is master of himself will also, I presume, be the slave of himself, and the slave will be the master'[81] – as both statements are made by the same person. In reality, the laughable expression is a symptom of the most serious matter: 'in man himself' (*en auto to anthrópo*) there is evidently a better and a worse side relating to the soul (*peri ten psychén*). This matter, which is no laughing one, emerges *in actu* in twofold fashion: in the reflections formulated here and in the life conditions they address. If the part that is by nature (*physei*) better rules over the worse part, one calls this being stronger than oneself or superiority over oneself and rightly praises it. If the situation is inverted, however, and the worse part – which is also the larger – overpowers the better – which is naturally smaller – one speaks of being weaker than or inferior to oneself, and rebukes it accordingly. The further applications of these reflections result from the maxim of all political psychology: as in the psyche, so in the polis.[82]

Two aspects are decisive for an understanding of this philosophy-historically fateful passage. Firstly: Plato here manages to integrate the affect of contempt, which appears in a crudely external way in Heraclitus, into the structure of the psyche, so that contempt becomes a regulative principle of the person and an agent of their self-direction. Whoever is able to feel self-contempt has already mastered the decisive aspect. Secondly: Socrates clarifies why the worse part can only take over after 'bad education' – whose criterion lies in leaving untethered (*akólaston*) something that requires tethering, and, if all were as it should be, could be tethered with ease. If one assumes that, for the Greeks, *paideía* was an amalgamation of insight and training – or, differently put, the result of intellectual instruction and physical drill – then the talk of the imminent takeover by the bad side unmistakably contains a call for more training, or a lament about the failure of the current scheme.

Naturally one could, in the style of the sociologizations still customary today, raise the objection that Plato's talk of self-superiority was a projection of Greek class structures onto the psyche. Then one could – in the mode of the utopianism that is no longer so common – add that in a classless society, the self-relations of the psyche would be rebuilt into flat hierarchies, or even complete anarchies without any above–below difference to speak of. These objections, however, miss the essence of *paideía*. The idea of restraint comes from an internalization of the differences between teacher and pupil, or trainer and athlete, possibly also between rider and horse, which have nothing to do with dominance in the usual sense. The relationship between the aristocracy and the rabble only provides a metaphor for these conditions, and to take it literally would be to misunderstand the autonomous laws of figurative speech. In truth, a manifestation of verticality emerges in *paideía* that cannot be depicted by, let alone reduced to, political dominance. That does not, of course, mean that the matter is automatically understood by its carriers, namely the operators and patients of training.

The basic confusion of Greek ethics, as well as the art of education connected to it, comes from the fact that it never managed to work out the difference between passions and habits with the necessary clarity – which is why it also never clearly articulated the corresponding difference between dominance and practice. The consequences are evident in over two millennia of ambiguity in European pedagogy – initially it often suffocated its pupils with authoritarian discipline by treating them as subjects, while later on it increasingly addressed them as false adults and released them from all discipline and practising tension. The fact that pupils are initially and mostly burgeoning athletes – not to say acrobats – who must be brought into shape was, because of the moralistic and political mystification of pedagogy, never pointed out as explicitly as a matter of such import would require.

For the time being, nothing seems simpler than the thought that existing passions, destructive intensities or obsessions demand restraining – that is, dominance – while habits are not given *a priori*, but must rather be built up in longer periods of training and practice; they grow through mimetic repetitive behaviour, but turn into a will-supported autonomous effort at a certain point in their development. As elementary as the distinction between habits and passions may seem, however, the association of these two factors has led to the most diverse confusions throughout the history of ethical thought. One could go so far as to say that along with the asceticisms themselves, the ambiguities in the understanding of *áskesis* constitute the 'broadest and longest fact that exists' on the 'ascetic planet'. In Europe, asceticisms and their misunderstandings are of more or less equal age – the incomparably more deeply thought-out universe of the Indian *asanas* simultaneously shows us that this long-lasting confusion is a regional fate, not a universal law. Once this has been grasped, one understands why the emancipation of practice from the compulsive structures of Old European asceticism – as I hinted at the start – may possibly constitute the most important intellectual-historical and body-historical event of the twentieth century.

Between Two Overpowerings: The Possessed Human

If we go back from Plato's reference to the vertical distinction within humans themselves to Heraclitus' aphorism, it is illuminating how the thinker of Ephesus treats the same problem with a logic that is still entirely elementary, almost destitute. Now one sees clearly how this archaic three-word wonder *ēthos anthrópo daímon* itself formally demonstrates what it is talking about: the word 'man' stands in the middle between the two all too easily confused ethical factors – habits on the left, passions on the right. Whatever other meanings *ēthos* can have, it unmistakably refers here to that which is habitual, moral and conventional, while the word *daímon* indicates the higher power, the overpowering and supra-habitual force.

If one accepts these semantic deliberations serving the illumination of the two opaque terms, two new ways of translating Heraclitus' phrase arise. The first would be: 'Among humans, bad habits are the overpowering force.' The second is: 'New good habits in humans can gain control over the most intense passions.' Naturally we cannot say which of these Heraclitus had in mind. His logic was archaic, in so far as the archaic is the condensed embodiment of the not-yet-differentiated, the pre-confused. While the confused re-entangles alternatives that have already been unfolded, the pre-confused contains not-yet-unfolded alternatives intertwined *contracte*. Here there are even fewer words than thoughts that need to be expressed. It therefore remains unsaid or 'folded in' whether the demonic manifests itself in the form of bad habits or noble passions. It need hardly be explained why the prestige of the pre-Socratics reached its zenith at the start of the twentieth century: never had the homesickness of the European intelligentsia for their pre-confused beginnings been so strong. At the same time, this homesickness was never exposed to a stronger temptation to increase confusion by seeking refuge in unsuitable simplifications.

The original ethical confusion in European philosophy manifests itself in two complementary and time-honoured errors that run through the history of reflections on the question of how humans should live: in the first, the restraining of passions is confused with the exorcism of base demons, and in the second, the overcoming of bad habits is confused with illumination through higher spirits. The Stoic and Gnostic movements, with their striving for apathy or a speedy escape to the world above, are representative of the former, and the Platonic and mystical traditions, with their inclination to kill off the flesh or pass over embodied existence, of the latter. That these attractive errors did not become the mainstream is due to the resistance of the pragmatic ethical systems, which were aided by the anonymous wisdom of everyday cultures. Both are sources drawn upon by the legacy of European knowledge about the art of living – as demonstrated most recently by Michel Foucault's late studies. The anti-extremist projects of Aristotelian, Epicurean and sceptic provenance mostly achieved a fruitful balance between vertical passion, that is to say the restraining of desires, and the horizontal effort, namely the imitation and cultivation of good habits. They surveyed the difficult terrain in which the two primary directions of movement, the spreadings and the ascents, make their demands.

If one reads the *ēthos–daímon* statement directly alongside Socrates' words about the restraining of passions, one understands better the path on which Old European thought found itself confronted with what was termed 'possession' in religious contexts. In its older usage, the word *daímon* reminds us that being human and being possessed were initially practically the same. Whoever has no *daímon* has no soul that accompanies, augments and moves them, and whoever lacks such a soul does not exist – they are merely a walking corpse, or at best an anthropomorphic plant. If one now places the terms *ēthos* and *daímon* so closely together that *anthrópo* is directly between them, one sees how the human being is fundamentally bound between two forms of possession. Possessed by habits and inertias, it appears under-animated and mechanized; possessed by passions and ideas, it is over-animated and manically overloaded. The form and degree of

168

its animation are thus entirely dependent on the mode and tone of its possession – and on the integration of the occupier into its own self. The majority of people throughout history have only acknowledged the latter, the psychistic or passionate side of possession (as apparent in ancient notions of accompanying demons, invasive demons, personal geniuses and evil spirits in a wealth of images); it observes with concern its negative, de-animation, dispiritedness, depression. The early philosophers, on the other hand, the first gurus and educators, increasingly concentrate, in the morning light of their art, on the second front, the 'habit creature' side of the human condition. One could speak here of the habitual or hexic forms of possession (from Latin *habitus*, 'habit' and Greek *hexis*, 'possession, inner property, habit'). It represents possession by a non-spirit, a taking over of humans by the embodied mechanism.

Paideía: Gripping the Roots of Habit

To understand how humanity's dual possession was brought to an end by the ethical-ascetic Enlightenment, one must consider that the history of anthropological and pedagogical thought in Europe was, in the long run, identical to a progressive secularization of the psyche – that is, identical to the conversion of the logic of possession into programmes of discipline. In the course of these programmes, possessions of the first type are reformulated as enthusiasms and sorted into advantageous – recall Plato's list of the four good forms of enthusiasm or madness in *Phaedrus*[83] – and harmful ones. Among the latter, wrath, thirst for fame and greed stand out; in Christian times, these were included among the Seven Deadly Sins.[84] As they are no longer official forms of possession, only their functional successors, they are no longer driven out through exorcism but rather tamed through discipline, using the crudest of methods if need be.

The statements of Aurelius Augustinus, nine hundred years after Heraclitus, can also be placed in this progressing line: in his text *On True Religion*, he calls on Christians to become 'men' by subduing (*subiugare*) the 'women' in themselves, these 'blandishments and troubles of desire'[85] – a task that faces women in analogous fashion, because they should likewise be man enough 'in Christ' to subjugate the womanly desires (*femineas voluptates*) in themselves. Here Augustine still clings firmly to the schema of the Platonic psychagogics of affect: dominate that which would otherwise dominate us; gain possession of that which would otherwise possess us. Because he embeds it in a theology of the devil, the tendency towards a re-demonization of the passions always remains present. It is palpable here how the repressive understanding of asceticism, as a dictator-ship over the 'inner nature', begins its triumphal march through the Christian centuries.

As far as the second type of possession, habit, is concerned, its secularization leads to the concept of self-education, which includes a discreet self-exorcism: the human being owned by its habits must succeed in reversing the conditions of ownership and taking control of that which has it by having it itself. This applies above all to the bad habits that are to be replaced by good ones. Thus Thomas à Kempis, still fully in the tradition of the first educators, writes: 'Habit overcomes habit.'[86] In the more radical spiritual practice systems, the demand for a breaking of habitual conditionings is still being expanded to the neutral, even 'good' habits – for example, in the theatre pedagogy of Constantin Stanislavski or the 'Institute for the Harmonious Development of Man' founded in October 1922 in Fontainebleau by George Ivanovich Gurdjieff. From the perspective of the radicals, the habitus basis of human existence is, as a whole, no more than a spiritually worthless puppet theatre into which a free ego-soul must be implanted after the fact, and through the great-est effort. If this fails, one experiences an effect in most people that is familiar from many athletes and models: they make a promising visual impression – but if one knocks, no one is at home. According to these doctrines, the adept can only rid themselves of their baggage by subjecting their life to a rigorous practice regime by which they can de-automatize their behaviour in all important dimensions. At the same time, they must re-automatize their newly learned behaviour so that what they want to be or represent becomes second nature.

Thinking and Wakefulness

For Heraclitus, the dark, early, pre-confused one, such differen-tiations and complications are non-existent. In his thought, the passions and habits could stay together in a single class – contained in the dimension of vagueness termed *ēthos anthrópeion* (human behaviour) in Fragment 119. On the other side are the supra-human factors: the divine, the fire of reason, the immeasurable psyche and the all-pervading logos. Compared to them, one reads, even the wisest human is a mere ape. One cannot yet speak of any *paideía*, but there is a statement by Heraclitus (Fragment 116, quoted by Stobaeus) that

170

heralds the 2,500-year empire of the educators as if in mockery: it tells us that essentially all people, including the uninformed masses, are capable of knowing themselves and having good sense.

Heraclitus enjoys an even greater privilege in being permitted, on the 'intellectual side' of his doctrines, to leave together what would have to be taken apart in a later culture of rationality, and even spread among different disciplines: being awake, having good sense and listening for the logos. Later generations and more distant periods assigned waking – alongside the phenomena of sleep and dream – to psychology and the security services, while good sense was handed over to practical philosophy and ethics, and a receptiveness to the logos to logic, mathematics and structural theories. If there is one strong characteristic of the pre-Socratics – assuming they are not simply an invention of modern compilers, for which there are indications – it seems to me that it lies in the pathos-filled equation of waking and thinking.

If one had to say in one sentence what constituted thought in the Ionic era, the answer would be: thinking means being sleepless in Ephesus – sacrificing one's nights in Miletus. One can almost take this literally, as the proximity of the Ionians to the Chaldean traditions of nocturnal celestial observation may also have bred in them a tendency towards intellectual night work; the contempt of the waking for the sleeping belongs to the basic inventory of intellectual athletism. As Heraclitus' fragments tell us, the distinction between diurnal and nocturnal activity is meaningless for waking thought. The waking that is unified with thinking performs the only asceticism that can help the first philosophy get into shape. As waking thought, it is pure discipline – an acrobatics of sleeplessness. If it does not virtually unify the thinker with the ever-wakeful logos, it certainly brings them close together. It is no coincidence that some of Heraclitus' harshest words deal with the dependence of ordinary people on sleep. For him, *hoi polloi* are none other than the people who do not awaken to the shared (*koinon*) in the morning, but instead remain in their private world, their dreamy idiocy, as if they had some special knowledge (*idían phrónesin*). These are the same who also sleep through religious matters, as it were – they think they are purifying themselves by soiling themselves with blood, 'just as if one who had stepped into the mud were to wash his feet in mud'.[87] Trapped in their own worlds, people do not hear what the non-sleepers have to say to them. If one speaks to them of the all-pervading logos, they merely shrug their shoulders. They see nothing of the One, even though they are submerged in it. They act as if they were seeking God, yet he is standing in front of them.

Thinking Without Waking, Waking Without Thinking: East–West Contrasts

Among twentieth-century thinkers, it was Heidegger who first sought to regain the privileges of pre-confused (contract-symbolic) thought through his secession from the 2,500-year philosophical tradition. In his way, he attempted – in opposition to his own time, yet keeping up with it in some respects – to restore philosophical activity to its 'pre-Socratic' state, when a unity of waking and thinking had temporarily been possible. The decline of pre-confused unity had already proved inexorable 2,500 years ago; the rapid progress in the formation of concepts split the basic terms of old into many partial meanings. Not all words survived this development intact – the archaic verb *sophronein* in particular, 'to be of good sense', the most elegant term of achievement in the ancient world, lost its penetrating energy and intimate appellative effect when it congealed into the noun *sophrosyne*, which refers to the virtue of prudence among a group of other virtues. However, Heidegger's interpretation of this process – the freezing of verbs into nouns and the move from event observation to conceptual concoction – as the fate incurred by forgetfulness of being (*Seinsvergessenheit*) contains an unacceptable exaggeration that contributes little to overcoming the problematic situation it touches upon.

The asymmetrical decay products of this process led to the far-reaching differences between the culture of rationality, or 'ethics', in the Occident and the Orient. While the Western path, generally speaking, saw the establishment of thinking without waking, devoted to the ideal of science, the Eastern path arrived more at a waking without science, which strove for illuminations without conceptual precision – based on a state store of wisdom figures that more or less belonged to all masters. Heidegger's attempt to circumvent the opposition of scientism and illuminism from a neo-pre-Socratic angle produced a concept of 'thought' that is clearly closer to meditative waking than to the construction or deconstruction of discourses. His late pastoral of being, which is closer to an exercise than a discursive praxis, points to the undertaking of transforming the philosophy of consciousness, after the shake-up of its passage through existential philosophy, into a worldly philosophy of wakefulness.[88] It is fair to assume that man, as the 'guardian of being', is subject to a sleeping ban. It does not become entirely clear in Heidegger's work, however, how the timetable for guarding being is planned. Nor is it easy to see how the guardians receive the night work permit in the laboratories of elite research. The bet is as plausible as it is demanding: it is now a matter of carrying out the transformation of thought into a wakefulness exercise envisaged by Heidegger without regressing below the level of the modern culture of rationality.

Whether Heidegger himself achieved this is doubtful for a number of reasons. His later doctrine became too much of an idyll amid the monstrous. Before Heidegger, it was only Oswald Spengler who presented a few provisional, but not insignificant sketches for a critique of the rationalist access to the world via a general theory of wakefulness; instead of pursuing this, however, he translated it into a speculative psychology of advanced civilizations and thus philosophically neutralized it. Furthermore, he distorted his subtle references to the fear-based constitution of wakeful existence – which resurfaced ten years later in Heidegger's inaugural address 'What is Metaphysics?' of 1929 – through the crudeness of his pragmatic faith in the precedence of 'facts'.[89] Taken as a whole, the philosophy of the twentieth century fails somewhat pitifully in the face of the imperative of a culture of wakefulness. It is not without reason that it lost the majority of its virtual clientele to the psychotherapeutic subcultures in which new, liveable stylizations of the relationship between wakefulness and knowledge had developed, not infrequently to the disapproval of those employed as civil servants to look after theory.

Against the background of theosophical amalgams of traditions from Eastern and Platonic sources, Jiddu Krishnamurti (1895–1986) developed the most radical doctrine of wakefulness presented in the twentieth century. Distancing himself from his early indoctrinations, he declared that it is always possible to exit the construct of the rational world from one moment to the next and burn all notions in the 'flame of attention'. For reasons that are not entirely clear, Krishnamurti refused to examine the connection between the capacity for constant wakefulness in the moment and working on oneself through practice, or the cathartic clarification of the psyche, in detail and to integrate the possible results of such studies into his theory, even though his own history of clarification is among the most dramatic and well-documented examples in the history of spiritual exercises.[90]

After Heidegger, it was above all Foucault who took up the bet and proved in his work how waking and thinking can once more be convincingly connected in a contemporary existential-intellectual project. From the circle of German thinkers who followed on from Heidegger and went to the limits of what was currently possible, Carl Friedrich von Weizsäcker is the most notable. It was he who probably came closest to the paradoxical ideal of a pre-Socratism at the level of contemporary knowledge. His late central work, *Zeit und Wissen* [Time and Knowledge][91] – possibly the most profound scientific-philosophical book of the late twentieth century – was ignored by the public and colleagues alike, even by those not of the opinion that they were amusing themselves to death.

— 4 —

HABITUS AND INERTIA
On the Base Camps of the Practising Life

One More Time: Height and Width – Anthropological Proportionality

The preceding reflections on Nietzsche, Wittgenstein, Foucault, Heidegger and Heraclitus leave us with a number of observations about the 'anthropological proportion' articulated by Binswanger. It was this Heidegger-inspired pioneer of psychiatric anthropology who elaborated the basic phenomenon of existential directedness into an elemental ethics of space or proportions – especially in his largely overlooked study on Ibsen from 1949. There he explains how human self-realization in ordinary life takes place above all in the polarity of *narrowness* and *width*, while the dramas of intellectual and artistic self-realization are mostly located in the dimension of *depth* and *height*.[92] In both cases one observes life's basic kinetic tendency, of which Goethe noted, 'we humans are dependent on extension and movement'.[93] While existential mobility in the horizontal is dominated by a relative symmetry of outward and return journeys, vertical mobility is often characterized by an asymmetry when the descent is not simply a mirror of the ascent, no application of the Heraclitean formula 'The way up and the way down are the same', but rather a fall – I have examined this relationship from the perspective of a key phrase from Binswanger's texts also adopted by Pravu Mazumdar: 'tragic verticality'. Binswanger does not, incidentally, comment on the natural objection that there is also a kind of fall in the horizontal, when the step into width becomes a forwards without return, as embodied by the Wandering Jew and the Flying Dutchman.

The tragic asymmetries observed by the psychiatrist in vertical movements do not concern height as such, either in the physical or in the moral sense. They are more related to the inadequate ability of the agent who climbs to a height at which he is unable to move. In general, one should assume that the same ability which allows a climber to reach the top would also bring them down again without any trace of 'tragic verticality'. Only if non-ability or non-consideration of the boundary conditions for ability interferes, as with the flight of Icarus, does a fall become likely. Otherwise, the degree of ability is more or less sufficient for the descent as well. The aviation industry, which is certainly a non-Icarian art form, proves this every day, as does disciplined alpinism. It is only upon advancing into the unmastered and unsecured that the problem of a fall arises – whether the protagonist undertakes something at their own risk for which they lack the technique, or attempts something new that they cannot have mastered by virtue of its untried nature. I shall refrain from elaborating on these reflections with reference to the situations of the artist, the criminal, the dictator and the merchant adventurer; they are all in situations that are unimaginable without an inherent inclination to fail – though not without a chance to learn something in the respective situation. With these in mind one can recall the saying, attributed to Oliver Cromwell, that a man never climbs higher than when he does not know where he is going.

At the Base Camp: The Last Humans

Following on from Binswanger's expositions on 'anthropological proportionality', we arrive at what I shall call the 'base camp problem'. Once again, Nietzsche must inevitably be considered its inventor. It appears at the moment when Zarathustra, the prophet of humanity's ascent beyond itself in a way that can no longer be conceived of Platonically, stumbles at the very start of his mission on the fact that the vast majority of people have no interest in becoming more than they are. If one investigates the average direction of their wishes, one finds that they simply want a more comfortable version of what they have. This state of the culture of wishes is where Zarathustra's words about the last human initiate his attack on the audience. His improvised second speech – the first had announced the *Übermensch* – is meant to describe the most despicable creature under the sun: the human without longing, the final stuffy bourgeois, who has invented happiness and gazes after the passing women while sunbathing by the pool – why else would he be squinting? In his address, however – which one could, incidentally, call the first virtual pop event in the history of philosophy – Zarathustra miscalculates: attempting to speak to the pride of his listeners, he reaches the conclusion that they have none, and are not interested in regaining it. Hence the enthusiastic response from the audience, which, after Zarathustra's failed provocation-therapeutic intervention, is: 'Give us this last human!'[94] Zarathustra has no reply to this. From that point on, he divides people into his audience and his friends. The audience consists of those able to ask themselves: 'What is in it for me if I exceed myself?'

Nietzsche's talk of the last human provides the first version of the base camp problem. It appears as soon as it becomes possible to claim programmatically that base camps and summits are the same thing – or, more precisely, when some can argue in all seriousness that the stay at the base camp and its prolongation render any form of summit expedition superfluous. I have already explained indirectly how such understandings of existence on the plateau of Mount Improbable became plausible from the nineteenth century on, both in Darwinism and in Marxism: they follow from the standard interpretation of evolutionary theory, where the human being in the status quo embodies the final stage of becoming – with the only unsolved matter being the redistribution of end-stage achievements. This is what is argued in the corresponding social-political programmes. The entire twentieth century is marked by equations of base camp and summit founded on different ideological justifications – from the early proclamations of design for a transformation of everyday life to the total coexistence of life forms in postmodernism. In a related spirit, Analytic Philosophy declared ordinary language the last language, and liberalism termed the amalgam of consumption and insurance the last horizon. It may be that ecologism, which is in the process of becoming the central discourse of the present day, constitutes the extrapolation of this tendency into the twenty-first century through the fact that it has proclaimed ecosystems and species the last natures, thus asserting the inviolability of their present state of development.[95]

One could therefore say that the philosophy of the twentieth century, especially in its social-philosophical varieties, offers – for the reasons already hinted at – nothing more than a series of statements about the base camp problem. The authors I have quoted also cast their votes on the matter – usually in a both/and form, with an emphasis on the basal side. Of these, Nietzsche is the only one who unconditionally embraced the primacy of the vertical. For him, the only justification for the base camp is as a starting point for expeditions to ever higher and more obscure summits. Closest to him are early and late Foucault and the heroistically inclined early Heidegger,

177

who had not yet understood that the national revolution with which he wanted to 'set out' into the German destiny was nothing more than a base camp gone wild. In Wittgenstein's *Tractatus* period too, where the author used his well-known disposable ladder, there are traces of the hope that one could climb over the horizontal universe of facts and proceed to the ethical summit through a vertical act. In later Wittgenstein, on the other hand, as well as middle-period Foucault and late Heidegger, there is an unmistakable shift to the horizontal. They perform, each in their own way and for very different reasons, a sort of *resignatio ad mediocritatem*. The playing of language games, the repeated study of the discourses of earlier power games and the late pietistic waiting for a new sign of being – these are all attitudes in a camp where the path evidently comes to an end, even if the authors have preserved some leftover aspirations to ascent. As far as Binswanger is concerned, it seems to me that he does not develop an opinion of his own on the critical question, instead contenting himself with a reference to the desirability of 'anthropological proportionality'. As he sympathized with the late Heidegger on the one hand, but on the other hand, as a member of the psychiatric mountain rescue corps, attempted to retrieve the 'extravagant', one can consider him one of the outposts of the base camp who, because of their profession, still had some understanding of the dynamics of verticality.

Bourdieu, Thinker of the Last Camp

Among the authors in the second half of the twentieth century, Pierre Bourdieu stands out for the problematic merit that in his work, the rejection of any notion of summit expeditions took on dogmatic proportions. He is, to put it pointedly, the sociologist of the definitive base camp – and even acted for a while as its intellectual prefect, comparable in this respect to Jürgen Habermas, whose publications on the theory of communicative action can likewise be read as pamphlets on the overall completion of base camps in flat areas. Bourdieu's appearance on the French intellectual scene had taken place in the early 1960s, when the theoretical 'field' – to take up one of its preferred concepts – was almost completely occupied by Marxistically coded forms of social critique. As a temporary assistant to Raymond Aron and a reader of Max Weber, Emile Durkheim and Alfred Schütz, he could not fail to see the inadequacies of Marxist approaches, especially in their fatal extrapolations by Lenin and Stalin. If he wished to earn a place in the success field of French critical culture, he would have to leave aside the implausible language games of impoverishment and exploitation critique, compensating for their lost offensive power through additional efforts in the area of power critique. This could only be achieved by progressing from a theory of direct domination to a logic of domination without dominators. Now it was anonymous and pre-personal agencies that gained the rank of a repressive sovereign. This constellation spawned all the turns and innovations that characterize Bourdieu's variety of 'critical theory' – and, as German readers know, 'critical theory' is a pseudonym for a Marxism abandoned by a faith in the possibility of revolution. In this situation, the theory itself – along with an art that behaves increasingly subversively – becomes a substitute for revolution.

The foremost characteristic of Marxist thought was the introduction of an anti-idealistic hierarchy of reality. According to this, the *base*, understood as a political-economical 'praxis', possesses a higher reality content – more power to bring about effects and side effects – than all other 'spheres', which accordingly had to content themselves with the role of a 'superstructure' determined by the base. As this demotion to secondary status concerned the state, the legal system, the educational system and all other articulations of 'culture', the political ontology of the basal made a deep caesura in the traditional ecology of the spirit. The most consistent realization of this approach could be observed in Stalinism, whose *modus operandi* can be summed up in a simple formula: destruction of the superstructure by connecting it to the base.

Habitus: The Class Within Me

Whoever wanted to found a 'critical theory' after 1945 could, in the light of Stalin's actions, only do so via an alternative understanding of reality as 'praxis'. It was therefore necessary to redefine 'praxis', and to show that it followed different laws from those described in economically bound standard Marxism. This only became feasible by moving the base lower down, and anyone who wanted to go deeper here had to climb down from the level of production processes to that of psychophysical realities. The zeitgeist did its bit to support this intention: from a theory-historical perspective, the rise of the 'body' began in the 1960s, when late Marxism realized how much its survival depended on proving that there was a substitute base. In Germany, the turn took place mostly in the form of studies on the deformed 'subjective factor', while in France, a form of ethnological

179

field research on the incorporation of class mentalities established itself. In truth, Bourdieu had become aware of the profound difference between an economy of honour and one of exchange since his investigations, begun in 1958, into the North Algerian agricultural societies of Kabylia; this led him to seek a new answer to the 'base' question.

This is where Bourdieu's most important conceptual innovation, the idea of habitus, comes into play. It undoubtedly constitutes one of the most fruitful tools of contemporary sociology, even though, as I will show, Bourdieu himself only uses it in a very restricted way. The greatest merit of the habit concept is that with its help, an *a prima vista* satisfying answer is provided to the two insoluble riddles of conventional Marxism: firstly, how the so-called base can mirror itself in the so-called superstructure; and secondly, how 'society' infiltrates individuals and keeps itself present within them. The solution is this: through class-specific psychosomatic forms of training, the social lodges itself in the individuals as a disposition at once produced and producing, unfolding an autonomous life that, while open to experience and life-historically active, is ultimately shaped indelibly by the past.

The analogy between habitus and language immediately catches the eye, for it too forms a structured and structuring social reality sedimented in the speakers. The structuralist zeitgeist of the 1960s may have ensured that Bourdieu temporarily engaged with the work of Ferdinand de Saussure, in which the matter at hand was thematized under the term *langue*. *De facto*, Bourdieu invoked an analogy between his concept of habitus and Chomsky's idea of grammar, in so far as one understands the latter as a system of conditioned spontaneities based on physically rooted deep structures. The possibility of comparison comes on the one hand from class-dependent behavioural dispositions, and on the other hand from grammar-dependent conditionings of speech. One could say that the habitus is the first language of the class training performed on me, and, however much individuals might strive for new content and competencies in the course of their lives, they remain shaped by their mother tongue in Bourdieu's eyes – and, because they are shaped, they in turn shape.

Base and *Physis,* Or: Where Is Society?

The habitus, then, is the somatized class consciousness. It clings to us like a dialect that never disappears, one that not even Henry Higgins would be able to drive out of Miss Doolittle. When Trimalchio, the freed slave who subsequently acquired wealth, tastelessly displays his wealth at his banquets, the members of the old elite recognize the typical slave in him. When Bourdieu, on the other hand, the grandson of a poor *métayer* and the son of a postman from Béarn, rose to become a master thinker and dominate the 'field' of academic sociology in France, the thought of the ineradicable habitus of his class helped him to allay the suspicion that he had betrayed his origins through his career. From this perspective, the theory of habitus has the inestimable advantage of serving the moral reassurance of its author: even if I wanted to betray my own class, it would be impossible, because its absorption into my old Adam forms the basis of my social being. Aside from that, the theory helps its users in the academic world and the open intellectual market alike to maintain the pretence of critique by providing them with a means of reducing the manifold vertical differentiations of 'society' to the simple matrix of the privileges of power – be they the prerogatives of the male sex or of capital owners, material or symbolic.

The price Bourdieu had to pay for lowering the base dimension into the psychophysical structures of the individual was much higher than he himself realized. Firstly, as already hinted, this habitus concept made him forfeit the better means for describing the play of vertical tensions in the numerous disciplinic fields of the social space with sufficient accuracy. *De facto*, Bourdieu's work as a writer is original and fruitful, for example in his analysis of the struggles for distinction and the ethnography of *Homo academicus* – not primarily through the application of the habitus concept, but rather through the author's intense attention as an outsider to rivalry-based ranking mechanisms where class influences play a certain part, but are not decisive. At his best, Bourdieu writes a satire without laughs about the *nouveaux riches* and the ambitious; where he thinks most profoundly, he touches on the tragic leftovers of the human condition.

A further weakness of the habitus concept, interpreted thus, is that it cannot grasp the individualized forms of existential self-designs. Bourdieu's analysis necessarily remains within the typical, the prepersonal and the average, as if *Homo sociologicus* were to have the last word on all matters. In a certain sense, Bourdieu parodies the analysis of the 'they' in Heidegger's *Being and Time* from an inverted perspective. While human Dasein is, for Heidegger, 'proximally and for the most part' [*zunächst und zumeist*] subject to the anonymity of the 'they', and only attains authenticity through an act of decisiveness, the authenticity of existence for Bourdieu lies in the habitus, over which a more or less random superstructure of ambitions, competencies and attributes of distinction accumulates. This reversal of the 'they' analysis follows almost automatically from agreement with the political ontology of practical thought, which states that the base is more real than the things that are superstructurally added. This would mean that humans are most themselves where their shaping through the habitus pre-empts them – as if the most genuine part of us were our absorbed class. The part of us that is not ourselves is most ourselves. The habitus theory provides a clandestine hybrid of Heidegger and Lukács by taking from the former the idea of a self dispersed among the 'they', and from the latter the concept of class consciousness. It builds the two figures together in such a way that the pre-conscious class 'in itself' within us becomes our true self. This corresponds to Bourdieu's division of the social space into diverse 'fields' – in which one naturally finds no 'persons', only habitus-controlled agents who are compelled to realize their programmes within the spaces offered by the field.

Whoever considers such suggestions acceptable may ultimately also find it plausible that in *Distinction*, Bourdieu's most successful book, the passing of aesthetic or culinary judgements of taste constitutes a reproductive medium of 'domination'. Word should have got around among sociologists that one can arrive at substantially more precise statements in these matters with a more horizontally than vertically differentiating theory of milieu, combined with an instrument for observing mimetic mechanisms, than with a theory of anonymous domination. As far as the base–superstructure schema as such is concerned, it has been refuted too often to merit any further comments. I would add that little effort would be required in order to show that the augmenting element often has no less power over reality than that which it augments – and sometimes even more. If this were not the case, humans would only seemingly be alterable and learning beings.

On the Genius of Habit: Aristotle and Thomas

The decisive weakness of the habitus concept in Bourdieu's version, however, is that it does not depict what it purports to be explaining, namely the region of 'habit', in a remotely adequate fashion. In this author's work, the great tradition of philosophical and psycho-physiological reflection on the role of habits in the formation of human existence shrinks to a remainder that is usable for the purpose of a critique of power. Instead of entering the panorama of effective subject-forming acts through practice, training and accustoming, habitus theory à la Bourdieu contents itself with that narrow segment of habits that constitute the sediments of the 'class within us' – it cheats its users of the wealth of that to which its name refers. Naturally Bourdieu, who adopted the term from Erwin Panofsky's study *Gothic Architecture and Scholasticism* of 1951, was generally aware of its philosophical history.[96] He knew that the *habitus* concept in Thomas Aquinas and the *hexis* concept in Aristotle had to play a substantial part in underpinning the establishment of an ethics within the framework of an aretological anthropology (that is, a theory which portrays human beings as the creatures capable of virtues), but consciously ignored the broad understanding of the *habitus* doctrine, restricting himself to those aspects which were suitable for his purposes.

Among the earlier authors one already finds the well-developed figure of habitus as an elastic mechanism of a two-sided, passive-spontaneous quality. The 'force of habit' was understood by the ancients not simply as being overwhelmed by routines, but as a pre-personally based generative principle of action. When the scholastics speak of *habitus*, they do not mean a Janus-headed disposition looking back with one face at the series of similar past acts in which it manifested itself, while the other face looks ahead to the next occasions on which it will prove itself anew. The *habitus* thus constitutes a 'potency' that is formed by earlier acts and 'updates' itself in new ones. Such a concept naturally came in handy for Bourdieu; as a sociologist, he was on the lookout for concepts that place human behaviour in a plausible intermediate position between excessive social determination and unlimited individual spontaneity. However, he only took over those elements of the classical *habitus* concept that could be integrated into his version of the base, which, as stated above, means the pre-conscious effects of the 'class within us'.

Both Aristotle and Thomas Aquinas, by contrast, had been concerned with explaining the possibility of the 'virtuous within us', or even the 'good within us'. They understood habit, in so far as it is good habit, as an embodied disposition that prepares the actor for virtuous actions – and indeed, in the case of bad habits, for bad deeds, though these are not the focus of their investigation. For the classical thinkers of practical philosophy, *hexis* and *habitus* are constantly on call: they are expected to leap up when the occasion arises and carry out the good and valuable as if it were the easiest thing in the world. It can only appear easy, however, if and because sustained practice has eroded the improbability of good in advance. As explanations for the challenging circumstance that humans, in so far as they act morally and aesthetically, are always determined by a state of having and being had, influencing and being influenced, disposing and being disposed, acting and having acted, *hexis* and *habitus* are anything but the mere auxiliary concepts of a critical sociology. They are anthropological concepts that describe a seemingly mechanical process in terms of insistence and intensification in order to elucidate the incarnation of the mental. They identify man as the animal capable of doing what it is supposed to if one has tended to its ability early enough. At the same time, they see the dispositions already attained growing further into new, heightened forms.[97] Thomas does not need to write any letters about the aesthetic education of the human race to achieve that – conceptual clarifications with instructions on how to be ready for good are entirely sufficient.

It is, in fact, already possible to read the classical theory of *habitus* as a theory of training. Whoever has practised properly overcomes the improbability of good and allows virtue to seem like second nature. Second natures are dispositions of ability that enable humans to stay on their level as artistes of *virtus*. They perform the near-impossible, the best, as if it were something easy, spontaneous and natural that virtually happens of its own accord. Good, to be sure, is not yet understood as an 'obligation', much less a 'value' dependent on my positing and evaluating it. It is the rope stretched out by God on which the artistes of overcoming must walk – and overcoming always means passing off the wondrous as the effortless.[98] That is why Jean Genet, in his crypto-Catholically inspired advice for the tightrope walker, recommended always keeping in mind that he owed everything to the rope.[99] Even if we can no longer think about 'good' in the same way, the classical analysis of *habitus* remains current; it can easily be translated, *mutatis mutandis*, into the languages of contemporary training psychology, neurocybernetics and pragmatics. With its help, the psychophysical conditions of possibility of correct, appropriate and skilled actions can be explained at a high standard with proximity to their subject. It certainly does not, as the crypto-Marxist interpretation of the 'base' would like, explain how the social enters the body. It rather states how the disposition for carrying out what is good, correct and appropriate can be incorporated into human existence. Allow me to add: 'good', 'correct' and 'appropriate' are names for the extraordinary, to whose nature it belongs to appear in the guise of the normal.

The older theory of *habitus* thus forms part of a doctrine of incorporation and in-formation of virtues. It is applied aretology, carried out in the form of a deep analysis of the force working within active people, the force that strives towards the act. An 'informed energy' of this kind carries its self-reinforcing principle within itself. Its optimization is not subject to any limits imposed from without. Even the saints, writes Prosper of Aquitaine, 'always have something left in which they must be able to grow' (*superest quo crescere possint*). Whoever takes up the *habitus* theory as formulated by Thomas is already halfway to an interpretation of being human as an artistry of good. This provides an anthropological concept for the effectiveness of inner technologies that subtly articulates the vertical tension inherent in every area of ability. It explains how precisely that which is already carried out fairly successfully feels the pull of something better, and why that which is performed with great skill stands in the attraction field of an even higher skill. The authentic form of the *habitus* theory describes humans in all discretion as acrobats of *virtus* – one could also say as carriers of a moral competency that turns into social and artistic power. That is the wide-open door through which the thinkers of the Renaissance only had to pass to transform the saints into the virtuosos.

Homo Bourdivinus: The Other Last Human

By this standard of analysis, Bourdieu's appropriation of the habitus concept seems like a wilful impoverishment. It resembles a regression to an involuntary pre-Socratism in which the division of possessions into tameable passions and formable habits has not yet taken place. *Homo bourdivinus* is like one possessed by class, riding both having and had in a circle on the broomstick of habitus. He is the human at the base camp who acts as if it were the goal of the expedition. For him, the journey upwards is over before it has begun. This youngest brother of the last human has been drastically shown that whatever distinctions he might acquire are never more than supplements to the habitus, pseudo-vertical differentiations within the camp population. What Bourdieu calls the class society is a base camp where all ascents take place internally, while ascents to external goals are strictly ruled out. As Bourdieu, like any member of a non-utopian left, secretly knows all too well that the 'classless society' cannot exist for a number of convincing reasons, critique at the base camp is limited to keeping up the appearance of critique – which makes sense as long as gains in distinction in the critical scene can thus be achieved. Hence Bourdieu's successes in the milieu populated by the 'conformists of being different'.[100] We have found the base, say the camp-dwellers, and blink.

It should hardly be necessary to emphasize here that these objections should not be mistaken for destructive criticism. Bourdieu's direct and indirect contributions to understanding human practice behaviour are, in some respects, as valuable as Wittgenstein's language game theory and Foucault's discourse analyses – but, like those projects, the habitus theory in the form propounded by Bourdieu needs to be turned around to release its stimulating potential for a general theory of anthropotechnics. For this, it is enough to disentangle the habitus concept, to separate it from the fixation on class phenomena, and restore the wealth of meaning it possessed in the Aristotelian and later the empiricist tradition. It only unfolds its full power, however, when combined with Nietzsche's programme of 'positivizing' asceticisms – this would be the equivalent in today's context of the somewhat inappropriate term used by Nietzsche, that of 'making natural'.

This demands a dissolution of the singular 'habitus' – one head, one habitus – and an uncovering of the multitude of discrete, habitual readinesses to act that accumulate in each individual. This brings to light the unsummarizable plurality of elaborable 'habits', or trainable ability modules, of which real individuals 'consist'. Bourdieu's 'habitus' is the 'ensemble of social relations' well known since the sixth thesis on Feuerbach, which can no longer be thought of as an abstract 'being', but is rather 'inherent' in the individual. Admittedly, even Marx had not conceived this inherence adequately, being even more of a slave to the stereotypes of power critique than Bourdieu. If class-specific aspects manifest themselves in the ensemble of disciplines and practice complexes that *de facto* constitute what is concretely 'inherent' in the individual, then all the better for us if we have learned from Bourdieu how to decipher them. Privileging this layer of the assimilated as the 'base' is more of a concern for sociologists.

Teaching as a Profession: The Attack on the Inertias

At this stage of our reflections, it can become clear why and with what intention the older tradition turned its attention to such topics as habit, *hexis* and *habitus*. The explication of behaviour, the habitual, the psychomatically assimilated is, as implied in the references to ethics as First Theory, a partial phenomenon of the process I termed the division of possession into passions and habits. This transformation took place under pressure from the first educators, who were naturally the most significant carriers of the ethical-ascetic attack on existing psychosocial conditions.

One can only grasp the true meaning of the two-thousand-year molestation of humanity by teachers if one examines the angle from which the knowing attack the not-yet-knowing. Only where the secularization of the psyche was on the daily agenda, for individuals and collectives alike, did the inner conditions of inertia among those to be taught become thematic for the teachers. These, as some now began to understand, are responsible for the fact that people cannot simply follow the directions of their new ethical directors without further ado. If the first philosopher-pedagogues spoke obsessively about habits, then, it was in the context of a resistance analysis: its purpose was to show how that already present within humans, namely the *hexis*, the *habitus*, the *doxa* (joined in the eighteenth century by prejudice), hinders or entirely prevents the absorption of the new, the philosophical ethos, the explicit logos, the purified *mathesis* and the clarified method. 'Habit', both the word and the matter, stands for the factual possession of the psyche by a block of already acquired and more or less irreversibly embodied properties, which also include the resilient mass of opinions dragged along. As long as the block rests inert, the new education cannot begin. That observations of this kind were also collected and documented in the Asian world is demonstrated by the well-known anecdote of the Zen master who, to the amazement of his pupil, poured a cup of tea and did not stop when it was full, rather continuing to pour: this was meant to show that a full spirit cannot be taught anything. The course of study, then, consists in pondering the question of how to empty the cup. Whether one should subsequently fill it anew or cultivate its emptiness, once reached, as a value of its own is another matter.

The early schools are, on the whole, base camps whose board members have impressive peak-scaling ambitions, even if the definitions of those peaks are school-specific. Each school spontaneously develops an internal verticality and, sooner or later, a system of levels that produces a 'class' society *sui generis* – one can still recognize the origin of the term 'class' from non-political gradations quite well here. But the early school, for the time being, retains a natural extroversion. It follows tasks that transcend its system, whether in the qualification of students for professions and offices, supra-curricular perfection in personality forming, illumination or the supremacy of philosophers – or whatever else the great shots in the dark might be called. The late school, by contrast, puts an end to transcendent pretensions and fends off the notion that there could be anything real outside the school. It then turns into the base camp whose inhabitants only study for shifts of location within the camp – just as it was Bourdieu's primary intuition to describe the games of ambition in class society as pseudo-vertical efforts to acquire more or less illusory gains in distinction.

Identity as the Right to Laziness

The world of pseudo-verticality is the playground of identities. An 'identity', after all, whether presented as personal or collective, can only become attractive and valuable if people wish to distinguish themselves from one another without the licence to set themselves apart hierarchically. In this view, the concept of identity circulating in contemporary sociology forms the generalized counterpart to Bourdieu's doctrine of habitus; with its help, inertia is elevated from a deficiency requiring correction to a phenomenon of value. My identity consists of the complex of my unrevisable personal and cultural inertias. While Sartre claimed: 'The totality of my possessions reflects the totality of my being. I am what I have',[101] the identity owners say: 'I am what has me.' The reality of my being is guaranteed by the sum of those things that possess me. The identicals take themselves as a ready-made; in the document folder, they step with themselves under the wide roof of values that have a claim to preservation. They introduce themselves as systems of inertia, demanding the latter's idealization by ascribing the highest cultural value to the inert deposited within themselves. While the Stoics of antiquity devoted their lives to the goal of erecting within themselves, through constant practice, the statue that crafted its best self from invisible marble, the moderns find themselves as finished inertia sculptures and set themselves up in the park of identities, regardless of whether they prefer the ethnic wing or the individualistic open-air space.

Next to habitus, therefore, identity is the central value of base camp culture – and if identity is augmented by a trauma, there is nothing left to obstruct the idealization of the value core. What is decisive is that the very thought of new heights must be frowned upon – if they were climbed, the deposited stores could lose worth. If and because previous achievements as such are placed under cultural protection, any expedition project in the vertical is sacrilege, a mockery of all framed values. In the regime of identities, all energies are de-verticalized and handed over to the filing department. From there they are passed on to the permanent collection, where there is neither 'progressive hanging' nor evolutionary gradation. In the horizon of the base camp, each identity is worth every other. Identity thus provides the super-habitus for all those who want to be as their local influences have made them and are content with that. In this way, the identicals ensure that they are out of earshot if the imperative 'You must change your life!' should unexpectedly sound again somewhere.

— 5 —

CUR HOMO ARTISTA

On the Ease of the Impossible

Catapults

In the course of these investigations, we seem to have reached a point at which it would be productive to take stock of the distance covered. It leads, pointedly put, from anecdotal steps to approach the planet of the practising to the emergence of the region we call 'habits' – and then from the appearance of habits to the leaps into the supra-ordinary. This term does not refer to the average improbability of nature- and social-historical specializations on the plateau of Mount Improbable, but rather to the above-average improbability that is reached as soon as individual people – whether alone or in the company of co-conspirators – begin to catapult themselves out of the habitus communities to which they initially and mostly belong. Once one has grasped the fatefulness of the abrupt and uncanny secession of the heightened from the inhabitants of the base camps, it becomes evident that cultural theory can only be meaningfully carried out as the description of catapults.

Here we once again see the explicifying movement that we know drives and accompanies the progress of civilizations towards cognitive self-display. Explication breaks up what is found in confused disclosedness, and augments the aggregate of the already-discovered with further discoveries. In the process, the boundaries between the commonplace and the unusual are shifted – people increasingly become the creators of self-performed miracles. As anyone would concede, nothing is more obviously natural than for humans to be 'entangled in habits'. Nothing could be less obviously natural, however, than for individuals who, not infrequently, later act as pioneers in questions of world-orientation for their collectives to find themselves in a secession from habits. Precisely this is the movement towards the supra-ordinary that can be observed in the ancient birthplaces of philosophy, in Greece as well as India and China. Cultural historians associate this process with such phenomena as urbanization and division of labour – which does little to elucidate the matter. What is genuinely thought-provoking is rather the question of how, in the course of this secession, the complex of acquired habits as such could become thematic, and the thought of supra-ordinary things powerful, within individual humans.

However one answers this question, one thing is clear: it is only in this separation that the human in advanced civilization discovers itself as the animal that is split, mirrored and placed beside itself, that cannot remain as it was. Difference within humans is now primed as difference between humans. It divides 'societies' into classes of which the theorists of class 'society' know nothing. The upper class comprises those who hear the imperative that catapults them out of their old life, and the other classes all those who have never heard or seen any trace of it – normally people who are quick to admire, and thus make it clear that higher efforts can exclusively be a matter for the admired, but certainly not the admirers.

This non-political division of classes initiates the history of the inner witness or 'observer'. Swimming in the waters of habitus, discourses and language games is one thing; getting out and watching one's fellow humans from the edge as they swim in the habitus pool is another. As soon as this difference develops a language of its own to become a doctrine and life form, those based on the shore distance themselves from the swimmers. When, therefore, the ancient Indians discovered the observer or witness consciousness and equated it with *atman*, the subjective world principle, they created routes of access to a surplus of attention that simultaneously silences and mobilizes them. And when Heraclitus deems it impossible to step into the same river twice, this may be a passing reference to the irreversible stream of becoming – which is how the dictum is often read, in convenient analogy to 'everything flows'. In reality, the opaque formula reminds us of a deeper irreversibility: whoever steps out of the water can no longer return to the first way of swimming.

With the emergence of consciousness from the habit nature of human behaviour, a boundary is reached that, once visible, must already be overstepped. One cannot discover the habits without adopting a certain distance from them – in other words, without getting into a duel that clarifies who dominates the ring. Not everyone wants to win this fight; conservatives of all periods feign weakness in order to be overcome by habit – and then to be allowed to serve it after its victory as if it were invincible. Others, by contrast, are convinced that habits are foreign rulers under which no real life can be lived. This is the position brought to light by Foucault among ancient authors in his late studies on 'self-concern'. 'Concern for oneself' is the attitude of those who have encountered the greatest of all opponents within themselves – the two-headed *daímon* which, as we saw, keeps humans in a state of possession: on one occasion as an impulse power, that is to say a complex of affects that rise up in me, and on another as an inertial power, that is to say a complex of habits that have sedimented themselves in me. The secularization of the psyche discussed in the same context consists in nothing other than the creation of a new handling art that turns possessions into manipulable dispositions. In this transition, the enchanters disenchant themselves and change into teachers. They are the provocateurs of the future, who build the catapults for shots into the supra-ordinary.

The Axial Age Effect: The Humanity of Two Speeds

The discovery of both passions and habits forms the psychological counterpart to the long-known process termed 'the discovery of the mind' by philosophers and philologists. Karl Jaspers summarized this complex with the somewhat mysterious title 'Axial Age' and named five places of 'breakthrough': China, India, Persia, Palestine and Greece. These, he states, are the locations in which advanced civilizatory progress in intellectualization took place first of all, and with unforgettable long-range effects. In the period between 800 and 200 BC, people in those cultures took the 'step into the universal' that we continue to this day in everything we do with an authentically civilizatory intention. According to Jaspers, the first outlines of what would later be called 'reason' and 'personality' became visible during that time. Above all, however, it was from that point that the divide between the most heightened individuals and the many grew immeasurably. Jaspers writes:

> What the individual achieves is by no means passed on to all. The gap between the peaks of human potentiality and the crowd became exceptionally great at that time. Nonetheless, what the individual becomes indirectly changes all.[102]

By advancing their exercises on the tightrope of humanization, the extremists introduce the duty for everyone to pass a test in intermediate acrobatics to remain in the practice community of the humanized. The simple people obtain their certificate if they admit that merely watching makes them dizzy.

In reality, the discovery of passions and habits cannot be separated from the discovery of opinions, for the same interruption that allows humans to step out of the river of emotions and habits also makes them attentive to the sphere of mental routines. This interruption, which signals the entrance of the observer, irreversibly creates new positions concerning the totality of facts, inside as well as outside. Stepping out of the river means abandoning the old security of the habitus in the inherited culture and ceasing to be a growth of the first cultural community. Now the aim must be to found a new world from the shore with new inhabitants.

For this reason, the Axial Age effect is not so much based on a sudden worldwide interest in increased intellectualization; it comes from the gigantic disturbance of habitus that followed the discovery, from the shore, of the inertias embodied in humans. The most important cause for this is the inner acceleration triggered by the early cultures of writing. This was responsible for the overtaking of the habitus of the non-writers by the brains of the writers – just as the bodies of ascetics, athletes and acrobats overtake the bodies of everyday humans. The velociferic power[103] of writing practice, which entails additional accelerating disciplines, makes the inertia of the old ethos sunk into the average bodies palpable. Where accelerating practice asserts its effects, cultural evolution becomes divided; the result is a humanity of two speeds.

It is this disturbance that forces the secession of an elite of learning and practising parties from the old commonalities. It leads to the construction of a new heaven over the old earth, and of a new *koinon* over the old communes. The *koinon* that must be conquered, that shared realm in which, since the Milesians, the stars, the logos and the polis have supposedly testified to one and the same order, is much too sublime and remote from everyday institutions to be accessible to all. It is from this that the basic paradox of all universalisms develops: a common system for all is set up in which most can only participate in the mode of non-comprehension. The paradigm for this is the division – which has been dominant for three thousand years and partially revised for barely two hundred – of humanity into its literate and non-literate factions. Virtually, after all, everyone could be able to write, but only few do actually write – and those few will unwaveringly believe they are writing for everyone else. The same applies to all figures of logical, ethical or medial socialism. Some might call the

193

setting of the universalism trap the intellectual side of the entrance into a class society, though the distinguishing criterion, admittedly, no longer consists in the power of an armed lord over his unarmed servant; it lies rather in the self-arming of the practising individuals against the inertias within themselves – through logic, gymnastics, music and art in general. In this practice-cultural turn, the role models of Axial Age spirituality are constituted: the wise men, the illuminated, the athletes, the gymnosophists, the sacred and profane teachers. It is with figures of this type that the people of advanced civilizations would concern themselves in the subsequent millennia (artists in the modern sense were not initially an issue). They would ensure that culture time became the time of intellectual role models.

Getting to the Other Side: Philosophy as Athletics

To continue the metaphor of stepping out of the river, humans who have accepted the task of explicating the inertia within them find themselves forced by the course of experience to switch to the other side of their self-findings no fewer than three times. By noting how passions are working within them, they understand that they must reach the other side of passion so that they do not simply suffer from the passions, but rather become skilled at suffering.[104] By noting to what extent they are controlled by habits, they immediately understand that it would be decisive to cross to the other side of habits so that they are not simply possessed by them, but rather possess them. And by noting that their psyche is populated with confused notions, it occurs to them how desirable it would be to arrive at the other side of the tumult of notions so that they are not simply visited by muddled thoughts, but develop logically stable ideas. Thought begins when the charade of associations ends that is currently being described as a competition of 'memes' for free capacities in the neocortex. This threefold change of sides forms the ethical programme in all activities grouped together by Plato under the invented term 'philosophy'.

The word 'philosophy' undoubtedly contains a hidden allusion to the two most important athletic virtues, which enjoyed almost universal popularity at the time of Plato's intervention. It refers firstly to the aristocratic attitude of 'philotimy', the love of *timè*, that glorious prestige promised to victors in contests, and secondly to 'philopony', the love of *pónos*, namely effort, burden and strain. It is no coincidence that the patron saint of athletes was Hercules, the performer of the twelve deeds that were preserved in the collective memory as archetypes of *pónoi* for an entire epoch. Just as philosophers after Plato would later portray themselves as friends of wisdom, gymnasts and philosophers presented themselves long before them as friends of the toil that makes men into men, and as lovers of the long, hard labour placed between them and victory by the gods. The Cynics in particular later claimed Hercules as their ancestor in order to underpin their thesis that they alone, the total ascetics among philosophers, were true athletes, while the sportsmen were no more than decadent musclemen chasing after ephemeral successes, without any notion of solid virtue or cosmos-suited reason.

The imperative 'You must change your life!' thus resounded in ancient Europe from the fifth century BC onwards not only from the countless statues that the Greeks, like people possessed by an unbridled pictorial compulsion, erected in temple precincts and squares as if they wanted to augment the mortal polis-dwellers with a population of statues – presumably to draw attention to the similarities between gods and victors.[105] It comes even more from the new knowledge situation, or rather the altered attitude of the knowing to their tasks in life. Changing one's life now means breeding, through inner activations, a practice subject that will eventually be superior to its life of passions, habitus and notions. This means that anyone who takes part in a programme for de-passivizing themselves, and crosses from the side of the merely formed to that of the forming, becomes a subject. The whole complex known as ethics comes from the gesture of conversion to ability. Conversion is not the transition from one belief system to another; the original conversion takes place as an exit from the passivist mode of existence in coincidence with the entrance into the activating mode.[106] It is in the nature of the matter that this activation and the avowal of the practising life come to the same thing.

These observations allow us to grasp more precisely what Nietzsche had seen when he characterized the earth as the *ascetic planet* in his reflections on *The Genealogy of Morals*. *Áskesis* became inescapable from the moment when an avant-garde of observers found themselves compelled to overcome their inner obstacles – more precisely, the three obstacles that faced them in the form of passions, habits and unclear ideas. In view of this compulsion to clarify and practise, this three-obstacle run that appears at the beginning of higher culture, one can justifiably take Nietzsche's statement further and speak of the earth as the *acrobatic planet*. This phrase would also have the advantage of doing even more justice to Nietzsche's most important moral-philosophical intuition: in seeking with all his might to free the concept of *áskesis* from the dismal spectacles of Christian penitential asceticism, and finally point out the misunderstood and indispensable asceticisms of toughening and advancement among the old elites, he gave the starting signal for a strictly artistic interpretation of human facts. If one refrains from the mistaken projection of the *Übermensch* into the future, it becomes evident what Nietzsche had realized: that, since the entrance of peoples into the phase of advanced civilization, every achiever acrobatically comes under tension.

Asceticism and Acrobatics

Acrobatics is involved whenever the aim is to make the impossible seem simple. It is not enough, therefore, to walk the tightrope and perform the *salto mortale* at a great height; the acrobat's decisive message lies in the smile with which he bows after the performance. It speaks even more clearly in the nonchalant hand gesture before his exit, the gesture one could take for a greeting to the upper tiers. In reality, it conveys a moral lesson: for our like, that is nothing. Our like – meaning those who have completed the course in impossibility, with making an impression as a subsidiary subject. Some of them remain in the arenas and stadiums until the end of their careers, others switch to *asketería* and climb religious ladders instead, many retire to the forests and deserts, a further faction tries their hand at the visual and musical arts, and others still speculate on high-ranking civil service, maybe even the highest of all. Plato famously sought to show that the art of governing states can also be learned to perfection, provided the political artistes prepare themselves for the impossible in a forty-year course of study, from the tenth to the fiftieth year of their lives. The ability to rule the state following ideas and not, as is usually the case, simply stumble from one situation to the next like a power clown – this too could, with the necessary will, be refined into a masterfully performed craft. One does not have to be born as a god, like the Pharaoh, to be a practitioner. It is sufficient for an enlightened Greek, with the right tuition, to practise themselves upwards psychotechnically to the pharaonic level.

Nietzsche's insights into the convergence of asceticism and artistry show him in step with the tendencies of the late nineteenth century, which I have described with such key phrases as 'athletic renaissance' and 'de-spiritualization of asceticisms'. If one has perceived these movements, it is easier to see why ascetic feelings of self-concern certainly do not begin from penitent self-humbling. Early practice

196

systems started from the elementary intuition that one must get to the other side of the three automatisms at all costs. Only thus did 'man' come into the focus of those sequences of exercises which change his 'nature' in order to realize his 'nature'. Here he becomes the animal that is condemned to direct, practise and think. Philosophical anthropologists have been wont to say since the start of the twentieth century, with meaningful emphasis, that humans cannot simply live their lives, but must 'lead' them.[107] That is not untrue, and expresses an important insight – though it would be even more valuable if one could explain why there is no other way, and how it is that countless people, especially in the addiction zones of the West, nonetheless make more of an unleading and unled impression.

Anthropotechnics: Turning the Power of Repetition Against Repetition

The answer is to be found in the emergence of anthropotechnics during the axial age of practice. As soon as one knows that one is possessed by automated programmes – affects, habits, notions – it is time for possession-breaking measures. Their principle, as already noted, consists in crossing to the other side of repeated events. Since the discovery of repetition itself as the starting point for its own harnessing, such a crossing has seemed practicable according to precise rules. This discovery was the premiere of anthropotechnic difference.

The explanation for this lies in the double-edged nature of the matter itself: with the power of repetition, one simultaneously grasps the dual nature of repetition as repeated repetition and repeating repetition. This highlights the distinction between active and passive in the subject of repetition with pathos. Now one understands: there is not only the affected, but also the affecting affect; not only practised, but also practising habit; not only imagined, but also imagining notions. Each time, the chance lies in the active present participle: in this form, the activated human is celebrated as one who is autonomously feeling, practising and imagining in opposition to the felt, the practised and the imagined. In this manner, a subject human gradually sets itself apart from the object human – if it is permissible to use these unsuited, overly modern and cognitively tinged terms here. In the second position, the human stays the same as before – the passive, repeated being overwhelmed without a fight – whereas in the first, it becomes the post-passive, repeating, battle-ready being. Choosing the first path produces the 'educated human', of whom Goethe still knew that it was formerly a mistreated one.[108] What this human leaves behind on the ascent to education is the *naïveté* that also once belonged to it – together with the twofold attitude towards it: contempt for the overcome cliché and homesickness for the unbroken.

The discovery of 'deep-seated' habit as a barely corrigible inertial principle, then, invokes the sum of measures that we still feel and continue today as the most far-reaching innovation of the ancient world: the turn towards the art of education, *paideía*, which initially means something along the lines of 'art of the child' or 'technique for training boys'. Children could, in fact, only come into view methodically as children after the emergence of habits: as those not yet possessed by habits, they attract the attention of the meanwhile lively instructors. In the twilight of the teachers, which is simultaneously an anthropological twilight, the child changes from a mere burgeoning phenomenon to a protagonist in the drama of upbringing.

One could almost say that before this turn towards 'guidance of boys', children were culturally invisible. Only after the discovery of the region of habit do they gain the privilege of visibility, which can be temporarily diminished – as in medieval Europe – but is never entirely lost. Now the young become objects of a concern that develops into a veritable art: the art of controlling habit formations and building up complex competencies on a base of automatized exercises. The advantage of being a child, however, the relatively unformed nature and openness to influence, comes at the price of a natural disadvantage, namely the strong emotionality and spontaneity of the young – the early educators would not have called themselves 'pedagogues', however, had they not believed that they would cope with this in the long run. Here, behind the educator, one recognizes the barely disguised figure of the animal tamer – just as there is grooming behind all teaching. That is why the true history of pedagogy also recounts the shared history of children and animals. But when the animal tamer succeeds in training elephants to walk the tightrope, as Pliny describes in his natural history, or to write Greek and Latin words with their trunks, as mentioned by a different author, the pedagogue should provide more than mere training and enable his pupils to recognize and choose their careers from the multitude of possible ones.

Pedagogy as Applied Mechanics

In short: because the inertial quality of the habitual had been explicitly understood in the twilight of the educators during the first millennium BC, this was naturally followed by the resolution to take control of habit *in statu nascendi* in order to turn the former principle of resistance into a factor of co-operation.

This brings us to the underlying principle of all early anthropotechnics. Every technical approach to humans – and that is precisely what pedagogy initially is – is based on the primal idea from classical mechanics of placing inertial forces in the service of the attempt to overcome inertia. This notion had its first triumph in the discovery of the lever principle. The smaller force can, if multiplied by the longer distance, move the larger force – a similar idea also underlies the pulley, which was known in antiquity. *Mechané*, Greek for 'cunning', therefore means nothing other than outwitting nature with its own means.[109] Pedagogical *mechané* grows from the considered decision to use habit for its own negation – one could also say it uses the probable as a medium for increasing improbability. One divests habit of its resistance qualities and turns it towards the purpose of achieving otherwise unattainable goals. This succeeds if the pedagogue is capable of gaining the greater pull – that is, getting to the root of conditioning through practising repetitions. From that point, one can say that *repetitio est mater studiorum*. Small human forces can achieve the impossible if they are multiplied by the longer distance of practice.[110]

The discovery of this mechanics triggers the euphoria that shapes the spiritual schools *in statu nascendi*, in Asia and Europe alike. Hence the high training aims typical of early school and practice systems as found in the esoteric core of Platonism, as also in most forms of Brahmanic training and Taoist alchemy. Naturally, running a school always involves exotericism and preparation for offices. In the hot core of the teaching, however, is the guidance of adepts towards the vertical wall on which to attempt the ascent to the impossible. Behind the theses of the school's advertising brochure, which states 'Virtue can be learned', lies an esoteric radicalism that can be summarized in the message 'The divine can be learned' (which is unutterable on Western soil). How – if the ascent to the gods could be mastered through secure methods? If immortality were just a matter of practice? Whoever believes that also thinks, like Plato, the Indian teachers and the immortals of Taoism, that they have a mandate to teach the impossible, albeit never beyond a small circle of suitable initiates. The teaching assignment includes the use of all suitable means for overcoming inertia. How far this goes is shown by the long line of spiritual and athletic extremists who have shaped the image of humanity in previous millennia.

Didactic Ascension: Learning for the Life of Life

Regardless of whether the early school presented itself exoterically or esoterically, however, it never considered itself the goal of its activity. The maxim of medieval schoolmasters – *non scholae sed vitae discimus*[111] – clearly meant: we are not learning for the base camp; all that counts is the expedition. As strait-laced as this declaration may sound, however, it took on monstrous dimensions in its interpretations. The word *vita*, on first reading, means no more than proving oneself on the outer front, in professions and offices; everyone involved in the lofty game realized, however, that this was only an initial step. In its deeper design, 'learning for life' was a maxim in favour of the most ambition projects of ascent – projects for which the divine was just high enough.

Such an equation of God and life was suitable for building up the most excessive vertical tension; it forced people to revise radically their conventional notions of the meaning of 'life'. It suddenly became possible to turn the attribute 'living' into a superlative and to multiply the noun 'life' by itself. Whoever says 'life' will sooner or later also say 'life of life'. Then, however, 'learning for life' means learning for pure surplus. In the course of studying the heightened life, one encounters the *vita vitalis*, which stands vertical in relation to the axis of empirical existence. This dictates the direction for the primary surrealism: the vertical pull effective in all advanced civilizations, which was given the unfortunate name 'metaphysics' in the West. Perhaps 'metabiotics' would have been a more suitable term, or on Latin soil the word 'supravitalistics' – though one must admit that both words would have deserved to die of sheer ugliness immediately. The term 'metaphysics' kept itself at the top of our curricula until that other terminological monstrosity, the doctrine of 'survival' so central for the moderns, gained the upper hand.

Dying Performance: Death on the Metaphysical Stage

The hardest test for the new subject of the practising power is death, as it is the factor that forces people most strongly into passivity. Whoever challenges death, then, in order to integrate it into the domain of ability, will – if successful – have proved that it is within the realm of the humanly possible to surmount the insurmountable – or become one with the terrible. That is why all exercises directed against the controlling of the soul by intense affects, unexamined habits and the illusions of the tribe and the forum lead ultimately and inevitably to measures against the subjugation of all subjugations, the possession of all possessions: the subordination of humans to the power of death. This can occur in two different ways: firstly through an asceticism, which leads to an artificially acquired attitude of being able to die. That is how the philosophical *ars moriendi* was read, whose primal scene is the death of Socrates, the most momentous dying performance in the Old European world; that is what was demonstrated by the Indian ascetics, who went through the art of leaving the body in numerous variations; and this was also demonstrated by the Japanese culture of suicide (*seppuku*), in which it was always extremely important to part with one's life as soon as there was a danger that it could outlast one's honour. Emancipation from the tyranny of death can also occur through the formulation of a myth that asserts the allegiance of the soul to the kingdom of the living God. In such cases – Egyptian doctrines of the afterlife and Christian Platonism provide the best-known examples – the soul's right of return is secured less through supplementary ascetic efforts than by living life with integrity.

Since the rise of the surrealisms of advanced civilizations, then, the climate on the ascetic planet has been subject to a constant change, something comparable to global warming through ever-increasing moral emissions. This forces the shift from simply 'living one's life' in the current of collective habitus to leading life under the influence of individualizing school powers. This new kind of guidance causes a defamiliarization of existence to the point where notions about the areas of school and life merge into that bizarre dogma that life itself is nothing more than one great pedagogical project that must be learned like an esoteric school subject – and along with life, the art of ending it in exemplary fashion. That is why what the Greeks called *euthanasía*, the art of the beautiful death, forms the secret centre of the acrobatic revolution; it is the rope over an abyss that the practising learn to cross in order to advance from life to meta-life.

Along with the death of Socrates as described by Plato, the Old European tradition has a second thanatologically momentous primal scene in which the emancipation of the intellectually practising from the tyranny of death could be observed at the greatest height: the death of Jesus as described in the gospels. In both passion stories, the emphasis is on the conversion of obligation into ability, an ability that transpires all the more impressively because circumstances impose a twofold passivity on the victims: firstly in the face of the injustice of the death sentence, and secondly in the face of the cruelty of the executions *more Romano*. In the case of Socrates it is particularly clear how the wise man's ability appropriates the external compulsion through the fact that he, condemned rightly in formal terms but wrongfully in factual terms, adapts the sentence to his own will and co-operates with the procedure imposed on him as if he himself were the organizer of the passion play into which he was forced.

The superordination of the voluntary over the compulsory is most brilliantly embodied by the allegory of the laws that speak to Socrates in the dialogue *Crito*. The personified laws tell the condemned man something along these lines: 'Everything would suggest, dear Socrates, that you liked it here in Athens more than anywhere else. We, the laws, and this city we rule, were clearly enough for you. You never went on travels, as many people do, to become acquainted with other cities and other laws. You praised the fate of existing under our leadership like no other – even at your trial, you proudly declared that you would rather die than be banished. You had seventy years in which to turn your back on us and this city, but you chose to stay with us. So if you wanted to flee from us now, in the face of the execution we have decreed, how could you ever repeat elsewhere what you never tired of saying here: that man must regard virtue and justice more highly than anything else? Do not, therefore, follow Criton's advice to flee, but rather ours, which is this: stay here and continue your path to its end!' Thereupon the wise man draws the only possible conclusion for him:

> 'This is the voice I hear murmuring in my ears, like the sound of flutes in the ears of Corybants. That voice prevents me from hearing any other. [. . .] I will follow the will of the gods.'[112]

To What Extent It Is Right for Jesus to Say: 'It Is Finished'

The absorption of external compulsion into the protagonist's own will is also staged powerfully in the Golgotha account in the gospels, and is all the more impressive because an execution in the Roman style is as far as one could imagine from the civilized setting of the Greek art of dying. As far as the subordination of the victim to external acts of compulsion is concerned, the Jesuan passion greatly surpasses that of Socrates, and yet it is there that the transformation of obligation into an inalienable ability was demonstrated to greatest consequence.

The scene of the final moments on the cross is itself loaded with exemplifying energies by the evangelists. While we are told in Mark

15:37 and Matthew 27:50 that Jesus died with a loud cry after drinking from the vinegared sponge, Luke 23:46 describes the same scene in latently ability-coloured transitional terms: 'Father, into your hands I commit my spirit', *et haec dicens expiravit*. John 19:30 adds a phrase that belongs fully to the sphere of ability: *tetélestai*, rendered in Latin as *consummatum est*, meaning 'It is finished.' As venerable as these translations may be, they scarcely do justice to the spirit of John's addition. For what John, the Greek apostle, undertakes at this point is no less than an athleticization of the saviour's death – which is why Jesus' last words should be reproduced more in the manner of 'Made it!' or even 'Mission accomplished!', even though such a turn of phrase would go against the conventional Christian view of the passion. The goal of the operation is unmistakable: Jesus must be transformed from the chance victim of wilful Judaeo-Roman justice into the fulfiller of a mission dictated by divine providence – and this can only be achieved if his suffering is completely 'sublated' as something foreseen, determined and desired. The same word with which Jesus breathes his last breath on the cross, *tetélestai*, is used by John shortly beforehand to posit the 'fulfilment' or completion of written predictions through the Golgothan documentation. The decisive point is that Jesus himself recognizes the 'fulfilment' of the mission on the cross and considers it completed (*sciens Jesus quia omnia consummata sunt*), so his final utterance does indeed contain a scriptural-messianic-athletic statement of achievement.

The acrobatic revolution of Christianity does not end with the conquest of death's passivity demonstrated on the cross. The triumph of ability over non-ability takes place between Good Friday evening and Easter morning – the most pathos-laden of all time spans. In this time, the slain Jesus carried out the most unheard-of act, that of *akro baínein* into hell – he walked through the underworld on tiptoe. With his resurrection 'on the third day', anti-gravitation celebrates its greatest victory: it is as if Christ, the first among God's acrobats, had got hold of a vertical rope that opened the way for him and his followers to an absolute vertical previously closed or only sensed mythically. Through his *salto vitale*, the risen one breaks open the world form characterized by a belief in the supremacy of the fatal interruption. From this moment on, all life is acrobatic, a dance on the rope of faith, which states that life itself is everlasting – and in an irrevocably proclaimed 'from now on'.

Klaus Berger remarks on the Athanasian theology of the evangelist: 'Staring at death is replaced by integration into the line of those who wander beyond death. For even physical death is exceeded; it is merely an immaterial part in the sequence of events.'[113] Death, an 'immaterial part' in the course of things: humanity had to wait a long time for the chance to hear such frivolities – or should one say, such delirious acquittals from the grip of finitude? As soon as such a doctrine is in the world, the psychopolitical *ancien régime*, the normal depression also known as realism, finds itself in palpable difficulty. The steady continuation of the anti-depressive campaign provokes history: it is subject to the law of the deceleration of the miracle. This results in what Alexander Kluge calls the immense 'time need of revolutions'.[114]

Death Athletes

The athleticization of the Christian death struggle hinted at by John reaches one of its climaxes during the persecutions of Christians in southern Gaul, initiated by Marcus Aurelius and continued by his successors, which flared up more heavily again around AD 202, under Severus. At this time, the North African Tertullian wrote his consolatory text *Ad Martyros*, a highly rhetorically stylized piece, which employs all the tools of ancient ascetology to make the prisoners in the dungeons of Vienne and Lyon aware of the parallels between their situation and that of soldiers before the battle – and even more that of athletes before the agon. The African reminds his Gaulish brothers and sisters, not without a degree of cynicism, that they should actually count themselves lucky to be sitting in a dungeon and awaiting their execution in the arena, as the outside world is a far worse prison for a true Christian.

> O blessed, consider yourselves as having been transferred from prison to what we may call a place of safety.[115]

This robust comforter's expectations of the martyrs have already become sporting to the point where he expects nothing less than peak performances from his fellow believers. These faith athletes owe it to Christ to provide a great match for their executioners.

> You are about to enter a noble contest [*bonum agonem*] in which the living God [*Deus vivus*] acts the part of superintendent [*agonothetes*] and the Holy Spirit is your trainer [*xystarchès*], a contest whose crown is eternity, whose prize is angelic nature, citizenship [*politia*] in heaven and glory for ever and ever. And so your Master [*epistates vester*], Jesus Christ, who has anointed you with His Spirit and has brought you to this training ground [*scamma*], has resolved, before the day of the contest, to take you from a softer way of life to a harsher treat-

ment [*ad duriorem tractationem*] that your strength may be increased. For athletes, too, are set apart for more rigid training [*disciplina*] that they may apply themselves to the building up of their physical strength. [. . .] They are urged on, they are subjected to torturing toils, they are worn out [*Coguntur, cruciantur, fatigantur*] [. . .] And they do this, says the Apostle, to win a perishable crown. We who are about to win an eternal one recognize in the prison our training ground [*palaestra*], that we may be led forth to the actual contest before the seat of the presiding judge [*ad stadium tribunalis*] well practised [*bene exercitati*] in all hardships.[116]

Tertullian continues his reflections by reminding the martyrs that profane humans from heathen peoples have defied death and voluntarily taken the most terrible ordeals upon themselves – like the philosopher Heraclitus, who reportedly covered himself in cow dung and burned to death, or Empedocles, who leapt into the flames of Mount Etna. In certain heathen cities, Tertullian tells them, young men have themselves flogged until they bleed, simply to demonstrate how much they are capable of enduring. If these people pay such a high price for mere glass beads, how much easier it should be for Christians to pay the price for the real pearl!

Admittedly, tortured Christians in Roman provincial theatres are anything but the ideal of the philosophical *savoir mourir*. Even in Tertullian's relentlessly drastic rhetoric, however, one can detect an echo of the agonal ethics which states that through *áskesis* and harshness (*sklerotes*) towards oneself, even immensely difficult feats can become easy.

Certum Est Quia Impossibile: Only the Impossible Is Certain

Tertullian's dauntless pep talk to the *morituri* of Lyon reveals the logic of Christian acrobatism with a clarity never attained again. It is the goodwill to carry out the strictly absurd, the boundlessly nonsensical, the completely impossible, that makes theology theology. This alone prevents it from gliding back into an ordinary ontology. In the kingdom of God, what appears in being as a discontinuity is pure continuity. If Christ is risen, then the world in which no one can rise from the dead is refuted. If we never see anyone resurrected here, however, we should switch locations and go where that which does not happen here does happen – being here is good, but being there is better. No self-respecting Christian, according to Tertullian, would appear in the circus arena and present any less than the opposite of what the profane people believe to be possible. Whoever believes must *épater la bourgeoisie*. In the best fighting mood, the author put the matter in a nutshell in his treatise against the Marcionites, *On the Flesh of Christ*:

> The Son of God was crucified; I am not ashamed because men must needs be ashamed of it. And the Son of God died; it is by all means to be believed, because it is absurd. And He was buried, and rose again; the fact is certain, because it is impossible.[117]

This *certum quia impossibile* underlies practically everything Europeans have known about vertical matters for the last two thousand years. In Simone Weil's superbly exaggerated thesis '*La vie humaine est impossible*' – human life is impossible[118] – we still hear a certainty that is also born of impossibility. What we call the truth is the result of the quarrel between gravitation and anti-gravitation. The Holy Spirit invoked by Christians was that art of wisdom which ensured that the extravagance of martyrs was tempered by the memory of horizontal motifs in their lives. In this sense, the Holy Spirit was the first psychiatrist in Europe – and the early Christians its first patients. Its tasks include defusing religious immune paradoxes, which break open at the moment when the untethered witnesses of faith weaken their physical immunity because they are overly sure of their transcendent immunity.

What happened in the arenas of Roman mass culture, at any rate, was no slave revolt in morality, to recall Nietzsche's problematic theorem once again – it was the outdoing of the gladiators by the martyrs. What took place here was the translation of the physical *agones* into an athletic insistence on the declaration *ego sum Christianus* – even if the declarers were thrown to those blond beasts so loved by the Romans, the lions. Even if one views martyrdom with suspicion, sensing in it the fundamentalist obstinacy of people who have nothing better to do with their lives than throw them away with the gesture of an irrefutable proof, one must admit that the acts of martyrdom in the era of persecution occasionally have some of the spirit of the original Christian acrobatism. In some old accounts of suffering one can still sense that will to cross over which people had begun to practise in the training camps of the higher life. The will to believe was not yet equated with the will to worldly success, as found in the Puritan varieties of Protestantism and in the most recent metamorphoses of 'American religion'.[119] Its symptom was a boisterous transvitalism. Wherever it was able to assert itself, the depressive reality principle, the belief in the supremacy of death, had to accept its worst setback. It was the faith in anti-gravitation that suspended the tragedy, and stretched the rope so tautly between the two states of life that many formed the daredevil plan of venturing a crossing.

Even the fallen tightrope walker from the prologue to Nietzsche's *Thus Spoke Zarathustra* profited from the tension between the rope ends on this side and the other side. And, although the more recent doctrine states that there is nothing to support life on the shore beyond, one still finds ropes in immanence with sufficient tension to carry the steps of those who cross. It almost looks as though one 'were walking on nothing but air'. They form a support that lacks all qualities of a solid ground – 'and yet it really is possible to walk on it'.[120] Every step on the rope has to be practised ten thousand times, and yet every step up there must be taken as if it were the first. Whoever trains for the rope subjects themselves to a *paideía* that removes the foundation of all ground habits. Walking on the rope means gathering all that has been in the present. Only then can the imperative 'You must change your life!' be transformed into daily sequences of exercises. Acrobatic existence de-trivializes life by placing repetition in the service of the unrepeatable. It transforms all steps into first steps, because each one could be the last. It knows only one ethical action: the superversion of all circumstances through the conquest of the improbable.

II

Exaggeration Procedures

A fervent and diligent man is ready for all things.
It is greater work to resist vices and passions than to sweat in physical
  toil. [. . .]
Watch over yourself, arouse yourself, warn yourself [. . .].
The more violence you do to yourself, the more progress you will make.
Thomas à Kempis, The Imitation of Christ

The road of excess leads to the palace of wisdom.
William Blake, Proverbs of Hell

BACKDROP

Retreats into Unusualness

If one had to summarize the main difference between the modern and ancient worlds and define the two states of the world in the same sentence, it would have to be the following: the modern era is the one that brought about the greatest mobilization of human powers for the sake of work and production, while all those life forms in which the utmost mobilization took place in the name of practice and perfection are ancient. This means that the 'Middle Ages' in Europe, contrary to their name, do not form an autonomous intermediate phase between antiquity and modernity but rather an unmistakable part of antiquity, even though, in superficial terms, their Christian colouring could make them seem post- or even anti-ancient. Because the Christian Middle Ages were far more an era of practice than work, there is no doubt about their status as belonging to the ancient regime from an activity-theoretical perspective. Living in antiquity and not believing in the priority of work or economic life – these are simply two formulations of the same state of affairs. Even the Benedictine *labora*, which some have occasionally sought to misconstrue as a concession to the spirit of work wrested from prayer, actually meant no more than an extension of meditative practice to the material use of one's hands. No monk could grasp the concept of work in the newer sense of the word as long as the monastic rule ensured the symmetry between *orare* and *laborare*. Furthermore, one should know that the emphasis on *labora* in the Benedictine Rule (which, according to tradition, came into being upon the founding of the monastery of Monte Cassino between 525 and 529) was a reaction to centuries of observing monastic pathologies: while the moderns compensate for their work-related illnesses with health cures and holidays, monks used work to remedy their contemplation-related ailments.

211

The thesis that antiquity was characterized in practical terms by exercise and modernity by work posits both an opposition and an inner connection between the worlds of practice and work, of perfection and production. This gives the concept of a renaissance a significantly altered meaning. If a phenomenon such as the rebirth of antiquity in a late Christian or post-Christian, or rather a post-work, world genuinely exists, it should make itself felt in the revitalization of the motifs of the practising life. There is no lack of indications for this. What characterizes both regimes is their capacity to integrate human powers into effort programmes on the grandest scale; what separates them is the radically divergent orientation of their respective mobilizations. In the one case the energies awakened are completely subordinated to the primacy of the object or product, ultimately even to the abstract product known as profit, or to the aesthetic fetish, which is exhibited and collected as a 'work'. In the other case, all powers flow into the intensification of the practising subject, which progresses to ever higher levels of a purely performative mode of being in the course of the exercises. What was once called the *vita contemplativa* to contrast it with the *vita activa* is, in fact, a *vita performativa*. In its own way, it is as active as the most active life. This does not, however, express itself in the mode of political action that Hannah Arendt, following the trail of Aristotle, wanted to see at the forefront of active life forms,[1] nor in that of work, production and economy, but rather in the sense of an assimilation by the never-tiring universal or divine being-nothing, which does and suffers more than any finite creature would be capable of doing or suffering. Like those creatures, however, it knows a form of self-enclosed, fulfilling and indestructible calm that, going on the accounts of initiates, in no way resembles the profane calm of exhaustion.

It is no coincidence, of course, that the rediscovery of the practising mode of life began at the very moment when the idolization of work (extending to the imperial German ethos of 'We are all workers') reached its climax. I am speaking here of the last third of the nineteenth century, for which I earlier suggested such ciphers as 'athletic renaissance' and 'de-spiritualization of asceticisms'. These two phrases refer to tendencies that point beyond the era of productivism. Since practice as an activity type – together with aesthetic play – stepped out of the shadow of work, a new ecosystem of activities has been developing in which the absolute precedence of product value is revised in favour of practice values, performance values and experiential values.

No one can be credible as a contemporary today, then, unless they sense how the performative dimension is overtaking the work dimension. Thus the sports system has developed into a multiverse with hundreds of secondary worlds, in which self-referential motion, useless play, superfluous exertion and simulated fights celebrate their existence somewhat wilfully, in the clearest possible contrast to the utilitarian objectivism of the working world – no matter how often a dull-witted sociology might claim that sport is merely a training camp for the factory and a preparation for the capitalist ideology of competition. One must admit, however, that those parts of the sporting world closest to the 'circus' in the ancient sense, especially in the vicinity of the Olympic industry and in the professional segments of football and cycling, have meanwhile become subject to a result fetishism that absolutely rivals the compulsive product-oriented thinking of the economic sphere. But what does that mean if, on the other hand, statistics show that in those sports there are ten thousand amateurs or more for every professional?

The tendency towards an exhibition of self-referentially practising acts articulates itself even more clearly in the art scene of the previous century: aesthetic modernity is the era in which the performative separates from the procedures and aims of the working world, erecting countless stages for completely autonomous presentations. The emancipation of art from its work-shaped nature has long since reached the point – in system-immanent terms too – at which the work is merged once more with the self-referential process of practising, or rather with a change in the shape of creative energies. It often no longer stands in the world as an autonomous result, eternally severed from its conditions of birth and transposed to the sphere of pure objectification through the label 'finished', but rather as a practice crystal frozen in the moment – an indication of a drift from one performative state to the next.

On the other hand, such great artists as Rodin have spoken of their activity of constant practising, albeit always geared towards the concrete product, as the highest form of 'work' – *toujours travailler* – as if to make it clear that art, despite its self-referentiality, is the most serious and selfless of matters. In doing so they revealed, in their own way, a secret among the old breed of craftsmen and fetish makers, namely that a well-made object is always imbued with the 'soul' of its maker, while he can only master his craft if he is constantly attentive to the voices of the material.

Alongside this, the countless psychotherapeutic systems that unfolded in the course of the twentieth century brought the ancient methods of practising introspection to life again, normally without realizing their kinship with the old models. Nietzsche's demand that if his readers wanted to understand him, they should not be modern people but rather meditators or 'regurgitators' initiated the return from the logic of work to the exercise. When Foucault, by contrast, brought the ancient discourse around 'self-concern' back into the contemporary discussion around 1980, this was a signal to conclude the era of therapeutic ideologies. What has been on the agenda since then is the retrieval of a generalized practice consciousness from the sources of ancient philosophy and modern artistic and bodily praxis. Here and there, people are beginning to comprehend that the therapeutism of the twentieth century was itself only the cloak for a shift of tendency with epochal traits. Let us recall: the key psychoanalytical term 'work through' is based on the discreet adoption of a Stoic practice principle, namely turning a notion or an affect this way and that in meditation, known in the Greek terminology of the school as *anapolein* or *anapóleisis* and in Latin as *in animo versare*. It is characteristic of the modern zeitgeist that sport and meditation are also often presented as 'work'.

The most far-reaching subversion of the faith in work and production took place on its own terrain when the Communist Party of the Soviet Union prescribed a course of modernization for the still largely agrarian economy of the former Tsarist empire after the October Revolution of 1917. In the course of this upheaval, the motivational foundations for modern employment, the obligation to pay debts in the credit system of property economy and the personal striving for prosperity were so profoundly wrecked that nothing resembling an efficient working culture in the modern sense was able to develop in the entire area. As the criterion of personal advantage was suspended *a priori*, the only options for working Soviets were either the attitude of the voluntary record producer or the self-ironic robot – in both cases, the predication of work on the primacy of the result was undermined and transformed into a more or less self-referential exercise. Essentially, the Soviet economy was an amalgam of a feudal temple economy in which a cynical state clergy absorbed the surplus product and a Gurdjieff group: it is well known that participants in such gatherings work day and night, to the point of exhaustion, on tasks assigned by the group leader, only to witness the product then being destroyed before their eyes – supposedly to further their inner ability to let go. In that sense, we can say that communism carried out a quasi-spiritual exercise with its populations that used the pretext of work while reducing work to absurdity: it exhausted the lives of three generations for the production of a political ornament

214

that was passed over by history. From a distance, its fate reminds one of how Tibetan monks craft large mandalas of coloured sand that are destined to be washed away by the river the day after their completion.

In this section, I will reconstruct various defining traits of the *explicitly* practising life. Considering the immensity of the material one would have to address here, I will have to content myself with outlines and anecdotal colourings. Following the course taken by the matter itself, I will begin with the separation – visible since antiquity – of the practising from the social continuum of life, and their fixation within an eccentricity requiring systematic consolidation in relation to their previous existence dictated by group pressures and organic inertias. This withdrawal from the collective identity – the practical matrix of every intellectual *epoché* – is one characteristic of the ascetic *modus vivendi* stylized in an endearing exaggeration by Helmuth Plessner, who created the doctrine of man's 'eccentric positionality', into a general trait of the human condition – as if all individuals stood beside themselves *a priori* and had always lived their lives in front of the mirror like actors of everyday life, natural hysterics or public relations managers. One should remember, however, that mirrors, though in use over two thousand years ago in rare cases, only gained wider distribution some two hundred years ago; when the mirror market finally reached saturation a hundred years ago, its omnipresence evoked a certain discreet eccentricity in the self-relationships of all men and women. They seduce their users into believing that they had always been reflexively 'beside themselves', whereas, from a historical perspective, mirrors only began to play their part as central egotechnic media of the modern, self-image-dependent human truly unmistakably very recently.

In the next section, I will show in what way the inner world of the practising is affected by ideal model forces, and also how the intuition of a distant, yet authoritative perfection leads to the build-up of strong vertical tensions. This produces a realm of idea-driven upswings and subtle attractors of which the moderns, generally speaking, only know as much as becomes visible through the caricatures circulating under the heading 'narcissism'. It yields insights into the temporal forms of an existence subject to the pull of perfection-oriented thinking. The temporal structure of being-unto-completion, whether in its Old European or Asian variations, can provide information about the power of perfectionism without which one cannot understand how the moderns could be seduced by the phantoms of the philosophy of history.

After various historical and systematic remarks on the indispensable figure of the trainer, which, depending on one's region, tradition or whims, is referred to as a master, guru, father, healer, genius, demon, teacher or classic, I shall consider anew the theologically well-examined phenomenon of conversions in order to show how the practising are not infrequently confronted with the difficulty of having to continue their work with a different trainer. Here it transpires that many who change subjects or levels had begun training with a wrongly formatted 'god', one that was too unsuccessful – like Wotan, who was eventually outstripped by Christ – or too serious, as could be observed in the modern transition from the eternally suffering Christ to cheerful Fortuna. We shall see why a dismissed trainer always has a good chance of finding a second life in the spiritual household of their former trainee as an idol, demon or *cattivo maestro*. This necessitates a revision in the supreme discipline of the sociology of religion, the theory of conversions. I would like to question the established model of conversion (even if I do not subscribe to Oswald Spengler's thesis that genuine conversions do not exist) by showing that true conversion occurs only upon entering an advanced-civilized discipline of the practising life (which I call secession), while a mere change of discipline or confession – like Paul's leap from Jewish zealotry to apostolic devotion – does not display true conversion character.

— 6 —

FIRST ECCENTRICITY

On the Separation of the Practising and Their Soliloquies

Uprooting from the First Life: Spiritual Secessionism

The step into the practising life takes place through ethical distinction.[2] This distinction is made by anyone who dares or is called upon to step out of the river of life and take up residence on the shore. The leaver cultivates a battle-ready attention to their own interior and retains a hostile suspicion towards the new exterior, which had previously stood for the surrounding world as such. All increases of a mental or bodily kind begin with a secession from the ordinary. This is usually accompanied by a forceful rejection of the past – not infrequently assisted by such affects as disgust, regret and complete rejection of the earlier mode of being. What people today, with a reverent turn of phrase, often call 'spirituality' is initially more like a holy perversion than a generally respectable inner praxis. The original awe of spiritual 'values' is always infused with a fear of perversion and a horror in the face of the mysteries of the unnatural, regardless of whether one is dealing with the monstrous performances of Indian fakirs, the petrifaction exercises of the Stoics or the ascension exercises of Christian extremists. If even an author as sympathetic towards the Stoa as Horace remarks that Epictetus was *atrox* – dreadful, gruesome – because of his severity, this tells us more about the climate of ancient spirituality than any esoteric warbling. Did Epictetus not teach, in fact, that when one kisses one's child, one should inwardly call out to it 'You will die tomorrow' in order to train letting go, and offset a pleasant notion with an unpleasant counter-notion?[3] We hear the same hardness in the speeches of Buddha, who encapsulated monastic perfection as follows:

He who cares not for others, who has no relations, who controls himself, who is firmly fixed in the heart of truth, in whom the fundamental evils are extinguished, who has thrown hatred from him: him I call a Brahman.[4]

To understand the depth of the rupture expressed in the words of the awakened, one must remember that only a few generations earlier, the Brahman's redemption depended entirely on his relatives, or more precisely on his paternal lineage and on the sacrificial arts cultivated by his family. One must therefore always take into account that the extremism found among Stoics, early Christians, Tantrics, Buddhists and other despisers of probability is not an illegitimate supplement invented later by morbid agitators in order to sour an essentially healthy and mild doctrine; in every case, it comes from the sources themselves.

To hear the original language of the radical secession dynamic, it is sufficient to look up Matthew 10:37:

'Anyone who loves his father and mother more than me is not worthy of me; anyone who loves his son or daughter more than me is not worthy of me.'

This is the *locus classicus* of aggressive vertical language in the Western hemisphere, a performative flash of lightning from a sky that causes apocalypses and forces farewells. The economic basis for the break with the first life is revealed in a dialogue recounted in Mark 10:28–30:

Peter said to him, 'We have left everything to follow you!'
'I tell you the truth,' Jesus replied, 'no one who has left home or brothers or sisters or mother or father or children or fields for me and the gospel will fail to receive a hundred times as much.'

The uprooting must be practised on this foundation until the adept understands that the triviality of earlier life is the most disgusting heresy; reality as such is a plague. Faith in this plague and its governing principle constitutes an immersion in miasma.

Though this be monstrous, yet there is method in it: the secessionism of the great transformative ethical systems seeks to assert once and for all that there is no salvation in the first life. The initial ties transpire as shackles that bind the souls to irredeemable circumstances. Once the region of possession, fallenness and hopelessness is uncovered, the exorcism of those spirits must stop at nothing. For the radicals, it is not enough to abandon one's village, fields and nets; one's old physical and mental self must also be left behind. For Patanjali, the mythical author of the Yoga Sutras, who is often identi-

218

fied with the grammarian of the same name from the second century BC, the ascetic purifications (*tapas*) preceding meditation evoke a curative disgust in the contemplator at their own body, urging them to interrupt any contact with the other bodies.[5] As soon as I see the world as a slough of filth, I am already halfway along the path into the open. The attitude of the correctly practising individual in relation to their earlier existence is described by Hindus as *vairagya*, which translates as 'detachment' and refers to a mildly disgusted indifference towards everyday pleasures and concerns.

Graeco-Roman Stoicism also knows and praises the break with the attachments and aversions of the first life – whoever wants to grow a thick skin to defend against fate must first wean themselves from their natural preference for the pleasant. Nietzsche remarks on this in a quietly parodying tone:

> The Stoic, on the other hand, trains himself to swallow stones and worms, slivers of glass and scorpions without nausea; he wants his stomach to become ultimately indifferent to whatever the accidents of existence might pour into it.[6]

Even more importantly than the indifference of the stomach, the aim of Stoic practice is the indifference of the eyes to random sights, of the ears to random sounds and of the spirit to random notions – that extends, as Marcus Aurelius notes in his cautionary aphorisms *To Himself*, to a fundamental refusal to be surprised by anything.

> How ridiculous and how much of a stranger in the universe is he who is surprised at anything which happens in his life.[7]

In this maxim, cold-blooded as it was intended to sound, we see a hint of the Stoic's anthropotechnic trick: in his deliberate equation of surprises and injuries, his concern is to immunize himself against the former and simultaneously acquire the necessary level of resistance to the latter.

The Splitting of the Entity through the Crusade Against the Ordinary

Let us reiterate: entering ethical thought means making a difference with one's very own existence that no one had previously made. If there were an accompanying speech act, it would be: 'I herewith exit ordinary reality.' Secession from the habitual world as the first ethical operation introduces an unknown division into the world. It not only divides humanity asymmetrically into the group of the knowing, who leave, and the unknowing, who remain in the place of vulgar doom; it also inevitably implies a declaration of war by the former on the latter. This results in the bloodless war of those who return as authorized teachers against all others, who now learn that they are students – and mostly poor students, lost students, even hopeless cases, unaware that they are playing with damnation: people of yesterday, from a time before the discovery of the great difference. At the same time, all cultures that experienced the outbreak of such a logical-ethical civil war have no shortage of mediators seeking to bridge the rupture. They bring those humiliated by the logos, insulted by the Noble Truths and excluded from the curative exercises closer to the party of attackers through sentimental, universalistic formulas of reconciliation – indeed, perhaps the 'great' religions, with their clerical apparatuses, their networks of organized escapism and their world-friendly schools, clinics and welfare services, are nothing but businesses for softening the hurtful overloads let loose by their founders. Wherever universalisms appear, their grand gestures of embrace provide more or less deceptive reparations for the attack of the radicals. The achievements of minorities, they regularly claim, are not privileges for the few but rather conquests for all. The truth is that universalism can never bring about more than the reformatting of an elect group. Sooner or later, this group expands and assembles a larger ring of new converts and sympathizers around the hard core. It is on such peripheries that the dreams of absolute inclusivity flourish. Viewed as a whole, abstract universalism – like 'man' in Sartre's definition – remains a futile passion, a consolation to the untrained and a phantom to the trained.

Going through with the secession means splitting the world. The operator is the one who, by leaving, cuts the world's surface into two initially irreconcilable regions: the zone of the leavers and that of the stayers. Through this cut, both sides learn first of all that the world, which previously seemed to be common to all people, a many-headed but inseparable and unconfrontable unity, is in truth a separable and confrontable phenomenon. The withdrawal of the ascetic is the knife that makes the cut in the continuum. From that point, the world appears in a completely new light – indeed, perhaps one can only posit the existence of a 'world', in the sense of moral-cosmic reaches for the whole that are coded in advanced-civilized terms, once it has been divided by the new class of deniers and reconstituted at a higher level. The whole, previously a confused multiplicity of forces with a vague basis for unity, now becomes a strained synthesis of the unequal parts produced by the cut. What Heidegger called the 'age of the world picture' does not begin only with the modern globes and atlases, but already with the visions of cosmos and empire in the Axial Age. A world from which the ethically best flee can no longer be a maternal container for all life forms. Owing to the exodus of the ascetics, meditators and thinkers, it becomes the site of a drama that fundamentally questions its ability to house ethically aroused inhabitants sufficiently: what is this world if the strongest statement about it is a withdrawal from it? The great world theatre deals with the duel between the secessionists and the settled, those who flee from the world and those who remain-in-the-world. Where there is theatre, however, the figure of the observer appears on the scene. If all the world becomes a stage, it is because there are secessionists who claim to be only visitors here, not participants. Pure theory is the reviewing of the world by reserved visitors. Its appearance creates an ethical challenge to the 'prevailing' through an observation from a quasi-transcendental position: these observers seek to describe from the 'edge of the world' what is the case in this amazing venue.

Spaces of Retreat for the Practising

With these observations, I am hinting at a spiritual form of spatial planning that negotiates over deeper borders than those which can be addressed by any geopolitics. The spaces created by the secessionists – we can think for the time being of the hermitages, the monasteries, the academies and other places of ascetic-meditative and philosophical retreat – would, in the better days of cultural Marxism, undoubtedly have been termed mundane bases of the 'spirit of utopia'. As utopias in the precise sense of the word are only narratively evoked images of better worlds that do not exist anywhere in the real world, however, this term is unsuitable to characterize the localities created via secession. Secession produces real spaces. It sets up borders behind which a genuinely different mode of being dictates its will.

Wherever secessionists dwell, the rules of actually existing surrealism apply. A monastery, whether at the foot of the Himalayas or on the outskirts of the Nitrian Desert, a few days' walk south of Alexandria, has nothing in common with a dreamt island in the Atlantic Ocean – it is a concrete biotope, populated by heavily tanned surrealists who follow a strict regime. The same applies to the caves of the Egyptian hermits, the forest and mountain refuges of the Indian *sannyasins*, as well as all other bases of meditative retreat or ascetic death to the world – in paradoxical fashion, even to the airy camps of the Syrian

Stylites, who, on platforms on the tips of their sacred pillars, staged charades lasting years that were in line with the expression 'to reach for the heavens'. It was a theatre of world-contempt before the eyes of the miracle-hungry masses, who poured from the cities to the desert ruins so that they would finally see something they could not believe.

It therefore seems more plausible to describe the space-forming results of the ethical secession with a term like 'heterotopia', which was coined by Foucault in a little-known lecture he gave in 1967 to an audience of architects, entitled 'Des espaces autres' [Of Other Spaces]. For him, heterotopias are spatial creations of an 'other place' that belong to the network of sites (*emplacements*) in a particular culture, yet at the same time are not part of the trivial continuum because their inner rules are stubbornly autonomous, often running counter to the logic of the whole. He names cemeteries, monasteries, libraries, high-class brothels, cinemas, colonies and ships as examples of heterotopias. One could easily extend the list by adding such phenomena as sports venues, holiday islands, places of pilgrimage, miracle courts, car parks[8] and different kinds of no-go areas. Among the heterotopian spatial inventions of the late twentieth century, the space station is probably one of the most important innovations – it would, furthermore, be easy to show that a specific form of astronaut spirituality has developed there whose repercussions on the inhabitants of the earth's surface have yet to be studied.[9]

The first real heterotopia is the spatial type that, building on the Heraclitean image of the river into which one never steps twice, I have called the shore. Places with shore qualities can be projected onto all corners of the inhabited earth – *de facto*, they come about wherever those practising parties who have resolved to secede step out of the river of habits. They constitute the first bridgeheads of eccentricity. Where the flight from the centre declared itself affirmatively, the great theories about the necessity of uprooting for redemption were born, such as the Buddhist doctrine of leaving one's house or the Christian ethos of pilgrimage. In a sutra of the *Digha Nikaya* (the 'Collection of Longer Discourses'), we are told of Buddha:

> But if he go forth from the household life into the houseless state, then he will become a Buddha who removes the veil from the eyes of the world.[10]

As far as the Christian topoi of life as *peregrinatio* and the believer as *Homo viator* are concerned, these are sufficiently well known today (as well as being refreshed and having their spiritual-touristic value increased by the current pilgrimage trend) for it to be sufficient to note their emergence from the break with the status quo. The only decisive thing about such figures is their secessionist point: as salvation is impossible to find in the first socialization, possessed by the old habitus and living under the idols of the tribe, tradition and theatre – in short, in the life under the spell of the beginnings – whoever realizes this must break with their old solidarities.

Houselessness and pilgrim existence create eccentric spaces through escape; the house-leaver, the pilgrim and the world-stranger constantly carry their own desert, their hermitage, their alibi around with them. A stay at the scene of the crime of ordinary life is no longer an option for these noble evaders. Whoever always has their escape space around them, on the other hand, no longer needs to leave physically. The metaphorization of the desert made it possible to temper the extremism of the first secessionaries and introduce a bourgeois variety of retreat for everyman. This trend was supported by the body of edifying literature, especially after the replacement of the weighty codices with the small book, which permitted readers from the fourteenth century onwards to keep their pocket desert to hand wherever they went.[11] In fact, the literary media of the early Modern Age in Europe made a strong practice medium available to laypersons. Open a book, read a line, and your one-minute anachoresis has been realized. For years, the book has served the contemplative as a vehicle for withdrawal 'to the country home of the self'.[12]

What Helmuth Plessner ascribes to 'man' in general, namely the 'eccentric positionality' of his self-relation, is in reality an effect of the use of egotechnic media in the Modern Age – media which, in the course of a few centuries, equipped virtually every individual with the necessary tools for a mild chronic being-outside-themselves: the prayer formula, the confessional mirror, the novel, the diary, the portrait, the photograph, newspapers and radio media, and not least mirrors on all sides. Provided with this equipment for self-techniques, individuals developed a second attitude towards their first position almost unnoticed. Barely any of the moderns who assert the human right for 'one's own space' are aware of the origin of this demand in a revision of social topology from the distant past.

The Deeper Distinction: Self-Acquisition and World-Relinquishment

Nonetheless, the previous references to the division of the world through ethical-ascetic secession prove unsatisfactory for a philosophical evaluation of original eccentricity. Certainly their starting point is the incontestable observation that a series of intellectual-historically far-reaching separation movements began in a number of advanced civilizations some three thousand years ago; even so, these observations are not adequate to highlight the agent of secession with sufficient clarity. This inadequacy has a methodological reason: it is impossible to explain from a sociological perspective alone how such a split could come about. Essentially, the motor of secessionary events remains untraceable from the outside. Its logical source only becomes evident if one reconstructs the opposition between the ascetics and the rest of the world according to the criteria of an ontological analysis. Only thus can one clarify how the totality of what exists was subject to something resembling a local government reorganization during which the competencies of 'man' for himself and the other things were radically redistributed. Yes, one can say that 'man' emerged from this cosmic reform, and was only thus created as the carrier of a chance at salvation in the first place. 'Man' comes about from the small minority of ascetic extremists who step out from the crowd and claim that they are actually everyone.

The division of the world by the secessionaries thus presupposes a deeper distinction; only through this distinction was the separation of those practising elsewhere from those continuing in the old place able to take on its full radicality. This distinction can be compared to cutting out a figure from a larger picture – or punching a piece of a certain shape out of some rolled-out dough. The primordial difference does indeed result from a form of subtraction where the thinking and practising individual removes themselves from their first surroundings ethically, logically and ontologically; were this not the case, they could not want to distance themselves physically and affectively too. This self-extraction is based on the distinction between two radically different spheres of influence in the existent: the sphere of influence of my own powers and the sphere of influence of all other powers. At first glance, this must result in a radically asymmetrical, almost self-annihilating division, as my power and my significance, compared to that of all other spheres and powers, are virtually zero.

On the other hand, this distinction assigns a significance to me – though not necessarily a power – that is virtually infinite, because, for the first time, my own sphere is placed as a counterweight to the sphere of the non-own, very much as if to convince me to set myself and what is mine again 'the rest of the world'. Through the ethical division, the minuteness of the own is placed in the difficult situation of having to balance out the monstrous block of the non-own.

Whatever one chooses to call this event – the invention of the inner human, the entrance into the inner-world illusion, the doubling of the world through introjection, the birth of psychologism from the spirit of the exterior's reification, the meta-cosmic revolution of the soul or the triumph of higher anthropotechnics – its concrete meaning is the invention of the individual through the isolating emphasis of its sphere of influence and experience from that of all other world facts. I shall use the word 'subject' for the agent that cuts itself out and the term 'subjectivism' for the cutting-out as such, without burdening them with loans from German Idealism or memories of Heidegger's critique of modern 'subjectivism'. It is sufficient to take a 'subject', as explained above, as the carrier of exercise sequences. The basic subject-forming exercise of which I will speak in the following is clearly none other than the methodically performed withdrawal from the complex of shared situations one calls 'life' or 'the world'. From now on, 'being in the world' will mean *suum tantum curare*: to care for what is one's own and nothing else, against all dissipation into the non-own.

By separating my power and its jurisdiction from all other powers and competencies, I open up a narrowly defined sphere of influence in which my ability, my wanting, but above all my mission to shape my own existence ascend, as it were, to autonomous rule. The critical distinction that enables this promotion made its first explicit appearance on Western soil among the Stoics, who, in a perpetual exercise, put all their energy into separating the things that depend on us from those that do not. Own or non-own – this is the question that provides the sharp-edged canon, the yardstick for measuring all circumstances. This cut divides the universe into two areas, from which the operator naturally only chooses their own half, the one that is decisive for themselves. That is why the typical axioms of the Stoics begin with 'It is in your power . . .'

One notorious passage from Epictetus' practice instructions recounts how an apprentice cuts himself out of the world in the workshop of self-acquisition and uncouples himself from the hubbub of daily affairs through conscious de-participation:

> As soon as you go out in the morning, examine every man whom you see, every man whom you hear, answer as to a question, What have you seen? A handsome man or woman? Apply the rule. Is this independent of the will, or dependent? Independent. Take it away! What have you seen? A man lamenting over the death of a child. Apply the rule. Death is a thing independent of the will. Take it away! Has the proconsul met you? Apply the rule. What kind of a thing is a proconsul's office? Independent of the will or dependent on it? Independent. Take this

away also; it does not stand examination; cast it away; it is nothing to you!

If we practised this and exercised ourselves in it daily from morning to night, something indeed would be done. But now we are forthwith caught half asleep by every appearance.[13]

'Take it away!' is the central maxim of the first Methodism. Anthropotechnic work on oneself begins with the evacuation of the interior through a removal of the non-own. We now see what is meant by the image of the ontological 'local government reorganization' used above: it shows the turn towards that which depends on me and the turn away from everything else. The student of wisdom starts from the intuition that their chance is based on the separation of the two regions of being. The clear distinction between them takes on the greatest significance for what they do or do not do in any given situation.

The first is the region of the own; the Latin Platonists termed it the realm of the 'inner human', and claimed that only there was the truth at home: *in interiore homine habitat veritas*,[14] usually under exclusion of one's own body, while the yogis and gymnosophists of the East incorporated it into the interior. Within my enclave, there is nothing to which I can be indifferent, as I bear responsibility for everything here, down to the smallest details; for me, it is simply a matter of not desiring anything I cannot have and not avoiding anything that is meant for me.

The second area encompasses the entire rest of the world, which is suddenly known as the outside, the *saeculum*, and faces me like an exile populated by random things. What begins thus is the long walk of the soul through an 'outside world' of which no one quite understands any longer why it has receded into the outlandish – namely, because of the ontological separation of the non-own and the congealment of the previously shared encompassing situation into an aggregate of objects that have now become distant and indifferent. In truth, the protagonists of the great secession are doing everything to alienate the world; but they remain incapable of understanding how their own contributions ensure that, in the panorama of sensory perception, the 'objects' emerge and an alien entity known as the 'outside world' comes about through the sum of these objects.[15] Marcus Aurelius tell us: 'Matters outside our doors stand there by themselves neither knowing nor telling us anything about themselves.'[16] Subject to poor sensuality and meagre materiality, the 'external' truly has no choice but to stop at the entrance to the separated ego. All it is good for now is serving as an opposite pole to withdrawal, flight and contempt (*anachoresis, fuga saeculi, contemptus mundi*) – at most, it becomes an object of disintegrative and disenchanting investigations. Perhaps in a later order of things, when the ideal of withdrawal moves to the second row, it will be 'rediscovered' as the target area for care, mission and spiritual conquest. The decisive aspect is that the increasing insignificance of the exterior following from the secessionary distinction releases an incredible surplus of self-referentiality in the individual. Channelling this surplus into occupational programmes is the purpose of existence in ethical separation. Indeed: once the outside world has been separated from me and has become distant, I find myself alone and discover myself as a never-ending task.

Birth of the Individual from the Spirit of Recession

What I am discussing here using the category of secession is thus founded on an inner act that, for want of a better term, I shall call 'recession'. This first of all means the withdrawal of each person from the mode of being that is immersed in the riverbed of worldly matters – or, to take up the oft-invoked image once again, an exit from the river of life to take up a position on the shore. Only the recessive self-insulation can give rise to the behavioural complex that Foucault, following on from the Stoic principle of *cura sui*, calls 'concern for oneself' (*souci de soi*). This can only develop if the object of concern, the self, has already stepped out of the situational river of social life and established itself as a region *sui generis*. Where retreat to the self is carried out – whether the practising person burns the bridges behind them, as monks of every kind usually do, or settles into the everyday back-and-forth between self-pole and world-pole, as characterizes the sages of the Stoic type – it reinforces the emergence of an enclave in the existent which, remaining within the metaphor, I shall call 'shore subjectivity'.

For millennia, this subjectivity has been fighting from its precarious position on the shore of the alienated river for a language that is suited to its confusing self-experience. Its attempts at articulation fluctuate between extremes: spiritual-heroic overcompensation on the one side, where the foreignness of the outside world is meant to be conquered through an alliance between the inner and the divine – as demonstrated by Heraclitus in his triumphant moments and by Indian thinkers during the Upanishad period – and the flight to contrition on the other side, as if the impossibility of staying in the river of life could only be explained by a profound personal guilt; that is the path first trodden by early Judaism before Christianity expanded it into an avenue. Subjectivity withdrawn into itself comes closest to the truth about its situation when it asks questions that seek to get to the bottom of its difficulty in dealing with a whole that has frozen into complexes of external facts. Thus Søren Kierkegaard alias Constantin Constantius, representing a procession of shore subjects from several millennia, asks:

> Where am I? What is the 'world'? What does this word mean? Who has duped me into the whole thing, and now leaves me standing there?[17]

The Self in the Enclave

In recession to themselves, humans develop a form of enclave subjectivity in which they are primarily and constantly concerned with themselves and their inner conditions. Each human transforms themselves into a small state for whose inhabitants they must find the right constitution. No one expressed the recession imperative, which calls upon the living to govern their own lives, as clearly as Marcus Aurelius:

> From now on keep in mind the retreat into this little territory within yourself. Avoid spasms and tensions above all.[18]

This pinpoints the origin of all imperatives of self-collection, without which the subjectivity of advanced civilization, in so far as it is a product of concentration, could never have assumed its familiar manifestations. At the same time, it is in the nature of things that the micropolis which I am will have to make do with an interim government for a long time. This polis, after all, is usually taken over by its sole inhabitant in a ruined, almost ungovernable state. Spirituality begins with clean-up work in an inner failed state, a failed soul – it was not by chance that the young Gautama, the later Buddha, began his path to asceticism when he came into contact with the suffering in the world and his youthful worldview crumbled. Or was this collapse merely a pious fiction, and was the root of the later enlightened one's secession in fact the ascetic revolt against the idiocy of the military nobility's way of life?[19]

Anyone who considers a modern account more credible than an ancient legend can read how Bernard Enginger (1923–2007), a young Frenchman on the edge of a nervous breakdown who had been morally and mentally wrecked by his experiences in a German concentration camp, found a new spiritual composure through his encounter with Sri Aurobindo and the 'mother' (Mira Richard) – as well as a second name: Satprem. Whoever joins the path of philosophical practice, or Dharma, or Christian *exercitationes spirituales*, does so not in full possession of their self-control, but because they realize a lack thereof – and at once in the hope, supported by actual role models, of one day mastering the art of self-governance (*enkrateia*). The Hindu title *swami* (from Sanskrit *svāmi*, 'own' or 'self'; compare Latin *suus*), which can belong to a chief in profane contexts, refers in its spiritual meaning to the 'master over oneself', the ascetic, who has achieved complete control over his own powers on the path of practice.

In the Microclimate of the Practising Life

Enclaved subjectivity thus constitutes itself as a provisional state in which self-concern comes to power. The practising life form is like an inner protectorate with a temporary government and an introspective supervisory authority. In practical terms, this *modus vivendi* can only be established through an ascetic pact with a teacher whom one supposes already to have achieved ethical reform.[20] In order to keep up the enclaved state, a constant guarding of borders and daily checks for infiltrations from the outside are indispensable. The most difficult part of the withdrawn subject's task is actually to interrupt the stream of information that joins the practising person to their former environment. There are two weak points that must be kept in mind especially here, and present a constant danger: firstly sensory openings, and secondly language connections, to the social environment. Without a strict regulation of both crisis areas, any attempt at a *vita contemplativa* is doomed from the start. On the subject of sensory contacts, more or less all systems of contemplation show how they work at the interruption of the perceptual continuum – they close the visual channels in particular (to say nothing of oral or tactile ones), and prescribe a systematic withdrawal of the practising person from all sensory fronts until complete disaffection has been achieved.

This is where Horace's *nil admirari*[21] has its basis in life, assuming that life and *exercitatio* are already synonymous. Seneca occasionally mentions that with time, the sight of an execution should leave us as indifferent as a view of an unprepossessing landscape. Images like the 'inner citadel' or the 'inner statue', which were used to provide the meditator with notions of goals for their vivid self-perfection, were able to follow on from such advice on progressive apathy. Without a certain acquired heartlessness, spiritual attitudes like apathy, peace of mind or detachment cannot be realized. The ethics of advanced civilizations produces an artificial inhumanity, resulting in an equally artificial benevolence being summoned up to compensate for it.[22]

An even more important factor is the removal of the subject from the language stream of the first society, which would keep it shackled to the foreign rule of everyday notions and affects even more firmly than the sensory channels do. That is why all practice communities develop symbolically ventilated microclimates in which the ascetics, meditators and thinkers hear and learn fundamentally different things from those they hear in the village square, the forum or the family. This does not mean that a secret language always needs to develop because of recession, though there is no shortage of such ideas in many spiritual subcultures.[23] Even where the spiritual teachers use the people's language with enlightened simplicity – as is said of Buddha or Jesus – there is an unmistakable tendency towards the development of closed language game circles.

The Rejection of Self-Concern: Consistent Fatalism

The recessive subject can only work out a liveable constitution for itself on two conditions: firstly, it must be filled with the conviction that ethical secession can genuinely open up a zone of successful self-concern activities, and secondly, it must find a mode of staying in dialogue with itself along the way and enduring itself in its provisional state. That the first of these conditions can by no means be taken for granted, although it has long constituted a form of common sense in practising circles, is demonstrated by the history of fatalistic thought systems. Though spiritual isolation from the life of the people may not be entirely out of the question for their followers – fatalists can be ascetics too – an effective recession would be impossible according to their views. To them, the division of the world into things that depend on us and those that do not is an illusion: for consistent fatalists, everything is absolutely independent of ourselves, even our own existence, which is pure thrownness by fate. All human striving to break away and be free is doomed to be inconsequential. One may consider this position defiant and gloomy, but it is not without an impressive consistency.[24]

It is certainly more than a coincidence that the strongest teacher on Indian soil of a strictly deterministic doctrine of doom, the *niyati* philosophy, was the very same Makkhali Gosala who provoked his contemporary Gautama Buddha to the only noticeably irate polemic known in the latter's lifetime. Buddha recognized in the teachings of his rival the most dangerous provocation of his own system, which was based entirely on the redemptive power of personal effort, and referred to the determinism of the *niyati* doctrine as a spiritual crime that lured its followers to their doom. In Gosala's philosophy, the division of the world and the isolation of the recessive subject would be impossible, because no creature, not even the human in search of redemption, is capable of having an original will:

> All animals ... creatures ... beings ... souls are without force and power and energy of their own. They are bent this way and that by their fate.[25]

Anyone looking for proof that the Buddhist doctrine, in precise analogy to the Stoic, is based on an ontological 'local government reorganization' that strictly separates what I can achieve from everything else can find it in Buddha's polemic against the teachings of Gosala. According to these, every creature automatically proceeds through all the evolutionary stages – the necessary 84,000 incarnations, or in other accounts even the same number of *mahakalpas* or world cycles. Every life form and stage of existence shows through itself how far the process has advanced for it; asceticism can therefore be a consequence of development at best, but never the reason for it. Buddha could certainly not accept this. By attacking Gosala's equation of being and time, or facticity and fate, he secured the space for his opposing doctrine based on the acquisition of redemptive knowledge – and thus for the acceleration of liberation. Only thus could he proclaim the elimination of the ontological blockade through insight. Needless to say, Buddha's insistence on the possibility of a more rapid emancipation was in keeping with the spiritual needs of his time. From then on, the time of inner exertion was meant to overtake the sluggish time of the world. Where more advanced civilization begins, people come forward who want to hear that they can do something besides waiting. They look for proof that they are moving themselves, not simply being carried along by the course of things like the rock on the imperceptibly flowing glacier.[26]

The doctrine of rigorous determinism must have offered its adepts a seductive gratification, for it lasted for almost two thousand years in the ascetic *Ajivika* movement before dying out in the fourteenth

231

century. One can imagine what made it attractive. In all cultures there are individuals who feel a sort of dark satisfaction when they are shown that there is nothing they can do – aside from accepting what is the case and watching things take their course. The asceticism of Gosala's companions consisted in keeping up their strike against all feelings of desire or ability for a lifetime; the general Indian rejection of the phantoms of the ego may have helped them in this. One notes with a degree of amazement that ancient India provided the setting for the appearance of the first positivists.

Solitude Techniques: Speak to Yourself!

The second of the aforementioned preconditions for existence in recessive subjectification, the regulation of language, must be strictly applied and constantly reaffirmed, as the adept can only sustain their efforts on the path to self-governance if there is a constant flow of stabilizing information from the closed language game circle of salvific and practice knowledge. This requirement is fulfilled through the establishment of a methodically regulated praxis of conversation with oneself. Here, incidentally, one can easily show how and why the practising life, contrary to what popular clichés about the mystical or supra-rational quality of spiritual processes might suggest, depends very significantly on rhetorical phenomena that have been turned inwards, and that a cessation of the endo-rhetorical functions – aside from such rare states of meditative trance as *samadhi* – brings about the end of spiritual life as such. What is known as 'mysticism' is, for the most part, an endo-rhetorical praxis in which the rare moments without speaking have the function of fuelling endless words about the wonders of the unspeakable.

From the universe of endo-rhetorical methods – which are augmented in theistic practice systems by prayers, ritual recitations, monologies (one-word litanies) and magical evocations, which do not concern us here – I shall highlight three types without which the existence of recessively stabilized practice carriers would be inconceivable. Thomas Macho's concept of 'solitude techniques' can be applied to all these forms of speech; the term refers to procedures whereby humans learn to keep themselves company in retreat.[27] With their help, the recessively isolated manage, as shown by the history of hermits and countless other secessionaries, not to experience their more or less rigid self-exclusion from the world as banishment. Instead, they mould their anachoresis into a salvatory concentration on what is now considered essential. The central trait of the solitude-technical procedure consists, as Macho shows, in the 'self-doubling' of the contemplator. It offers an indispensable stratagem for all who are halfway along the practice path: it shows them a way to be in good company after withdrawing from the world – at least, in better company than would be available to the withdrawn individual if they remained alone with themselves undoubled.

Self-doubling only makes sense if it does not produce two symmetric halves – then the contemplator would encounter their own identical twin, who would confront them again with their muddled state in a superfluous act of mirroring. Those who practise successfully rely without exception on an asymmetrical self-doubling in which the inner other has the association of a superior partner, comparable to a genius or an angel, who stays close to its charge like a spiritual monitor and gives them the certainty of being constantly seen, examined and strictly assessed, but also supported in case of a crisis. While loneliness makes the conventional depressive sink into the abyss of their insignificance, the well-organized hermit can profit from a privilege of notability, as their noble observer – Seneca sometimes calls it their *custos*, guardian – constantly supplies them with the feeling of having a good companion, in fact the best, albeit while under strict supervision. In the Benedictine Rule, the friars were reminded that a monk must know that he is watched (*respici*) by God at every moment, that he must take into account that his every action is witnessed from a divine observation point (*ab aspectu divinitatis videri*) and constantly relayed upwards (*renuntiari*) by the angels.[28]

This plausibly shows how recessive subjectivity can develop into a forum for intense dialogues, even passionate duels between the self and its intimate other. As the Great Other only gains a clearer presence through retreat from the multiplicity of daily themes – a procedure from which psychoanalysis and related therapeutic techniques also profited in the twentieth century – the withdrawn individual gains mental intensity by isolating themselves monothematically. They learn from their inner other who they themselves are meant to be, and their daily self-examination tells them what state they are in. One must admit, however, that in this arrangement they remain a split subject for the meantime – they live as a solitary, perhaps not quite *coram Deo*, but under the gaze of the master or angel whom they fear disappointing. At this level of concern for oneself, one cannot yet speak of any unification with the Great Other or a dissolution of the duality between real and ideal self, as taught in Neoplatonism and the Indian schools of non-duality.

Endo-Rhetoric and Disgust Exercises

There are essentially three forms of speech that can be given at the inner forum as part of the recessive subject's psychogymnastic exercises: firstly, separation speeches, which are devoted to reinforcing the recession; then training speeches, with which the practising person seeks to improve their spiritual immune situation; and finally vision speeches, which enable the contemplator to direct their gaze at the whole and to the heights – and from imaginary heights back down to the depths.

Speeches of the first type are especially important for the stabilization of the recession, as they fight the practising person's inclination to regress to the experiential mode of the worldlings. It is clear enough that the position of exclusive self-concern is existentially far more improbable, and thus in far greater need of cultivation, than the formerly practised lifestyle of unspoilt participative pluralism, where individuals were allowed to unburden themselves via group drift, collective curiosity and mediocre diversion. Heidegger, following Kierkegaard's example of a philosophical insulting of the audience,[29] famously described the *modus essendi* of this form of self in his analysis of the 'they' in *Being and Time*: everyone is the other, and no one is themselves. He went in search of a path to authenticity that would no longer lead through a withdrawal to the enclave, but rather through a renewed participation in the historic 'event' that is elevated to the call of being. As long as the spiritual call to withdrawal applies, however, nothing must be fought more ardently than the constantly reappearing inclination to find ordinary life with its little refuges and communitary anaesthetics attractive. Whoever starts dreaming of the joys of ordinariness again after their withdrawal is spiritually lost. That the primitive truth of existence in normal situations, the participative embeddedness in natural and co-personal circumstances (as post-metaphysical spherological analysis explains with comprehensive descriptions), must be sacrificed is part of the price of life under increased vertical tension. This context demands the denaturing of normality and the transformation of the improbable into second nature.

Attacks of homesickness for the lost normality can be remedied through endo-rhetorical exercises from the angle of disgust arousal. They are effective because they fight the root causes of the temptation to find, on occasion, the external world left behind attractive. Thus Marcus Aurelius notes:

> Just as taking a bath seems to you a matter of oil, sweat, dirt, scummy water, all of it offensive, so is every part of life and every kind of matter.[30]

This shows in a highly suggestive manner how the genesis of the external also includes ethical and affective distancing mechanisms. Sensory disgust arousal is assisted by disillusioning and disenchanting analysis:

> Altogether, human affairs must be regarded as ephemeral, and of little worth: yesterday sperm, tomorrow a mummy or ashes.[31]

In this context, ancient atom theories find their moral place: they show how all phenomenal life is based on momentary groupings of particles. In the long run, only the spiritual soul can confront the *vanitas* of the particle flurries. One need hardly point out how much Buddhism owes to the use of the atomic theory, and more generally to the analytics of the composite – and how strongly the obligatory motifs of disgust arousal and disillusionment affected it. The doctrine of the not-self (*anatman*) so characteristic of Buddhism likewise has less of a theoretical than an aversive purpose: it persuades its adepts to accept that even if there were such a thing as the self or the soul, these would be dissoluble – which is meant to put us off the whole thing from the start.

The contemplation of organic metamorphoses goes a step further:

> Observe every object and realize that it is already being dissolved and in process of change, and, as it were, coming to be from decay or dispersion, and how each is born, in a sense, to die. [32]

In this context one can appreciate Ovid's achievement, the poetic retrieval of transformative phenomena. It was the honour of poetry to protect the space of normality from devastation by a disillusioning analysis that had got out of control. In addition, there is a wealth of self-admonitions intended to render any affective attachment to the non-own impossible through constant exercises in separation and disaffection – recall Epictetus' suggestion to parents not to kiss their child without bearing in mind that death could take it away from them the very next day. The practising person had to have such maxims of self-admonition and self-training 'to hand' day and night, like a spiritual first aid box – in the terminology of the school, such mentally handy material was called the *procheíron*, and whoever still speaks today of having some thing or other 'ready' is quoting the conventions of a lost practice culture from a distance.

Endo-rhetorical phrases with comparable tendencies can be found in abundance in the practice systems of Hinduism, Buddhism, Christianity, spiritual Islam and others. We are all familiar with images of Indian *sadhus* meditating next to pyres on cremation grounds (*shmashâna*). For the notorious Aghori, who fall into a trance state while sitting on corpses, the cemetery symbolizes 'the totality of psychomental life, fed by consciousness of the "I"'.[33] Shaivite extremists insist on eating and drinking from the skulls of Brahmans – and noisily bearing witness to it. One can easily imagine what they say to themselves in their inner monologues on the charnel ground: 'You must transcend all this.' Those with a Catholic upbringing will remember the Ignatian exercises, which constitute one great rhetorically structured persuasion of the meditator to participate in the passion of Christ and turn away from the recklessness of worldly life. In the Protestant camp, in Puritanism, the believer's day is structured by admonitions to withdraw from worldly temptations. Most people are familiar with the ominous processions in Shi'ite Iran, where grown men walk through the streets of their cities lamenting and bleeding, striking their heads with broad knives amid monotonously tormenting monologues to commemorate the martyrdom of Husayn.

There is no need to list examples for the methods of immunization and training speeches, or for vision and worldview speeches directed at one's own intellect. The two are closely connected, as the striving for a transvital self-securing beyond death aims directly for the highest-level symbolic immune system. In Stoic doctrines, this is presented as the totality of nature: dissolving into it must be viewed as the highest form of integration, even if it is accompanied by the disintegration of that conglomerate of atoms which I provisionally think of as my body. In Christianity, by contrast, death is understood as a transition from this life to eternal life. In those spheres dominated by the idea of karma, the final immunity is attained by disabling the guilt-driven causal impetus; thus only a life that had completely ceased to produce suffering would be safe from the repercussions of those products. In this sense, *Nirvana* refers less to a place than to a state in which all injury and contamination by the effects of being has ceased.

To consider such ideas of dissolution, transition and final immobilization existentially plausible, the practising would constantly have to call to mind their own finitude and endo-rhetorically anticipate its sublation into absolute immunity in keeping with the conventions of their cultural area. In doing so, they speak to themselves from the position of perfect teachers attending to this student as if there were no others. Recessive subjectivity always takes private tuition from the universe, from God, from Nirvana. The three absolutes would be bad teachers if they did not encourage their students to view the impossible as if it were close enough to touch; but they would be equally bad if they did not occasionally threaten to end the tuition if there were no clear improvements in performance.

The practising life is thus a continuum of self-persuasive acts. Without these, nothing whatsoever can happen among the practising, not even those who have devoted themselves to a largely non-verbal mode of practising, as is the case in the majority of Asian school systems. Many doctrines incessantly emphasize the vast difference between the desired inner states and the rational level with its linguistic reference points. Nonetheless, the cult of non-verbalizable states drifts towards an endless stream of speeches on stages and nuances of ascent. All exercises, be they of a Yogic, athletic, philosophical or musical kind, can only take place if carried by endo-rhetorical processes in which acts of self-admonition, self-testing and self-evaluation – in line with the criteria of the respective school tradition – play a decisive part, and with constant reference to the masters who have already reached the goal. Were this not the case, recessively isolated subjectivity would return to its diffuse initial situation in a very short time, mingling once more with uncultivated conditions.

The Inner Witness

One of the particularities of enclaved subjectivity, as noted above, is the technique of self-division that made anachoresis grow into the borderline case of an inwardly withdrawn art of being in good company. A deeper self-analysis by the withdrawn subject, however, shows that the doubling of the practising person to yield the observed self and the observed Great Other cannot be the final state. The dyadic relation between the recessively isolated soul and its inner partner transpires as a figure predicated on an anonymous consciousness underlying both poles. The dialogue between the ego that subjects itself to the exercise and its mentor, who supervises it, also includes the inner witness, which is always already present at the exchange of the two as a third factor. The discovery of the mental space's triadic structure simultaneously initiates the integration or transfusion of the Great Other into the ego. For it would always be hopelessly ahead of the dyad's ego pole if there were not some bridging third element, that field-shaped witness consciousness which spreads itself neutrally across the poles of the inner dyad.

Through continuous practice under the gaze of the Great Other, the pathological ego of the anachoretic beginner, who can initially only be a nuisance, a source of suffering and a quasi-external object to themselves, increasingly gains a share in the presence of the witness. It is this presence that is reinforced in the meditative exercises of the adepts. The autoplastic effect of practising ensures that the witness consciousness ingrains itself ever more deeply in the contemplator's bodily memory. By increasingly liberating itself from its pathological traits and de-reifying or de-objectifying itself (which comes to the same thing), the initial ego gets the unconditional presence of the witness on its side. With time, therefore, it can shed the pathological habitus of being seen by the Great Other. Among the advanced, this extends to the point where it might seem to them as if their first ego had died off and been replaced by a self that is at once supra-personal and more native.

One thing, at any rate, is certain: only a strengthening of the witness can bring about the integration of the meditator and prevent their regression into possession by the Great Other. The history of fanaticisms shows that such regressions are the order of the day in 'religions'. Fanaticism makes the triadic field implode – with the pathological ego eliminating the witness by directly appropriating the position of the Great Other in order to act in its name. In the light of this diagnosis, it becomes clear how far our claim is valid that 'religion' is nothing but a misunderstood mental practice system, and often a psychodynamically derailed one based on half-price asceticism, where beginner's mistakes and aspects of pathological subjectivity are elevated to the essence of the matter. The two expansionist monotheisms are naturally most at risk from such fanaticism, in so far as they do not make their quality as practice systems sufficiently clear to their adepts. They often present themselves on the didactic surface as a purely confessional matter, thus opening the door to pathogenic error: then desertion from the failed ego formation leads straight into possession by the Great Other. Whenever one sees monotheistic populism at work, it is another case of a mental practice system concealing its true character: once again, a training programme has passed itself off as a 'religion'. Then it is hardly surprising if agitation outstrips introversion. Indeed, one can wonder whether the modern effect known as 'religion' perhaps ensues only when an ethical practice programme is turned to the purpose of collective identity formation; in this way, spiritual exercise changes from a demanding form of withdrawal into the cheap form of possession known as confession. This 'faith' is hooliganism in the name of God.

Inquisition Against the Ego

In the same context, we can expound a common trait of all practice systems developed from the position of recessive subjectification – I am thinking of the ubiquitous, dramatic warning to apprentices to avoid the temptation that comes from an excessive ego relation. One could almost speak of a worldwide inquisition common to the Mediterranean and Middle Eastern monotheisms as well as the Indian and East Asian systems. Since the emergence of ambitious forms of existential acrobatics, there are notably unanimous warnings in East and West alike of the danger that humans could get stuck to their ego – or 'little I', as some call it – and thus fail to take their true place in both the cosmic hierarchies and their own social contexts. The global spiritual conspiracy against the ego is not without a certain irony, as it stems from the same movements that spawned the ego phenomenon in the first place. If there has ever been an ego that made itself the measure of all things, there can be no doubt that it was first and foremost in the radius of the egotechnic procedures described here – and only secondarily on the side of the world-people who fall prey to games of power and prestige.

The oft-cited ego is itself the shadow of enclavement – and plausibly enough, it steps into view because, after the ontological local government reorganization, the excluded self as such becomes conspicuous. As soon as the recessively isolated subject turns around, it becomes aware of its shadow – which falls, understandably enough, on the entire 'rest of the world'. If this is noted, it is inevitable that the individual will be shocked and accuse itself of casting such a monstrous shadow. As soon as priests and master teachers seize this observation, the accusation is passed on to all mortals – even the majority of poor devils to whom it has not even occurred to have an ego.

As far as the ordinary vanity of mortals is concerned, something that is so eye-catching for spiritual persons, it is generally not an indication of an increased ego relation, but rather of the possession of individuals by collective idols and their more or less naïve efforts to become like them. In reality, the phenomenally conspicuous 'egotism' of world-people shows an overwhelming of the psyche through an illusory image of the other – which is why it is usually simply a misunderstood form of invasive altruism, an obsessive need to shine in the eyes of their parents or the tribal elders.

The egotism programmes that are genuinely hazardous, by contrast, conceal themselves in the actual spiritual practice systems that are founded on enclavement – extending all the way to systems of 'subjective idealism'. Small wonder that they could only flourish under the protection of the archaic class order – most obviously in ancient India, where the tendency to flee from social restraints took on epidemic proportions early on, and could only be calmed through the integration of spiritual withdrawal into the normal course of life, as a form of retirement. Thus it was part of the standard Brahman's career that the married father or the mother of a family, once they had fulfilled their duties as students and parents, prepared in the third phase of their life for 'withdrawal to the woods' (*vanaprastha*), then finally leading the life of a wandering beggar (*bhikshu*).

In Christian times, the evasions of recessive subjectivity had to be balanced out with strong communitary counterweights, in particular the obligatory exercises in humility, whose basal paradox – reaching the top through degradation – is all too familiar. It was therefore indispensable for the internal stabilization of spiritual egotisms that they resolutely, even fanatically deny being such programmes from the start. One identifiable symptom of this denial is the beggar's existence, which became characteristic in both the East and the West of the antisocial or 'houseless' ways of life. In this historic compromise between withdrawal from the world of humans and participation in its surpluses, the radically practising had found the suitable form to persuade themselves that their methodical isolation was in fact a mode of living in the humblest possible way.

Entirely in keeping with this, the cutting-out of the inner region from the continuum of the existent marks the beginning of a pathos-laden compensation programme against both spiritual and profane egotism, without making ethical secession credible or even merely tolerable either for itself or in social terms. In short: the recessive subject has scarcely been successfully excluded and elevated to its exceptional ontological status before it becomes the object of a tireless propaganda of humility and self-abdication. Here one should no longer imagine that before which it humbles itself – the divine, the universe, the whole, the universal monad of life, nothingness, etc. – in the meanwhile problematic form of the external. The great humility-demanding entity can now only appear from the side of the self: as a god from within, a cosmos from within, as a not-self from within.

Hence the typical two-stage structure of subjectivity in the advanced-civilized space. In this structure, an everyday and illusory Little Ego must be set apart from a true and real Great Ego, and it goes without saying that the former is meant to be 'consumed' by the latter. If the so-called outside world still has any significance, it is as a parable of the power of the all-causing monad of life, as a source of transcendental metaphors of strength and a sparring partner of the soul, which wants to test how many things already leave it indifferent – thus there were monks who enjoyed boasting that they could spend an entire night lying next to a young woman without being tempted. As soon as the psyche has followed the imperative to change its life by embarking on recession to itself, it hears the corrective command to change the change. Successes in the striving to become holy must therefore not penetrate too far into the self-awareness of the holy, otherwise they lose their exemplary role for others. The paradox of this position is systematically obscured everywhere: that the holy man must not know about his own situation, even though he is the first who should know. Holiness seems attainable only at the price of mental shallowness, as it is incompatible with self-reflective individuality – a trait that, as a remark by Luhmann states, the saint shares with the hero of the modern novel.[34]

Rehabilitating Egotism

I shall conclude these reflections on the original emergence of the practice space through the secessionary movements and the recessive withdrawal of the subject as a practice carrier with a recollection of Nietzsche's efforts towards a rehabilitation of egotism after millennia of denigration. These drew above all on two critical observations that were frequently ignored in the history of the inquisition against the ego: firstly, that criticism of egotism was highly premature for most people, because they were not yet faced with the task of forming an ego that could cast a negative shadow in the first place. Secondly, that even among those who had developed an ego by recessively taking over themselves, this certainly did not always merit the humbling imposed on them by the agents of the anti-egotism inquisition.

This inquisition, as we now understand, means nothing other than an indispensable measure for darkening the basal paradox that the saint must not know that they are a saint, or, technically speaking, that the old-style religious 'virtuoso' – to use Schleiermacher's fatal term – remains condemned to conceal their virtuosity from themselves. Perhaps the right hand should not know what the left is doing – but the brain that knows what the left hand is doing has always also been aware of the right hand's activities.

Nonetheless, the saints could be plagued by the demon of self-reference without noticing its presence. This is revealed by a passage from Thomas of Celano's second life of St Francis (1246/7). In this account the young man, still 'unconverted', was imprisoned after a skirmish between the citizens of Assisi and Perugia and predicted his future in an exalted tone to his depressed fellow inmates: he himself was not downcast, for he knew that he would 'yet be venerated as a saint throughout the whole world'.[35] We note in passing that to avoid further evidence of such spiritual career reverie, the stigmatization with the wounds of the Lord, following St Francis of Assisi's great example, was the only tolerable form of pretension to holiness during one's lifetime, because it bypassed the self-awareness of the candidate, as it were, and presented the status of sanctification as an objective passion fact. The question of the stigmatized party's own contribution to producing the sacred marks has always remained taboo within pious circles.[36]

As soon as one understands that the subject itself is nothing other than the carrier of its own exercise sequences – on the passive side an aggregate of individuated habitus effects, and on the active a centre of competencies that plays on the keyboard of callable dispositions – one can join Nietzsche in calmly admitting what was unspeakable for millennia: egotism is often merely the despicable pseudonym of the best human possibilities. What, by the light of the *humilitas* hysteria, resembles a sinfully exaggerated self-relation is usually no more than the natural price of concentrating on a rare achievement. How else should the virtuoso reach and maintain their level if not through the ability to evaluate themselves and the state of their art soundly? Only where the self-relation keeps running idly can one speak of an out-of-control exercise. In such cases one should speak of an aberration rather than a sin, a malformation rather than a malicious act. Something that theological authors considered a major factor, namely the desire to be evil purely for the sake of it – including the oft-cited Augustinian *incurvatio in seipsum* – is presumably as rare as perfect holiness. Where people supposed egotism, and accordingly condemned it in brief malediction procedures, closer inspection shows the matrix of the most exceptional virtues. Once this is revealed, it is the turn of the humble to explain what they think of the outstanding.

— 7 —

THE COMPLETE AND THE INCOMPLETE

How the Spirit of Perfection Entangles the Practising in Stories

In the Time of Completion

The remoulding of humans as carriers of explicit practice programmes in the more advanced civilizations not only leads to the eccentric self-relation of existence in spiritual enclaves. It also imposes a radically altered sense of time and the future on the practising. In reality, the adventure of advanced civilizations consists in lifting an existential time out of the cosmic, universally shared time. Only in this framework can one call upon humans to cross over from the even years of being into the dramatic situation of a project time. The acceleration whereby existence frees itself from the inertias of the course of the world is characteristic of existential time. Whoever takes the step into the practising life wants to be faster than the whole – whether they seek liberation still 'in this life' or still aim for 'heavenly exaltation' (*exaltatio caelestis*) *in vita presente*. If even Benedict of Nursia, the master of Western monasticism, spoke of a *rapid* ascent to God, this was not indicative of his personal impetuousness. He was acting entirely in keeping with the rules of life in the time of the spiritual project. His instructions for a holy life followed on consistently from the apocalyptic 'soon' (*mox*)[37] and the apostolic 'quickly' (*velociter*).[38] Because recessively isolated existence itself constitutes an anti-inertia programme, its élan is always ahead of the general evolution. Existing and hurrying (*festinare*) are the same thing, just as the coercion to hurry and the will to perfection belong together.[39] This is where the seemingly patient East and the manifestly impatient West converge. Just as Buddha advises his followers to lead this life as if it were the last, the Christian doctrine, bringing together Jewish and Mediterranean thought, convinces its adepts that this life

243

is the only one they will ever have, and each day a part of the last chance.

I have attempted elsewhere to show how the longing for justice and alleviation of suffering in the first pre-Christian millennium led to the establishment of a temporal structure with a new tension, marked by the purpose of delayed revenge.[40] This temporal connection ensues because the pain of injustice suffered produces an individual and cultural memory that does everything in its power to inflict an equivalent punitive pain on those responsible. This leads to an existentialized time with a clear retributive finality. As not everyone who suffers injustice is in a position to gain satisfaction by their own actions, however, a large part of the retributive energy must be passed upwards and managed by a divine economy of balancing out suffering. This results in the moralized conceptions of world time in Christianity and Hinduism. In the former system, world time is compressed into the relatively short span between creation and the impending Final Judgement, where wrongful deeds will return to their perpetrators; in the latter, the stored mass of injustice itself propels the karmic process, which, like a permanent martial law, ensures that the moral balance of each individual's deeds expresses itself in that life during its early embodiments. In both cases, the lifetimes can be integrated more or less plausibly into the process of moralized world time.

In the following, I shall explain how this derivation of existential time from retributive tension, or from the transcendentally heightened demand for suffering to be balanced out, must be augmented by a second derivation from practice tension, or from the anticipation of completion. This is only possible if one can show the existence of a clear finality running through the entire lifetime of the practising. This condition is unmistakably fulfilled by the classical forms of the practising life. Just as the time of revenge is structured by anticipation of the fulfilled moment in which pain catches up with the one who caused it, the time of practising is structured through the imaginary anticipation of the arrival of the practising at their distant practice goal – be it virtuosity, illumination or alignment with the highest good. The temporal form of the practising life also inalienably includes the more or less situationally or concretely envisaged fantasies of arrival without which no beginner could set off on their path, and no advanced adept remain on course. If one can describe the temporal structure of a life subject to retributive intentions as a being-unto-revenge, the temporal mode of the practising life is a being-unto-the-goal – or directly a being-to-completion. It is characteristic of a 'goal' in the ancient sense of the word that it is already visible from a distance – hence the Greek word *skopós*, which emphasizes the recognizability of the 'target' from afar. The irony of the goals, namely that they lose concreteness as one draws closer to them, is usually only explained to advanced adepts.

Movedness by the Goal

One characteristic of the structure of the practising and zealous life in its initial phase is the ability to be moved by its goal-image from any distance. It provides the most vivid example of what is listed as the fourth causal type in Aristotle's doctrine of causes (after material, formal and efficient causes) – the final cause (*causa finalis*): while the other *causae* 'carry' the effect or push it along in front of itself, as it were, the final causality has the property of contributing to the effect in question through a pulling tension acting from above or in front. By this logic, goals resemble magnets, which irresistibly draw in suitable objects located within their radius of attraction. The only way to imagine this is that the goal is, in some opaque way, already planted within the body that is drawn towards it – whether through what Aristotle called *entelecheía* (which literally means 'inward purposefulness' and refers to being moved *a priori*), native to all organisms, or because a creature capable of desire is, at a given moment, shown a goal it did not previously know about, or of which it was not consciously aware, towards which it subsequently strives like a goal that can never be abandoned.

This second form of goal-directedness, this phenomenon of being moved by a goal recognition *a posteriori*, implies the activation of a latent ideal of perfection or the promise of an irresistible prize in case of victory – comparable to the *athlon* fought over by Greek athletes. What Christian martyrs called the wreath of victory, *stéphanos* (also a crown, and later a bishop's mitre), constitutes such a reward. Nowhere is the predication of one's own behaviour on a motivating prize expressed more clearly than in the well-known athletic metaphors of St Paul, who, referring to his later apostolic vigour, writes in 1 Corinthians 9:26:

> Therefore I do not run like a man running aimlessly; I do not fight like a man beating the air.

Here Christian determination is connected with remarkable directness to the athletic focus on success. This does not mean that Paul was especially familiar with the customs of the athletic world; he simply adopted the *athlon* motif in order to explain to his fellow believers the unusual notion of an immortal winner's prize as vividly as possible.

Concerning the Difference Between a Wise Man and an Apostle

What counts is the fact that the apostle himself is not speaking from the position of one who has achieved the goal, but from that of a practising person halfway there – or, in modern terms, someone committed – who is almost as far away from the goal as those to whom he turns as spiritual mentors. This makes him testify all the more emphatically to the significance of being moved by the idea of the goal. What early Christianity meant by 'faith' (*pistis*) was initially nothing other than running ahead and clinging to a model or idea whose attainability was still uncertain. Faith is purely anticipatory, in the sense that it already has an effect when it mobilizes the existence of the anticipator towards the goal through anticipation. In analogy to the placebo effect, one would have to call this the movebo effect. This is precisely what Paul is referring to in his exhortation to the Corinthian readers of his first letter: 'Follow my example, as I follow the example of Christ' (1 Cor. 11:1). The speaker's imitation-worthiness here lies not in the successes he has achieved, but rather in his movedness by the goal. Whoever imitates such an imitator of Christ is running behind a runner.[41]

This approach outlines the minimum for a culture of practice. It implies the elementary three-step structure without which there can be no organized guidance of practising beginners towards higher goals. The leader of the field is naturally the one who has fully reached the goal, the perfect one: in this case the God-man, Christ in person, 'belief' in whose perfection is already equivalent to faith in his relative imitability – as believing and anticipating, as noted above, mean the same thing in this context. The paradox of pedagogy in advanced civilizations, namely that it teaches the imitation of the inimitable, is discussed at greater length below.[42] In the middle of the field, here and everywhere else, one finds the figure of the advanced adept – in this case the apostle – who places himself as a first-degree successor in front of the main field, consisting of beginners and second-degree imitators, in this case the spiritually frail members of the young community in Corinth, who require guidance and inspire the apostle through their neediness.

What matters is that this primitive logic of stages, which lays out the simplest hierarchy, offers a project sketch that is intended to be realized in actually lived time. The things lying on top of one another in the illustration are projected onto the time axis, after which the beginner's position can be identified with the Now, the advanced position with the Later and the position of perfection with the Finally. From now on, onwards and upwards mean the same thing. One can say that encompassing practice histories are not only teleologically directed; they also show a latently eschatological structure. In this field, imaginary goals and last things show a tendency to merge. As soon as the practising person is concerned not simply with the learning of an art or craft as a process that can be concluded with the attainment of mastery, but rather with the existential art in which life as a whole strives for elevation and transfiguration, death and perfection inevitably come into contact. This trait is shared by paths of spiritual practice in the most diverse cultures; what sets them apart from one another are the codings of the highest and last, the modes of approach, the number of steps to complete, and the shaping of the different degrees of harshness against which the advanced must fight. The being-unto-death that the young Heidegger sought to attribute purely to the thrown Dasein's awareness of finitude had been known to apprentices of withdrawal since time immemorial – though they admittedly understood it as a being-to-completion. Consistently, their existential was not thrownness; that, as we know, is only true of those who cling to the world. Their existence was entirely centred on being drawn to the highest.

Paul's call for the Corinthians to be his imitators, just as he imitated Christ, makes it clear how the formation of stages is controlled from the middle. The middle is what lies below the perfect and ahead of the beginnings. Unlike in the Indian world, however, where the licence to teach is made dependent on the master's own complete realization, Stoicism and Christianity know the phenomenon of the imperfect teacher, who overrides his weaknesses by incorporating them into his teachings. To the extent that Paul felt able to teach virtues he himself did not possess, he could only present himself to fellow believers as a role model in the sense of a particular committed 'runner'. This indicates less, as is sometimes claimed, a proximity to the thought forms of Greek sports – something that he, as an educated zealot, must have loathed – than his talent for transforming himself into his addressees when writing. So here, speaking to Greeks, he experimentally became a Greek, just as he became a Roman when he needed to speak to Romans. It was, furthermore, quite clear to him that the perfection vital for goal magnetism could not come from his own person, only from the great model he himself was emulating – which is why he carried out his magisterium as a stand-in, in the name of the one who would really have been authorized to teach, had he still been willing and able to act *in praesentia* after the resurrection. Paul was painfully aware of his lack of personal charisma, and he was always aware that his slight appearance made little impression on others. Logically enough, he therefore shifted his claim to authority to hysterical apostolic speech acts from afar. He was able to incorporate such addresses uncontradicted into his letters of instruction, which are dated to the years between AD 48 and 60.

In analogous fashion, Seneca discovered the position of the advanced adept as a literarily fruitful starting point for a philosophical lectureship, and likewise distinguished himself from AD 62 onwards as a writer of instructive epistles. Formally, these were addressed to a certain Lucilius, a younger man of uncertain personal profile who had resolved to devote his life to philosophical exercises, but they were aimed beyond him at a larger audience from the start. In formal terms, Seneca approached his own role as an apostolic orator by speaking up as the intermediary of a doctrine of completion; he too drew on halfway experiences to initiate the beginner into the *exercitationes spirituales* of the school and attract a wider audience at the same time. He knew that he was still on the way to perfection, with a substantial distance still ahead. Nonetheless, his advanced degree of maturity allowed him to speak with authority about the highest good, which lay beyond his present status. Thus he asked, 'What can augment the complete?', directly giving the answer himself: 'Nothing – unless that which it augmented was not perfect.' 'The ability to improve is a sign of something imperfect.'[43] If growth suggests imperfection, then reduction does so all the more.

Death Exam: Wisdom Teaching as Training for the Theatre of Cruelty

Seneca's concept of wisdom as a goal of perfection is infused in its every fibre with the Roman principle of reality, which understands the reality of the real as the harshness of life. Thus education to reality always meant preparation for an examination in tolerating cruelties. While Roman power is exerted as a collaboration with fate, Roman wisdom can only be proved as an unwavering resistance to the power of fate; this especially concerns the type of fate that people suffer through the wilfulness of others. No other culture was so skilled at turning terror into theatre and placing the taking of life at the centre of public rituals. Where else could one observe such a unity of entertainment and massacre?

Where one conceives the world after the image of a theatre of cruelty, the wise man can only be presented on such a stage as an actor. No simulations are permitted on this stage, as the games appear realer than life itself. While life is only cruel on occasion, the Roman arena elevates cruelty to a central principle and a routine, extending to the actual butchery in the sand and the genuine tortures at the ramp. On a world stage of this type, there is only one difference that makes a difference: that between the standing, who will still be upright at the end, and the falling, who stay fallen.[44] Consequently, wisdom can only be invoked here with the image of standing upright – if there was ever a substance prior to Hegel that needed to be developed as a subject, it is the one that presented itself in the figure of the Stoic seer. This is why Seneca says that it is not surprising if someone who is not tested goes about their life quietly; what is amazing is when 'someone stands up (*extolli*) while everyone allows themselves to be kept down (*deprimuntur*), and stays standing while everyone is lying on the ground: *ibi stare ubi omnes iacent*'.[45] The only risk posed by torture is that it could break the organ of upright stance, namely the spirit. The completely wise man, however, is the epitome of intransigence: 'He stands there upright under any given load. Nothing makes him smaller, nothing that has to be carried displeases him [. . .] he knows that he lives to carry a burden.'[46]

Like Paul, Seneca requires a solid embodiment of perfection in an exemplary individual for the credibility of his message, even though he cannot point – like the apostle – to a master of constancy whose *stabilitas* extended beyond death. Thus the author contents himself with invoking the ideal, which would still be equally binding for us if there had never been a perfect sage. The Stoics' victories over death require the participation of the practising person in a different mode of perfection: they aim for a non-Christian *savoir mourir*. Their appeal is directed at a *summum bonum* that resides in the developed human mind (*mens*). As long as this mind has not worked its way to complete self-confidence, it continues to know uncertainty and fleetingness (*volutatio*). If it is perfect, it enters a lasting state of immobile solidity (*immota stabilitas*)[47] – and in the Roman context, as noted above, *stabilitas* always means resistance to torture in the death exam. In this criterion alone lies the difference between a completely wise (*sapiens*) and an advanced (*proficiens*) individual. If Seneca considered himself one of the latter, it was undoubtedly because he could look back on decades of serious philosophical practice. Even after so long a time, however, he was forced to admit that he had so far only been able to talk himself (*suadere*) into believing what was best for him; in all those years, he did not manage to achieve a complete persuasion (*persuasio*). And even successful self-persuasion would still, as he knew, not have brought him to his goal, for this would only be achieved when his wisdom teaching had become completely ingrained in him and available (*parata*) in any situation, even the most adverse. It is not sufficient, he emphasized, to colour (*colorare*) the mind with wisdom; it must be pickled (*macerare*) in it, as it were, soaked in it (*inficere*), and entirely transformed by it.

Seneca's testimony not only offers an insight into the endorhetorical procedures of Latin Stoicism; it also shows an incipient theory of stages, with the typical three-stage structure comprising the beginners, the advanced and the perfect – though the peak of the final stage is hidden by clouds. As usual, the operative essential is in the middle, for only here can work on the assimilation of the improbable take place.

Seneca the teacher is charming enough to take his own imperfection together with that of his student. Hence the admonition to both: 'More than we have overcome so far still lies before us, but the most important factor in advancing is the will to advance.' The way is long, for what we want to win are not victories in the Persian Wars, but victories over the forces that have defeated the greatest peoples: greed, ambition and fear of death.[48]

Elsewhere (especially in letters 72 and 75), Seneca develops the outline for a five-stage pyramid by dividing the advanced adepts in the middle zone (*medii*) into three groups and levels (*gradus*): those who are finding their feet like convalescents; those who have already made significant progress (*profectus*), though there is still a long way to the highest level (*multum desit a summo*); and the third kind (*tertium genus*), for whose members complete wisdom is already within reach (*in ictu*) – 'they are not yet on dry ground, but have reached the harbour' (*nondum in sicco, iam in portu*). With each level of ascent, the practising person comes closer to the *summum bonum*, of which it is said that our desire inevitably pauses before it, 'for there is no other place above the highest' (*quia ultra summum non est locus*).[49] The higher the ascent to perfection, the more stable one's anchoring in a final immunity.

In its doctrine of the final goals of life, Stoic theology adopts elements of Plato's theory of spirit, in which humans, having a share in the noetic sphere, take part in its indestructibility. The work of practice purely concerns the task of turning listless sharing into clear co-ownership and minimizing the proportion of the corruptible in relation to the non-corruptible. The chance for humans is the transformation of an unstable *methexis* (share) into a stable *hexis* (possession, habit). They are meant not only to touch the higher sphere occasionally, but to settle there firmly and irreversibly. How this can be achieved is explained through the conventional circle of perfection: we could never perfect ourselves without already having a share in perfection; indeed, we could not even want to approach the *summum bonum* were it not already within us as a target image, albeit only darkened and broken. The purpose of all practice is to break this breaking, to clear the darkening, and to correct the deviation of the perfect into the imperfect that has been imposed by fate.

Curriculum Vitae a Priori

The wise man, then, is not an artist with visions of something new, but rather a conservator in search of the original state. The restoration of a concealed archetype is his passion. Whether the conservation succeeds is another matter, as Western apprentices of the *cura sui* have only a fraction of the resources known in the Orient at their disposal – they must seek redemption primarily in the automatization ensured by countless repetitions that are meant to ingrain the improbable habitus of inner peace in the bodily memory. Whether this meets the requirements of an *ars moriendi* worthy of the name remains uncertain – *in extremis*, it is the psychophysical constitution that is most decisive, while the lifelong habit of suppressing the fear of death and preventing our fantasies from making things even worse than they already are only plays a collaborative part.

The simple three-stage schemata already show how the lives of the practising are integrated into plans for ascent. Recessively excluded subjectivity can no longer participate in the conventional lives of the worldlings, and must therefore rely on special curricular paths. As the fates of the external human are to become indifferent, while inner development demands full attention, it is not surprising if the practising being-in-the-world consistently takes the form of an ascent on a spiritual or anthropotechnic ladder – and the advances in the field of subtle physiology, especially in Indian practice forms, must also always be taken into account. Regardless of whether one looks at Eastern or Western systems, however, it is evident everywhere that the act of withdrawal as such only marks the very beginning of a career. The real difficulties of existence on the shore of observation reveal themselves in the working-out of curricular steps. These ensure the division of the practising life into meaningfully experienceable sequences and the structuring of the journey towards the high goal in stretches that are congruent with the aspirant's self-experience. The chapters of this *curriculum vitae* correspond to the intermediate rounds and daily legs of lived life (and in bio-mimetic sports events such as tournaments and major bicycle races).

As soon as the motif of being-unto-completion takes hold of existence, it causes the projection of the vertical ladder schema onto the time axis. That is why ascent can be understood as progress, and movement on the *scala* as the course of life. Being-unto-completion thus becomes the most powerful 'biography generator' – to adopt a technical term from recent literary criticism.[50] It causes curricular effects not only in the sense that occasionally, ascetic projects indeed produce careers that seem worth recounting in retrospect; rather, the generative energy of perfection-driven life projects already refers to future life stories, as if these had already been recounted in advance. The practising person would then only need to enter their personal or spiritual name and the local particularities of their practice life in the biographical form. The schematization of existence in the step-based systems of practice paths extends so far that a person could only give their story an individual touch through an admission of failure, or by a description of how they fell short of the requirements for asceticism. The 'path' they have taken, furthermore, seems like a *curriculum vitae a priori*. All it needs in order to match its factual content with the schema is actually to be lived.

Needless to say, the dominance of the schema over lived life is by no means specific to spiritual lives; it appears equally often in the biographies of the other 'classes'. For as long as humans can remember, societies layered in classes have understood the fulfilment of the type as the fulfilment of the individual. Only where new fate-generators such as greater vertical mobility, differentiated educational paths, social unrest and epidemic neuroticism (with its side effect, the compulsion to compensatory self-invention) ensure greater variation on the side of lived life can recounted life increasingly deviate from the schematicism of advance biographies. This shift of emphasis manifested itself in late medieval Europe in the emancipation of the novella from the legend. It was above all the modern novel that articulated the needs of individuals for non-schematic biographies between the seventeenth and twentieth centuries – not without creating schemata for deviating life stories, which in turn provoked new distinctions.

Wherever individuals submit to the call of being-unto-completion, the absolute imperative 'You must change your life!' is concretized into the ascetic or perfectionist imperative: 'Always behave in such a way that the account of your development could serve as the schema for a generalizable history of completion!' This call to an exemplary life takes its addressees out of the natural and people's histories once and for all, placing them instead under the star of completion. This may have been called the star of redemption in some spiritual communities – it is the same heavenly body, and approaching it follows the same law of existence in the vertical. Hence approaching a star – and only this! – is the primary motto of existence in the time of completion. Heidegger, however – to whom we owe this turn of phrase – concealed this star behind a seemingly impenetrable cloud cover in his early work and camouflaged the indirect approaching thereof under the pseudo-fatalistic formula 'being-unto-death'. In reality, even the young Heidegger had not entirely lost sight of the noble death that faces the individual as a death of completion, and the only substantial concession to modernity's breakdowns of meaning that he was prepared to make in the shadow of the World War consisted in showing the impenetrable facticity of the end as emphatically as that of the beginning: where there are thrown people, there are also fallen ones. Consequently he ascribed a certain purpose of completion to premature and externalized death, so that every death implicitly revealed an element of complete incompletion or incomplete completion.[51]

In the older traditions, approaching the star of completion (or the ascent to the summit of perfection – *ad celsitudinem perfectionis*[52]) took place under a protocol documented as much by the manifold monastic rules and books of exercises in the Christian hemisphere as the incomprehensibly multi-variant spiritual curricula of the Indian world, regardless of whether they belong to the Yogic, Tantric or Vedantic schools. In both universes, the practising life *per se* takes the form of a grand narrative. The concern is the same in both cases: the assimilation of the split-off individual to the absolute.

Benedict's Ladder of Humility

Such similarities come about in two forms of asymptotic movement: on the one hand along the *via perfectionis*, through a constant increase in the powers that make us resemble the *summum bonum* or final life monad, and on the other hand along the *via humilitatis*, where the adept discards their self on the assumption that the old ego will sooner or later be replaced by the absolute self or nothingness. The first movement is translated into a novel of achievement with a markedly forward-striving finality – I attempted earlier on to show elements of this in the two great death scenes of Old Europe, the death of Socrates and the crucifixion of Christ in John's account; by contrast, the second movement must, in a sort of backward motion, be recounted as the history of a progressive self-evacuation. While the first form is intended to 'realize' the hidden God-man beneath the mask of trivial humaneness, the second depends on taking the sensory or empirical human to the point where their 'own' entirely disappears and is replaced by the Great Other, or great not-self.

I would like to show with an example from the early days of Western monasticism how the exchange of the profane subject for the higher self was envisaged in the Christian tradition. In the decisive seventh chapter of his *Regula*, 'On Humility', Benedict of Nursia outlines a twelve-step de-selfing course that he presents as a monastic analogy to the ladder that appeared to Jacob in a dream. This exercise in humility is described as a paradoxical ladder which the monk ascends to the extent that he learns to denigrate himself – or rather the natural human within him. While both ascending and descending angels can be seen on Jacob's Ladder, in keeping with the different angelic functions, Benedict rather wilfully equates the descending angels with hubristic souls – of which, following the oldest spiritual suggestion, one can then say that their downward motion is the just punishment for *superbia* – with no further thought for the possibility that descending angels could be selfless messengers in field service. The only true verticality is that which allows the practising to ascend self-humbling (*humilitate ascendere*).[53]

On the first step – in fear and trembling – the pact with the observer beyond is sealed and the decision to renounce personal will is resolutely made. On the second, the abandonment of one's own will (*propria voluntas*) is put into action. On the third, the inner submission of the adept to the higher authority is completed – comparable to a first instalment of the *imitatio Christi*. The fourth step serves to heighten obedience, not least in situations where the natural self tends to rebel against unjust treatment. On the fifth, all evil and base stirrings of the heart are confessed to the abbot: the beginning of sacred psychoanalysis. On the sixth, the monk reaches the moment when he is satisfied with the thought that he is the lowest and last of all. With a first light of insight, he now repeats the words of the prophet: 'I have become nothing and know nothing' (*Ad nihilum redactus sum et nescivi*). The seventh step sees the *monacus* entirely infused with the truth to which his lips testified on the sixth. He now says openly: 'I am a worm and not a man' (*sum vermis et non homo*). On the eighth step, the monk has learned to be no more than an organ of monastic life: he does only what the rule demands – not in the mode of service according to regulations, but rather in the spirit of highly motivated availability. On the ninth, tenth and eleventh steps – described by Benedict with conspicuous haste, and written after one another without any real sense of progression (presumably because he took these passages, like some of the preceding ones, somewhat mechanically from the analogous sections of Cassian's *Regula*) – it is emphasized how important it is to reinforce silence and suppress unruly laughter. This means that whoever values the *imitatio Christi* must reduce their words until nothing issues from their mouth except what is exemplary and necessary for salvation.

Finally arriving at the goal, the twelfth step, the monk who has emerged from the Benedictine mould has become the perfect image of monasticism, his gaze ever lowered to the ground, a sinner and accused at every moment, bent and humbled, *incurvatus et humiliatus*.[54] And yet, by the end of the course, love is supposed to have driven out fear; the lightness of the detached would have replaced constant effort. This lightness is the signature of spiritual success: where there was fear and trembling, there shall now be effortlessness. Instead of fearing hell, one is now a friend of the Lord.

At this point – to label the culmination – we encounter the central anthropotechnic principle of *bona consuetudo*: good habit. Tellingly, the ending of this treatise on perfection contains not a word about illumination, completion or transfiguration. The description 'perfect' can no longer be applied to the human carrier, only to their most important quality, the love of God (*caritas dei*), of which it is said that because it is perfect (*perfecta*), it wards off all fear. The word *timor* stands for the sum of pathological affects by which the beginner felt possessed; one who has reached the goal will no longer discover any trace of them in himself. He has ceased to be the psychopath of God, and is now himself godlike through the easiest availability, pure kindness and collected spontaneity – though the creative, expressive dimension is excluded by the unflinching precept of *taciturnitas*.[55] If he has come to resemble the Highest, it is not on the side of the father but of the son, obedient to the end. The transformation of the monk into the living statue of the penitent guarantees that he ascends to the highest *gradus* on the *scala* without any danger of pride. This is the level at which the impossible has become easy, the wondrous has become habit, and detachment has become everyday: *velut naturaliter*, the monk is already living here as if he were yonder.

Scala Paradisi: Anachoretic Psychoanalysis

Perhaps too little attention has been paid to how far the Benedictine Rule fostered an implantation of the Orient into the path of the West. The immeasurable successes of this monastic rule led to that translation of the desert without which the older European culture of subjectivity would be inconceivable. It was only with Luther's Reformation that the Orient was driven out of newer Christianity – and along with it the priority of monastic strivings for salvation over lay spirituality. The anachoresis of the patriarch Antonius was certainly Eastern, for he transformed the desert into a spiritual palaestra, a training hall for demonic agons; the gymnosophic and semi-Yogic excesses of the Syrian pillar saints, whose reputation extended to Britain and India, was Eastern; the transformation of hermitdom in the rigid monastic barracks system of the early cenobites (from *koinos bios*, 'shared life'), which provided the matrix for obedient communism, was Eastern;[56] the idea of unconditional obedience, which followed from the transformation of the spiritual teacher into the *dominus*, the sole ruler of the soul, was Eastern; and, not least, the over-enthusiastic idea of forcing salvation during one's lifetime, as evident in the crypto-angelistic concepts typical of the time, which stated that it was possible to exchange the profane ego for a holy selfness at the end of laborious asceticisms, was Eastern.

The master of early Catholic orientalism was undoubtedly St John Climacus (*c*.525–605), abbot of the monastery on Mount Sinai from around 580 onwards, author of the *plákes pneumatikaí* – 'spiritual tablets' – whose first scribes gave the name *klimax*, 'the ladder', which in Latin became the *scala*, that is to say the *Scala Paradisi*. The work stands out from the flood of monastic literature not only through the power of its language and its conceptual confidence, but even more through its masterful overview of monastic psychagogics. It offers no less than a sum of the anachoretic psychoanalyses that had developed in the Christian East in the wake of Athanasius' *Life of Anthony*, in a learning process that spanned several centuries. In the psychagogic analyses, everything revolves around uncovering and heightening the awareness of sin, struggling against the resistance of pride, avoiding depression (*akédia*) and greed (*gastrimargía, gula*), as well as healing the soul through the complete elimination of pathological fear. Here too, the fact that completion is described with the term *apátheia*, or *transquillitas animi*, testifies to the continuities that tie the monastic practice system back to the ascetic arts of pre-Christian practical philosophy and metaphorized athletism. In both cases, the life of the complete remains an *anabasis* unto death.[57]

This text shows as scarcely any other document does that Christian Methodism comes from the desert, unlike the Greek, which was at home in the palaestra, the stadium and the schools of the rhetoricians; and unlike the Roman, which never denied its origins in the Field of Mars – it is no coincidence that Cicero, among others, had already pointed to the connection between the name of the army (*exercitus*) and its specific training, the drill (*exercitatio*). And naturally the connection to Jacob's dream image in Bethel cannot be omitted. In the *Spiritual Tablets*, the monastic mystical narrative of the long migration of the soul also appears, beginning with the obligatory exodus from Egypt – and Egypt is to be found wherever there is a conceptually, morally and emotionally alienated 'outside world' – ending with 'the resurrection of the soul before the general resurrection'[58] and its retreat to the heaven of apathy, in the closest possible similarity to the image of God (*homoíosis theou, similitudo Dei*).

The thirty *logoi* or chapters of the *scala* were already equated early on with the steps (*gradus*) of the heavenly ladder, even though the order of chapters does not always form a systematically developing curriculum – otherwise it would scarcely be imaginable that the prayer on which John writes such exalted words is only mentioned on the third-last step. As in the chapter on humility in the Benedictine Rule, the *scala* of the Sinaite monks constitutes a ladder of humbling whose first rungs consist in the renunciation of worldly life, the discarding of social cares and the embarking on a pilgrimage – the *peregrinatio* is here simply equated with flight from the times (*fuga saeculi*) and the entrance into 'religious life'.[59] This, furthermore, makes it clear once again that when earlier authors use the epithet *religiosus* they are referring exclusively to the monastic and ascetic *modus vivendi*, with the modern scarecrow 'religion' far in the distance. Even as late as Diderot, the nun was simply called *La religieuse*, which meant a person who has chosen world renunciation as their profession – with tragic consequences in this particular case. If there is anything that must be completely frowned upon at this stage of incipient detachment from the trivial world, it is any hint of homesickness for Egypt.

257

If someone wants to become a stranger (*xenos*) to the world, they will regard the whole of it as a strange land. Whoever turns around will be turned into a statue, like Lot's wife.[60]

While the three introductory *logoi* dealt with the curative secession from the outside world, the fourth chapter sees the author summoning his readers to God's training camp: this cannot occur under any other heading than 'blessed obedience' (*de beata obedientia*). These expositions are not so much a step in a curriculum as the platform for the entire existence of these 'fist-fighters and athletes of Christ', whose aim is 'to shatter the iron breastplate of habit'.[61] This demonstrates that flight from the world remains insufficient if not assisted by self-flight. Obedience is the monastic code word for those techniques that are suitable for renouncing the old human self by every trick in the book. The collection of examples provided by John in this chapter, by far the longest of all, testifies to the procedural awareness of the old abbots who were entrusted with supervising the monastic metamorphoses. Here one sees how far the old self-experiential knowledge is cumulative in its constitution: after two hundred and fifty years of psychagogic experiments in the desert, the treasury of monastic empiricism was full to the brim. Those responsible for maintaining this knowledge knew clearly that all further ascents among their adepts would depend on the instruction they received in the first term of heavenly studies – hence their strictness, inconceivable by today's standards, in which the inhuman and the superhuman came into contact.

If there is a mandatory progression at any point on John's ladder, it is at the transition from the fourth step to the fifth, which concerns penitence and detention. Contemporary readers cannot help finding analogies between the description of penitential exercises and the harsher forms of modern group therapy, while the pathos of the sections on the prison room is closest to modern regression methods such as primal therapy, rebirthing and the like – though in both cases, the possibility of breaking the patients mentally through excessive tests is accepted with pious or pseudo-salvatory ruthlessness. The old and modern cathartists are also surprisingly close together in how they view the meaning of tears; the Desert Fathers had already celebrated the gift of tears as a redemptive dowry.[62] Sin, we are told, is not a single isolated fact; the entire old human being must be called thus.[63] In what follows, we consistently re-encounter the concepts of *áskesis* and *pónos* familiar from athletic and philosophical contexts.[64] Even the Stoic concern only for one's own things (*sua tantum curare*) receives a suitable place in the monastic code; it ensures that whoever cares only for themselves damns no one but themselves. That the sixth step on the paradoxical ladder leads directly to meditation on death follows naturally from the logic of contrition. The pre-emptive destruction of the destructible promises these lost labourers at perfection the possibility of approaching their goal, no matter how great the distance. The first semblance of a lightening, however, comes on the seventh step, in the reflections on the lamentation (*pénthos, luctus*) that creates joy. Needless to say, sorrow at one's own corruption will accompany the monk until the higher steps.

Theomimetic Radiance

I would like to dispense with a full description of the *scala* (which, in its further course too, remains more of a handbook of monastic psychology than a plausible novel on a journey of the soul) and content myself with a brief glance at the final steps. On the twenty-seventh step of ascent one reads of holy calmness (*peri hieras hesychías*), which is meant to be achieved after shedding profane selfdom. This is the state alluded to by the expression 'walking in the Spirit'. Nonetheless, one must still be wakeful; justified fear of relapse is found even in the cells of the most advanced practising. This is followed by remarks on prayer that are notable not only for their heightened tone, but above all for their late appearance, as if adepts were only permitted to receive this powerful instrument at the last minute – and yet the monks practise it from the very first day. The twenty-ninth step sees the triumph of the central term of monastic anthropotechnics: perfection (*teleiótetes, perfectio*). No other word can contribute more to the definition of this anthropotechnics than the 'theomimetic apathy' already mentioned in the title of this *gradus* – the calmness that imitates God. It is only with reference to this state that John can resort to so conventional and effusive a phrase as God's 'inhabitation' in the mortal human vessel,[65] though not without reassuring himself with the Pauline formula for the integral change of subject: 'I no longer live, but Christ lives in me.'[66] Apathy leads to detachment not only from human matters of every kind, but even from the memory of these. In perfect Platonic fashion, it grants the gift of seeing immortality in beauty.[67]

A meditation on the three evangelical virtues of faith, hope and love is reserved for the thirtieth and final step. Here, the human body is transformed into a living monstrance: 'For where the heart is joyful, the face blossoms.'[68] Some monks forget to eat and drink on this step – like Moses, who enjoyed the privilege of seeing God, they are surrounded by glory. Flooded with divine love, the entire being emits a bright glow. Now one can even use the phrase *status angelicus*, which puts Christian supremacism in a nutshell – and simultaneously explains how aspects of the highest can be present in the non-highest. Because the ontological difference between God and humans remains in force to the end, an intermediate element is required to ensure the participation of the lower in the higher. Assuming that angels are closer to God than to the human world, the angelization of a human being is synonymous with removing them from the human condition and transferring them to the trans-human register of being. At the same time, angelic individuation – if the spiritual authors have their way – is no more than the return of humans to what they would always have been and remained if the corruption of their nature through the *imitatio diaboli* had not interfered.

Perfectionism and Historicism

After these overly hasty remarks on various manifestations of 'occidental teleology',[69] one thing is plain: in the early days of the perfection motif, the focus on perfection exclusively concerned the lives of the wise men and saints.[70] The question of how the perfectionist tendency was extended to the 'people' and the human race as a whole, occasionally even to the universe, is something that should be addressed in the necessary detail elsewhere. At present, what is missing is a critical account of the shared history of perfectionism and universalism. Hints in this direction have been circulating for two hundred years under such broad terms as 'Enlightenment' or 'evolution', and in the corresponding grand narratives. Scarcely anyone would suspect in these the continued effects of anonymous ideas of perfection, hatched in the Christianized desert under strictly individual auspices and concerning the individual soul. It was only because the soul had gained a history there that the church, the ferry to the beyond, could conquer an analogous historicity. As church history could not keep its secret of perfection to itself, it was disclosed to world history and published by philosophy.[71] 'Let us hasten to make philosophy popular' – Diderot's slogan would become the password of the anonymous perfectionists who, calling themselves Enlightenment thinkers, continued an old narrative form.

What we call historicism would then only superficially be the observation of all things from the perspective of becoming; in its deeper meaning, it is essentially the same as the progressive extension of the perfectionist infection to larger units – extending to the actually existing maximum, whether one calls it a people, humanity or the universe. As the curriculum leading to perfection consists of a sequence of purifying ordeals, the extension of the idea of perfection from the individual to the church community, and from the community to the species, amounts to a constant increase in the format of the collective that is to be cathartically tested. It was initially the hermits who discovered the desert as the stage for the individual purgatory; they were followed by the cenobites as the inventors of the group purgatory, known first as the *asketería*, then later the *monasterium* and cloister – the first training camp for group perfection and centre of religious communism. The high Middle Ages then popularized the notion of a 'third place' (as Luther called it) in the beyond, which was now officially dubbed 'purgatory' and in which – an early manifestation of democracy – the Christian majorities received follow-up treatment.[72] Here we see a transcendent transitional society taking on its first contours. The Enlightenment, finally, invented progressive 'history' as an inner-worldly purgatory in order to develop the conditions of possibility of a perfected 'society'. This provided the required setting for the aggressive social theology of the Modern Age to drive out the political theology of the imperial eras. What was the Enlightenment in its deep structure if not an attempt to translate the ancient rhyme on learning and suffering – *mathein pathein* – into a collective and species-wide phenomenon? Was its aim not to persuade the many to expose themselves to transitional ordeals that would precede the great optimization of all things?

Our experiences with 'history' and its goddess 'society' offer so little encouragement, however, that one can find the anti-teleological reaction pervading the postmodern (or post-perfectionist) zeitgeist understandable in every sense, including its exaggeration as the intoxication of aimless drift. Against the background of this disenchantment we can appreciate Chateaubriand's profound observeration: 'Purgatory surpasses heaven and hell in poetry, because it represents a future and the others do not.'[73] In the eyes of the Romantic, the future means the dimension in which the poetry of imperfection unfolds. This can be shared in by those who resist the temptation of both perfection and inertia – the hellish parody of arrival. Need we still say that Nietzsche was the last true historicist? It was he who, in a century of shallow general education, guarded the eremitic secret of individual purgatory, which produces the greater human being.

261

Indian Teleology

I would like to conclude with an overview of the elementary forms of Indian perfectionism and its relationship to the temporal structures of the practising existence. If there has ever been a form of thought that left even the escalations of the occidental being-unto-the-goal behind, it is the Eastern teleology that developed on the Indian subcontinent. It is a truism that the magnetism of perfection has had more powerful effects in ancient and modern India than in any other civilization. Indian spirituality is the planetary granary of narcissism – assuming one can free up this term, coined by psychoanalysis but no longer monopolized, for a new description of spiritual self-relationships in general

While Narcissus, the egotechnically unenlightened youth, leans over the water's edge and seeks to embrace his delightful mirror image – causing him to lose his balance, topple forwards and drown – the Indian contemplator bends over their inner self and begins to ascend. They waste little time with the reflections looking back at them, rather being careful to open their field of consciousness for the presence of the transcendent witness, though here too, it is initially and mostly amalgamated with the figure of the Great Other. In a culture where the number of gods exceeded that of humans, spiritual life inevitably became an endless tournament of Great Others – the pre-Socratic dictum that everything is full of gods applies far more to Indian than Greek conditions.[74] The consequence of divine overpopulations is that elements of imagining thought are superimposed on the pure expectation of the witness self. The theological phantasm involuntarily steps in front of the imageless presence of the all-encompassing soul in the individual soul. Removing such superimpositions and burning up the residues of pathological individuality from earlier life and current childhood in the 'flame of attention' is the declared purpose of all the spiritual techniques developed on Indian soil; gaining an adequate sense of their wealth of forms, peaks and nuances *in extenso* is an almost equally futile undertaking for Indians and non-Indians alike.

The beginnings of Indian anthropotechnics refer back to an archaic mental and psychagogic process that can be traced to the pre-Aryan period. It is no coincidence that one of the oldest names for the ascetic is *shramana*, 'the toiler' – a word that directly recalls the Greek *pónos* and the athletes who prided themselves on their *philoponía*. Supposedly the word *ashramas*, which is traced to the

Sanskrit root *shram* and collectively refers to the four stages of the Brahmanic path,[75] initially referred to the exercises of the ascetics and forest hermits; this also seems to be the origin of the term 'ashram', which originally denoted a hermitage, an ascetic's place of practice, before branching out to all manner of venues for meditative retreat, including the monastery-like settlements in the vicinity of a spiritual teacher. The parallels with the phenomenon of Christian eremitism are plain to see – and the affinity between athletic-somatic practice and Yogic and spiritual self-concern is obvious. The reverence shown towards silence both in India (where the holy man is known as the *muni*, meaning 'silent man') and in the Egyptian deserts points in the same direction. In both centres of asceticism, people had understood that any form of ordinary speech amounted to a profanation that entangled the soul once more in the very thing from which their withdrawal was meant to free them.

A brief glance at the vocabulary with which those contemplators had articulated their spiritual goals since ancient times already shows how radically Indian spirituality is based on the elaboration of secession motifs. The four basic terms of spiritual life – *mokṣa, apavarga, nirvṛtti* and *nivṛtti* – all belong to the verbal field of withdrawal, turning away, disappearance, desisting and expiry, each with an extensive apparatus of anthropotechnic procedures responsible for the assimilation of recessive qualities. Without further commentary, I shall follow Heinrich Zimmer's overview of the semantic fields of the highest goal-related words:

> *Mokṣa*, from the root *muc*, 'to loose, set free, let go, release, liberate, deliver; to leave, abandon, quit', means 'liberation, escape, freedom, release; rescue, deliverance; final emancipation of the soul'. *Apavarga*, from the verb *apavṛj*, 'to avert, destroy, dissipate; tear off, pull out, take out', means 'throwing, discharging (a missile), abandonment; completion, end; and the fulfilment, or accomplishment of an action'. *Nirvṛtti* is 'disappearance, destruction, rest, tranquillity, completion, accomplishment, liberation from worldly existence, satisfaction, happiness, bliss'; and *nivṛtti*: 'cessation, termination, disappearance; abstinence from activity or work; leaving off, desisting from, resignation; discontinuance of worldly acts or emotions; quietism, separation from the world; rest, repose, felicity'.[76]

If one wishes to follow the development of Indian practice cultures from the perspective of high abstractions, one should ask here too in what mode the original ascetic secession and the development of cultures of recessive subjectification took place. The fates of Indian anthropotechnics only differ very fundamentally from their Western counterparts in one respect: because of the caste system, secession is more or less inherited as a family legacy by the eldest Brahmans, and therefore does not initially need to be acquired through an individualized reaction to the absolute imperative. The answer to the call 'You must change your life!' is inherent in the Brahmanic life as such, which in its sum represents nothing other than a collective secession. In essence, it is the implantation of a caste of god-men, or rather man-gods, amidst and above the non-Brahmanic populations. From this point of view, the oldest Brahmanic existence promises a quiet growth into a firmly established structure of hereditary superhumanity. Just as one could define the ordinary Westerner as 'so politic a state of evil',[77] to use a Shakespearean phrase, which does not permit the influx of a single virtue, then the *modus vivendi* of the Brahmanic man-god could be described as a stable republic of unaugmentable merits.

The Secret of the Second Secession: Karma-Darkening and Striving for Liberation

Even in such a culture, however, the question of the personal appropriation of the legacy arises – especially in the time of social change, when the first individualization began in the early cities. Just as being born into a priestly house did not automatically solve the spiritual problems experienced by the sons of Protestant vicars, descent from a Brahman family could not remove all the uncertainties of life that might accompany the existence of a Brahman's progeny. The individualization of a sense of class superiority demanded by this can, according to the logic of the matter, only be achieved through an additional secession of the single member from the seceded group. This necessity of a second secession was the evolutionary motor of ancient Indian culture. Its initial paradox was that it alleged a seemingly unsurpassable peak as the starting point for further differentiations. Consequently, the only dimension of Brahmanic existence suitable for heightening and surpassing was the area of negative statements on life and the world. Certainly the earliest Brahmans were already familiar with a degree of world-distance; this came from the emphasis on the ecstatic departure from the world of senses – praised since time immemorial as the royal road to experiencing the final reality – but the priestly and familial ties affecting the heads of Brahmanic households, together with their divine self-assurance, set palpable limits to an actually realized flight from the world. If members of the younger generations aspired to a deeper appropriation of the ecstatic legacy, they were directed almost automatically towards the radicalization of withdrawal – not only in the second half of life, after fulfilling one's Brahmanic procreative duties and passing on the divine secret to one's descendants, but in the first, discarding the procreative urge and ignoring the previously unassailable passing on of the holy fire from father to son. It is above all through this – more than through the oppressive real plight that had always affected India – that the pessimistic blurring of judgement concerning the totality of existence was able to gain the upper hand.

Only in this context can one make sense of the otherwise barely explicable opening of Indian culture to the wheel of rebirths, an image still unknown to the Vedic singers. The mysterious success of the doctrine of rebirth can only be appreciated if one views it as the means chosen by the ascetics to advance the necessary darkening of the worldview in the spirit of the second secession. It provides the ontological foundation for the asceticism of the early leavers; only this asceticism could have an interest in describing the universe as a trap for the soul, a penal and illusionistic institution in which those who are conceived and born are all reconceived and reborn beings who move forward from one imprisonment to the next. From this perspective, the doctrine of rebirths not only articulates a sublime metaphysics of self-propagating guilt – in this sense the functional equivalent of the Egyptian-Christian judgement myths, and hence to an extent a vehicle for metaphysicized *ressentiment* – but is also the *conditio sine qua non* for the secession of a class of young professional ascetics. These rebels adopted the chronic resistance to the curse of procreation once it occurred to them to understand it directly as the procreation of the curse. From that point on, the reality of the real could not be defined alone by the misery that humans synchronically inflict upon one another; it equally asserted itself diachronically as a proliferation of stored guilt. Henceforth, the great watchword 'liberation' (*mokṣa*) referred less to the possibility of following on from the original ecstasy; instead, it changed into the password for the flight from impure and hopeless being.

One can see how liberation had to mutate into a phenomenon of *longue durée* under such conditions. As such, it was not yet suitable to be heightened into an existential project – for 'existential' is always synonymous with 'manageable in this life'. As long as individuals wander on the long tracks of karmic time, the pilgrimage to liberation is dominated by inert rhythms. Although, after the infiltration by the doctrine of rebirth, all substantial time was recognized as a time of salvation – and salvation should always be thought of strictly in terms of the individual soul – it was only the teachings of the historical Buddha that sought to exceed the limits of the inert karmic machine and ensure its standstill in this life. What is decisive, however, is that Indian asceticism, like that of the Christian desert, ultimately knows only individual-purgatorial tests and individual-eschatological salvations. If it were capable of conceiving something resembling a world salvation time, it would perhaps be most feasible under the image of a thick rope of countless karmic threads with varying length, colour and purity. India's immunity to temptation by the idea of a history common to all stems from the fact that its culture of meditation had already dissolved the phantom of a universally shared world time into millions of invidualized salvation histories early on – an operation that would only present itself to the socio-holistically enchanted Europeans, *mutatis mutandis*, through the post-Enlightenment of the twentieth century. Though it was deeply perfectionist, and in this sense historicist, it never occurred to Indian culture to acknowledge collective perfections as serious options. Its indifference to the ideas of progressive salvation politics was repaid by Western ideologues with the label 'ahistorical'.

Against this background, one can understand the mounting negativism that took over Indian spirituality from the days of the early Vedic man-gods onwards, finally maturing into the complete systems of mutually reflected world- and life-denial during the generation of Buddha and Mahavira (in the fourth century BC, according to recent dating). At the time of these great teachers, the impulse of ascetic secession had long spread to the other castes and infected them with the spirit of radical negation – certainly always against the background of the old, generally Indian concern for purifying sequences of acts and touches. Naturally such evaluations are always based on an element of authentic existential disposition. One does not need to deny the distress of the young Siddhartha upon his first departures from his father's palace, when he first saw the ills of the world in the shape of the sick, the old and the dead with his own eyes, nor his fascination with the ascetic, whom he supposedly met last when he left the palace by the north gate, and whose sight pulled Siddhartha onto the path of redemption. We must be allowed to surmise, however, that he saw the ascetic first, and that this encounter indicated to him the necessity of liberating oneself from sickness, age and death. No prince outside of legend would ever think of relating the sight of poor or sick people to himself. Only someone whose interest in asceticism had

266

already been awakened, and who is consequently in search of empirical arguments in its favour, would behave in such a way. A ruler's son does not ask for vaccines against the ills of existence; he is interested in a fight where victory seems nobler than a royal inheritance. The great systems of pessimism are less concerned with idiosyncratic tendencies coming from the existential disposition of the protagonists than with the laws of second-degree ethical secession, or the break with worldly life from the non-Brahmanic position. For ascetics who had chosen this gesture, the path to the negativization of existence was the only one still open.

These circumstances are expressed in all varieties of Indian perfection projects in post-Vedic periods. The highest goal – the unification with absolute reality, whether this was taken as the final self or not-self (in a systemically defamiliarized version: the striving for total immunity in being or nothingness) – is fixed *a priori*, and it is correspondingly stereotypical to state that people should go to whatever lengths necessary to attain it. It is therefore more than justified to speak of 'Eastern teleology'. Where such a high level of goal-awareness, even supremacist frenzy, belongs to the basic characteristics of a practice culture, it is inevitable that there will be greatly differing notions of these goals.

The Slow and Fast Paths

The fundamental division of Indian thought in terms of the conception of final goals was summed up most plainly by Mysore Hiriyanna: 'So far as the nature of the goal of life is concerned, the Indian systems may be divided into two classes – those which conceive of it merely as one of absolute freedom from misery and those which take it as one of bliss also.'[78] (The author makes no mention of the altruistic turn in Mahayana Buddhism, presumably because he views the elevation of sympathy to one of the highest goals in life as an element that is foreign to the basic Indian tendency.) In general, one can probably say that the more developed the motifs of world-denial and release from the compulsion to be are in a practice system, the more decisively it espouses the former option (which corresponds typologically to Stoic *apátheia*), while the world- and life-affirming movements naturally tend more towards a culmination of asceticism in a divine, even supra-divine rapture. Similarly, the affinity of negatively redemptive systems with a quick solution that can still be attained in this life is just as plausible as the compatibility between doctrines of final bliss and the slow progress of souls in the class-rooms of reincarnation.

With regard to the temporal profiles of practising life, no other system displays such extreme variations as Buddhism: wherever it mingles with traditions of archaic shamanic magic, as in Tibet, it reaches excesses of ascetic negativity that are unmatched in the world – here the salvific impatience of early Buddhism lost virtually all influence, while the fatalism of rebirth triumphantly returned, infused with the darkest manifestations of a life-swallowing sacrificial mentality. Even the most extreme contemplators, including those entombed alive and other athletes of self-elimination, are here faced with the prospect of numerous returns. Even with the harshest of asceticism, then, progress can only take place in small steps. At the other end of the scale are the reflections, typical of Zen Buddhism, on the question of whether enlightenment comes suddenly and soon, or gradually and late. Concerning this, the Chinese master Huineng (638–713) tells us in the *Platform Sutra*: 'Good friends, in the Dharma there is no sudden or gradual, but among people some are keen and others dull.'[79] The question left unanswered by this remark, however, is whether the detachment takes place in minutes or decades. But regardless of whether a school of Zen Buddhism favours the sudden or the gradual line, the movement as a whole, due to its basic therapeutic and atheoretical attitude, proves sufficiently impatient to be attractive for the spiritual aspirations of Western people, who only know life as a finale.

It would be futile to examine the procedural details of Indian self-technologies in the present context – firstly, because this subject would open up an ocean of differentiations whose exploration would require more time and energy than any interested mortal has at their disposal, and secondly, because almost every technical term in this field poses virtually insurmountable semantic difficulties for Western observers. What nonetheless seems familiar about the Indian practice doctrines is the fact that they too, like their Western counterparts, are almost universally arranged in step-based systems. Among these, the eight *angas* or 'limbs' from Patanjali's Yoga Sutras, to name only one example, have acquired a particular reputation: (1) the tamings (*yama*), (2). the disciplines (*niyama*), (3). the body positions (*asana*), (4) breath control (*pranayama*), (5) the withdrawal of the senses from objects (*pratyahara*), (6) concentration (*dharana*), (7) meditation (*dhyana*), (8) enstatic trance (*samadhi*).[80] As in all systems of progressive habitualization, the dispositions acquired in the earlier steps – especially the first two, which amount to a moral propaedeutic, as well as the third and fourth, which provide something like an elementary course in physical self-control – are taken along to the higher-level exercises, providing the base that can, and should, remain athematic *in actu*.

Analogous ascents are known from Buddhist self-technology as expounded in the *Potthapada Sutta*.[81] This nine-step itinerary of the spirit into Nirvana leads via the four elementary *jhana* or meditations (purification, concentration, emptying, purity), as well as the four higher *samapatti* or 'attainings', up to the final state, which is described as stasis in absolutely empty enstasy.[82] Naturally the law of escalation is visible in Indian step systems, which are prone to exaggeration at any time; according to this law, any formulation of a final step, however high, can be taken further through additional ordeals, iterations and increases in abstraction without anyone being able to say by some criteria – perhaps not verifiable, but at least utterable ones – whether any concrete content can be assigned to the additionally invented degrees of height. In Mongolian Lamaism, *samadhi*, which admittedly only nominally recalls the legendary final stage of Indian immersion exercises, is divided into 116 steps – an employment programme for numerous very full reincarnations.[83] One is inclined to suspect that some of the perfect grew too bored of perfection to put their hands in their lap after attaining it. Just as the Western world knows the horror of unemployment (the sociological name for depression), the Eastern knows that of an absence of practice. So what could be more natural than to raise the level of transfiguration? Nothing seems simpler than to 'reach' a Nirvana-and-a-half after Nirvana. Another motive for the inflation of perfections is undoubtedly to be found in the psychodynamic instability of the final states; Western monastic literature also had a few things to say about this in the categories of 'temptation', 'testing' and 'relapse'.

As far as the semantic side of Indian practice terminology is concerned, its complications go far beyond the familiar discrepancy between perception and communication. The world of meditation-induced states is a broad country, or rather a galaxy with unsecured routes and uncertain borders. Whoever travels through it can never be sure whether other travellers have seen or visited the same stars in the same Milky Ways. Though the masters insist that they have reliable maps for the expanses of the meditative space, only contradictory things have been heard about their art of map-reading. We would be falling prey to mystification if we assumed that the routes to completion all led to the same goal. In fact, meditation – in a comparable way to dreams – opens up a sphere of unobservable observations, such that here, as with dreams and their interpretation, one remains dependent on secondary reports and tendentious modifications after the fact. In addition, it is characteristic of mystical states that their carriers privilege silence as a form of communication. It would certainly be a mistake to conclude that silence indicates illumination. In terms of sheer non-communicability, any dim-wittedness can compete with an ascent to the third heaven.

Perhaps the misfortune of Indian spirituality was that it detached the culture of inner states too early and too willingly from the sphere of expression – this suggests that it was overcome by the immunitary imperative, *vulgo* by 'religion', which, as we have seen, one encounters wherever the interest in final insurance sabotages the affective and aesthetic charging of penultimate things. One can imagine how the alternative to this might have been when listening to classical Indian music: here one finds the most suggestive analogy to the chromatics of illuminations, in that it develops entirely from a dynamic of moods, swellings, cataracts and calmings. Though there are no concrete notations for the artificially produced inner states of ascetics, it seems clear that they contain manifold endospheres that remain as inaccessible for us as the dreams of strangers. We would know absolutely nothing about them if we were not ourselves capable of dreaming and gliding between the musical keys of mental life.

8

MASTER GAMES

Trainers as Guarantors of the Art of Exaggeration

Cura and *Cultura*

In its least muddled definition, the term 'culture' refers to grooming systems for the transmission of regionally essential cognitive and moral principles to subsequent generations. Because this transmission is always the source of serious intelligence work, all actually successful cultures sufficiently capable of reproduction develop a form of central ontological organ that passes judgement on the vital or non-vital status of 'things' – six thousand feet beyond the philosophical distinction between the substantial and the accidental. Thus 'things' are always already matters for negotiation in the forum of survival intelligence – in a related sense, Bruno Latour presented a groundbreaking reformulation of the 'thing' concept for the agenda of a world of plural parliaments.[84] In this organ, which in earlier times was consistently administered presbyterocratically – in councils of elders – and in more recent times with democratic tendencies – that is, drawing on a mixture of institutional intelligence, expert opinion and popular opinion – resides an unspecialized 'totipotente' power of judgement that attends to its duties long before the separation of reality fields into ethical, political and aesthetic. For the sake of calibration with reality, it presides over the two most important categories of practical reason: the judgements of emergency and priority. That is to say, it recognizes states of emergency and decides on the order in which the most important things should be taken care of. The fact that fallibility is one of its working conditions in no way devalues the activity of this power of judgement.

The 'cultivation' dimension of *cultura* here refers to the concern for the eternal return of the similar in subsequent generations. Where

271

cura and *cultura*, concern and cultivation, appear, they initially serve the purpose of similarity. Similarity demands that the members of a population always behave in such a way that the sum of acts in the group can produce a sufficient number of similar juniors. Whoever behaves in an unconcerned or non-cultivating fashion here permits uncontrolled growth that will more often seem decadent than original. In this context, we should once again recall the basic neophobic mentality of older cultures.[85] The wonder of later, liberally opened civilizations can be expressly defined against this background: it is the possibility for a given population to have become sufficiently sure of its reproductive capability, its didactic techniques and the attractiveness of its mode of life to be able to afford to dispense with the long-standing suppression of unwelcome variation and instead embrace the new, hazardous habitus of a broad tolerance for variation. This leads to the typical late cultural problems that occupy us daily today – they grow from the non-peaceable coexistence of variation-hostile and variation-friendly groups within a civilizatorily asynchronous state population.

Stabilized Improbability: The Erection of Models

Against this background, the appearance of early advanced civilizations seems all the more amazing. To define them, I shall fall back on my reflections on the stabilization of high vertical tensions in secessionarily isolated groups. On the basis of these, advanced civilization means nothing other than a system for the reproduction of hyperbolic or acrobatic functions in spaces of retreat for elites – whose general form appears in an ethics of stabilized improbability. Hence the acrobat, both in the literal and in the figurative sense of the word, takes centre stage as the carrier of a long-term near-impossibility – at the expense, incidentally, of the conventional equation of aristocracy and elite. It was Nietzsche who first noted that true aristocracy reveals itself in the way that, in the spiritual leader, the 'tremendous impossibility' of the task is translated into a refined bodily posture.[86]

We know, admittedly, that the stabilization of extreme improbabilities can generally only take place via the erection of models. Understandably, these are not only intra-familially transferable, but must be passed on via the collective imaginary, that is to say through the mental practice and ranking systems of a culture (short cuts only exist in milieus where family and advanced civilization coincide: among Brahmans and rabbis, and in Protestant vicarages). When we speak of models, we should think first of all of the exemplarily embodied types of the heroic, sacred and sporting *agon* – that is, the heroes of the battlefield, the god-men in the forests and in the reddish dust of field tracks, the saints of the desert and the monastery, and the athletes in the palaestra, the stadium and the arena. They all still have some of the aura of their predecessors, the miracle men of archaic times, the wizards and magical diplomats who negotiated with the powers and the demons: they had been the first to captivate those around them as rebels against the block of reality. It was only much later that artists were added to this list, each one of them a miracle maker in their own genre, and thus a blasphemer against the principle of impossibility.

With these figures, the roles and spaces of stabilized improbability in advanced civilization are sketched out sufficiently clearly. Once they are established, it is necessary to explain the modes in which the translation of the improbable and unrepeatable into the probable and repeatable – and thus the setting-up of the original field of tuition – can take place in each individual area. Initially, only one thing is certain here: what would be called 'school' in later times was at first less of a pedagogical than a thaumaturgical phenomenon. First the miracle, then education; hence the close link between ethics and artistry. When Plato and Aristotle assure us that philosophy begins with amazement (*thaumazein*), they are just managing to grasp the very end of an order in which all higher achievements were measured in relation to the unbelievable; it was only much later that half-price trivializations and imitations would be able to dictate the agenda. At first, certainly, the introduction to the improbable has nothing to do with guiding children; it is directed at adults who realize halfway through their lives that ordinary human existence is no longer enough. The beginning was not education but seduction by the amazing. The effects that move humans to secede come purely from the school of wonder.

Paradoxes and Passions: The Genesis of the Inner World through Chronic Overstraining

Advanced civilization, then, is by no means what Oswald Spengler claimed, namely the result from the encounter between a landscape and a group soul – or the amalgam of a climate and its trauma. Nor, however, is it simply 'richness in problems', to quote Egon Friedell's witty definition of culture in the sense of education. Rather, each advanced civilization is rooted in its robust ownership of a paradox that has been made capable of transmission. It stems from the cruel *naïveté* with which the basal paradox embodies itself in its early stages. The *naïveté* of early advanced civilizations is cruel to the extent that it enforces its demand for the enabling of the impossible against its adepts. Only once such hard starting paradoxes have relaxed to form problems can they be enjoyed like riches and collected like educational objects. In their early states, paradoxes are suffered as passions rather than experienced as treasures.

Let us say clearly where the basic paradox of all advanced civilization lies: it follows from its orientation towards hyperbolic or acrobatic excesses, which are always viewed on the assumption that they are only suitable for imitation or normalization. By elevating exceptional achievements to conventions, advanced civilizations create a pathogenic tension, a form of chronic altitude sickness to which sufficiently intelligent participants in the paradoxical game can only respond with the development of an internal space of evasion and simulation, and thus a 'soul', a *ba*, a *psyché*, an *atman* – or, more generally speaking, an inner world that is permanently reflexively unsettled.

The soul emerges as the entity in which the impossible must be called to mind like a possibility that constantly has to be considered. 'Soul', in the sense of a microcosmic or inner-world organ for doubling the existent as a whole, is by no means a timeless entity in which the being-for-oneself of humans from all times and peoples manifests itself. It only comes about as the symptom of an over-stimulation by an inescapable paradox – a demand that can neither be met nor ignored. The 'human interior' then ceases to be merely the transit space for 'upsurging' affects, something one can still observe clearly in the Homeric view of *thymós*, for example;[87] nor is it any longer simply the reception hall for the visits of demons, dreams and 'ideas'. It is more like a chronic inflammation of the self-perception, provoked by the imposition that the desire of the individual should align itself with examples that cannot possibly be imitated. The paradoxical inflammation and the stabilized for-oneself are the same age. Conversely, advanced-civilized ethics only becomes attractive by learning to advertise itself with the highest fascinations, with the physically and morally wonderful. The wonderful is the smile of the impossible.

It is only through the transformation of the unbelievable into the exemplary that the working climate of advanced civilization can stabilize itself: when it speaks to its own, it always forgets to mention the complete, who become recommendable for imitation precisely through inimitable achievements. As soon as the *akro baínein*, the gaze-commanding walk on the rope over the abyss, moves from the physical field to the moral, the paradox comes into play: vertical tensions of the most exuberant kind come about through the elevation of the inimitable to the status of the exemplary.

Twilight of the Trainers

Against this background, the figure of the trainer can be explained as the one who leads the way into improbability. In systemic terms, they have the task of making invisible the paradox of advanced civilization, where precisely that which is impossible to imitate is employed as an incentive to the most intense imitation. Here the strategy presented by Edgar Allan Poe in 'The Purloined Letter', where the most visible surface provides the best hiding-place, proves effective. It is characteristic of the heroic-holy-athletic complex that it conceals its seduction to the impossible under an elaborate legendary noise: first and foremost, this purely serves the purpose of making the contradictory nature of its message – which is immediately noticeable to the calm observer – invisible and inaudible through overexposure and overemphasis. Its second function is to mobilize the mimetic instincts, which cannot tolerate praise for virtues in others that are supposedly lacking in one's own existence. Aretological propaganda fulfils its purpose if, when faced with the question: 'What does the other person have that I supposedly do not?', it provokes the answer: 'We will see!' Admiration is the great vehicle of jealousy, which tolerates no absolute preferential treatment – and if there is one thing that goes profoundly against its nature, it is the private ownership of triumphs over impossibility accumulated by a supposedly inimitable other. The early attempts to scale the heights of improbability, therefore, are by no means psychodynamically helpless. All explicit advanced civilizations fuel themselves with a mimetic mobilization whose intention is no less than the dispossession of the model. Here too, silence is the first working condition: just as undisturbed 'cultural activity' precludes any exposure of its basal paradox, the driving forces of emulation also remain unconfessable.

Only on these premises can one consider the performances of the first trainers with the necessary scenographic attentiveness. Initially, the

275

only people eligible for such a role are the exceptional humans themselves, those who have achieved self-mirabilization, the transformation into the actually existing monstrosity. They radiate the numinous
aura that surrounds the highest magisteria. Because the teaching itself
is embodied by teachers in their mirabilic otherness at this stage, they
display a new form of authority – it is no longer the gravity of the
elders, but rather the luminosity of the pure exception that seduces
as soon as it is seen and felt. This results in the new, distinguished
pedagogical tone: 'I am the way and the truth and the life';[88] 'I and
the Father are one';[89] 'I am I, but also the other. [. . .] I am devoid of
honour and dishonour, I am without attributes, I am Shiva, I am free
from duality and non-duality, I am free from the pairs (of opposites).
I am he.'[90] A corona of pupils soon gathers around the firstborn of
the unheard-of, seeking to embody the privilege of emanating directly
from the exception.

The first round of the transference experiment had already seen
the appearance of a phenomenon that accompanies all foundings of
schools as an almost tragic shadow: the separation of the suitable
from the unsuitable. The efficient spiritual trainer not only develops
the prudence of the ancient doctor, who stays away from incurable
cases; they also develop the specific perception unique to the fisher of
men, who senses those with a natural affinity with the spirit of the
teaching among the merely interested. In scholastic times they would
be called talented, in the bourgeois era gifted – and, for understandable reasons, the abstractly universalistic *ressentiment* would one day
be up in arms about the concept of 'talent' as such.[91] It is not only old
Manto who loves those who desire the impossible;[92] everyone who
embodies advanced-civilized élan does so. What is more important
than loving the one who desires the absurd, however, is picking them
out from the countless cases in which it would be a waste of effort to
attempt a nurturing of the eros of the impossible within an individual.
Like Charon, the ferryman of the underworld who conveys a Faust
lusting after Helena, all the great trainers accompany those students
who will not cease desiring on their way 'across'.

Ten Types of Teacher

In the following, I shall sketch five types of spiritual trainer of which
each, in their own way, fulfils the task of giving exaggerations
that are *prima vista* unliveable and aim to give the supra-real the
semblance of feasibility and liveability. First comes the guru of the

Brahmanic-Hindu tradition, then the master of the Buddhist doctrine of liberation, then the apostle or abbot as *imitatores Christi*, next the philosopher as a witness to the search for truth, and finally the sophist as a polytechnician of the *ars vivendi*. It should scarcely be necessary to explain why each of these types embodies a variety of teaching licence at the enthusiastic faculty of our anthropological polytechnic. Going through these even more quickly, I shall assign to these figures an analogous five-member set of pragmatic or artistic trainers – the athletic trainer, the master of a craft or virtuosic artistic feat, the academic professor, the mundane teacher and the Enlightenment author. It is clear enough why one should expect shallower and more anonymous forms of vertical tension from the start among this group of certified teachers: they are all involved in the popularization and standardization of *mirabile* effects and, in one way or other, already on the way to what modernity – after the triumphant initial successes of general alphabetization – would later make its cause under the catchword of 'general education'. Nonetheless, these teachers also purvey a notion of peak performance, albeit one that requires increasing justification: democracy, they implicitly state, is not as such a valid reason to do away with all forms of vertical tension. They remain in effect, though in an altered mode – even if only for the power-ecological reason that even in a world with a strictly egalitarian constitution, not everyone will be able to do everything, let alone do everything equally well.

The Guru

The first in this list is the figure of the Indian *guru* – a name that is rarely used without irony in the contemporary Western context, as if one wanted to denote a person who gives their followers opportunity to overestimate them, and presumably not without succumbing to self-overestimation first. Naturally this habitual irony tells us absolutely nothing about Indian conditions, but a great deal about the anti-authoritarian change of mentality among Westerners in general, and about the decline in the standing of their teaching professions in particular. It reveals the scepticism that has been epidemic in the Old World for some time towards the notion that any mortal could have more insight than another into the basic conditions of the world and life – not merely in the sense of a coincidentally greater knowledge based on longer experience, but thanks to a deeper penetration of the concealed structures of existence. Just as the concept of the master is

277

ruined in Europe – the *maestro* in musical life being the one exception – so the idea of any higher teaching licence in existential matters has practically lost all credit. When Martin Heidegger occasionally used the expression 'master of reading and living' to describe Meister Eckhart, the archaic tone was already unmistakable at the time. In doing so, he was going very palpably against the newer consensus that the discipline of life is under no circumstances open to mastery.

The scandal of the guru function is easy to pinpoint: it implies a mode of teaching and learning based on an initiation, and thus a crossing-over to the sphere of sacred or non-public knowledge – it is precisely this aspect that makes the guru-centred study model of ancient India unacceptable for the modern learning culture of the Occident. We have introductions to this or that area of knowledge to offer, but do not allow any initiations – quite aside from the fact that enlightenment is not envisaged as the conclusion to a course of study. We also presuppose among our students the continuity of person from school enrolment to matriculation to graduation, while learning with a guru entails two discontinuous aspects: one at the initiation into the *modus essendi* of the pupil, which implies a form of symbolic death, and the other upon the prospective attainment of the highest goal, which Indian convention describes as the insight – gained psychosomatically and via certain states – into the identity of the individual soul and the world soul. This shows how the dramaturgical form of initiatic learning, beyond its trimming through the narrative form of a step-based life, is nested in a schema of rebirth – which is why its goal must be sought not so much in a qualification as in a transformation.

For Western sensibilities, the convivial or virtually promiscuous constitution of the Indian master–pupil relationship is even more scandalous than the initiatic alliance that accompanies it. As a rule, devotion to a master in a stationary Brahmanic context implied joining his household, usually for a period that could scarcely be shorter than twelve years – this was usually the time required merely to memorize the Vedic texts whose internalization was expected of adepts, regardless of which practical exercises (*asanas*) were used to carry out the psychophysical work of transformation. This household element of the master–pupil relationship implied an openly psycho-feudal dependency. Here the pupil not only had to receive knowledge from the master, but also to fulfil various servant duties – hence the Sanskrit name *antevasin*: 'the one who accompanies the guru and waits upon him'. More often, the pupil is referred to as a *shisia* or *chela*, which denotes one who 'sits at the feet of the master' – a word that calls to mind the memory of a lost world before the invention of the universal anthropotechnic device of the Modern Age, namely the school desk. From an attitude-historical perspective, incidentally, modernity is synonymous with a dependence on chairs or other seating furniture, and *eo ipso* the dying-out of the ability to sit on the floor without feeling burdened by one's own body.[93]

The true meaning of the guru-centred learning model, admittedly, does not consist in the cosy homely aspects, which from a distance recall the life forms of medieval craftsmen's households in Europe. Hence also the threat of terrible consequences for any pupil who dared embark on an affair with the master's wife – although this does not seem entirely outlandish given the informal situation of courtly love: a noble lady and a lowly aspirant in the closest proximity, separated by a strong taboo and with the attention of each drawn to the other. Its purpose only reveals itself when one takes into consideration the psychodynamic aspect of the master–pupil relationship: this is, after all, no less than a contract for the regulation of a hyperbolic transaction. As soon as the guru takes an *antevasin* or *chela* into his following, he has implicitly made a form of perfecting contract with him. This means a simultaneously metaphysical and pragmatic alliance with the goal of advancing at least a few steps along the path to actually existing impossibility, or even of realizing the *magnum opus* as such: deification in one's lifetime and transformation into the *jivanmukti*, the one who is saved here and now. The guru and his student thus enter an alliance perhaps not of life and death, but certainly of life and hyper-life.

Viewed by the light of recent occidental psychological knowledge, this singular relationship is a magnetopathic or psychoanalytical rapport – that is to say a stabilized state of emergency in the soul field where the master makes himself available for the most intense idealizations on the part of the pupil. In contrast to the magnetistic or psychoanalytical situation, however, where, in accordance with the prevailing norms of sobriety, the long-term goal is the dissolution of an idealizing transference, the guru–*antevasin* relationship aims not for the end, but rather for the clarifying amplification of that idealization – and at once an identificatory intensification that, if carried out in an orthodox and proper fashion, should be driven forwards into the supra-pictorial, pre-objective and pre-personal register. From the guru's point of view, the pupil's idealizing anticipations are not wrong because they aim too high; rather, the pupil is only condemned to a form of indispensable error in the sense that he cannot yet know how much higher the real goal is located than his dreamy anticipations are capable of imagining. Nonetheless, identification is the most important affective resource that is available for use in transformative work – which is why one part of the craft of guru pedagogy is to keep the fire of the beginner's illusion burning for as long as possible. That an institutionalized art of the impossible cannot be judged by the standards of Western trivial ontology, with the corresponding psychological constructs of normality, is understandable enough.

Such references to the hyperbolic dimension in the transformation contract between masters and pupils cannot, of course, refute scepticism towards the guru-centred form of studying. It is therefore anything but coincidental that a large part of Western writings, but also of the growing native literature on the guru phenomenon – not infrequently penned by disconcerted psychiatrists, committed social psychologists and nervous sect advisers[94] – is devoted to the problem of false masters and the psychological abuse of those dependent on them. The authors consistently postulate the reinforcement of quality control for products on the religious markets. They usually view the situation as if the process of globalization had also cast the spiritual world market into a state of upheaval. Just as some dangerous pathogens today profit from the facilitation of worldwide travel, the memes of the 'God delusion' can also spread more easily beyond the borders of their source regions. Even more disturbing is the impression that psychosis has got carried away, and is now aiming to change its status from a classified illness to a misunderstood form of fitness. Most provocative of all, admittedly, is the epidemic of mystical amoralism which, thanks to the missionary successes of Hinduizing masters, began to spread through the overly receptive Western hemisphere. The virus, which has nestled in correspondingly arranged classes since then, consists in the dangerous realization that lack of conscience and illumination are, from a certain point of view, identical.

The truth is most probably that the world of enlightenment games too has been affected by mediatization, and the appearance of performance talents among the teachers of well-tempered impossibility was only a matter of time. No guru's life from the last decades demonstrates this shift more clearly than that of the Indian enlightenment preacher and sect founder Bhagwan Shree Rajneesh (1931–90), alias Osho, who, despite his controversial status, constitutes – along with Ramana Maharshi, Jiddu Krishnamurti and Sri Aurobindo Gosh – the fourth figure of Indian spirituality in the twentieth century whose aura emanated across the world. His exceptional standing is clearest in the adoption of Western performance techniques among the forms of spiritual instruction, which were otherwise steeped in pious routine. Like a Duchamp of the spiritual field, he transformed all the relevant traditions into religious playthings and mystical ready-mades. It was not least a testament to his lucidity that, at the pinnacle of his success, he turned himself into a ready-made and, showing a clear awareness of the change in the zeitgeist, distanced himself from his Hinduizing past. As he recognized just in time, this past was tied too strongly to the mentality wave of Euro-American post-1968 romanticism. In assuming the Japanese-tinged name Osho in 1989 – 'the joke is over' – he quick-wittedly connected to the recently developed neo-liberal, Buddhophile mood in the West and invented a label for himself with a promising future. This gesture announced that in the field of guru-centred anthropotechnics too, the age of re-branding had begun.

The Buddhist Master

As far as the Buddhist varieties of the teacher's image are concerned, they took part in two evolutionary shifts that profoundly modified the meaning of teaching: in ancient times in the change of emphasis from the elitist self-redemptive art of the *Hinayana* (Small Vehicle) to the compassionate populism of the *Mahayana* (Great Vehicle), and in more recent times the epochal shift from a position of radical world- and life-denial to one of fundamental world- and life-affirmation. The most important information about the profile of the first teacher on the path of the new teaching probably comes from the enlightenment legend itself, as told in its Sri Lankan version: in this account, the awakened one waited under the Bodhi Tree for seven days in silence, untouched by everything around him, and 'experienced the joyful feeling of awakening'; he then arose and immersed himself in his detachment for another seven days under a different tree, then the same again under a third tree. The message of the tale is unmistakable: what took place here is beyond all teaching. No path with signposts leads to such a goal; the event rendered the attempt to produce it obsolete. The bond between truth and method was broken.

Nonetheless, this episode and Buddha's later decision to act as a teacher formed the point of departure for the most widely ramified scholastic phenomenon in the history of civilization. The teaching grows from the paradoxical act of breaking a silence in full awareness of the fact that the spoken words can never be taken merely at their propositional value, but predominantly as therapeutic directives. The pronouncements of the spiritual teacher are 'indirect messages' of a more hygienic than dogmatic tendency. Equipped with a starting paradox of such power, Buddhism sought to sow the seeds of the incommunicable and unfolded into one of the most loquacious movements in global spiritual culture.

In its first half-millennium, it remained the only thing its starting framework would have allowed: a matter for the few, who would nonetheless, under Indian and Indo-Chinese conditions, inevitably become numerous. Though, viewed from a distance, the Buddhist trainers, abbots of monasteries and advisers of those seeking help seemed merely to embody the continuation of the guru system by slightly different means, closer inspection reveals that they were in many respects the opposite. They entered the stage of intellectual history as a movement of therapists who, in keeping with their healing mission, were not concerned so much with the transmission of a religious doctrine, an esoteric worldview or a mystical visionary art. What they had in mind was purely to do away with the conditions of suffering – resolutely beginning with one's own entanglement in the mental processes that create suffering. By taking the salvific motif dominant throughout North India since 500 BC to the extreme, they infiltrated – feeling the zeitgeist fully on their side – the caste-based foundations of Brahmanism and its metaphysical 'superstructure'. Only in terms of the central civilizatory tendency, namely that towards a progressive internalization and subtilization of the sacrifice, can Buddhism also be considered an evolutionary unfolding of late Brahmanic potentials. While older times were dominated by the equivalence of the human and the sacrifice,[95] the sacrifice was now shifted entirely inwards – and ultimately, it would appear as if nothing had been sacrificed at all; for when humans relinquish the things to which they cling, they part with something that was never substantially their property in any case. One could see this as an internalization of conventional ascetic nudism, where it is not the body that walks in a garment of air – as practised by the *Digambara* – but rather the soul that paradoxically reveals its non-being in nakedness.

Admittedly, a number of Buddha's pupils only a few generations after his death fell prey to the most extreme fetishism in their interpretation of the monastic rule – the first significant schism, as is well known, took place partly as a result of an embittered debate between abbots over such questions as whether a monk is permitted to store salt in a buffalo horn – which amounted to a violation of the rules for storing food – or whether a monk's sleeping mat is allowed to have loose threads – which would have broken the rule concerning the size of mat.[96] Disputes of a philosophical kind also led to schisms in the schools, such that a few centuries after the master's passing, the well-known eighteen 'classical schools' took shape, each one of them divided into numerous subgroups and sectarian fringes which, in keeping with the universal laws of narcissism, pursued conflicts over the smallest differences.

I shall restrict myself here to the question of how Buddhist masters and pupils deal with their contracts about the impossible. Essentially, all the motifs that we know from the relationship between the guru and his disciple return here, complicated by the increase in negativity that characterizes Buddhist teaching in comparison to Brahmanic doctrine. While the guru can act as an accomplice to the pupil's projection for much of the time, the Buddhist teacher has the duty of distracting the projection from his person and deflecting it to the Dharma, the redemptive doctrine, in keeping with the principle of the not-self. The fulfilment of the impossibility contract here gains an additional dimension of crypticism, as the school workload requires that the adepts break even more profoundly with their folk-ontological intuitions.

In schematic terms, one could say that the guru initiates the student into the simple counter-intuitive truth that the great self of the world and the small ego-self are identical – a realization that undoubtedly presupposes intense modifications on the follower's part. The Buddhist teacher, on the other hand, is faced with the difficulty of making a doubly counter-intuitive truth seem plausible to the pupil: the identity of world-not-self and private not-self. The execution of this equation is synonymous with enlightenment *more buddhistico*. By its nature, it demands a form of tuition in which students are constantly thrown back to the self-referential nature of their search. They have to learn to find the liberating nothingness in themselves, and then to see through the world as a nothingness and finally recognize the two nothingnesses as one and the same. Every encounter should give them an opportunity to bid farewell. Where others settle and gather themselves, they must learn to give away and move on. Hence the abundant use of paradoxes that can be observed among many Buddhist teachers. While religious orthodoxies show their interest *ex officio* in dissolving paradoxes and making their doctrine reasonable – the most recent example being the much-noted Regensburg speech by Benedict XVI – one often recognizes Buddhist instruction – assuming it has not itself been corrupted in a religioid fashion – by its efforts to push its paradoxical character to the threshold of self-refutation, not infrequently to the point where the Dharma is termed a mere mirage.[97] Verbal paradoxes are all projections of the basic ascetic paradox whereby one conveys to the adept the message that there is 'nothing to attain' – but that to understand this, they must first of all sit in meditation for ten years, ideally for fourteen hours a day.

Alongside the paradox, the most striking stylistic means of recent Buddhism is probably the tautology, especially its Japanese varieties, which are often palatable to the contemporary individualism of the West – though probably only because we tend to confuse the tautologies of negativism in the doctrine of the not-self with those of our positivism. A rose is a rose: in the occidental context, this celebrates monovalence – or one could call it the idiocy of being – in which the intellect rests. That this cherry blossom is this cherry blossom, on the other hand, means that a manifestation of weak nothingness, a pink transience, comes into momentary contact with a transient eye, another manifestation of weak nothingness, both against the background of strong nothingness.

Intermezzo: The Critique of Illumination

I shall note in parentheses why the concept of illumination has lost its meaning for European philosophers of modernity. In typological terms, only two philosophically notable forms of illumination have become known: on the one side the illumination of the 'substance'-ontological or spirit-ontological type as present in the Hindu systems, as well as in Platonism and its Christian derivatives. Here, the equation of the world soul and the individual soul, or the infinite and the finite intellect, takes place in a varyingly thorough fashion. On the other side, we encounter enlightenment of the Nirvanological type, as known from Buddhist traditions. Here, the essential identity of the selflessness of the world and the absence of a substantial soul is 'realized' in the individual.

Modern analysis has decisive objections to both of these patterns: in the case of the first variant, the problem is that it ascribes more intelligence and soul to the world than is its due. As far as the inorganic sphere is concerned, its share in the mental and intellectual capacity was judged very reservedly. But the organic world too, going on everything one sees of it, is more a battlefield of confusedly distributed life-will points than a reason-animated whole. If people were able to ascribe to it something resembling a comprehensive animation, it was only by means of a transparent projection. This was achieved by taking out a loan from the self-evident animation of the animal-noetic sphere and passing this on – multiplied by the value

284

'infinity' in the imaginary realm – to the world-whole. In this respect, ancient India and Old Europe are partners in an alliance who understand each other blindly: as far as the soul is concerned, both of them have always wanted too much, and incur massive expenses to keep alive the welcome confusion of totality with animation by the world soul. On the other side, one sees how Buddhism, starting from the partly plausible selflessness and soullessness of the world machine, which it takes for granted thanks to its sober view of the game of constitutions and dissolutions, postulates the selflessness and soullessness of the human interior. This looks like a complementary fallacy: in the same way one borrowed soul from human self-experience to lend it to the 'cosmos' without sufficient securities in the first case, one borrows not-selfness from the 'outside' world in the second case in order to transfer it to the human self-relationship at the risk of losing its most precious quality, finite animation, and inducing it to speculations in which it can only lose – assuming there are no gains elsewhere, such as high ethical sensitizations, to compensate for the losses. I shall conclude this digression by noting that for a contemporary philosophical psychology, the only path that remains is the middle one, equidistant from the Hindu and Buddhist over-non-animation; it would therefore advise neither a leap into being nor a leap into nothingness. Instead of promoting self-sacrifice on one side or the other, it argues for the connection between effort and self-experience. This alliance opens up the paths of increase and transformation on which the moderns seek their optimizations.

The Apostle

Against such a background, it is not difficult to make the third figure of spiritual trainerdom, which is responsible for the Christian transmission of the impossible to ever new generations of adepts, understandable. Its basic form is that of apostolic succession, in which the art of immortality coded as 'faith' is passed on. As illustrated above with the example of Paul, no illumination need be presupposed for this; the result of movedness and commitment is sufficient. The two highest forms of the *imitatio Christi* are on the one hand martyrdom, which was understood by its observers as a direct transition into the kingdom of God (which is why, according to some authors, martyrs were exempted from any form of further purification in the beyond), and on the other hand the Christomorphic transformation of man that was meant to lead to the point where the logos and *caritas* take possession of the entire human person. What distinguished the greatest performance artist of the high Middle Ages, St Francis of Assisi, was his resolve to unify the two extremes of *imitatio* in his person, which could only be achieved by equating life in utter poverty with the martyr's *agon*.[98]

The general form of the Christian *imitatio* contract can be seen in the choice of apostolic existence as such, which is always based in some way on a change of subjects. Its schema was defined by Paul in the statement from Galatians 2:20: 'I no longer live, but Christ lives in me.' This identifies the *imitatio* as a two-sided relationship in which one can distinguish between an *imitatio subiectiva* and an *imitatio obiectiva*. Via subjective imitation, the imitator refers to Christ himself, or to a first-degree imitator of Christ, such as a martyr or miracle-working saint. By imitating the inimitable, the Christian zealot can himself become an object of imitation by third parties. In the position of the imitable imitator, he follows the call to be exemplary and subordinates his own existence to the formal law of exemplary life. It is in this sense that Eugippus, in the introduction to his *Vita Sancti Severini* – the life of the fifth-century saint from Mautern an der Donau, in the Austrian Krems district – quotes Peter's command to his deacons: 'Be an example to the flock' (*forma estote gregi*), as well as Paul's instruction to Timothy: 'Be an example to the faithful' (*forma esto fidelibus*); in the original Greek, *forma* is replaced by *typos*. Hence the Christian teacher is destined not only to be an imitator of Christ himself, but also to take the position of the imitable and make himself available to the communities of believers as a 'formant', a shaping 'type'. Hence the dictum: a Christian is one who makes others Christians. The secular duplicates of this cliché lead to the theses that only those who guide others to education are themselves educated, and that only those who spread enlightenment can be called enlightened. Through the two-sided *imitatio*, apostolic succession takes on the form of a pyramid game, in which each participant is at once imitator and imitated – except for the simple believers at the base, who only imitate without being imitated; it is their prerogative to fund the advanced with material contributions. They are naturally furthest from the tip of the pyramid, where the advanced jostle one another in the art of the impossible. Among these, next to the declared saints and miracle workers, one also finds the 'type' of abbot, of which the Benedictine Rule states that he has taken over the duty of guiding souls (*animas regere*), and must one day give account for his wards in fear and trembling. The statesmanship of the monastic director, we read, consists in doing the right thing at the right time, which means combining flattery with terror, and the severity of the Lord with the kindness of the Father.[99]

The Philosopher

If we now cast a glance at the fourth trainer figure in our list, represented by the philosopher, we are immediately struck by its fragmentation into the erotic, statuary and gnostic types. As Pierre Hadot has shown very eloquently, Socrates embodies the first of these, Marcus Aurelius the second – and, if anyone were suitable to represent the third type alongside these, it would be Plotin, the master of logical ascents above the physical world. We are also indebted to Hadot for a clear reconstruction of the Socratic procedure as seduction in the service of the ideal: by feigning, with a responsible irony, love for his pupil, he gains the latter's love in return – and proceeds to direct it from his person to the insight as such.[100] He himself can only love 'upwards', and wishes to teach this way of loving as the only truthful one. While the students train with the master, the master trains with the *ágathon*. By conveying a love for the love for the absolute, he resembles – from a distance – certain psychoanalysts who seek to liberate their patients world-immanently to their insane love. Hence: 'Love your symptom as yourself',[101] and: 'Never retreat from its desire' (Lacan). The erotic *imitatio philosophi* could only be stimulated to the extent that the master represented a sufficiently impressive *typos* of philosophical life. In this sense, one could speak of the birth of philosophy from the spirit of performance – the death of Socrates wholly confirms this diagnosis.[102] Whereas modern aesthetic performance generally remains as self-referential as it is inconsequential, and scarcely encourages imitation,[103] the classical form aims entirely for the exemplary. Nietzsche was still able to say that a master only takes himself seriously with regard to his pupils.

The contours of philosophical mimesis come to light even more clearly among the statuary philosophers, who largely identified themselves with the Stoic movement – Seneca usually calls them simply 'our people'. They embody that type of practical philosophy in the ancient style which made the greatest impression on the public: the figure of the ascetic sage who, against the background of an ontology of world-divinity, works on equating the ability to live with the ability to die. It was in Stoicism, after all, that the metaphorical equation of philosophical concern for oneself and sculptural work on the inner statue enabled a veritable training consciousness to ensue.[104] Seneca does not simply appropriate the successful results of this work for himself; he simultaneously claims, only half in jest, a copyright on the intellectual progress of his pupil – he even tells him to his face: *meum opus es*, 'you are my work'.[105] Hence the pupil is doing nothing wrong in offering himself to the teacher as a 'great gift' (*ingens munus*).[106] At the same time, he reminds his student of the principle that teachers are not our masters, but leaders (*non domini nostri sed duces*).[107] The Stoic teachers hardly ever permit doubts as to the necessity of studying with a master, even though one can feel the beginnings of the idea of internalizing the master principle clearly within reach.[108] This could be taken up by more modern schools, which declared the external master merely a temporary augmenter of the inner one.

The Sophist as Universally Able

It may seem bewildering to conclude this summary overview of trainer figures in the field of the élan of impossibility with that of the Sophist. This confusion is easily removed as soon as one calls to mind that the Sophists, going on their achievements and their own self-image, were by no means simply the intellectual lightweights portrayed in the Platonic counter-propaganda. If one leaves aside the caricatures, it transpires that sophistry, in its essence, was an artistry of knowledge – one could even say an artistic doctrine of knowing everything and being capable of anything, without which the attractiveness of the philosophical life form in antiquity could not be so readily explained. As contradictory as it might sound: by seeking to make the impossible teachable – far beyond the Socratic-Platonic promise to capture virtue (*areté*) within a school framework – it produced, as far as Western tradition is concerned, the first comprehensive science of training in the narrower sense of the word. It did this by consistently relating the processual side of upbringing (*paideía*) and tuition (*didaskalía*) to the form of training (*áskesis* and *meléte*). It thus pointed energetically to a principle of progress: the gradualness of increases in achievement, as well as the imperceptible yet effective growth into the more improbable habitus. Because they viewed learning more as being shaped through interaction and repetitive practice than an active mental grasping of the material, the Sophists were probably the first to place an emphasis on early education in order to ensure the naturalization of the improbable from childhood onwards.

All ability is thus trapped in a circle of diligence: one only does what one is able to do, and one is only able to do what one constantly repeats. In this purely 'hexic' analysis, however – that is, one oriented towards an active formation of habit – the agent of increase in the praxis of repetition, namely the only recently discovered network of neuro-rhetorical rules, remains unacknowledged, and is only drawn upon implicitly. For the time being, all didactics is summed up by the admonition: 'Practise, practise, practise!' – a slogan whose echo one still hears in Lenin's 'learn, learn and learn again', and to which even Rodin's sublime *toujours travailler* responds from afar. Sophist theory can therefore only constitute a practising praxis of thinking and imagining. The paradigm of an ability wholly embedded in constant practice is the mother tongue, which we could not master if we had not always been in a seemingly obvious and natural, but in truth quite miraculous circle of ability and application, practice and improvement. This can serve to demonstrate the miracle that is intended to become the school subject: everyone has always spoken in some way or other, but only the Sophist makes an art of his speech like no other – about everything, in every situation, always well and mostly victoriously. That is why it is necessary to climb, with the right teacher, from within the mother tongue to the all-encompassing tongue.

The nub of the Sophist learning model is demonstrated in the Sophist's leap from language competency to general life competency, even applied omniscience. Through the constant company of an artist of ability, the speaking and living master of his school, who knows everything because he speaks about everything, and can in fact do anything that belongs to the higher ability to live, the practising of universal ability increasingly rubs off on the adept, until he too is ready to enter public life as a pan-technically shaped individual who knows everything and can do anything. The things that cannot be anticipated by practice alone, the situative imponderabilities, are heard by the true man of skill in the spirit of the moment (*kairós*), and even this balancing on the tip of the favourable moment can, within limits, be trained.

In its own way, then, Sophistic education goes beyond the physical – its concept of 'metaphysics' is unmistakably a form of artistry. Sophistic artistry formulates the existential antithesis of helplessness. The cultivation of never-helpless individuals is the goal of all such *paideía*. Nothing comes closer to the practical ideal of the polis citizen, and even more the polis politician, than the image of a human who is always in training and knows how to help themselves in any situation. This is why, if we look closely, we always enjoy watching circus artistes: they spread the good news of the invincible mobility of the body – and for the same reason, a well-built and effectively delivered speech always concerns us. It reminds us of the humanly possible in the closest proximity. While the untrained human falls silent in their lack of means, the Sophistic teacher shows the trained adept how to find the words to overcome suffering due to *amechanía*, lack of means and helplessness, in any situation.[109]

As much as this education places the emphasis on gradual growth into artistic superiority to all challenges, it is equally a performative, indeed a theatrical matter. Nowhere is this clearer than in an anecdote about Gorgias: one day he came to the theatre in Athens, which was fully booked, ready to improvise a random speech, and boldly called out to the audience: 'Name any subject!' (*probállete*).[110] To understand the meaning of this appearance, one must realize that Gorgias acted very self-confidently, but in no way inappropriately, as he was genuinely willing and able to give a sample of his pan-sophical and pan-rhetorical skill in any given situation. It was with a similar gesture that until the end of the eighteenth century, some pianists would appear and elaborate spontaneous dissertations in notes for their audiences on random 'themes', like sophists at the piano – in this sense, the young Mozart was one of the great sophists in music history, albeit one who largely called out his own themes, assuming he did not leave this to the librettist. Franz Liszt too, the inventor of the solo piano recital (1839), was still wont to improvise on spontaneously chosen themes before a large audience. For the piano sophists, the nature of their profession and the manner of its exercise meant that all learning had to be wholly embedded in the praxis of practice.[111] As far as the magic of the pan-sophical and pan-technic habitus cultivated by the Sophists is concerned, it extended very much further than one would think after Plato's defensive battles against the challenge of their position. It was Aristotle, no less, who did the Sophists' pretensions the honour of taking their aim of saying something about everything at face value – in this sense, he was more an imitator of Gorgias than Plato. He paid tribute to his own teacher by replacing the pan-rhetorical habitus by the pan-epistemic one.

I shall conclude these observations by noting that the Sophistic idea of universal ability experienced an unexpected resurrection in the twentieth century – in the form of the deconstruction developed by Jacques Derrida. This, in its basic procedure, is nothing other than a reinstatement of sophistic omniscience in the form of omni-commentary or immanent omni-refutation. As we know, the key to the Sophistic art of omniscience lay in the artful trick (*mechané*) of always letting the other speaker forge ahead with a thesis, an elaborated speech, even an entire theory, and subsequently employing the technique of rebuttal (*antilégein*) – this, as Plato showed, was also the method of Socrates. *Antilégein* starts from the foundation of knowing-equally-well – which is already secured through the other's exposition, though often only borrowed from it – and directly ascends to the level of knowing-better. This is always simple to attain if one considers how easily one can prove the inevitable existence of weak points in the first text; such passages can be found almost effortlessly, even in the discourses of the masters, by recalling the selection that underlies every decisive thesis. It seems that Gorgias, the all-knowing, and Socrates, the all-not-knowing, were reunited in Derrida to launch a neo-acrobatic form of sophistic knowledge art, or a philosophistical sophism that required constant practice and existed only in practice. It was as good as certain that a new academic reaction would resist this.

The Profane Trainer: The Man Who Wants Me to Want

It is only a short way from the figure of the noble sophist – which, for the reasons detailed above, I wanted to place closer to the spiritual-artistic teachers than the pragmatic ones – to the second group of trainers. I will speak briefly here of such teachers who concern themselves with passing on more specialized techniques and praxis-related complexes of abilities. It is an obvious choice to begin with the athletic trainer, as this embodies the most striking figure in the field of technically transmittable improbability. Like every trainer, the athletic one has a supportive procedure best described as the technique of interlocking motivation. While every athlete has a decent portion of will to success of their own accord, it is nonetheless the trainer's duty to implant in this will a second will – their own, which heightens the first and helps it to rise above its crises. Through the alteration of the willing will by such a willed will, the athlete can be carried to heights of achievement that could never have been reached without the interlocking of the two wills. Athletism, then, is the original practice field of harnessed spontaneity that later – in a mono-theistic context – bore such strange fruit as the scholastic discussions on free or unfree will (*de libero vel servo arbitrio*). This problem was solved on the sports field long before philosophers entangled themselves in it. Theologians who, seeking to penetrate the mystery of the contradiction between human freedom and divine omnipotence, teach that we should freely want what God wants us to want, generally no longer understand that in doing so, they have made God a successor to the athletic trainer. The definition of the trainer is that they want the athlete to want what they, the trainer, want for them.[112] Needless to say, the athlete is meant to want something that is not entirely impossible, but fairly improbable: an unbroken series of victories.[113]

The Master Craftsman and the Two Natures of the Work of Art

The second type in the pragmatic field is embodied by the craftsman, or, philosophically put, one in command of a professional-everyday *techné*. With aptitudes of this type, one no longer sees once they have been routinized and trivialized (and on Greek soil, even 'Philistinized') that every single one of them came from a slow, cumulative revolt against helplessness, a quiet rebellion against the forlornness, lack of means and lack of cunning for which the Greeks coined the profound word and spirit name Amechania – absence of *mechané*, lack of tricks and *truc*, of leverage and tools. In this sense, all craftsmanship constitutes a collective and anonymous counterpart to one of the twelve labours of Hercules, these pan-technic acts of heroism whose unmistakable purpose was to prove that it is in man's nature – or a demigod's, in this case – to master seemingly insurmountable tasks. Whoever has no interest in craftsmen should therefore be equally silent about heroes. From the perspective of the ability to do something, heroes, craftsmen and finally also politicians belong much closer together than the Old European doctrines of action, which were usually aristocratically inclined, were able to recognize – even Hannah Arendt's book *The Human Condition* (1957/8), admirable in all other respects, paid far too great a tribute to traditional distortions by pushing the activity of making, let alone of mere working, rather grossly into the second and third positions, far behind action, that is to say the political behaviour of humans.

In the light of this, it had to be considered not merely a great academic, but in fact intellectual-historical deed when Richard Sennett recently attempted to liberate the crafts from the disdain they were shown by philosophical theory, and restore to these fundamental, yet unnoticed factors their due rank among the phenomena of the *vita activa*.[114] The principle of craft is based on the coincidence of production and practice – finally recognizing this again is what makes Sennett's venture on activity-theoretical terrain so significant.

Whoever defends the crafts *eo ipso* shields repetitive learning, with all its slowness and lack of originality. Such a gesture presupposes that one can give repetition, much maligned in modernity, a new mark of honour. Anyone who attempts this must prove the reconcilability of the repetitive-mechanical and the personal-spontaneous – an undertaking that leads directly to a praise of individually embodied memories, and thus what one could, quoting Nietzsche, call 'incorporation' [*Einverleibung*], or, invoking Ravaisson, the system of acquired abilities.

Anyone who remembers the curriculum of the older craft professions knows that no one is born a master. According to this curriculum, an apprentice had to be initiated into the techniques of his profession for at least seven years before he could take the final examination. After this, the journeyman perfected his art for another five to ten years, and only after twelve to eighteen years of teaching and practising could he consider the production of his final masterpiece. According to an old rule of thumb, at least ten thousand hours of practising 'praxis' are required to become a decent craftsman or a reasonable musician;[115] if one includes higher levels of mastery, one can safely double or even triple that number. Until recently, what we call 'genius' merely referred to cases in which these average practice times were spectacularly shortened – recall musical child prodigies: the music history of the last three centuries would be barely conceivable without them. In the end, a genius-aesthetic plague befell entire populations of artists who were anything but *Wunderkinder*, yet wanted to push this shortening as far as the complete omission of practice.

The phenomenon of craftsmanly mastery is of paradigmatic significance for an understanding of both the ancient and the modern *vita activa*, as it marks the beginning of the process whereby the artistic *mirabile* became commonplace. Whether the craft is ship-building – a discipline Plato enjoys weaving into his discussion of the nature of *techné* – surgery, pottery or goldsmithery (Sennett, as a critic of the modern fragmentation of abilities and demoralization of mere job work, is especially fond of the last of these[116]), the respective craftsmen are producers of artifices that overstep the circle of natural things in varyingly conspicuous ways. Because of their standardized, serial and everyday character, these works of 'art' have mostly ceased to be an object of admiration, though that does not stop their production from requiring a substantial amount of practice, experience, care and vigilance. This activity in the field of an anonymized and degraded artificiality provides the ideal conditions for a type of production

located precisely on the threshold between fabrication and meditation. It stimulates a practising work in which the agent reproduces
and expands their competence to perform this very work to the same
extent that they immerse themselves in the production of the object or
effect.[117]

This explains why every conscientiously performed work of craftsmanship can be of spiritual surplus value. When, in the European
cities of the late Middle Ages, a massive wave of lay religiosity developed that would culminate in the *devotio moderna* of the fourteenth
century and the Reformation of the early sixteenth century, this was
scarcely connected to the supposed affinity between capitalism and
Protestantism of which Max Weber had made too much in his well-
known study, and far more to the blatant analogies between monastic
exercises and those found in the workshops. The practising work of
the crafts – the Parisian *Livre des métiers* listed over one hundred
and fifty guild-based artisan 'professions' as early as 1268[118] – had to
produce a type of personality that would become increasingly aware
of its potential spiritual equality with professional clerics. Just as *ora
et labora* had long been the rule for most monks, the more up-to-date
maxim *labora et ora* presented itself urgently to the secular brothers of
artisanal life. There are also many sources documenting direct moves
of individual craftsmen from monastic workshops to urban ones,
meaning that the transfer of the spiritual habitus – the self-moulding
of the actor in regular, vigilant activity – to the larger artisanal milieu
could even take place by the shortest route on occasion. In this sense,
the workshops are not simply the places where pure 'equipment'
[*Zeug*] is called into existence; they are at once plantations for a form
of subjectivity suspended between production and contemplation,
mints for self-assuredly pious singularities. Occasionally this spark
flies back into the religious field, as with the British Methodists, who
applied the craft of devout enthusiasm to their own psyche.[119]

From here, it is only a short way to the secession of the arts from
the crafts – that most activity-theoretically relevant spectacle of the
Modern Age before the onset of the one even greater drama: the crys-
tallization of modern 'labour as such, labour *sans phrase*',[120] the
labour without qualities in which Marx found the systemic definition
of the proletarian condition as an illusion-free self-sale of the universally available 'commodity of labour power'.[121] Like all secessions,
this one too serves the purpose of a heightened subjectification, in
this case the boosting of the craftsman's ability to that of the artist.
What distinguishes art from craftsmanship is its resolve to display the
ability to art as such in the piece of work (*opus*). Sennett illustrates

this leap from the simple consumer item to the work-narcissistic dimension with Benvenuto Cellini's famous salt cellar (the Vienna *Saliera*, 1540-3), which he crafted for Francis I in over three years of work. Such objects no longer tolerate everyday use; they force the user to yield to the compulsion to admire that is fashioned into them.

It was only after protracted dogmatic quarrelling that the two natures of the work of art were laid down with the appropriate clarity: wholly craft or wholly *mirabile*. With the one side each work remains the creation of the profession through and through, and with the other it testifies to the irruption of the supra-artisanal into the workshop. The two natures exist unmixed alongside each other and are recognized through different receptive capacities. All the upgradings of both the master status and the concept of the masterpiece that have animated discussions about art and artists since the Renaissance are connected to this. Just as art means the re-conquest of the wonderful from the position of the workshops, the artist's existence implies restoring the creative, almost godly competency within the workshop – with the side effect that for almost half a millennium, Europeans have been subject to a constant inner mission by theologians of creativity and their critical deacons, though also a slightly later Arian[122] or humanistic-materialistic counter-mission whose message is that even the greatest works of art are no more than higher products – that is to say, simulations of something higher – and even the greatest artists are only human.

Professors, Teachers, Writers

I shall conclude this overview with a summary description of the three remaining types of pragmatic teaching licence: the university professors, the teachers at the primary and secondary schools of modern nations, and finally Enlightenment writers and politico-culturally committed journalists. From a historical perspective, these authorized teachers and speakers are largely involved in a drama that could be described as the progressive self-abolition of the privilege of education, or the democratization of the elites. In a process drawn out over several centuries, many of them – never without opposing tendencies complicating and deflecting the course of the development – devoted themselves increasingly explicitly to the aim of rendering the trainer obsolete through the training. They reinforce the depersonalizing tendency of toughening exercises by shifting the emphasis from the person of the teacher to the learning field (the faculty, the school, the press) – a tendency that, since the growth of Internet communities, the most immediate illustration of the phenomenon today, becomes easier to identify retrospectively as early as Gutenberg's time, even in the age of manuscripts.

If one looks back at the figure of the Old European professor, one immediately notices that he was never meant to be, nor ever wanted to be, more than a character mask of his subject, and how little he was initially expected to make any original contribution to the advancement of his science. Until recently, an original professor was a contradiction in terms – and still is today, essentially, except that the contradictions now have slightly better living conditions, especially in the humanities, where teachers are allowed to speak not only professorially, but also (within limits) enthusiastically and expressively. The name 'professor' already indicates the vocation to reproduce and pass on whatever the state of the art required, and if the bearer of such a title received an honorarium from the state, it was in acknowledgement of the energetic unoriginality with which he was able to teach his subject as a whole. Professors belong to an economy of ordinated secular knowledge in which the professorial chair is strictly superior to its holder, just as, at the next highest level, the priority of the faculty over the chair is never in doubt. The faculty is the impersonal self of a discipline, whereas the individual professors act *de facto* and *de jure* as mere personifications of a teaching and learning process that has long been supra-personally institutionalized. If the chairholders can look back on qualification processes of twenty to thirty years, they constitute the average in their discipline. In their totality they form a collective subject that, at the start of the Modern Age, was given – not without reason – the title *res publica litteraria*, the scholars' republic.[123] To explain the nature of its task, one would first have to point to the expanded reproduction of cognitive capitals with which academic life concerns itself. One would perhaps have to emphasize even more that this *res publica* ultimately constituted a crypto-Platonic political body: the replacement of the simple pyramid of the 'philosophers' kingdom' with the complex polyhedron of the 'philosophers' republic'. The former sought to guide a city that would have been governable via a completed science of principles against the background of a static nature; the latter is based on the self-administration of a polity exposed, both in terms of principles and nature, to an unforeseeable dynamization.

If one is prepared to understand the faculty, the university and the scholars' republic as collectivizations, anonymizations and perfections of the master function – and this means judging the 'Enlightenment' more highly than it usually judges itself – then one can make analogous statements about the next two steps of pragmatic trainer functions, namely writers and journalists. They carry the toughening process on which the *res publica* of the knowing is based to the respective wider levels – first into the classrooms, from which tomorrow's literate individuals capable of judgement and action will emerge, and then into the public media that serve the communication among today's society of the knowing. From this perspective, the teachers are character masks of the school system, just as journalists are personifications of the press – so they too, if they wanted to see themselves in that way, would serve a positive dynamic of collectivization that sought to expand a particular quality to the level of 'society' as a whole, a quality long believed to be afforded only to the few: that of mastery, be it the solving of a factual problem or the art of living as such. But as long as the collectivization of mastery – in philosophical terms, the self-determination of 'society' (as if 'society' could possess a self) – does not take place, individuals would do well to continue practising as if they were the first who will reach the goal.

9

CHANGE OF TRAINER AND REVOLUTION

On Conversions and Opportunistic Turns

The Science of Reversal

To conclude this investigation into the structure of orthodox retreats to the practising and artistically heightened life, I shall cast a brief glance at a phenomenon without which the ascetic radicalisms discussed here would remain a mystery: I mean those moments of existential concentration, self-collection and reversal that, from a religion-historical perspective, one calls *conversions*. It should be clear by now that these certainly cannot be considered merely 'religious' events. Rather, they belong to the overall inventory of ascetic behaviour from the recessive position – that is to say from the stance that develops in response to the absolute imperative. They take on a 'religious' semblance through the combination of practising or radical-ethical behaviour with the language games of the sacrifice, regardless of whether one performs these outwardly or inwardly. Sacrifices of the first kind have always been made with blood and fire, and those of the second kind as the renunciation of the will and transformation of desires.[124] While sacrificial thinking supplies the symbolic code for operations of violent exchange, the practising life as such provides the foundation for all civilizations, especially those based on internalized forms of sacrifice.

In the following, I shall cast a second glance at the processes that I have described in terms of secession and recession, detachment from the social environment and withdrawal into oneself. Dealing more closely with the phenomena, it now transpires that these categories are not adequate for identifying the first ethical movement. The spokesmen of the great ascetic caesura were never content to label their behaviour as mere distancing, as a retreat (*epoché*) to the shore of observation or an evasion of the real, even though their own statements of intent do not lack such turns of phrase – recall such widespread distancing metaphors as flight from the world (*fuga mundi*), flight from the times (*fuga saeculi*), passionlessness (*apátheia*), detachment (*vairagya*) or refuge in the Dharma path. The last great symbol of distance of this type is the 'Angel of History' in Walter Benjamin's interpretation, which backs away step by step from the flood of disasters, its eyes fixed in disbelief on the world scene. The concern of the most resolute secessionaries is not simply a fascinated retreat from a reality that no longer invites participation, but rather a complete reversal – a turn away from the superficially manifest, which means a turn towards something that is better, true and real on a higher level.

What I would like to sketch here cannot be more than a small preliminary study towards the general science of reversal that was inseparably bound to the older radicalisms of the practising life. Only through this doctrine of philosophical and ascetic conversion do secessionary and recessive operations gain an object and a direction, and it is no secret that even modern revolutionary teachings still constitute the more distant derivatives of the oldest statements on beneficial turns and salvatory changes of direction. This means that there is a movement of all movements without which the concept of truth, according to this tradition of thought, cannot be adequately conceived.[125]

This movement, which is not only retreat but also turning, was first accounted for in the ancient occidental tradition by Plato. In his account, the critical movement initially appears as a purely cognitive act meant to lead from the corrupt sensible world to the incorruptible world of the spirit. To carry it out, a change of sight from the dark to the light is required, a change that cannot take place 'without turning the whole body' (*hólo to sómati*).[126] This marks the first explicit reference to the motif of the integral turn. Analogously, the same faculty must 'be wheeled round, in company with the entire soul' (*hóle te psyché*), from seeing to becoming, until one has learned to pay attention only to the eternally existent, and to prefer and endure the brightest part (*phanótaton*) thereof: the sun of good. Needless to say, the 'turned' soul takes the whole human being with it in its subtle movement. This redirection of sight and existence must not occur by chance and merely once, however, but be developed into a veritable 'art of turning around' (*techné periagogés*), or an asceticism of complete existential reversal. This is based on the assumption that those to be turned have their full cognitive apparatus, but that this is initially and mostly 'turned in a wrong direction' due to an age-old bad posture. The philosopher knows about this from his own experience, for he has discovered the cave's exit. He understands what it means to have turned himself around and ventured outside. What he has achieved should not, he feels, be impossible for his fellow humans. Never is he, the first orthopaedist of the spirit, more generous and more of a stranger to the world than when, as here, he projects his own character onto others.

All Education Is Conversion

The implications of these seemingly harmless reflections are literally monstrous: they constitute no less than the first sketch for a doctrine of subversion which holds that pedagogy *more platonico* must virtually be defined as an integral science of revolution. The licence to teach in this field is acquired thus: an individual pioneer of the new way of seeing escapes from the collective cave into the open, and subsequently – initially with inevitable reluctance, overcoming himself – feels ready to descend once more to the wrongly directed in the shadow cinema and explain to them how to access these liberations. In this sense, Platonic pedagogy is a pure art of conversion – revolutionary orthopaedics. Purely because the philosopher is already a 'convert', one who has been turned around and the first of his kind, can he make it his task to pass on the turn to others. If he simply remained enlightened on his own behalf, he could bask in his private happiness; if he is seized by concern for the state, however, he must abandon privatism and seek to share his illumination with the many.

Pierre Hadot calmly encapsulates the surplus flowing from radical reversal: 'All education is conversion.'[127] One must add: all conversion is subversion. In the instruction to this movement lies an inexhaustible 'revolutionary' potential, at least as long as it does not content itself with individual reversal. At the start, after all – because of the strict parallelism between the psyche and the polis – it always had to be concerned with the universalization of turning, and sought to include virtually all members of the commune it meant to reform in the other way of living. It was only the later philosophical schools – the Stoics, the Epicureans and the Neoplatonists – that made private tuition a central concern. For them it became a sign of wisdom to content oneself with the conversion of individuals and give up on the incorrigible many – hence their belief that there is no wisdom without resignation, and no resignation without a certain consent to the 'cruelty of life'. They abandoned the plan to reform the souls and the state at once – not only because they no longer wanted to believe in the parallelism between the two factors, but also because they began to recognize in the state that cold monster which, they were convinced, could not possibly be the valid analogue of the soul.

There were good reasons for the timing of the individualistic retreat from Plato's over-enthusiasm, from this excess of missionary zeal that denizens of the Modern Age would term 'utopian'. The doctrine of *periagogé*, the turning around of the soul (which was later often combined with the term *epistrophé*), was in fact the first explicit version of the absolute imperative 'You must change your life!', framed in the exhortation to turn one's entire being towards the spiritual side. This imperative was first formulated in a holistic variation that led to numerous severe misunderstandings. In its deep structure, the Platonic doctrine of learning by the sun of truth had remained an occulted sacrificial theory – related in this respect to the ascetic systems appearing in Asia at the same time – as the turning around of the soul could ultimately only be defined as a relinquishment of the particular in favour of the general.[128] The consequence was that this version of the absolute imperative was affected by two profoundly misconstruable factors. The first was the verb, in that 'change' here meant something along the lines of 'sacrifice oneself to the general', and the second lay in the possessive pronoun, in that the adepts were secretly dispossessed of 'their' lives, which were instead handed over to the true whole that was yet to be created. You are in the world for the sake of the whole, not vice versa – this is the corresponding admonition in Plato's *Nomoi*. 'We do not belong to ourselves', we are still told today in traditions of this type. This is the origin of anthropotechnic tendencies that pervert the absolute imperative by reading 'life' instead of 'your life' – though here, on the terrain of antiquity, the word 'life' admittedly has more political than bioscientific implications. Compared to this, the apolitical spiritual systems of late antiquity were absolutely right to insist that individuals should be taken seriously as individuals. Only for that reason had they been concerned to initiate them into the craft of life, concern for oneself, *lege artis*. Like an ancient anticipation of the modern restriction of the right to arrest (the Habeas Corpus Amendment Act of 1679), they undo the individual's helplessness before the whole and assert its inalienable claim to a self-determined life, even if, as prisoners of reality, they are forced to accept certain curtailments of their right to freedom.

It would take a millennium and a half until the holistic coup of the Christian post-Christian Neoplatonist Hegel and his materialistic followers put the idea of universal conversion back on the agenda of modernity, with the known consequences – predominantly bloody consequences that, taken as a whole, go back to the amalgamation of the Graeco-Germanic philosophy of liberation and the ideas of the French Revolution. I will show in chapter 11 how his amalgam led to an anthropotechnics that was intended to help produce the New Human Being, this time as the product of a political conversion that did not rule out the rebuilding of the body – and still, questionably enough, in line with holistic concepts of 'society', where it is only ever a small step from the over-elevation of the whole to the sacrifice of the part.

The Catastrophe Before Damascus

In the meantime, the motif of reversal – which had initially been primarily the domain of political theory and the philosophical art of living – had been monopolized by religious interpretations. Their paradigm was the conversion of Paul on the road to Damascus, commented upon countless times. There are two accounts of this defining moment in the Acts of the Apostles: once in autobiographical form as part of Paul's defence speech before the Jews in Jerusalem (Acts 22), and once in the third person (Acts 9). Both versions emphasize that Paul was 'turned around' through the event on the road to Damascus, transformed from a persecutor of Christians to an envoy of Christianity. In the personalized version, the story is as follows:

> 'About noon as I came near Damascus, suddenly a bright light from heaven flashed around me. I fell to the ground and heard a voice say to me, "Saul! Saul! Why do you persecute me?"
>
> '"Who are you, Lord?" I asked.
>
> '"I am Jesus of Nazareth, whom you are persecuting," he replied. My companions saw the light, but they did not understand the voice of him who was speaking to me.
>
> '"What shall I do, Lord?" I asked.
>
> '"Get up," the Lord said, "and go into Damascus. There you will be told all that you have been assigned to do."' (Acts 22:6–10)

The third-person account of the same events, which is located near the beginning of the *acta apostolorum*, contains only one substantial variation: it emphasizes that the companions stood by speechless because they heard the voice, but saw no one (Acts 9:7).

Considering this tale, one thing is clear: even here, we are already light years away from the sublime Platonic reflections on the turning of the soul and its guidance from the cave of collective sensory illusions. There is no reference to the concerns of Greek rationalism or the turn towards the sun of truth. The light that dazzles the zealot on the road to Damascus is a mixture of midday demon and hallucination. The story is already set firmly on the terrain of a magical conception of the world (Spengler even assigned it to the atmospheric space of the 'Arabian' cultural soul) whose mood is defined by apocalyptic expectation, salvation panic and a miracle-hungry supra-naturalistic hermeneutics. Most of all, it displays the spirit of a zealotry that is ready to leave for any destination, and which barely seems to care whether it heats up in one direction or another. Placed against the background of the philosophical concept of *conversio* or *epistrophé*, Paul's experience is by no means a conversion, which would have completely changed his personal habitus. Nor was it for a moment a realization, but rather the encounter with a divine voice that has no qualms about manifesting itself in this world. Taken as a whole, what happened to Paul is no more than the 'reprogramming' of a zealot in the precise sense of the world. The term is justified because the 'operating system' of Paul's personality could continue to be used more or less unchanged after the reversal, but now freed up for an extraordinary theological creativity.

The conversion of Paul therefore belongs in an entirely different category of 'turnings' that display an apostolic-zealotic character, not an ethical-'revolutionary' one. The theological tradition provides the term *metánoia* for this, whose general tendency is best formulated as 'change of heart', with 'penitence' as the heightened Christian form.[129] From a psychodynamic perspective, the term belongs in the force field of the inner collection that seems appropriate before or after great events – whether after a personal or political defeat that forces a re-evaluation of one's decorum, one's guiding maxims in life,[130] or in anticipation of an imminent event that is apocalyptically foreshadowed. Metanoia is above all a panic phenomenon, in that it goes hand in hand with the gesture of pulling oneself together in a crisis and getting serious before the looming end. It is no coincidence that the era of the European Reformation, which was swarming with people who wanted to get serious, was another heyday of the dark belief in astral influence and the fear of end times. The *modus operandi* of metanoia is not the turning around of the personality, but rather the collection and heeding of the long-known, which, for lack of an immediate occasion, one had previously avoided examining in full depth. This applies especially to Paul, who, while pursuing the Jewish dissidents who had joined the Jesuan sect, would have had ample opportunity to understand that they essentially had the more coherent interpretation of the tradition already, and that they were the ones who had given the messianic element of Jewish doctrine the most exciting of all possible readings.

What Paul experienced on the road to Damascus, then, was a metanoetic episode that led to a reorganization of consciousness from the perspective of a newly formed centre of the highest conviction. This constitutes a process that William James, in the chapters devoted to 'conversions' in his classic *Gifford Lectures* of 1901 ('The Varieties of Religious Experience'), sought to interpret using a suggestive general schema: in the subliminal consciousness of the subject, a new epicentric personality core prepares itself and merges with the hot spot of operative self-awareness at an opportune moment, bringing about an intense transformative experience.[131] The application of this model to the case of Paul immediately yields a consistent picture; in practice-theoretical terms, he had already 'trained with the opponent' for some time. His exercises in hostility towards the Jesuans had put him in sufficient form to cross over to the position of his previous adversary at the right moment. He had long formed a clear, albeit still unwelcome idea of this adversary's strengths on the pre-conscious level. In this context, it seems significant that in the 'autobiographical' version of the scene on the road to Damascus, he already addresses the speaker who calls him from above as 'Lord' (*kýrie*), even before he has identified himself as the Jesus he had been persecuting. Everything would suggest that his second person was waiting for this interjection.

From this point of view, Paul was not a convert, let alone a 'revolutionary', as is claimed in recent neo-Jacobin interpretations of the Pauline phenomenon,[132] but rather an opportunist – in the sense of Machiavelli's theory of opportunity – who, in spite of himself, had long since recognized the high spiritual chances of the new doctrine he had initially fought. He had understood, at first intuitively and later explicitly, that only a messiah who genuinely came could help the politically hopeless and intellectually stagnating Judaism of his time to escape from its rut. Naturally he had never remotely intended to found or set in motion 'universalism', or even a subjective variation thereof; he simply applied himself to reformatting an elect group (much like the professional revolutionary of the Leninist cast, who were always more elitist exterminists than inclusion-friendly universalists, and like the no-longer-numerous successors of Robespierre in France). It is characteristic of 'conversions' of this type that they occur more in the mode of yielding to an already pre-consciously recognized self-evidence than of adopting a completely new doctrine – James quotes extensively from the accounts of heavy drinkers who, through a form of religious self-collection (usually in a Protestant environment with strong conversion stereotypes), had managed to ally themselves with their existing, but previously powerless better judgement and thus distance themselves from their addiction.

There Is No Conversion: The Augustinian Paradigm

In this context we have an opportunity to re-evaluate Oswald Spengler's strong thesis that essentially, conversions do not exist – only re-occupations of vacant positions in the fixed structures of a culture's field of options.[133] The basal soul atmosphere of an advanced-civilized complex remains identical through all superficial changes of confession, he argues, and what seems like a U-turn from the outside can, in reality, never be more than an ultimately arbitrary variation (albeit occasionally a far-reaching one for present and future generations) within a clearly demarcated space of possibility. Hence in spiritual matters too, the saying applies: *plus ça change, plus c'est la même chose.*

The suggestiveness of this claim can best be explained using the example of the second conversion hero in Christian tradition, Aurelius Augustinus, who, in his *Confessions*, famously stylized the entire story of his youth as a protracted hesitation before his 'conversion' in 386. In his case, Spengler's theorem seems supremely plausible. One can easily use his life story – like those of countless analogous confession-changers and serious-getters – to show that no trace of a 'conversion' ever took place in the deep structure of his personality. Rather, within an age-old orientation towards the world above, he simply changed addresses, or the Great Other, the transcendent trainer, several times – from Manichaeism to Platonism, from Platonism to philosophical Christianity, from philosophical Christianity to a theocentrically darkened cult of submission. He was no anomaly in this; as early as the second century AD, 'conversions' to philosophy had taken place among the educated members of the Roman ecumenical community, and these were organically continued in adoptions of Christianity – in the case of Justin the Martyr, for example, the Catholic patron saint of philosophers.

At no point in these multiple rebuildings of his edifice of convictions did Augustine go through a complete *epistrophé*; he simply radicalized the break with worldly life already foreshadowed in his Manichaeic beginnings bit by bit, until he attained a personally condensed and completely embodiable form of ascetic rejection of 'this world'. Nor did the famous 'take up and read' [*tolle lege*] contain any new discovery, merely a reminder of familiar motifs that had ripened within his 'epicentric personality' for the inner takeover. Thus, in ideal-typical purity, he embodied the qualities of the 'sick soul' or the depressively 'divided self', of which William James showed how, not infrequently, it also achieves the collection of its powers in a gradual or sudden unification without any religious turn.[134] In psychological terms, what converts have often described as the effect of grace manifests itself above all as a personal energy gain as a result of increased integration. Such integration takes place when the entire system of mental drives is subordinated to a unified perspective of purpose. It is due to this effect that all partial forces now work together under the direction of a previously latent new centre of conviction. Such a 'united' subject experiences itself as simultaneously called-upon and moved: the movebo effect[135] manifests itself in it with twice the strength. In the case of Augustine, the 'unification' seemed to have been reached at the moment when he achieved the concentration of all partial energies in the gesture of Christian-Platonic self-abandonment. The candidate's long hesitation, furthermore, proves that during his time, a complete conversion to Christianity had to be undertaken as an entrance into a training camp surrounded by ascetic horrors, the Byzantine *asketería* or the Western *monasterium*. It was thus never purely a matter of the 'faith' so often invoked by Paul, but rather the total subordination of the person to the harsh practice law of the *imitatio* with fatal results – or the monastic metaphorization thereof. It seems only consistent, then, if the initial eutonic balance between philosophy and religion in Augustine's early writings gave way in time to his bleaker late theology.

The originality of Augustine's 'conversion' is only evident in the determination with which the convert managed to elevate his transformation to the exemplary level. His *Confessions* are the first model of Christian performance literature – the transformation of a life story into a lesson in grace. What helped Augustine most to carry out this performative turn was his Christian radicalization of the Platonic doctrine of the psyche's original malposition. In Augustine's vision, what Plato had described merely as the factual fixation of those trapped in the cave on the shadow play on the cave walls – in neutral terms: the priority of empirically oriented perception over reflective insight among worldlings – is immediately declared a consequence of original sin: a repetition of the first 'perversion' in which the creature turned away from its creator, preferring itself to its origin. From that point on, sinful egotism governs all actions, as life in perversion always means idolizing the things one should be using (sensual and worldly things) and using the things one should honour (spiritual and godly things).[136] The perverted creature, according to Augustine, cannot perform the complementary reversal to undo the resulting metaphysical damage by its own strength – it would remain incurably fixed in its fallen position, its abandonment of origin, if God Himself did not accommodate it in the person of Christ and enable its re-conversion.

Spengler was certainly exaggerating when he rejected the possibility of conversion within a given culture out of hand, but there were good reasons for his objection, as the vast majority of actual conversions take place not in the mode of an epistrophic total reversal, but of a transition to a more or less natural alternative; ultimately, a truly radical change only occurs upon taking the advanced-civilized path as such, which trains mortals for the high forms of vertical tension by injecting them with the madness of longing for the impossible.

Seneca defines the individual-revolutionary character of this turn late on, but clearly, when he declares: *Desinamus quo voluimus velle!* 'Let us cease wanting what we previously wanted!'[137] The will to want differently sets in motion the permanently tense concern for the new, unaccustomed and improbable stance. One could say something similar about the doctrine of Epicurus, which, in its way, meant practising the break with the vulgar *modus vivendi*. Because wisdom implies emancipation from the mistaken faith in the predominance of Tyche or Fortuna, it aims for a radical departure from ordinary concerns: where there was fear of the gods, there shall now be fearlessness. This already heralds the Enlightenment – the conversion of the spirit to a use of one's own life without religious intimidation. Religiously encoded conversions, on the other hand, usually only display the character of a switch to an alternative cult system with rearranged compulsions. This process can generally be imagined as a shallow operation – even the striking inversion figure 'Burn what you worshipped and worship what you burned' in no way makes the procedure more inward; it merely formulates the directive to give Christ the ritual attentions previously reserved for Wotan, or whatever forest, wind and mountain gods one used to follow. With numerous other religiously coded conversions too, one observes most of all the metanoetic shifts of emphasis within a heavily prestructured field.

Even in the psychoanalysis of the twentieth century, incidentally, one can still hear echoes of the ancient *conversio*. From a distance, the Freudian maxim 'Where there was id, there shall be ego' reveals its membership in the group of metanoetic practices where the change of living habits is accompanied by a change of subject, that is to say a reallocation of the guiding figure to the place of the Great Other. Here the id corresponds typologically to the murky category of demonic possession, and the ego to monotheistic brightening.

Conversion as Change of Trainer: St Francis and Ignatius

From a practice-theoretical perspective, conversions of the meta-noetic type amount to a change of trainer, as the converts generally submit not only to an altered moral regime – and *eo ipso* a new Great Other – but also a new practice plan. The personality structure as such, however, is usually kept throughout the change. Thus the long-habitualized zealotry of Paul 'after Damascus' was reassigned from Pharisaic to Jesuan principles – and subsequently expanded with Christological supplements of his own making. Certainly it makes a difference whether one trains with Gamaliel, the rabbinical teacher, or with Jesus, the resurrected. One would be doing an injustice to the people's apostle if one reduced the *opus Christi* he set in motion exclusively to its zealotic element. In submitting to Christian doctrine in the matter of love (*agapé* or *caritas*), Paul had experienced a notable expansion of his personality. And the success story of Christianity would simply be unthinkable without Paul's stretching of the horizon of chosenness (which, as noted above, must not be confused with universalism).

The metanoetic forms of reversal would consistently prove the most far-reaching for the further development of Christianity as the most important practice field and habitus generator in the transitional space between antiquity and the Middle Ages. Alongside these, the real initiatic sacrament – baptism – remained a momentary and external matter. An effective remoulding of human beings does not depend on a singular gesture; it can only succeed as a result of lasting self-curatorial efforts. The interpretation of baptism as rebirth lends the act a symbolic depth that does not have any adequate correlate in terms of internalization.

The extent to which Christian metanoia amounts to a change of practice system and trainer figure is shown not least by the two most popular conversion legends of the high Middle Ages and early Modern Age: those of St Francis of Assisi and Ignatius of Loyola. If one examines the turn of the young Francis, it was anything but a sudden leap into the Christian camp. In a certain sense, the youth had long been prepared for the later turn, whose immediate cause was the well-known conflict of authority with his father, since internalizing a robust form of knightly idealism and an elegant, quasi-Provençal rhetoric of courtly love – commentators often refer in this context to his mother's French descent. It was when Francis seemingly turned 'against his own origins' in his spectacular renunciation of paternal authority that he began to consolidate them all the more. In the symbolic area, it was only a small step from the noble dames of troubadour poetry to the 'Lady Poverty' whom he now served, and similarly, the elegant upper-class Platonism underlying the courtly cult of ladies and honour (which had visibly affected the middle classes of Assisi) was not far from the people's Platonism offered by late ancient and medieval Christianity.

Once again, the novelty lies purely in the decision – in the focus on the one thing that collects individual power where 'there is need'. The young Francis was unmistakably seized by the zeitgeist: the Christianity of the early urban period was looking for a superstar. With the role of poverty's troubadour, he had found a position that allowed him to transpose the *imitatio Christi* into an allegory of courtly love. By learning to draw sweetness from bitterness, he gained leeway for the release of mental energy to compensate for the constant depression of the coming centuries: the growing scandal of involuntary poverty in an era that was increasingly devoting itself to wealth. By practising self-denial for the sake of Lady Poverty, he created surplus powers from the weakest point – albeit at a price that already made his contemporaries shudder. He paid this price in the form of a triumphant self-chastisement that would not rest until total imitation, the emulation of the crucified through the duplication of his wounds, had been achieved. Thomas of Celano put his finger on the critical point: 'Nothing else could spring up in that soil, since from the first that wonderful cross claimed it for its own.'[138] For the *imitator Christi*, this inevitably meant that he must live no longer than his model: without the imperative of following the Lord even in the duration of his life, his deliberate self-attrition would have been inconceivable. The pantomime of his death shows how much he was still thinking in the traditional terms of the ascetic *agon* and Christian athletism:

309

For, worn down by his serious illness that was being brought to an end with every suffering, he had himself placed naked upon the naked ground, so that in that final hour when the enemy could still rage against him, he might wrestle naked with a naked enemy. He waited without fear for his triumph, and with his hands clasped he was grasping a *crown of justice*.[139]

For Francis and his followers, the thought form of *imitatio* went so deep that the small congregation surrounding the dying man even celebrated the Last Supper – coming dangerously close to blasphemous parody. In this imaginative field, the reappearance of the deceased to some friars in a transfigured state was naturally a must: it was recognized that his person and that of Christ had merged into one and the same person – an indication that intense supra-naturalisms appear in the form of fields and develop in spaces of synchronously practised suggestibility.

The case of Ignatius of Loyola also shows all the hallmarks of a classic change of trainer under the sign of metanoia. Although these are already distant from the sacred expressionism of the performance artist Francis, the conversion mechanism manifests itself here in strictly analogous forms. In keeping with the code of honour during that period, the structure of the young noble's personality was fully developed, and his horizon of ambition saturated with the popular concepts of knightly life and the lady cult. After the catastrophe of the battle of Pamplona in 1521, which left the thirty-year-old officer crippled and removed him from the ranks of the pretenders to worldly fame, he too was seized by the spirit of the age, which this time suggested an *imitatio Christi* in militant forms. Ignatius changed trainers, switching from Amadis of Gaul, the hero of the chivalric novel, to Christ – who now appears in the form of a divine general who can only be imitated by earthly elite troops.

I have discussed the unforeseeable consequences of the Ignatian turn for the further history of Catholic and more general forms of subjectification at greater length elsewhere.[140] They are inseparable from the modernization of practice – in this case, from the transference of the military training principle to the new roles of religion-political achievement, which were formed on the battlefields of the Counter-Reformation. What makes Loyola's place in the history of subject techniques so exceptionally significant is that all earlier layers of autoplastic practice had successively been sedimented within it in complete clarity: what began with the drill of the Greek and Roman soldiers, and was continued by athletes and gladiators before

Christian hermits and cenobites appropriated the ascetic secrets of these agonists – all this returned after 1521 in the existence of the failed soldier, leading to the strongest surge in newer psychotechnic exercises. This time, however – corresponding to the humanistic milieu with its neo-rhetorical rupture – it was in the form of a theatre of the imagination in which the practising person, following strict instructions, convinces themselves of their own worthlessness and immeasurable guilt before the saviour. In their time, the Jesuit exercises, this autogenic training in contrition over thirty hard days and nights of utmost concentration, obviously formed the newest layer in the stratigram of Old European practice cultures, whose older and most ancient layers lead back to the beginnings of heroism and athleticism. Recent neuro-rhetorical research, incidentally, shows that the 'artificial' affects produced in exercises are physiologically indistinguishable from natural ones.

The almost instrumental grab of the Jesuit technique for the trusting psyche, which itself turned meditation into a training camp, explicitly heralded the beginning of what would later be called the 'Modern Age'. Its inhabitants developed into 'modern people' to the extent that they convinced themselves they had discovered the secret of self-determination in exchanging absolute dependence on God for human self-assertion. We will see that nothing could be further from the truth.

III

The Exercises of the Moderns

For indeed this is the time above all ages that are past both to hope, and to attempt, greater things.

John Amos Comenius, *A Reformation of Schooles, 1642*

PROSPECT

The Re-Secularization of the Withdrawn Subject

On the Power of the Slogan

'To hope, and to attempt, greater things':[1] one of the strengths of the modern world is that it was never at a loss when it came to proclaiming slogans through the mouths of its protagonists by which participants in excessive crusades could identify one another. Now, two hundred years later, what the Florentine goldsmith and humanist Lorenzo Ghiberti said to his co-conspirators in the early fifteenth century, at the start of their argonautical journey to the shores of universal art – 'Men can do all things if they will'[2] – has almost become self-evident to the artistic and technical virtuosos, the modern people of skill, the entrepreneurs of their own lives, as well as the increasingly numerous prefects for the life of the others. Despite all periodically recurring cycles of historical discouragement and calls for self-reduction, the proud motto of the Modern Age would never be entirely forgotten; even the Soviet educators from the time of change around 1920 still repeated this revolutionary-optimistic thesis in every register, though perhaps adding the qualification that aside from the resolute will to act, the social conditions must also be given.

The great Comenius (1592–1670), founder of Baroque pedagogy and idea provider for the construction of modern large-scale learning machines, knew what it meant to undertake greater things after so many wasted centuries: grace is great, but technology applied to man is even greater; and election takes us a certain distance, but the new art of education takes us further. Where there had been the exception, there would now be the rule. Now was the time to apply the letterpress to young souls and print annual volumes of students who would emerge like prize specimens from the erratum-free human publishing

315

house. It was no coincidence that the visionary educator spoke of his school project as a *typographaeum vivum*, a live typesetting apparatus that would populate the world with masterpieces of human print. He thus presented an idea that could be newly acknowledged by the media theorists of the late twentieth century – although these would speak less of the subject being printed in a press than of its mental formatting. The early twentieth century revealed its concerns when Leon Trotsky lectured in the style of the enthusing hardware ideologue:

> Once he has done with the anarchic forces of his own society, man will set to work on himself, in the pestle and retort of the chemist. For the first time mankind will regard itself as raw material, or at best as a physical and psychic semi-finished product.[3]

According to the revolutionary cult of science, completion could only take place in the mints of the New Human Being which the Soviet state was planning to create. The periods after Trotsky showed that work on the human being continued in quite different treatment centres. The semi-finished product man has its dangers that resist reprocessing, whether into educated man, the 'overman' or the New Human Being. But at least, since the end of the Second World War, the news has been all over town: 'Man has reached the point of treating the human race as material.'[4]

The New Zeitgeist: Experiment with Humans

The path to the age of production, which culminated in the production of the producer, began long before the twentieth century. Whenever there was progress along this route, it was announced with great pomp that humans were becoming 'accessible' to themselves. It seems that the effective centre of modern currentnesses consists in continuous reports on the growth of the radius of human availability to oneself and one's kind. Such novelties have always – below the level of general rejection stemming from their potentially disturbing nature – evoked affirmative and negative passions. Indeed, the appearance of anything truly new on this front was followed by apocalyptic declarations, most recently around the year 2000, when the decoding of the human genome was imminent. *Tempus est*, Comenius wrote on the wall in fiery letters in 1639: 'It is time' – this formula continues to determine agendas for the futurized world to this day. The most pressing item on these agendas is the systematic production of human beings who meet the highest standards of anthropomorphism – we are speaking of the seventeenth century in Europe, when the zeitgeists of change were becoming strong (though the word *Zeitgeist* only entered the modern German vocabulary around 1800). 'Anthropomorphism' – at the time, this still meant an unimpaired image of God. For the passionate reformatory theologian, it encompassed universal knowledge of the three great books of being: nature, the human soul and the Holy Scripture.[5] Humanity was now to go into serial production in order to populate every area of this continent – and later the planet – with individuals at the level of the humanly possible. Patience with the old inadequacies had come to an end: it was time for humans to cease being an outgrowth of moral coincidence. We, the meanwhile impatient self-sculptors and man-sculptors of the technological centuries, could no longer wait until some individual deigned to break with their conventional existence and create a heightened, exemplary life through metanoia, asceticism and study. In future, the young creatures in the human gardens of the Baroque state would be cultivated on high trellises to become well-formed specimens of their kind.[6]

The new educators believed that they knew how to overhaul each individual's coincidental weariness of their previous life: the whole system of moulding humans was arranged metanoetically – indeed, the basic order of the 'pedagogical province' itself bespeaks the impulse to pre-empt the late remorse of individuals through the early training of all. This 'anthropogogics' reveals a naïve perfectionism whose élan still fed the later Enlightenment. Here discipline is aligned with the quest for perfection, duty with voluntary agreement, and study with inner surplus. It is only a secondary concern to reflect on the necessity of facing the wilder outgrowths of humanity with the means of guarding and punishing.[7]

It is high time to clear up a misunderstanding to which Foucault contributed: it is not in the prisons and places of oppressive supervision but in the frequently strict schools and academies of the Modern Age, along with the craftsmen's workshops[8] and artists' studios, that the main human orthopaedics of modernity is carried out – that is to say, the moulding of the young by the standards of Christian-humanist discipline. The real aim of the departure to the age of arts and technologies was to train ever new generations of virtuosos. Certainly, the disciplinary imperative shows its second face in the 'heterotopic' background inhabited by the droves of 'infamous humans' (in the age of absolutist population politics, they inevitably constitute a massive group) – and this face must be mentioned by anyone seeking to reconstruct the 'birth of the prison' from the spirit

317

of responsibility for the human surplus. It would be absurd, however, to reduce the concept of disciplining in general to the penitentiary, repressive and surveillance-state meanings on which Foucault placed such deliberately exaggerated emphasis in the writings of his middle period.[9]

Anyone wishing to acquaint themselves with all phases of the production of the New Human Being, at any rate, must probe as far back as the seventeenth century, even to the turbulences of the Reformation – and further still, to their preludes in late medieval mysticism. Whoever wanted, like the young Gorky – clearly under Nietzsche's influence – to 'write "man" in capital letters' almost unknowingly joined a tradition that had begun with the recruits of Christ in the Egyptian desert monasteries and the Pauline communities in Greece and Asia Minor, those pneumatic aggregations through which the Holy Spirit, supported by the exercises in crucifixion of the flesh, was meant to bring about a 'new creation'.[10]

The early Christians began to transform their whole lives into an experiment in order to resemble the God-man: *nos autem in experimentis volvimur*, Augustine writes in his *Confessions* – only God always remains identical to himself, whereas we are tossed from trial to trial.[11] Modern humans augmented the ascetic experimentalism of the ancients with technical and artistic, then finally political experimentalism. The task they set themselves, in all seriousness, was to rewrite the text of the human condition – partly with updated Christian-humanist procedures, partly following the guidelines of post-Christian and post-humanist schemes of existence. The essay and the experiment are not merely literary and scientific procedures; they shaped modernity's style of existence as a whole – and, after 1789, also that of major politics and the national and global economy. An experimenter is someone who takes a chance every time, convinced that the new is always right. Needless to say, the American president Theodore Roosevelt placed himself in the same tradition when he invoked the 'great work of uplifting mankind' in 1899, exchanging the Christian world mission for civilizatory messianism.[12]

Modern Unrest

The beginnings of the turn towards greater things were already several centuries in the past when Comenius launched the campaign of universal education (*panpaedia*) in response to the apocalyptically interpreted confusion of the Thirty Years War. In the human zoo of

the burgeoning Modern Age, the Black Death of 1348 had been followed by an unrest that would never be calmed. There has been much
speculation as to the origins of the new zeitgeist and *Weltgeist*. Some
sought to locate them in the mysticism of Northwest European towns
or in the early capitalist economy; connections have been posited with
the development of the clockwork mechanism, or with the double-
entry bookkeeping of the Venetians, propagated by the Franciscan
priest Luca Pacioli in his 1494 book on arithmetic, which was read
throughout Europe. The Faustian soul was taken as the metaphysical
source of modern restlessness, while Doctor Faustus, that man of infinite skills and 'far-famed Sorcerer and Master of the Black Art' who
pawned his soul for the sake of heightened self-enjoyment, was conversely declared the personification of credit, that fifth essence which
grips honest debtors to the marrow and drives them over land and
sea in ever-expanding trajectories. Modern unrest was also attributed
to the shock of spatial expansion resulting from Atlantic seafaring
and the discovery of the New World, as if the global mobility of the
floating capital on the oceans had reproduced itself in the attitude
towards life in the most obscure mainland towns. 'The primary fact
of the Modern Age is not that the earth revolves around the sun, but
that money flows around the earth.'[13]

In the following, I will show that the specifically modern unrest in
the field of shaping humans – which, in its most recent offshoots, is
still and more than ever ours – stems most of all from endogenous,
that is to say practice-historically or ascetologically relevant sources.
Looking back on the programmes and workshops of the practising life in the premodern world, it becomes clear: the realization
among Marx and the Young Hegelians that 'man produces man' can
only be understood in all its ramifications if one looks behind the
word 'produce', which was borrowed one-sidedly from the modern
working world and its industrial procedures, and also perceives the
universe of practising behaviour, training and routines of conscious
and unconscious keeping-in-shape, among which, ironically enough,
one must also include the phenomenon of getting-out-of-shape
through the wrong training and exercises in neglect. This concession seems more acceptable in the case of athletes and monks than
farmers, factory workers or handymen. Nonetheless, even the most
intense activities of a working type constitute one of the many masks
of the practising life. Whoever lifts it sees through the mystifications
of the productivistic era and sees the omnipresence of the practice
aspect amidst work phenomena. Then it becomes demonstrable,
down to the smallest detail, how the active mould themselves through

319

regularly repeated activities. It is necessary to understand why and through what repercussions on his own existence man can effectively be considered the producer of man.

Autoplastic Action: *Circulus Virtuosus*

The basic information about the production of humans through humans is made explicit via study of the *vita activa*; the pragmatists of the nineteenth century realized this. By studying the active life, they uncovered the basic anthropotechnic law: the repercussions of all actions and movements on the actor. Working places the worker in the world and marks them with the stamp of their own acts by the short route of a practising self-shaping. No activity evades the principle of retroactive influence on the operator – and whatever reacts to earlier events also affects later ones. The act produces the actor, the reflection the reflected, the emotion the feeler, and the test of conscience the conscience itself. Habits shape the virtues and vices, and complexes of habits form 'cultures'. The European seafarers who circumnavigate the world are still discovering peoples with their own ways of life, some of them bizarre, on the most distant islands; the anthropologists on board recognize the power of practice systems in the local customs and describe these autoplastic rules of human shaping, in analogy to corresponding European phenomena and, for want of a better term, as 'religious' rituals.

The practising life is not limited to a simple reproduction of actors by their actions, however. All expansions of ability circles, all increases extending to the furthest caves of artistry, take place on the basis of self-shaping through practice.

The mystery of why achievements tend towards growth under certain circumstances has not been fully solved to this day; for some forms of ascending spirals, however, more precise descriptions are available. In the field of physical strength increase, for example, the explicit description of the supercompensation mechanism in modern sport physiology has brought about a far-reaching expansion of understanding. The newer sciences of training have been able to show in detail how, after heavy strains, the muscular apparatus can restore its strength to a level higher than its original fitness status – assuming it is granted the necessary recovery time. The rhythms of regeneration hold the secret of the overexertion that leads to higher performance levels. This phenomenon has been intuitively comprehensible since time immemorial, and had already been exploited for intensive training sessions in antiquity; on the other hand, the ancients were also familiar with the phenomena of overtraining that appear if regeneration rhythms are disregarded.[14] With increases in mental and fine motor performance, supercompensation is augmented by a form of superadaptation. This ensures that nervous and kinetic systems accommodate certain regular stimulations through a form of pre-emptive willingness to execute – thus even highly improbable movements such as *prestissimo* runs on the piano or a conjurer's tricks ('prestidigitator' literally means 'fast-fingerer') can be imprinted on the bodily memory and stabilized as a virtuosic habitus. Here it is the anticipatory intelligence in particular that is stimulated. Recent research in the fields of learning theory, neuro-motorics, neuro-rhetoric and neuro-aesthetics consolidate and vary didactic intuitions that originate in early asceticisms and artistries. All somewhat advanced civilizations make use of the observation that every active person is dyed in the lye of their activities until the miracle of 'second nature' takes place and they perform the near-impossible almost effortlessly.[15]

The highest theorem of explicit training theories, then, is that ability subjected to persistent furthering tension produces, almost 'of its own accord', heightened ability. Through exact descriptions of the *circulus virtuosos*, it becomes explicable how accomplishment leads to higher accomplishment and success to expanded success. The Jesuan axiom 'everyone who has will be given more'[16] is not evidence of an early Galilean capitalism, but rather one of the oldest formulations of the circle of success, also known in sociology as the 'Matthew effect'. Whoever is able will be granted more ability. It is not without reason that successful people from the most diverse fields believe they can learn from one another at a distance; they intuit that virtuosos from all kinds of disciplines emerge from comparable circles of increase. They see humans standing at the crossroads which all forms of positive feedback must pass. Together, they thus become carriers of able virtue, which is often only a short distance away from giving virtue – this observation creates the possibility of affirming the medieval doctrine of the *connexio virtutum* on a modern foundation.[17] Everyday intuitions already tell us that non-leisure is the beginning of virtue. Conversely, Christian monks recognized lethargy as the mother of despair – accompanied by its other unattractive daughters: digression, verboseness, aimless curiosity, lack of restraint and inconstancy.[18] It is the daily line of writing that forms the artist, the daily self-denial that forms the ascetic, the daily encounter with the power needs of other humans that forms the diplomat, and the daily joy at the willingness of children to be stimulated that forms the teacher.

Anyone who subjects themselves to rituals and regularities develops *nolens volens* into their representative. What is a carrier of culture if not a guardian of repetition? Just as practice makes perfect, training makes the subject – provided that we understand subjectivity in the light of the general theory of practice as the carrier of its activity sequences, the apprentice of trainable modules and the holder of its habitual acquisitions, without having to deny the relative validity of the usual interpretation of subjectivity as the epicentre of expression, reflexivity and innovation. As soon as one realizes how every gesture carried out shapes its performer and determines their future state from the second occurrence on, one also knows why there is no such thing as a meaningless movement.

Repetition lost its innocence in the anthropological Enlightenment: as people now explicitly understood, the continuance of the world depends on it – which does not say anything against the unique, except that we abuse it by dancing around the Golden Calf of the 'event'. It is in the nature of natures to be systems of repetition for the established, and this applies almost equally to cultures. God Himself has to carry out most things via the routines of nature, and can only occasionally make use of His ontological secret weapon, the miracle. Kierkegaard was already speaking from the perspective of modern reflexive knowledge when he stated:

> If God Himself had not willed repetition, there would never have been a world. [. . .] This is the reason there is a world. The world consists of repetition. Repetition is actuality and the earnestness of existence.[19]

Nietzsche adds to this what he learned through long experiments on himself: style is indeed man himself, provided one is aware that style is a cultural manifestation of repetition. Anyone with style will even see happiness as the good habit of being happy.[20] Even genius is simply a group of good habits whose collision makes sparks fly.

In order to uncover the matrix of Old and New European techniques for shaping humans, one must first examine the training centres scattered across the whole continent in which those who practise with Christ prepare for their highest *agones*, brought into shape by their abbots, pastors, saints and learned mentors. And those who have been called 'professors' since the sixteenth century were initially no more than trainers at schools of transfiguration, and those later termed 'students' were first of all seekers in whom the eros of impossibility was at work *more academico*. They yielded willingly to the illusion that is indispensable for all advanced civilizations: that the inimitable is imitable, and the incomparable repeatable. As soon as the utmost ambition had taken root within them, they came under the spell of the paradox without whose constant re-enactment no culture can securely fix its upper pole. For them, therefore, 'You must change your life!' meant nothing other than the call to follow the godly or god-manly models under whose influence the boundaries between the possible and the impossible are blurred.[21] With the advent of modern times, the absolute imperative changed the direction of its impact. In future, it would be: 'You must act at all times in such a way that within your person, you anticipate the better world in the worse.' It will not be long before the meaning of this directive is twisted into an instruction for 'external application': 'You must change the world so that, if it is reshaped in the correct sense, you can adapt to it with a clear conscience.' Modernity is the time in which those humans who hear the call to change no longer know where they should start: with the world or with themselves – or with both at once.[22]

The Discovery of the World in Humans

The forms of unrest that began to manifest themselves in the fourteenth century stem primarily from the surpluses of subject energy that were bred in the thousand-year empire of withdrawals from 'this world' *more philosophico* and *more christiano*. One could almost speak of an original accumulation of capital comprising concentrations, intensities and readinesses to act that one day had to look for suitable forms of investment. The centuries following the Black Death in Europe in fact belonged to an unprecedentedly novel economy in which new means of practice – machines, tools, media and funds – brought about new circumstances of practice: first of all schools and more schools, then artists' studios, theatres, concert halls, barracks, factories, clinics, prisons, speakers' pulpits, markets, places of assembly, stadiums and sport studios. What began in the Modern Age was no less than a new form of large-scale anthropotechnic regime, a fundamentally changed battle formation of disciplines. Need we repeat that it was Foucault whose studies on the history of modern disciplinary procedures, which had no models to speak of, sensitized us to this previously almost unnoticed field?

The decisive changes primarily concern the traditional division in the world of the practising life, which I call the 'ontological local government reorganization'. In the course of this process, the practising of antiquity, the adepts of the philosophical *modus vivendi*, and later the monks, the pentitential warriors and athletes of Christ, had withdrawn from worldly matters in order to devote themselves exclusively to what each viewed as 'their own'. Their whole existence revolved around the concern for their own ability to remain intact in the midst of the ominous century. Their aim was no less than the final immunization of their own lives in the face of the constant threat of injuries and ubiquitous distractions. *Suum tantum curare* had been the salvific formula for the era of self-discovery in retreat from the world, applying to both philosophical and religioid life plans.

One cannot remotely claim that the Modern Age disabled the world-averse and radically metanoetic forms of religiously or philosophically coded *cura sui* overnight. Nothing would be more deluded than to believe that in early modernity, the escapists of yesterday suddenly turned into new worldlings who regretted their gloomy absences. The legend of the 'modern individual's' suddenly recovered affirmation of the world and life should be approached with suspicion. More than a few sound thinkers of the Modern Age placed their lives programmatically under the sign of Saturn – the planet of distance from the world. The *homines novi* who entered the stage in the fourteenth century, the early virtuoso era, were not runaway monks who had abruptly embraced the joys of the extroverted life, as if they wanted to erase the memory of their thousand-year recession like some regrettable episode. They normally clung doggedly to their ontological exile, indeed claimed more than ever a noble exterritoriality in relation to impoverished ordinariness. Even an exemplary new human like Petrarch – one of the first moderns to wear a poet's crown, the emblem of a new type of aristocracy – had very strong personal reasons to hide in his refuge in the Vaucluse for so many years, searching for a non-monastic form of *vita solitaria*. Where else could he shelter his noble sickness, the world-hatred of the man of black-galled constitution, the evil discovered and fought by the abbots in the Egyptian desert under the name *akédia*, if not in his study cell, far from vulgar concerns?

For the early moderns, devotion to the spiritual sphere still assumed a refusal to participate in profane affairs. And yet they, the proto-virtuosos, vacillating between the older monks' cells and the newer studios of the humanists,[23] found themselves drawn into a heightened learning dynamic. They were pulled along by a drift towards self-intensification that only formed a contradictory unity with conventional monastic de-selfing courses. This intensification resulted in tendencies towards a restricted new participation of spir-

itual persons in the world. Using a term coined by the neo-phenomenologist Hermann Schmitz, albeit in a modified fashion, I call this
return a 're-embedding' of the excluded subject.[24] The first embedding enables individuals to participate directly in their situations;
through re-embedding, they find their way back to these after phases
of estrangement. Whoever affirms an immersion in the situation is on
the way to becoming what Goethe, referring to himself, occasionally
called 'the worldling in the middle' [*das Weltkind in der Mitte*].[25]

Nonetheless: even at the start of the Modern Age, the exiles of the
practising were chosen just as resolutely as in antiquity, when the
ethical distinction began to take effect. How else can one explain
the popularity of the icon of St Jerome, which inspired countless variations on the joys of retreat in the early Modern Age? The scholar
with the lion at his feet still testifies to the attraction of the contemplative life on the outskirts of a convivially transformed, in fact a bour-
geoisified desert – and in a turbulent time that, one might think, was
knowledgeable about everything but deserts and refuges. But note:
the escapism of the moderns was as urgently motivated as it was in
the days of the earliest disgust at circumstances. It still gave hope to
those without worldly hope, still offered those with no social prospects the prospect of an alternative existence. Nonetheless, the newer
retreats often accumulated worldly meanings with a value and scope
of their own, to the point where recessively excluded subjectivity,
within its enclave of self-concern, emerged as a figure of the world in
its own right. Now, from the starting point of a methodically sought
unworldliness, a virtuoso industry blossomed. Its masters took themselves up as workpieces of the art of living, moulding themselves into
humane valuables. What Nietzsche's confession in *Ecce Homo* – 'I
took myself in hand' – renders audible, as well as the auto-therapeutic
impulse of a chronically ill man, are overtones that recall the turn of
the early moderns towards a transformation of themselves into living
artifices. Perhaps the habit[26] maketh not the monk, but study gets
the scholar in shape, writing exercises make the humanist skilled at
his subject, and *virtù* allows the virtuoso to shine. In the midst of a
subjectivity excluded through regression into itself, the practising discover a distant coast within themselves – the promise of an unknown
world. More than a hundred years before the actual continent, a symbolic America appeared on the horizon: its coast is the place where
the practising of modernity set foot in the small world of themselves.

Hence what Jacob Burckhardt, following the trail of Michelet,
had presented as the formula for the Renaissance – 'the discovery
of the world and man' – was initially, seemingly paradoxically, an

inner-world event. It led to the discovery of the world in humans, or rather the discovery of the human being as a model of the world, a microcosmic abbreviation of the universe. Friedrich Hebbel still had a notion of this phrase when he noted in his journal: 'Great men are humanity's tables of contents.' The secret of the humane ability to be whole would no longer be founded on the biblically certified image of God: it pointed equally to the image of the world, which makes suffering, active and contemplative humans view themselves as universal mirrors and cosmic oracles. This launched the train that would not stop until it arrived at the Baroque equation of God and nature – with the human being as a copula and living sign of equality. For the subject of the Modern Age, this meant that it had to understand itself as a reality-hungry potential. From that point on, being human meant running oneself as a workshop of self-realization.

Homo Mirabile

The re-interpretation of the human potency for totality transformed escapism, flight from the world, into the most world-filled mode of being thus far encountered by the individuals of our cultural area. The enrichment of withdrawal into a life form that displays no less wealth or diversity than extroverted existence produces the unlimitedly cultivatable self-structure addressed with the anthropological catchword of the Modern Age: 'personality'. Modern personalities: these are the microcosmic works of the art of living that result from the time-honoured position of recessive self-formation – except no longer in the spirit of monastic *humilitas* or the mystical art of dying, but rather driven by an encyclopaedic artistic dynamic that leads to interminable virtuosities and virtualities, jaw-dropping results of an inward extroversion. The imperative 'You must change your life!' now implies taking oneself in hand and moulding one's own existence into an object of admiration.

Where humans themselves are meant to become the *mirabile*, the living *artificia* admired by those around them (and that means far more than respect, love or sympathy), they cannot remain in their escapist retreat forever; one day they must go on the stage and turn their inward performance into an outward one. Petrarch was forced to leave his refuge when he was crowned poet laureate on the Capitoline Hill in Rome – on 6 April 1341, a key date in the history of 'modern fame'. Much of what conventional Renaissance scholars have produced to document the 'modern individual' depended on the outing of the intelligent human being in the new forums of admiration – it is not without reason that Burckhardt had already emphasized the correlation of fame and the culture of individuality as a characteristic of the era. What has more recently been termed 'the archive' was initially no more than a collecting point for fame and the famous in the cultural memory, a function that, for reasons yet to be established, had to be come under the control of the modern state – or, more precisely, the semantic state banks, museums and major libraries whose duty it is to look after the balance of meanings and 'cultural values'.[27] What seems like a Vanity Fair is, in truth, the state treasury of prestige and excellence, the nucleus of a new economy based on the creation of cultural value. The fact that these secular collections challenge the status of the church's salvific treasury testifies to the attractiveness of this new system of value.

We recall: in the sphere of monastic anthropotechnic forms, the monks worked on transforming themselves into the status of the monk, the exemplary sculpture of servient obedience whose legend was *incurvatus et humiliatus sum*, evidence of the effects of the Holy Spirit on human material.[28] Under divine observation (the angels, after all, pass on all information upwards) and monastic supervision (the abbot acknowledges all his flock's movements), the spiritually practising sought to become like the archetype of their *modus vivendi*, the suffering God-man. The complete transformation into the saint, admittedly, required the intervention of the world above – which is why it is only permissible to admire the miracle, which breaks through earthly regularities. Only the beyond was empowered to grant the transfigured human a certification from above.

The rules are entirely different in the sphere of courtly, humanistic and artistic anthropotechnics – to say nothing of the mass-media, neo-athletic and biotechnical age. They stand under the sign of the man-made wonderful (*mirabile*), which no longer addresses faith, but rather educated artistic taste. They appeal to a second-degree faith that expresses itself as an expertise in mastered unbelievabilities.

Modern 'culture' came about when the appreciation of miracles gave way to an appreciation of the miraculous. As one can easily see, this culture could no longer be a matter for saints and the silent, who interpret all higher things as signs from the world above. The turn towards the wonderful marked the debut of the society of the spectacle, which Guy Debord mistakenly dated to the twentieth century. It extends back into the late Middle Ages, when virtuosos stepped out of the shadow of the saints. The golden age of admiration for art continued for as long as the willingness to be astonished applied equally to works of art and art-creating humans – presumably opera is the last art form today in which sublime confusion has survived. Every festival summer proves that there is still a disposition towards honouring singing goddesses and listening to the *acuti* of tenors as if they were sonorous proofs of God. The modern type of virtuosity came from the invitation to encounter the man-made *mirabile* – it was the appeal to the welcome confounding of art and life, and the equally welcome mingling of heroes, saints and artistes.

Now, knowledge of human nature was only possible as insight into the complexities of the strategically folded and artistically heightened life. Humans are 'structurally' superior to themselves, and carry within them an asymmetry in which they mould and are moulded – these two insights, consolidated in the course of the modern centuries, revealed an eccentric potential in humans that could no longer be attributed to the coarse facts of the political 'domination of man by man', to recall the tired formula of the Saint-Simonists. In the course of anthropological enlightenment, it became clear just how far every individual was caught up in vertical tensions and hierarchical effects of an apolitical type. If existence means the personal realization of chances at ability, then everyone is always already on a ladder of more or less, where they position themselves through the results of their own efforts and cannot dismiss those ahead of them as oppressors. Now the individual seems more like a trainer who oversees the selection of talents and drives the team of his habits. Whether one calls this 'micropolitics' the 'art of living', 'self-design' or 'empowerment' is purely a matter of taste.

Homo Anthropologicus

The unstoppable growth of the knowledge of human nature into the theory of the artiste can be taken to explain the tendency towards anthropology that has formed the manifest centre of modern philosophical activity since the eighteenth century. The phenomenon of anthropology indicates and declares: technical explication has brought about a situation in which humans must be explained to humans again from scratch. It is no longer enough to be a human as one was supposedly spawned by nature; the dream of simple self-foundation via the origin is over. The first edition of humanity is now only of ethnological interest – Rousseau's idyllic excursions were powerless to change this. An even weightier factor is that the methods known since antiquity for ascetic revolt against the old Adam in us,[29] who is ruled by habits, passions and mental inertias, and the boosts in being-human through religious, philosophical and athletic exercises are no longer adequate. The spiritually interested of our time should acknowledge that the great teachers of mankind from Lao Tzu to Gautama Buddha, from Plato to Jesus and – why not? – also Mohammed, are, strictly speaking, no longer our contemporaries.[30]

In anthropological explication, humans come into a morally and epistemologically ecstatic – Plessner calls it 'eccentric' – position towards themselves. A more precise description of this position yields the picture of an ontological hybrid: it shows a theatre director who has been condemned to a practising self-reference from early on, and now faces the task of realizing the script of their own existence on stage and observing how others observe them. One can now say it explicitly: in *Homo artista*, the agent and the observer merge to form a single dynamic dual. The early ascetics had already elucidated these conditions; modernity sought to make the corresponding insights binding in its discursive style, and with technical accessories. Henceforth, it was resolved, no one could be human without simultaneously being an anthropologist, indeed an anthropotechnician. This title is bestowed on those who take responsibility for their form and appearance. In the late twentieth century, the translation of the anthropological axiom that humans do not simply live, but 'must lead' their lives, was the medially ubiquitous call to turn one's own self into a project and the project into a business, including self-bankruptcy management.[31]

At the first climax of the great subjective armament cycle, in Baltasar Gracián's 'pocket oracle' *The Art of Worldly Wisdom*, the most astute training manual for men of the world, published under a pseudonym in 1647, the author was still able to put forward a comprehensive maxim for life in the book's final paragraph:

> In one word, be a saint. Virtue is the link of all perfections, the centre of all the felicities. She makes a person prudent, discreet, sagacious, cautious, wise, courageous, thoughtful, trustworthy, happy, honored, truthful, and a universal hero.[32]

One would be hard pressed to find a passage in the literature of modernity where the phrase 'be a saint' is used in as artfully misleading a fashion as here. What is called a 'saint' here is the mask worn by the returned sage of Stoic provenance, who is himself a cover for the yet uncomprehended modern human, the virtuoso, the success artist, the entrepreneur, in fact the epitome of the man – and woman – with far-reaching intentions and complex ulterior motives. In the age of the one-person company, it is perhaps interesting to remind ourselves that what we think of today as fitness could be recommended as saintliness in early modernity. The first sentence of *The Art of Worldly Wisdom* gives a clearer sense of the true quality of the new personality structure than the last:

> Everything is at its peak of perfection. This is especially true of the art of making one's way in the world. There is more required nowadays to make a single wise person than formerly to make the Seven Sages of ancient Greece, and more is needed nowadays to deal with a single person than was required with a whole people in former times.[33]

— 10 —

ART WITH HUMANS

In the Arsenals of Anthropotechnics

Passion Plays

In the light of all this, the moral-historical caesura of the Modern Age gains emphasis: this era saw the change from individual metanoia to the mass rebuilding of the human condition 'from the root'. Modernity, which could never be anything but radical, secularized and collectivized the practising life by breaking the long-standing asceticisms out of their spiritual contexts and dissolving them in the fluid of modern societies of training, education and work. Needless to say, this pulls the ground out from under the venerable *vita contemplativa*. The activism of the moderns pushed the monastic way of life to the margins; the Reformation drove the Orient out of Christianity. Leftovers of contemplation survived in the art system, where faith was converted into amazement and prayer into admiration. Here individuals learn to experience the effects of the great masters' works on them, with varying reverence, as artistic enjoyment. In the fifteenth century, the *devotio moderna* moved from the monasteries to the cities as a popularized mysticism. It expressed the idea that in future, ordinary citizens should also have the right to be crucified alongside the Lord – as a form of the ability to suffer, the imitation of the God-man on the *via crucis* set up a sublime attractor for the laity. At the start of the artistic age, the will to passion changed camps: now it expressed itself as admiration for artistes whose performances show suffering and ability merging into each other. What is art if not the ability-form of suffering that is simultaneously the suffering-form of ability? The empathetic sharing in the virtuoso's suffering and ability became the foundation of modern applause. The old style of crucifixion is given less attention in a world full of artists.

The post-medieval world was therefore filled with passions that did not name, or no longer knew, their origins. This perhaps explains why the ascetic methods of modernity hid behind a triple pseudonym – art, education and finally work – only presenting themselves in an almost uncovered state in the field of sport, now modernized as training. Wearing these masks, the disciplinary imperatives of modernity established themselves on all fronts of human self-intensification. The exercises that moulded the artist, the educated person and the working person already met the condition formulated by Nietzsche when he addressed the supposedly revolutionary prospect of making asceticisms natural again. If the wanderer of Sils Maria called for the abandonment of Christian exercises in mortification and de-selfing – leaving open the question of whether he had understood the nature of Christian asceticism correctly – in favour of an asceticism of improvement, exercises in self-domination and development training, he was speaking neither as a caller on the mountain who had rushed ahead nor as an eccentric prophet on the periphery, but from the mainstream of the tendency that had grown since the start of the virtuoso era in fifteenth-century Europe. The event of Nietzsche remains epochal not because the author said completely new things about the human condition – after all, the call for an over-elevation of man, whether individual or collective, had been in the air since antiquity and had constituted the fluidum of Christianity for a millennium and a half,[34] and it continued to be the first self-evident truth of all enlightened communications about the course of the world, even if the pessimistic conservative motto 'man is always the same' had chronically opposed it since the French Revolution. Nietzsche's intervention remains significant because it raised the level of articulation in the process of anthropotechnic explication – and this explication, I repeat, is for us the technological and epistemological form of destiny. Because the human being is now understood as the *animal technologicum*, every further advance in technology for application to itself contains an inescapably binding *pro nobis*.

Inoculation with the Monstrous: Nietzsche as Immunologist

Nietzsche is connected to the little-understood central logical event of the nineteenth and twentieth centuries: the transformation of metaphysics into General Immunology – an event that modern philosophy, theology and sociology have all failed to comprehend to this day.[35] By revealing immunity as a system and principle, humans are explained anew to themselves. They explicate themselves as beings that must secure themselves in the monstrous – in-the-world, Heidegger says – even at the price of terrible alliances. Clarifications of this type should have had an immediate effect on the status of 'religion' as the most comprehensive immunitary praxis of the symbolic kind (next to the legal system) –and yet it took an entire century for newer forms of cultural theory and theology to make use of the new potentials for reflection.

The course had already been set in German Romanticism, however: if religion, according to Schleiermacher's semi-modern definition, is to be understood as a 'sense and taste for the infinite', what this means against the background of the immunological turn is nothing other than the option of a maximum symbolic immunity, a version of final insurance that stabilizes itself in the greatest possible – so it must accordingly grow with the scale of the injuries. Schleiermacher is close enough to logical modernity to understand that this result can only be achieved through a new operationalization of religious acts: an inoculation with the infinite, as it were. This is precisely what Romanticism had discovered concerning consciousness: according to Novalis, romanticizing is identical to the art of giving infinite meaning to the finite; hence religion was now considered the general application of the Romantic procedure. Consistently with this, the reciprocal transitions from art to religion and vice versa were a clear fact for Novalis and his colleagues. Now one could also show retroactively what motivated people in their first 'religious' actions: they primarily carried out diplomatic procedures in order to form alliances against harmful powers. Thus it always had to be ensured that more energy flowed into salvation than disaster: God is greater. In particular, the greatest expected damage to life – absolutely certain and probably violent death – had always been opposed through the possibility of a reinsurance in an indestructible life. In order to promise such a thing, it seemed natural to ally oneself with a principle that could overcome death. This forming of alliances has appeared in countless variations in virtually all cultures. It was recoded with the Roman term *religio* to give the alliance between humans and God, who had refuted death, its definitive form. Hence Christianity's claim to be the 'true religion': it is the alliance that offers the highest insurance benefits.

Nietzsche, who was one step ahead in the explication of these phenomena, termed the procedure of infinitization 'inoculation with madness'.[36] For him, however, its purpose was not only to insure against life's risks, but also to raise the stakes. Inoculating humans with madness means making each individual dissatisfied with their status quo and provoking a reaction of the will to give trivial existence a non-trivial meaning. Since Nietzsche, it has been possible to know why functional explanations of the 'religious' phenomenon remain incomplete: like the practice system of art, the practice system of 'religion' does not simply react to deficits. It solves no problems, instead manifesting surpluses that cannot be exhausted in any real task. The pious say: 'There are not only uses – there are also blessings.'[37] Those who are less pious translate it thus: there is not only lack – there is also excess.

The religioid act *par excellence*, which Schleiermacher conventionally calls 'faith', consistently goes hand in hand – *folie oblige* – with a suspension of empiricism. Only someone who is able to decide against the authority of appearances, in this case the appearance of finitude and in Fichte even the apparent primacy of the objective, can believe. Whoever cannot go mad – or become childlike, one could say – within certain boundaries has no place among believers. The reason for this is clarified by an understanding of the function of symbolic immune systems: they separate out individuals from the continuum of prosaic data. Their basic operation aims to rehearse the most improbable as the most certain. We recall Tertullian's words: *certum est quia impossibile*.[38] There can be no immunity to setbacks without separation from the principle of reality, and without the will to faith there can be no confidence that the mountains standing here today could already appear elsewhere tomorrow.[39]

The European Training Camp

In sketching the drama of the explication of human existence through technological and symbolic additions in a few of its central aspects, it is not my intention to tell the whole story of newer forms of anthropotechnics – such a project would occupy a team of researchers for decades or longer. I cannot promise more in this chapter than a provisional attempt to name a few minimal logical and factual preconditions for an understanding of the questions discussed.

The complex of phenomena that I would like to expose displays its discouraging complexity at first glance, and its uncanniness at second glance. It encompasses no less than the conversion of Europe into a training camp for human improvements on a multitude of fronts, whether in the school and military context, the world of workshops or the idiosyncratic universes of newer medicine, the arts and the sciences. When sport, accompanied by hygienism and numerous gymnastic systems, joined this group in the mid-nineteenth century, it augmented the familiar spheres of praxis with an autonomous discipline comprising no less than the pure representation of modern heightening behaviour in specific theatricized forms. In sport, the spirit of competitive intensification found an almost universally comprehensible, and hence globally imitated, form of expression. It not only completed the 'rebirth of antiquity', but also provided the most concrete illustration of the performative spirit of modernity, which is inconceivable without the de-spiritualization of asceticisms. De-spiritualized asceticism is known as 'training',[40] and corresponds to a form of reality that demands fitness as such, fitness *sans phrase*,[41] of individuals.

Training is Methodism without religious content. Hence the predominance of the West in the evolution of world society in the nineteenth, twentieth and early twenty-first centuries came not only from widely and rightly criticized 'imperialism'; the deeper reason was that it was the people in this part of the world who, because of their head start in practice, forced all other civilizations on the planet to join in with the training systems they had introduced. The proof: among the outpaced nations, only those that knew how to implant a sufficient degree of didactic stress through a modern school system managed to leap forwards. This succeeded most where, as in Japan and China, an elaborated system of feudal conditionings facilitated the transition to modern disciplines. Meanwhile the tiger states of practice have caught up, and while the modernism of the West haughtily turns up its nose at imitation and mimesis, new competitors all over the world have built their success on the oldest learning principle. Westerners will probably only understand how much an old great power of practice like China owes to this principle when the Confucian institutes of the new global power have penetrated the furthest corners of the earth.[42]

The aforementioned groups of disciplines form a constellation that can only be understood within the framework of a general history of systemic intensifications. As noted above, this shares some elements with Foucault's studies on the history of ordering and disciplinary systems, but integrates them into a broader horizon. One can only do justice to the Modern Age as a whole if one relates it to a mental, moral and technological change that has never been adequately portrayed: the existence of the moderns shows aspects of a global fitness exercise in which what I have termed the 'ethical distinction', the intense call to elevate life – heard by very few in premodern times –

has been transformed into a universally addressed and multifariously answered metanoetic imperative. Its transmitters were primarily the modern state and the corresponding school,[43] at first supported energetically by the clergy of all confessions. In addition, other agencies, not least the writers of the Enlightenment, appropriated fragments of the mandate to call for a change in life. 'Culture is a monastic rule' – for the moderns, this meant constantly facing the task of integrating themselves into an order of achievement that imposed its rules on them, with the notable detail that far from entering the order of their own volition, they were born into it. Whether they liked it or not, their existence was embedded in ubiquitous disciplinary milieus from the outset – with no breakaway movements, romanticisms of laziness or great refusals to oppose it. As if to prove that it was serious about its imperative of achievement, the order of achievement that donned the mantle of civil 'society' also has something resembling confirmations for the élan of the young: certificates, examinations, doctorates and bonuses.

As soon as the absolute imperative takes broader effect, the age of propaganda begins. It was not only the Christian faith that strove for universal dissemination and penetration (the goal which the infamous *Congregatio de propaganda fide*, set up by the Counter-Reformation Pope Gregory XV in 1622, set itself); it was rather the imperative of human getting-into-shape in general that put training pressure on European populations, guided by their clerical and worldly mentors. And the antagonism between confessions had always included a compulsion to heighten the tonicity of faith. Belonging to a religious camp implied – particularly in times of war – an increased level of coercion to religion-polemical being-in-form. Even the Ignatian exercises constituted only one of many varieties of early modern fitness imperative in the religious field. The widespread Jesuit schools, famous both for their severity and for their teaching success, were the most tangible document of corresponding advances on the pedagogical front.

As soon as affecting larger populations through morally and artistically demanding vertical tensions is put on the cultural agenda, one must resort to unaccustomed methods in order to popularize asceticisms. This entails abandoning the elitist beginnings of asceticism. Thus the exercises of the moderns broke open the monasteries, cathedral schools and medieval armouries to create new practice centres. In time, the renovated training units transformed society as a whole into a training association affected by the stress of increase: what had once largely been the province of escapists now shifted to the centre of the system. Hermitages were now elegant places of retreat or moody palaces on the banks of cold rivers, but even those who could afford such higher varieties of relaxation could not escape the dictate of fitness. One could take the great departures to pedagogical utopias in the seventeenth century as indicating the transitional 'saddle period' of the new universalism of achievement – indeed, even the prompters of the current 'information society' who trumpet the motto of 'lifelong learning' are still performing an unconscious continuation of Baroque mobilizations. To understand why the Modern Age transpired as the era of technology and simultaneously anthropological self-explanation one must note the fact that the main sociohistorical, or rather lifestyle-historical, event of this epoch was the transformation of 'societies' into practising associations, stress-driven mobilization groups and integral training camps – spanning all their differentiated subsystems. Here, constantly renewed technologies are configured with humans who constantly have to learn anew about themselves. These associations are of an 'interdisciplinary' constitution, as the diverse practice systems are intertwined via both close and loose connections – like the different weapons in a military association or strategic roles within a team. What we call labour-divided 'society' is *de facto* the practice-divided competency field of a modern achievement collective entering the stress field of 'history'. Writing history turns into reporting on competing communities of fate under shared stress. One should never overlook, however, how much the national formats of the new European performance culture have been foiled by the internationalism – initially taken for granted – of the arts, literatures, sciences, military drill procedures and, more recently, also sporting athletisms.

Speaking of the Modern Age, then, means addressing the cultural production of an all-pervading bracing climate of performance increase and ability development – a climate that had established itself in the absolutist states long before the social Darwinist proclamation of competition as the supposed law of natural history. It is characterized by a constant externalization of practice goals and the transformation of self-collection into fitness.

The current key term for these externalized increases in outward application is 'enhancement',[44] a word that expresses the shift of emphasis from the previous practising-ascetic self-intensification (and its bourgeois translation into 'education') to the chemical, biotechnical and surgical heightening of individual performance profiles. The enhancement fever of today articulates the dream – or the illusion – of a modernization that does not stop at formerly internal zones in human self-relationships. From Arnold Gehlen's

337

perspective, the diagnosis of this trend would be that the principle of relief has penetrated to the core areas of ethical behaviour. By relieving oneself of the ego, one supports the suggestion that it is possible and desirable for individuals to access their own lives like an external datum, without having to bother shaping their existence themselves through practice. A glance at the most recent effects of the enhancement industry operating worldwide – with its departments of plastic surgery, fitness management, wellness service and systemic doping – retroactively suggests that the exercises of the moderns had possibly only ever aimed for the perfect externalization of 'concern for oneself' and the avoidance of the subject in the definition of its fitness status. Where the enhancement idea is dominant, the raising of the performance level is used like a service where the effort made by the individual is restricted to purchasing the most up-to-date procedures. The classical practice subject, which sought to adapt to the law of the cosmos in protracted asceticisms or made space for God within itself through de-selfing (an 'aesthetic of existence' like the one Foucault believed he had discovered never existed in antiquity, however, and the Middle Ages could never have invented such a thing), is replaced by the lifestyle subject, which does not want to forgo the conventional attributes for representing existential autonomy.[45]

Second History of Art: The Executioner as Virtuoso

In the following, I shall present elements of a second history of art that tells of applied art. It deals with the art that takes humans themselves as its material – in Trotsky's words, by seizing on the human being 'as a physical and psychic semi-finished product'. I shall leave aside the most obvious phenomena of 'art with humans' – especially the well-known practices of tattooing and the manifold varieties of body painting, cosmetics and decorative deformation. Nor will I discuss the fantastic world of status-indicating headwear such as crowns, hats and helmets, although these would be fruitful for the observation of 'put-on' art with humans.[46] As far as the reservoir of clothing fashions, jewellery and accessories is concerned, I shall merely refer to the corresponding literature.[47] This literature, on a passing note, shows that the history of vestimentary modernization can only be told as a history of people and their wardrobes.

Instead, I shall begin at the macabre extreme of a craft exercised on human beings: the profession of executioner. It should be beyond doubt that Michel Foucault had the gruesome penal rituals of the early Modern Ages in mind when he presented his equally famous and problematic definition of biopolitics in older and newer times, stating that biopower in classical times expressed itself in the approach 'let live and make die', while modernity supposedly prefers to 'make live and let die'. It is no coincidence that the author of *Discipline and Punish: The Birth of the Prison* opens his discipline-historical investigation with a fascinated and fascinating account of the most opulent execution spectacle ever presented to an eighteenth-century audience – the torture, quartering and burning of the would-be royal assassin Robert François Damiens in 1757 before the royal household on the Place de Grève in Paris. Foucault's description brings back memories of the era of the *châtiment spectacle*, which ended with the *ancien régime*, when punishment was staged as the triumph of the law over wrongdoing and the exclusion of delinquents from moral society – a further reason to date the 'society of the spectacle' back to classical, or perhaps medieval, even archaic statehood.[48]

Among the French Restoration authors, none perceived more clearly that the *art de punir* later uncovered again by Foucault indeed had an artistic character in its own right than Joseph de Maistre, author of those notorious pages in *Soirées de St. Petersbourg* (1821) devoted to that shunned pillar of social order, the executioner. Here he reminds the reader – targeting the spirit of the bourgeois age with Catholic-royalist defiance – of the forgotten and frowned-upon punitive art of pre-revolutionary times:

> A dismal signal is given. An abject minister of justice knocks on his door to warn him that he is needed. He sets out. He arrives at a public square packed with a pressing and panting crowd. He is thrown a poisoner, a parricide, a blasphemer. He seizes him, stretches him out, ties him to a horizontal cross, and raises his arms. Then there is a horrible silence; there is no sound but the crack of bones breaking under the crossbar and the howls of the victim. He unties him and carries him to a wheel. The broken limbs are bound to the spokes, the head hangs down, the hair stands on end, and the mouth, gaping like a furnace, occasionally emits a few bloody words begging for death. He has finished; his heart is pounding, but it is with joy. He congratulates himself. He says in his heart, *No one can break men on the wheel better than I.*[49]

De Maistre's executioner appears as a master of his craft who anticipates the Romantic artist: like the latter, he must forgo daily conviviality, as his art alienates him from human relationships; like the artist, he develops a specific detachment (Flaubert's *impassibilité*) that enables him to carry out his profession matter-of-factly, and as with the artist, his self-approval precedes the judgement of the masses –

provided he has a successful work to attribute to his *savoir faire*. His loneliness goes deeper than that of the artist, as it is not even broken by collegial conversation. He does not receive any guests who could give him advice on how to perfect his craft; there is no chance of a visit from an 'earnest traveller' with greater knowledge – one who 'humbly leaves with us another craftsman's trick'.[50] The executioner is a virtuoso of an art applied to humans whose focus is the exhibition of a body twisted in agony. Anthropotechnics is involved, in so far as the delinquent appears as starting material for artful manipulations – a semi-finished product that is transformed into a fatal end product within a few hours.

The Beginning of Biopolitics: Even the Classical State Had Already Made Humans Live

At first glance, it might appear that there is no more convincing con- firmation of Foucault's first version of the biopower formula – 'let live and make die' – than the performances of the 'theatre of terror' in the penal rituals of the early Modern Age.[51] In reality, the early modern state was precisely *not* content to 'let' its subjects 'live'. On the contrary, it is clear from even the most fleeting glance at the demographic policy of the sixteenth and seventeenth centuries that in its incipient absolutist phase, the state was equally determined to 'make' its subjects 'live' – to a degree that makes the 'biopolitics' of the nineteenth and twentieth centuries, which supposedly 'makes live and lets die', seem like a helpless postlude, helpless especially in the face of the main demographic trend in twentieth-century Europe: the abrupt decrease in reproduction, stemming from the return of con- traceptive art in combination with the new rise of private procreative considerations.

In truth, the state of the pre-classical and classical age was prima- rily a life-making state, for the equally simple and fatal reason that, as a mercantile state, a tax state, an infrastructure state and a state of standing armies, it strove for a form of sovereignty that presumed the discovery of the demographic mass law: that power, in its more recent inflection, primarily means dominion over the greatest possible number of subjects – with the subject already conceived consistently within the expanding property economy as a non-enslaved worker, an epicentre of value creation and a taxable self-interest headquar- ters. As the modern state knows, it shares a fateful alliance with this centre – macro-egotism cannot thrive without blossoming micro-

340

egotisms. Under such premises, a suitably modern exercise of power involves the state – supported by its providential accomplice, the church as guardian of family values – gaining control over the source of populousness. It intervenes in the generative behaviour of its subjects via suitable measures, specifically by terrorizing the bearers of contraceptive knowledge, namely midwives, to ensure the highest possible number of reproductively able people.

The measure of all measures in this field is the state- and church-sanctioned maximization of 'human production' – even Adam Smith, in his main work of 1776, speaks calmly of the 'production of men', which is governed by the 'demand for men'.[52] It was set in motion by the systematic destruction of the informal balance between the manifest patriarchy and the latent matriarchy, and thus by the annulment of the historic compromise between the sexes that, under the mantle of the church's life-protection ethics, had become established in Europe since late antiquity and remained in force until the late Middle Ages. Hence the unprecedented offensive to enslave women to the imperative of reproduction and the systematic destruction of knowledge about birth control, which went down in history under the misleading name of 'witch hunts'. As Gunnar Heinsohn showed decades ago in co-operation with Otto Steiger and Rolf Knieper,[53] the misogynistic excesses of the sixteenth and seventeenth centuries in Europe, with their numerous live burnings of women, should not be understood as a regression of modern 'society' into medieval 'barbarism', nor as an epidemic sexual neurosis, as psychoanalytical commentaries usually claim. They were rather the hallmark of early modernity itself, which followed its main impulse in accordance with the new demographic imperative: to ensure an unlimited availability of subject material.[54]

With its terror against midwife-witches, the early nation-state handed its business card to 'society' as the latter modernized itself. The question of whether one can genuinely ascribe a 'highly developed expertise' to the 'wise women' of that time in matters of contraception will perhaps remain open; supposedly, however, over a hundred procedures for the prevention of unwanted offspring were known before the repression began – procedures whose effectiveness may, in some cases, be open to doubt. But apart from this, the consequences of 'witch oppression' were soon plain to see – and represent statistically. During a long period of rigid demographic policies, the modern state in alliance with the Christian clergy refused to tolerate the conventional controlling function of wives over the 'source of humans' at all, let alone respect it. The guided sensibility of early modernity declared infanticide the exemplary crime against humanity and a direct attack on the national interest; here one finds a rare case of total congruence between family and state morality.

It is anything but coincidental, then, that the greatest modern state theorist after Machiavelli, the jurist Jean Bodin (1530-96), a former Carmelite monk, distinguished himself as one of the most rabid witch hunters of all time. The writer of the epochal *Six livres de la république* (1576) was at once the author of the most brutal witch-hunting tracts of all time, published in Paris in 1580 under the title *De la démonomanie des sorciers*.[55] What he wanted to achieve in his dual function as the founder of the modern theory of sovereignty and master thinker of the inquisition against reproductively able but self-willed women is plain to see. The crux of the matter had already been revealed a century earlier by the authors of *Malleus Maleficarum*, alias *The Hammer of the Witches*: 'No one does more harm to the Catholic faith than midwives.'[56] From now on, Catholic faith implied an unconditional subjugation of married persons to the consequences of marital intercourse, regardless of whether they were in a position to ensure a sufficient inheritance, and thus a productive future, for their offspring – without consideration, even, for the question of whether one can expect workers with no property of their own to bring up children at all. The policy of 'capital expansion through population increase' calmly passed over objections of this kind. In truth, the population explosion of the Modern Age was triggered in part by the extensive incorporation of the propertyless workers, the subsequently much-discussed and usually wrongly declared 'proletariat', into the family and procreative praxis of late aristocratic-bourgeois 'society'.

In matters of procreation, the attitude of most Reformation theologians was even more Catholic than that of the papacy. Martin Luther, who produced half a dozen children with Katharina von Bora, taught – intoxicated by the élan of his own faith – that Christian men should rest assured that if they increased the numbers of the faithful, God would not withhold the material means to nurture them as long as they were sufficiently diligent. Heinsohn and his colleagues incisively sum up the maxim behind such thinking: 'Generalization of individual irresponsibility in the form of responsibility to God.'[57] One should note here that the concept of responsibility is significant neither in theology nor in classical moral philosophy; it only moved to the centre of ethical reflection in the course of the twentieth century, when the explosively grown problem of actions and their unintended consequences gained a large part of the moral attention.

It is undeniable, however, that to this day, Christian sexual ethics – in its official Catholic form – shows a resolute blindness to consequences that would like to be mistaken for trust in God. Because of their commitment to the protection of unborn and born life, an honourable thing in itself, Modern Age churches of all confessions acted as *de facto* accessories to the most cynical biopolitical operation of all time.

Human Overproduction and Proletarianization

In its boundless longing for subjects, the new Leviathan decreed the most massive deregulation ever seen in the history of human reproductions, excepting the demographic explosions during the twentieth century in the Islamic sphere and various zones of what was once called the 'Third World'. Within a few generations, thanks to consistent 'witch policies' from both above and below in the leading European nations (which, moreover, were still looking back fearfully on the depopulation catastrophe in the thirteenth century and the periodically returning plagues), birth rates first increased steadily, then exploded. Within barely more than a quarter of a century, the effects of absolutist biopolitics accumulated (though temporarily restricted by the consequences of the Thirty Years War) into a human tsunami whose crest broke in the nineteenth century – one of the conditions not only for the growth of a 'proletariat' damned to frustration, a class of propertyless workers who had to sell their services on markets outside of family businesses, but also for a disproportionate human exportation, mistakenly termed 'imperialism' by Marxists, that supplied the personnel to populate three continents with Europeans – South America, North America and Australia – as well as a partial occupation of the remaining continents.[58]

The same demographic tidal wave flooded European 'societies' with countless unusable, unruly and unhappy people absorbable neither by the labour market nor by regiments, let alone the navy or overseas destinations. It was they who, from the seventeenth century on, brought about the first precursors of the welfare state, the *Etat providence*, and provoked intervention. It was their fates that Foucault stumbled upon in his studies on the history of the modern disciplinary system. It is no insult to him if one notes that the explanatory value of his investigations is lessened by their insufficient consideration for the demographic dimension of his topic – a disconcerting observation on a scholar whose present renown is based almost entirely on his supposed discovery of biopower mechanisms.

What is demographic policy but the application of biopolitics? It is perhaps time to point out calmly that Foucault, especially at the start of his disciplinological research, fell prey to an enormous optical illusion when he sought to attribute the state's capture of irretrievable surplus humans, whose existence is often documented by no more than a note in the records of the absolutist administrations,[59] to the effects of a fundamentally repressive, state-based disciplinary power. In reality, the measures taken by the early modern state on the poverty-political front can only be grasped if recognized as a more or less mechanical defence against its own excessive successes in the field of human production. What seems like a quintessential manifestation of 'disciplinary power' from the perspective of the genealogy of the prison was, from a state-functional perspective, already a form of the caring power that would constitute the modern welfare state[60] – long before the nineteenth century raised any capitalism-specific 'social question'. In fact, the measures to discipline the poor in the classical period already contained the concession to the central principle of anthropological enlightenment: it is not nutrition that makes humans, but rather incorporation into the symbolic order – 'socialization', in the jargon of the twentieth century. What is socialization, however, but one of the masks worn by the practising life in an age bewitched by work and domination?

The culture-pathological consequences of deregulated human production in Europe between the sixteenth and nineteenth centuries were unforeseeably far-reaching. They culminated in a modernization of cruelty that surpassed even the purposeful brutalization training of antiquity. Even here, however, one should not confuse side effects with intentions. Gunnar Heinsohn and his colleagues point out the early Modern Age's 'inability to fine tune itself',[61] which guaranteed that it would fall prey to its lack of regulation sooner or later.[62] It is generally doubtful, in any case, whether demographic policy can already be viewed as a concise form of modern anthropotechnics, as it quite obviously lacks the technical aspect, the mastering of the procedure that brings about the desired result in discrete, explicit and controlled steps. There is no doubt that it turns human beings into raw material for further processing, political and otherwise. It is equally evident that it is committed to the experimental style of modern 'great politics' already identified by Nietzsche: the dynamism and futurism of the new civilizatory model are inconceivable without a significant element of chance. From this perspective, the absolutist style of demographic policy was a form of project-making on a grand scale – something halfway between technique and gamble that was typical of its time.[63]

The Birth of Social Policy from the Problem of Human Surplus

In our context, all that matters is that the populationist policies of the early modern state triggered the impetuous development of numerous concrete forms of anthropotechnics, whether these manifested themselves on the education-political, pedagogical, military, police or welfare state fronts. The demographic policy based on unconditional growth led to the typical modern vicious circle in which the incessant, soon apparently fateful overproduction of humans caused a massive overtaxing of upbringing potential in families, and hence a higher risk of epidemic child neglect. The response to this disastrous situation was, for understandable reasons, usually to appeal to the modern school system – not only so that it would provide the modern community with the necessary numbers of achievers, but also in the hope that the vast group of hopeless and superfluous people might form something resembling useful, or at least harmless members of society after all – a task at which the educators of the early modern state were doomed to fail.[64] When the toughening disciplines of school and the integrative effects of professional life fail, a second rescue system is required to 'catch' the surplus individuals. It is in this regime of administrative severities that the Foucauldian phenomena – the disciplines of custody, sedation and correction in the classical state – developed.

What we call social policy today is initially nothing but the modern state continually tracing its self-created vicious circle. 'Capitalism' only contributed to it after the Industrial Revolution of the late eighteenth century, by beginning the never-ending crusade to lower the cost of the labour factor. This all-too-successful campaign is still giving the postmodern therapy and redistribution state a chronic headache, as it does not know what to make of the confusing simultaneity of high unemployment and low birth rates; *de facto*, this points to the excessive success of the economic system in its search for ways to reduce labour costs – a success that inevitably leads to the mass dismissal of workers, yet can only be attained at the expense of the social system. But even the absolutist state, which 'made live' too much from the start by producing substantially more humans through its control over sexual parameters than it – or rather the families, schools and factories – could equip with humanizing qualifications and chances of economic employment, was damned to erect its ever higher-towering pyramids of polytechnical virtuosity over a substrate of impoverished and over-numerous humans. For them, compulsive disciplining was the only way to achieve some form of completion, however pitiful. Looking only at these phenomena, however, is not enough to understand the disciplinological adventure of the Modern Age as a whole – neither in its artistic and artisanal dimensions nor in its scholarly, epistemological and engineering aspects, to say nothing of the neo-athletic and anthropo-political departures in the late nineteenth and complete twentieth century.

Educational Policy Under the Absolute Imperative

Modern pedagogy reacted to the new order situation in its own way: it took advantage of the state's chronic need by making itself indispensable to the modern body politic for centuries. It sharp-wittedly rose to become the discipline of all disciplines. It single-mindedly combined the crude education-political imperative – supplying the modern state with usable human beings – with a modern form of the absolute imperative: 'Instead of changing your life later on, you should let us change you from the start.' At the start of their offensive, educators were committed almost without exception to this rule, as they almost all came from church traditions – or, in our translation, from the institutionalized practice forms of ethical difference. They knew from venerable sources and early-morning introspections that man is the being which needs to be brushed the wrong way. The era in which Rousseau and the anti-authoritarians would spread their confusion had not yet dawned; it had not occurred to anybody that one need only let children follow their own inclinations in all matters for free citizens to emerge. Even the most terrible *fouetteur d'enfants* – to use the epithet Rabelais coined for Pierre Tempête, master of the Parisian Collège de Montaigu (where Ignatius of Loyola studied), who became legendary for his brutality towards students – was absolutely convinced that he was merely doing what was necessary, as a Christian and schoolmaster, to turn little monsters into adults with character. In the certainty that idleness is the beginning of all vice, the pious educators of that time did everything in their power to ensure that the devil had no chance of finding a pupil's mind unoccupied.

Emendatio Mundi

Perhaps this was the only way for the absolutely unexpectable to occur. From the modern state's initiation of human production

emerged, through the intervention of the educators, the most powerful idea of the last five hundred years: the notion of world improvement appeared on the scene when the Baroque school accepted the
task of warding off the human catastrophe triggered by the early
modern state through its policy of unfettered human production.
In this situation, improving the world meant improving humans *en
masse*. As this was no longer practicable as the self-improvement of
an ascetic minority, it required improvement of the many through
educational institutions. Hence the pedagogues of early modernity,
for the first time, applied the metanoetic imperative directly to children. Only then did the meaning of the thesis that all education is
conversion truly become clear. The later totalitarian systems would
be heir to the invasive schools, reclaiming the prerogative of completely capturing the young.

With the support of the human production state, which was
demographically competent (and hence strong) but pedagogically
incompetent (and hence in difficulties), educators on the eve of the
Enlightenment realized that they could only perform their duty successfully on one condition: they would have to reach for the whole
human being in each student: they already saw the child as the future
citizen. They consequently decided to pre-empt metanoia, the ethical
revolution in mid-life, by planting the seed of change at the beginning.[65] Because of this disposition, the early modern school became
the cell of ambition for the world that was to be changed – indeed, the
incubator for all later 'revolutions'. It not only wanted to prepare for
the better world while still in the worse; it sought to pull the world as
a whole onto the better side through the production of graduates who
were too good for the world as it was. School had to become the place
where the adaptation of humans to deficient reality was thwarted. A
second overproduction was to compensate for the damage caused by
the first.

Implanting the change of life in the beginnings of each life demanded,
to begin with, no less than the transference of monastic discipline to
the school setting; this was the minimum price for the project of
modernity. From the start, its goal was nothing but the correction
of the erroneous world text – the *emendatio mundi*. It consisted in
the replacement of the current depraved wording with a lost original
version that could only be rendered legible once more by theologians,
philosophers, and now also educators. This idea – which could only
have occurred to the typesetters and printers, the correctors and publishers of the Gutenberg era and their accomplices, the schoolmasters
and educators of adults, who would call themselves members of the

347

Enlightenment soon afterwards – could be applied most plausibly to the souls of children in the burgeoning age of print. School transpired early on as the moral distillation flask of modern 'society', being the place where the metanoetic appeal to retreat from the world was to be taken up by a secular institution and turned towards profane ends. Here it was always important to maintain the semblance of subordination to the state mission – no publicly funded school in the time between Erasmus and Hartmut von Hentig has ever stated openly that its aim was the production of socially unusable characters, let alone modern hermits. Nonetheless, it is fair to say that every educator of quality had thoughts about the true goals of their profession that did not exactly coincide with the expectations of statehood.

This, then, proved to be the highest form of art with humans in the age of Christian humanism and its school projections: the availability of procedures for incorporating imperatives of humanization into education and imprinting the watermarks of the ideal indelibly upon the souls of the youngest. The premises for this change lie in the dissonant alliance between state and school: the mercantilist state of the early Modern Age identified the movements of monastic flight from the world, which were still massive, as an unwelcome tendency, almost a subversive evasion of potential workers from the spreading dictate of universal usefulness. It believed it was acting circumspectly and in its own interests by giving educators the power to take the young by the hand early on, and thus commit them to a curriculum of general usability from their first steps on. Its miscalculation would become evident in subsequent centuries; whoever relies on pedagogues to produce citizens should be prepared for unexpected side effects.

School Interest Versus National Interest

The trick of pedagogical reason articulated itself in the fact that while the modern school trained its pupils nominally with a view to the state and 'society', it secretly, sometimes even manifestly, bypassed the state and 'society'. This error was crystallized in the resonant German word *Bildung*.[66] The special status of 'culture' in the modern construction of reality cannot be understood without the organized deviation of education from its external purpose. One could already see a hint of the incipient 'differentiation of subsystems' – the trivializing sense behind the talk of differentiation, admittedly, would be clearer here than elsewhere. Just as modern demographic policy fails at fine tuning its demographic instruments, state-controlled pedagogy fails at fine tuning its educational measures. Because school has a logic of its own, modern culture was flooded with an enormous surplus of dead-end idealisms – personalism, humanism, utopianism and moralism being the official varieties.[67] This excess provoked a series of culture-pathological reactions, from escapism and inner retreat to Romanticism, revoltism and immoralism. The character mask of the cynic conquered the late aristocratic and bourgeois stage from the eighteenth century on – the Mozart–da Ponte operas would be quite incomplete without the figure of the hard-boiled philosopher who, wrapped in his foul-smelling donkey hide, always expects the worst of humans.[68] At the same time, the modern novel unfolded a veritable phenomenology of private reason turned bad. Hegel's philosophy, at its didactic core, is nothing other than a machine for processing frustrated idealism; for what he calls 'education' is essentially disappointment management. It refers not to the decentred wandering of bourgeois curiosity between this and that thing, as today's equation of 'culture' with leisure implies. *Bildung* demands the hard later conditioning of the flaring-up idealistic subject, which must abandon the illusion that the world owes it any adjustment to its morally exaggerated expectations. Needless to say, the sensible Protestant Hegel was defeated across the board in his struggle with modern protest culture.

No one who wanted to write a reasoned history of modern pedagogy could avoid examining the deepest systemic rupture within the semantics of the Modern Age: the divergence of school interest and national interest. The pseudo-symbiosis of school and state holds some of the most baffling dysfunctionalities of modern culture – it causes frictions whose dissonant potential goes beyond the old symbiotic dualism of church and state. A retelling of this dangerous liaison would not only have to show how, to this day, countless graduates of the modern school systematically dream in directions unrelated to the conditions of the 'working world'; it would also have to explain the state's chronic attempts to defeat the single-mindedness of the 'pedagogical province' for pragmatic and utilitarian reasons. Such attempts would provide the running thread leading to a history of school as a history of school reforms – always from the ideal school to the real one, of course. University reforms in Germany during the twentieth century, whether those of 1933 or those from the late 1960s – to name only the most symptomatic caesuras – form a coherent picture if one sees in them the undisguised will of the state to reconquer the commanding heights of cognitive human production in the service of the working world and power politics. Had Wilhelm II not already claimed, in front of German secondary school teachers, that what was needed at German schools were not new Greeks but young German men? Naturally the 'education planners' could only succeed in their neo-realistic plan if they took suitable steps to eliminate the humanism still blooming in the faculties, especially the humanities – assuming the reorganized departments did not initiate the necessary adjustments of their own accord: for decades, pre-emptive dismay has been the zeitgeist itself.[69]

All the World's a School

Whoever wants to teach becomes a member of the modern world's most powerful organization: teachers without borders. If world time and school time converge in future, it is due to their actions. No author of the burgeoning era of teachers formulated with more élan, more comprehensively or more radically how pervasive the new pedagogy had become than John Amos Comenius. His works give the impression that he wanted to correct Shakespeare's statement, 'All the world's a stage / and all the men and women merely players',[70] replacing it with the counter-thesis that all the world is a school – and all humans merely pupils. We are inhabitants of a creation in which everything revolves around instruction.

> 2. That it is right to call the world a school is shown first of all by the matter itself [. . .] for what is a school? It is generally defined as *a company of persons who teach and learn what is useful*.[71] If this is true, then the world is a school, since it is entirely made up of an order of teachers, learners, and disciplines.
> 3. For everything that exists in the world teaches or learns, or it does both alternately . . .
> 5. Therefore everything is filled with *disciplines*, i.e. with various tools for admonishing, advising and driving on: therefore it is not wrong to call the world a *house of discipline*.[72]

For human beings, the created world is a 'prelude to eternity': it offers a preparatory course that we must attend before we are admitted to the heavenly academy.[73] Comenius has no doubts about the material that has to be covered during the stay in the house of discipline: the world-pupil must work through three books to acquire the necessary wealth of knowledge:

> The first and greatest book of God is the visible world inscribed and illustrated with as many characters as there are creatures of God to be

seen in it. The second book is man himself, made in the likeness of God. [. . .] But God has given into man's hands a third book [. . .] the Holy Scripture.[74]

If one takes into account the depraved nature of man, it is hardly surprising that mortals have so far, for the most part, made no proper use of the aids given to them. They rejected the universal books granted to them thanks to the free availability of divine teaching tools. They wilfully insisted on imaginary special knowledge, causing them to sink into darkness and eternal quarrelling. As a result, there is no redemption in the world, only a civil war between the pseudo-knowledgeable and the ignorant. At the time he wrote these statements, Comenius was not only looking back on the Thirty Years War, which he had experienced in its entirety; he could also see the beginnings of the never-ending cold war that modern experts in international law whitewash as the 'European state system' established in the Peace of Westphalia and rationalized by the *Ius publicum europaeum*.

Pre-Enlightenment: The Way of Light

For Comenius, the enthusiastic mastermind of the Bohemian Brethren, the way to heal the world's sickness was not to be found at the peace conferences of potentates. It could only be gleaned from the eternal philosophy and from revelation. The path of salvation for the decrepit world could only be the *Way of Light* – thus the title of Comenius' chiliastic manifesto of 1668, whose most significant parts had been written in London over twenty years earlier. In this epochal treatise, he stirred up conventional Neoplatonic thought figures (such as the doctrine of the threefold action of the primal light, comprising inner stasis, emanation through creation and the satisfying return to the source) in the spirit of a pedagogical apocalypticism. Here the main motifs of the later Enlightenment – in so far as it is based on a barely disguised totalitarianism of the school – are plain to see in their original Christian-millenarian form.

In our context, it is instructive to observe how for the great school man, the way of light prefigures the way of school, while the way of school points to the perfection of the book. Thus he answers the question, 'How can the greatest light of understanding be kindled for the world?'[75] with the information that one must unify the three sources of light – self-communicating nature, the inborn ideas of the human soul and the Holy Scripture – in a single over-bright flame. Through its reflected rays, this universal light of the mind can communicate itself step by step to all peoples of the world: because it already shines in the new books, and will shine even brighter in the future once improved books are available, the 'absolutely necessary books can be translated into the common languages'.[76] Thanks to the timely inventions of the letterpress and deep-sea navigation, the spreading of that strongest and most radiant light which overcomes all resistance from darkness is now only a 'matter of time': the omens of future pan-harmony are shining on the horizon of the present. Among these is the widespread human longing for a better world. Comenius would not have been a metaphysicist in the classical tradition if he had not taken the presence of that longing as a sign that it could be fulfilled – God would not have implanted this yearning for good in us if He had not already ensured its attainability. Analogously, Ernst Bloch, the last great-naïve thinker of world improvement, saw hope itself as an agent of realizing the hoped-for.

The top form of Modern Age art with humans is evident in the over-enthusiastic project of turning every student into a pupil of pansophy. This term, common among encyclopaedic scholars since the sixteenth century, is probably best translated as 'the art of omniscience'. In our century, though probably since the days of Diderot and his colleagues, it has been forgotten that the world knowledge of the Modern Age had begun its reproduction cycles under the catchword of omniscience – a word whose history of decline indicates the oft-cited 'clarification of Enlightenment' [*Abklärung der Aufklärung*]. The syllabus of the student of omniscience (and other students are, for the moment, not worth mentioning) is based on the aforementioned premises: whoever wishes to learn must learn everything, in keeping with the three keys to totality or 'books' which the creator, according to Comenius' doctrine of source, provided for mankind. Hence every single pupil must transform into an artwork of omniscience, printed in the typographic workshops of the new pan-disciplines. Comenius, one of the grand masters of pansophy alongside Athanasius Kircher and Leibniz, never tired of constantly inventing new subdivisions and variations to augment the mother discipline: *panpaedeia* (universal education), *panurgia* (universal technique), *panglottia* (doctrine of universal language), *panorthosia* (doctrine of universal reform), *pannuthesia* (universal warning), *panergesia* (universal appeal) and *panaugia* (universal light). The definition of school in Comenius' *Orbis sensualium pictus* [The Visible World] – the first schoolbook of the Modern Age, published in Nuremberg in 1658 – as a 'workshop in which young minds are formed in accordance with virtue'[77] is therefore incomplete. Institutions of this kind had long ceased to deal merely with the *virtus* of the schoolchild trained to behave well in life; their goal was to transform the pupil's soul into a speaking mirror of totality. To graduate, the student had to become a *Gesamtkunstwerk* of world knowledge and cognizance of godly things.

In the light of such monumental aims, one would suppose that their author himself had the greatest doubts as to their feasibility. But the undaunted pedagogue of totality insisted on proving by all means that it was indeed time to hope and strive for the 'greater'. Hence the six learning steps of mankind summarized by the author in chapter 13 of *Via Lucis* – one of the first outlines of a stage theory of the human race, from Adam and Eve to Gutenberg and Magellan – had to be augmented by a seventh: the step into the global society of light. It is not hard to recognize the euphoric original state of the disenchanted 'society of knowledge' in this vision. For Comenius, this final manoeuvre contains the mission and adventure of the now. Whoever completes it supports the operative light in its current work: they further the breakthrough to total didactics, which promises without false modesty to convey *everything to all in a universal fashion.* Here sounds the battle cry of pedagogical millenarism: *omnes omnia omnino*, which runs through Comenius' work – unwaveringly maintaining the balance between enthusiasm and method for forty years.

With the call to universal education, Comenius announced that the apocalyptic call was the order of the day in this 'evening of the world': because not much time was left, it was high time to gather up what had been scattered, and collect all summations in summations of summations.[78] The agenda of the age called for a new book of books, a hyper-Bible that would meet the needs of the Gutenberg era. A book of this kind, a form of Newer Testament that would test our ability to count to three with the Holy Scriptures too, would by its nature have to be the definitive, or even final, book. It would have to contain everything a prudent person should know – heavenly and earthly, natural and artificial things alike.[79] It is meant to hold the evangelic potential of profane knowledge.

What is peculiar here is that world knowledge, whose scope is wide, and salvific knowledge, which demands a restriction to the one essential thing, suddenly find themselves in a state of unimpaired harmony. One can, in fact, view the balanced coexistence of encyclopaedism and apocalypticism as the intellectual miracle of the seventeenth century. Something of this kind would not reappear until the spiritual lightning flash prior to the Russian Revolution, namely in the work of Nikolai Fedorov (1829–1903), the creative mind of the Russian cosmists, who not only postulated an all-encompassing world museum and a universal cemetery for all the dead of mankind, but also predicted the resurrection of the dead of all eras with the help of the life sciences, which would be founded specifically for this purpose. For him, true universalism consisted in the rejection of death, the final cause of asynchronicity, finitude and disconnection.[80]

Something distantly comparable also applied in the apocalyptic thought of the Baroque: Christians were able and expected to be encyclopaedists once the conflict between the theomorphism of the soul and the cosmomorphism of the whole human being had ceased to exist. *One* universe, *one* book, *one* psyche: the book-shapedness of the world permits the literate soul to embrace its world-shapedness fully. This is the ultimate reason why the great practisers of modernity no longer retreated to the desert. In future, it would suffice for them to live by the rule *nulla dies sine pagina*. Many pages form a chapter, and many chapters create the world. The immersion of scholars in the total book created a polyvalent movement in which withdrawal and exodus coincided: modern being-in-the-world realized a third way between flight into the world and flight from the world.

This movement, which always points forwards and upwards, contains the original gesture of world improvement.[81] Improving the world means comparing the corrupted text to the intact one and correcting it to restore it to its original state. If there is no access to an original world text, improvers must rely on the dialectical assumption that the negation of the wrong will automatically produce the right. Against this background, it is clear why the Critical Theory of the early Frankfurt School, especially after its reduction to a negative dialectics, was not only a camouflaged Marxism without a revolutionary perspective; at the same time, it constituted a late daughter product of Baroque world-improving idealism – or, more precisely, its regression to a 'sad science'. Need we still add that during its best years, Baroque idealism carried out the transference of the Reformation from matters of faith to matters of knowledge? According to this idealism, we should be saved not only by faith, but also through knowledge. Enlightenment begins as pedagogical gnosis.

For those producing art with humans in the seventeenth century, the mission of *emendatio mundi* entailed a wealth of further conclusions: they quickly had to produce universal books (the plural is used here merely as a formality), universal schools, a universal college and a universal language. 'In this, no corner of the earth, no people, no language and no class of society will be neglected.'[82] The books of light, schools of light, colleges of light and languages of light are urgently required in every corner of the universe; the unforced force of self-evidence will win out everywhere, in accordance with the Comenian motto: *Omnia sponte fluant, absit violentia rebus.*[83] The primal light and the technical light campaign for the same cause: books are the lamps of world-illumination, schools the lamp-bearers, scholars the lamp-lighters, and languages the fuel for the flame of universal illumination.[84]

Words and things are still so close together here that one can easily cross over from one side to the other. The world is the orderly tableau of essences, and as such it is easily understandable as a whole; that is why the encyclopaedias of the early Modern Age were still a form of atlas reproducing all the continents and countries of being 'topically' in clear maps. God and humans share the same 'conception of the world'. The lexica of the late eighteenth century, on the other hand, abandoned the aim of metaphysical overview, mirroring the disintegration of the whole in unrelated or weakly connected keywords.[85] Hence the newer 'reference works' since Zedler's *Universallexikon* and the French *Encyclopédie* have opted to string articles together alphabetically. One should not underestimate the formative effect of alphabetically 'ordered' lexica of the eighteenth century; for later ones, they provided exercises in incoherentism. Their mere structure reinforced the implicit conviction of the moderns that the world was an aggregate of isolated details; to this day, no form of holism has been able to overcome this influence – be it the ecological or the philosophical variety.

Comenius' manifesto of the pedagogical international uncovered substantial premises for world-improving action: for those who choose the way of light, haste is as necessary as the conviction that they can pass on universal knowledge. A hundred years later, one of the editors of the *Encyclopédie* took up the impulse provided by Comenius. Diderot's vigorous call *Hâtons-nous de rendre la philosophie populaire* can therefore also be reversed: to make philosophy popular and effective requires an acceleration. Only by its haste can one recognize that progress is apocalypticism under a bourgeois guise. For the philosophical apocalypticist, the way to the light is the way of light itself: it is the absolute in history. It has accepted performing the work of world-pervasion since the beginning of all creation, and in our time the enterprise has entered its final phase. If there has ever been a version of the 'project of modernity' in plain terms, it can be found in the work of Comenius.

The postulate of omniscience recalls a time from which we have long since been alienated, when knowledge was viewed as something almost exclusively qualitative and grounded in the nature of things. It viewed itself as essential knowledge and claimed to offer penetrating insight into the structure of the rounded cosmos of essences. It referred to an effectively complete, but phenomenally disordered world in need of repair, and thus seemingly incomplete – but nonetheless reparable. At that time, the world-improvers were any who wanted to give the world back its original perfection – whereas today, one must assume that every repair causes new imbalances, new imperfections. For the pansophists of the sixteenth and seventeenth centuries, there was nothing presumptuous in the call for omniscience; it merely drew the inescapable conclusions from the basic assumptions of classical metaphysics, which rested on an ontology of the perfect and comprehensible world. This could at most be augmented by a therapeutics that enabled humans to heal into the whole.

These assumptions echo in the admonition of Comenian pedagogy to build the new school on the summation of all summations, so that future tuition would be based on a universal book. Even omniscience can be given a child-friendly form. The pan-pedagogical intention is unmistakably based on other premises than the ancient way of practising towards omniscience. For the Sophists, it did not come from an overall insight into the circle of knowledge joining the world, but rather the decree that the artiste in the eternal rhetorical training camp should be able to speak spontaneously and triumphantly on any given subject.[86]

Eccentric Positionality: The Human Automaton as a Provocation of Anthropology

The modernity of Comenius' school projects is clear not so much from its limitless optimism, which seems decidedly antiquated today; it comes from the radically technical definition of school as an integral learning machine. It is not without reason that Comenius emphasized that the reformed school, this workshop (*officina*) of humaneness, must function in the manner of an *automaton*. To understand this term, one must take into account that the seventeenth century began to honour God Himself as the first builder of automata. The later equation of automatism and soullessness – undoubtedly the greatest success of anti-modern semantics after 1750 – was still a remote notion for the engineers of the time. For his own part, Comenius aimed to construct a *perpetuum mobile*. As his notes reveal, he was determined to make such an object public – assuming he succeeded in producing it – as a new proof of God's existence via technology; he therefore prayed to heaven that it might grant him, not least in his own interests, the completion of the perfect machine.[87] Here the adventure of cognitive modernization hinges on the identification of nature as the epitome of the God-built automaton. It formed the basis of the prediction that man, viewed by Comenius as the *co-operator Dei*, could soon embark in earnest on the reconstruction of natural machines.

Barely a century later, the anthropomorphic automata from the workshops of Baron von Kempelen (who had been appearing with his purportedly mechanical Chess Turk since 1769), Pierre Jacquet-Droz (who presented his immortal androids the Writer, the Draughtsman and the Musician in 1774) and Friedrich Kaufmann (who displayed his automatic trumpeter to the public) were on everyone's lips. From that point on, Romantic literature, including opera, raved about the possibility of confusing humans with statues, dolls or machines – with nothing to suggest that this motif could ever be abandoned again in technological civilization.[88]

As early as the seventeenth century, then, or the eighteenth at the latest, anthropotechnics opened up a second front by projecting the impulse of artificial human moulding onto android machines. For Comenius there was no doubt: school had to become a machine. Its task was to send perfect reproductions of humans into the world – as genuine, well-formed humans. Anyone curious as to the things of which pedagogy once dared to dream can obtain the necessary information here. Here we also witness the reactivation of a disposition that was already familiar to the Stoic teachers: when they gave the students who chose the philosophical way the task of working on their 'inner statue', this contained the suggestion that the empirical human should step aside for the ideal figure.

The popularity of anthropology from the eighteenth century on was triggered not least by the doubling of humans as androids and their human observers. If one takes this into account, it becomes clear why Plessner's 'eccentric positionality', correctly understood, is not merely a trivial self-transposition to the place and view of others, or the familiar human phenomenon of stepping out of oneself in front of the mirror. It not only reflects the increased demands of multi-situative 'societies' on the art of role playing; in addition, it is irreducible to the disadvantage of being seen, as illuminated by Blumenberg, let alone to an attempt to turn the disadvantage of visibility into an advantage. As much as this observation might offer a plausible explanation for the essential theatricality of cultures: theatre is the flight from visibility as the flight *into* visibility.[89]

The awareness of eccentricity among the moderns primarily rationalizes the shock of the ability to produce human automata; at the same time, it mirrors the amusement that can be derived from playing with mechanical doppelgangers. The statue is alive, it may harbour unpredictable intentions, it is moving towards humans – the modern theory of the human being is unimaginable without these suggestions. If the moderns still erected statues, it was no longer simply to set up moral and cultural models; they also did so to learn new things from within the statues. Were not the anatomical maps of Vesalius, in fact, macabre statues that revealed what the 'factory of the human body' looks like from the inside – though the viewer of the Vesalian plates would be reminded less of a workshop than of a ballroom acting as a venue for modernized *danses macabres*, performed by men composed of blood vessels and organs in all possible cuts and projections? Was not the message of the human skeletons appearing in the scientific collections of the nobility, and later also as demonstration objects in publicly funded schools, primarily an anthropological one, as they were presenting the basic framework of the android? And did not the plastinates of the Beuys imitator Gunther von Hagens, which have caused a worldwide furore since 1996 under the name 'Body Worlds', merely clarify the idea of the modern statue – the statue that exposes the inner android?

The plausibility of the anthropological mode of reflection from the eighteenth century onwards stemmed from the fact that every individual was now confronted with the stimulus of understanding themselves as a composite of android and real human.[90] Thus the venerable body–soul distinction presented itself in a new state of matter. The heyday of body discourses in Europe for the last two hundred years makes this constellation clear to this day. Following the publication of La Mettrie's *L'Homme machine* in 1748, the recipients of the physiological Enlightenment could see what happens when automata learn to speak and machines become nervous. It is not without reason that somnambulism – alongside the fear of being buried alive[91] – was the central psychopathological symptom of the nineteenth century. The sleepwalker presents the inner android acting independently after the subtraction of the ego's consciousness, while live burial evokes the complementary phenomenon: the pure ego as it appears to itself after the interment of its body. The psychoanalysis of the early twentieth century (a contemporary mask of practising life in a world where even mourning is described as a form of work) still attempted to map the interaction between the two factors onto the internal relationship between the ego and the id.[92]

The constant back and forth between the poles of the android id and the human ego gave rise to the soul drama of the mid-Modern Age, which was simultaneously a technical drama. Its topic is best summarized in a theory of convergence, where the android moves towards its animation while increasing parts of real human existence are demystified as higher forms of mechanics. The uncanny (which Freud knew something about) and the disappointing (on which he chose to remain silent) move towards each other. The ensoulment of the machine is strictly proportional to the desoulment of humans. As explained in the first and so far only philosophically elaborated theory of technology, that of Gotthard Günther, the draining away of transcendently misunderstood subjectivity into the outer world was the key metaphysical event of the Modern Age.[93] The most commonplace observations already show how humans come under pressure on two fronts at once: not only have humans constituted a tiny minority compared to images for some time – for every Western person in the twentieth century there are countless visual documents and reproductions – they are also becoming a minority in relation to anthropomimetic cognition-mimetic machines, namely computers.

The Interdisciplinary Continent

It was one of the terminologico-historical mishaps of the Modern Age that it reserved the word 'scholasticism' for the higher education of the Middle Ages and its philosophical-theological treatises. By now it is unmistakably clear how far modernity itself gave rise to a scholastic world form determined by didactic-disciplinary impulses, far beyond what medieval school culture, which was *de facto* only a marginal element in its time, could hope to achieve. Modernity is hyper-scholasticism. It is based on the universal invasiveness of the school, as well as the reciprocal transfer of disciplines between the subsystems of 'society'. We have already hinted at the transfer of monastic discipline to school life. Its consequence was a transforma- tion of humans into pupils, one that continued through all temporally conditioned forms of pedagogy – including the school-hating move- ments in the twentieth century.

A sufficiently complex civilization history of the Modern Age would, furthermore, have to show how all systems of social action interlock in a constant play of discipline transfer:[94] thus it is not only the monastic *modus vivendi* that is translated into the scholastic one, for military discipline also retroactively affects religious discipline – the most famous example being the amalgam of monastic grooming and sublimated combat training in the companies of the *Societas Jesu*. All three areas of disciplines – the monastic, the scholastic and the military – not only act as matrices for the ordering projects of the 'police' and the professional shaping of the civil service,[95] but also radiate into the sphere of craftsmen's studios, factories and trading companies. Those who had known the strict alliance of discipline and compulsion in these areas could experience the harmonious coexistence of discipline and freedom in the arts. In this sense, Europe was the interdisciplinary continent from the virtuosity boom in the fifteenth and sixteenth centuries onwards, and has remained it to this day. As such, it forms a network of total schooling. The constant stimulation of the skilled by competitors was one of the effects of the network's increasing density. Educators have often overlooked the fact that one's rival is the most important teacher of all.

The new media of the Gutenberg era contributed to the expansions of practice zones. Thanks to increasing literacy, all nation-states saw the growth of reading populations who were exposed to insistent media fitness training: they embodied the equation of humans and readers. They were joined in the twentieth century by the telephone and radio peoples, who were subsequently sublated into the world people or the Internet. Media fitness is the element in which modern populations elaborate both their global and specific fitness. Why passive media consumption leads almost inevitably to unfitness (in technical terms: how the stimulating connection described by Comenius between seeing for oneself, *autopsia*, and doing for oneself, *autopragmasia*) would have to be explained via an analysis of negative training.

Art History as Asceticism History

Without the ubiquitous modern *fluidum* of disciplinary increase, it would have been impossible for the art industry of the Renaissance and subsequent centuries to function. It is time that the frequently told history of the visual and musical arts in the Modern Age was presented as the history of artistic asceticisms. This would not only show the phenomenon of art in a different light; it would also cast a new spotlight on the art of mid-modernity, which can be understood in significant aspects as the production of an increasing suspension of artistic and craft disciplines. If what I have termed the 'second history of art' concerns art with humans, in particular the art of pushing them towards higher achievements, one of its most important chapters deals with the production of artists in the early modern 'house of discipline'. Suffice it to recall Richard Sennett's remarks on the ethos of the crafts, specifically his excursus on the goldsmiths of the Renaissance.[96]

Only in the area of art singing and instrumental music does one find an unbroken and self-evident tradition of practice awareness that has survived all changes of style, taste, compositional technique and performance tradition from the Renaissance to postmodernity. Ironically, it is the great instrumentalists who stand in the limelight almost daily, trained in 'decent impudence' before the audience, who wallow in applause and thus feed the welcome illusion of that high artistic freedom which one likes to imagine first at the mention of repressive discipline. Because of their overwhelming practice workload, these virtuosos seem more open to Foucauldian analogies than almost any other disciplined group. Many of them see the parallels when one compares their practice rooms to prison cells, and the torment of etudes to solitary confinement at the instrument.[97] One cannot, however, deny the relatively voluntary nature of their suffering through discipline.

Though it may, at first glance, seem plausible to present the history of newer instrumental music as a classic case of 'disciplinary power', it actually forms a chapter in the metamorphosis of passions. If one looks from Czerny's notorious didactic piano works, such as *The School of Velocity* op. 299, *Forty Daily Exercises* op. 337 or *Nouveau Gradus ad Parnassum* op. 822, to the didactic devotional texts of the fifteenth and sixteenth centuries, such as Thomas à Kempis' *De imitatio Christi* (written anonymously around 1418) or the *Exercitationes spirituales* by Ignatius of Loyola (published in Spanish in 1533, in Latin in 1541), they give an idea of the wide-ranging changes in the willingness among modern humans to accept passion in the course of barely more than four centuries. They extend from the instrument-less passion of the spiritually co-crucified, co-dead and co-resurrected, who follow mystical instructions, to the instrumental virtuoso culture of the early nineteenth century that embodies the Romantic compromises between the artiste's bravura and a de-selfing in the face of the instrument's demands – to say nothing of the interpretative requirements of the works themselves. Whoever scans this stretch will immediately realize why the art history of the Modern Age cannot be understood solely as a history of works. In addition, it always constitutes the history of passion exercises and their transformation into artistic passions.

What I call the second history of art, then, is primarily responsible for the training procedures of artists in their disciplines. It thus also deals with the process of de-disciplining in more recent art history. With this dual focus, it shifts the focus from the work to the artist by defining the production of art producers as an independent dimension of art history – which, incidentally, is the opposite of conventional biographism. This re-focused art history thus becomes a branch of the general history of practice and training. Firstly, it gives technically precise answers to the question of high art's creation, in so far as this is possible through the analysis of practice forms. Secondly, it can offer new ways to interpret the paradoxes of mass culture, for example the phenomenon that some international stars in the pop music scene still cannot sing after decades on the stage – which is only mildly surprising if one knows that a mere fraction of their practice time is invested in singing, whereas they automatically assume that less than three hours of working out at the gym are insufficient for their stage show.

If one transposes the history of art into the framework of a history of asceticisms, one gains not least a new perspective on the complex of phenomena which Hans Belting presents as a 'history of the image before the era of art' in his study *Likeness and Presence*.[98] This knowledgeable synopsis of iconic painting from late antiquity to the Renaissance is not so much concerned with venturing into a zone 'before art' – this would mean delegitimizing the secular artist and subordinating him to the artist-priest. In his book on icons, Belting rather discovers the possibility of rethinking art history as the medium for a history of art-bearing asceticisms. The author stops halfway, admittedly, subsuming art history *à contre cœur* under a general 'image history' – for him, one of the few resolute art essentialists today, this was certainly only a provisional solution, in which the sense of different qualities had not yet been sufficiently explored.

In reality, it is not the liquidation of art history in favour of a general image history that is the order of the day – otherwise, the mass photographing of everything and everyone would be the culmination of the history of image productions. What needs to be made explicit is rather the historical alliance of art and asceticism, which has thus far only been discussed indirectly. If one accepts this thematization, iconic painting can offer the most plausible starting point for a grand narrative of the procession of image-creating energies through the ages – not because one considers it a form of artless pictoriality, but because the icon embodies the exemplary work of asceticism: here art is applied asceticism, and high asceticism sometimes high art. The sacred image is not only an object of selfless prayer and meditation; the very act of painting from which it ensues is one of the most concentrated forms of prayer, meditation and de-selfing. The reason why generations of icon painters have devoted themselves to a single motif for their entire lives is that, in the spirit of Hellenistic-Eastern Christianity, they were obliged to keep submitting anew to a transcendent image that would then materialize through their work. This monothematicism shows that the image is only permissible in the service of salvation; hence there is no question of a free choice of motif. Through its restriction to a few archetypes, spiritual painting is capable of furthering flight from the world or ethical secession. Icon painters could never entertain the belief that they had created the perfect image; it was a sign of Satanic temptation to think that the divine archetype had chosen them in order to take on a worldly manifestation through their work. Only the transcendent archetype could exhibit the fullness of perfection, not its inner-worldly projection – let alone the painter, a subordinate iconopoiete, however dissolved his ego.

Icon painting thus embodies art at its ascetic maximum – and the minimum connection to the world. Once this point has been fixed, post-iconic European art history can be presented as a multi-stage process entailing a shifting, expansion, loosening and dissolution of art-enabling asceticisms. In the disappearance of the monopoly held by religious themes, it was the visual art of the Renaissance that literally opened new windows. The liberation of polythematicism was the true mission of the 'art of perspective'. Seeing perspectively, after all, means affording the world the third dimension, depth, and with it the dignity of contemplability. Now the icon was everywhere: any image could be a sacred one, and every window opened on a true manifestation. Salvation no longer meant liberation from the temptations of the world, but rather liberation to experience the wealth of earthly wonders. The world became everything worthy of being shown.

The encounter between the most elaborated discipline and the most comprehensive attention to the world created the conditions for extreme culminations of artistic success. The possibility of such heights is not limited to the classical centuries, of course, being essentially present in all later periods too – including the present. As is well known, however, this creates a less favourable environment for new peak productions, as the all-infiltrating phenomenon of mass culture, thanks to its victorious mixture of simplification, disrespect and intolerance, is averse to any normative notion of height – let alone heights to which it is supposed to compare.

It is unnecessary to trace the problematic role of twentieth-century visual art in the dissolution of 'standards', even – and especially – in its advanced-civilized wing. One of its passions, after all, was the propagation of an art without disciplinary premises: the topic 'Duchamp and the consequences' will continue to occupy art critics for a long time, and it is by no means certain whether the reputation held by the church father of art after art will survive such examination intact.[99]

On Military Drill

A significant side branch of newer art with humans, one that only receives scant interest and even scanter sympathy among contemporary audiences, is evident in the military world of the early Modern Age. We know that soldierly practice extends back to the early periods of Mesopotamian and Mediterranean state forms – the famous Greek phalanx and the Roman legions were already considered marvels of combat training and the overcoming of psychological probability (that is, the human inclination to flee in the face of mortal danger) in their own time. Nor was Cicero's connection of the Roman word for the army, *exercitus*, to its main function of daily weapons practice, *exercitatio*, ever completely forgotten in Europe. In addition, ancient accounts describe how in battle, group fitness – demonstrated in impressive formations and coherent collective movements – far outweighed individual fitness in man-to-man combat. Although the medieval military system could not ignore this information, knighthood established an entirely different notion of battle and victory, and it was only in the early Modern Age that a new type of warfare on the basis of resolute formation training emerged once more. Without this, it would be impossible to understand the controlled 'evolutions' of troops, both on the battlefield and on the drill ground, between the seventeenth century and the innovations of Napoleonic mobile warfare.

In the common descriptions of early modern reconnections to Greek and Roman cultural patterns in the fields of architecture, visual art and literature, it has often been overlooked that this was almost contemporaneous – displaced by a few generations – with a military 'return of antiquity'. It is associated in particular with the work of the army commander Maurice of Nassau (with contributions from William of Orange and his brother, John VI of Nassau-Dillenburg), which, next to contemporary military-theoretical impulses, was based most of all on the renewed interest in ancient military writers. Thanks to his sound knowledge of classical languages, Maurice was able to study the original texts of authors such as Xenophon, Polybius and Onasander, as well as Caesar, Livy and Suetonius, but most of all the tactical writings of Aelianus and the Byzantine emperor Leo VI. From these works he took precise instructions for the development of modern training rules. In the military reform he carried out for the Dutch troops in the anti-Spanish war of liberation after 1589, he drew particularly on the instructions – already tested by the Greeks – to set up soldiers in rank and file, a division whose effects could still be observed on the barrack squares of the twentieth and twenty-first centuries. In a sort of involuntary Platonism, Greek and Roman warriors alike had adopted the central principle of the *Republic*, namely that the 'state' is nothing but a great man (*makránthropos*) – unabashedly equating the 'state' (*polis*) with a disciplined military troop. Such ideas suited the intuitions of Renaissance strategists, because they permitted the projection of geometric figures and homogeneous movements (evolutions) onto larger masses of 'political organisms'.

Consistently with this, Maurice took the descriptions – some of them extremely precise – of the 'elementary movements' of army groups from the ancient tactical manuals, including such figures as about-turns, wheeling, countermarches and others. Here the soldier is shaped into the lateralized human being, who must not confuse left and right under any circumstances. Furthermore, the ancients had already discovered the significance of a simple and effective language in which commands could be conveyed unambiguously to the troops. Under this influence, all armies of the burgeoning European nation-states followed the Orange-Nassau model and developed their own native military codes, consisting of short one-word commands that would be internalized on the barrack squares and subsequently followed on the battlefield. The sections of the new rule books devoted to the use of arms, in particular the still-unwieldy firearms – a subject on which the pioneers of the Orange reform could not learn much from the ancients – even contain first descriptions of complex movement sequences whose ergonomic precision would only return in the positivistic investigations of early sport science in the nineteenth century, as well as the instructions for production-line workers in the era of Taylorism.[100] These studies were not surpassed until the last third of the twentieth century, when quantified sport physiology and training science made motion studies with imaging procedures, diagrams showing the metabolic rates of top athletes, and individualized training instructions for sporting disciplines of all kinds and levels the order of the day.

Human-Fitters in General

We have seen how the privilege of conveying the absolute imperative gradually left the hands of religious speakers and passed to a number of secular agencies at the start of the Modern Age. Notable examples of these were the early modern prince as a patron of human production, the Baroque educator as an expert on the pansophic moulding of humans, and the Renaissance commander as a classically schooled virtuoso of massed human arrangements in the war of formations. In time, these were joined by throngs of advisers and prompters who no longer addressed their fellow humans as messengers of the metanoetic imperative, but as bringers of practical innovations that concerned technical advantages more than moral improvements. I call these the human-fitters of the Modern Age. They were highly significant in the moulding of the 'human material' of their time, for, unlike some philosophers, they never succumbed to the ideology of the unequipped, absolute human being.[101] The new fitters chose the pragmatic way to access humans: they saw them primarily as clients, that is to say as participants in the world of goods and things who were surrounded by obtainable objects, were stimulated by objects and practised with objects. They never spoke of the single necessity as long as they could promote useful innovations. They suggested to their contemporaries that they should change their life through participation in current artificialities and raise their existential tonicity, and not least their competing power, through new means of information, comfort and distinction. This new market undermined the archaic either/or of ethical difference: now fundamentalists could transform themselves into customers, believers could become readers, and escapists could turn into manifest media users. Whoever wanted to change their life found themselves amidst an ever-widening horizon of life-augmenting and life-increasing accessories – these are the strongest attractors in the modern deluge of commodities, which is often unjustly described only in terms of consumerism. Their acquisition is tied to a share in elevated fitness chances and expanded gratifications. This extends from the first editions of humanist authors to flat rates for the networked world, from spices harvested on the Moluccan Islands to Parker-graded *Grands Crus du Médoc*, from the crude prosthetic hands of Götz von Berlichingen's day to the hi-tech implants of the present, from the coaches of Emperor Maximilian's time to the luxury jeeps for the mobility elite of the last petroleum years.

The human-fitters are no mere sellers or market criers peddling accessories for an up-to-date life. If one takes their function as seriously as is absolutely necessary in the face of their significance for the material equipping of modern existence, one observes that what they offer is frequently no less than world improvement in discreet amounts – such as the late medieval invention of eyeglasses, without which reading and living in the Gutenberg era would have been inconceivable.[102] Even Petrarch, it is written, already made use of such a reading aid from the age of sixty. Modern paper also falls into the category of world improvements from the production line; this is the source of the pandemonium of commodities that are brought to the modern audience via printers, publishers, newspaper makers, cartographers, writers, scholars and journalists. Members of the paper-based professions here act as discreet drill instructors for modern humans. They change the life of every individual without reaching for their whole existence.

The anthropotechnic effects of these services and products – the competence-elevating dynamic and the expansion of the operational horizon – are generally only granted full approval in their early days. At the beginning of an innovation it is the difference between users and non-users that is most apparent, while in the phase of market saturation, its entropic and abusive effects attract attention. That is why Comenius and Karl Kraus could not hold the same opinion about the blessings of the Black Art. As long as no more than a small minority are capable of reading and writing, universal alphabetization seems like a messianic project. Only once everyone has this ability does one notice the catastrophe that almost no one can do it properly.

This background enables us to understand a fact that is symptomatic of the current phase of saturation: there are countless people who want to withdraw from the omnipresence of advertising, who even avoid it like the plague. Here too, it is helpful to distinguish between the states before and after. From the perspective of the burgeoning modern world of products, advertising could be justified by the argument that spreading the word about the existence of new means of life improvement was indispensable, as the populations of industrial and trading nations would otherwise have been cheated of major knowledge about discreet improvements to the world. As the ambassador of new bringers of advantage, early advertising was the general training medium for contemporary performance collectives thoughtlessly denounced in culture-conservative milieus as 'consumer societies'. The aversion to advertising that pervades the saturated infospheres of the present, however, is based on the correct intuition that, in most of its manifestations, it has long since become a form of downward training. It no longer passes on what people should know in order to access advantageous innovations; it creates illusions of purchasable self-elevations that *de facto* usually lead to weakenings.

Finally, we should speak of modern bankers, who, because of their role as lenders for people who seek to improve their situation, and, as business actors, often actually do so, prove the most effective motivators for an intensifying change. Their work shows how a substantial part of the improvement imperatives under which the moderns live stem from the *arcanum magnum* of the modern property economy. If one formulates it explicitly, one stumbles on the categorical imperative of debt service: economize in such a way that, through an efficient use of resources, you can always be sure of being able to repay credit on time. The credit stress that forces growing populations of debtors into shape is a source of willingness to innovate that no theory of creativity has yet adequately acknowledged. As soon as one understands that modern disciplinings are based neither on the relationship of 'master and slave' nor on the opposition of 'capital and labour', but rather on the symbiotic antagonism of creditors and debtors, the entire history of money-driven 'societies' must be rewritten from scratch.

— 11 —

IN THE AUTO-OPERATIVELY CURVED SPACE

New Human Beings Between Anaesthesia and Biopolitics

In Praise of the Horizontal

In modernity, the metanoetic imperative increasingly changed into a prescription of 'outward application'. Its dissemination from the philosophical and monastic sphere into late aristocratic and bourgeois circles, and later also into proletarian and lower middle-class groups, reinforced the tendency towards de-spiritualization, pragmatization and finally the politicization of the dictate of change. Thus countless individuals in the centuries of modernization could follow the call to change their lives by opening the door to the typical products of their time. The magical paper products of the Gutenberg era – Bibles and non-Bibles alike – reached many, if not all, households over the years, decades and centuries. Whoever dealt with them seemed *eo ipso* on the better path. Printed texts accustomed their users to the dynamic of their time, which was still entirely opaque to them: that new media spread old content until different circumstances provide new content. This is in turn kept in circulation by the ageing media until the appearance of newer ones, which recycle the old media along with their old and new content.

What is decisive in all that followed is the observation that the demand for self-change and reversal no longer affected the change-disposed consciousness only from above: it need not always be the light from the vertical that casts the zealot to the ground before Damascus. The bright streak on the horizon towards which we wander on the ground now takes on a new spiritual and moral value. If the east is red, it cannot be a mistake to walk in that direction. The Reformation abolished the spiritual privileges of monastic life, as every point in the world is equidistant from grace. This changed the preconditions for a radical rejection of the world in their most sensitive point. If the ascetics in their strict orders were no closer to the light than the laymen in public offices and workshops, the latter could also find opportunities to advance spiritually by worldly means. The Enlightenment was able to follow on directly from this. And more than this: since the beginnings of the lighting policies that gave rise to the *lumières*, one could imagine the path to the illumination of all things as a gentle upward slope on which anyone with a vaguely good will who understood the signs of the times could move forwards. An inarticulate urge from within was now to be sufficient in order to find the right path; where there is an urge, there is a way forwards. From the eighteenth century on, a constant striding along moderately rising paths was rationalized as the authentic mode of progress. *Cultura non facit saltus.*[103] World improvement is the good thing that needs time.[104]

It is impossible to overstate the consequences of the shift towards a moderation of ethical standards; the tempering of aims restored an awareness of the moral chromaticism of the real. The ethical distinction moved to the level of nuances. It not only gave tepid Christians back their clear conscience; it even granted the worldlings precedence in the quest for the good life – in fact, it made it possible after millennia of spiritual discrimination to rehabilitate the worldly life as a positive movement in the horizontal, provided it showed a certain upward tendency. Whoever denied or dismissed this tendency was immediately reactionary; whoever was not content with it would dream sooner or later of a vertical exit from anything that seemed horizontal, continuous or foreseeable: of revolution.

Progress as Half-Price Metanoia

Thus the idea of progress and development in modernity transpires as the worst enemy of old-style radical metanoia. It deprives the steep old-ascetic vertical of its plausibility, relegating it to the domain of 'fanaticism'. This change lies behind the thousandfold repeated misreading of modernity as the era of secularization. Certainly Christianity lost its predominance in Europe from the eighteenth century onwards, but only a few Enlightenment zealots established a form of 'humans alone' movement that slammed shut all doors to the beyond and sought to transfer everything unconditionally to the realm of immanence. The general populace had always retained a vague awareness of transcendence, even in the supposedly secular centuries – William James called the popular tendency towards the simultaneously credulous and incredulous supposition of a higher reality 'piecemeal supranaturalism', applying it also to himself. This disposition was perfectly suited to the pragmatic immanentism of the Modern Age, as well as the good logical manners of academia and the educated audience, and it is this familiar attitude that is attracting attention once more in the rumours currently circulating of a 'post-secular society'.

The central moral-historical event of this epoch was therefore not secularization, but rather the de-radicalization of the ethical distinction – or, if one prefers, the de-verticalization of existence. This is precisely what is meant by the once-great word 'progress'. The discreet spiritual sensation of the Modern Age was that the middle paths were now the ones leading to salvation. The moderation of demands for a radical disavowal of ancient Adam and his corrupt milieu gave worldliness a new dignity. They contributed to bringing about the cultural climate change in favour of a fundamental neophilia. It is unnecessary to demonstrate here how the inclination to welcome the new gave the Modern Age its futurist orientation. Since Hans Blumenberg's central work, its debt to the rehabilitation of curiosity has been known.[105]

In its quieter periods, especially 1648–1789 and 1815–1914, and once more from 1945 to the present day, the newer era was, all in all, an age of half-price metanoia. In these times one could safely go along with the 'development' driving forwards *grosso modo* and let old Adam live in a bourgeois guise. To consider oneself one of the justified, one of the good, it was sufficient to be in step with the times and follow the general trend of progress. From a critical point onwards, the reversal of consciousness was even supposed to take place for free, simply by remembering one's natural goodness: Rousseau even managed to proclaim Adam the true human being and denounce all attempts by civilization to educate him, better him and make him strive upwards as aberrations. To this day, we do not know what caused the deeper culture rupture in recent centuries – Rousseauism, with its doctrine that true nature is free for all, or Leninism, with its fierce re-raising of the price for changing the world and humans. The latter spawned activists who prided themselves on large-scale killing for the good cause, while the former seduced countless educated men of the nineteenth and twentieth centuries into believing that one could restore the human being's inner truth by doing away with all cultural trappings and artistic superstructures.[106]

The half-price metanoia that defined the moral *modus operandi* of progressive, semi-secular 'society' from the Baroque onwards enabled the historic compromise between self-improvement and world improvement. While the former was still entirely the business of the change-willing individual, the latter depended on the perform-ances of the teachers, inventors and entrepreneurs who populated the social field with the results of their activity – pedagogical results on the one side, technical and economic results on the other. As far as changes of method are concerned, one notes how the emphasis increasingly shifts from the practising self-influence of the individual to the effects of teachers and inventors on the many from without. When Seneca wrote to his only student, *meum opus es*, this was barely more than a motivating turn of phrase, not to mention a charming expression of pedagogical eros. He himself knew best of all that even in the demanding relationship between master and student, everything ultimately depends on the latter's willingness to mould themselves.

Things look rather different when the modern school and the guild of human-fitters set about their work: their life-changing intentions are undeniable, but their angle of attack is chosen in such a way that there can be no doubt as to the primacy of the outside influence. The early school drill has always pre-empted the student's own perform-ance; syllabuses lay down the courses of study before it can even occur to pupils that they might have an interest of their own in this or that subject; and for the buyers of competence-expanding devices, a possible contribution of their own is essentially meaningless from the start compared to the performance on offer. Each time it is the optimization from without that keeps the upper hand, even when the inner sediments of tuition and the habitual use of life-heightening means – works of art, prostheses, vehicles, communication media, luxury items etc. – become second nature for students and users.

World Improvement as Self-Improvement

These observations can be translated into a distinction: in the prac-tising life of the spiritual-ascetic, virtuosic or athletic type, the agent has a self-improving influence on themselves via the direct route of daily training. On the path of world improvement, by contrast, they become a user of objective optimization tools that modify their ethical status indirectly at most, albeit not insignificantly. This dis-tinction directly concerns the way in which the call to change one's life modifies the existence of the individual. As we have seen, where the metanoetic imperative is accepted at its full price – to retain our business jargon – existence comes under a steep vertical tension: it imposes the passion form of the individually chosen field on life, whether that of the 'religious', artistic, political or sometimes also the sporting sphere. If, on the other hand, the half-price imperative is adopted, as in the shallower forms of enlightenment, progressive thought and starry-eyed idealism, a mode of existence is established whose aims are facilitation of life, breakdown of vertical tension and avoidance of passion.

As long as the moderate tendency succeeds in presenting itself as the reasonable that is in the process of becoming the real, and thus claims universal validity, it is not overly problematic to compare and perhaps even equate technological progress with moral and social progress. For conventional progressism, the journey forwards and upwards is one that does not need to be completed under one's own steam; it is like a current that we can allow to carry us. Coming from distant sources, it has flowed through entire epochs; our ship of progress would not have travelled so far had it not been drifting on this current – though we have only recently started guiding it towards the port. Shame on anyone who has trouble imagining rivers that flow uphill! Today one calls complex masses in qualified movement 'evolving systems' to neutralize the paradox in the requirement that forwards should simultaneously mean upwards.[107] The postmoderns sheepishly note down the pale remnants of progress under the heading 'complexity increase'. As long as the early Enlightenment looking ironically over the shoulders of the 'positive religions' itself functions like a religion, however – as an illusion-training club for groups, and as a practice system for internalizing surrealistic assumptions among individuals – it is the duty of every decent human being to promote the conviction that there are indeed rivers which flow uphill.

Having-Oneself-Operated-On: The Subject in Auto-Operative Curvature

It is necessary to insist on these essentially familiar and established observations because the complications that will concern us in the following can only be understood against this background. They relate firstly to the intense frictions between the strong and weak forms of the metanoetic imperative in modernity, and secondly to the relationship between the optimizations I carry out on myself and the life improvements which, as a contemporary of advanced inventions and services, I arrange for others to perform. I shall refer to the first mode of action as 'self-operation', which makes the phrase 'having-oneself-operated-on' a logical choice for the second. Together, they refer to competing modes of anthropotechnic behaviour. In the first, I am moulded as an object of direct self-modification through measures of my own; in the second, I expose myself to the effects of others' operating competence and let them mould me. The interplay of self-operation and having-oneself-operated-on encompasses the entire self-concern of the subject.[108]

Modern conditions are characterized by the fact that self-competent individuals increasingly draw on the operative competence of others for their acts on themselves. I call the referring-back of having-one-self-operated-on to self-operation the auto-operative curvature of the modern subject. It is based on a strongly evident fact: whoever lets others do something directly to them is indirectly doing something for themselves. This leads to an altered way of integrating suffering into actions. The competent subject must not only attend to the expansion of its own radius of action; it must also extend its responsibility for 'treatments' through others.

It is easy to see why this is the only possibility in a modernized world. Individuals are not only unable to take the entire work of changing the world upon themselves – they cannot even take care of everything required for their own personal optimization by themselves. By exposing themselves to the effects of others' ability to act, they appropriate a form of passivity that implies a roundabout or deferred way of acting themselves. The expanded passivity competence of the moderns expresses itself in the willingness to have oneself operated on in one's own interests.

The Treated Self

Welcome passivity takes on numerous forms: having oneself informed, having oneself entertained, having oneself served, having oneself supplied, having oneself aroused, having oneself healed, having oneself edified, having oneself insured, having oneself transported, having oneself represented, having oneself advised, or having oneself corrected. Unwelcome forms of passivity supplement this series, beginning with letting oneself be blackmailed – through the dimension of disadvantageous employment contracts, for example, as examined by Marx, who took them as indicating a state of 'exploitation'; it follows from this, incidentally, that as soon as exploitation becomes chronic, it does not continue without a degree of consent on the passive side. Finally, we shall mention letting oneself be deceived: it becomes relevant in situations where the subject cannot cover its need for self-deception alone and, in order not to relent in its desire, turns to a qualified illusion provider who can supply what is needed.

Whatever the subject lets others do to it, it not only appropriates the 'treatments' after the fact, but seeks them of its own accord and integrates what is done to it into what it does to itself. From this perspective, one can see through Sartre's worn-out statement that we must make something out of what has been done to us as a one-eyed version of the passive–active interconnection. As is well known, Sartre always emphasized the act of self-appropriation, which puts an end to the previous acceptance of heteronomy. With this act, the subject breaks away from its being-object-for-others, thus realizing its freedom; at the same time, it does away with the bad faith that made it pretend to be a powerless something: whoever claims to be a thing among things has originally deceived themselves. It is not hard to recognize the model of *résistance* being applied to the philosophical analysis of existence here – and one can even discern the dramatic shadow of the French Revolution in the projection's background. In addition, this accelerated the shift towards the externalization of the dictate of change, as its ambivalent outcome called into existence the modern forms of radicalism: dissatisfaction with the results of the revolution produced the concrete desire for its repetition; dissatisfaction with the repetitions produced the abstract longing for its permanence. Sartre was lucid enough to transfer the chronic dissatisfaction from the outer front back to the inner one. The consequences speak for themselves: if self-realization is presented as a rejection of passivity that must constantly take place anew, the ghost light of permanent revolution takes hold of the individual's self-relationship – and Sartre, referring to Trotsky, in fact spoke of true morality as a *conversion permanente*.[109] This approach could only produce one result: the simultaneous destruction of politics *and* morals.

What is decisive, in fact, is the free cultivation of the passive elements in the individual's self-relationship, corresponding to the auto-operative constitution of modern existence. For this we certainly do not need to choose the perverse exploitation of the suffering position, masochism, where the sexual relationship is embedded in a game of domination. In one of the most impressive sections of his early central work, Sartre showed this mode of having-oneself-operated-on as the paradigm of a cunning, voluntary becoming-object-for-others – brilliant in literary terms, but factually misleading.[110] The field of personal interest in skilled passivity is far more extended than the perverse contract of the pain-seeker with the appointed abuser expresses; it is also much broader than one can grasp via the critique of power and domination. If I arrange for a transport company to take me from A to B, I take on board the driving service offered as an acceptable suffering – rides in hired vehicles only actually turn into masochistic ordeals on certain days. If I go to see my doctor, I usually also welcome the unpleasant examinations which his special-ized competence enables him to grant me; I subject myself to invasive treatments as if I were ultimately performing them on myself. If I switch on a preferred channel of mine, I *nolens volens* accept being flooded by the current programme. McLuhan's punning remark that *message* is *massage* makes philosophical sense if one recognizes it as a competent statement on the 'question of the subject' in the media age. Having oneself massaged symbolizes the situation of all those who act on themselves by allowing others to act on them.

In all cases of voluntarily sought passivity, it is easy to show how the passive aspects connect back to independent activity. This involves suspending that activity for the duration of the outside influence without abandoning the prospect of its resumption. The result is the phenomenon I here term the auto-operative curvature of actions in a highly labour-divided, or rather competence-divided and practice-divided, space of action. From the subject's perspective, its insertion into the curvature determines its actions through the ability to suffer. It does not mean submitting to domination, but rather sharing in a foreign competence. If the operation endured leads to the desired result, the suffering subject will believe that it performed an act of self-concern by handing the law of action to the operator. The statement 'I took myself in hand' is now replaced by a more complex formulation: 'I put myself in other hands so that, after completed treatment, I would once more be able to take myself in hand.'

If it were possible to keep its pietistic connotations at bay, one could mark this figure of a passivity underpinned by independent activity as the manifestation of 'calmness'[111] that is constitutive of modernity. Calmness means passivity competence – it is the small change of ability that carries greater passions. It comes into play in situations where the subject is ready and willing to take the position of a client and profit from the *savoir-faire* of the operating partner. It is thus more a mode of prudence than the modern substitute for wisdom that Heidegger wanted to see in it. We recall: the philosopher had recommended 'calmness' [*Gelassenheit*] so that the modern human being, dazed by its own ability to act, could expose itself once more to treatment by Being itself. In reality, passivity-competent behaviour is part of the game intelligence of humans in an elaborated networked world, where it is impossible to make a move without simultaneously allowing others to play with one. In this sense, calmness is inseparable from the self-conception of experienced actors for whom the philosophical chimera of the subject residing at the centre of its circles of action has faded – or rather, has lost its utility value as the self-description of the day. It is replaced everywhere by concepts for agents who operate and are operated on, 'prosumers' and users of technical interfaces.[112] Bazon Brock had already anticipated the figure of 'passivity competence' in the field of art observation decades ago: from 1968 on, he set up 'visitors' schools' at the 'documenta' in Kassel, and has meanwhile developed these further into the fourfold concept of the certified consumer, the certified patient, the certified voter and the certified recipient.

In the Operative Circle: Medical Calmness

One of the most important modifications of calmness comes into play when the subject visits its 'treating' physician. Although the recent culture of having-something-done-to-oneself – which I shall here call a general form of having-oneself-operated-on – generalized the figure of the client, the medical field contains an older form of passivity for which one normally reserves the word 'patient'. It would not be surprising if it disappeared from the vocabulary of the medical system in the course of the twenty-first century, surviving only in conservative subcultures where sickness is viewed as a chance and the accident as a medium of self-experience. *De facto*, this area too has been subject to clientization for some time, assisted not inconsiderably by the juridicization of the doctor–patient relationship. But whatever one calls the relationship between the doctor and their counterpart, it becomes acute when the latter entrusts themselves to the former for a surgical operation. Now one conventionally speaks of having-oneself-operated-on, meaning that faced with a serious diagnosis, the patient must be prepared for subjection to an invasive treatment. The content articulated in the old medical maxim *vulnerando sanamus* – we heal by wounding – translates on the patient side into a hypothesis: by allowing the infliction of skilled injury on myself, I contribute to my recovery. Although the asymmetry between the roles of patient and operator is great here, there is no doubt that the patient is an indirect co-actor, and thus meets the criteria for action in the auto-operatively curved space.

The curvature is rounded into a complete circle if the operator is the operated – a rare exception, but one that appears several times in medical history. A notable example is the doctor Leonid Rogozov, who was forced to perform an appendectomy on himself in 1961 during a stay at Novolazarevskaya Station, a Russian research station in the Antarctic. A famous photograph shows him lying on a table wearing a surgeon's gown with a face mask, having just opened his lower right abdominal wall. An even more sensational case was that of the American mountain climber Aron Ralston, who performed a spectacular self-amputation: following an accident during a mountain hike in Utah in April 2003 in which his right arm was trapped under a dislodged boulder, he decided, after attempting in vain to free himself for five days, to break his lower arm bone and sever the flesh with a blunt pocket knife. Afterwards he travelled the world as a speaker, describing his unusual act of self-concern to packed venues. In 2000, there was considerable attention in the media to the case of the then twenty-nine-year-old British performance artist Heather Perry, who performed a trepanation on her own skull using a local anaesthetic and a special drill – supposedly to cure her chronic fatigue and attain a higher level of consciousness. Furthermore, we know from the life story of the Indian wise man Ramana Maharshi (1873–1950) that he underwent surgery several times towards the end of his life for a cancer on his arm, and each time turned down the anaesthetic in favour of a Yogic form of pain neutralization. For an illuminated man of the old school, it was clearly out of the question to accept a treatment by Western methods that violated the spiritual axiom of constant wakefulness.

As a rule, the auto-operative self-reference that enables the subject to tolerate technical modifications to its body displays a gentler curvature. Since around the eighteenth century, it has expressed itself in the extensive use of stimulants among enlightened Europeans. Their application increased from the twentieth century on, to the point of a massive use of doping agents in every possible discipline. It is no secret how dependent authors like Voltaire and Balzac were on caffeine, or how much Sigmund Freud owed to his nicotinism. Equally, connoisseurs of Sartre's later career know of the extremes brought about by his alternating alcoholism and amphetamine addiction. In all these cases, the decisive question was obviously what the stimulated parties made out of what the stimulants had made of them. Sartre's addiction to amphetamines was not without a certain irony:

it made him dependent on a substance that was intended to create a feeling of complete independence.

October Revolution: The Ether Anaesthetic

From the mid-nineteenth century on, surgical operations saw the inclusion of anaesthesia, without which having-oneself-operated-on in the narrower sense would be inconceivable today. Its appearance on the stage of medical options was accompanied by one of the most profound modifications of the human self-relationship in modern times. If there has ever been a technical innovation that merited the use of the word 'revolution', it was the reintroduction of the general anaesthetic. Its first successful application was on 16 October 1846, in the operating theatre of the Massachusetts General Hospital, where it was administered to the patient Gilbert Abbot with the aid of a specially constructed spherical ether inhaler for the removal of a neck tumour. The operation took place in the presence of the Boston medical elite, who constituted a rather sceptical audience after the failure of a similar attempt in the same auditorium using laughing gas. Once William Morton, the constructor of the ether ball, had induced the patient to take a few deep breaths from it, the surgeon, Dr Warren, carried out the operation in just under three minutes (before the reintroduction of the general anaesthetic in surgery, speed was of the essence), with no pain whatsoever felt by the patient. After completing the demonstration, Warren supposedly turned to those present with the words: 'Gentlemen, this is no humbug.' Thus the strongest neo-evangelic message in medical history was conveyed by the greatest understatement.[113]

This surgical 14 July, which entered the annals of medicine as 'ether day', changed the anthropotechnic situation of modernity more radically than any individual political event or technical innovation since – including the biopolitical experiments of the Russian Revolution, as well as all attempts at genetic manipulation thus far. While the Bastille was immediately torn down as a supposed 'symbol of despotism' (the 'patriot' Palloy, a quick-witted building contractor who had appeared on the scene with a demolition crew as soon as the fortress was stormed, supposedly received the commission to demolish it as early as 16 July), the American doctors reverently preserved the scene of the rebellion against the tyranny of pain. The 'Ether Dome' at Massachusetts General Hospital can still be visited in its original state today. A painting by Robert Hinckley from 1882 captured the

379

scene. Within a few days, the news from America reached the Old World by sea mail in almost twenty separate messages. European doctors received it with almost universal enthusiasm, welcoming it like a secular gospel and imitating it to massive success; only a group of sceptics and algophilic traditionalists, who defended pain as part of the human condition, initially refused to consider the new method for disabling pain. Among the vast majority, there was a wave of emulation based not on mimetic rivalry, but on a long-felt need for deliverance from an epochal evil.

The 16th of October 1846 is the key date in the history of the operable human being: since then, the rediscovered possibilities of having-oneself-anaesthetized have enormously expanded the radius of having-oneself-operated-on by surgeons. Through the development of such new anaesthetics as Evipan (1932) or Propofol (1977), as well as highly effective opium derivatives, professionalized anaesthesia has for some time also had efficient short-term narcotics at its disposal, enabling a significant reduction of wake-up time. Thanks to intensive research, the depth of the narcosis can now also be closely controlled, and the constant improvement of the necessary equipment rounds off the optimization of anaesthesia.

What made these rediscovered possibilities was the fact that between 1490 and 1846, European medicine almost entirely forgot the anaesthetic techniques of antiquity and the Middle Ages, especially the formally well-known and frequently used 'soporific sponges', which contained highly effective extracts from poppies, henbane, mandrake and hemlock. This amnesia, which is still virtually inexplicable, was a factor in the harsh climate of reality throughout the Modern Age until the mid-nineteenth century: in this era, surgical operations were almost always torturous affairs that amounted to agonies for the patients.

On the Human Right to Unconsciousness

In philosophical terms, the reintroduction of complete anaesthesia marked a caesura in the self-relationships of modern humans. Not only because the contemporary subject's attitude towards its physical body and its operability is simply incomprehensible if one does not take into account the new possibility of consenting to the disabling of its sensitivity to pain. As self-awareness is often extinguished along with it, the subject faces the dramatic choice of temporarily resigning from its being-for-itself and entirely adopting the position of

380

an unconscious in-itself. It not only agrees to this injury in its own interests – the precondition for all having-oneself-operated-on in the stricter sense – but also affirms artificial unconsciousness to gain an advantage. This is significant because it explicitly articulates a previously unimaginable thesis: that humans can no longer be expected to endure every state of wakeful being-in-the-world. In this context it is worth mentioning that before the term 'anaesthesia' was officially established in the early nineteenth century, one sometimes spoke of suspended animation. This better expressed the central principle of the general anaesthetic: liberating the patient for the duty of 'animated' passion.

One could say that in October 1846, the human right to unconsciousness was established – the right of not-having-to-be-present in certain extreme states of one's own psychophysical existence. The claim to this right had been prepared by a fashionable gesture of the late eighteenth and early nineteenth centuries: the proverbial phenomenon of fainting due to over-stimulation, which was accepted in particularly sensitive people – those of the female sex – as a mark of cultivated weakness, and flourished in the hysterical symptoms of the late nineteenth century. Furthermore, the techniques of animal magnetism and artificially induced somnambulism, both discussed throughout Europe after 1785 and both early forms of what became known as 'hypnosis' in 1840, enabled modern subjects to become familiar with the advantages of suspended animation. These methods, which became common from the late eighteenth century on under the name of Mesmerism – also in the context of social vaudeville entertainment – occasionally served among doctors after 1800 as a forerunner of chemical anaesthesia. Mesmerism enjoyed an intensive reception by the Romantics and German Idealists, as it could be interpreted as the royal road to the realm beyond everyday consciousness, almost a form of experimental theology.[114]

This play with artificial unconsciousness reached its pinnacle in the 1830s, when laughing gas became the party drug of the British upper class. At the same time, elegant opium eaters and educated narcomaniacs could be sure that their confessions would be read attentively by a public interested in anaesthetics of all kinds. Even two generations later, the propagandists of the Theosophical Society (founded in 1875) – Helena Blavatsky (1833–91), Annie Besant (1847–1933) and Charles Leadbeater (1847–1934) – who showed a precise feeling for the spiritual market in mixing European mysticisms with Indian psychotechnics, found an audience that longed more than ever for instruction in the art of self-renunciation in the service of the self.

Typically modern techniques for expanding one's passivity competence were rehearsed in all these forms of conditional self-renunciation,
though not always with ego-strengthening prospects. The element of
auto-operative curvature manifests itself most clearly in the medically
required general anaesthetic, as it constitutes a borderline case of temporary not-being-oneself in the service of being-oneself. It indicates
a liminal zone that can only be shifted to regions even more distant
from the self through an artificial coma – provided that the prospect
of a controlled return to waking life is assured. Consent to this type of
suspended animation means the last possible level of calmness.[115]

Revolutionary Un-Calmness

Alongside the subjective appropriation of technological and social
progress in the context of calmness culture, or the system of conditional passivities, modernity brought forth a culture of un-calmness based on the declared unwillingness to await the results of
slow progress. It includes a profound distrust towards most forms
of letting-something-be-done-to-oneself. This regularly brings the
domination-critical motif into play, namely that power and its abuse
are synonymous. Un-calmness and the general rejection of passivity
are the root of the extremisms that began to take hold in Western
Europe and Russia in the nineteenth century and led into the 'revolutions' of the twentieth century.

Medical progress, on the other hand, aligned itself with the gradual
model of the bourgeois Enlightenment. This taught its adepts to view
every improvement achieved as the starting point for further optimizations. This applied not least to anaesthesia-supported surgery,
which, despite its great leap forwards around the middle of the nineteenth century, generally remained a case of cumulative skill increase
on the path of progressive moderation.

The simultaneity of optimism and realism in the standard concept
of progress was tied to an ambitious cultivation of the feelings of the
time: at every moment, satisfaction at what had been achieved was
meant to balance out impatience at what still had to be achieved –
everything already possible had to be viewed in relation to the prospect of the not-yet-feasible. In any case, participation in the 'great
work of uplifting mankind' was unattainable without constant training in patience and impatience. Both attitudes were based on the tacit
assumption that the path to further civilization was itself a civilized
journey.

The un-calm of modernity was responsible for demonstrating what can happen if this precondition is rejected. The adherents of extremist positions refused to participate in the balancing exercise between patience and impatience, voting instead for radical acceleration. According to them, the truth lay in imbalance: good, for them, was one-sided and partisan. Never give up impatience – this was the axiom of the desire committed to radicality. According to the purveyors of the extreme, the only respectable form of progress – the one that would tackle the social question at its roots – does not come gradually, but must rather constitute a sudden and irreconcilable rupture in the usual way of things. It is not an additional step on a prescribed path – more like a wild ride through uncharted terrain. The revolution builds its own roads in the direction it chooses; no slip road from the past can dictate where it should go. In the conquest of the improbable, yesterday's realists are out of place as route planners.

The followers of such ideas rely on the objection that one must not be taken in by the illusion of the necessary gradualness of progress, for it conceals the reprehensible slowing of development by a class of ruling preventers who are secretly determined to keep the people waiting until the end of time. They say 'progress', but what they mean is the perpetuation of the status quo. The most familiar version of this thesis is the Marxist one, which states that only the 'greed for profit' of the capital owners prevents the general release of 'productive powers' in favour of the workers, who are usually blithely equated with the 'people'. Another popular idea was the anarchist maxim that the preventers were first and foremost among the representatives of the states and its notorious ally, the church, which meant that only direct violence against both could bring about the necessary destabilization of the situation. Only dead souls accept the principle of gradual progress. Whoever is still morally alive listens to the voices testifying here and now to the intolerability of the prevailing conditions. These voices give the individual in revolt the mandate of immediate overthrow. The young Marx unforgettably formulated the categorical imperative of the revolution: it is the absolute duty of the activist 'to overthrow all conditions in which man is a debased, enslaved, neglected, contemptible being'.[116]

Radical Metanoia as the Will to Overthrow

In reality, the rejection of the gradualness model of standard Enlightenment, to which the liberals of the nineteenth and twentieth

centuries clung as much as the social democrats and Christian democrats, by no means stemmed solely from the pressure of social crises.
It occurred because of a moral option whose inherent logic demanded
a break with the existing state of things. This choice constituted the
political continuation of the original ethical distinction between the
own and the non-own as made since the beginnings of ascetic secession. The central nuance lies in the fact that everything which is now
to be viewed as non-own is assigned to the past, while the own lies
exclusively in the future. The ethical distinction is temporalized, splitting the world into things past to be rejected and future things to be
welcomed. There is no hope in the present and the continuous – that
applies in equal measure to ancient escapism and to the modern
devaluation of all old regimes. But after the ontology of the finished
existent was abandoned and the becoming of a 'different world' transpired as increasingly plausible, indeed inevitable, the future became
an attractive home for those who made the great ethical distinction
anew.

Thus it becomes deplorable to seek the attainment of satisfying
conditions via the gentle slopes of bourgeois world improvement.
Whoever chooses this pass has essentially already decided to leave
everything as it was, no matter how many changes of detail might
give the impression that the affirmability of conditions is on the
increase. In truth, the primacy of the past remains in force as long
as the relationship between the vertical and horizontal dimensions is
defined by the dominance of the latter. What the world lacks are not
people willing to go along with changes on the plain; what it needs are
people in whom an awareness of the vertical is reawakening. A few
years before the October Revolution, one of the most distinguished
authors of biopolitical utopianism in the early Soviet Union, the poet
Alexander Svyatogor (1899–after 1937), had founded a group whose
programme included the abolition of death, the scientifically achieved
resurrection of the dead and the technological domination of the
cosmos; the group called itself the 'Verticalists'.

Only those who take the idea of world improvement utterly seriously will arrive at the view that world improvement is not enough.
Identification with the principle of externalized metanoia leads to
the insight that the existing world, that is to say the given 'social'
order, will remain incorrigible until its basal construction flaws –
class society and the unequal distribution of material and immaterial
wealth – are rectified. Thus the world of the 'existent' must not be
progressively improved but revolutionarily eradicated. With the help
of reusable elements from the old construction, the new construction

can begin after the great rupture in the spirit of equality before the 'achievements' – past and futures ones alike. Conventional progressism must be rejected so that the good intentions underlying it can take effect. It seems that the *naïveté* of the progressives has been seen through once and for all: they sincerely believe they are doing a service to freedom by opting for small, controlled steps. In reality, they are allying themselves with what is quintessentially bad – with the conditions based on the private property of world-improving means.

The notion that property is the means to all other means was ruled out by the new radicals. The deep-seated *ressentiment* towards private property, indeed towards anything private, blocked the conclusion that follows from any impartial examination of wealth-producing and freedom-favouring mechanisms: an effective world improvement would call for the most general possible propertization. Instead, the political metanoeticians enthused over general dispossession, akin to the founders of Christian orders who wanted to own everything communally and nothing individually. The most important insight into the dynamics of economic modernization remained inaccessible to them: money created by lending on property is the universal means of world improvement. They are all the blinder to the fact that for the meantime, only the modern tax state, the anonymous hyper-billionaire, can act as a general world-improver, naturally in alliance with the local meliorists – not only because of its traditional school power, but most of all thanks to its redistributive power, which took on unbelievable proportions in the course of the twentieth century. The current tax state, for its part, can only survive as long as it is based on a property economy whose actors put up no resistance when half of their total product is taken away, year after year, by the very visible hand of the national treasury for the sake of communal tasks. What the un-calm understand least of all is the simple fact that when government expenditures constitute almost 50 per cent of the gross national product, this fulfils the requirements of actually existing liberal-fiscal semi-socialism, regardless of what label is used to describe this situation – whether people call it the New Deal, 'social market economy' or 'neo-liberalism'.[117] What the system lacks for total perfection is a homogeneous worldwide tax sphere and the long-overdue propertization of the impoverished world.

Against the background of the beginnings of a history of the ethical distinction outlined above, it is immediately apparent how the offensive articulation of communist and anarchist radicality opened a new chapter. It deals with the breakthrough of the metanoetic imperative into the political dimension. Its most ambitious manifestation coincides with the strongest tendency to external application. This is why the twentieth century was the age of the 'commissars' who believed in changing the world by external and extreme means – we recall Arthur Koestler's essay 'The Yogi and the Commissar', which was published in 1942, in the heart of Europe's darkness, and in 1945 supplied the title for a volume of essays on the moral situation of the time that gained international recognition.[118]

Political Verticalism: The New Human Being

On the eve of the Russian Revolution, then, 'verticalism' could no longer assume its original form, in which it would purely have concerned individuals. Since the beginnings of ethical secession, it had been entirely down to them to force the impossible and remould themselves through tireless asceticism into wise men, god-men, new human beings – preferably alone, or in co-operation with other like-minded individuals if absolutely necessary. Even the wise men on the throne – Antoninus Pius and Marcus Aurelius in the West, Milinda and Ashoka in the East – did not think for a second of turning their individual philosophical metanoia into a state metanoia, a reversal for all. Even Paul, whose message was of the end of the world of death, was only actually speaking to the few who, through concern for their salvation, would be capable of joining the ranks of the saved before the imminent end.

In the course of its progress through the age of immanence, the absolute imperative turned into the dictate 'You must change the world – down to the very last elements of its construction, and with the involvement of everyone.' Whoever sought to execute this dictate as a mere constant progression – through the synergy of school, the market and technology – would be falling prey to the most dangerous of all temptations from the start. They would be succumbing to the siren song of the bourgeoisie to choose the path of conformity, on which the old state remains intact beneath the semblance of constant improvement. The revolutionary, however, has themselves tied to the mast like Odysseus. Undaunted, they traverse the ambivalent zones where liberal and social-democratic sounds tempt them. The better they know what they are refusing, the more cold-bloodedly they remain committed to their mission.

The great change, then, can only be brought about by a categorical renunciation of the shaping principle of the old world: a decisive rejection of mankind's division into the privileged and the non-privileged, the haves and the have-nots, the knowing and the unknowing, the rulers and the ruled. This new version of the metanoetic imperative directly affects the agents who submit to it: what it demands of them is no less than a complete break with their previous lives and a transformation into revolutionaries. This cannot be achieved by those who content themselves with electing a party that loudly proclaims rebellious slogans, and least of all by those who think it is enough to harbour secret satisfaction when the bourgeois media report bloody acts of 'revolutionary violence'. The revolution demands an integral discipline whose absorptive energy absolutely matches the great asceticisms of antiquity and the Middle Ages.

Above all, becoming a revolutionary is not simply a decision: one cannot transform oneself into the human of the future overnight. The New Human Being is a great not-yet for itself, even if it is brought near by the most feverish anticipations. Entrance into the revolutionary process, therefore, is initially merely the beginning of a protracted self-renunciation. Whoever opts for the revolution as a new form of belonging must first admit that they are still human through and through – infused with the hereditary injustice of the entire history of mankind, filled with the inner sediments of class society, spoiled by the mis-conditioning of all previous generations, perverted and distorted even in the most intimate elements of their sexuality, their taste and their forms of everyday communication. They also remain the old human being in their continuing inability to be brotherly – most of all because they still exist as the victim of a distorted life instinct or, as Trotsky wrote, 'a pinched, morbid, hysterical fear of death',[119] the deepest source of non-solidarity among mortals. The only difference between the revolutionary and the old human being is that the former has realized the nature of themselves and others, while the rest either suffer mutely or succumb to one of the countless self-delusions that historical humanity developed in order to accommodate itself to its situation.

The choice of an existence in revolution rules out both muteness and accommodation. Because it prefers the arduous path, it is comparable to an adept's flight to the Dharma path or a novice's entrance into a Christian order. Perhaps the elite of Lenin's professional revolutionaries proves the validity of this analogy, at least in ideal-typical terms; the difference, however, is a significant one: for the latter activists, there was never a binding monastic rule, unless one counts the abstract imperative of total self-instrumentalization. An even greater difference is that all worldly or transcendent ethical authorities which could have assessed the course of the revolution according to universally valid criteria were disabled within their respective jurisdictions. The actually occurring revolution claimed ethical sovereignty, thus immunizing itself to all verdicts from without. If the party was always right, this was because the revolution is always right; consequently, those who actually carried out the revolution were right. Hence even their perversions were meant to be subject only to their own interpretations. No one who was not themselves at the forefront of the revolution was entitled to a judgement about the means it should choose. It alone could know how much killing was necessary for its success; it alone could decide how much terror would guarantee the triumph of its principles. It was Georg Lukács who, amidst the war between white and red terrorists, coined the phrase 'Second Ethics' for the free choice of means by the bearers of the revolution.

This resulted in a situation where the revolution taking place could only be understood by its current leaders. The statement 'I am the revolution' was only true in theoretical and practical terms of Lenin and Stalin, who lived in the hot spot of the event, while none of the others, even seasoned fighters, could be sure of understanding the revolution. They all lived with the constant risk of suddenly being exposed as counter-revolutionaries. It was no longer enough to be orthodox in one's adherence to revolutionary principles; now one also had to be an orthodox believer in the incomprehensibility of the daily manoeuvres of one's leaders. Even when it arrested, tortured and shot dead its most faithful followers, the revolution still claimed to be right. The believers who allowed themselves to be subjected to such things were not witnesses whose memories were collected in a Moscow martyrology; they resembled mystics who undertook that most demanding of spiritual exercises, the *resignatio ad infernum* – the attempt to want nothing except what God or Stalin wants, even if it is my damnation.[120]

Communist Production of Humans

In our context, there is no need to address the 'religious' or religion-parodying dimensions of the Russian Revolution.[121] It is sufficient to hint at how the revolutionary complex of events took up the motif of human production, which had been virulent since the Enlightenment, and pushed it to its (provisionally) greatest heights. It was characteristic of the communist experiment that from the outset, it fought on both anthropotechnic fronts simultaneously in order to connect the spiritual-ascetic and biotechnical components as directly as possible. One must keep this strategy in mind whenever the frequently invoked formula of the New Human Being is used.

This production took place firstly in the elite cadres of the 'party', the training centres of revolutionary morals: these were the collecting places for individuals who, after an initial act of radical metanoia, were working on the eradication of the old human in themselves. It is hardly necessary to show in detail how the dispositions of orthodox spirituality still in effect here, with their thousand-year culture of de-selfing, became important. Anyone who postulated the New Human Being after 1917 only had to cover a small part of the moral evidence for this demand with the modern arguments that had circulated in Russia since 1863, the year in which Chernyshevsky's epoch-defining light novel *What Is to Be Done?* was published – Rakhmetov, one of the book's heroes, was a modern ascetic who slept on a bed of nails, trained his muscles and strictly monitored his diet. How many replicas of Rakhmetov were at work in the Russia of Lenin and Stalin is a question to which we will never find a clear answer. The only certainty is that whoever demanded the utmost of themselves in the face of the revolutionary upheavals stood in a tradition that extended back from *The Philokalia* – the belated Russian counterpart of *The Imitation of Christ* – to the Desert Fathers and the monasteries of Athos, and still had a virulent reservoir available for metanoetic procedures.

Secondly, the call for the New Human Being is formulated in socio-technical and biotechnical language. Because the productive powers invoked by Marxism are, according to their moral potency, powers of world improvement, the revolution states that they can and must be applied to human material. If one wants to establish socialism according to plan, its architects must themselves be produced according to plan. Bukharin's well-known claim in 1922 that the true aim of the revolution must be 'to alter people's actual psychology'[122] clarifies the dimensional leap in revolutionary anthropotechnics: with the production of the producer, the producing collective reaches the stage of reflexiveness. What was once transcendent morality becomes part of a circuit: the eternally unchanging group of asceticisms is replaced by a cybernetic optimization system.[123]

Many authors, including Trotsky, did not content themselves with the call to rebuild the psyche, and also held out the prospect of the genetic reconstruction of humans, even their cosmic reform: the foremost revolutionary demand was the physical optimization of humans through an elimination of sick and inferior variants – much the same as in the contemporaneous social-democratic, bourgeois and *völkisch* programmes. This was to result in the improvement of mental qualities – here the parallels with the breeding speculations of 'scientific racism' during the Nazi dictatorship in Germany are particularly clear.[124] The final perfection of the great reform, however, was presented in ideas of which no mere 'eugenicist' of either leftist or rightist persuasion could have dreamed: the emancipation of humans from space and time, from gravity, from the transience of the body and from conventional procreation. Ultimately, then, revolution means disabling the second law of thermodynamics.

Even in the most utopian of concepts, one can easily see how the figure of action in the auto-operatively curved space affects the level of great politics to produce a revolutionary passivity along with the revolutionary culture of activity: whoever has grand plans must also endure a great deal. In truth, everyday life after 1917 already forced the masses to be prepared for having-themselves-operated-on by the functionaries of the revolutionary state. The New Human Being could only be forced into existence if the current ones were willing to undergo major operations. The role of surgical metaphors in the language of the revolutionary leaders would merit a study of its own. They clarify the price of every political holism: whoever conceives of 'societies' as organisms will sooner or later be confronted with the question of where to apply the amputation instruments.

It is only in this context that the role of the aesthetic avant-garde in the Russian Revolution should be acknowledged: it committed itself to the titanic task of raising the passivity competence of the impoverished masses within a few years to the historically necessary level. The principal agitative quality of revolutionary art stemmed from the intoxicating project of proclaiming, for the first time in history, the passion for all. This is the meaning of the didactic turn evident in the manifold varieties of committed revolutionary art: peak performances of suffering were now offered by the 'commissars' to the many, who had previously known only vulgar suffering. No one was to be denied the right to crucifixion, though the technical matters of burial and resurrection were not settled in every detail. To convey what was on offer on a sufficiently broad scale, the fiction was spread that every single national comrade had entered a contract of treatment with the revolution, stating that they were ready and willing to endure and affirm whatever they were subjected to for their own good by the agencies of the great change. Only in the light of this hypothesis can one grasp the unfathomable passivity with which countless people bore the hardships of the 'transitional time' between the legendary storming of the Winter Palace and Stalin's death. The most important 'shared task' of the revolutionaries was undoubtedly that of enduring the revolution and furthering it in the mode of suffering under it. No one can deny the great achievements of the Russians and the peoples associated with them in this field.

Even if the theory of the 'religious' nature of revolutionary ideology has been repeated *ad nauseam* in the relevant literature, it must nonetheless be emphasized that by its design, the Russian Revolution was not a political event but an anthropotechnic movement in a socio-political guise, based on the total externalization of the absolute imperative. Its contribution to making the nature of 'religion' explicit is of lasting significance – placing it in the group of synthetic illusion-practising organizations in modernity of which I showed above, using the example of the Church of Scientology, how they go about the production of auto-hypnotically closed counter-worlds. In both cases, the individually effective psychotechnic aspect was combined with mass-psychological effects based on leader cults and group narcissism. In undertaking a large-scale attempt to seize power over conditions, the communist experiment demonstrated what activists should believe in – and what they must allow to be done to themselves for the old human to be remoulded into the new one.

De facto, the communist upheaval triggered the second emergency of extensive biopolitics in the Modern Age – we discussed the first above in our recollections of the early modern state's demographic policy. The latter had failed spectacularly in the fine tuning of its methods, with consequences whose darkness requires no further elaboration here. The biopolitics of the Russian Revolution could likewise not be sure of its results, albeit for entirely different reasons. While the early modern state sought to produce the greatest number of subjects and took on board an enormous surplus of unusable ones, the revolutionary state strove for an organic collective of convinced individuals – and accepted the risk of losing all others. The first biopolitics sought the solution to its problems in the mass export of humans and extensive internment, while the second found the solution in mass internment and even more massive extermination of humans.[125]

The Biopolitics of the Miracle and the Art of the Possible

We have thus articulated the anthropotechnic secret of the 1917 revolution, and numerous authors have revealed it in different formulations. In the course of its appropriation by the Russian intelligence, the Western idea of political revolution underwent a metamorphosis that moved it towards depoliticization and remoulded it into a radical-metanoetic experiment. One must almost call it a subversion of politics through orientalization – but not only for the sake of portraying the Soviet state power as an 'oriental tyranny'. 'East' in this case refers to the tendency towards the supremacy of the spiritual factor. It seems that a revolution on Russian soil could only take place without becoming analogous to a conversion. The result was the enormous spectacle of a conversion from without.

Conversion means spiritually resetting one's life; revolution implies the gesture of redesigning the world from zero. It transforms historically congealed reality into a mass without qualities that could literally turn into anything in the reconstructive phase. In the chemical flask of revolution, the matter frozen into qualities is transformed into a totipotent potential that can be used by new engineers for free projects. Where world improvement is the priority, the New Human Being must be imagined as a function of a New Society. The New World comes about as the production of revolution and technology. The call for the technical repetition of the miracle is the most intimate agent of great change. For an enterprise on this scale, the reassignment of faith from the miracle to the miraculous is not enough. While the Christian and Yogic traditions reserved the impossible for the few in their cults of saints and living-saved figures, the spiritually subverted revolution reclaims the impossible for all.

The definition of politics as the art of the possible – thus my premise – passed its historical test *grosso modo*. The German Chancellor Otto von Bismarck, to whom we owe this formula, was presumably unaware that he had coined a phrase that momentarily put him on a level with the classics of political theory. He knew exactly what he was talking about, however, as he witnessed the opposing position – the politicization of the impossible and the remoulding of daydreams into party programmes – on a daily basis in all varieties from left to right, in the Berlin Reichstag as well as contemporary German and European journalism. From the second half of the nineteenth century on, equations of the desirable with the realizable constituted the preferred procedure of the 'zeitgeist' for disseminating its slogans. At the same time, the mass press had recognized its most important task in the transport of illusions to its customers – in the era of mass circulation, the media are in fact not so much organs of enlightenment for an audience of learners as service providers in the auto-operatively curved space of mass having-oneself-deceived.

Only in contrast to the laconic thesis of the last German *realpolitiker* can one understand what happened in Russia in the wake of the October Revolution: it created a platform for politics as the art of the impossible. In full awareness, it abandoned the standard model of rational realism in favour of an unabashedly surrealistic praxis, even when it donned the bloodstained mantle of a *'realpolitik* of revolution'. Though it presented itself as gruesomely realist in order to secure its initial victory, it knew that it could only survive as long as there was a light shining on it from far above: it could only gain its justification in the steepest vertical. 'Verticalists' were no longer simply the utopian poets around Svyatogor, who had published his *Verses on the Vertical* already in 1914 – the entire revolutionary elite was inspired by verticalist commitments.

The Era of Abolition

After the victorious civil war against the leftovers of the old 'society', the ascension of the revolution could truly begin. It rushed from one abolition to the next, from one securing measure to the next – the era of abolition was inevitably also a heyday for measures of all kinds. As far as abolitions were concerned, the élan of the intellectuals naturally exceeded that of the new lords of the Kremlin, though these too did what was necessary to earn their stripes as abolitionists. Not long after seizing power, they declared the abolition of private property; in their understanding of communism, this change in the legal system laid the foundation for all further resolutions. The abolition of bourgeois liberties ensued, and this was to be followed by that of the bourgeoisie themselves. The functionaries had understood why state overthrow could only be stabilized through a cultural revolution, meaning the liquidation of the bourgeois individual and its curricula. For them, the bourgeois was not only the class enemy who monopolized the means of world improvement and perverted *de jure* shared property into *de facto* private property; he was the embodiment of gradualness who unified all the errors of conventional realism and all the vices of self-centred rationalism.

The first preliminary stage of the New Human Being was the non-bourgeois moulded in political revolution, who had left behind the purportedly natural egocentricity of the old human being. Along with it, the 'preform' of the future human being also discarded the ethics of historical advanced civilizations concerned with the prohibition on human sacrifice – or more generally the prohibition on taking

393

innocent life. The abolition of moral inhibitions regarding killing was a decisive step on the way to producing the post-bourgeois personality. What resulted from this was no less than the figure of the saint devoid of conscience – the most original contribution of the Bolshevik revolution to universal moral history.

Being and Time – the Soviet Version

In his book *Soviet Civilization*,[126] Andrei Sinyavsky illustrates the prototype of the New Human Being using the figure of Felix Edmundovich Dzerzhinsky (1878–1926), chief of the notorious Cheka, the early Soviet secret police. He describes the feared model functionary – who had spent eleven years in banishment and Tsarist prisons, those training camps for those determined to stop at nothing, between 1897 and 1917 – as a man of steel 'with a soul as clear as crystal'. He assumed the role of the Soviet Union's chief executioner not because of cruel inclinations, but rather because he was prepared to sacrifice not only his own life but also his conscience on the altar of the revolution. As a consummate Leninist, he had internalized his teacher's doctrine that the revolutionary knowingly gets his hands dirty: only by sullying himself morally could he express his loyalty to the great cause. Like many historically aroused contemporaries in the 1920s, including those from the camp of non-Bolshevik 'revolutions', Dzerzhinsky had learned to interpret being as time. As a result, he wanted to do only what time wanted to do through him. With the obedience of the 'calm' person he listened out for its signals, which could seemingly be received unencrypted at the time: 'And if He orders you, "Lie!" – do so. / And if He orders you, "Kill!" – obey.'[127]

In this context, it almost seems to follow a legendary template that this man, who was responsible for the liquidation of hundreds of thousands, had wanted to be a monk or a priest in his youth. It may be a tendentious fabrication that, as a crypto-Catholic, he secretly prayed to the Virgin Mary between cruel interrogations, or perhaps even after days full of executions. His wife stated plausibly that Dzerzhinsky, the selfless activist who worked around the clock, who slept in a narrow iron bed in his office and died of exhaustion at the age of forty-eight, had spoken of one day resigning from his office as Chief Executioner of the revolution, and, as People's Commissar for Education, devoting himself to the education of children and young people for the coming 'society'. Sinyavsky comments: 'Isn't that a wonderful prospect – in the spirit of communist morality – the chief executioner converted into chief educator?'[128] And yet: the transition from the extermination of unusable and unconvinced humans to the breeding of usable and convinced ones seems far less absurd if one takes into account the logic of acting from zero underlying both of these functions. What distinguishes the Soviet executioner from de Maistre's executioner is that one cannot possibility imagine him secretly saying to himself: 'No one liquidates better than I.'

Immortalism: The Liquidation of Finitude

In the eyes of the philosophically radical among the representatives of the revolutionary intelligentsia, such phenomena as those described above were reduced to surface effects of the kind that had to be accepted *nolens volens* in a time of fundamental transformations. This group of ontological utopianists included, next to the aforementioned Alexander Svyatogor, Konstantin Tsiolkovsky (1857–1935), an esoteric and rocket scientist who became famous as the father of Russian space travel; Alexander Yaroslavsky (*c.*1891–1930), an exponent of a 'cosmic maximalism'; Valerian Muraviev (1885–1931), who postulated the overcoming of time and a technology of resurrection (anastatics); and Alexander Bogdanov (1873–1928), an advocate of 'physiological collectivism' and the founder of a movement for the 'struggle for vitality'.[129] For them, the metaphysical revolutionaries, almost all of whom were followers of Nikolai Fedorov (though some, like Svyatogor, negated his influence), who had laid the foundation for a politics of immortality with *The Philosophy of the Common Task*, the Bolshevik beginnings of the cultural revolution were scarcely more than a crude, albeit limitedly useful prelude to the true 'world revolution' whose premises, prospects and methods these authors explored in their writings of the 1920s.

If the revolution made it possible to climb up the ladder of the abolition of traditional social problems, the abolition of 'private property of production means' and the bourgeois personality were productive, albeit provisional – not to say inferior – stages in a programme of ascent whose heights none of those caught in the turbulences of the great change could imagine. Yet these two operations, as momentous as they seemed to both the perpetrators and the victims of change, merely constituted the continuation of the bourgeois revolution of 1879, which had barely achieved more than the abolition of aristocratic privileges, the release of bourgeois ambitions and double-edged human rights rhetoric. From the Russian perspective, they continued the Tsarist reforms of 1861. To the metaphysical revolutionaries, these achievements were at most preparatory episodes for a revolt of an entirely different scope.

After the era of preliminary attempts, the time was ripe for an *opus hominis* on a larger scale. The rule of humans over humans had become offensive, but was only the epiphenomenon of a far older and more comprehensive enslavement. Had mortal man not lived under the tyranny of outer and inner nature since time immemorial? Was not nature itself the biopower that wilfully created life on the one hand while letting it die equally wilfully on the other? Did its universal domination not provide the matrix for all secondary forms of domination? Was it not necessary, then, to put the abolition of death on the agenda of a metaphysical revolution – and simultaneously an end to the fatalism of birth? What was the use of doing away with the absolutist state as long as one continued to pay tribute to the divine right of nature? Why liquidate the Tsar and his family if one did nothing to overturn the immemorial crowning of death as the lord of finitude?

Ending the Epoch of Death and Bagatelles

The speculative avant-garde of the Russian Revolution thought it had understood that one must begin directly at the highest rung on the abolition ladder if one wants to make the decisive difference. Otherwise the elimination of abuses and inequalities among people, even the abolition of the state and all repressive structures, would be provisional and in vain. If anything, they only sharpen the awareness of the absurdity that afflicts egalitarian 'society' as long as it fails to abolish death – including all forms of physical imperfection. Whoever wishes to eliminate the final cause of harmful privacy in human existence must do away with the enclosure of each individual in their own little piece of lifetime. This is where the renewed 'common task' must begin. The true commune can only be formed by immortals; among mortals, the panic of self-preservation will always dominate. The equality of humans before death only satisfies that international of reactionary egalitarians who enjoy seeing the rich and powerful perish 'like cattle'. People of this kind have always sympathized with death in the role of the grand leveller – as presented annually at the Salzburg *Jedermann* production since 1920, dressed in the kitsch of the time. What none of these friends of the just end for all want to admit is the simple fact that death is the ultimate reactionary principle.

396

Each memento only pushes humans down further under the yoke of nature. The ideologues of death incessantly corrupt modern 'society' by tirelessly inculcating it with the formula 'death is inevitable'. They provide the fuel for individualism, which encourages greed – in so far as one can apply this term to the striving to maximize experiences and advantages of being within the narrow window of existential time.

There could only be such a thing as a 'being-unto-death', which Heidegger emphasized as a structural feature of existence in his principal work of 1927, because even the most radical thinkers of the 'agonizing bourgeoisie' had not participated in the furthest-reaching revolution of the present day. In 1921, Alexander Svyatogor postulated a new agenda, beginning with the contention:

> The question of the realization of personal immortality now belongs on the agenda in its full scope. It is time to do away with the inevitability of natural death.[130]

In these words, we once again hear the *tempus est* with which Christian apocalypticism turns into the project of history: time itself has reached the point of supplying the password for the final historical enterprise: do away with time! Whoever has understood the spirit of the age must ensure that there will soon be no more talk of finitude. The 'epoch of death and bagatelles' was coming to an end – what was beginning was 'the era of immortality and infinity'.[131] 'Biocosmism alone can define and regulate society as a whole.'[132] One year later, Alexander Yaroslavsky announced the birth of Cosmic Maximalism, which incorporated immortalism, interplanetarism and the suspension of time, while Alexander Bogdanov simultaneously published his ideas on a 'Tectology of the Struggle Against Old Age'. He enthused over the notion that one could realize socialism physically by turning entire populations into artificial kinship circles and immune alliances through extensive reciprocal blood transfusions. With this physicalization of brotherliness, 'blood' – usually the domain of the right – transpires as the medium of an actual communist circulation.[133]

'Anthropotechnics'

Among the authors of the metaphysical revolution in the 1920s, if I am not mistaken, it was Valerian Muraviev who examined the question of producing the New Human Being most extensively, thinking through its technological aspects from the widest possible perspective. Naturally the contemporary thought form of the 'production of the producer' was an omnipresent cliché in the entire Soviet sphere – not least in the working world, where the imperative of forced modernization presented itself most nakedly. It dictated the mass production of socialist proletarians as the most pressing planned task; if they did not exist before, the supposed carriers of the revolution should at least be brought into being after the event. The language game of human production was equally firmly established in Soviet pedagogy. As far as we know, however, it was Muraviev – whose writings of the early 1920s contain the first use of the term 'anthropotechnics', largely synonymous with the word 'anthropurgy', coined at the same time – who aimed more for the production of a higher form of human.[134] Owing to his study of Eastern and Western spiritual traditions, Muraviev saw the connection between the ascetic and the technical revolt against nature more clearly than other authors with biocosmist-immortalist tendencies. In his view, the achievements stemming from conventional forms of 'asceticism and the Yogi movement' inevitably reached their limit because, through the age-old idealistic contempt for the material sphere, they remained defined by 'neglect of the bodily aspect'. The 'remoulding of human beings', however, 'was not conceivable merely in mental and moral terms'.[135] It now had be built on entirely new foundations – that is, on technical, serial and collectively guided procedures. Among these, Muraviev states, eugenics would only have a secondary function on account of its clumsiness. Certainly, he writes, the eugenic procedures of the present go far beyond the primitiveness of Paracelsus' attempts to breed homunculi in calves' stomachs or pumpkins; nonetheless, they remain tied to the awkwardness of sexual reproduction and the ugly excesses of natural birth, which can only be viewed as an 'extraordinarily complicated, painful and imperfect process'.[136] Eugenics through breeding, which produces favourable results with plants and animals, can only be transferred to humans to a limited degree.

Consequently, Muraviev continues, one must think about new procedures in which the division of humanity into men and women becomes meaningless. The abolition of birth and the production of humans in the laboratory must lead to a 'fourth method for recasting the human being' – the other three being ascetic-didactic, therapeutic-medical and eugenic-breeding measures. Here the idea of what would later be called cloning momentarily appears ('budding'), which, according to Muraviev, should by no means only be considered the domain of lower life forms. If such a procedure were applied to more advanced creatures too, and ultimately to *Homo sapiens*, humans would no longer be the result of a sexual relationship between two more or less narrow-minded individuals, but rather the work of a research community committed to the highest goals. When this community devotes itself to the production of humans, it celebrates a technical sacrament – in free synthesis outside of the old nature.

The appearance of New Human Beings would mean that of new bodies which could subsist on light and would no longer be subject to gravitation. At the same time, the new technology for creating humans would bring an unheard-of level of individualization within reach. In time, the template human of today would disappear, and the basis for vulgarity would be eliminated not only socially and aesthetically, but also biologically. Then artists of Shakespeare's and Goethe's calibre would no longer create dramas, but humans and groups of humans – anthropic singularities and social sculptures that would make the works of earlier art history look like lifeless preliminary exercises.[137]

The principal operation of biopolitical utopianism in Russia can be expressed in a simple formula: what had previously seemed possible only in the imagination would now be realized in technical procedures. Where there were man-made works, there would now be man-made life. Modern technology tears down the boundary between being and phantasm, and transforms impossibilities into schemata of the actually possible – empty sets that would now begin to be filled with actually existing entities. The term 'anticipation', which forms a common thread running through Marxist commentaries on the 'achievements' of earlier cultural periods, would now refer to planned phantasms. This same transgression of limits, incidentally, forms the basis of the American mass culture flourishing at the same time, which, especially since the flooding of the Hollywood 'dream factory' with European émigrés, had been producing one variation after another on the motif of dreams come true.[138] Aron Zalkind (1889–1936), a Soviet psychologist who sought to combine Freudian and Pavlovian approaches in his 'pedology' of the 1920s (in order to reclaim the field of education for the widely used theory of 'conditioned reflexes', and to annex cultural theory as a field of application for higher reflexology), calls this 'scientifically based fantasizing'.[139] It provides the foundation for the art of socialist prognostics.[140] This is the concrete utopian counterpart of Oswald Spengler's equally pretentious attempt to place the narratability of the future on a scientific footing through insight into the processual laws of 'cultures'. In his report on the psychosocial future of socialist humans, Zalkind predicted that they would be transformed through revolutionary treatment into ever more stable, more productive, more vital and fundamentally sociophilic beings; they would develop a form of holistic immune system in which self-preservation would become a function of communal preservation – unlike in Western society, where individualist disintegration proceeds inexorably. The blurring of boundaries between didactics, therapy and politics is characteristic of Zalkind's opportunistic-optimistic argumentation: it conceives of communist humans as unlimitedly flexible patients of change who can only win if they allow unlimited operations on themselves. What Zalkind does not reveal are the methods of communist anaesthesia. Lenin knew: state terror is the functional equivalent of general anaesthetic in difficult operations on large collectives.

Post-Communist Postlude: Revenge of the Gradual

I shall refrain from commenting on the empirical fate of the immortalist and biocosmist impulses in the early phase of the Russian Revolution; no one should be surprised if the gulf between the programmatic and the pragmatic is dramatic in such projects. If there were a pantheon of Icarian phenomena, the Russian bio-utopians would have a claim to a chapel of their own. Almost all of these protagonists of the highest abolition perished in the turbulences of the revolution they had so vigorously affirmed: except for Konstantin Tsiolkovsky, who, co-opted and honoured by Soviet officials 'as a brilliant son of the people', died at an advanced age in 1935, all other protagonists of the biopolitical revolt met an end more typical of the time. Svyatogor disappeared in a 'corrective labour camp' in 1937, at the age of forty-eight. Muraviev's trail ends around 1930, when he was roughly forty-five, in a detention camp – probably on the infamous Solovetzky Islands in the White Sea. Yaroslavsky was shot dead while trying to escape from said camp in December 1930, aged around thirty-five. Bogdanov died in 1928 at the age of fifty-five after performing a blood transfusion experiment on himself. Zalkind died of a heart attack at forty-eight, in 1936, upon receiving the news that the Central Committee of the Communist Party had condemned and banned his 'pedology' as 'anti-Marxist pseudo-science'.

It seems equally superfluous to explain at length why, after the end of the Second World War – and all the more after the implosion of the Soviet Union and the Eastern Bloc around 1990 – virtually no one in the East or the West had the slightest interest in a revolt against the human condition, the old Adam, the unconscious and the entire syndrome of finitudes – except in the simulation rooms of the unrestricted modern museum, where there is a curator for every revolt. It would be a grave error, however, to conclude from the global anti-utopianism after 1945, which was only broken up by the third youth movement of the twentieth century – the international student revolt – that the system of modern 'societies' had lost its 'forward' orientation and its quality as a universal training camp for ever-growing virtuosities, or 'qualifications' and 'competencies'.

In reality, the global system after 1945 simply carried out the necessary course correction. It eliminated the mode of revolution from its catalogue of operative options, instead deciding entirely on that of evolution. The appearance of neo-revolutionary discourses around 1968 was merely an expanded romanticism that appropriated such historical figures as Lenin, Stalin, Mao, Brecht and Wilhelm Reich as ready-mades. In the principal current of the time, the gradualness party came to power once more – led by an elite of determined professional evolutionaries. Behind the exterior of the general anti-revolutionary mood, which articulated itself discursively as anti-totalitarianism or anti-fascism, lay a return to the progressive traditions of the Baroque and the Enlightenment, whose pragmatic core is the relatively constant, rationally supervised expansion of human options. In order to take part in these optimization movements, it was no more necessary for progress to be writ large than to feign belief in the goddess of history.

The development of the Western civilizatory complex after 1945 seems to provide almost complete confirmation for the moderate. It led to the saturation of one's surroundings with easily accessible means of world improvement for most. Their distribution occurred partly through free markets, partly through services of the redistributive state and the overgrown insurance system – the two apolitical operationalizations of the solidarity principle, which do more for the practical implantation of leftist motifs than any political ideology could.

The most important intellectual-historical realignment, however, lay in the fact that metanoia changed its direction yet again: after an era of bloody slogans and malign abstractions, the commonplace seemed like something one could 'bring back' once more. Countless people realized that the here and now was a remote island on which they had never set foot. This supplied one of the preconditions for the rediscovery of the ethical distinction in its original form – the distinction between concern for oneself and attention to everything else. Nothing was more helpful for the disenchanted revolutionaries than the re-actualization of this distinction. In Jean-Luc Godard's film

Passion (1982), a figure utters the key sentiment of the time: 'One does not save oneself by saving the world.' After half a century of militant youth movements, a creature that had been absent from the scene for a long time resurfaced: the adult. Its reappearance gave life to offensive pragmatisms that filled empty word-shells like 'democracy', 'civil society' or 'human rights' with actual content. Thus the awareness of what had been achieved was accompanied by a broad agenda outlining the next optimization steps for countless targets of progressive praxis. Today, this is the real working form of a decentralized international that articulates itself in tens of thousands of projects in the traditions of world improvement élan – without any central committee that would have to, or even could, tell the active what their next operations should be.[141]

The all-pervasive pragmatism of the post-war years must not, therefore, be dismissed as restoration, as the eternal Jacobins would like. Nor does it express any return to modesty. In reality, the complex of Western 'societies' under the leadership of the USA has constantly raised the level of economic and technical evolution since the 1960s – to the point where the ability of populations to keep up with their fleeting financial and media system became problematic. This became manifest primarily after the neo-liberal coup against the semi-socialism of the 'mixed economy' that dominated the West after 1945 until the Thatcherist-Reaganist caesura of the late 1970s.[142] Through this aggravation of the climate, global capitalism transpired as the agency of 'permanent revolution' demanded in vain by the ideologues of the communist command-based economy. The mixed economy was popular as long as a capitalism domesticated by the welfare state could present itself as the power that more or less kept the promises of declared socialism. In the meantime, the accelerated permanent revolution known for the last twenty years as 'globalism' is compelling countless people to work once more on the expansion of their passivity competence – much to the displeasure of the last devotees of 'permanent revolution' in Europe, who dream incessantly of the lost comfort of Rhine Capitalism.[143] Exposed to the cruelties of the expanded world market, they feel the compulsion to have an operation again – this time to improve their competing fitness on the now unpredictable world markets. In the great financial crisis of 2008, however, the necessity of having operations also caught up with the operators.

The supra-epochal tendency of modernity towards a de-verticalization of existence continued under the present conditions. At the

402

same time, the symbolic immune systems demanded fine tunings that would break through some of the automatisms of overly crude secularism. This is the origin of the widespread new interest in 'religious' and spiritual traditions – and the discreetly reawakening awareness of vertical imperatives. In fact, a resolute anti-verticalism established itself in the dominant forms of the zeitgeist after 1945: in existentialism as the cult of finitude, in vitalism as the cult of overexertion, in consumerism as the cult of metabolism, and in tourism as the cult of changing location. In this de-spirited time, top athletes took over the role of guarding the holy fire of exaggeration. They are the *Übermenschen* of the modern world, beheaded *Übermenschen* who strive to reach heights where the old human being cannot follow them – not even within themselves. It is the inner androids that now constantly exceed themselves. All that the old human being inside the athletes themselves can offer is a dull commentary on the performances of the *Über*-androids they embody.

— 12 —

EXERCISES AND MISEXERCISES
The Critique of Repetition

Damned to Distinguish Between Repetitions

The ethical distinction took effect from the moment in which repetition lost its innocence. The appearance of ascetics and asceticisms in the twilight of the advanced civilizations revealed a difference that had not been open to explicit development in earlier stages of civilization: in choosing to withdraw, the early practising ethicists broke with the conventional forms and attitudes of life. They abandoned the established repetition sequences and replaced them with different sequences, different attitudes – not arbitrarily different, but rather redemptively different ones. Where the original distinction between high and beneficial life forms on the one hand and hopelessly ordinary ones on the other hand makes its cut, it does so in the mode of a neuro-ethical programming that turns the entire old system against itself. Here there are initially no intermediate forms. Body and soul reach the other shore together – or not at all. 'The whole man must move at once.'

The radical separation of ascetics, saints, sages, practising philosophers, and later also artists and virtuosos from the mode of existence of those who continue in the average, approximate and unqualified, shows that the human being is a creature damned to distinguish between repetitions. What later philosophers called freedom first manifests itself in the act with which dissidents rebel against the domination by inner and outer mechanisms. By distancing themselves from the entire realm of deep-seated passions, acquired habits and adopted or sedimented opinions, they make space for a comprehensive transformation. No part of the human can stay as it was: the feelings are reformed, the habitus remodelled, the world of thoughts

404

restructured from the bottom up, and the spoken word overhauled. The whole of life rises up as a new construction on the foundation of favourable repetition.

A first enlightenment came about when the spiritual teachers showed that humans are not so much possessed by demons as controlled by automatisms. They are not assailed by evil spirits, but by routines and inertias that force them to the ground and deform them. What impair their reason are not chance errors and occasional errors of perception – it is the eternal recurrence of the clichés that render true thought and free perception impossible. Next to Gautama Buddha, Plato was the first epidemiologist of the spirit: he recognized everyday opinion, the *doxa*, the pestilence that does not kill, but does occasionally poison entire communities. Empty phrases that have sunk down into the body produce 'characters'. They mould humans into living caricatures of averageness and turn them into incarnated platitudes. Because existence in the ethical distinction begins with the annihilation of empty phrases, it inevitably leads to the negation of characters. Part of the charm of free humans is that one can see in them the caricature they might have become. Whoever sought to eradicate it would be the human without qualities, free for an absence of judgement, character and taste. Such a person would, like Monsieur Teste, state: '*La bêtise n'est pas mon fort.*' [Stupidity is not my strong suit.] They would be the human who had killed the marionette inside them. The transformation occurs through mental de-automatization and mental decontamination. Hence the use of silence in many spiritual schools to empty the cliché depot – a procedure that usually takes longer than a major psychoanalysis. Pythagoras supposedly demanded a five-year silence of his pupils at the beginning of their studies. Nietzsche was still acting in this tradition: 'Every characteristic absence of spirituality, every piece of common vulgarity, is due to an inability to resist a stimulus – you *have to* react, you follow every impulse.'[144] The spiritual exercise is the one that disables such compulsion.

This de-automatization, this liberation from infection by the blindly reproducing unexamined, must be accompanied by the methodical erection of a new spiritual structure. Nothing could be more alien to the pioneers of the ethical distinction than modern spontaneism, which cultivates shock, confusion and the interruption of the habitual as aesthetic values *per se*, without asking what should replace the interrupted. The original ethical life is reformatory. It always seeks to exchange harmful for favourable repetition. It wants to replace corrupt life forms with upright ones. It strives to avoid the impure and immerse itself in the pure. That these binary oppositions entail costly simplifications is, for now, beside the point. All that matters is that in this framework, individualized freedom emerges in its oldest and most intense form. It results from an awkward discovery: there is a choice that changes all the factors influencing human behaviour. The first ethicists faced the decision between a life in the usually unnoticed iron chains of involuntarily acquired habits and an existence on the ethereal chain of freely accepted discipline. The most erroneous possible conclusion one could draw from this is that the appearance of genuine practising awareness concerned purely the active. Let the sadhus torture themselves in their lonely forests with complicated breathing exercises; let the Stylites feel closer to heaven on their absurd pillars, and let the philosophers sell their second coats and sleep on the ground – the average mortals will cling nonetheless to the opinion that these extravagant distortions of the ordinary are meaningless for them, the business of a sacred-perverse private meeting between the incomprehensible God and his artiste followers. Whoever is unable to participate can continue in their old habitus, which, though not perfect, seems good enough for everyday life.

The Creature that Cannot Practise

In reality, the secession of the practising places the entire ecosystem of human behaviour on an altered foundation. Like all acts of rendering things explicit, the appearance of the early practice systems brought about a radical modification of the respective area – that is, of the whole field of psychophysically conditioned actions. Explicit exercises, whether the *asanas* of the Indian yogis, the Stoics' experiments with letting go of the non-own, or the *exercitationes spirituales* of Christian climbers on the heavenly ladder, cast a shadow on everything that lies opposite them on the implicit side: this is no less than the world of old Adam, the gigantic universe of unilluminated conventionalities. The shadow zone encompasses the area dominated by repetitions of an undeclared practice character. We can leave open the question of whether the psychoanalytical insult to humans claimed by Freud – triggered by the purportedly unwelcome discovery that the ego is not the master of its own house – ever really existed. There is certainly no doubt about the reality of the behaviouristic insult to humans, which could equally be called the ascetological one. It follows from the observation that 99.9 per cent of our existence comprises repetitions, mostly of a strictly mechanical nature. The only way to deal with this insult is to imagine that one is still more original than plenty of others. If one subjects oneself to more probing self-examination, one finds oneself in the psychosomatic engine room of one's own existence, where there is nothing to be gained from the usual flattery of spontaneity; and freedom theorists would do better to stay upstairs.

In this investigation, one advances into a non-psychoanalytical unconscious encompassing everything belonging to normally athematic rhythms, rules and rituals – regardless of whether it stems from collective patterns or idiosyncratic specializations. In this area, everything is higher mechanics, including intimate illusions of non-mechanics and unconditioned being-for-oneself. The sum of these mechanics produces the surprise space of personality, in which surprising events are actually very rare. Humans live in habits, not territories. Radical changes of location first of all attack the human rooting in habits, and only then the places in which those habits are rooted.

Since the few have been explicitly practising, it has become evident that all people practise implicitly, and beyond this that humans are beings that cannot practise – if practising means repeating a pattern of action in such a way that its execution improves the being's disposition towards the next repetition. Just as Mr K. is always preparing his next mistake, humans as a whole are constantly taking the necessary steps to ensure that they will remain as they have been up until this minute. Whatever is not repeated sufficiently often atrophies – this is familiar from everyday observations, for example when the musculature of static limbs begins to degenerate after a few days, as if concluding from its temporary disuse that it has become superfluous. In truth, one should probably also keep the non-use of organs, programmes and competencies for exercises in steady decline. Just as there are implicit fitness programmes, there are also implicit unfitness programmes. That is why Seneca warns his pupil: 'A single winter relaxed Hannibal's fibre.'[145] Other states of weakening may follow years of neglecting-work.[146]

From this it follows that even a simple maintenance of bodily – or rather neurophysical – form can only be comprehended as an effect of undeclared training. This comprises routines whereby the standard movements of an organ complex are, through inconspicuous procedures, employed often enough to stabilize the complex at its current fitness status. The self-activations of organisms in sequences of undeclared practice programmes, sequences that constantly have to be run through anew, culminate in a mute autopoiesis: the element in live creatures that seems like mere self-identity is *de facto* the result of a perpetual self-reproduction by overcoming invisible training programmes. The nocturnal activities of the brain, part of which one experiences as dreams, are probably first and foremost back-up processes for the self-programme in its state prior to the last waking phase. The self is a storm of repetition sequences beneath the roof of the skull.

Personal identity, then, offers no indication of a mental essence or inert form; it rather shows the active overcoming of a probability of decline. Whoever remains identical to themselves thus confirms themselves as a functioning expert system specializing in constant self-renewal. For surprise-friendly creatures of the *Homo sapiens* type, even triviality is not futile. It can only be attained through a constant cultivation of identity whose most important aid is inward and outward self-re-trivialization. Re-trivialization is the operation that enables organisms capable of learning to treat something new as if they had never encountered it – whether by equating it mechanically with something familiar or by openly denying its didactic value. Thus the new, initially and mostly, has no chance of integration into the apparatus of operating gestures and ideas because it is assigned either to the familiar or to the insignificant.[147]

If, in turn, the neolatric culture of modernity posits meaning in the new *per se*, this causes a brightening of the global learning climate; the price of this is a historically unprecedented will to be dazzled that gives unlimited credit to illusions of the new. Even manifest stupidity, incidentally, cannot be taken as a simple datum: it is acquired through long training in learning-avoidance operations. Only after a persistent series of self-knockouts by the intelligence can a habitus of reliable mindlessness become stable – and even this can be undone at any time through a relapse into non-stupidity. Conversely, every learning-theoretical romanticism should be viewed sceptically, even if it appears under classical names. Aristotle was speaking as a romantic when he stated in the first line of his *Metaphysics*: 'All humans strive for knowledge by nature.' In fact, every striving for knowledge – understood by Aristotle above all as primary visual enjoyment – encounters its limits as soon as something new appears that one does not want to see. Such things are usually sights that are irreconcilable with the imperative of preserving identity. Then the much-lauded thirst for knowledge among humans turns in a flash into the art of not having seen or heard anything.

The ethical distinction not only uncovers the hidden practice character of ordinary life; it also reveals the gulf between the previous existence in the accustomed and the metanoetic life forms that must be newly chosen. This distinction demands cruelty towards oneself and others; it leads to overload in its most naked state. We hear its original voice when Jesus says: 'Anyone who loves his father and mother more than me is not worthy of me.'[148] 'Any of you who does not give up everything he has cannot be my disciple.'[149] 'I did not come to bring peace, but a sword.'[150] The blade of distinction is the apocalypse that takes place now or never.

The Re-Exercising of All Exercises

Just as a person's unexpected suicide calls their entire social environment into question, an individual's conversion to philosophy or their entrance into an ethical group problematizes the *modus vivendi* of all those with whom they had previously lived under the same roof – bound by the same customs, impregnated with the same habits, entangled in the same stories. Every conversion implies the speech act: 'I herewith leave the shared reality', or at least the statement of intent, 'I wish to leave the continuum of the false and harmful.' To do this, the adept does not need to board the ship that would take them to the island of Utopia. The destinations are often only a few hours' travel from the hopeless villages or a day's walk from the agitated city. Whoever seeks out these heterotopias knows that once they arrive there, they will have to undertake far longer inner than outer journeys.

If an applicant is taken up into a community of the practising, their further life consists in the systematic revaluation of values. The Cynics called this procedure 'defacing the coin' (*paracharáttein to nómisma*), which also means 'changing one's customs'. Thus a counterfeiter's metaphor provides the keyword in the history of higher morals. The ethical mints are training camps for the ethos in need of remoulding. For the cynics of the fourth century BC, this meant renouncing all forms of behaviour based on arbitrary human rules and henceforth listening only to the *physis*. These unabashed dissidents were probably the only wise men to believe that one could do such a thing in the middle of the city – provided one could find a vacant barrel. The other adepts of ethical difference knew very well that it is best to turn one's back on one's usual abode. As ethos and topos belong together, a different ethos calls for a different residence – one can only return to the origin if one is so deeply rooted in the new place and the changed habitus that there is no risk of relapsing into the old one. Until one reaches that point, it is good to inhabit a protected space in which the things considered right by the many – *ton pollon doxa*[151] – bounce off the better knowledge of the few. Among the early Greek Christians, one openly named a remote training centre after the activities that went on there: *asketería*, or sometimes *hesychastería*, a place for exercises in silence. The Indian word *ashram*, still in frequent use today, refers to the 'place of exertion'. *Sannyasin*, on the other hand, the Indian name for the world-abstinent, literally means 'one who has cast off all things' – including the ties to a profane abode. It is said that the Indian wise man Tota Puri (*c.*1815–75), Ramakrishna's teacher, who bore the epithet 'the naked' (*nagka*), never wore clothes, never slept under a roof and never stayed in one place for more than three days in his entire life. For Nietzsche, only a generation younger than the evasive Indian, the other place was Sils Maria, at the foot of mountains that are mirrored in the severe smoothness of Lake Silvaplana, 'six thousand feet beyond man and time'.

The ethical distinction brings about the catastrophe of habits. It exposes humans as beings that grow accustomed to anything. 'Virtue' is one possibility of habituation among others. Humans are equally able, however, to make the worst their own until it seems incontestably self-evident. Any inhabitant of a somewhat freer country today who looks at conditions in overt dictatorships will find ample evidence of this, whether in the daily news or in the archives. One has to have seen a Nuremberg Rally, a Moscow parade on 1 May or a mass gymnastic performance in Pyongyang to have an idea of how far an attachment to the abhorrent can extend. From the perspective of the Greek *asketería*, the Indian *ashram* or the Upper Egyptian hermitage, however, the entire empirical world of humans was already nothing but a corrupt training camp early on, one in which comprehensive wrongness exercises were performed day and night – under the guidance of semi-lucid kings with the rank of gods, pseudo-knowledgeable elders and gloomily severe priests who only knew how to pass on conventional rules and idle rituals: they translated external necessities into holy customs, which they then defended like holy necessities. The rest is 'culture' – in so far as this means the copier that guarantees the self-preservation of the convention complex (in newer jargon: a memeplex) through the transference of prevailing patterns from one generation to the next and the one after that.

All moral philosophy is superficial, then, if it is not based on a distinction between habits. Even a *Critique of Practical Reason* relies on unguaranteed conditions as long as the most important anthropological question has not been settled: can human beings even be taken out of fixed bad habits, and under what circumstances do they succeed in finding a new rooting in good ones? Kant's well-known argument from the text on peace, that even 'a race of devils', if it has a modicum of sense, must find a passable *modus vivendi* by establishing a legal order uncannily similar to a civil constitution, is flawed because he fails to understand anti-moral gravitation: 'being a devil' – whether poor or evil is unclear – is only a metaphor for an actor's trapped state within an ignorant habitus, and it is precisely the undoing of this that Kant makes too easy for himself in his appeal.[152] The Kantian devils are merchants who know how much they can go too far, well-behaved egotists who have attended their rational choice seminars. A true race of devils embodies a collective of fatalists where de-disciplining has reached the fundamentalist level. They do not merely live in the squalid cellars of St Petersburg; they are at home in every dead-end *banlieue* and every chronic battle zone. In such circumstances, individuals are convinced that nothing is more normal than the hell they have provided for one another as long as anyone can remember. No devil without its circle, and no hell without the circle made of circles. Whoever grows accustomed to hell becomes immune to the call to change their life – even if it is in their own interests. The meaning of own interests is already trapped by running in the harmful circle. Under such conditions, it is almost irrelevant what instructions one gives the inmates of these personal *circuli vitiosi* to bring them to their senses, for failure is certain whatever one does: one should neither hope for any results from the inner 'moral improvement of man', which Kant too wisely abandoned, nor from the external 'mechanism of nature working through the self-seeking propensities of man',[153] whose reciprocal neutralization the philosopher considered a way to achieve at least an enforced peace. Experience shows that peace between inhabitants of infernal circles comes not from a mutual tempering of 'self-seeking propensities', but from concrete asymmetries. These can result from one-sided exhaustion or a resounding victory by one party. That is why systemicists say that the one of the tools of evil is the inability to win.

The Source of Bad Habits: On the Metaphysics of the Iron Age

Before we settle the matter of whether humans can be uprooted from bad habits, and if so, by what method, we should recapitulate

411

how they were able to take root in them in the first place. Instead of *unde malum?* we now ask: *unde mala habitudo?* The classical moral-theological answers exist as catalogues of vices, of which the seven-part list by Gregory the Great from the late sixth century enjoyed the greatest success.[154]

These state that bad habitus is the consequence of an evil decision, born of leisure and encouraged by arrogance. Some mythical answers go deeper, looking beyond the individual and relating bad habits to the necessity of inhabiting a barren world. If this were a culture-historical investigation, a passage on the natural history of need and its translation into the human sphere would have to follow here. In our context, it is sufficient to note that the earliest articulations of the difficulty of being a human date from the era of Mesopotamian and Mediterranean empires. One finds anonymous authors speaking for the first time of an unease in the world that points beyond any unease in culture.[155]

Instructive statements about the genesis of negative habitualizations are provided by the two great myths about the human condition that mark the beginnings of the ancient Western civilizatory complex: on the Judaeo-Christian side the biblical tale of the expulsion of the first human couple from Paradise, and on the Graeco-Roman side the doctrine of the Golden Age – which, owing to a dark causality of deterioration, had led to the present Iron Age via the intermediate stages of the Silver and Bronze Ages. Both narratives share the intention of explaining the normality of the bad; what sets them clearly apart from each other is the means they use to achieve this. The former explains the stay of post-Paradise humanity in a chronically unsatisfying reality using a moral catastrophe model known as the Fall of Man; the latter attributes the difficulties of the human race to a law of destiny that defines the present as the third stage of decay in a providential worsening process. While the moralistic model explains the unfavourable status quo as a consequence of overstepping a single boundary, the myth of the Ages of Man needs three descending steps to interpret mankind's unbalanced state as a result of the adverse conditions of the Iron Age.

I will not linger on the conclusion that the fatalistic interpretation far exceeds the moralistic one in terms of contemplative breath and historico-philosophical substance, whereas the moralistic version has a stronger personal effect on addressees due to its invasive tendency. From a systemic perspective, the biblical account contains a signifi-cant element of 'moral insanity', as it twists the knife even deeper into the chronically burdened humans in order to read their situation as an inherited debt and well-deserved punishment. At the same time, there is a certain psychagogical prudence in the culpabilistic arrangement, for humans, as empirical findings show, become substantially more resistant to suffering when they are presented with a clear sense of 'what for' – or, failing that, at least a 'why' and a 'from where'. The Christian reception of the tale describing the expulsion from Paradise produced a civilization whose members cannot experience hardship without thinking they deserve it. We regularly display our willingness to take the blame for our suffering, as if making a contribution to a semantic health insurance – in fact, what was viewed as a commitment to the Christian 'religion' was often no more than our mandatory contribution to this guilt system.

In the present context, however, what concerns us is the shared dedication of the Jewish and Graeco-Roman narratives to interpreting the situation of humans in the world as a permanent stay in a malign milieu. The point of departure for both is the evidence that human existence in its present manifestation is fundamentally a being-in-need – including the necessity of adapting to need. Together they support the complementary evidence that the current state of affairs can only be understood as a fall from an originally completely different state. The chronic misery only appears as a consequence of epochal deteriorations, whether gradual and repetition-based or singular and catastrophic. In both cases, habitualized misery is experienced differentially: in the real domain it contrasts with the *modus vivendi* of happy individuals, who are still better off than most others, and in the imaginary domain with the notions of times in which things were better for everyone. This difference provides the matrix for the search for the other condition. 'Where life itself is a withdrawal treatment, it provides fertile ground for addiction.'[156] The connection between addiction and search is explained by etymologists and psychologists.[157]

Realism, Scarcity, Alienation

According to the oldest behavioural theories, adaptation to a chronically inappropriate climate creates a habitus that could, in a non-philosophical sense, be termed realism; it is best described as a reinforced perseverance under chronic pressure. In the biblical account the emphasis is placed on holding out in a bowed state – 'by the sweat of your brow' under the constraints of agriculture – while the Mediterranean tales of the Ages of Man focus more on the new compulsion to lead an existence in permanent conflict with hostile and corrupt neighbours. The most important results of banishment, according to the Book of Genesis, are the curse of work and the hardship of birth, and in Hesiod's version the chronically unreliable nature of social relationships and the perversion of neighbour-ethical norms.[158]

Both models contain rudimentary social philosophies and elementary hermeneutics of need that can be mapped onto modern theories of alienation: according to the former, the fall from the paradisaic non-working world to the sphere of forced work through the traumatic advent of scarcity. The necessity of living in a milieu of scarcity results from humanity's primal guilt: no one who has sinned will ever get enough. Because of an unforgivable transgression, the primal habitus of enduring in the face of constant lack is burned into the notion of the world entertained by man, the supposedly 'deficient being'.[159] It constitutes a primary disciplining elevated to a prevailing mood. From this follow primal resignation, which leads to realism as an inner regulator of hardness, and primal escapism, which postulates the establishment of imaginary wealth enclaves.

This places the stranger in the role of the one who dramatizes scarcity by threatening to consume that on which my survival and the self-assertion of my group depend. The first stranger is the master on whom I have become dependent and who keeps me alive, but takes away every surplus that would improve my lot if I could keep it; he is my exploiter and my rescuer at once. The second stranger is the enemy, who takes until there is nothing left. One is alienated, then, if one has a master and an enemy – regardless of whether, as in psychopolitical set pieces, one joins forces with the master against the enemy in an emergency or with the enemy against the master – as can be observed in the dissolution of loyalties in palace revolts, rebellions and revolutionary wars.

What Sartre writes in his investigations of alienated 'praxis' on the 'man of scarcity' (*l'homme de la rareté*)[160] is, in essence, merely an exegesis of the biblical expulsion myth, read through a Hegelian conceptual grid. Scarcity imposes the impossibility of coexistence on the collective. Sartre locates this infernal existential one dimension too deep to reconcile it with the Marxist concept of exploitation; likewise, he places competition and mutual reification through the evil 'gaze' in such depths that no reconciliation or befriending could ever overcome them, either inside or outside the sphere of scarcity. Thus he not only fails to see the possible productivity of competition; he also overlooks the factual departure from the world of lack through the modern property economy. The project of recuperating Marxism by enriching it with existentialist motifs was thus doomed to miss the mark from the outset. The deepest source of Sartre's failure, however, is not his pandering to the internally flawed critique of political economy; it is rather his philosophical equation of the human being with the epicentre of nothingness. It is where he draws most resolutely on metaphysical jargon that he becomes most remote from the present state of human knowledge. The human being is not negativity, but rather the point of difference between repetitions.

Hesiod emphasizes the disintegration of social cohesion in his statements on the Iron Age. What strikes him most is that the habitus of disloyalty predominates in the current race of humans, even among relatives and apparent friends. The 'natural' parameters of good and bad, honour and dishonour etc., all seem to have been inverted in the Iron Age. From a culture-historical perspective, this shows a pragmatic general climate in which populations with a rural character are obliged to learn unaccustomed urban-strategic life forms. In this change, individuals must learn to switch from mentality to success; they are forced to exchange recognition from their relatives and neighbourhoods for recognition from public markets and power cliques. They have to abandon the intuitive sense of right and wrong they have developed and become accustomed to the primacy of institutionalized court procedure. Together these adjustments amount to a change of habitus that followers of older values, like the farmer-poet Hesiod, could only view as training for a world gone wrong. I shall add in passing that the Koran, despite coming into existence twelve hundred years later, shares several aspects of Hesiod's worldview as described in *Works and Days*. Here the farmer's distrust of the incomprehensible new world of traffic has grown into the desert-dweller's apocalyptic hatred of large cities, which were impenetrable for the old mindset. Here, what some call prophetism is the fiery form of saying no to heightened complexity.

The Ascetic Suspension of Alienation: The Five Fronts

These considerations enable us to define the consequences of the ethical distinction more precisely: it aims for the systematic weaning of the subject from the reality effects of the Iron Age. Contrary to one's first impression, it questions the finality of the post-paradisaic condition. To separate the practising individual from the dominant reality bloc, the ascetic revolt consistently attacks its opponent's strongest point. The great weaning process, as the history of asceticisms shows, is directed at the five main fronts of need: material scarcity, the burden character of existence, sexual drive, alienation and the involuntary nature of death. In these fields, the early explicitly practising life proves that it is possible to compensate for even the most widespread existential deformations – albeit at a price that leads most to accept the ills instead. It is not only the fear of something after death, as Hamlet says, 'that makes calamity of so long life'; even more, it is the hesitation before breaking out of a well-rehearsed and accepted misery. Given the choice between acquired deformation through reality and the feared deformations through asceticism practised *lege artis*, the majority has always chosen the former. They preferred to wait for a comfortable revolution that, so they were told, would come as an 'event'. People have always recoiled from the inconvenient realization that nothing happens unless one brings it about oneself.

Against Hunger

Historical evidence shows that the earliest asceticisms developed on the poverty front: the ancient Indian practice masters were probably the first to discover the principle of voluntary withdrawal that, one could say, takes the subject to the other side of suffering. As early as the earliest Brahmans, an extremism of abstinence came about, driven by the fantastic belief that the metabolism is but one of the illusions with which Maya, the sensuous veil maker, makes fools of humans. By expanding abstinence from food to a somatic-spiritual technique, they transformed hunger into a voluntary act of fasting; they turned a humiliating passivity into an ascetic action. The disempowerment of hunger led directly to the emancipation from the compulsion to work. Whoever chooses abstinence exits the producing life and knows only exercises. The early cultures of beggar monks in Asia and Europe prove that for their fellow humans, the spectacle of the spirit's superiority to the minimized body was worth a sacrifice: alms were the entrance fee for the theatre of spiritual triumphs. One could say that those who made donations to the monks were falling for priestly deception, but the psychological reality was very different. The ancient beggar economy belongs to the realm of the search for autonomy, even for the poorest of the poor: someone who has almost nothing, yet shares the most frugal meal with someone else, participates in the ascetic victory over the law of scarcity. In the case of St Francis of Assisi, the defeat of hunger appears clothed in the relationship of courtly love to Lady Poverty – some Europeans, perhaps not the most morally insensitive, are impressed to this day by this transformation of a misery factor into a gallant allegory. Let us note that the old workers' movement in Europe still knew something about the first rebellion against the tyranny of need. Whether starving or eating: solidarity . . .

Against Overtaxing

The second expansion of the autonomy zone is due to the early athletes and their forerunners in the military nobility. They found a way to disable the law of permanent overtaxing to which the great majority of people in class societies submit. While the normal response to chronic strain is a mixture of hardenings and little escapes that wear individuals down sooner or later, warriors and athletes develop the opposite response: they gain degrees of freedom from the burden character of existence by consistently outdoing the difficult through the even more difficult. They show that a state of great effort is no sufficient reason not to make an even greater effort. The image of Hercules at the crossroads is the primal ethical scene of Europe: this ultimate hero of being-able-to-do-something embodies the rule that one becomes human by choosing the difficult path. For this, it is necessary to favour the austerity of *areté* over the sweetness of depravity.

Athletic irony pushes the boundaries back into the unbelievable – where there was nobody-can-do-this, there is now I-can. This expansion of the ability horizon also has a direct influence on the general sphere. Even the vulgar curiosity of the audience at athletic and circus performances contains a solidarity with the actors that has anthropologically far-reaching implications. Like the hunger artist, the athletes have a message for the psychologically poorest and the physically weakest that is worth sharing in: the best way to escape from exhaustion is to double the load. Even someone who cannot imagine following this maxim literally should still draw inspiration from it. The theory that there is always room to go higher is one that concerns everyone.

It is in this context that one must assess the future of modern sport. Like a Herculean collective, it is standing at a crossroads. Either the athlete continues to act as a witness to the human ability to take forward steps at the threshold of the impossible – with unforeseeable transference effects on all who involve themselves in the appealing spectacle[161] – or they continue along the path of self-destruction that is already marked out, where moronic fans shower co-moronic stars with admiration from the very bottom, the former drunk and the latter doped. One might recall in this context that Euripides already considered the athletic scene in the fourth century BC, which had taken on a decadent life of its own, a plague. 'Of all the countless evils in Greece, none is worse than the race of athletes (*athleton génous*).'[162]

Against Sexual Need

On the third front, the activists turn their attention towards the tensions of sexual drive. As the libido was usually condemned to a long wait in many older cultures, especially those with strictly patriarchal rules for marriage and family relations – decades often passed between the reaching of sexual maturity and possible legalized sexual activity – eros was experienced by countless people as an unliveable dilemma. For so many, the kindest of all the gods thus transpired as the cruellest. If one yielded to one's urges, one could easily descend into disorder; if one resisted them, one faced constant torture from within. Thus the despair at sexuality became a constant factor of the unease in civilization. The widespread outlet institutions of prostitution, concubinage, letting off steam with slaves, masturbation, licences for the young etc. alleviated the problem, but did not solve it. The ascetic response to the challenge of the sexual drive was to transform the constant excess of specific pressure into an aspecific élan to strive for higher goals. The procedure for this, to use a more recent term, was sublimation. Plato revealed its schema by describing the ladder on which sensual desire ascends to a spiritual motivation – from one beautiful body to another, and from the plurality of beautiful bodies to the singularity of the beautiful. This ultimately transpired as the side of the good itself that shines in sensuality. In its conventional manifestations, philosophical critique of sexuality merely accuses it of sabotaging the ascent – whether it creates a fixation on frustrating fantasies when it is unfulfilled or, when fulfilled, drains off mental energy and gets caught in the small-scale cycle of tension and relaxation. Monastic critique of sexuality takes a far more direct approach from the outset by virtually demonizing physical desire – but with the same aim: to create perpetual desire and keep it at the necessary temperature. What this infinitized desire – which still haunted the shame-faced metaphysics of the twentieth century under the name *désir* – has most cause to fear is the relapse into finitude that brings about the return of tepid prose. This finitude is dominated by trivial inner states, depression, lack of élan, as well as the banal excess drive that does not lead to any goal-achieving or boosting programmes. The uninspired psyche is unable to feel encompassed by an absolute – this spawns the gloom which the early abbots called *akédia*, the midday demon that paralyses the monk's soul with indifference to God and everything else. *Akédia* appears in the list of Seven Deadly Sins as 'sluggishness' or 'sloth', and those who know it well almost fear it more than the queen of all vices, *superbia*.[163] In modernity, infinite desire separated from humans and migrated to the economic system, which produces its own restlessness, while individuals increasingly discover that they can no longer follow the perverse imperative of always desiring and enjoying more.

Against Domination and Enmity

On the fourth front, the ascetic revolt puts an end to alienation by showing that humans can never be forced to have a master and an enemy. Here too, the method of liberation is a voluntary exaggeration of the evil: the ascetic enslaves themselves so radically that no empirical enslavement can touch them any longer. They choose their master in the highest heights to free themselves from all second-class masters. Hence Abraham breaks free of the visible gods by avowing his invisible God; hence the Cynic-Stoic wise man submits to the law of the cosmos, which emancipates him from arbitrary human regulations; hence Christ sarcastically recommends giving unto Caesar what is Caesar's, for loyalty belongs to the God of the faithful and the relationship with Caesar can therefore be no more than external. Thus Paul reminds the Romans that they were once slaves of sin, but now, as slaves of righteousness, are free.[164] He even introduces himself in his opening salutation as a chosen slave of God – and for that very reason a free man. Modern references to the 'rule of law' still recall the language of the oldest supremacism, which held that freedom could only exist under the law. Coercion by the highest downgrades all other compulsions to second-order factors. The dominion of the general is a medium of asceticism against the dominion of the concrete. Consequently, any universalism worth taking seriously presupposes an ascetic mode of access to the sphere of norms. Anyone who wishes to have universalism without the work of renunciation, as if it were an omnibus to equality, has understood nothing about the cost of high generalizations.

At the same time, the ascetic emancipates themselves from the compulsion to have an enemy by choosing a universal enemy within, who can only appear in the outside world in second-rate projections. Whoever knows that the devil dwells inside them no longer needs an external malicious partner. Hence the advice to turn the other cheek, and hence the Buddhist caution that the torture victim must not lose sympathy for their torturer. Moral asceticism takes away the enemy's power to make us strike back. Whoever moves beyond the level of reacting to enmity breaks the vicious circle of violence and counter-violence – albeit often at the price of remaining the suffering party.

Moral hyperbole of this kind only draws small audiences in modernity, while the majority once again demands the licence to strike back. The cause of this is primarily the change in the prevailing mood: the anti-thymotic psychopolitics of Christianity, which cautioned people for almost two thousand years to conduct an inner inquisition against all stirrings of pride and self-affirmation, no longer has a footing in the 'achieving society' of today.[165] Let us not forget that every advanced legal system implies a scaled-down reproduction of ascetic abstinence from direct governance, because it forces the wronged party to seek redress via the indirect path of a third party's judgement structured as court proceedings.

Against the Necessity of Dying

On the fifth front, the heroes of the ethical distinction attack death by transferring it from the sphere of abstract and fatal necessity into that of personal ability. They abolish the terrorism of nature to which mortals have been subjected since time immemorial. This does not have to go as far as a physicalization of the immortality idea as found in the writings of Paul, then once more of the Russian biocosmists,[166] and currently among the American techno-gnostics, whose ambition is to absorb theology into physics.[167] The conversion of necessity into ability presupposes a strong notion of continuum that spans the boundary between life and death – this can be seen in the two great scenes of the art of dying in Old Europe, the death of Socrates and that of Jesus.[168] Through demonstrations of composure in death, the end of life exemplarily changes into a symbolic order with a strong sense of continuum, as if 'crossing over' were no more than a change in the state of matter.

An able and nurtured death is a direct revolt against the animal-like perishment of which Job said that it is nonetheless the fate of humans. It equally contradicts the naked killing that pervades Homer's world, which virtually overflows with second-class dead who are left lying on the ground without honour to become food for the dogs and vultures, while the incomparable slayer Achilles finds a place in Hellenic memory. The symbolically nurtured death in Christianity extends the memorial function to the saved, who remain unforgotten in a divine memory and thus become immortal. One could describe the work of ascetics on the life–death continuum as an original accumulation of civilizatory energy that allows even the most external compulsion to be embedded in the interior of the symbolic order. A modern trace of this civilization is visible in the growing suicide movement in the West. It has dismantled the metaphysical exuberance of the ascetic art of dying, but works on the meanwhile secure evidence that humans are always entitled to experience their death in culturally tended forms. The sound arguments of contemporary movements advocating a dignified death aim to break up the alliance between a reactionary religion and a progressive technological medicine, which together barely allow more than a higher form of bucket-kicking. Instead, the goal is to make the achievement of ascetic cultures – embedding death in a shared ability – accessible also to non-ascetics.

The Post-Metaphysical Legacy of the Metaphysical Revolt

Looking back at the ascetic revolts against the reality principle of the Iron Age permits a clearer definition of what I call the de-spiritualization of asceticisms. It shaped a significant stretch of the path to modernity, in so far as this epoch was characterized by the pragmatic levelling of metaphysical upswings. This process forces the excesses into the arts, as well as the adjustment that Gotthard Günther terms the transition 'from the truth of thought to the pragmatics of action'.[169] In this sense, modernity constitutes a strong substitute programme for the ethical secession. Its precondition is the demonstration that on the five fronts of the old need, one can still win by other means than those used in battle by the practice heroes of earlier times. This was precisely the motto proclaimed by the pansophists of the Renaissance and the pioneers of explorative thought: humans can do anything of their own accord as soon as they want to. They opened the door to the post-miserablist age – which, for the same reason, is also a post-metaphysical one, as it reacts to existential compulsion with inner-worldly answers. Thinking and acting post-metaphysically means getting beyond the burdens of the old human condition with the aid of technology and without extreme ascetic programmes. The only modern-day ascetics whose victories one wishes to be authentic are athletes – whereas the spiritual victors over the old human condition have been stripped of their authority through the culture of suspicion. Anyone who heard a voice from a burning thorn bush after forty days in the desert would be taken for a victim of a psychedelic episode. Anyone who claimed to transcend sexuality without ever having known it could be sure of being diagnosed neurotic. And modern observers of religion consider Buddha Amida, who reveals himself to Japanese monks after one hundred nights of sleep deprivation, a local psychosemantic effect.

Because of its egalitarian design, modernity feels compelled to reformulate all truths that were previously accessible only to the few into truths for the many – and neglect whatever is lost in translation. This eliminates the foundation of practical ascetic extremism, but affirms its tendencies in all aspects: it is indeed necessary to set up a strong antithesis to the misery-based definition of reality in the agro-imperial age – if this can now also be articulated by non-metaphysical and non-heroic means, then all the better. Every one of these translations ensued after the technical caesura of the Modern Age. The principle of their success is displayed by the fact that during the last three hundred years, an unprecedented civilizatory learning cycle has been active that fundamentally changed the laws of existence from the Iron Age – and continues to change them. At times, this cycle has helped the dream of a return to a Golden Age or a restoration of Paradise to political power, and even if the dream was never going to come true, the dream tendency as such already tells us something about the prevailing mood of the newer era. It was based on the intuition that the principle of reality had become a malleable plasma. Communist maximalism, which would accept nothing short of total renewal, has lost its psychological plausibility; it only lives on indirectly in the weary hatred which ex-radicals and their imitators in the third and fourth generation show towards our more moderate conditions. Nonetheless, the idea of returning to the second best still has great practical charm.

In fact, Europeans and Americans, to use Hesiod's terms, catapulted themselves into a renewed Silver Age in the second half of the twentieth century. Within the 'Crystal Palace', they created conditions for the majority that differed not gradually but epochally, or rather aeonically, from everything that had been the case a few centuries earlier. Let us recall once again the October Revolution of 1846 – the epochal date in the history of pain.[170] We should also emphasize the de-agrarianization of economic life, and thus the end of the 'idiocy of rural life'.[171] To the historian, it is beyond doubt that virtually all inhabitants of the Crystal Palace profit, at least in material and infrastructure terms, from unprecedented improvements in living conditions[172] – a fact that is augmented and confirmed by the equally unprecedented blossoming of a culture of additional demands. The spiral of resignation from the Iron Age has been reversed and turned into an upward spiral of desire. In this situation, philosophy loses its mandate to rise beyond the static world of need that, as the theoretical wing of the ethical distinction, it administered for two thousand years. It changes into a consultant to assist in explaining the advantage of no longer living in the Iron Age. It becomes a translation agency for transforming heroic knowledge into civil knowledge. It stands surety for the esoteric remainder with its own assets.

In Defence of the Second Silver Age

It was Richard Rorty who promoted this translation work most coherently and appealingly in the last decades – appealingly primarily because, despite his Dewey-inspired advocacy for the priority of democracy over philosophy, he made no secret of his sympathy for the exaggerations of heroic thought (which he also called romantic or inspiring thought). What places the American Rorty in the better traditions of European Baroque philosophy and the British-French-German Enlightenment is his unshakeable fidelity to the idea of world improvement, a fidelity that finds its most old-fashioned and stimulating manifestation in his book on the improvement of America.[173] Rorty was, next to Hans Jonas, the only thinker of the last half-century from whom one could learn why a philosopher with an understanding of the times must have the courage to strive for simplicity: only in a jargon-free language can one discuss with one's contemporaries why we, as members of modern civilization, may not have entered a Golden Age, but should not still view ourselves as citizens of the Iron Age either. When discussing this subject, philosophy and non-philosophy become one, and historico-philosophical theories and everyday intuitions merge into one another. The grandiloquent conservatives, who continue to cultivate the idiom of the Iron Age as if nothing had happened, must be challenged in a language of the middle.[174] The same tone must be used to counter the far left ideologies still virulent at a local level, which, out of disappointment at the failed return to the Golden Age, do everything in their power to smear the Silver Age as a farce. Only in such a conversation could the reasonable element in the claims of the 'end of history' after the collapse of the Soviet Union, which are presented somewhat exaggeratedly and rejected even more exaggeratedly, be reiterated.[175] The end of history is a metaphor for the disablement of the dominant reality principle of the Iron Age following non-heroic measures against the five needs. These include the industrial-political switch from scarcity to oversupply; the division of labour between the top achievers and the moderately working in business and sport; the general deregulation of sexuality; the transition to a mass culture without masters and a politics of co-operation without enemies; and attempts towards a post-heroic thanatology.

None of these measures are flawless; not one of them can move entirely beyond the level of lesser evils, and in some aspects they are even perceived as greater evils of a new type. That is why countless inhabitants of the second Silver Age, which does not understand itself, tend towards a defamation of this new state. What we call postmodernity is largely no more than the medial exploitation of unease at the second best – including all the risks that go with luxury pessimisms. The fateful question is whether one succeeds in stabilizing the standards of the episodically materialized Silver Age, or whether a regression is imminent to an Iron Age of whose currentness both old and new realists are convinced – not least considering the fact that over two thirds of the human race have never left it. Such a regression would not be fate, but rather a consequence of wilful reactions to the paradoxes of existence in the subpar.

The decision about the further course of events depends on whether the learning context of modernity can get through all technical, political, economic, cultural, epistemological and sanitary crises and be expanded into a sufficiently stable continuum of improvement knowledge and optimization ability. How little this continuum can be taken for granted is evident in the fact that the history of ideas in the nineteenth and twentieth centuries produced an endless series of rebellions initiated by hostility to civilization and anti-technical *ressentiment*, regardless of whether these came about in the name of faith, the soul, life, art, national character, cultural identity or diversity of species. These outbursts constituted terminations of training that did grave damage to modernity fitness – and the danger of new terminations has not passed, as the omnipresence of far left, far right, conservative and ecological fundamentalisms proves. The 'discourse of modernity' – and not only the philosophical one – demands a constant clarification of its agenda and defence against the wrong curricula. Every generation must choose between escapisms and forms capable of becoming traditions. To ensure even the possibility of an effective learning continuum, an intensive filtering of contemporary idea production is indispensable – a task once entrusted to 'critique', which has been entirely gutted in the meantime. Critique is replaced by an affirmative theory of civilization, supported by a General Immunology.[176]

Canon-Work in Modernity

More than any form of civilization before it, modernity relies on sorting out what deserves to be passed on and foreshortening maladaptive developments – even if the necessary warnings are perceived by the protagonists of a current generation that basks in expressive malformations as oppressive infringements. Being allowed to bask in short-lived maladaptations, incidentally, is a significant factor in the appeal of modern life forms. It defines their aroma of freedom and lack of consequences; it liberates the present from the burden of creating role models – it is no coincidence that modernity is the Eldorado of youth movements. Its greatest temptation is to abolish the future on the pretext of being the future. Whoever restricts themselves to 'single-age' ways of life does not have to worry about conveying role models in multi-age processes.[177] As self-evidently maladaptive forms also tend towards reproduction under liberal conditions, and go on to haunt subsequent generations, it is important for the civilizatory process to musealize such variants as soon as possible – at the latest, one generation after the resignation of the protagonists.[178]

In truth, one of the most important functions of the modern cultural archive is to render superfluous the index of forbidden books and works of art, which has meanwhile become counterproductive. The archive reverently preserves all important and interesting errors, all projects with no future and all unrepeatable departures forever.[179] Its collections are recruited from strictly outside of the canon in which the real generational process continues to work. Otherwise, preservation in museums runs the risk of being confused with setting an example for successors – which is, incidentally, the favourite mistake of contemporary artists: following the end of the museoclastic movements, they view the public museum as a collection of normative works and fail to recognize its new function as the final destination of singularities, that is to say as a depository for productions that can neither be followed up nor repeated. They likewise misunderstand the function of private collections, which is ultimately merely to withdraw pseudo-transcendent works from circulation. In addition, the paralysis afflicting the humanities today stems from the fact that its protagonists have, for the most part, settled into the archive as free-floating observers – Rorty slightly contemptuously calls them 'detached cosmopolitan spectators' – and left all programmatic work on the crafting of a civilizatory code with a future to chance and fanaticism.

Malign Repetitions I: The Culture of Camps

Following on from these observations, I shall point out a few mala-daptation phenomena that shaped the civilizatory process of the twentieth century. From today's perspective, they should be read as symptoms of the triumph of malign repetition in recent sequences of traditions, and therefore constitute emergencies for an intervening science of 'culture'. I shall begin – continuing from the reflections of the previous section – with the culture of political murder in the pseudo-metanoetic politics of the twentieth century; then deal with the weakening of the imitative factor in contemporary pedagogy; and finally address the illusory rejection of imitation in modern aesthetics.

As far as the externalization of metanoia in the revolutionary politics of the twentieth century goes, there is little to add to the earlier deliberations on the biopolitics of Bolshevism. The attempt to force, by political-technical measures for large collectives, what could previously barely be achieved even through extreme ascetic exercises by highly motivated individuals inevitably led to a politics of absolute means. Because the elimination of sluggish fellow humans seemed a logical choice as the means of all means for projects with this level of ambition, the first half of the twentieth century saw the birth of the most historically unheard-of form of a maladaptive culture: the culture of camps.[180] It served repression on the pretext of re-education, extermination on the pretext of work, and finally eradi-cation without any pretext. One initially hesitates to apply the term 'culture' to such phenomena. If one considers the scale of the camp worlds, however, their ideological premises, the logistical efforts they demanded, their personnel requirements, their moral implications, their habitus-forming effects and their mental side effects among those running the camps,[181] the word 'culture' cannot be avoided, even for these professionally learnable, routine-anchored monstrosities. Although one tends, initially, to assume that the longer-term prospects of transmission for camp norms must have been poor, it is undisputed that during most of the twentieth century, there was an entrepreneurial culture of internment, selection and elimination that survived for longer than one would ever have believed possible, either on moral or on culture-theoretical premises. Crime organized by the revolutionary party state reached the Weberian stage in the Soviet Union and China – in the sense of a transition from a state of emergency to bureaucratization. A maladaptive reversal with such long-term effects can also be observed in the life forms of the Parisian miracle courts in the seventeenth and eighteenth centuries, those counter-worlds of thieves, beggars and gypsies immortalized in novels of the nineteenth century – above all Victor Hugo's *The Hunchback of Notre-Dame*. In these too, something resembling a stable-perverse counter-culture had come into being with unduly high chances of continuance. It constituted a parallel culture of the metropolitan poor that had been born out of need. The long-term camp culture of the twentieth century, on the other hand, was exclusively the work of pseudo-metanoetic states that invoked the French Revolution and took over the Jacobin sanctification of terror.

The birth date of modern exterminism as an entrepreneurial form and an institution can be precisely determined: 5 September 1918, when Lenin's decrees on Red Terror stated expressly that one must incarcerate the enemies of the Soviet system in concentration camps and eliminate them step by step. This approach, intended as provisional in the first years, was maintained on a massive scale well into the 1950s, and in smaller forms until the 1980s – finally in collaboration with Soviet psychiatry, which was based on the axiom that dissatisfaction with the life forms of actual socialism was a symptom of severe mental illness.

The facts speak a clear language: the world of Nazi camps lasted for just under twelve years, those of the Soviet Union almost seventy years, and those of Maoism at least forty years – with a protracted aftermath in the prison system under the authoritarian capitalism of present-day China. This means that Soviet exterminism could spread its copies as far as a third generation, and in the case of Maoism a second, whose effects are still felt today: the system of *laogai* – literally 'reform through labour' – affected over fifty million people and wiped out over a third of these. We owe a debt of gratitude to anti-fascism of all stripes for the insistence with which it denounced the hyper-maladaptive atrocities of the Nazi state – the Holocaust, that German synthesis of amok and routine. What remains notable is the asymmetry of 'coming to terms with' the past: 'anti-fascists' of Soviet and Maoist dispositions have always evaded the question of why they showed so much more discretion when it came to the excesses in their own history, which were quantitatively even greater. To this day, knowledge of its true proportions is anything but widespread – despite Solzhenitsyn, despite Jung Chang, and despite *The Black Book of Communism*. While the denial of Nazi crimes is rightly treated as a punishable crime in some countries, the atrocities of the Marxist archipelago are still considered peccadilloes of history in some circles.

We learn from this that lies do not always have short legs. If maladaptation forms on such a scale are able to develop a second and third generation, their legs are rather longer than those of ordinary lies; it is worth pondering what enabled them to become so long. This concerns not only the autonomous creation of laws in dictatorial state formations, which tend to become retreats into abnormality, but also the foundations of modernism: with its advent, the gulf between demoralizing success and legitimate exemplariness known from older cultural stages opened up with unprecedented virulence. If a thinker of Sartre's calibre resolved to keep silent about the facts of the Soviet camp world well into the 1950s despite knowing of its origins, its dimensions and its consequences, and even went so far as denouncing Western critics of the camps – including Albert Camus – as mendacious lackeys of the bourgeoisie, it is evident that the greatest maladaptive anomaly in the political history of humanity cast its shadow on the power of judgement of eminent intellectuals. The most culture-theoretically relevant information lies in the dates: Sartre's vow of silence accompanied the transition of Soviet camp culture to the third generation. He supported the perverse change of a 'measure' into an institution. If one acknowledges this irrefutable meaning or secondary meaning in Sartre's reference to his 'companionship' with socialism, it is undeniable that in his person, which seemed to embody the moral oracle of his generation, the archetype of the false teacher had entered the stage – though cultivators of the critical memory prefer to discuss it with reference to the person of Heidegger. Heidegger may have been a false teacher against modernity in some respects; the later Sartre was in all respects the false teacher in favour of modernity.[182] Only in the context of a strict musealization can one refer to authors of this calibre to distinguish between greatness and exemplarity.

Malign Repetitions II: The Erosion of the School

As far as the decline of practice culture and the awareness of disciplines in the pedagogy of the second half of the twentieth century are concerned, this forms the most recent chapter in the long history of antagonistic co-operation between the modern state and the modern school. I have shown how the liaison and the contradiction between state semantics and school semantics in Europe from the seventeenth century on, if not earlier, inevitably led to chronic tensions between the internally differentiated 'subsystems'. If the state's traditional request to the school to produce usable citizens is translated by the latter into an order to develop autonomous personalities, constant friction is preordained – as creative dysfunction on the one hand, and as a source of chronic disappointment on the other. Generally speaking, one can say that bourgeois advanced civilization emerged from the surpluses of school humanism via the state education mission.[183] One can virtually speak of a *felix culpa* on the part of the older bourgeois education system: it gave its more talented pupils infinitely more cultural motifs than they would ever be able to use in their civil functions. In this context, it may be productive to note that some of the greatest phenomena of spiritual surplus in recent intellectual history – Johann Gottlieb Fichte as the reinventor of the theory of alienation and Friedrich Nietzsche as the modernizer of the Christian superhuman idea – passed through the same school, the Thuringian Pforta near Naumburg, which was known in its time as one of the strictest secondary schools in Germany: Fichte from 1774 to 1780[184] and Nietzsche from 1856 to 1864. It is hardly necessary to explain how the Tübingen seminary over-fulfilled its training mission with the pupils Hölderlin, Hegel and Schelling. The question of what the pupil Karl Marx, who graduated in 1835, owed to his formative years at the gymnasium in Trier, the former Jesuit Trinity College, has been answered with rather modest information by revolutionary historiography.[185]

In the most recent phase of school history, the creative maladaptation of the classical school has been perverted into a malign maladaptation that can be called modern in so far as it resulted from an epoch-typical disturbance of role model functions and the accompanying decline in practice consciousness. In the wake of this, school approaches a point of twofold implosion at which it produces neither citizens nor personalities. It heads towards a state beyond conformization and production of surpluses that bypasses all aspects of direct usefulness and indirect creation of consequences. Year after year, it releases more and more cohorts of pupils whose adaptation to a school system that has got maladaptively out of control is increasingly evident, without any blame whatsoever being attached to individual teachers or students. The two are joined in an ecumene of disorientation scarcely paralleled in history – unless one wishes to point to the long night of education between the collapse of the Roman school system in the fifth century and the rebirth of a Christian-humanist school culture in the wake of the Alcuinic-Carolingian reforms during the eighth century.

To diagnose the malaise, one would have to show in detail how the current school takes part in the process that Niklas Luhmann calls the differentiation of subsystems. Differentiation means the establishment of strictly self-referentially organized structures within a subsystem or 'praxis field' – in evolution-theoretical terms, the institutionalization of selfishness. Luhmann's ingenious impulse was to show how growth in the performance capacity of subsystems in modern 'society' – whether in politics, business, law, science, art, the church, sport, pedagogy or the health system – depends on a constant increase in its self-referentiality, to the point of its transition into a state of complete self-referential closure. In moral-theoretical terms, this implies the remoulding of selfishness at the subsystemic level into a regional virtue. For 'social' critique, this means that helpless protest against the cynicism of power is replaced by system enlightenment – that is to say, a clarification of enlightenment.

The systemically conditioned revaluation of values presupposes the de-demonization of self-preference that one can observe in the texts of the European moralists between the seventeenth and nineteenth centuries.[186] It is hardly surprising, then, that one encounters a neutralized perversion at the centre of every subsystem. It is not only the offensive deviation of the 'blasphemer' from the moral norm that appears perverse, but far more the openness of the admission that the subordinated system is ultimately only concerned with itself, not its possible mandates in a larger framework.[187] Thus there is a close connection between cynicism and perversion – cynicism, after all, as enlightened false consciousness, speaks the truth about the false, provided that it helps immorality to become blatant. This breakthrough to blatancy – the *alétheia* of systems – first occurred in the field of politics, when Machiavelli disclosed the autonomous laws of political action and recommended its emancipation – long considered scandalous – from general morality. This was followed by economic theory after the advent of mechanical production in the late eighteenth century. Early liberals like Mandeville and Adam

Smith had already understood: first comes amortization, then morality. The industrial system openly recognized that its task was to gain profits for its managers so that they could service their loans, make new investments and cover salary costs. In short: within the system, 'social' factors can only be taken into account via calculations of side effects. The argument that business is of most use to the social environment when it concentrates on what it does best, namely generating profits, is correct across the board – and yet it does not manage to acquire more than a vague plausibility, for the evident success of the one side is accompanied by growing evidence to the contrary: the selfishness of the economic system ignores too many other interests, whether one describes these as the interests of the whole or not.

The remaining subsystems are naturally forced far more strongly to hide their selfishness and justify themselves with the aid of vague holistic rhetoric.[188] This does not alter their factual development into 'selfish systems'. Each of them produces so-called experts who explain to the rest why things have to go the known way They have to make it clear to the sceptical audience why the all-too-visible self-interest of the subsystem is outweighed by its usefulness for all. But one can still not imagine a health system openly stating that it primarily serves its own self-reproduction. Nor has one heard any utterances from churches to the effect that their only goal is to preserve the churches, even though open speech is considered a virtue among the clergy. There is even less reason to expect the school system's one day becoming sufficiently perverse to declare that its only task is to keep itself running somehow, in order to ensure that its profiteers – teachers and administrative employees – have secure positions and solid privileges.

Where one cannot expect confessions, one must rely on diagnoses. Diagnoses remould perversions into structural problems. It is obvious that the problem of today's school system is not only that it is no longer able to fulfil the state mission to breed citizens because the definition of the goal has become too blurred amid the demands of the current professional world; it is even clearer in the abandonment of its humanistic and artistic surplus in favour of devoting itself to a more or less de-spirited industry of pseudo-scientifically founded didactic routines. Because, in recent decades, it has no longer summoned the courage for dysfunctionality it had persistently shown since the seventeenth century, it changed into an empty selfish system. It produces teachers that only remind one of teachers, school subjects that only remind one of school subjects, and pupils that only remind one of pupils. In this process, school becomes 'anti-authoritarian' in an inferior fashion without formally ceasing to exercise authority. As the law of learning through imitation cannot be disabled, the school risks becoming exemplary for the next generation in its own reluctance to represent exemplarity. This means that the second and third generations will be populated almost entirely by teachers who no longer do any more than celebrate the self-referentiality of the tuition. The tuition taking place is self-referential because it is in the nature of the system for it to take place. The internal differentiation of the school system brings about a situation in which there is only a single main subject left in school: that of 'school'. Accordingly, there is only one external goal to tuition: graduation with the corresponding qualification. Whoever completes a career at such a school has spent up to thirteen years learning not to take the teachers as examples. Through adaptation to the system, they have learned a form of learning that dispenses with the internalization of the material; they have virtually irreversibly rehearsed working through it without any acquisitive practice. They have learned the habitus of a pretend learning that defensively makes various objects its own in the system-immanently correct belief that the ability to adapt to the given forms of tuition is, for the time being, the aim of all pedagogy.

In the light of these phenomena, radical school thinkers have called for a dissolution of the entire system – whether, as with Ivan Illich, in the postulation of a 'de-schooling of society' or, as among current reform educators, through the suggestion of abolishing the whole established system of subjects and turning school during the formative years into an open training camp for the polyvalent intelligence of young people. Such demands are in keeping with the great shift from book culture to network culture that has taken place over the last two decades. Its practical application would lead to something resembling a reintroduction of intelligence into the wild that could be described as a controlled jungle pedagogy. In this context, there are notable findings indicating that young people who spend a great deal of time with computer games and junk communication show considerable training effects in dealing intelligently with data clutter. Steven Johnson has summarized these developments under a title that should catch the attention of parents and systems theorists: *Everything Bad Is Good for You*.[189] It presents the thesis that almost any form of strong inculturation is better than going along with a maladaptive selfish system that can only offer parodies of the previous education. The problem of the false teacher, which I illustrated in the philosophical context using the example of Sartre, returns at the systemic level as the problem of the false school.

Malign Repetitions III: The Self-Referential Art System of Modernity

Observations of this type and this tendency are pushed yet further as soon as one turns to the art system of modernity. It is clear to anyone who examines the history of art from 1910 to the present day that the catastrophe of the visual arts took place during this time – both in the process-theoretical and in the colloquial sense of the word. The three decisive generations of artists in the visual arts – from 1910 to 1945, 1945 to 1980, and 1980 to 2015 – expanded the field of their profession in a dizzyingly rapid advance towards new procedures. In the process, however, they forgot how to follow on from the highest artistic standards of the previous generation. The vast majority of them gave up the continuation of the golden chain of thematic, technical and formal imitations at the level of modernly unrestricted art experiments.

The catastrophe of art transpires as the catastrophe of imitative behaviour and the training consciousness associated with it, which had spanned the previous three thousand years of 'art history' as a proliferation, however fragmented, of masteries and trade secrets. After a sequence of some eighty to a hundred generations of *imitatio*-based copying processes in premodern art, the imitation of content and technique was almost entirely stripped of its function as a substantial cultural replicator within a mere two changes of generation. As imitation constitutes the decisive tradition-forming mechanism, however, even in a culture that disavows imitation in favour of a suggestive and dubious ideology of creativity, the imitation carried out by the moderns concerns the only aspect of art still suited to imitation without the imitators having to notice, let alone cultivate, the tendency of the imitation themselves. This aspect consists in the fact that works of art are not only produced, but also exhibited.[190] The shift from art as a power of production (along with the 'baggage' of the old masters) to art as a power of exhibition (along with its freedom of effects) gives pre-eminence to a form of imitation that turns its back on the workshop and puts the place of presentation at the centre of events. In this way, an uncontrollably exaggerated element of selfishness enters not only the art world, but also the works themselves. From each decade to the next, one can see more clearly that they are ever less interested in their production character and ever more interested in their exhibition character.

In his essay *Countdown: 3 Kunstgenerationen*, Heiner Mühlmann uses evolution-theoretical arguments to reconstruct the free fall of the art system into a state of rigorous self-referentiality. In this X-ray image of aesthetic evolution from 1910 to the present day, it becomes clear how the systematic misjudgement of imitation and the training element leads to paradoxical imitations and perverse forms of training. Paradoxical imitations and perverse training forms are ones in which malign qualities – which one would have termed 'vices' in earlier times – reproduce most successfully. In the imitation-blind subculture of modern visual art, on the thresholds between generations, works and artists established themselves in which one could observe the next highest level of self-referentiality; yet contemporary observers proved unable to conclude from this that a self-referential work is simultaneously one that denies its own existence. Rather, the consummate malignity of the modern art scene is evident precisely in the fact that even the most shrilly self-referential cynicism can be taken as proof of the transcendent nature of art.

The art system has meanwhile taken over the best place in the sun of selfishness unchallenged. Although Martin Heidegger had taught that the work of art establishes a world – at the very time when art began its descent into pure self-referentiality. In reality, the work of art in the selfish system of postmodernized art has no intention of establishing a world. Rather, it presents itself as a sign that it is showing something which does not refer to any world: its own exhibited state. The work of art in the third generation of blind selfishness-imitation has anything but an explicit world-relation. What it establishes is its manifest remoteness from everything outside its own sphere. The only thing it knows about the world is that it contains people who are full of longing for experiences of meaningfulness and transcendence. It relies on the fact that many of them are prepared to gratify their yearning in the empty hermeticism of self-referential works, in the tautology of self-referential exhibitions, and in the triumphalism of self-referential museum buildings. Like all pseudo-religions, it aims for transcendence without for a second taking its eyes off its mundane interests.

When it comes to exhibiting its lack of concern for external references, the art system has even surpassed the financial one. It has already achieved what the economic system can only dream of: it has sacralized its selfishness, and now displays it like a seal of election. Hence the irresistible temptation emanating from the art system for the financial system and all other domains of self-referential activity. The curators, who organize self-referential exhibitions, and the artists, who act as self-curators and self-collectors,[191] are the only ones from whom the protagonists of speculative business can learn

434

anything. Their lesson is this: one can never take selfishness too far, as long as the audience is prepared to react to art as if it were a manifestation of transcendence – and how else should it react in a time when any added meaning is dressed up as a religious experience?

Everything suggests that the same audience will also react to extreme wealth as if it were transcendence. The future of the art system is thus easy to predict: it lies in its fusion with the system of the largest fortunes. It promises an illustrious exhibitionistic future for the latter and a transition to the princely dimension for itself. After the emergence of the artistic power of production in the Renaissance, which made the artist great as the master of the landscape, the portrait and the apocalypse, and after the emergence of the power of exhibition in early modernity, which began with the exhibition of a urinal and culminated in the self-exhibiting museum, we are currently experiencing the emergence of art market power, which places all the power in the hands of the collectors. The path of art follows the law of externalization, which proves the power of imitation precisely where imitation is most vehemently denied: it leads from the artists, who imitate artists, via the exhibitors, who imitate exhibitors, to the buyers, who imitate buyers. Before our eyes, the motto *l'art pour l'art* has turned into 'the art system for the art system'. From this position, the art system develops into the paradigm for all successful maladaptations – indeed the source of malign copying processes of all kinds. The problem of the false school returns as the problem of seduction through the rewards provided by the art system for examples of pseudo-culture.[192] The conclusion is an obvious one: in future, there will hardly be any perversion that does not take the current art system as an example. Derivative trading was long established there before the financial world began doing the same. Like the doping-corrupted sport system, the art system is at a crossroads: either it goes all the way on the path of corruption through imitation of the extra-artistic effect in the world of exhibitions and collections, exposing art once and for all as the playground of the last human, or it remembers the necessity of bringing creative imitation back to the workshops and re-addressing the question of how one should distinguish between what is worthy and what is unworthy of repetition.

RETROSPECTIVE

From the Re-Embedding of the Subject to the Relapse into Total Care

If one looks back from these current, all too current perceptions to the long way travelled by modern forms of subject-forming practice from their beginnings in urban mysticism, the workshops of artistes and craftsmen, the studios of scholars and the offices of the early Renaissance to the educational institutions, art galleries, fitness centres and genetic laboratories of the present, we arrive – beyond the unsummarizable wealth of divergent lines of development – at a problematic overall finding. Certainly the Modern Age fulfilled one of its promises: for the escapist ethicists populating the millennia between Heraclitus and Blaise Pascal, between Gautama Buddha and Tota Puri, it opened up the possibility of a new existence as world-lings. In keeping this promise, however, it simultaneously took away from humans what many had considered most valuable: the possible of distinguishing oneself radically from the world.

One cannot deny that modernity ended the alienation between the enclaves of the secessionists[193] and the wasteland of externalities, and provided a new description of the discrepancy between humans and being in partly pathological, partly political and partly aesthetic terms. It offered therapies on the first track, social reforms on the second, and emergences into creativity on the third. Do we still need to point out that these main directions of world improvement and self-improvement are simultaneously the modes that helped us to resolve most of the misunderstandings concentrated in the concept of 'religion'? When it comes to correcting the disproportion between humans and the world, the most powerful mediators are medicine, the arts and democracy (better described as the politics of friendship). And when the concern is to redirect the forces of escapism towards a beneficial immanence, a fulfilling world on this side provides enough light to outshine the special effects of the beyond.

But regardless of whether modernity sought to adapt humans to the demands of the conditions or vice versa, its aim was always to bring back those who had voluntarily become estranged from the world in their secession from the 'country home of the self' to 'reality'. Its ambition was to imprint on them a single citizenship that gives and takes everything: being-in-the-world. It binds us to a communal life that knows no more emigration. Since living there we all have the same passport, issued by the United States of Ordinariness. We are guaranteed all human rights – except for the right to exit from facticity. Hence the meditative enclaves gradually become invisible, and the residential communities of unworldliness disband. The beneficial deserts are abandoned, the monasteries empty out, holidaymakers replace monks and holidays replace escapism. The demi-mondes of relaxation give both heaven and Nirvana an empirical meaning.

The re-secularization of the ascetically withdrawn subject (which is erroneously elevated to a substance) is undoubtedly one of the tendencies in modernity that merits close philosophical attention. In fact, it initiated a change that can be followed with sympathy, as it held out the prospect of nothing less than a reconciliation of humans and the world after an era of radical alienation. The 'age of balance' made the negation of ancient oppositions its mission – the spirit and life wanted to come together again, while ethics and the everyday wanted to form a new alliance. Millennia had passed in which the individuals resolved to embark on secession split the totality of the world into inner and outer, own and non-own parts; now they would be re-embedded in the milieu of a multi-dimensional whole, each one in its place and grasping itself as the 'worldling in the middle', to draw once again on Goethe's cheerful self-description. When the Enlightenment drove forward the disenchantment of metaphysics, it did so not least with the aim of freeing those indoctrinated with notions of the beyond from their extravagant immersion in worldless fictions. What made the critics of the religious illusion so sure of their cause was the conviction that the alienated human race could only achieve emancipation and true happiness by renouncing all imaginary happiness.

Taken together, these efforts form the complex of forms of the practising life I have outlined here under the classification 'exercises of the moderns'. Their key figures were the technical, artistic and discursive virtuosos who, in extensive practice cycles, managed to produce themselves as worlds in the world, as microcosms, as 'personalities'. These elaborated, stylized and documented individuals could be sure of experiencing the wide world inside their own person. All of them still profited from a metaphysical reinsurance that made the turn to worldliness appear as a gain on the account of the heightened and spared ego. For them, experience was synonymous with development. They could still enjoy the glowing isolation that guaranteed the separated subject a seemingly inalienable right of domicile in the realms of the soul and the mind; from there, they organized their journeys into the open – conquistadors and beautiful souls in one. It was at them that Goethe directed his pronouncement: 'No time there is, no power, can decompose / The minted form that lives and living grows.'[194]

The rest is quickly told, for it is untellable: the radicalized enlightenment of the twentieth century broke open the enclosures of 'personalities' immunized as figures or with reference to the beyond. Along with the soul that it posited for itself, it simultaneously drove out its *daímon*, the eerie companion from which Goethe borrowed the confidence that every individual life follows its inner primal form, in accordance with 'the law presiding at your birth'.[195] This expulsion too initially occurred for the sake of inner-worldly bliss, which was entitled to demand the sacrifice of various illusions. A particular concern was to end the priority of the soul, which had become a prison for the body.[196]

The true price of the epochal operation is revealed by the aberrances of the last century. If one were to compress this era into a film script, its title would have to be 'The Secularization of the Inner World', or 'The Revenge of the World on Those Who Thought that They Could Remain Untouched by It'. It would demonstrate that humans are destined for mass consumption as soon as one views them as a mere factor in the game of world improvement. The plot would be centred on the symmetrically interrelated primary ideologies of the nineteenth and twentieth centuries, which advanced the re-translation of humans from world-flight into world-belonging: naturalism and socialism – one could, because of their close kinship, also say social naturalism and natural socialism. Both systems strove to reclaim humans, along with their physical foundations, entirely for the 'ensemble of social relations' and to prevent their flight into supposed inner worlds or counter-worlds – to say nothing of religious backworlds. Both approaches are inseparable from an elemental pragmatism which states that a thing is only real if it can be treated in social actions and technical procedures. It is augmented by a relentless moralism, indeed an inclination towards moral-demonic excess: if humans can no longer succeed in distancing themselves spiritually from worldly conditions, then countless people at least do everything they deem necessary so that, under the given conditions, they can count themselves among the good, the morally superior.

The decisive blow to the mere possibility of an existence capable of world-flight did not come from the pragmatic side, however, but from the renewed 'revolution in the way of thinking' in the early twentieth century associated with the young Heidegger. He turned the clock of philosophical reflection back more than two and a half millennia when he decided, in his principal work *Being and Time* (1927), to let philosophical thought begin anew in the situation of Dasein as being-in-the-world. He thus reversed the step into the aloof realm of theory, and with it the securing of the self in a distant observing position, the step that – reusing Heraclitean images – I described as stepping out of the river of life and conquering the shore.[197] On the shore, we saw the appearance of the observer whose gaze transformed the world into a spectacle – an undignified one, of course, from which the ethically motivated intelligence must turn away.

Through this new approach in the midst of the comprehensive situation that is being-in-the-world, the greenhouses of the inner-world illusion were shattered and the lodges of pure observation sank in the flood. The separated subject found itself demoted to Dasein and stripped of its theoretical privilege, namely its similarity to the observer gods. It was immersed anew in the sea of moods that open up and colour pre-logically the whole in which we reside. This brought to light once more how far the human being, as an 'organ' of existence, is disposed towards being-outside-oneself. Its mode of being is self-forfeiting, as it always already occurs as being-among-things and being-with others. In its spontaneous quality, the human being is a marionette of the collective and a hostage of situations. Only at the 'second reading', after the event and exceptionally, does Dasein return to itself and its possible mandate of self-being, and all attempts to elevate this later discovery to a first substance, a primal form, a world axis rising from the ego, show traces of subtle forgeries. Just as Proudhon declared, 'Whoever says "God" seeks to deceive', we can conclude from Heidegger: 'Whoever says "I" seeks to deceive themselves.' Through their symptomatic prematurity, these over-elevations of the self betray an interest in rescue from the torrential flow of time. Is it necessary to emphasize that the longing for rescue does not in itself prove the possibility of rescue?

The consequences of the shift are as unforeseeable as the conditions of the coming age, which, whatever else it might be, can only be referred to as the age 'after' this one. One observation, at least, does suggest itself: the re-secularization of the withdrawn subject did not fulfil the expectation that abstaining from imagined bliss directly contributes to physical or actual happiness. The reason for this can be found in Heidegger's description of the Dasein re-embedded in the worldly situation. The price for the new beginning of a thinking orientation from the position of being-in-the-world is inevitably a loss of distance, whose main symptom is the handing over of humans to concern and their immersion in the lived situation. Whoever turns the 'subject' back into 'Dasein' replaces the withdrawn with the included, the collected with the scattered, the immortalized with the de-immortalized,[198] the redeemed with the un-saved. What Heidegger calls concern [*Sorge*] is the concession of humans to the world that they cannot seal themselves off against its infiltration. The shore on which the observer wanted to establish themselves is not a genuine rescue. Factical existing is 'always also absorbed in the world of its concern'.[199] However it might attempt to protect and isolate itself – as *atman*, as the noetic psyche, as *Homo interior*, as an inhabitant of the inner citadel, as a soul spark, as an underlying subject, as a present ego, as a personality, as an intersection of archetypes, as a floating point of irony, as a critic of the context of delusion and as an observer of observers – its constitutive being-outside-itself in fact means that it is always already in the grip of concern; only the gods, and fools with them, are without concern in themselves. Dasein is colonized by worldlinesses from the start. Because it is always already absorbed in concern, it must draw up lists of priorities and work through them as if this were its innermost aim. Attempts to gain distance can never be more than secondary modifications of a self-delivering that anticipates everything else. The externalities Marcus Aurelius claimed stand outside our doors have, in reality, occupied the house. Its supposed master is possessed by the guests, and he can count himself lucky if they allow him a corner to which he can retreat.

Thus everything suggests that after three millennia of spiritual evasions, human existence has been taken back to the point where the secessions began, and is little the wiser for it – or at least, barely faces less difficulty. This impression is simultaneously correct and incorrect: correct in so far as the exuberance of surreal ascents, hungry for a world beyond, has neither stood the test of time nor stood up to analysis; and incorrect because the treasuries of practice knowledge are overflowing, despite being rarely frequented in recent times.

Now it is time to call to mind anew all those forms of the practising life that continue to release salutogenic energies, even where the over-elevations to metaphysical revolutions in which they were initially bound up have crumbled. Old forms must be tested for reusability and new forms invented. Another cycle of secessions may begin in order to lead humans out once again – if not out of the world, then at least out of dullness, dejection and obsession, but above all out of banality, which Isaac Babel termed the counter-revolution.

OUTLOOK

The Absolute Imperative

See what large letters I use as I write to you with my own hand!

Galatians 6:11

Who Is Allowed to Say It?

'You must change your life!' The voice Rilke heard speaking to him at the Louvre has meanwhile left its point of origin. Within a century, it has become part of the general zeitgeist – in fact, it has become the last content of all the communications whirring around the globe. At present, there is no information in the world ether that cannot be connected to this absolute imperative in its deep structure. It is the call that can never be neutralized into a mere statement of fact; it is the imperative whose effects are unhindered by any indicatives. It articulates the motto that arranges the innumerable chaotic particles of information into a concise moral form. It expresses concern for the whole. It cannot be denied: the only fact of universal ethical significance in the current world is the diffusely and ubiquitously growing realization that things cannot continue in this way.

Once again, we have reason to recall Nietzsche. It was he who first understood in which mode the ethical imperative must be conveyed in modern times: it speaks to us in the form of a command that sets up an unconditional overtaxing. In so doing, he opposed the pragmatic consensus that one can only demand of people what they are capable of achieving in the status quo. Nietzsche set the original axiom of the practising life against it in the form established since the irruption of ethical difference into conventional life forms: humans can only advance as long as they follow the impossible. The moderate decrees,

442

the reasonable prescriptions, the daily requirements – in all cases, their fulfilment presupposes a hyperbolic tension that stems from an unrealizable and inescapable demand. What is the human being if not an animal of which too much is demanded? Only those who set up the first commandment can subsequently present Ten Commandments In the first, the impossible itself speaks to me: thou shalt have no other standards next to me. Whoever has not been seized by the oversized does not belong to the species of *Homo sapiens*. The first hunter in the savannah was already a member; he raised his head and understood that the horizon is not a protective boundary, but rather the gate for the gods and the dangers to enter.

In order to articulate the current overtaxing in keeping with the state of the world, Nietzsche took the risk of presenting the public with 'a book for everyone and nobody' – a prophetic eruption, six thousand feet beyond mankind and time, spoken with no consideration for any listeners, and yet allied in an invasive fashion with each individual's knowledge of his intimate design for the not-yet. One cannot simply let the *Übermensch* programme rest if one knows that it stands for vertical tension in general. Its proclamation became necessary once there was no longer sufficient faith in the hypothesis of God to guarantee the anchoring of upwards-pulling tension in a transcendent pole. But even without God or the *Übermensch*, it is sufficient to note that every individual, even the most successful, the most creative and the most generous, must, if they examine themselves in earnest, admit that they have become less than their potentiality of being would have required – except for those moments in which they could say that they fulfilled their duty to be a good animal. As average *Über*-animals, tickled by ambitions and haunted by excessive symbols, humans fall short of what is demanded of them, even when they wear the winner's jersey or the cardinal's robe.

The statement 'You must change your life!' provides the basic form for the call to everyone and nobody. Although it is unmistakably directed at a particular addressee, it speaks to all others too. Whoever hears the call without defences will experience the sublime in a personally addressed form. The sublime is that which, by calling to mind the overwhelming, shows the observer the possibility of their engulfment by the oversized – which, however, is suspended until further notice. The sublime whose tip points to me is as personal as death and as unfathomable as the world. For Rilke, it was the Dionysian dimension of art that spoke to him from the disfigured statue of Apollo and gave him the feeling of encountering something infinitely superior.

Today, on the other hand, the authoritative voice can scarcely be heard in works of art. Nor do the established 'religions' or church councils possess any commanding authority, let alone the councils of wise men, assuming one can still use this phrase without irony.

The only authority that is still in a position to say 'You must change your life!' is the global crisis, which, as everyone has been noticing for some time, has begun to send out its apostles. Its authority is real because it is based on something unimaginable of which it is the harbinger: the global catastrophe. One need not be religiously musical to understand why the Great Catastrophe had to become the goddess of the century. As it possesses the aura of the monstrous, it bears the primary traits that were previously ascribed to the transcendent powers: it remains concealed, but makes itself known in signs; it is on the way, yet already authentically present in its portents; it reveals itself to individual intelligences in penetrating visions, yet also surpasses human understanding; it takes certain individuals into its service and makes prophets of them; its delegates turn to the people around them in its name, but are fended off as nuisances by most. On the whole, its fate is much like that of the God of monotheism when He entered the stage scarcely three thousand years ago: His mere message was already too great for the world, and only the few were prepared to begin a different life for His sake. In both cases, however, the refusal of the many increases the tension affecting the human collective. Since the global catastrophe began its partial unveiling, a new manifestation of the absolute imperative has come into the world, one that directs itself at everyone and nobody in the form of a sharp admonition: 'Change your life! Otherwise its complete disclosure will demonstrate to you, sooner or later, what you failed to do during the time of portents!'

Against this background, we can explain the origin of the unease in today's ethical debate, both in its academic and in its publicistic varieties. It stems from the discrepancy between the monstrosities that have been in the air since the Cold War era after 1945 and the paralysing harmlessness of all current discourses, whether their arguments draw on the ethics of attitude, responsibility, discourse or situations – to say nothing of the helpless reanimation of doctrines of value and virtue. Nor is the oft-cited return of 'religion' much more than the symptom of an unease that awaits its resolution in a lucid formulation. In reality, ethics can only be based on the experience of the sublime, today as much as since the beginning of the developments that led to the first ethical secessions. Driven by its call, the human race of two speeds began its campaign through the ages. Only the sublime is capable of setting up the overtaxing that enables humans to head for the impossible. What people called 'religion' was only ever significant as a vehicle of the absolute imperative in its different place- and time-based versions. The rest is the chatter of which Wittgenstein rightly said that it should be brought to an end.

For the theologically interested, this means that the one God and the catastrophe have more in common than was previously registered – not least their trouble with humans, who cannot rouse themselves to believe in either. There is not only what Coleridge called the 'willing suspension of disbelief' in the fiction whose absence would render aes- thetic behaviour impossible. An even more effective approach is the willing suspension of belief in the real whose absence would prevent any practical accommodation with the given situation. Individuals barely ever cope with reality without an additional element of de- realization. Incredulous de-realization, furthermore, makes little dis- tinction between the past and the future: whether the catastrophe is a past one from which one should have learned or an imminent one that could be averted by the right measures, the reluctance to believe always knows how to arrange things in such a way as to achieve the desired degree of de-realization.

Who Can Hear It?

When it comes to man-made catastrophes, the twentieth century was the most instructive period in world history. It demonstrated: the greatest disaster complexes came about in the form of projects that were meant to gain control of the course of history from a single centre of action. They were the most advanced manifestations of what philosophers, following Aristotle and Marx, called 'praxis'. In contemporary pronouncements, the great projects were described as manifestations of the final battle for world domination. Nothing happened to the humans of the age of praxis except what they or their fellow humans had instigated. Hence one could say: there is nothing in hell that has not previously appeared in programmes. The sorcerer's apprentices of planetary design were forced to learn that the unpredictable is an entire dimension ahead of any strategic calculus. Small wonder, then, if those good intentions did not rec- ognize themselves in the bad results. The rest was in line with psy- chological probability: the militant world-improvers withdrew from their self-induced debacles and attributed whatever was too much for them to disastrous fate. The most convincing interpretation of this behavioural pattern was penned by a sceptical philosopher: after fatal undertakings, the failed protagonists indulge in 'the art of not having been the one'.

Analogous patterns are at work in the run-up to the announced catastrophe: before fatal developments, the actors on the political stage demonstrate the art of not having understood the signs of the times. Western people have long been well rehearsed in this behaviour – one could call it universal procrastination – through deep-seated cultural practices: ever since the Enlightenment demoted God to a moral background radiation in the cosmos, or declared Him an outright fiction, the moderns have shifted the experience of the sublime from ethics to aesthetics. In accordance with the rules of the mass culture existing since the early nineteenth century, they internalized the belief that one survives merely imagined horrors completely unharmed. In their eyes, shipwrecks only ever occur for the viewers, and disasters only so that they can enjoy the pleasant feeling of having escaped. They conclude from this that all threats are simply part of the entertainment, and warnings an element of the show.

The return of the sublime in the shape of an ethical imperative that is not to be taken lightly catches the Western world – to leave aside all others – unawares. Its citizens have become accustomed to viewing all indications of imminent disaster presented in the tone of reality as a form of documentary horror genre, and its intellectuals are doing justice to their reputation as 'detached cosmopolitan spectators' by deconstructing even the most serious warnings as a discursive genre and portraying their authors as busybodies. But even if it were not an aesthetic genre, they would remain pragmatic in the belief that they could take their time taking the information seriously. Furthermore, surely someone who wished to take the signs on the horizon personally would immediately collapse under such worries?

Nonetheless, these contemporaries will ascertain sooner or later that there is no human right to non-overtaxing – any more than there is a right to encounter only such problems as one can overcome with on-board resources. It is a misunderstanding of the nature of the problematic if one only puts such matters in that category as have a prospect of being solved during the current term of office. And it shows an even greater misjudgement of the nature of vertical tensions in human existence if one assumes a symmetry between challenge and response. Overtaxing on one side, surpluses on the other – and no guarantee that the two go together like a problem and its solution.

Who Will Do It?

Whatever is undertaken in the future to confront the dangers identified, it is subject to the law of increasing improbability that dominates our overheated evolution. We can deduce from this observation why the socially conservative propaganda circulating between Rome, Washington and Fulda does not provide any suitable answer to the current world crisis – aside from possible constructive effects in smaller circles. For how should timeless 'values', which have already proved powerless and inadequate in the face of comparatively small problems, suddenly gain the necessary power to bring about a turn for the better when confronted with greater difficulties?

If the answer to the current challenges were genuinely to be found in the classic virtues, it would be sufficient to follow the maxim formulated by Goethe in his *Divan* poem 'The Bequest of the Ancient Persian Faith': 'Solemn duty's daily observation / More than this, it needs no revelation.' Even if one is willing to admit that this – beneath the oriental mask – is the greatest utterance of the European bourgeoisie before its historic failure, it is clear that we cannot be helped merely by a rule of preservation. Next to the indispensable concern for taking established traditions with us, after all, what impresses us most is the novelty of situations that demands bold answers. Even in Goethe's Weimar home, there would be more talk today of solemn duty's daily *invention*, before doing away with the adjective 'solemn' – firstly because it goes against the taste of the time, and secondly because something that is invented daily is not suitable for a solemn sense of duty. After further reflection, one would also remove the preceding noun and speak of tasks rather than duty. Finally, one would issue a statement with the impenetrable suggestion that the well-intentioned people in the Harmonious Society find a fruitful way of combining the old and the new. If one studies the instructions from Rome, one will note that they consist of equally inscrutable formulas.

The law of increasing improbability opens up the perspective of two overtaxings in one: what is happening on the earth at this moment is, on the one side, an actual integration disaster in progress – that of globalization, launched by Columbus' voyage in 1492, set moving by the Spanish conquest of the Aztec empire in 1521, accelerated by world trade between the seventeenth and nineteenth centuries, and driven along to the point of an effective synchronization of world events thanks to the quick media of the twentieth century. These synchronize the previously scattered factions of humanity – what we

447

call cultures – into an unstable collective torn by inequalities at a high level of transaction and collision. On the other side, a disintegration disaster is in progress, heading for a crash whose time is uncertain, but which cannot be delayed indefinitely. Of these two monstrosities, the second is far more probable, as it is located on the line of processes that are already under way. It is furthered above all by the conditions of production and consumption in the world's wealthy regions and developing zones, in so far as they are based on a blind overexploitation of finite resources. The reason of nations still extends no further than preserving jobs on the *Titanic*. The crash solution is also probable because it offers a large psychoeconomic price advantage: it would save us from the chronic tensions affecting us as a result of global evolution. Only happy minds experience the piling up of Mount Improbable to the heights of an operatively integrated world 'society' as a project that vitalizes its participants. They alone experience existence in the present as a stimulating privilege and would not want to have lived at any other time. Those with less cheerful natures have the impression that being-in-the-world has never been so tiring. What, then, could be more logical than the principle of mass culture: making entertainment the top priority, and accepting that as far as everything else is concerned, things will happen as they must?

It was the philosopher Hans Jonas who proved that the owl of Minerva does not always begin its flight at twilight. Through his remoulding of the categorical imperative into an ecological one, he demonstrated the possibility of a forward-looking philosophy for our times: 'Act in such a way that the effects of your actions can be reconciled with the permanence of true human life on earth.' Thus the metanoetic imperative for the present, which raises the categorical to the absolute, takes on sufficiently distinct contours for the present. It makes the harsh demand of embracing the monstrosity of the universal in its concretized form. It demands of us a permanent stay in the overtaxing-field of enormous improbabilities. Because it addresses everyone personally, I must relate its appeal to myself as if I were its only addressee. It demands that I act as if I could immediately know what I must achieve as soon as I consider myself an agent in the network of networks. At every moment, I am to estimate the effects of my actions on the ecology of the global society. It even seems that I am expected to make a fool of myself by identifying myself as a member of a seven-billion-person people – although my own nation is already too much for me. I am meant to stand my ground as a citizen of the world, even if I barely know my neighbours and neglect my friends. Though most of my new national comrades remain unreachable for me, because 'mankind' is neither a valid address nor a thing that can be encountered, I nonetheless have the mission of taking its real presence into consideration at every operation of my own. I am to develop into a fakir of coexistence with everyone and everything, and reduce my footprint in the environment to the trail of a feather.

The situation of overtaxing is fulfilled by these mandates as much as by the Old European *imitatio Christi* or the Indian *mokṣa* ideal. As there is no escaping this demand – except by fleeing into narcosis – one faces the question of whether one can describe a sensible motif with whose aid the gulf between the sublime imperative and the practical exercise can be bridged. Such a motif – if one leaves aside the phantoms of abstract universalism – can only be gained from a consideration of General Immunology. Immune systems are embodied or institutionalized expectations of injury and damage based on the distinction between the own and the foreign. While biological immunity applies to the level of the individual organism, the two social immune systems concern the supra-organismic, that is to say the co-operative, transactional, convivial dimensions of human existence: the solidaristic system guarantees legal security, provision for existence and feelings of kinship beyond one's own family; the symbolic system provides security of worldview, compensation for the certainty of death, and cross-generational constancy of norms. At this level too, the definition applies that 'life' is the success phase of an immune system. Like biological immune systems, the solidaristic and symbolic systems can also pass through phases of weakness, even near-failure. These express themselves in human self-experience and world-experience as an instability of value consciousness and an uncertainty as to the resilience of our solidarities. Their collapse is tantamount to collective death.

The strong hallmark of systems of this type is that they no longer define the own in terms of organismic egotism, but rather place themselves in the service of an ethnic or multi-ethnic, institutionally and intergenerationally expanded self-concept. This enables us to understand why evolutionary approaches to an animal-like altruism, which manifest themselves in the natural readiness for species to procreate and care for one's brood, develop among humans into cultural altruisms. The rationale for this development lies in the magnification of the own: what seems altruistic from the individual's perspective is actually egotism at the level of the larger unit; to the extent that individuals learn to act as agents of their local culture, they serve the wider own by making concessions in the narrower own. This implicit immunological calculus forms the basis of sacrifices and taxes, manners and services, asceticisms and virtuosities. All substantial cultural phenomena are part of the competitions between supra-biological immunitary units.

This reflection necessitates an expansion of the concept of immunity: as soon as one is dealing with life forms in which the *zoon politikón* man participates, one must reckon with the primacy of supra-individual immunity alliances. Under such conditions, individual immunity is only possible as co-immunity. All social organizations in history, from the primal hordes to the world empires, can, from a systemic perspective, be explained as structures of co-immunity. One finds, however, that the distribution of concrete immune advantages in large layered 'societies' has always shown considerable inequalities. The inequality of access to immune chances was already felt early on as the deepest manifestation of 'injustice'. It was either externalized as an obscure fate or internalized as a consequence of dark guilt. During the last millennia, such feelings could only be balanced out through supra-ethnic mental practice systems, *vulgo* the higher 'religions'. Through sublime imperatives and abstract universalizations of salvific promise, they kept the paths to equal symbolic immune opportunities open for all.

The current state of the world is characterized by the absence of an efficient co-immunity structure for the members of the 'global society'. At the highest level, 'solidarity' is still an empty word. Here, then as now, the dictum of a controversial constitutional law theorist applies: 'Whoever says "humanity" seeks to deceive.'[200] The reason for this is plain to see: the effective co-immunitary units, today as in ancient times, are formatted tribally, nationally and imperially, and recently also in regional strategic alliances, and function – assuming they do – according to the respective formats of the own–foreign difference. Successful survival alliances, therefore, are particular for the time being – in keeping with the nature of things, even 'world religions' cannot be more than large-scale provincialisms. Even 'world' is an ideological term in this context, as it hypostatizes the macro-egotism of the West and other major powers and does not describe the concrete co-immunitary structure of all survival candidates on the global stage. The subsystems still exist in mutual rivalry, following a logic that repeatedly turns the immune gains of some into the immune losses of others. Humanity does not constitute a super-organism, as some systems theorists prematurely claim; it is, for the time being, no more than an aggregate of higher-level 'organisms' which are by no means already integrated into an operational unity of the highest order.

All history is the history of immune system battles. It is identical to the history of protectionism and externalization. Protection always refers to a local self, and externalization to an anonymous environment for which no one takes responsibility. This history spans the period of human evolution in which the victories of the own could only be bought with the defeat of the foreign; it was dominated by the holy egotisms of nations and enterprises. Because 'global society' has reached its limit, however, and shown once and for all that the earth, with its fragile atmospheric and biospheric systems, is the limited shared site of human operations, the praxis of externalization comes up against an absolute boundary. From there on, a protectionism of the whole becomes the directive of immunitary reason. Global immunitary reason is one step higher than all those things that its anticipations in philosophical idealism and religious monotheism were capable of attaining. For this reason, General Immunology is the legitimate successor of metaphysics and the real theory of 'religions'. It demands that one transcend all previous distinctions between own and foreign; thus the classical distinctions of friend and foe collapse. Whoever continues along the line of previous separations between the own and the foreign produces immune losses not only for others, but also for themselves.

The history of the own that is grasped on too small a scale and the foreign that is treated too badly reaches an end at the moment when a global co-immunity structure is born, with a respectful inclusion of individual cultures, particular interests and local solidarities. This structure would take on planetary dimensions at the moment when the earth, spanned by networks and built over by foams, was conceived as the own, and the previously dominant exploitative excess as the foreign. With this turn, the concretely universal would become operational. The helpless whole is transformed into a unity capable of being protected. A romanticism of brotherliness is replaced by a co-operative logic. Humanity becomes a political concept. Its members are no longer travellers on the ship of fools that is abstract universalism, but workers on the consistently concrete and discrete project of a global immune design. Although communism was a conglomeration of a few correct ideas and many wrong ones, its reasonable part – the understanding that shared life interests of the highest order can only

451

be realized within a horizon of universal co-operative asceticisms – will have to assert itself anew sooner or later. It presses for a macrostructure of global immunizations: co-immunism.

Civilization is one such structure. Its monastic rules must be drawn up now or never; they will encode the forms of anthropotechnics that befit existence in the context of all contexts. Wanting to live by them would mean making a decision: to take on the good habits of shared survival in daily exercises.

NOTES

1 *Incende quod adorasti et adora quod incendisti*: according to the chronicle of Gregory of Tours, the bishop of Reims, *Remigius*, spoke these words while Clovis I, king of the Franks, convinced of Christ's hand in his victory, stepped into the baptismal font 'like another Constantine' after the Battle of Tolbiac.

2 Translator's note (henceforth: TN): the reference is to Thomas Mann, in *Tonio Kröger* (*Death in Venice, Tonio Kröger and Other Writings*, ed. Frederick Alfred Lubich [New York: Continuum, 1999], p. 12).

3 Reflections on the concept of practice can be found below in the sections on the discovery of pedagogy (pp. 197ff), the formation of habit (pp. 182ff), the *circulus virtuosus* (pp. 320ff), and in the first three sections of ch. 12 (pp. 404–11).

4 TN: this phrase refers to the apocryphal fourteenth-century Austrian bailiff (*Landvogt*) Albrecht Gessler, who ruled the town of Altdort in a tyrannical fashion. It is said that he raised a pole in the market square, and all who passed it were obliged to bow before it (William Tell's legendary archery task was a result of his refusal to do so). In contemporary German usage, it denotes an arbitrary postulate that is blindly obeyed.

5 Edward Herbert of Cherbury (1583–1648), author of *De Veritate* (1624), *De Religione Gentilium* and *De Religione Laici* (1645), can be considered the founding father of what was later termed 'philosophy of religion'.

6 A typical example is Oswald Spengler, who claims in *The Decline of the West* that Nietzsche's turn towards an awareness of life as art was symptomatic of a 'Climacteric of the Culture'. He saw in it an example of the decadence that characterizes the 'civilisatory' phase of cultures: during this, the sublime metaphysical worldviews degenerate into mere guides for individuals in their everyday and digestive worries. Oswald Spengler, *The Decline of the West*, trans. Charles Francis Atkinson (New York: Knopf, 1939), p. 359.

7 TN: the phrase 'life form' refers throughout the text to a form or way of life, not a living creature. The latter are usually termed 'organisms' here.

8 Concerning the legal system 'as society's immune system', see Niklas Luhmann, *Social Systems*, trans. John Bednarz Jr. (Palo Alto: Stanford University Press, 1995), pp. 374f.

9 Problems of this type are the domain of the new science of psychoneuroimmunology, which deals with the interplay of several systems of messenger substances (nervous system, hormone system, immune system).

10 Concerning the significance of cultural science for survival in the global context, see the section 'Outlook' below, pp. 442f.

11 See Peter Sloterdijk, 'Rules for the Human Zoo', trans. Mary Varney Rorty, *Environment and Planning D: Society and Space* 27 (1), pp. 12–28. The term was, incidentally, already in use during the heroic years of the Russian Revolution; it can be looked up in the third volume of the *Great Soviet Encyclopedia* of 1926, where it refers especially to speculatively anticipated possibilities of biotechnical manipulations of human genes.

12 The underlying dichotomy of self-improvement and world improvement is explained in ch. 3, where I discuss the increasing externalization of the metanoetic imperative in modernity.

13 TN: the word for 'humanities', *Geisteswissenschaften*, literally means 'sciences of the spirit'; hence the author implying that they are merely so-called, not genuine, sciences.

14 Carl Friedrich von Weizsäcker, *Der Garten des Menschlichen: Beiträge zur geschichtlichen Anthropologie* (Munich: Hanser, 1978).

15 Concerning extended parliamentarianism, see Bruno Latour and Peter Weibel (eds.), *Making Things Public: Atmospheres of Democracy* (Cambridge, MA: MIT Press, 2005), as well as Bruno Latour, *Politics of Nature: How to Bring the Sciences into Democracy*, trans. Catherine Porter (Cambridge, MA: Harvard University Press, 2004). On the general programme of civilizing cultures, see Bazon Brock, *Der Barbar als Kulturheld* (Cologne: DuMont, 2002).

16 See also below, pp. 164f.

17 See Thomas Macho, 'Neue Askese? Zur Frage nach der Aktualität des Verzichts', *Merkur* 54 (1994), pp. 583–93, in which, with reference to the culture-historically powerful alternative of satiation and hunger, the central distinction of full versus empty is examined.

18 Friedrich Nietzsche, *The Birth of Tragedy and Other Writings*, trans. Ronald Speirs (Cambridge: Cambridge University Press, 1999), p. 75.

19 The best example being Heinz-Theo Homann, *Das funktionale Argument: Konzepte und Kritik funktionslogischer Religionsbegründung* (Paderborn: Schöningh, 1997).

20 See Detlef Linke, *Religion als Risiko: Geist, Glaube und Gehirn* (Reinbek: Rowohlt, 2003).

21 See Dean Hamer, *The God Gene: How Faith Is Hard-Wired into Our Genes* (New York: Anchor, 2005).

THE PLANET OF THE PRACTISING

1 Paul Celan, in *Gesammelte Werke*, vol. 3 (Frankfurt: Suhrkamp, 1983), p. 181.

2 Wolfgang Brückle, *Von Rodin bis Baselitz: Der Torso in der Kunst der Moderne* (Ostfildern: Hatje Cantz, 2001).

3 Trans. Edward Snow, in *The Art of the Sonnet*, ed. Stephen Burt and David Mikics (Cambridge, MA: Harvard University Press, 2010), p. 230.

4 'People did not speak to him. Stones spoke', Rilke had already written in his essay on Rodin. Rainer Maria Rilke, *Werke*, vol. 3 [2]: *Prosa* (Frankfurt: Insel, 1980), p. 369.

5 Ibid., p. 359.

6 Written in February 1921, published posthumously in 1933.

7 See Beat Wyss, *Vom Bild zum Kunstsystem*, 2 vols. (Cologne: Walther König, 2006).

8 TN: the word *Reformhaus* refers to a health food shop.

9 See Aaron Antonovsky, *Unraveling the Mystery of Health* (San Francisco: Jossey-Bass, 1987).

10 Nietzsche, *The Genealogy of Morals*, trans. Horace Barnett Samuel (Mineola, NY: Dover, 2003), p. 84 (translation modified).

11 Ibid., p. 90.

12 Ibid., p. 100. These notes acted as a stimulus for Alfred Adler's individual-psychological approach to psychotherapy, where neurosis is defined as a costly means of securing the inferior's illusion of superiority.

13 A reminder: under pressure from the politically correct zeitgeist, the well-known initiative of the German disability society, 'Aktion Sorgenkind' [Operation Problem Child], founded in 1964, was renamed 'Aktion Mensch' [Operation Human Being] in March 2000.

14 Carl Hermann Unthan, *Das Pediskript: Aufzeichnungen aus dem Leben eines Armlosen, mit 30 Bildern* (Stuttgart: Lutz' Memoirenbibliothek, 1925), p. 73.

15 Ibid., p. 147.

16 Ibid., p. 97.

17 Ibid., p. 306.

18 Ibid., p. 307.

19 Ibid.

20 Ibid.

21 Ibid.

22 TN: another reference to *Tonio Kröger*, where the narrator characterizes gypsies as living 'in a green caravan' (p. 17).

23 Unthan, *Das Pediskript*, p. 72.

24 Nor is Würtz mentioned in the most significant recent study on the subject: Klaus E. Müller, *Der Krüppel: Ethnologia Passionis Humanae* (Munich: C. H. Beck, 1996).

25 H. Würtz, *Zerbrecht die Krücken: Krüppel-Probleme der Menschheit. Schicksalsstiefkinder aller Zeiten in Wort und Bild* (Leipzig: Leopold Voss, 1932), p. 101.

26 Ibid., p. 88.

27 Ibid., p. 97.

28 Ibid., p. 31.

29 Ibid., p. 4.

30 Ibid., p. 49.

31 Ibid., p. 11.

32 Ibid., p. 18.

33 The smaller-scale variety of the *Homo compensator* doctrine became known in Germany through the work of Joachim Ritter, Odo Marquard and Hermann Lübbe.

34 Ibid., p. 67.

35 Ibid., p. 37.

36 Thus the title [*Siegreiche Lebenskämpfer*] of an earlier book by Hans Würtz from 1919, when the problem of born cripples was somewhat overshadowed by that of war cripples.

37 Otto Perl, *Krüppeltum und Gesellschaft im Wandel der Zeit* (Gotha: Leopold Klotz, 1926).

38 Concerning the problematics of masters and trainers, see ch. 8, pp. 291f.

39 TN: the football coach Giovanni Trapattoni became particularly well known in Germany during the 1990s, as coach of Bayern Munich.

40 Würtz, *Zerbrecht die Krücken*, p. 50.

41 Ibid., p. 63.

42 Ibid., p. 34.

43 Ibid., p. 36.

44 These ideas are developed into a general theory of existence in insulated spaces in the third volume of my *Sphären* project. See *Sphären III. Schäume: Plurale Sphärologie* (Frankfurt: Suhrkamp, 2004), pp. 309–500.

45 Peter Schneider, *Erhinken und erfliegen: Psychoanalytische Zweifel an der Vernunft* (Göttingen: Vandenhoeck & Ruprecht, 2001).

46 Edmund Husserl, *The Crisis of European Sciences and Transcendental Phenomenology*, trans. David Carr (Evanston, IL: Northwestern University Press, 1970).

47 Nietzsche, *Thus Spoke Zarathustra: A Book for Everyone and Nobody*, trans. Graham Parkes (Oxford and New York: Oxford University Press, 2005), p. 18.

48 Ibid.

49 See Reiner Stach, *Kafka: The Decisive Years*, trans. Shelley Frisch (New York: Houghton Mifflin Harcourt, 2005).

50 *The Zürau Aphorisms of Franz Kafka*, trans. Michael Hofmann, ed. Roberto Calasso (New York: Knopf Doubleday, 2006), p. 3.

51 These disclosures, which amount to the uncovering of a doping fraud, are laid out by Sergio Luzzatto in his book *Miracoli e Politica nell'Italia del Novecento* (Turin: Einaudi, 2007). See Dirk Schümer, 'Ein Säurenheiliger', *Frankfurter Allgemeine Zeitung*, 26 October 2007.

52 Franz Kafka, *The Complete Stories*, trans. Nahum Norbert Glatzer (New York: Schocken, 1995), p. 251.

53 Ibid., p. 258.

54 Ibid.

55 Ibid., p. 259.

56 See the descriptions of the first two modules on pp. 23ff. above.

57 Concerning Tertullian, see pp. 205f. below.

58 In *Biographia Literaria* (1817). According to the author, this act creates 'poetic faith'.

59 Kafka, *The Complete Stories*, p. 268 (translation modified).

60 Ibid.

61 Ibid., p. 271.

62 Ibid., p. 276.

63 Ibid.
64 Ibid., p. 277.
65 Concerning the ascetic revolt against hunger, see pp. 416f. below.
66 TN: 'enlightenment' written in lower case should be considered synonymous with illumination, *satori*.
67 The metaphor is misleading, as it is based on the confusion of oral and pre-oral searching intentions. The central distinction that applies to the hungry world, that of empty versus full, does not cover the whole field of searching: for the most spiritually demanding among them, the distinction between homeostatic-beyond-concern and restless-in-concern is a more applicable one.
68 With the combination of hunger genocide policies, forced collectivization and kulak persecution, Stalin's policies led to some 14 million deaths between 1929 and 1936 alone.
69 Nietzsche, *Beyond Good and Evil*, in *Basic Writings of Nietzsche*, trans. Walter Kaufmann (New York: Modern Library, 2000), p. 271.
70 Nietzsche, *The Genealogy of Morals*, p. 100.
71 Emile Cioran, *Cahiers, 1957–1972* (Paris: Gallimard, 1997), p. 14.
72 Quoted in Bernd Mattheus, *Cioran: Portrait eines radikalen Skeptikers* (Berlin: Matthes & Seitz, 2007), p. 83.
73 Cioran, *Cafard: Originaltonaufnahmen 1974–1990*, ed. Thomas Knoefel and Klaus Sander, with an afterword by Peter Sloterdijk (audio CD) (Cologne: supposé, 1998).
74 Bernd Mattheus, *Cioran*, p. 130.
75 Cioran, *A Short History of Decay*, trans. Richard Howard (London: Quartet, 1990), p. 168.
76 See Robert Spaemann, *Das unsterbliche Gerücht: Die Frage nach Gott und die Täuschung der Moderne* (Stuttgart: Klett-Cotta, 2007).
77 I would like to remind the reader *en passant* of the three aforementioned modules of religioid inner operation: the assertion of a subject in the location of the thing; the assumption of a metamorphosis that enables the latter to 'appear' in the former; the modal positing by which the possibility of a matter follows from its impossibility. The fourth module mentioned here is the genuinely artiste-like one. It can be applied both to notions of artistic perfection and to the ideals of holiness. The fifth module consists in calling to mind the overwhelming; that is, in the inner operations with which one meditates upon the destructibility of one's own existence and its engulfment by the oversized. This is discussed further on pp. 332f below.
78 See ch. 7 below.
79 He sometimes defines clear-sightedness as a 'vaccine against the absolute', though not without admitting that he occasionally succumbs to the first available mystery. See Cioran, *All Gall Is Divided*, trans. Richard Howard (New York: Arcade, 1999) p. 97.
80 Bernd Mattheus, *Cioran*, p. 210.
81 Ibid., p. 219.
82 Cioran, *All Gall Is Divided*, p. 95.
83 See Cioran, *Entretiens avec Sylvie Jaudeau* (Paris: Librairie José Corti, 1990).
84 See pp. 54f above, as well as ch. 8, pp. 291f.
85 I remind the reader of the hypothesis discussed in the introduction (pp. 8f)

that humans have not one immune system but three, with the religious complex located almost entirely in the functional circle of the third.

86 Cioran, *All Gall Is Divided*, p. 92.

87 TN: the word *Angebot* both means 'offer' and 'supply', especially in the phrase *Angebot und Nachfrage* ('supply and demand'). It is usually translated as 'supply' in this section, but sometimes 'offer' has been used to stress the gesture of giving implicit in the German word.

88 In his aforementioned essay ('Neue Askese?'), Thomas Macho argues that Catholic Christianity is essentially a 'hunger religion' organized around the question: what fills people?

89 This would mean that Protestantism is no longer a 'hunger religion' but a 'fitness religion', a spiritual surplus for the sated.

90 See Karl Barth, *Die Theologie Schleiermachers: Vorlesung Göttingen Wintersemester 1923/24*, ed. Dietrich Ritschl (Zurich: Theologischer Verlag, 1978). Here the author derides his favourite enemy as a parliamentarian with a white flag in his hand, speaking to the educated *about* religion instead of declaring himself a Christian (p. 438). There is noticeable contempt when he quotes Schleiermacher's definition of being a Christian: seeking 'the utter lightness and constancy of pious excitements', and clear sarcasm when he quotes Schleiermacher's early characterization of himself as a 'virtuoso of religion', presenting him as a cross between Paganini and Jeremiah. Concerning Schleiermacher's definition of religion, see pp. 333f below.

91 After the Middle Ages had only spoken of *religio* to refer to the virtue of believers and the life form of professional ascetics in the holy orders, the Reformation introduced the word 'religion' to brand Catholicism a falsification of the 'true religion'. The Enlightenment finally generalized the concept of 'religion' to give a reasonable order to the tangle of confessions that culminated in the Thirty Years War, and the multitude of cults reported by seamen. Before 'religion' could be declared a private matter, it had to be generalized into an anthropological constant and defined as a natural talent.

92 François-Alphonse Aulard, *Le culte de la Raison et le culte de L'Etre Suprême (1793–1794)* (Paris: Alcan, 1892).

93 De Coubertin occasionally refers to Olympism as a *ruskianisme sportif*.

94 See Walter Borger, 'Vom "World's Fair" zum olympischen Fair Play – Anmerkungen zur Vor- und Entwicklungsgeschichte zweier Weltfeste', in *Internationale Einflüsse auf die Wiedereinführung der Olympischen Spiele durch Pierre de Coubertin*, ed. Stephan Wassong (Kassel: Agon, 2005), pp. 125f.

95 Pierre de Coubertin, *Olympism: Selected Writings*, ed. Norbert Müller (Lausanne: International Olympic Committee, 2000), p. 319.

96 See Sloterdijk, *Sphären III*, pp. 626–46: 'Die Kollektoren: Zur Geschichte der Stadion-Renaissance'.

97 Concerning the phenomenon of gods of the moment, see Hermann Usener, *Götternamen: Versuch einer Lehre von der religiösen Begriffsbildung* (Frankfurt: Klostermann, 2000), pp. 279f.

98 See pp. 406f below.

99 De Coubertin, *Olympism*, p. 201.

100 Ibid., p. 405 (translation modified).

101 Willi Daume, foreword to the German edition of de Coubertin's memoirs, in *Olympische Erinnerungen* (Frankfurt and Berlin: Ullstein, 1996), p. 10.

102 See Hermann Cohen, *Religion of Reason out of the Sources of Judaism*, trans. Simon Kaplan (New York: F. Ungar, 1972); Mark Lilla recently described the modern religion of reason as the cult of a stillbirth in *The Stillborn God: Religion, Politics and the Modern West* (New York: Vintage, 2008).

103 Karl Marx and Friedrich Engels, *Werke*, vol. 1 (Berlin: Akademie, 1976), p. 544.

104 As demonstrated by a number of Bible theme parks in the USA.

105 Documents whose authenticity we have no reason to doubt show that in 1943, while serving in the navy as an office worker, he suffered from psychotic states in the form of severe depressions with suicidal tendencies, which led him to file a request for treatment with an army medical authority. Allegedly he was severely wounded by a grenade shortly before the war's end, was temporarily blinded, but healed himself. No details are known about his convalescence or methods of self-treatment, but they are said to have contributed to his conviction that the mind forms matter. A report authored by Australian specialists from the 1960s confirms Hubbard's presentiments: it attests to an abnormal personality structure with strong paranoid and schizophrenic traits.

106 Gotthard Günther, 'Seele und Maschine', in *Beiträge zur Grundlegung einer operationsfähigen Dialektik*, vol. 1 (Hamburg: Meiner, 1976), pp. 75f.

107 It is not an absolute debut, however, as is shown by analogous, often more brilliant projects in the avant-garde movements of the Russian Revolution, especially the writings of the Immortalists and Biocosmists. See *Die Neue Menschheit: Biopolitische Utopien in Russland zu Beginn des 20. Jahrhunderts*, ed. Boris Groys and Michael Hagemeister in collaboration with Anne von der Heiden (Frankfurt: Suhrkamp, 2005). In addition, they can be taken as proof that communism, for its part, was a form of applied social science fiction.

108 The Church of Scientology is only an anachronism in one aspect: it repeats the historically overcome forms of compulsory membership in a cult collective, indeed takes them so far that the organization virtually consumes its members cannibalistically. On the open market, by contrast, the 'religious experience' has itself become a kind of event commodity or consumable special effect.

109 The phrase 'politics fiction' has been used in a different context by Philippe Lacoue-Labarthe, in *Heidegger, Art, and Politics: The Fiction of the Political*, trans. Chris Turner (Oxford: Blackwell, 1990).

110 See Dana Goodyear, 'Château Scientology: Inside the Church's Celebrity Center', *New Yorker*, 14 January 2008.

111 In 1979, L. Ron Hubbard himself was convicted of fraud *in absentia* by a French court and sentenced to four years in prison. The FBI also found incriminating information in the sect's financial records; Hubbard's wife was sentenced to several years in prison in the USA during the 1970s.

112 Concerning the role of pseudo-transcendence in the modern art system, see Heiner Mühlmann, *Countdown: 3 Generationen* (Vienna and New York: Springer, 2008).

113 See Gotthard Günther, *Die amerikanische Apokalypse*, ed. and intr. Kurt Klagenfurt (Munich and Vienna: Profil, 2000), p. 277.

114 See John Carter, *Sex and Rockets: The Occult World of Jack Parsons* (Los Angeles: Feral House, 2005).

1 I made provisional reference to the enclosure constituted by the culture of writing, and its opening via post-literary techniques, in 1997 using the metaphor *Menschenpark* [human zoo].

2 See the section 'Remote View of the Ascetic Planet' above, pp. 29–39.

3 Nietzsche, *Thus Spoke Zarathustra: A Book for Everyone and Nobody*, trans. Graham Parkes (Oxford and New York: Oxford University Press, 2005), pp. 60f.

4 It was presumably to avoid such semantic baggage that Gregory Stock, one of the promoters of human genetic engineering in the USA, presented his vision under the title *Metaman: The Merging of Humans and Machines into a Global Superorganism* (New York: Doubleday, 1993).

5 TN: 'onward propagation' is a literal rendering of *Fortpflanzung*, which is the standard term for procreation; Nietzsche was modifying a common word rather than presenting two idiosyncratic phrases.

6 See Terrence W. Deacon, *The Symbolic Species: The Co-Evolution of Language and the Brain* (New York and London: Norton, 1998).

7 Jean Genet, 'The Funambulists', trans. Bernard Frechtman, *Evergreen Review* 32 (April–May 1964), p. 47.

8 TN: the German word *Prominenz* is most often used with reference to celebrities, so its connotations are somewhat more media-related than those of its English cognate.

9 TN: 'being there' and 'being up there' correspond in this case to *Dasein* and *da oben sein*.

10 See Deacon, *The Symbolic Species*, pp. 325–51.

11 Nietzsche, *Thus Spoke Zarathustra*, p. 180.

12 Richard Dawkins, *Climbing Mount Improbable* (New York and London: Norton, 1996).

13 TN: the connection is more obvious in German, as the word for 'survival' is *Überleben*.

14 Dawkins, *Climbing Mount Improbable*, p. 236.

15 From this moment on, the metaphysical misinterpretation of slowness, its consignment to the realm of transcendence, can be abandoned. See Heiner Mühlmann, 'The Economics Machine', in *5 Codes: Architecture, Paranoia and Risk in Times of Terror*, ed. Gerd de Bruyn (Basle, Boston and Berlin: Birkhäuser, 2006), p. 228. See also Peter Sloterdijk, *God's Zeal: The Battle of the Three Monotheisms*, trans. Wieland Hoban (Cambridge: Polity, 2009), pp. 5–7.

16 Concerning the take-off of innovation affirmation in the European Renaissance, see pp. 334f below.

17 Nietzsche, *Thus Spoke Zarathustra*, p. 181.

18 Nietzsche, *Will to Power*, ed. Walter Kaufmann, trans. Walter Kaufman and R. J. Hollingdale (New York: Vintage, 1968), p. 483.

19 Ibid.

20 Moroccan circus troupes also have a famous pyramid tradition, in which up

to fifteen artistes form towers of five or six 'storeys'. Catalan artistes are famous for erecting human pyramids with up to eight or nine storeys. The Canadian Cirque du Soleil has even featured tightrope-walking pyramids.

21 The grammatical comparative stands for a logical superlative of the adjective *deinon*, which was used in rhetoric to refer to the wonderful and alarming (*mirabile*). Heidegger modernized the translation tradition by giving the word back its meaning with his choice of *unheimlich* [uncanny] – which permits numerous connections to the discourses of philosophical topology, psychoanalysis, architectural theory and systems irritation theory.

22 Concerning the motif of city-overstepping and over-giftedness, see Peter Sloterdijk, 'Die Stadt und ihr Gegenteil: Apolitologie im Umriss', in *Der ästhetische Imperativ: Schriften zur Kunst*, ed. Peter Weibel (Hamburg: Philo Fine Arts, 2007), pp. 221–4.

23 Scheler's astute term was later taken over by the speech therapy based on the work of Victor Frankl (Frankl himself used it from 1938 onwards) and twisted into a retort against the methods of Freud et al. – in line with the solid paternal maxim that complicated people should do more and think less; assistance in doing more is here called 'healing', and assistance in thinking less 'de-reflection'.

24 TN: all biblical quotations are taken from the New International Version.

25 See Thomas Macho, 'Himmlisches Geflügel – Betrachtungen zu einer Motivgeschichte der Engel', in *Engel: Legenden der Gegenwart*, ed. Cathrin Pichler (Vienna and New York: Springer, 1997), pp. 83–100.

26 See Giorgio Agamben, *Il Regno e la Gloria* (Vicenza: Neri Pozza, 2007).

27 Nietzsche, *Thus Spoke Zarathustra*, p. 21.

28 As well as this, Nietzsche coined some twenty other terms with the prefix *über-*.

29 TN: again, all words with the prefixes 'super-' or 'over-' listed here begin with *über-* in German.

30 Even Martin Luther still saw the Areopagite as his enemy, the trainer of ecclesiastical high acrobatics. In his early writings he sought to co-opt him for his own simplistic mysticism of darkness, inspired by the *Theologia Germanica*: 'Unde in Dionysio frequens verbum est hyper quia super omnem cogitatum oportet simpliciter in caliginem entrare.' Later he understood that Pseudo-Dionysius was not concerned with a quick entrance into pious darkness, but with a higher-order logic created for virtuosos of religion that bore firm marks of exclusivity. From that point on, Luther had a horror of the founder of negative theology, and viewed him more as a Platonist than a Christian. See Thomas Reinhuber, *Studien zu Luthers Bekenntnis am Ende von De Servo Arbitrio* (Berlin: de Gruyter, 2000), p. 102. A word like 'hyper-Marxism', by contrast, which Foucault coined to describe French ideology in the 1960s and 1970s, was always satirically intended.

31 See Ernst Benz, 'Das Bild des Übermenschen in der Europäischen Geistesgeschichte', in *Der Übermensch: Eine Diskussion*, ed. Ernst Benz (Stuttgart: Rhein-Verlag, 1961), pp. 21–161.

32 This would be no simple task: for antiquity, because we have enough information about the gymnastic and agonal disciplines to appreciate the immensity of the manifestations of athletism, but too little to put together an authentic picture; and for the Middle Ages, because the history of

monasticism exceeds the capacity of any descriptive attempt in its breadth and its wealth of details.

33 Hugo Ball, *Byzantinisches Christentum: Drei Heiligenleben*, ed. Bernd Wacker (Göttingen: Wallstein, 2010), p. 271.

34 Peter Sloterdijk, *Rage and Time*, trans. Mario Wenning (New York: Columbia University Press, 2010).

35 Ludwig Wittgenstein, *Culture and Value*, ed. G. H. von Wright, trans. Peter Winch (Oxford: Blackwell, 1980), p. 83e (translation modified). See Thomas Macho, '"Kultur ist eine Ordensregel": Zur Frage nach der Lesbarkeit von Kulturen als Texten', in Gerhard Neumann and Sigrid Weigel (eds.), *Lesbarkeit der Kultur: Literaturwissenschaft zwischen Kulturtechnik und Ethnographie* (Munich: Fink, 2000), pp. 223–44.

36 Eckhard Nordhofen, *Der Engel der Bestreitung: Über das Verhältnis von Kunst und negativer Theologie* (Würzburg: Echter, 1993), p. 144.

37 Paul Engelmann, *Ludwig Wittgenstein: Briefe und Begegnungen* (Vienna and Munich: Oldenbourg, 1970), p. 32.

38 Wittgenstein, *Culture and Value*, p. 84e.

39 Allan Janik and Stephen Toulmin, *Wittgenstein's Vienna* (New York: Simon & Schuster, 1973), p. 236 (translation modified).

40 Wittgenstein, *Culture and Value*, p. 10e.

41 Ibid., p. 33e.

42 Ibid., pp. 34e–35e.

43 Ibid., p. 76e.

44 See Macho, 'Kultur ist eine Ordensregel', p. 229.

45 Janik and Toulmin, *Wittgenstein's Vienna*, p. 99.

46 Ibid.

47 Karl Kraus, 'Nachts' (1919), in Burkhardt Rukschcio (ed.), *Für Adolf Loos* (Vienna: Locker, 1986), p. 27.

48 Wittgenstein, *Culture and Value*, p. 27e.

49 Ibid., p. 12e (translation modified). Concerning the relationship between Wittgenstein and Socratic teaching, see Agnese Grieco, *Die ethische Übung: Ethik und Sprachkritik bei Wittgenstein und Sokrates* (Berlin: Lukas, 1996).

50 Wittgenstein, *Culture and Value*, p. 56e.

51 Ibid., p. 77e.

52 See pp. 78f above.

53 Wittgenstein, *Culture and Value*, p. 7e.

54 *The Rule of Saint Benedict*, ed. and trans. Leonard Joseph Doyle (Collegeville, MN: Liturgical Press, 2001), p. 25.

55 See n. 30 above.

56 Michel Foucault, 'The Masked Philosopher', in *Politics, Philosophy, Culture: Interviews and Other Writings 1977–1984*, ed. Lawrence D. Kritzman (London and New York: Routledge, 1990), p. 324.

57 Foucault, 'Dream, Imagination and Existence', in Michel Foucault and Ludwig Binswanger, *Dream and Existence*, ed. Keith Hoeller (Atlantic Highlands, NJ: Humanities Press, 1993), p. 53.

58 Ibid., p. 54.

59 Ibid., p. 55.

60 Ibid., p. 62.

61 Ibid., p. 69.

62 The *locus classicus* for this is Augustine, XXXIX, 72: 'Do not go outside. Return within yourself, for truth dwells in the interior man. If you find that your interior nature is mutable, then transcend yourself too [*transcende et te ipsum*]. But remember that when you transcend yourself, you must even transcend yourself as a reasoning self [*Sed memento cum te transcendis, ratiocinantem animam te transcendere*].'

63 TN: the original phrase for 'going beyond oneself' is *über sich hinausgehen*; it thus uses the same word, *über*, that elsewhere means 'over'. In this particular paragraph, 'beyond' is used briefly for the sake of congruence.

64 See Jacques Lacarrière, *L'envol d'Icare suivi de Traité des Chutes* (Paris: Seghers, 1993).

65 Concerning height fantasies in general, see Gaston Bachelard, *Air and Dreams: An Essay on the Imagination of Movement*, trans. Edith and Frederick Farell (Dallas: Dallas Institute for Humanities and Culture, 1988).

66 Michel Foucault, *Remarks on Marx: Conversations with Duccio Trombadori*, trans. R. James Goldstein and James Cascaito (New York: Semiotext(e), 1991), p. 173. TN: the second sentence is not included in the English edition, but appears in the German translation cited by Sloterdijk.

67 Ibid., p. 31.

68 Ibid., p. 171.

69 Michel Foucault, *The History of Sexuality*, vol. 2: *The Use of Pleasure*, trans. Robert Hurley (New York: Vintage, 1990), p. 11.

70 Wittgenstein, *Culture and Value*, p. 72e.

71 Ibid., p. 56e.

72 Michel Foucault, 'The Return of Morality', interview with Gilles Barbedette and André Scala, in *Politics, Philosophy, Culture*, p. 249.

73 Foucault, *Remarks on Marx*, p. 174.

74 See Foucault's allusion to the builder Solness in his introduction to *Dream and Existence* (quoted above, p. 150). I do not know whether Foucault had read Binswanger's book *Henrik Ibsen und das Problem der Selbstrealisation in der Kunst* (Heidelberg: Lambert Schneider, 1949).

75 This is a key term in Gaston Bachelard's work *Air and Dreams*.

76 Ludwig Binswanger, *Drei Formen missglückten Daseins: Verstiegenheit, Verschrobenheit, Manieriertheit* (Tübingen: Niemeyer, 1956), p. 6.

77 Ibid., p. 4.

78 Martin Heidegger, 'Letter on Humanism', trans. Frank A. Capuzzi with J. Glenn Gray, in *Basic Writings*, ed. David Farrell Krell (San Francisco: Harper & Row, 1977), p. 233.

79 Ibid., p. 234.

80 Admittedly, Heidegger's rendition of *daímon* in the singular as 'God' is supported by the synonymy – since Homer – between *daímon* and *theos*. In the present context, however, this translation does not strike me as very plausible.

81 Plato, *Republic*, trans. John Llewelyn Davies and David James Vaughan (Ware: Wordsworth Classics, 1997), p. 126.

82 The ontological and theological variations on this political psychology are: as in being, so in the city, and as in heaven, so on earth.

83 Prophetic divination, divinely inspired healing, the poetic madness (*manía*) fuelled by the muses, and the love sent by the gods (see *Phaedrus* i 244a–245b).

84 These passions were still described as demons – albeit only metaphorically – by Dio Chrysostom (second century AD), whose account of the quarrel between Diogenes and Alexander is described at length by Foucault in *Six Lectures on Discourse and Truth* (1983, at www.lib.berkeley.edu/MRC/foucault/parrhesia.html, accessed 14 May 2012). See Plutarch, *On the Daimonion of Socrates*, ed. Heinz-Günther Nesselrath (Tübingen: Mohr Siebeck, 2010), p. 61, which describes the recycling of the *daímones* in the beyond.

85 St Augustine, *Of True Religion*, ed. Louis O. Mink, trans. John H. S. Burleigh (Washington, DC: Regnery Gateway, 1991), p. 75.

86 Thomas à Kempis, *The Imitation of Christ*, trans. Aloysius Croft and Harold Bolton (Mineola, NY: Dover, 1983), p. 18.

87 Fragment 5.

88 Concerning the suspension of the liaison between thought and waking in nineteenth- and twentieth-century anaesthetic practice, see pp. 380f below.

89 Oswald Spengler, *The Decline of the West*, trans. Charles Francis Atkinson (New York: Knopf, 1939), pp. 4ff.

90 See Pupul Jayakar, *J. Krishnamurti: A Biography* (London: Arkana, 1986).

91 Carl Friedrich von Weizsäcker, *Zeit und Wissen* (Munich: Hanser, 1992).

92 Binswanger, *Henrik Ibsen*, p. 48.

93 Ibid., p. 50.

94 Nietzsche, *Thus Spoke Zarathustra*, p. 16.

95 See Slavoj Žižek, *In Defense of Lost Causes* (London and New York: Verso, 2009), ch. 9, 'Unbehagen in der Natur'.

96 Erwin Panofsky, *Gothic Architecture and Scholasticism* (New York: Meridian, 1957).

97 The significance of habit as a starting point for ever more shifts within the system of our constituted faculties is highlighted especially by the French philosopher Félix Ravaison. See Ravaisson, *Of Habit*, trans. and intr. Clare Carlisle and Mark Sinclair (London and New York: Continuum, 2008).

98 This is precisely what the modern ethics of obligation rejects. The decisiveness with which Kant shifted from the concern for skill to pure obligation in his ethics is shown, among other things, by his rejection of the idea of a habitus that assists the performance of duty. For then virtue would be 'a mere mechanism of applying power. Rather, virtue is *moral strength* in adherence to one's duty, which never should become habit but should always emerge entirely new and original from one's way of thinking.' Immanuel Kant, *Anthropology from a Pragmatic Point of View*, trans. Robert B. Louden (Cambridge: Cambridge University Press, 2006), p. 38. If man can only be rescued by duty, all help from one's disposition or inclination falls by the wayside.

99 Genet, 'The Funambulists', p. 47: 'It is not you who will dance, but the rope.'

100 See Norbert Bolz, *Die Konformisten des Andersseins: Ende der Kritik* (Munich: Fink, 1999).

101 Jean-Paul Sartre, *Being and Nothingness: An Essay on Phenomenological Ontology* (London: Routledge, 1969), p. 591.

102 Karl Jaspers, *The Origin and Goal of History*, trans. Michael Bullock (New Haven: Yale University Press, 1953), p. 4.

103 See Manfred Osten, *'Alles veloziferisch' oder Goethes Entdeckung der*

Langsamkeit (Frankfurt: Insel, 2003). This word, coined by Goethe, points to the fact that from the start of the nineteenth century, a second overtaking process began in which non-scriptural pacemakers left behind the classical script-based *humanitas*. Humanists cannot see that the latter, from the perspective of pre-literate life forms, had itself already constituted a devilish acceleration. See also Peter Sloterdijk, 'Rules for the Human Zoo', trans. Mary Varney Rorty, *Environment and Planning D: Society and Space* 27 (1), pp. 12–28.

104 TN: the proximity of passion and suffering is especially close in German, where the word for the former, *Leidenschaft*, is based on that for the latter, *leiden*.

105 See Babette Babich, 'Die Naturgeschichte der griechischen Bronze im Spiegel des Lebens: Betrachtungen über Heideggers ästhetische Phänomenologie und Nietzsches agonale Politik', in *Internationales Jahrbuch für Hermeneutik*, vol. 7, ed. Günter Figal (Tübingen: Mohr Siebeck, 2008), pp. 127–90.

106 Concerning the difference between conversion and opportunistic turnaround, see below, ch. 9, pp. 298f.

107 See recently Dieter Henrich, *Denken und Selbstsein: Vorlesungen über Subjektivität* (Frankfurt: Suhrkamp, 2007).

108 See the motto of *Poetry and Truth*: *Ho mé dareis anthrópos ou paideuetai*, meaning 'The man who is not mistreated is not educated.'

109 See Peter Sloterdijk, 'Der andere Logos oder: Die List der Vernunft. Zur Ideengeschichte des Indirekten', in Achim Hecker, Klaus Kammerer, Bernd Schauenberg and Harro von Senger (eds.), *Regel und Abweichung: Strategie und Stratageme. Chinesische Listenlehre im interdisziplinären Dialog* (Münster: LIT, 2008), pp. 87–112.

110 As well as pedagogical training through enlightened repetitions, a technique that cultures have always also had at their disposal is training via terror, or the imprinting of a norm by branding a sacred scene on the psyche through shock. See Heiner Mühlmann, *Jesus überlistet Darwin* (Vienna and New York: Springer, 2007), in which the author shows how the memoactive fitness of a collective can be increased through killing dramas (sacrifices) that are carried out together. In the light of this analysis, the Christian mass appears as a double conditioning form: on the one hand a constantly repeated killing drama, and on the other hand a rehearsing of the blood sacrifice's replacement by the symbolic game.

111 This is the inversion of Seneca's satirical statement *non vitae, sed scholae discimus* [we are learning not for life, but for the school] (*Epistolae morales ad Lucilium* 106, 12), with which he declares that the decadence of the school constitutes the system of learning. The true school programme, the learning of the divine, must therefore be copied onto other media, for example the philosopher's correspondence with a younger friend. It is therefore likely that Seneca was inverting an older, undocumented saying – which would make the return of the medieval schoolmasters to the version *non scholae sed vitae discimus* entirely justified.

112 *Plato's Euthyphro, Apology, Crito, and Phaedo*, trans. Benjamin Jowett (Millis, MA: Agora, 2005), p. 62.

113 Klaus Berger, *Theologiegeschichte des Urchristentums: Theologie des Neuen Testaments* (Tübingen and Basle: Francke, 1994), p. 661.

114 Alexander Kluge, *Tür an Tür mit einem anderen Leben: 350 neue Geschichten* (Frankfurt: Suhrkamp, 2006), pp. 341f.
115 Tertullian, *Disciplinary, Moral and Ascetical Works*, trans. Rudolph Arbesmann, Sister Emily Joseph Daly and Edwin A. Quain (Washington, DC: CUA Press, 1959), p. 20.
116 Ibid., p. 23.
117 Tertullian, *On the Flesh of Christ*, trans. Peter Holmes (Whitefish, MT: Kessinger, 2004), p. 12.
118 Simone Weil, *Gravity and Grace*, trans. Emma Crawford and Marion von der Ruhr (London and New York: Routledge, 2002).
119 See Harold Bloom, *The American Religion: The Emergence of the Post-Christian Nation* (New York: Simon & Schuster, 1992).
120 Wittgenstein, *Culture and Value*, p. 84e.

II EXAGGERATION PROCEDURES

1 See Hannah Arendt, *The Human Condition* (Chicago and London: Chicago University Press, 1998). For a critical response to this from a student of Arendt, see Richard Sennett, *The Craftsman* (London: Allen Lane, 2008); see also p. 292 below.
2 See pp. 163f. above.
3 Paul Rabbow, *Seelenführung: Methodik der Exerzitien in der Antike* (Munich: Kösel, 1954), based on Epictetus, *The Enchiridion*, 3. One finds the same motif in Marcus Aurelius, *The Meditations*, book 11, ch. 34.
4 Albert Schweitzer, *Indian Thought and Its Development*, trans. Mrs Charles E. B. Russell (Boston: Beacon, 1960), p. 110.
5 Patanjali, Yoga Sutra II, 41.
6 Nietzsche, *The Gay Science*, trans. Walter Kaufmann (New York: Vintage, 1974), p. 245.
7 Marcus Aurelius, *The Meditations*, trans. G. M. A. Grube (Indianapolis: Hackett, 1983), p. 124.
8 See Jürgen Hasse, *Übersehene Räume: Zur Kulturgeschichte und Heterotopologie des Parkhauses* (Bielefeld: transcript, 2007).
9 See Peter Sloterdijk, 'Strong Observation: For a Space Station Philosophy', in *Native Land, Stop Eject*, ed. Raymond Depardon and Paul Virilio (Arles: Actes Sud, 2010), pp. 29–36.
10 *Digha Nikaya* 5.
11 In this context one should recall Petrarch's well-known letter of 26 April 1336, in which he claims to have been reading a pocket edition of Augustine's *Confessions* at the summit of Mont Ventoux.
12 See Rabbow, *Seelenführung*, p. 93.
13 Epictetus, *The Enchiridion*, III, 3, 14; quoted in Rabbow, *Seelenführung*, p. 135.
14 Augustine, *De vera religione*, XXXIX, 72.
15 One possible version of the philosophical counter-movement to the age of objectivism and the illusion of the outside world is presented in my *Spheres* trilogy (Frankfurt: Suhrkamp, 1998–2003). In English so far: *Spheres*, vol. 1: *Bubbles*, trans. Wieland Hoban (Los Angeles: Semiotext(e), 2011).
16 Marcus Aurelius, *The Meditations*, p. 90.

17 Søren Kierkegaard, *Repetition and Philosophical Crumbs*, trans. M. G. Piety (Oxford and New York: Oxford University Press, 2009), p. 60.
18 Marcus Aurelius, *The Meditations*, p. 26.
19 See p. 266 below.
20 This is treated in greater detail in ch. 8, pp. 277–84.
21 Horace, *Epistles* I, 6, 1.
22 This could be shown especially clearly using the evolution of Buddhism and the adaptation of the *arhat* ideal of the Hinayana to the *bodhisattva* ideal of the Mahayana.
23 On 'riddle language' or 'intentional language' in Tantrism, see Mircea Eliade, *Yoga: Immortality and Freedom*, trans. Willard R. Trask (Princeton: Princeton University Press, 2009), p. 249.
24 In the first part of *The Vocation of Man* (1800), Johann Gottlieb Fichte demonstrated the deterministic-fatalistic position with a perfect simulation in order to evoke the despair that drives us forwards to practical idealism.
25 Quoted in Eliade, *Yoga*, p. 189.
26 In this respect, Buddha is 'simultaneous' with Greek Sophism, which, in terms of its overall direction, must be viewed above all as a humanistic exercise programme. It views a helpless letting-oneself-go as the worst form of behaviour and fatalism as an assault on *areté*, the willingness to self-help.
27 Thomas Macho, 'Mit sich allein: Einsamkeit als Kulturtechnik', in Aleida and Jan Assmann (eds.), *Einsamkeit (Archäologie der literarischen Kommunikation* VI) (Munich: Fink, 2000), pp. 27–44.
28 *Regula Benedicti* 7, 13 and 7, 28.
29 Kierkegaard, *A Literary Review*, trans. Alastair Hannay (London: Penguin, 2001).
30 *The Meditations*, p. 78.
31 Ibid., p. 35.
32 Ibid., p. 103.
33 Eliade, *Yoga*, p. 296.
34 See Niklas Luhmann, 'Die Autopoiesis des Bewusstseins', in *Selbstthematisierung und Selbstzeugnis: Bekenntnis und Geständnis*, ed. Alois Hahn and Volker Knapp (Frankfurt: Suhrkamp, 1987), pp. 64f.
35 Thomas of Celano, *First and Second Life of Saint Francis, with Selections from the Treatise on the Miracles of Blessed Francis*, trans. Placid Hermann (Chicago: Franciscan Herald Press, 1963), p. 84.
36 Critics of the miracle of stigmata have formulated the taboo-breaking question of why the wounds in the hands of Francis and his imitators appeared in the palms rather than the historically accurate place, namely the wrist bones. Their reply: because Francis was himself imitating the painted and sculpted crucifixes of his time, in which nails through the palms had long since become the norm. This does not answer the question of whether the wounds came about through pious deception, self-harm, or some physiologically inexplicable autoplastic achievement of the holy body. The first option is espoused with regard to Francis of Assisi by Christoph Türcke, who considers the saint the greatest actor, or most determined faker, of the Middle Ages: see Türcke, 'Askese und Performance: Franziskus als Regisseur und Hauptdarsteller seiner selbst', *Neue Rundschau* 4 (2000), pp. 35f. By analogy, the Indian mystic Ramakrishna, a worshipper of the Great Mother, claimed that she gave him the gift of menstruation as a sign of grace.

37 *Regula Benedicti* 7, 67.
38 Ibid., 7, 5.
39 That is why the *Regula Benedicti* contains such formulations as 'hasten to the perfection of the monastic ways' (73, 2) and 'hurrying forward to your heavenly fatherland' (*ad patriam caelestem festinare*) (73, 8).
40 Peter Sloterdijk, *Rage and Time*, trans. Mario Wenning (New York: Columbia University Press, 2010), pp. 69f.
41 In the later mystical theology of Gregor of Nyssa, this dynamized mimesis is pushed further to the thesis that Christian desire, because it follows a boundless object, can never rest, only lead into a paradoxical unity of movement and standstill.
42 See pp. 272f.
43 *Epistolae morales ad Lucilium*, 66, 9. *Crescere posse imperfectae rei signum est.*
44 See Peter Sloterdijk, *Sphären II. Globen, Makrosphärologie* (Frankfurt: Suhrkamp, 1999), pp. 326–39 (Excursus 1, 'Später sterben im Amphitheater: Über den Aufschub, römisch').
45 *Epistolae morales ad Lucilium*, 71, 25.
46 Ibid., 71, 26. *Scit se esse oneri ferendo.*
47 Ibid., 71, 27.
48 Ibid., 71, 37.
49 *Epistolae morales ad Lucilium*, 71, 11. While Stoic doctrine can only conceive of a perfection that is static and satisfying, Christian mysticism opened up the perspective of a perfection without a loss of desire. Thus Karl Rahner states in his summary of Gregory of Nyssa's mysticism of ascent: 'The only true sight of God is that which does not offer a final satisfaction of longing.' See Marcel Viller and Karl Rahner, *Aszese und Mystik in der Väterzeit: Ein Abriss der frühchristlichen Spiritualität* (Freiburg: Herder, 1989), p. 144.
50 See *Selbstthematisierung und Selbstzeugnis*, pp. 12f.
51 The last example of an existence under the star of completion is provided by the autobiography of Jean-Paul Sartre, *Les mots* (1964), where the young Sartre's flight into the artist's career is deconstructed *a priori* as a neurotic fabrication.
52 *Regula Benedicti* 73, 2.
53 Ibid., 7, 7.
54 Ibid., 7, 66.
55 Concerning the monk's silence, see *Regula Benedicti* 6, 1–8 and 7, 9–11.
56 The similarities between the early *asketería* (i.e. the monastic training camp) and a military facility are discussed by Marcel Viller and Karl Rahner in their work *Aszese und Mystic in der Väterzeit*, pp. 92f. This leads to a second derivation of the ideal of obedience from religiously overcoded soldiership. A third derivation would address imperial and ecclesiastical functionary ethics; concerning the ecclesiastical side, see Giorgio Agamben, *The Kingdom and the Glory: For a Theological Genealogy of Economy and Government* (Palo Alto: Stanford University Press, 2011), and on the imperial side, see Sloterdijk, *Sphären II*, pp. 729f.
57 S. *Joannis Abbatis vulgo Climaci opera Omnia editore et interpreto Mattheo Radero* (1633), in *Patrologiae Cursus Competus*, ed. Jean-Paul Migne, *Series Graeca* 88 (Turnhout: Brepols, 1967), col. 1152. In the following, I shall use both the Greek original and the Latin translation.

58 Ibid., col. 1147.

59 Ibid., col. 663.

60 Ibid., col. 674.

61 Hugo Ball, *Byzantinisches Christentum: Drei Heiligenleben*, ed. Bernd Wacker (Göttingen: Wallstein, 2010), p. 28.

62 At the same time, the monastic psychagogues knew the difference between the false tears of self-pity and the true ones of remorse or devotion. By analogy, see *The Questions of King Milinda*, trans. T. W. Rhys Davies, ed. F. Max Müller (London: RoutledgeCurzon, 2001).

63 *All' hólos ho palaiós ánthropos hamartía kaleitai. Non enim unum est peccatum, sed totus vetus homo peccatum appellatur* (col. 781/2).

64 Joannis Climaci, *Scala Paradisi*, col. 782.

65 Ibid., col. 1149/50.

66 Galatians 2:20.

67 Joannis Climaci, col. 1153/4.

68 Ibid., col. 1157/8.

69 See Jacob Taubes, *Occidental Eschatology*, trans. David Ratmoko (Palo Alto: Stanford University Press, 2009).

70 The corresponding literature certainly pays lip service to the possibility of 'perfection outside of monasticism', but if one sees how quickly even authors such as Viller and Rahner, the Jesuits cited several times above, get through the subject in their outline of early Christian spirituality (§36), the truth of the matter is clear enough. Before the start of *devotio moderna*, what applies in practice is this: *nulla salus* outside the order.

71 Löwith's commentary on this is still central: Karl Löwith, *Meaning in History* (Chicago and London: Chicago University Press, 1957).

72 See Jacques le Goff, *The Birth of Purgatory*, trans. Arthur Goldhammer (Chicago and London: Chicago University Press, 1984).

73 Quoted (as a motto) in ibid., p. v.

74 In his book *La vie de Ramakrishna* (1929), Romain Rolland points to the moment of demographic parity between 300 million gods and the same number of living Indians.

75 See pp. 231f above.

76 Heinrich Zimmer, *Philosophies of India*, ed. Joseph Campbell (Princeton: Princeton University Press, 1969), p. 41.

77 William Shakespeare, *Much Ado About Nothing*, Act 5, Scene 2.

78 Mysore Hiriyanna, *Essentials of Indian Philosophy* (Delhi: Diamond Pocket Books, 1996), p. 102.

79 Huineng, *The Platform Sutra of the Sixth Patriarch*, ed. and trans. P. B. Yampolsky (New York: Columbia University Press, 1967), p. 137.

80 See the comprehensive commentary of B. K. S. Iyengar, *Light on the Yoga Sutras of Patanjali* (London: Thorsons, 2002).

81 See *Digha Nikaya*, 9.

82 See Eliade, *Yoga*, pp. 169–73.

83 A. M. Podznejev, *Dhyana und Samadhi im mongolischen Lamaismus* (Hanover: Lafaire, 1927).

84 See Bruno Latour and Peter Weibel (eds.), *Making Things Public: Atmospheres of Democracy* (Cambridge, MA: MIT Press, 2005), ch. 4, 'From Objects to Things', pp. 250-95.

85 See pp. 119f above.

86 Nietzsche, *Daybreak: Thoughts on the Prejudices of Morality*, trans. R. J. Hollingdale (Cambridge: Cambridge University Press, 1997), p. 37.

87 See Bruno Snell, *The Discovery of the Mind in Greek Philosophy and Literature*, trans. T. G. Rosenmeyer (Mineola, NY: Dover, 1982), ch. 1, 'Homer's View of Man', pp. 1–22.

88 John 14:6.

89 John 10:30.

90 *Maitreya Upanishad* III-1, 4.

91 A symptomatic example of this is the essay 'Les "dons" n'existent pas' by the Marxist educational theorist and psychologist Lucien Sève, *L'Ecole et la Nation* (October 1964).

92 Johann Wolfgang von Goethe, *Faust II*, l. 7488.

93 TN: in German, the equivalent of 'school desk' (especially in its metonymic sense) is *Schulbank*, which actually translates as 'school bench'.

94 There is also no shortage of mocking journalists: see Gita Mehta, *Karma Cola: Marketing the Mystic East* (New York: Vintage, 1994).

95 See the chapter 'The Salvation of Identifications' in Axel Michaels, *Hinduism: Past and Present*, trans. Barbara Harshav (Princeton: Princeton University Press, 2004), pp. 325–44.

96 See Michael von Brück, *Einführung in den Buddhismus* (Frankfurt: Verlag der Weltreligionen, 2007), pp. 188f.

97 See the collection of statements by Kodo Sawake (1880-1965), one of the most striking Zen masters of recent times: Kosho Uchiyama, *The Zen Teaching of 'Homeless Kodo'* (Kyoto: Kyoto Zen Center, 1999).

98 See pp. 308f below.

99 *Regula Benedicti* 2, 24: *miscens temporibus tempora, terroribus blandimenta, dirum magistri, pium patris ostendat affectum.*

100 Pierre Hadot, 'The Figure of Socrates', in *Philosophy as a Way of Life: Spiritual Exercises from Socrates to Foucault*, trans. Michael Chase (Oxford: Blackwell, 1995), pp. 147–78.

101 Slavoj Žižek, *Liebe dein Symptom wie dich selbst! Jacques Lacans Psychoanalyse und die Medien* (Berlin: Merve, 1991).

102 See pp. 200f above.

103 A contemporary exception to this is the Socratic performance philosopher Bazon Brock; see Peter Sloterdijk, 'Der Jahrhundertmensch', in Bazon Brock, *Lustmarsch durchs Theoriegelände: Musealisiert Euch!* (Cologne: DuMont, 2008), pp. 6–24.

104 See Pierre Hadot, *The Inner Citadel: The Meditations of Marcus Aurelius*, trans. Michael Chase (Cambridge, MA: Harvard University Press, 1998).

105 *Epistolae morales ad Lucilium*, 34.

106 Ibid., 35.

107 Ibid., 33.

108 The same tendency appears in some younger schools of Buddhism.

109 Concerning the complex of Sophistic *paideía* as training for universal ability, see Thomas Buchheim, *Die Sophistik als Avantgarde des normalen Lebens* (Hamburg: Meiner, 1968), pp. 108–27; concerning the Sophists' approach to *kairos*, see pp. 82f.

110 Ibid., p. 114.

111 Concerning the history of the piano recital and its increasingly sterile character, see Kenneth Hamilton, *After the Golden Age: Romantic Pianism and*

Modern Performance (Oxford and New York: Oxford University Press, 2007).

112 See pp. 54ff above.

113 The most successful athlete in antiquity, Milo of Croton (*c.*556–510 BC), managed to remain undefeated for over a quarter of a century, from the sixtieth to the sixty-seventh Olympiad (540-512 BC).

114 Richard Sennett, *The Craftsman* (London: Allen Lane, 2008).

115 Ibid., p. 20.

116 Ibid., pp. 59ff.

117 This function of 'craftsmanly' and factory-work activity, which in turn affects the practising-producing person, had already been grasped by Lucien Sève in his studies towards a Marxist personality theory, though he made them virtually unrecognizable through a one-sided productivistic terminology. See Lucien Sève, *Marxism and the Theory of Human Personality*, trans. David Pavett (London: Lawrence & Wishart, 1975). The essay also contains notable ideas for a theory of subjective capital and the 'rise in the organic composition of the personality'.

118 Sennett, *The Craftsman*, p. 57.

119 See Robert E. Cushman, *John Wesley's Experimental Divinity: Studies in Methodist Doctrinal Standards* (Nashville: Kingswood, 1989).

120 Karl Marx, *Grundrisse (Introduction to the Critique of Political Economy)*, trans. Martin Nicolaus (New York: Vintage, 1973), p. 104.

121 Ibid., p. 51. Marx emphasizes in the same context that there is 'a devil of a difference' between uncivilized Russian slaves who allow themselves to be used for anything and 'civilized people who apply themselves to everything' (p. 105). This is the difference that, according to Marx, one cannot understand without having grasped the entire development of abstract labour in the system of capital.

122 The doctrine of the Alexandrine presbyter Arius (*c.*260-336) was condemned as heresy by the First Council of Nicaea in 325. It claimed that Christ was begotten, and subordinate to God the Father; some of his successors derived the theory of the purely human, albeit illuminated nature of Christ from this.

123 See *Res Publica Litteraria: Die Institutionen der Gelehrsamkeit der frühen Neuzeit*, ed. Sebastian Neumeister, 2 vols. (Wiesbaden: Harrassowitz, 1989).

124 The former sacrifices belong to the universe of older religions of equilibrium, which strive for 'theocosmic' balance; in them, the totality of the world is at once the first immune system (hence the barely suppressible interest of 'worldlings' in a 'perfect world'); the second belong to the religions of imbalance, which call for an abandonment of the imperfect world for the sake of saving the soul; in them, the refuge of the soul forms the highest immune alliance with God. One recognizes these theocentrists and their successors, the agents of 'critical consciousness', not least by their striving to make the very idea of a 'perfect world' seem ridiculous at all costs.

125 See Peter Sloterdijk, 'Absturz und Kehre: Rede über Heideggers Denken in der Bewegung', in *Nicht gerettet: Versuche nach Heidegger* (Frankfurt: Suhrkamp, 2001), pp. 12–81.

126 Plato, *Republic*, trans. John Llewelyn Davies and David James Vaughan (Ware: Wordsworth Classics, 1997), p. 229.

127 Pierre Hadot, 'Conversion', in *Exercices spirituels et philosophie antique* (Paris: Etudes Augustiniennes, 1987), p. 176.
128 See Peter Sloterdijk, *Sphären III. Schäume: Plurale Sphärologie* (Frankfurt: Suhrkamp, 2004), pp. 261ff.: 'Nicht Vertrag, nicht Gewächs. Annäherung an die Raum-Vielheuten, die bedauerlicherweise Gesellschaften genannt werden'; for arguments towards a critique of political holism, see in particular pp. 277f.
129 Concerning the difference between *epistrophé* and *metánoia*, see Hadot, 'Conversion', and Michel Foucault, *The Hermeneutics of the Subject: Lectures at the Collège de France 1981–1982*, trans. Graham Burchell (New York: Palgrave Macmillan, 2005).
130 Concerning a generalized concept of decorum, see Heiner Mühlmann, *The Nature of Cultures: A Blueprint for a Theory of Culture Genetics*, trans. R. Payne (Vienna and New York: Springer, 1996). On metanoia from a political perspective, see also Peter Sloterdijk, *Theorie der Nachkriegszeiten: Bemerkungen zu den deztsch-französischen Beziehungen nach 1945* (Frankfurt: Suhrkamp, 2008).
131 William James, *The Varieties of Religious Experience* (Cambridge, MA: Harvard University Press, 1985), pp. 157–209.
132 See Alain Badiou, *Saint Paul: The Foundation of Universalism*, trans. Ray Brassier (Palo Alto: Stanford University Press, 2003).
133 Oswald Spengler, *The Decline of the West*, trans. Charles Francis Atkinson (New York: Knopf, 1939), pp. 345f.
134 James, *The Varieties of Religious Experience*, pp. 139f.
135 See p. 246 above.
136 Concerning the reversal of *uti* (to use) and *frui* (to enjoy) in Augustine, see *Augustinus-Lexikon*, ed. Cornelius Mayer, vol. 3, fasc. 1/2 (Basle: Schwabe, 2004), col. 70-5.
137 *Epistolae morales ad Lucilium*, 61.
138 Thomas of Celano, *First and Second Life of Saint Francis*, p. 143.
139 Ibid., pp. 201f.
140 Peter Sloterdijk, *Im Weltinnenraum des Kapitals: Für eine philosophische Theorie der Globalisierung* (Frankfurt: Suhrkamp, 2006), ch. 11, 'Die Erfindung der Subjektivität – Die primäre Enthemmung und ihre Ratgeber', pp. 93f.

III THE EXERCISES OF THE MODERNS

1 *Maiora einem post omnia anteacta saecula et sperandi et tentandi tempus est.* J. A. Comenius, *A Reformation of Schooles, 1642* (Menston: Scolar, 1969), p. 22.
2 Quoted in Jacob Burckhardt, *The Civilisation of the Renaissance in Italy*, trans. S. G. C. Middlemore (London: Penguin, 1990), p. 103.
3 Leon Trotsky in a speech given to representatives of a Danish student organization on 27 November 1932: *In Defense of the Russian Revolution* (New York: Pioneer Press, 1933), p. 40.
4 *L'homme en est venu à traiter l'humanité comme une matière.* Quoted in Lucien Gauthier, *Von Montaigne bis Valéry: Der geistige Weg Frankreichs* (Reutlingen: Continental, 1949), p. xxvi.

5 A number of seventeenth-century authors inspired by Paracelsus have been identified as sources of Comenius' three-book doctrine: the authors of the Rosicrucian manifestos, Johann Heinrich Alsted, *Theologia Naturalis* (1615), as well as Benedictus Figulus, *Pandora Magnalium Naturalium* (Strasbourg: Zetzner, 1608). See Comenius, *The Way of Light*, trans. E. T. Campagnac (Liverpool and London: Liverpool University Press/Hodder & Stoughton, 1938). Regarding Comenius' pedagogical metaphysics in the run-up to the Enlightenment, see also pp. 350f below.

6 Comenius' impatience can be attributed to the apocalyptic expectations of the late Reformation; that of his successors already presupposed the shift from the apocalypse to the philosophy of history, and hence both the bourgeoisification of apocalypticism and its revolutionary defusing, while the ideologues of revolution preached neo-apocalyptic escalation.

7 TN: the original French title of Foucault's *Discipline and Punish* is *Surveiller et punir* – 'Supervise and Punish', rendered accurately in the book's German title *Überwachen und Strafen*, which Sloterdijk echoes here.

8 Concerning the formative effects of craftsmanly and instrumental exercises, see pp. 292f above.

9 See pp. 148f above. The tendency to associate the concept of discipline with despotism is not, incidentally, unique to the post-1945 or post-1968 zeitgeist. It is already evident in the work of Johann Friedrich Herbart, Kant's successor in Königsberg, who discarded the term 'discipline' used in so carefree a manner by Kant, only to choose an even more problematic replacement like 'government', a suggestion that recalls Foucault's idea of self-government. See Christopher Korn, *Bildung und Disziplin: Problemgeschichtlich-systematische Untersuchung zum Begriff der Disziplin in Erziehung und Unterricht* (Frankfurt: Lang, 2003), pp. 105f.

10 Galatians 6:15 and 5:24.

11 Augustine, *Confessiones*, book IV, ch. 5; *Confessions*, trans. Francis Joseph Sheed, ed. Michael P. Foley (Indianapolis: Hackett, 2006), p. 60.

12 Hamilton Club Speech, Chicago, 10 April 1899.

13 Peter Sloterdijk, *Im Weltinnenraum des Kapitals: Für eine philosophische Theorie der Globalisierung* (Frankfurt: Suhrkamp, 2006), p. 79.

14 As late as the nineteenth century, spokesmen for popular hygienic and gymnastic systems stirred up the fear of exhaustion and overtaxing (*fatigue, surmenage*) through excessive exercises – not only because of their bias towards notions of equilibrium, but also because they did not yet understand the principle of supercompensation. See Philipp Sarasin, *Reizbare Maschinen: Eine Geschichte des Körpers 1765–1914* (Frankfurt: Suhrkamp, 2001), pp. 317f.

15 See Peter Sloterdijk, 'Die Färbung der Bürger', in Bruno Latour and Peter Weibel (eds.), *Making Things Public: Atmospheres of Democracy* (Cambridge, MA: MIT Press, 2005).

16 Matthew 25:29.

17 See Peter Nickl, *Ordnung der Gefühle: Studien zum Begriff des habitus* (Hamburg: Meiner, 2005), pp. 48f.

18 See Josef Pieper, *Faith, Hope, Love* (San Francisco: Ignatius Press, 1986), pp. 113–23.

19 Søren Kierkegaard, *Repetition and Philosophical Crumbs*, trans. M. G. Piety (Oxford and New York: Oxford University Press, 2009), p. 4.

20 Sartre contradicts this with his thesis that there are no good habits, because habits are inertias and thus bad *per se*.

21 See pp. 272f above.

22 This can be seen most clearly in one of the most influential works of moral philosophy in recent decades: Alasdair MacIntyre, *After Virtue: A Study in Moral Theory* (Notre Dame, IN: University of Notre Dame Press, 1981). The author has often been praised for a beneficially corrective return to a neo-Aristotelian ethics of virtue – which, it is argued, is a welcome development amidst the moral confusion of modern societies. If one takes MacIntyre's closing statement into account, however, where he asserts the necessity of unifying St Benedict and Trotsky in a single person in order to find a new guideline, it becomes clear that one is dealing here with anything but an over-coming of confusion; neither Benedict nor Trotsky can make any contribu-tion to a return to virtues. Both are subject to the eros of the impossible: the first in the mode of holiness, the second in the mode of political crimes in the service of good. One must be grateful to MacIntyre for revealing that behind the neo-Aristotelian *juste milieu* discourse, the ethics of holy excess from early Catholicism is still in effect. No figure could expose modern indecision more clearly: the Benedict–Trotsky hybrid would never be able to decide whether it should work on self-improvement in the monastery or strive to better the world through terrorist activities. The constructive impulse of MacIntyre's reflections, therefore, cannot be absorbed into a restorative ethics of virtue. What is on the agenda is rather a training ethics in response to the sublime metanoetic imperative of our time. See pp. 442f below.

23 Concerning the transitions between the monastic and the humanistic spheres in the fifteenth and sixteenth centuries, see Harald Müller, *Habit und Habitus: Mönche und Humanisten im Dialog* (Tübingen: Mohr Siebeck, 2006).

24 The term also appears in English-language sociology, where some authors refer to embedding, disembedding and re-embedding in the relationship between the individual and traditional life forms. See in particular Anthony Giddens, *The Consequences of Modernity* (Palo Alto: Stanford University Press, 1990).

25 Johann Wolfgang von Goethe, 'Diné zu Coblenz im Sommer 1774', in *Sämtliche Gedichte* (Frankfurt: Insel, 2007), p. 326.

26 TN: 'habit' here refers exclusively to the monk's attire; no double meaning is intended.

27 Concerning the foundation of non-monetary banking phenomena, see Peter Sloterdijk, *Rage and Time*, trans. Mario Wenning (New York: Columbia University Press, 2010), pp. 135f. On the philosophical deduction of the idea of the world museum, see Beat Wyss, *Trauer der Vollendung: Von der Ästhetik des Deutschen Idealismus zur Kulturkritik an der Moderne* (Berlin: Matthes & Seitz, 1985); on the metaphysics of the archive, see Boris Groys/Thomas Knoefel, *Politik der Unsterblichkeit* (Munich: Hanser, 2002); on the transformation of immortality into a practical idea, see the references to Nikolai Fedorov on pp. 353 and 395f below.

28 'Bent am I and humbled', *Regula Benedicti* 7, 66–70.

29 Concerning the triad of habits, passions and mental inertias (also known as 'opinions') and their overcoming through the first ethical distinction, see p. 167 above.

30 I hint below (pp. 421–5) why their teachings all relate to conditions during the Iron Age as defined by Hesiod, whereas modern civilization must be understood as a second Silver Age; this poses other questions and searches for other answers.

31 See Ulrich Bröckling, *Das unternehmerische Selbst: Soziologie einer Subjektivierungsform* (Frankfurt: Suhrkamp, 2007).

32 Baltasar Gracián, *The Art of Worldly Wisdom*, trans. Joseph Jacobs (Boston and London: Shambhala, 1993), p. 171.

33 Ibid., p. 1.

34 The word *superhomo* (from the Greek *hyperanthropos*) first appeared in a papal document from the late thirteenth century, the canonization bull for Louis IX issued by Boniface VIII in 1297.

35 Only Luhmann's systems theory, thanks to its metabiological approach, integrated the immunological imperative into its foundations. See Niklas Luhmann, *Social Systems*, trans. John Bednarz Jr. (Palo Alto: Stanford University Press, 1995), pp. 369f.

36 Nietzsche, *Thus Spoke Zarathustra: A Book for Everyone and Nobody*, trans. Graham Parkes (Oxford and New York: Oxford University Press, 2005), p. 13.

37 See Heinz-Theo Homann, *Das funktionale Argument: Konzepte und Kritik funktionslogischer Religionsbegründung* (Paderborn: Schöningh, 1997).

38 Concerning Christian surrealism, see pp. 205f above.

39 Trotsky took up this motif to explain the intended direction of socialist technology: 'Faith merely promises to move mountains; but technology, which takes nothing "on faith," is actually able to cut down mountains and move them [. . .] according to a general industrial and artistic plan.' Trotsky, *Literature and Revolution*, ed. William Keach, trans. Rose Trunsky (Chicago: Haymarket, 2005), p. 204.

40 The word, which can be traced back to the 1820s, caused (along with its object) a furore from the mid-nineteenth century on (in French *entraîne-ment*, in German usually the same word as in English, though initially also *Trainirung* on occasion).

41 Concerning the kinship between abstract labour and abstract fitness, see the Marxian thesis (cited in part II, n. 120 above) on the difference between slavery and jobbing. The author sees in this difference a historical move-ment whose interpretation requires the entire apparatus of a critique of production conditions; to understand the emergence of abstract fitness requires no less than a comprehensive reconstruction of practice conditions.

42 See Manfred Osten, 'Konfuzius oder Chinas neue Kulturrevolution', in *China: Insel-Almanach auf das Jahr 2009* (Frankfurt: Insel, 2009), pp. 266–97.

43 Concerning the antagonistic alliance of state and school, see pp. 348f below.

44 TN: the author uses the English word in this context.

45 The current state of the enhancement debate is described from a pragmatic perspective by Bernward Gesang in *Perfektionierung des Menschen* (Berlin: de Gruyter, 2007).

46 TN: the double meaning of 'putting on' is intended.

47 See Barbara Vinken, *Fashion Zeitgeist: Trends and Cycles in the Fashion System*, trans. Mark Hewson (Oxford and New York: Berg, 2005).

48 Concerning the connection between the symbolic order of 'society' and the theatricization of law, see Pierre Legendre, *La fabrique de l'homme occidental* (Paris: Mille et une nuits, 1996).

49 Joseph de Maistre, *Petersburg Dialogues, Or, Conversations on the Temporal Government of Providence*, trans. Richard A. Lebrun (Montreal: McGill-Queen's University Press, 1993), p. 19.

50 Rainer Maria Rilke, *The Book of Hours*, trans. Annemarie S. Kidder (Evanston, IL: Northwestern University Press, 2001), p. 33.

51 See Richard van Dülmen, *Theater des Schreckens: Gerichtspraxis und Strafrituale der Neuzeit* (Munich: C. H. Beck, 1995).

52 In ch. 8 of the first book of *The Wealth of Nations*, he writes that 'the demand for men, like that of any other commodity, necessarily regulates the production of men.' Adam Smith, *The Wealth of Nations*, ed. Jonathan B. Wight [Petersfield: Harriman House, 2007], p. 53. What Smith views as an effect of the market is in fact a consequence of demographic policy.

53 Gunnar Heinsohn, Rolf Knieper and Otto Steiger, *Menschenproduktion: Allgemeine Bevölkerungslehre der Neuzeit* (Frankfurt: Suhrkamp, 1979). The authors' thesis did not go uncontested, especially their argument that the documentation of the witch trials shows more denunciation of witches by neighbours and fellow villagers than by state investigators and inquisitors. This does not change the truth of the observation that the creation of the witch-hunting climate stems from clericocratically based political measures.

54 TN: 'subject' is used here purely in the sense of subordination to power.

55 The German translation by Johannes Fischart appeared as early as 1591 under the title *Vom ausgelassenen wütigen Teufelsheer* (Graz: Akademische Druck- und Verlagsanstalt, 1973 [reprint]). See Gunnar Heinsohn and Otto Steiger, *Inflation and Witchcraft or The Birth of Political Economy: The Case of Jean Bodin Reconsidered* (Bremen: Institut für Konjunktur- und Strukturforschung, 1997).

56 Heinrich Kramer and James Sprenger, *The Malleus Maleficarum*, trans. Montague Summers (New York: Cosimo, 2007), p. 66.

57 Heinsohn et al., *Menschenproduktion*, p. 78.

58 For a macro-historical description of Europe's demographic anomaly between the sixteenth and nineteenth centuries, see Gunnar Heinsohn, *Söhne und Weltmacht: Terror im Aufstieg und Fall der Nationen* (Munich: Piper, 2008).

59 Michel Foucault, 'Lives of Infamous Men', in James D. Faubion (ed.), *Essential Works of Foucault*, vol. 3: *Power* (New York: New Press, 2000), pp. 157–75.

60 See James L. Nolan, *The Therapeutic State: Justifying Government at Century's End* (New York: New York University Press, 1998).

61 Heinsohn et al., *Menschenproduktion*, pp. 70-7.

62 In this context, they point out that Foucault's analysis of the 'microphysics of power' contains a dating error that, restricted by the methodological barriers of discourse analysis, he was no longer able to correct with its own methods. He directed questions at the eighteenth century that had already been answered by the sixteenth; for this reason, almost all of Foucault's statements about modern biopower are impaired in decisive aspects by anachronisms and explanatory gaps.

63 See Markus Krajewski (ed.), *Projektemacher: Zur Produktion von Wissen in der Vorform des Scheiterns* (Berlin: Kadmos, 2004).

64 This failure is described by Herbart in *The Application of Psychology to the Science of Education* (1832): 'the less useful an individual is, the less the State will trouble itself about him. Its schools are to provide it with those whom it requires. It chooses the most useful; the rest may look after themselves.' Johann Friedrich Herbart, *The Application of Psychology to the Science of Education*, trans. Beatrice Charlotte Mulliner (New York: Scribner's, 1898), p. 19.

65 It is no coincidence that the greatest metanoetic account to come from medieval Europe, *La Divina Commedia*, states that the poet's initiation into unearthly matters began when he lost his way in a forest at the midpoint of his life (*nel mezzo del cammin di nostra vita*).

66 TN: *Bildung*, from the verb *bilden*, 'to form' or 'to educate', usually refers to the academic aspect of education, as opposed to *Erziehung*, which conveys more the sense of upbringing or conditioning. Nonetheless, the word's origin suggests a moulding of character (as evident in the *Bildungsroman*).

67 Arnold Gehlen often pointed harshly to the tendency towards intellectual hyper-morality, accompanied by a massive moralizing disloyalty to the general interest. Niklas Luhmann speaks more detachedly of such phenomena: see Luhmann, 'The Morality of Risk and the Risk of Morality', *International Review of Sociology* 3 (1987), pp. 87–107.

68 See the *pelle di asino* aria in Act 4 of *Le nozze di Figaro*.

69 See Paul Konrad Liessmann, *Theorie der Unbildung: Die Irrtümer der Wissensgesellschaft* (Vienna: Zsolnay, 2006); concerning the implosion of school in postmodernity, see pp. 429f below. TN: there is a play on words concealed by the translation. *Entgeisterung*, meaning 'dismay' or 'dumbfoundedness', literally indicates a 'de-spiriting', in contrast to the *Geist* of *Zeitgeist*.

70 William Shakespeare, *As You Like It*, Act 2, Scene 7.

71 *Docentium et discentium utilia coetus*.

72 Comenius, *Via Lucis, Der Weg des Lichtes*, ed. and trans. Uwe Voigt (Hamburg: Meiner, 1997), pp. 21f. TN: because the aforementioned English translation is out of print and not accessible online, the author's references to the German edition have been retained and the corresponding passages newly translated.

73 Ibid., p. 23.

74 Ibid.

75 Ibid., p. 93.

76 Ibid., p. 95.

77 *Schola est officina, in qua novelli animi ad virtutem formantur*; from Comenius, *Via Lucis*, p. 206.

78 Ibid., p. 124.

79 Comenius offers a para-Baconian argument on this subject: 'But neither should the artificial be ignored. For the arts express nature, or even place it under pressure or keep it captive, forcing it to confess its secrets gradually to us. Hence these secrets become ever more well known. In addition, the arts serve to multiply the comforts of life (and in the Age of Illumination, there would surely have to be a wealth rather than a lack of such comforts).' *Der Weg des Lichtes*, pp. 110f.

80 See Nikolai Fedorov, 'Das Museum, sein Sinn und seine Bestimmung', in *Die Neue Menschheit: Biopolitische Utopien in Russland zu Beginn des 20. Jahrhunderts*, ed. Boris Groys and Michael Hagemeister in collaboration with Anne von der Heiden (Frankfurt: Suhrkamp, 2005), pp. 127-232.

81 In her otherwise admirable book *The Human Condition* (1958), Hannah Arendt failed to grasp the modernity-constituting relationship between flight from the world and flight into the world, and her misinterpretation of the new mode of futurized worldliness led her to the completely absurd conclusion that modern humans suffered from an unprecedented degree of 'worldlessness'.

82 Comenius, *Der Weg des Lichtes*, p. 125.

83 'Everything flows of its own accord – compulsion is absent from things.' This shows the after-effects of Quintilian's conclusion that all learning is based on the will, but this will cannot be forced.

84 Comenius, *Der Weg des Lichtes*, p. 126.

85 See Wilhelm Schmift-Biggeman, 'Enzyklopädie und Philosophia Perennis', in *Enzyklopädien der Frühen Neuzeit: Beiträge zu ihrer Erforschung*, ed. Franz M. Eybl, Wolfgang Harms, Hans-Henrik Krummacher and Werner Welzig (Tübingen: Niemeyer, 1995), pp. 15f.

86 See the section above on Sophism as a rhetorical version of the art of omniscience, pp. 288f.

87 See Klaus Schaller, *Die Maschine als Demonstration des lebendigen Gottes: Johann Amos Comenius im Umgang mit der Technik* (Hohenghren: Schneider, 1997).

88 See Klaus Völker (ed.), *Künstliche Menschen: Dichtungen über Golems, Homunculi, Androiden und Liebende Statuen* (Munich: Hanser, 1971).

89 See Hans Blumenberg, *Beschreibung des Menschen* (Frankfurt: Suhrkamp, 2006), part 2: *Kontingenz und Sichtbarkeit*, pp. 473-895.

90 In his youthful satire of 1798 – 'Einfältige, aber gutgemeinte Biographie einer neuen angenehmen Frau von bloßem Holz, die ich längst erfunden und geheiratet' – Jean Paul derived the possibility of legal bigamy from this circumstance: 'any man can marry two women at once, if one of them is made purely of wood'. Quoted in Völker, *Künstliche Menschen*, p. 140.

91 Henri F. Ellenberger, *The Discovery of the Unconscious: The History and Evolution of Dynamic Psychiatry* (New York: Basic Books, 1981).

92 This is one reason why psychoanalysis could only seem plausible in Western cultures with a historically grown technical awareness, while its reception was virtually impossible in Japan, China or Africa – that is, in cultures without significant ego–id polarizations or indigenous traditions of higher mechanical engineering.

93 See Gotthard Günther, *Das Bewusstsein der Maschinen: Eine Metaphysik der Kybernetik* (Baden-Baden: Agis, 1963). For Günther, it is still uncertain whether the draining of subjectivity into the second machine should be read as a mere emptying of the inner world or as a deepening of subjectivity via its mirroring in spirit-mimetic machines of increasing complexity. See also Günther, *Die amerikanische Apokalypse*, ed. and intr. Kurt Klagenfurt (Munich and Vienna: Profil, 2000).

94 One aspect of this has been mentioned by Bourdieu in his observations on habitus transfer.

95 See Foucault, *Discipline and Punish*, and François Ewald, *L'Etat providence* (Paris: Grasset, 1986).

96 See pp. 295f above.

97 See Grete Wehmeyer, *Carl Czerny und die Einzelhaft am Klavier oder Die Kunst der Fingerfertigkeit und die industrielle Arbeitsideologie* (Kassel and Zurich: Bärenreiter & Atlantis, 1983), especially pp. 151-80.

98 Hans Belting, *Likeness and Presence: A History of the Image Before the Era of Art*, trans. Edmund Jephcott (Chicago and London: Chicago University Press, 1997).

99 Concerning the decline in the awareness of imitation in the visual art of the twentieth century, see pp. 433f below.

100 An example of this is a sequence of forty-three movements for musket training, with the corresponding commands, dating from the early seventeenth century; quoted in Werner Hahlweg, *Die Heeresreform der Oranier und die Antike: Studien zur Geschichte des Kriegswesens der Niederlande, Deutschlands, Frankreichs, Englands, Italiens, Spaniens und der Schweiz vom Jahre 1589 bis zum Dreissigjährigen Kriege* (1941) (Osnabrück: Biblio, 1987), pp. 34f.

101 For a presentation of the opposing argument, see Friedrich W. Heubach, *Das bedingte Leben: Theorie der psycho-logischen Gegenständlichkeit der Dinge. Ein Beitrag zur Psychologie des Alltags* (Munich: Fink, 1987), as well as Bruno Latour, *We Have Never Been Modern* (Cambridge, MA: Harvard University Press, 1993).

102 See Chiara Frugoni, *Books, Banks, Buttons and Other Inventions*, trans. William McCuaig (New York: Columbia University Press, 2005).

103 Dieter Claessens, *Das Konkrete und das Abstrakte: Soziologische Skizzen zur Anthropologie* (Frankfurt: Suhrkamp, 1994).

104 TN: a reference to a popular German saying whose meaning is equivalent to 'Rome wasn't built in a day.'

105 Blumenberg, *Die Legitimität der Neuzeit* (Frankfurt: Suhrkamp, 1988) (expanded edition).

106 See Bernard Yack, *The Longing for Total Revolution: Philosophic Sources of Social Discontent from Rousseau to Marx and Nietzsche* (Berkeley: University of California Press, 1992).

107 Concerning evolutionary theory as a general way to make counter-intuitive assumptions about the 'current' of events plausible, see the passage about Nietzsche's combination of artistry and nature theory on pp. 121f above.

108 This difference strikes me as a suitable replacement for Foucault's power-critical reflections on the autonomizing reversal of being dominated into self-domination. I am convinced that this translation is closer to the author's intentions than the formulation which his own terminological framework permitted. As a whole, the field of exercises and reflexive praxes must be moved away from the naïve over-politicizations underlying the common ways of discussing 'biopolitics'. At the same time, this also refutes the feminist criticisms of Foucault's late works, which seize on his misleading choice of terms without noting the emancipatory perspective of his work for both sexes. For example: Lin Foxhall, 'Pandora Unbound: A Feminist Critique of Foucault's History of Sexuality', and Amy Richlin, 'Foucault's History of Sexuality: A Useful Theory for Women?', both in David H. J. Larmour, Paul Allen Miller and Charles Platter (eds.),

Rethinking Sexuality: Foucault and Classical Antiquity (Princeton: Princeton University Press, 1998).

109 See Jean-Paul Sartre, *Notebooks for an Ethics*, trans. David Pellauer (Chicago and London: Chicago University Press, 1992), p. 4. On the same page, he writes: '*Good* habits: they are never good, because they are habits.'

110 Jean-Paul Sartre, *Being and Nothingness: An Essay on Phenomenological Ontology* (London: Routledge, 1969), pp. 377f.

111 TN: the word used here, *Gelassenheit*, is related to the verb *lassen*, meaning 'to let', in the sense both of allowing and of arranging for something to be done (it also combines with numerous prefixes to produce other verbs related in different ways to leaving and letting). This dialectic is reflected in the entire section on 'operating', where the German for 'having oneself operated on' is *sich operieren lassen*.

112 Bruno Latour acted on this by abandoning the object of classical sociology, 'society' as an association of subjects, and replacing it with networks of agents. See Latour, *Reassembling the Social: An Introduction to Actor-Network Theory* (Oxford and New York: Oxford University Press, 2005).

113 *Illustrierte Geschichte der Anästhesie*, ed. Ludwig Brandt (Stuttgart: Wissenschaftliche Verlagsanstalt, 1997), p. 63.

114 See Peter Sloterdijk, *Spheres*, vol. 1: *Bubbles*, trans. Wieland Hoban (Los Angeles: Semiotext(e), 2011), ch. 3: 'Humans in the Magic Circle: On the History of the Fascination with Closeness', pp. 207–62.

115 The only context in which even this step is exceeded is that of science fiction literature – for example, when human actors have themselves transformed from matter into energy in order to be projected to other locations in the universe via beaming.

116 Karl Marx, *Critique of Hegel's 'Philosophy of Right'*, trans. Annette Jolin and Joseph O'Malley (Cambridge: Cambridge University Press, 1977), p. 137.

117 One could then constructively adopt Friedrich August von Hayek's anti-socialist arguments from *The Road to Serfdom* (1944), and use them for a positive structural diagnosis of the modern welfare and therapy state.

118 Arthur Koestler, *The Yogi and the Commissar, and Other Essays* (New York: Macmillan, 1945).

119 Trotsky, *Literature and Revolution*, p. 207.

120 Concerning the exemplary fate of Stalin's chief torturer Yagoda in 1938, see Bazon Brock, *Lustmarsch durch Theoriegelände: Musealisiert Euch!* (Cologne: DuMont, 2008), pp. 141–3.

121 The subject has been examined from many different angles by Arthur Koestler, Albert Camus, Aleksandr Solzhenitsyn, Alexander Vat, Andrei Sinyavsky, Boris Groys and most recently Michail Ryklin, to name only a few outstanding analysts. I added a footnote of my own to this literature with my essay *God's Zeal: The Battle of the Three Monotheisms*, trans. Wieland Hoban (Cambridge: Polity, 2009), in which I interpret communism as a fourth monotheism, or more precisely as the practical realization of Rousseau's 'religion of man'.

122 Quoted in Saral Sarkar, *Eco-Socialism or Eco-Capitalism?* (London: Zed, 1999), p. 58.

123 An echo of the new stage of anthropotechnics could still be discerned in the preference of the DDR elites for cybernetics and its further development in all areas.

124 See Peter Weingart, Jürgen Kroll and Kurt Bayertz, *Rasse, Blut und Gene: Geschichte der Eugenik und Rassenhygiene in Deutschland* (Frankfurt: Suhrkamp, 1988).

125 The third biopolitical emergency, that of National Socialism, combined the populationism of the Modern Age with exterminationism on the contemporaneous Soviet model to form an operative complex – with weak results in the former category and devastating consequences in the latter. By comparison, the 'constructive' attempts to cross humans with apes that had already been carried out in Stalin's time (after preludes in the colonial era) were merely episodes, barely different from the attempts to produce biologically correct offspring in certain breeding centres run by the SS. The historical evidence indicates that both the USSR and the Nazi state pursued the most large-scale policies of elimination, liquidation of 'unusable elements' and eradication of 'life unworthy of life', but never eugenics in the true sense of the word. The factually indefensible equation of eugenics and extermination policy (conveyed in Germany via the intermediate step of 'racial hygiene') still defines current polemics against the humanistic genetic-therapeutic research conducted today, which stands accused of being a 'liberal eugenics'.

126 Andrei Sinyavsky, *Soviet Civilization: A Cultural History*, trans. Joanne Turnbull (New York: Arcade, 1990).

127 Two lines from the poem 'TBC' (1929) by the Soviet poet Eduard Bagritsky, dedicated to the memory of Dzerzhinsky. Quoted in Peter Barenboim and Boris Meshcheryakov, *Flanders in Moscow and Odessa: Poet Eduard Bagritskii as the Till Ulenspiegel of Russian Literature*, at http://baruchim.narod.ru/Bagritsky.html (accessed 29 November 2011). Anyone seeking evidence for the explicit abolition of the commandment against killing in the twentieth century will find the first pieces among the intellectual analysts of the Russian Revolution.

128 Sinyavsky, *Soviet Civilization*, p. 126.

129 A selection of writings by these authors was edited and published – almost a century after the event – as part of the project 'The Post-Communist Condition', directed by Boris Groys, funded by the Kulturstiftung des Bundes and under the patronage of Peter Weibel at the Karlsruhe Centre of Art and Media Technology, under the title *Die Neue Menschheit: Biopolitische Utopien in Russland zu Beginn des 20. Jahrhunderts* (see n. 80 above).

130 *Die Neue Menschheit*, p. 393.

131 Ibid., p. 395.

132 Ibid., p. 403.

133 Concerning Bogdanov's politics of blood, see Margarete Vöhringer, *Avantgarde und Psychotechnik: Wissenschaft, Kunst und Technik der Wahrnehmungsexperimente in der frühen Sowjetunion* (Göttingen: Wallstein, 2007), pp. 173–229; also, by the same author, 'Im Proletformat – Medien für Transformationen und Transfusionen im Russland der 20er Jahre', in *Transfusionen: Blutbilder und Biopolitik in der Neuzeit*, ed. Anja Lauper (Zurich and Berlin: Diaphanes, 2005), pp. 199–210.

134 The *Great Soviet Encyclopedia* included the term 'anthropotechnics' in its third volume as early as 1926; it defines it as an 'applied branch of biology whose aim is to improve the physical and mental characteristics of humans

with the same methods used in zootechnics to improve and breed new races of pets'. Quoted in *Die Neue Menschheit*, p. 54. As early as 1922, the former Neoplatonist Pavel Blonski had told the public in his widely disseminated text 'Pedagogy': 'Education [. . .] should take its place along with veterinary medicine and phytoculture [plant breeding].' Quoted in Alexander Etkind, *Eros of the Impossible*, trans. Noah and Maria Rubens (Boulder, CO: Westview, 1997), p. 265.

135 *Die Neue Menschheit*, p. 466. In this argument, Muraviev passes over what he knows about the bodily dimension of Indian practice systems – evidently under the influence of the dominant technicism, which ignores the difference between self-operation and having-oneself-operated-on, relying exclusively on external treatments. The one-sidedness of this option is denied through simultaneous insistence on 'psychophysical' methods in the 'rebuilding of the human being'.

136 Ibid., p. 468.

137 Leon Trotsky made the analogous Nietzsche-inspired claim that through communist 'psychophysical self-education', 'the average human type' would 'rise to the heights of an Aristotle, a Goethe, or a Marx. And above this ridge new peaks will rise.' 'The human species, the coagulated *Homo sapiens*, will once more enter into a state of radical transformation, and, in his own hands, will become an object of the most complicated methods of artificial selection and psychophysical training.' Trotsky, *Literature and Revolution*, pp. 207 and 206.

138 Concerning the role of European émigrés in the restructuring of the American illusion industry, see Neil Gabler, *An Empire of Their Own: How the Jews Invented Hollywood* (New York: Crown, 1988).

139 Aron Zalkind, 'Die Psychologie des Menschen der Zukunft' (1928), in *Die Neue Menschheit*, p. 612.

140 In the aforementioned text, Zalkind provides ambivalent examples of this art: on the one hand, he foresees 'colossal progress in transportation and communications technology, an unusual dynamization of life' (p. 645); on the other hand, he ventures the prediction that the socialist human being will be so infused with *joie de vivre* that the last otherworldly stirrings of 'mysticism' will die out, just as the tails of their primate ancestors disappeared (p. 647). The upward trend in human development, he argues, no longer stems from competition between humans; it comes firstly from the declaration of outer space as the new 'cruel class enemy', and secondly from the systematic stimulation, through socialist education, of the indispensable discontent of all subsequent generations with the living standard of the previous ones. The motor of history must continue to run at full steam, but egotisms will be replaced by sociophilic forces (pp. 650f).

141 See Jean Ziegler's essay 'Gier gegen Vernunft', in *Tugenden und Laster: Gradmesser der Menschlichkeit*, ed. ZDF-Nachtstudio (Frankfurt: Suhrkamp, 2004), pp. 252f: 'Where is there hope? Completely new social movements and a powerful civil society [. . .] are coming into being. Opposition fronts are setting out everywhere on the planet. They all have different fighting methods, but their motivation is the same: the moral imperative. [. . .] Over 100,000 people from five continents – representing over 8,000 farmers' syndicates, industrial unions, women's movements and non-government organizations fighting for human rights, the environment,

and the end of torture and hunger – gathered last January (2004) for the World Social Forum in Mumbai. With no hierarchy, no central committee and no sophisticated imperative programme. As a brotherhood of the night, a living figure of solidarity. We know exactly what we do not want.'

142 The existence of the 'mixed economic system' from the New Deal years to the beginning of the Thatcher era is frequently overlooked in ideologically distorted criticism of 'capitalism'. Ironically enough, the 1968 movement, which brought about a shift from Stalinism to Maoism or alternative leftist positions, appeared in the heyday of actually existing Rhine semi-socialism. See Daniel Yergin and Joseph Stanislaw, *The Commanding Heights: The Battle Between Government and the Marketplace That Is Remaking the Modern World* (New York: Simon & Schuster, 1998), pp. 19–91.

143 Studying the party programmes of the three Trotskyist candidates in the 2007 French presidential election – Olivier Besancenot, Arlette Arguiller and Gérard Schivardi, who received a total of 2.2 million votes – yields a paradoxical result: all of them argue for the suspension of the permanent revolution of capital and for the return to the age of social security.

144 Nietzsche, *Twilight of the Idols*, in *The Anti-Christ, Ecce Homo, Twilight of the Idols, and Other Writings*, trans. Judith Norman (Cambridge: Cambridge University Press, 2005), p. 190.

145 *Epistolae morales ad Lucilium*, 51.

146 See Emil Szittya's account of a peculiar holy man in Ascona around 1910 who, to visible success, declared that humans must work on rotting alive. In *Das Kuriositäten-Kabinett* (Constance: Kraus, 1923).

147 Consequently, Alasdair MacIntyre's 'narrative concept of selfhood' (*After Virtue*, p. 217), which is meant to establish the possibility of personal identity, cannot fulfil its promise, because only a small part of this identity is based on conscious and narratable changes, while the largest part is based on automatic and non-narratable refusals to change, as well as unconscious and mimetic adaptations.

148 Matthew 10:37.

149 Luke 14:33.

150 Matthew 10:34.

151 See Julian the Apostate, *Oratio* 7, 225 D–226 A.

152 In the passage mentioned, at least. In his earlier lectures on pedagogy, Kant looks deeper by dealing at certain points with pre-logical conditions for being able to take on reason. In Rink's transcript, we read in Article 7: 'Whoever is not cultivated is crude; whoever is not disciplined is savage. Neglect of discipline is a far greater evil than neglect of culture, for one can still compensate for the latter; but savageness cannot be done away with, and an omission in discipline can never be balanced out.' See Immanuel Kant, *Werke*, ed. Wilhelm Weischedel (Frankfurt: Suhrkamp, 1977), vol. 12, p. 700 (quoted in Christopher Korn, *Bildung und Disziplin*, pp. 100f).

153 Immanuel Kant, *Perpetual Peace: A Philosophical Essay*, trans. Mary Campbell Smith (New York: Cosimo, 2010), p. 26.

154 It encompasses the five spiritual vices – *superbia* (pride), *acedia* (sloth) or *tristitia* (depression), *avaritia* (greed), *invidia* (envy) and *ira* (anger) – as well as the two carnal vices, *luxuria* (lust) and *gula* (gluttony).

155 TN: a reference to Freud's *Civilization and Its Discontents*, whose German

title, *Das Unbehagen in der Kultur*, actually translates as 'Unease in Culture'.

156 Peter Weibel in collaboration with Loys Egg, *Lebenssehnsucht und Sucht* (Berlin: Merve, 2002), p. 32.

157 TN: in German, the two words are connected: 'addiction' is *Sucht*, while 'search' is *Suche*.

158 'There will be no favour for the man who keeps his oath or for the just or for the good; but rather men will praise the evil-doer and his violent dealing. Strength will be right and reverence will cease to be; and the wicked will hurt the worthy man, speaking false words against him, and will swear an oath upon them.' Hesiod, *Works and Days* l.190-4.

159 For a rebuttal of the ideology of the deficient being, see Peter Sloterdijk, *Sphären III. Schäume: Plurale Sphärologie* (Frankfurt: Suhrkamp, 2004), ch. 3: 'Auftrieb und Verwöhnung. Zur Kritik der reinen Laune', pp. 671–859.

160 See Sartre, *Critique of Dialectical Reason*, vol. 2, trans. Quintin Hoare (London and New York: Verso, 2006).

161 Outstanding reflections on this can be found in Hans Ulrich Gumbrecht, *Lob des Sports* (Frankfurt: Suhrkamp, 2007); the lost poetry of early cycling is evoked in Philippe Bordas, *Forcenés* (Paris: Fayard, 2007).

162 Stefan Müller, *Das Volk der Athleten: Untersuchungen zur Ideologie und Kritik des Sports in der griechisch-römischen Antike* (Trier: Wissenschaftlicher Verlag, 1995), p. 5.

163 See Pieper, *Faith, Hope, Love*, pp. 113f.

164 Romans 6:17–18.

165 See Sloterdijk, *Rage and Time*.

166 See pp. 395f above.

167 See Frank J. Tipler, *The Physics of Immortality: Modern Cosmology, God, and the Resurrection of the Dead* (New York: Doubleday, 1994).

168 See pp. 200–5 above.

169 Günther, *Die amerikanische Apokalypse*, pp. 277f.

170 See p. 379 above.

171 Karl Marx and Friedrich Engels, *The Communist Manifesto* (London: Penguin, 2002), p. 224.

172 See Sloterdijk, *Im Weltinnenraum des Kapitals*, pp. 265f.

173 Richard Rorty, *Achieving Our Country: Leftist Thought in Twentieth-Century America* (Cambridge, MA: Harvard University Press, 1998).

174 This applies to all authors of the various conservative revolutions in the twentieth century. For a recent example of this tendency, see the bellicist tract of the American neoconservative Robert D. Kaplan, *Warrior Politics: Why Leadership Demands a Pagan Ethos* (New York: Vintage, 2002).

175 It is in this language that Rorty formulated the most intense manifesto of the late twentieth century for a renaissance of the idea of world improvement, drawing on the American civil religion of Whitman and Dewey: see the chapter 'A Cultural Left' in Rorty, *Achieving Our Country*, pp. 73–107. This document no longer had any chance of effect after the rupture in the discursive field, both in the USA and in the rest of the world, in the wake of 11 September 2001; today it reads like a liberal utopia from a bygone age.

176 See pp. 449f below.

177 The contrast between single-age and multi-age phenomena forms the basis

of Eugen Rosenstock-Huessy's sociological and language-philosophical studies.

178 In this context, the critical distance assumed by Peter Weibel in his texts with regard to Viennese Actionism and the drug culture of the 1960s and 1970s is of fundamental significance: it cancels the axiomatics of selfish art. The representatives of art history have thus far reacted to the triumphs of maladaptive art mostly with jargon-heavy cluelessness. At the same time, the enormous œuvre of Bazon Brock is still waiting to be explored: he seems to be the only contemporary artist and art theorist who has concisely formulated the necessity of re-civilizing art in an art-immanent fashion.

179 See Ilya and Emilia Kabakov, catalogue for the large-scale installation *Palast der Projekte* in the Zollverein cokery in Essen, 2001, where a humorous summary of utopian modernity was presented in sixty-five separate projects under three headings: 'How can one improve oneself?', 'How does one improve the world?' and 'How does one simulate the creation of projects?'

180 See Giorgio Agamben, *Homo Sacer: Sovereign Power and Bare Life*, trans. Daniel Heller-Roazen (Palo Alto: Stanford University Press, 1998).

181 Count Harry Kessler notes in his journal (*Tagebücher 1918–1937*, ed. Wolfgang Pfeiffer-Belli [Frankfurt: S. Fischer, 1982], p. 689) the observations of the *Corriere della Sera* correspondent Caffi: 'Apparently no Bolshevik executioner has lasted more than two years . . . They have been in all the asylums; the sanatoriums on the Crimean coast are full of executioners who have gone mad.'

182 See the study by Luuk van Middelaar, *Politicide: De moord op de politiek in de Franse filosofie* (Amsterdam: Van Gennep, 1999), in which he accuses Sartre and the majority of French philosophers of contributing to the destruction of the political future.

183 See pp. 348f above.

184 See Stefabo Bacin, *Fichte in Schulpforta: Kontext und Dokumente* (Stuttgart: Frommann-Holzboog, 2007).

185 Concerning the socio-idealistic surpluses of the German university system in the nineteenth century, see Matthias Steinbach, *Ökonomisten, Philanthropen, Humanitäre: Professorensozialismus in der akademischen Provinz* (Berlin: Metropol, 2008).

186 Niklas Luhmann, 'Am Anfang war kein Unrecht', in *Gesellschaftsstruktur und Semantik*, vol. 3 (Frankfurt: Suhrkamp, 1993).

187 The connections between the theological, psychoanalytical and systemic theories of perversion have not been clarified. That psychoanalytical contributions to this object are usually scarcely more than translations of the Christian critique of egotism into different terminology is clear from studies such as those by Janine Chasseguet-Smirgel, *Anatomie der menschlichen Perversion* (Stuttgart: Psychosozial Verlag, 2002).

188 Because they can ultimately only use 'embedded' experts, these disciplines do not produce any genuine sciences, instead making the transition to the level of a non-self-serving formation of theories more difficult.

189 Steven Johnson, *Everything Bad Is Good for You* (London: Penguin, 2006).

190 TN: though it is not particularly significant, there is a certain play on words here, as 'to produce' is *herstellen* and 'to exhibit' is *ausstellen*.

191 See Boris Groys, *Logik der Sammlung: An Ende des musealen Zeitalters* (Munich: Hanser, 1997).

192 For a definition of this term, see Heiner Mühlmann, *The Nature of Culture: A Blueprint for a Theory of Culture Genetics*, trans. R. Payne (Vienna and New York: Springer, 1996).

193 Concerning the phenomenon of secession, see ch. 2, 'Culture Is a Monastic Rule'.

194 Johann Wolfgang von Goethe, 'Daemon', in *Selected Works*, trans. Nicholas Boyle (New York: Knopf, 2000), p. 1123. See Hermann Schmitz, *Goethes Altersdenken im problemgeschichtlichen Zusammenhang* (Bonn: Bouvier, 2008 [reprint]), pp. 217f and 264f.

195 Ibid.

196 See Alfred Schäfer, 'Die Seele: Gefängnis des Körpers', in Alfred Pongratz et al. (eds.), *Nach Foucault: Diskurs- und machtanalytische Perspektiven der Pädagogik* (Wiesbaden: Verlag für Sozialwissenschaften, 2004), pp. 97–113.

197 This was academicized as a 'step back' in Husserl's doctrine of *epoché*, or 'bracketing' of the existential judgement. Concerning the 'shore' and 'shore subjectivity', see pp. 227f above.

198 See Eugen Rosenstock-Huessy, *Die Sprache des Menschengeschlechts: Eine leibhaftige Grammatik in vier Teilen*, vol. 2 (Heidelberg: Lambert Schneider, 1964), pp. 15–197: 'Wenn eine Ewigkeit verstummt. Erinnerungen eines Entewigten'. TN: the German word for 'to immortalize', *verewigen*, literally means 'to eternalize'.

199 Heidegger, *Being and Time*, trans. John Macquarrie and Edward Robinson (Oxford: Blackwell, 1978), pp. 236f.

200 TN: the words of Carl Schmitt.

INDEX